Explaining Consciousness
— The 'Hard Problem'

Explaining Consciousness
— The 'Hard Problem'

Edited by
Jonathan Shear

A Bradford Book

The MIT Press
Cambridge, Massachusetts
London, England

Second printing, 1998

Copyright © 1995–7 by the Journal of Consciousness Studies
Imprint Academic, PO Box 1, Thorverton EX5 5YX, UK

This book was set in Times New Roman by Imprint Academic.

Printed and bound in the United States of America.

Library of Congress Cataloging-in-Publication-Data

Explaining consciousness: the "hard problem" / edited by Jonathan Shear.
   p.   cm.
   "A Bradford book."
   Includes bibliographical references.
   ISBN 0-262-19388-4 (alk. paper)
   1. Consciousness.   I. Shear, J. (Jonathan)
   B808.9.E86   1997
   126—dc21   97–8302
                                                                          CIP

Contents

Physics

Neuroscience and Cognitive Science

Rethinking Nature

First-Person Perspectives

Response

Jonathan Shear

Introduction

In the view of modern science, the universe is fundamentally physical and existed and evolved for billions of years without any consciousness present in it at all. Consciousness, on this now commonplace view, is a very recent addition, a byproduct of the complex chemical processes that gave rise to sophisticated biological organisms. The question thus arises of how consciousness ever came to be.[1] For it is clear that science describes the world purely in terms of spatial distributions of dynamic potentials to occupy and influence regions of space, without any reference whatsoever to the colours, sounds, feelings, anticipations, meanings, and thoughts with which our consciousness is so wonderfully filled. Moreover, the experiential qualities of our subjective awareness are so different *in kind* from the colourless, soundless, non-conscious spatio-temporal struc-tures described by the physical sciences that it seems impossible to understand how such experiential qualities could ever be produced by the interactions of purely physical systems. This radical difference between the *qualia* (experiential qualities) of our sub-jective awareness and the *qualia-free* nature of non-conscious physical systems thus produces what David Chalmers calls, in the keynote article of this volume, the

> 'hard problem' of explaining how any physical system, no matter how complex and well-organized, [could] give rise to experience at all . . . Why is it that all this processing does not go on 'in the dark', without any subjective quality? . . . This is the phenomenon that makes consciousness a real mystery.

The underlying premise of the 'hard problem', that the universe can exist and unfold independently of the existence of, and interaction with, consciousness of any sort, while appearing commonsensical in today's scientific world, was of course not always taken for granted. The first paragraph of *Genesis*, for example, proclaims that it was God's 'spirit' that enlivened the formless 'depths' to unfold into the created universe, and this notion is echoed in the subsequent theological doctrines that insist God's active partici-pation is required for the continued existence of the universe. Outside the realm of faith, the pre-Socratics, Anaxagoras and Heraclitus, were famous for their claims that mind is the foundation of the activities of the natural world and 'steers all things through all things'. Plato argued that the very intelligibility of the universe presupposes the existence of a pure transcendental intelligence underlying the structural and dynamical order of the universe. And even the empirically-minded Aristotle argued that purpose permeates the inanimate as well as the animate universe, and that a transcendental intelligence, the Unmoved Mover, underlies all the activity in nature. Although there were also of course

[1] This is to be distinguished from the question of *why* consciousness arose, that is, what evolution-ary purpose it serves.

materialists such as Democritus, the Greek founders of Western thought, operating in a pre-scientific context, were not much occupied with the 'hard problem' of accounting for consciousness in a fundamentally physical universe that seems so difficult to us today. Indeed, as Plato's dialogues repeatedly show, the existence of mental entities unexplainable in physical terms were likely simply to be taken as evidence for the independent existence of mind, rather than as perplexing anomalies in a materialistic world.

With the rise of the materialistic-mechanical viewpoint characteristic of modern science, all of this changed, of course. But this viewpoint gained dominance only after a protracted struggle with the Aristotelian and neo-Platonic descendents of the ancient Greek views, as the notion of what we today call 'science' evolved during the sixteenth century. Each of these worldviews had a very different basic paradigm for understanding nature. The Aristotelian view, which had dominated during the middle ages, relied on the notion of *organism* as its basic explanatory image. The neo-Platonic view took *mind*, emphasizing mathematics and creative activity, as basic. The materialist-mechanistic view relied on the notion of *machines* unfolding automatically and unconsciously. The materialist-mechanistic view won out, of course. Before this happened, however, empirical science was forced to internalize a major component of the neo-Platonic perspective, newly reintroduced to European thought in the late fifteenth century. From our own vantage point, nothing could seem more natural to the empirical scientific approach than its extensive reliance on mathematics for formulating the laws of nature and evaluating their experimental status. But, surprising as it may seem today, fifteenth and sixteenth century scientific investigators at first often resisted the mathematizing approach emphasized by the neo-Platonists. For numbers, algebra and mathematical formulas are obviously not physical entities; they are purely mental and not objectively observable. Consequently early observation-oriented investigators tended to reject their use as an escape from the real world, more appropriate to neo-Platonic mysticism and metaphysics than to hard-boiled empirical science.[2] But the success of mathematics, based on its usefulness both in the formulation of theory and in the articulation of precisely testable predictions, was so great that it became seamlessly integrated into the evolving, ultimately mechanistic scientific paradigm, and the early objections to its inclusion in empirical science on the grounds of its mentalistic nature became largely forgotten. Indeed, by the mid-seventeenth century we find mathematics even came to be seen as *defining* the objective physical world in contrast to the generally non-mathematizable subjective world of consciousness, as formalized, for example, in Descartes' influential mind–body distinction.

Thus the modern scientific worldview, regarding the universe as material in nature and unfolding like a machine according to precise, mathematically articulatable laws gained ascendency and became the context of much of our Western intellectual discourse. Nevertheless, the largely forgotten early puzzle about the role of the mathematics in the physical sciences remained and has continued to draw the attention of influential physicists.[3] For mathematics appears to be paradigmatically non-physical. Its objects are

---

[2] For an account of the interactions between the three approaches in the early development of modern science, see Hugh Kearney, *Science and Change: 1500–1700* (New York: McGraw-Hill Book Company, 1971).

[3] See, for example, Eugene Wigner, 'The unreasonable effectiveness of mathematics in the natural sciences', in *Symmetries and Reflections* (Bloomington: Indiana University Press, 1967).

characteristically *universal* in nature, in sharp contrast to the complete *particularity* of all physical entities and empirical observations; it is discovered within the realm of thought, not in the physical world; and the truth of its theorems are almost always evaluated completely mentally, rather than by objective scientific investigation.[4] Thus as physics becomes progressively more mathematized, its objects often seem puzzlingly to become more mental than physical.

This is not, of course, the only problem with the standard materialist worldview that has come to the attention of philosophers of science. For it is obvious that insofar as it is observation-dependent, science is also to a degree dependent on the subjectivity of the observing scientific investigators. Consequently, philosophers of science came up with the notions of *intersubjectivity* and *intersubjective corroboration* to recognize the role of subjectivity in empirical science, and over the last half century this terminology has found widespread currency in scientific as well as philosophical discourse. It has also become apparent that our observations in general, and our scientific observations in particular, are characteristically (and even, it is often argued, always) theory impregnated. This has often been taken (especially by writers associated with 'postmodern' thought) to imply that the notion of 'objectivity independent of subjectivity' is simply incoherent. To the extent that this observation is correct, the notion of a purely physical object or universe, free from any admixture of mind, also becomes problematic.

Advances in physics, the paradigmatically materialist discipline, have sometimes seemed to reintroduce the notion of consciousness as well. The most extreme example is that of quantum mechanics, where the role of the 'observer' paradoxically seemed to become essential not only for *knowing* the discrete phenomena of nature, but even for their very *existence as* discrete phenomena. For on many well-known interpretations of quantum mechanics it has seemed that it is the act of observation itself which somehow causes the 'collapse' of the wave function (describing the probabilities of a particle manifesting in any particular location throughout the universe) and the consequent localized existence of the particle in question. These interpretations are of course radically counter-intuitive, calling the materialist paradigm directly into question. The problems involved here are clearly illustrated by Schrödinger's famous 'cat in the box' paradox. Schrödinger invites us to consider a physical system consisting of a cat in a box; until someone observes it, the equations of quantum mechanics imply that this system *can be* in a variety of states — including those in which the cat is dead and others in which it is alive — but that it *is not in fact* in any one of these states until it is actually observed. Consequently, it is *incorrect* to think that the cat *is either* alive *or* dead until an observation that collapses the quantum probabilities into a particular state (in which the cat is either alive or dead) takes place. Thus for the time (a day or a week, etc.) during which the cat remains unobserved it is *neither* dead *nor* alive, despite the fact that once the system is relevantly observed one will be able to say definitively that it *had been* one or the other during this time. Thus, problematically, the state (including even the location) of objects in the universe appears to be significantly undetermined until a conscious act of observation takes place. And even after this act takes place it remains

---

[4] Computer assisted evaluations of proofs too lengthy to be calculated by hand are arguably a partial exception to this general rule.

paradoxical, for one is compelled to hold that even though the cat *was neither* dead *nor* alive prior to being observed, after the observation takes place one can be sure that exactly one of these two alternatives *had been* the case, namely, that it *had* been alive (if it was alive on the subsequent observation) or that it *had not*. Clearly this logical dilemma, too, poses a deep problem for our commonsensical materialistic-mechanistic conception of objective reality.

It also demonstrates significant inadequacies in our notion of consciousness. For an obvious rejoinder to the 'cat in the box' paradox is that the *cat* should 'know' if it were alive. For the cat, when conscious, would often be observing its environment, and the specificity of its perceptions would imply that the wave functions had already collapsed prior to our own (human) observations. But could a *cat's* consciousness cause the collapse of the wave function? Would *its* observations be relevant to the formalisms of quantum mechanics? Would they provide the relevant 'information' or 'knowledge'? If not, why not? And if a cat's awareness could do this, what about that of an amoeba? For amoebas clearly display information-driven behavior. Or is an amoeba not conscious at all, or not relevantly information-responsive? Again, if not, why not? Are there different *types* of consciousness, and only some of these relevant to quantum-mechanical collapse? If so, what are they, what are their distinctive differences, and how do these differences relate to the dynamics of quantum mechanical processes? In short, the 'cat in the box' paradox, in addition to highlighting the puzzle of observation-driven quantum mechanical 'collapse' and the paradox of states simultaneously existing-and-not-existing, also suggests that such paradigmatically mental phenomena as 'consciousness', 'knowledge' and 'information' need to be analysed with much finer discrimination before their roles in — and overall relation to — physical systems can be properly understood.

Thus, after three centuries of dominance, the standard materialist paradigm has been forced by advances in quantum mechanics to wrestle once again with what appears to be a major anomaly: the nature and role of consciousness in physical systems. The emergence of the 'hard problem' of consciousness into the forefront of philosophical discourse can be understood as part of this reexamination process. How, in a basically material universe, are we to understand even the bare *existence* of consciousness? How could it ever have emerged?

We should remind ourselves, however, that alternatives to the materialist perspective have of course been developed and defended throughout the history of modern Western philosophy. Descartes' dualism split the universe into two distinct, independent types of 'substance', comprising, respectively, the mathematically-describable objective physical-spatial realm studied by science,[5] and the subjective spiritual realm of mind or consciousness, properly the domain of religion.[6] Spinoza split the universe into the same two realms, but argued monistically that they were both attributes of a further, underlying substance. Leibnitz developed a 'panpsychic' theory of pre-spatio-temporal monads in which every thing, no matter how merely physical and nonconscious it might seem,

[5] Descartes' work in this area was, of course, a major factor in the development of the now standard materialistic-mechanistic paradigm.

[6] Indeed, the very fact that the 'hard problem' seems so hard today is often held to be the legacy of Descartes' dualism, and the problem itself is often formulated in terms of the difficulty of reconnecting causally and ontologically what Descartes so forcefully divided.

actually had at least some faint degree of sentience and perception. And Hegel developed an idealistic theory of the universe evolving dialectically out of 'Spirit' or consciousness itself. From the perspective of each of these theories, of course, the 'hard problem', if articulatable at all, would certainly not be the central philosophical anomaly it is today. For since none of them take matter as basic, none need be constrained to attempt to account for consciousness as arising from matter. But, for a variety of reasons — not the least being their emphasis on metaphysical entities quite outside the realm of scientific enquiry and corroboration — these views have all dropped by the wayside in our modern scientific world, and the materialist view has come to be so dominant that it is generally regarded as simple common sense. In this context the hard problem of explaining consciousness has come to be recognized as a very hard problem indeed.

The materialist view, however, has often resolved what had seemed to be insurmountable obstacles. The physical sciences have repeatedly been successful in incorporating realms and processes once thought to be necessarily outside their scope. Newton's demonstration that the same gravitational and mechanical laws apply to both celestial and terrestrial phenomena, and contemporary explanations of biological processes in terms of DNA, RNA and molecular chemistry are notable examples. Such past successes have led many influential defenders of the standard paradigm to insist that, whatever the conceptual difficulties, consciousness and its phenomenal content will ultimately turn out to be explicable as and reducible to purely physical phenomena, even if we cannot now foresee how this will happen. However, to others the gap between the qualia-free material world of the physical sciences and the qualia-filled contents of phenomenal awareness at present remains so great that this insistence appears to be little more than an act of faith.[7]

The enduring difficulty of the 'hard problem' has accordingly prompted a number of otherwise hard-headed, scientifically-oriented thinkers to go outside the standard context of discourse in the search for unconventional solutions. The articles of the present volume, which originally appeared in a multi-part special 'hard problem' issue of the *Journal of Consciousness Studies* (JCS),[8] reflect this diversity. Indeed, the editors of JCS were surprised at how many of the papers submitted to the special issue developed theories containing distinctly non-standard suggestions, ranging from discussions of the foundations of quantum-mechanics to panexperientialist theses in which all of nature, no matter how seemingly non-sentient, actually has a phenomenal-experiential component. There were, of course, also quite a few papers that defended the standard paradigm and attempted to explain the 'hard problem' away as being not such a hard problem after all.

The present book consists of a keynote paper by David Chalmers, 'Facing Up to the Problem of Consciousness', followed by twenty-six papers, twenty-four of which were written in response to the keynote, and Chalmers' reply to the responses. The responses have been grouped into six categories. The categories are, to be sure, somewhat arbitrary, for a number of the papers could easily fit in more than one. Nevertheless, some organization seemed to be in order, especially to help readers who were not yet conversant with the diversity of serious approaches to the topic.

---

[7] For a useful overview see Güven Güzeldere 'Consciousness: what it is, how to study it, what to learn from its history', *JCS*, **2** (1), 1995, pp. 30–51; and 'Problems of consciousness: a perspective on contemporary issues, current debates', *JCS*, **2** (2), 1995, pp. 112–44.

[8] The one exception is the short commentary by Crick and Koch from *Scientific American*.

The keynote paper begins by defining the 'hard problem' as the problem of accounting for the existence of phenomenal experience, and discusses why this problem is so hard. Chalmers differentiates this problem from the relatively 'easy' problems of understanding the structural and functional properties of cognitive processes, arguing that these are at least in principle amenable to conventional scientific theories and methodologies, while the former problem does not appear to be. He then suggests that to resolve the 'hard problem' we need to postulate experience as a fundamental feature of nature alongside the more conventional features such as space-time, mass, and charge. On this view, a final theory of consciousness will consist of a set of fundamental 'psychophysical' laws accompanying the fundamental laws of physics. Chalmers then offers a preliminary outline of such a theory, centred on a 'double-aspect' (phenomenological and physical) view of information.

The papers in 'Deflationary Perspectives' argue that the problem of phenomenal consciousness is nowhere near as hard as it might seem; they argue, for example, that it is a pseudo-problem, that materialist reduction will dissipate the problem, and that it is simply premature, in our present ignorance of how consciousness and the brain work, to talk about any uniquely 'hard' problem. Those in 'The Explanatory Gap' argue, on the other hand, that the problem is very hard; several analyze further aspects of the problem that Chalmers didn't contemplate, and some take the position that the problem will necessarily remain unresolvable. The papers of the next four sections, however, argue that it ought to be resolvable, and offer a variety of possible resolutions. Those in 'Physics' base their suggestions on a reexamination of relationships between consciousness and the objective world in the light of contemporary physics, especially quantum mechanics. The papers in 'Neuroscience and Cognitive Science' contain suggestions, ranging from conservative to highly speculative, about how consciousness and the nervous system may be related. Those in 'Rethinking Nature' explore implications of the radical hypothesis that consciousness ought to be understood as a pervasive feature of the objective universe. Finally, the papers in 'First-Person Perspectives' argue that resolving the hard problem will require development of a new science of the subjective phenomena of consciousness, complementing our existing studies of the objective material universe.

The articles in this volume are thus quite diverse, and contain a variety of non-standard components, as well as those from within the usual scientific paradigm. This sort of creative diversity is of course what should be expected as we wrestle with what has come to be recognized as a serious challenge for standard materialism, namely the existence of consciousness itself.

Acknowledgments

I would like to thank a number of people for their help in preparing this book: Keith Sutherland, publisher of *Journal of Consciousness Studies* who had the original idea for the book, Anthony Freeman, JCS managing editor; David Chalmers, for his keynote and response articles and his ongoing encouragement; Jean Burns, another editor of JCS, for her help with the scientific submissions; Gene Mills of Virginia Commonwealth University, for his feedback on many of the early papers; the other referees, too numerous to cite here, for their careful analyses; my sweet wife Patricia, for more than I can express; and, of course, all the contributing authors.

The
Hard Problem

David J. Chalmers

Facing Up to the Problem of Consciousness

I: Introduction*

Consciousness poses the most baffling problems in the science of the mind. There is nothing that we know more intimately than conscious experience, but there is nothing that is harder to explain. All sorts of mental phenomena have yielded to scientific investigation in recent years, but consciousness has stubbornly resisted. Many have tried to explain it, but the explanations always seem to fall short of the target. Some have been led to suppose that the problem is intractable, and that no good explanation can be given.

To make progress on the problem of consciousness, we have to confront it directly. In this paper, I first isolate the truly hard part of the problem, separating it from more tractable parts and giving an account of why it is so difficult to explain. I critique some recent work that uses reductive methods to address consciousness, and argue that these methods inevitably fail to come to grips with the hardest part of the problem. Once this failure is recognized, the door to further progress is opened. In the second half of the paper, I argue that if we move to a new kind of nonreductive explanation, a naturalistic account of consciousness can be given. I put forward my own candidate for such an account: a nonreductive theory based on principles of structural coherence and organizational invariance and a double-aspect view of information.

II: The Easy Problems and the Hard Problem

There is not just one problem of consciousness. 'Consciousness' is an ambiguous term, referring to many different phenomena. Each of these phenomena needs to be explained, but some are easier to explain than others. At the start, it is useful to divide the associated problems of consciousness into 'hard' and 'easy' problems. The easy problems of consciousness are those that seem directly susceptible to the standard methods of cognitive science, whereby a phenomenon is explained in terms of computational or neural mechanisms. The hard problems are those that seem to resist those methods.

The easy problems of consciousness include those of explaining the following phenomena:

* This paper was originally published in the *Journal of Consciousness Studies*, **2**, No.3 (1995), pp. 200–19. The arguments are presented in much greater depth in my book *The Conscious Mind* (Chalmers, 1996). Thanks to Francis Crick, Peggy DesAutels, Matthew Elton, Liane Gabora, Christof Koch, Paul Rhodes, Gregg Rosenberg, and Sharon Wahl for helpful comments.

- the ability to discriminate, categorize, and react to environmental stimuli;
- the integration of information by a cognitive system;
- the reportability of mental states;
- the ability of a system to access its own internal states;
- the focus of attention;
- the deliberate control of behaviour;
- the difference between wakefulness and sleep.

All of these phenomena are associated with the notion of consciousness. For example, one sometimes says that a mental state is conscious when it is verbally reportable, or when it is internally accessible. Sometimes a system is said to be conscious of some information when it has the ability to react on the basis of that information, or, more strongly, when it attends to that information, or when it can integrate that information and exploit it in the sophisticated control of behaviour. We sometimes say that an action is conscious precisely when it is deliberate. Often, we say that an organism is conscious as another way of saying that it is awake.

There is no real issue about whether *these* phenomena can be explained scientifically. All of them are straightforwardly vulnerable to explanation in terms of computational or neural mechanisms. To explain access and reportability, for example, we need only specify the mechanism by which information about internal states is retrieved and made available for verbal report. To explain the integration of information, we need only exhibit mechanisms by which information is brought together and exploited by later processes. For an account of sleep and wakefulness, an appropriate neurophysiological account of the processes responsible for organisms' contrasting behaviour in those states will suffice. In each case, an appropriate cognitive or neurophysiological model can clearly do the explanatory work.

If these phenomena were all there was to consciousness, then consciousness would not be much of a problem. Although we do not yet have anything close to a complete explanation of these phenomena, we have a clear idea of how we might go about explaining them. This is why I call these problems the easy problems. Of course, 'easy' is a relative term. Getting the details right will probably take a century or two of difficult empirical work. Still, there is every reason to believe that the methods of cognitive science and neuroscience will succeed.

The really hard problem of consciousness is the problem of *experience*. When we think and perceive, there is a whir of information-processing, but there is also a subjective aspect. As Nagel (1974) has put it, there is *something it is like* to be a conscious organism. This subjective aspect is experience. When we see, for example, we *experience* visual sensations: the felt quality of redness, the experience of dark and light, the quality of depth in a visual field. Other experiences go along with perception in different modalities: the sound of a clarinet, the smell of mothballs. Then there are bodily sensations, from pains to orgasms; mental images that are conjured up internally; the felt quality of emotion, and the experience of a stream of conscious thought. What unites all of these states is that there is something it is like to be in them. All of them are states of experience.

It is undeniable that some organisms are subjects of experience. But the question of how it is that these systems are subjects of experience is perplexing. Why is it that when our cognitive systems engage in visual and auditory information-processing, we have visual or auditory experience: the quality of deep blue, the sensation of middle C? How can we explain why there is something it is like to entertain a mental image, or to experience an emotion? It is widely agreed that experience arises from a physical basis, but we have no good explanation of why and how it so arises. Why should physical processing give rise to a rich inner life at all? It seems objectively unreasonable that it should, and yet it does.

If any problem qualifies as *the* problem of consciousness, it is this one. In this central sense of 'consciousness', an organism is conscious if there is something it is like to be that organism, and a mental state is conscious if there is something it is like to be in that state. Sometimes terms such as 'phenomenal consciousness' and 'qualia' are also used here, but I find it more natural to speak of 'conscious experience' or simply 'experience'. Another useful way to avoid confusion (used by e.g. Newell 1990, Chalmers 1996) is to reserve the term 'consciousness' for the phenomena of experience, using the less loaded term 'awareness' for the more straightforward phenomena described earlier. If such a convention were widely adopted, communication would be much easier. As things stand, those who talk about 'consciousness' are frequently talking past each other.

The ambiguity of the term 'consciousness' is often exploited by both philosophers and scientists writing on the subject. It is common to see a paper on consciousness begin with an invocation of the mystery of consciousness, noting the strange intangibility and ineffability of subjectivity, and worrying that so far we have no theory of the phenomenon. Here, the topic is clearly the hard problem — the problem of experience. In the second half of the paper, the tone becomes more optimistic, and the author's own theory of consciousness is outlined. Upon examination, this theory turns out to be a theory of one of the more straightforward phenomena — of reportability, of introspective access, or whatever. At the close, the author declares that consciousness has turned out to be tractable after all, but the reader is left feeling like the victim of a bait-and-switch. The hard problem remains untouched.

III: Functional Explanation

Why are the easy problems easy, and why is the hard problem hard? The easy problems are easy precisely because they concern the explanation of cognitive *abilities* and *functions*. To explain a cognitive function, we need only specify a mechanism that can perform the function. The methods of cognitive science are well-suited for this sort of explanation, and so are well-suited to the easy problems of consciousness. By contrast, the hard problem is hard precisely because it is not a problem about the performance of functions. The problem persists even when the performance of all the relevant functions is explained.[1]

To explain reportability, for instance, is just to explain how a system could perform the function of producing reports on internal states. To explain internal access, we need to explain how a system could be appropriately affected by its internal states and use information about those states in directing later processes. To explain integration and

---

[1] Here 'function' is not used in the narrow teleological sense of something that a system is designed to do, but in the broader sense of any causal role in the production of behaviour that a system might perform.

control, we need to explain how a system's central processes can bring information contents together and use them in the facilitation of various behaviours. These are all problems about the explanation of functions.

How do we explain the performance of a function? By specifying a *mechanism* that performs the function. Here, neurophysiological and cognitive modelling are perfect for the task. If we want a detailed low-level explanation, we can specify the neural mechanism that is responsible for the function. If we want a more abstract explanation, we can specify a mechanism in computational terms. Either way, a full and satisfying explanation will result. Once we have specified the neural or computational mechanism that performs the function of verbal report, for example, the bulk of our work in explaining reportability is over.

In a way, the point is trivial. It is a *conceptual* fact about these phenomena that their explanation only involves the explanation of various functions, as the phenomena are *functionally definable*. All it *means* for reportability to be instantiated in a system is that the system has the capacity for verbal reports of internal information. All it means for a system to be awake is for it to be appropriately receptive to information from the environment and for it to be able to use this information in directing behaviour in an appropriate way. To see that this sort of thing is a conceptual fact, note that someone who says 'you have explained the performance of the verbal report function, but you have not explained reportability' is making a trivial conceptual mistake about reportability. All it could *possibly* take to explain reportability is an explanation of how the relevant function is performed; the same goes for the other phenomena in question.

Throughout the higher-level sciences, reductive explanation works in just this way. To explain the gene, for instance, we needed to specify the mechanism that stores and transmits hereditary information from one generation to the next. It turns out that DNA performs this function; once we explain how the function is performed, we have explained the gene. To explain life, we ultimately need to explain how a system can reproduce, adapt to its environment, metabolize, and so on. All of these are questions about the performance of functions, and so are well-suited to reductive explanation. The same holds for most problems in cognitive science. To explain learning, we need to explain the way in which a system's behavioural capacities are modified in light of environmental information, and the way in which new information can be brought to bear in adapting a system's actions to its environment. If we show how a neural or computational mechanism does the job, we have explained learning. We can say the same for other cognitive phenomena, such as perception, memory, and language. Sometimes the relevant functions need to be characterized quite subtly, but it is clear that insofar as cognitive science explains these phenomena at all, it does so by explaining the performance of functions.

When it comes to conscious experience, this sort of explanation fails. What makes the hard problem hard and almost unique is that it goes *beyond* problems about the performance of functions. To see this, note that even when we have explained the performance of all the cognitive and behavioural functions in the vicinity of experience — perceptual discrimination, categorization, internal access, verbal report — there may still remain a further unanswered question: *Why is the performance of these functions accompanied by experience?* A simple explanation of the functions leaves this question open.

There is no analogous further question in the explanation of genes, or of life, or of learning. If someone says 'I can see that you have explained how DNA stores and transmits hereditary information from one generation to the next, but you have not explained how it is a *gene*,' then they are making a conceptual mistake. All it means to be a gene is to be an entity that performs the relevant storage and transmission function. But if someone says 'I can see that you have explained how information is discriminated, integrated, and reported, but you have not explained how it is *experienced*,' they are not making a conceptual mistake. This is a nontrivial further question.

This further question is the key question in the problem of consciousness. Why doesn't all this information-processing go on 'in the dark', free of any inner feel? Why is it that when electromagnetic waveforms impinge on a retina and are discriminated and categorized by a visual system, this discrimination and categorization is experienced as a sensation of vivid red? We know that conscious experience *does* arise when these functions are performed, but the very fact that it arises is the central mystery. There is an *explanatory gap* (a term due to Levine 1983) between the functions and experience, and we need an explanatory bridge to cross it. A mere account of the functions stays on one side of the gap, so the materials for the bridge must be found elsewhere.

This is not to say that experience *has* no function. Perhaps it will turn out to play an important cognitive role. But for any role it might play, there will be more to the explanation of experience than a simple explanation of the function. Perhaps it will even turn out that in the course of explaining a function, we will be led to the key insight that allows an explanation of experience. If this happens, though, the discovery will be an *extra* explanatory reward. There is no cognitive function such that we can say in advance that explanation of that function will *automatically* explain experience.

To explain experience, we need a new approach. The usual explanatory methods of cognitive science and neuroscience do not suffice. These methods have been developed precisely to explain the performance of cognitive functions, and they do a good job of it. But as these methods stand, they are *only* equipped to explain the performance of functions. When it comes to the hard problem, the standard approach has nothing to say.

IV: Some Case-Studies

In the last few years, a number of works have addressed the problems of consciousness within the framework of cognitive science and neuroscience. This might suggest that the analysis above is faulty, but in fact a close examination of the relevant work only lends the analysis further support. When we investigate just which aspects of consciousness these studies are aimed at, and which aspects they end up explaining, we find that the ultimate target of explanation is always one of the easy problems. I will illustrate this with two representative examples.

The first is the 'neurobiological theory of consciousness' outlined by Francis Crick and Christof Koch (1990; see also Crick 1994). This theory centers on certain 35–75 hertz neural oscillations in the cerebral cortex; Crick and Koch hypothesize that these oscillations are the basis of consciousness. This is partly because the oscillations seem to be correlated with awareness in a number of different modalities — within the visual and olfactory systems, for example — and also because they suggest a mechanism by which the *binding* of information contents might be achieved. Binding is the process whereby separately represented pieces of information about a single entity are brought together to be used by later processing, as when information about the colour and shape of a perceived object is integrated from separate visual pathways. Following others (e.g. Eckhorn *et al.* 1988), Crick and Koch hypothesize that binding may be achieved by the synchronized oscillations of neuronal groups representing the relevant contents. When two pieces of information are to be bound together, the relevant neural groups will oscillate with the same frequency and phase.

The details of how this binding might be achieved are still poorly understood, but suppose that they can be worked out. What might the resulting theory explain? Clearly it might explain the binding of information contents, and perhaps it might yield a more general account of the integration of information in the brain. Crick and Koch also suggest that these oscillations activate the mechanisms of working memory, so that there may be an account of this and perhaps other forms of memory in the distance. The theory might eventually lead to a general account of how perceived information is bound and stored in memory, for use by later processing.

Such a theory would be valuable, but it would tell us nothing about why the relevant contents are experienced. Crick and Koch suggest that these oscillations are the neural *correlates* of experience. This claim is arguable — does not binding also take place in the processing of unconscious information? — but even if it is accepted, the *explanatory* question remains: Why do the oscillations give rise to experience? The only basis for an explanatory connection is the role they play in binding and storage, but the question of why binding and storage should themselves be accompanied by experience is never addressed. If we do not know why binding and storage should give rise to experience, telling a story about the oscillations cannot help us. Conversely, if we *knew* why binding and storage gave rise to experience, the neurophysiological details would be just the icing on the cake. Crick and Koch's theory gains its purchase by *assuming* a connection between binding and experience, and so can do nothing to explain that link.

I do not think that Crick and Koch are ultimately claiming to address the hard problem, although some have interpreted them otherwise. A published interview with Koch gives a clear statement of the limitations on the theory's ambitions.

> Well, let's first forget about the really difficult aspects, like subjective feelings, for they may not have a scientific solution. The subjective state of play, of pain, of pleasure, of seeing blue, of smelling a rose — there seems to be a huge jump between the materialistic level, of explaining molecules and neurons, and the subjective level. Let's focus on things that are easier to study — like visual awareness. You're now talking to me, but you're not looking at me, you're looking at the cappuccino, and so you are aware of it. You can say, 'It's a cup and there's some liquid in it.' If I give it to you, you'll move your arm and you'll take it — you'll respond in a meaningful manner. That's what I call awareness. ('What is Consciousness?', *Discover*, November 1992, p. 96.)

The second example is an approach at the level of cognitive psychology. This is Bernard Baars' global workspace theory of consciousness, presented in his book *A Cognitive Theory of Consciousness* (1988). According to this theory, the contents of consciousness are contained in a *global workspace*, a central processor used to mediate communication between a host of specialized nonconscious processors. When these specialized processors need to broadcast information to the rest of the system, they do so by sending this information to the workspace, which acts as a kind of communal blackboard for the rest of the system, accessible to all the other processors.

Baars uses this model to address many aspects of human cognition, and to explain a number of contrasts between conscious and unconscious cognitive functioning. Ultimately, however, it is a theory of *cognitive accessibility*, explaining how it is that certain information contents are widely accessible within a system, as well as a theory of informational integration and reportability. The theory shows promise as a theory of awareness, the functional correlate of conscious experience, but an explanation of experience itself is not on offer.

One might suppose that according to this theory, the contents of experience are precisely the contents of the workspace. But even if this is so, nothing internal to the theory *explains* why the information within the global workspace is experienced. The best the theory can do is to say that the information is experienced because it is *globally accessible*. But now the question arises in a different form: why should global accessibility give rise to conscious experience? As always, this bridging question is unanswered.

Almost all work taking a cognitive or neuroscientific approach to consciousness in recent years could be subjected to a similar critique. The 'Neural Darwinism' model of Edelman (1989), for instance, addresses questions about perceptual awareness and the self-concept, but says nothing about why there should also be experience. The 'multiple drafts' model of Dennett (1991) is largely directed at explaining the reportability of certain mental contents. The 'intermediate level' theory of Jackendoff (1987) provides an account of some computational processes that underlie consciousness, but Jackendoff stresses that the question of how these 'project' into conscious experience remains mysterious.

Researchers using these methods are often inexplicit about their attitudes to the problem of conscious experience, although sometimes they take a clear stand. Even among those who are clear about it, attitudes differ widely. In placing this sort of work with respect to the problem of experience, a number of different strategies are available. It would be useful if these strategic choices were more often made explicit.

The first strategy is simply to *explain something else*. Some researchers are explicit that the problem of experience is too difficult for now, and perhaps even outside the domain of science altogether. These researchers instead choose to address one of the more tractable problems such as reportability or the self-concept. Although I have called these problems the 'easy' problems, they are among the most interesting unsolved problems in cognitive science, so this work is certainly worthwhile. The worst that can be said of this choice is that in the context of research on consciousness it is relatively unambitious, and the work can sometimes be misinterpreted.

The second choice is to take a harder line and *deny the phenomenon*. (Variations on this approach are taken by Allport 1988; Dennett 1991; Wilkes 1988.) According to this line, once we have explained the functions such as accessibility, reportability, and the like, there is no further phenomenon called 'experience' to explain. Some explicitly deny the phenomenon, holding for example that what is not externally verifiable cannot be real.

Others achieve the same effect by allowing that experience exists, but only if we equate 'experience' with something like the capacity to discriminate and report. These approaches lead to a simpler theory, but are ultimately unsatisfactory. Experience is the most central and manifest aspect of our mental lives, and indeed is perhaps the key explanandum in the science of the mind. Because of this status as an explanandum, experience cannot be discarded like the vital spirit when a new theory comes along. Rather, it is the central fact that any theory of consciousness must explain. A theory that denies the phenomenon 'solves' the problem by ducking the question.

In a third option, some researchers *claim to be explaining experience* in the full sense. These researchers (unlike those above) wish to take experience very seriously; they lay out their functional model or theory, and claim that it explains the full subjective quality of experience (e.g. Flohr 1992; Humphrey 1992). The relevant step in the explanation is usually passed over quickly, however, and usually ends up looking something like magic. After some details about information processing are given, experience suddenly enters the picture, but it is left obscure *how* these processes should suddenly give rise to experience. Perhaps it is simply taken for granted that it does, but then we have an incomplete explanation and a version of the fifth strategy below.

A fourth, more promising approach appeals to these methods to *explain the structure of experience*. For example, it is arguable that an account of the discriminations made by the visual system can account for the structural relations between different colour experiences, as well as for the geometric structure of the visual field (see e.g. Clark 1992; Hardin 1992). In general, certain facts about structures found in processing will correspond to and arguably explain facts about the structure of experience. This strategy is plausible but limited. At best, it takes the existence of experience for granted and accounts for some facts about its structure, providing a sort of nonreductive explanation of the structural aspects of experience (I will say more on this later). This is useful for many purposes, but it tells us nothing about why there should be experience in the first place.

A fifth and reasonable strategy is to *isolate the substrate of experience*. After all, almost everyone allows that experience *arises* one way or another from brain processes, and it makes sense to identify the sort of process from which it arises. Crick and Koch put their work forward as isolating the neural correlate of consciousness, for example, and Edelman (1989) and Jackendoff (1987) make related claims. Justification of these claims requires a careful theoretical analysis, especially as experience is not directly observable in experimental contexts, but when applied judiciously this strategy can shed indirect light on the problem of experience. Nevertheless, the strategy is clearly incomplete. For a satisfactory theory, we need to know more than *which* processes give rise to experience; we need an account of why and how. A full theory of consciousness must build an explanatory bridge.

V: The Extra Ingredient

We have seen that there are systematic reasons why the usual methods of cognitive science and neuroscience fail to account for conscious experience. These are simply the wrong sort of methods: nothing that they give to us can yield an explanation. To account for conscious experience, we need an *extra ingredient* in the explanation. This makes for a challenge to those who are serious about the hard problem of consciousness: What is your extra ingredient, and why should *that* account for conscious experience?

There is no shortage of extra ingredients to be had. Some propose an injection of chaos and nonlinear dynamics. Some think that the key lies in nonalgorithmic processing. Some appeal to future discoveries in neurophysiology. Some suppose that the key to the mystery will lie at the level of quantum mechanics. It is easy to see why all these suggestions are put forward. None of the old methods work, so the solution must lie with *something* new. Unfortunately, these suggestions all suffer from the same old problems.

Nonalgorithmic processing, for example, is put forward by Penrose (1989; 1994) because of the role it might play in the process of conscious mathematical insight. The arguments about mathematics are controversial, but even if they succeed and an account of nonalgorithmic processing in the human brain is given, it will still only be an account of the *functions* involved in mathematical reasoning and the like. For a nonalgorithmic process as much as an algorithmic process, the question is left unanswered: why should this process give rise to experience? In answering *this* question, there is no special role for nonalgorithmic processing.

The same goes for nonlinear and chaotic dynamics. These might provide a novel account of the dynamics of cognitive functioning, quite different from that given by standard methods in cognitive science. But from dynamics, one only gets more dynamics. The question about experience here is as mysterious as ever. The point is even clearer for new discoveries in neurophysiology. These new discoveries may help us make significant progress in understanding brain function, but for any neural process we isolate, the same question will always arise. It is difficult to imagine what a proponent of new neurophysiology expects to happen, over and above the explanation of further cognitive functions. It is not as if we will suddenly discover a phenomenal glow inside a neuron!

Perhaps the most popular 'extra ingredient' of all is quantum mechanics (e.g. Hameroff 1994). The attractiveness of quantum theories of consciousness may stem from a Law of Minimization of Mystery: consciousness is mysterious and quantum mechanics is mysterious, so maybe the two mysteries have a common source. Nevertheless, quantum theories of consciousness suffer from the same difficulties as neural or computational theories. Quantum phenomena have some remarkable functional properties, such as nondeterminism and nonlocality. It is natural to speculate that these properties may play some role in the explanation of cognitive functions, such as random choice and the integration of information, and this hypothesis cannot be ruled out *a priori*. But when it comes to the explanation of experience, quantum processes are in the same boat as any other. The question of why these processes should give rise to experience is entirely unanswered.[2]

---

[2] One special attraction of quantum theories is the fact that on some interpretations of quantum mechanics, consciousness plays an active role in 'collapsing' the quantum wave function. Such interpretations are controversial, but in any case they offer no hope of *explaining* consciousness in terms of quantum processes. Rather, these theories *assume* the existence of consciousness, and use it in the explanation of quantum processes. At best, these theories tell us something about a physical role that consciousness may play. They tell us nothing about how it arises.

At the end of the day, the same criticism applies to *any* purely physical account of consciousness. For any physical process we specify there will be an unanswered question: Why should this process give rise to experience? Given any such process, it is conceptually coherent that it could be instantiated in the absence of experience. It follows that no mere account of the physical process will tell us why experience arises. The emergence of experience goes beyond what can be derived from physical theory.

Purely physical explanation is well-suited to the explanation of physical *structures*, explaining macroscopic structures in terms of detailed microstructural constituents; and it provides a satisfying explanation of the performance of *functions*, accounting for these functions in terms of the physical mechanisms that perform them. This is because a physical account can *entail* the facts about structures and functions: once the internal details of the physical account are given, the structural and functional properties fall out as an automatic consequence. But the structure and dynamics of physical processes yield only more structure and dynamics, so structures and functions are all we can expect these processes to explain. The facts about experience cannot be an automatic consequence of any physical account, as it is conceptually coherent that any given process could exist without experience. Experience may *arise* from the physical, but it is not *entailed* by the physical.

The moral of all this is that *you can't explain conscious experience on the cheap*. It is a remarkable fact that reductive methods — methods that explain a high-level phenomenon wholly in terms of more basic physical processes — work well in so many domains. In a sense, one *can* explain most biological and cognitive phenomena on the cheap, in that these phenomena are seen as automatic consequences of more fundamental processes. It would be wonderful if reductive methods could explain experience, too; I hoped for a long time that they might. Unfortunately, there are systematic reasons why these methods must fail. Reductive methods are successful in most domains because what needs explaining in those domains are structures and functions, and these are the kind of thing that a physical account can entail. When it comes to a problem over and above the explanation of structures and functions, these methods are impotent.

This might seem reminiscent of the vitalist claim that no physical account could explain life, but the cases are disanalogous. What drove vitalist scepticism was doubt about whether physical mechanisms could perform the many remarkable functions associated with life, such as complex adaptive behaviour and reproduction. The conceptual claim that explanation of functions is what is needed was implicitly accepted, but lacking detailed knowledge of biochemical mechanisms, vitalists doubted whether any physical process could do the job and put forward the hypothesis of the vital spirit as an alternative explanation. Once it turned out that physical processes could perform the relevant functions, vitalist doubts melted away.

With experience, on the other hand, physical explanation of the functions is not in question. The key is instead the *conceptual* point that the explanation of functions does not suffice for the explanation of experience. This basic conceptual point is not something that further neuroscientific investigation will affect. In a similar way, experience is disanalogous to the *elan vital*. The vital spirit was put forward as an explanatory posit, in order to explain the relevant functions, and could therefore be discarded when those functions were explained without it. Experience is not an explanatory posit but an explanandum in its own right, and so is not a candidate for this sort of elimination.

It is tempting to note that all sorts of puzzling phenomena have eventually turned out to be explainable in physical terms. But each of these were problems about the observable behaviour of physical objects, coming down to problems in the explanation of structures and functions. Because of this, these phenomena have always been the kind of thing that a physical account *might* explain, even if at some points there have been good reasons to suspect that no such explanation would be forthcoming. The tempting induction from these cases fails in the case of consciousness, which is not a problem about physical structures and functions. The problem of consciousness is puzzling in an entirely different way. An analysis of the problem shows us that conscious experience is just not the kind of thing that a wholly reductive account could succeed in explaining.

VI: Nonreductive Explanation

At this point some are tempted to give up, holding that we will never have a theory of conscious experience. McGinn (1989), for example, argues that the problem is too hard for our limited minds; we are 'cognitively closed' with respect to the phenomenon. Others have argued that conscious experience lies outside the domain of scientific theory altogether.

I think this pessimism is premature. This is not the place to give up; it is the place where things get interesting. When simple methods of explanation are ruled out, we need to investigate the alternatives. Given that reductive explanation fails, *nonreductive* explanation is the natural choice.

Although a remarkable number of phenomena have turned out to be explicable wholly in terms of entities simpler than themselves, this is not universal. In physics, it occasionally happens that an entity has to be taken as *fundamental*. Fundamental entities are not explained in terms of anything simpler. Instead, one takes them as basic, and gives a theory of how they relate to everything else in the world. For example, in the nineteenth century it turned out that electromagnetic processes could not be explained in terms of the wholly mechanical processes that previous physical theories appealed to, so Maxwell and others introduced electromagnetic charge and electromagnetic forces as new fundamental components of a physical theory. To explain electromagnetism, the ontology of physics had to be expanded. New basic properties and basic laws were needed to give a satisfactory account of the phenomena.

Other features that physical theory takes as fundamental include mass and space-time. No attempt is made to explain these features in terms of anything simpler. But this does not rule out the possibility of a theory of mass or of space-time. There is an intricate theory of how these features interrelate, and of the basic laws they enter into. These basic principles are used to explain many familiar phenomena concerning mass, space, and time at a higher level.

I suggest that a theory of consciousness should take experience as fundamental. We know that a theory of consciousness requires the addition of *something* fundamental to our ontology, as everything in physical theory is compatible with the absence of consciousness. We might add some entirely new nonphysical feature, from which experience can be derived, but it is hard to see what such a feature would be like. More likely, we will take experience itself as a fundamental feature of the world, alongside mass, charge, and space-time. If we take experience as fundamental, then we can go about the business of constructing a theory of experience.

Where there is a fundamental property, there are fundamental laws. A nonreductive theory of experience will add new principles to the furniture of the basic laws of nature. These basic principles will ultimately carry the explanatory burden in a theory of consciousness. Just as we explain familiar high-level phenomena involving mass in terms of more basic principles involving mass and other entities, we might explain familiar phenomena involving experience in terms of more basic principles involving experience and other entities.

In particular, a nonreductive theory of experience will specify basic principles telling us how experience depends on physical features of the world. These *psychophysical* principles will not interfere with physical laws, as it seems that physical laws already form a closed system. Rather, they will be a supplement to a physical theory. A physical theory gives a theory of physical processes, and a psychophysical theory tells us how those processes give rise to experience. We know that experience depends on physical processes, but we also know that this dependence cannot be derived from physical laws alone. The new basic principles postulated by a nonreductive theory give us the extra ingredient that we need to build an explanatory bridge.

Of course, by taking experience as fundamental, there is a sense in which this approach does not tell us why there is experience in the first place. But this is the same for any fundamental theory. Nothing in physics tells us why there is matter in the first place, but we do not count this against theories of matter. Certain features of the world need to be taken as fundamental by any scientific theory. A theory of matter can still explain all sorts of facts about matter, by showing how they are consequences of the basic laws. The same goes for a theory of experience.

This position qualifies as a variety of dualism, as it postulates basic properties over and above the properties invoked by physics. But it is an innocent version of dualism, entirely compatible with the scientific view of the world. Nothing in this approach contradicts anything in physical theory; we simply need to add further *bridging* principles to explain how experience arises from physical processes. There is nothing particularly spiritual or mystical about this theory — its overall shape is like that of a physical theory, with a few fundamental entities connected by fundamental laws. It expands the ontology slightly, to be sure, but Maxwell did the same thing. Indeed, the overall structure of this position is entirely naturalistic, allowing that ultimately the universe comes down to a network of basic entities obeying simple laws, and allowing that there may ultimately be a theory of consciousness cast in terms of such laws. If the position is to have a name, a good choice might be *naturalistic dualism*.

If this view is right, then in some ways a theory of consciousness will have more in common with a theory in physics than a theory in biology. Biological theories involve no principles that are fundamental in this way, so biological theory has a certain complexity and messiness to it; but theories in physics, insofar as they deal with fundamental principles, aspire to simplicity and elegance. The fundamental laws of nature are part of the basic furniture of the world, and physical theories are telling us that this basic furniture is remarkably simple. If a theory of consciousness also involves fundamental principles, then we should expect the same. The principles of simplicity, elegance, and even beauty that drive physicists' search for a fundamental theory will also apply to a theory of consciousness.[3]

VII: Toward of a Theory of Consciousness

It is not too soon to begin work on a theory. We are already in a position to understand some key facts about the relationship between physical processes and experience, and about the regularities that connect them. Once reductive explanation is set aside, we can lay those facts on the table so that they can play their proper role as the initial pieces in a nonreductive theory of consciousness, and as constraints on the basic laws that constitute an ultimate theory.

There is an obvious problem that plagues the development of a theory of consciousness, and that is the paucity of objective data. Conscious experience is not directly observable in an experimental context, so we cannot generate data about the relationship between physical processes and experience at will. Nevertheless, we all have access to a rich source of data in our own case. Many important regularities between experience and processing can be inferred from considerations about one's own experience. There are also good indirect sources of data from observable cases, as when one relies on the verbal report of a subject as an indication of experience. These methods have their limitations, but we have more than enough data to get a theory off the ground.

Philosophical analysis is also useful in getting value for money out of the data we have. This sort of analysis can yield a number of principles relating consciousness and cognition, thereby strongly constraining the shape of an ultimate theory. The method of thought-experimentation can also yield significant rewards, as we will see. Finally, the fact that we are searching for a *fundamental* theory means that we can appeal to such nonempirical constraints as simplicity, homogeneity, and the like in developing a theory. We must seek to systematize the information we have, to extend it as far as possible by careful analysis, and then make the inference to the simplest possible theory that explains the data while remaining a plausible candidate to be part of the fundamental furniture of the world.

Such theories will always retain an element of speculation that is not present in other scientific theories, because of the impossibility of conclusive intersubjective experimental tests. Still, we can certainly construct theories that are compatible with the data that

---

[3] Some philosophers argue that even though there is a *conceptual* gap between physical processes and experience, there need be no metaphysical gap, so that experience might in a certain sense still be physical (e.g. Hill 1991; Levine 1983; Loar 1990). Usually this line of argument is supported by an appeal to the notion of *a posteriori* necessity (Kripke 1980). I think that this position rests on a misunderstanding of *a posteriori* necessity, however, or else requires an entirely new sort of necessity that we have no reason to believe in; see Chalmers 1996 (also Jackson 1994; Lewis 1994) for details. In any case, this position still concedes an *explanatory* gap between physical processes and experience. For example, the principles connecting the physical and the experiential will not be derivable from the laws of physics, so such principles must be taken as *explanatorily* fundamental. So even on this sort of view, the explanatory structure of a theory of consciousness will be much as I have described.

we have, and evaluate them in comparison to each other. Even in the absence of intersubjective observation, there are numerous criteria available for the evaluation of such theories: simplicity, internal coherence, coherence with theories in other domains, the ability to reproduce the properties of experience that are familiar from our own case, and even an overall fit with the dictates of common sense. Perhaps there will be significant indeterminacies remaining even when all these constraints are applied, but we can at least develop plausible candidates. Only when candidate theories have been developed will we be able to evaluate them.

A nonreductive theory of consciousness will consist of a number of *psychophysical principles*, principles connecting the properties of physical processes to the properties of experience. We can think of these principles as encapsulating the way in which experience arises from the physical. Ultimately, these principles should tell us what sort of physical systems will have associated experiences, and for the systems that do, they should tell us what sort of physical properties are relevant to the emergence of experience, and just what sort of experience we should expect any given physical system to yield. This is a tall order, but there is no reason why we should not get started.

In what follows, I present my own candidates for the psychophysical principles that might go into a theory of consciousness. The first two of these are *nonbasic principles* — systematic connections between processing and experience at a relatively high level. These principles can play a significant role in developing and constraining a theory of consciousness, but they are not cast at a sufficiently fundamental level to qualify as truly basic laws. The final principle is a candidate for a *basic principle* that might form the cornerstone of a fundamental theory of consciousness. This principle is particularly speculative, but it is the kind of speculation that is required if we are ever to have a satisfying theory of consciousness. I can present these principles only briefly here; I argue for them at much greater length in Chalmers 1996.

1. The principle of structural coherence

This is a principle of coherence between the *structure of consciousness* and the *structure of awareness*. Recall that 'awareness' was used earlier to refer to the various functional phenomena that are associated with consciousness. I am now using it to refer to a somewhat more specific process in the cognitive underpinnings of experience. In particular, the contents of awareness are to be understood as those information contents that are accessible to central systems, and brought to bear in a widespread way in the control of behaviour. Briefly put, we can think of awareness as *direct availability for global control*. To a first approximation, the contents of awareness are the contents that are directly accessible and potentially reportable, at least in a language-using system.

Awareness is a purely functional notion, but it is nevertheless intimately linked to conscious experience. In familiar cases, wherever we find consciousness, we find awareness. Wherever there is conscious experience, there is some corresponding information in the cognitive system that is available in the control of behaviour, and available for verbal report. Conversely, it seems that whenever information is available for report and for global control, there is a corresponding conscious experience. Thus, there is a direct correspondence between consciousness and awareness.

The correspondence can be taken further. It is a central fact about experience that it has a complex structure. The visual field has a complex geometry, for instance. There are also relations of similarity and difference between experiences, and relations in such things as relative intensity. Every subject's experience can be at least partly characterized and decomposed in terms of these structural properties: similarity and difference relations, perceived location, relative intensity, geometric structure, and so on. It is also a central fact that to each of these structural features, there is a corresponding feature in the information-processing structure of awareness.

Take colour sensations as an example. For every distinction between colour experiences, there is a corresponding distinction in processing. The different phenomenal colours that we experience form a complex three-dimensional space, varying in hue, saturation, and intensity. The properties of this space can be recovered from information-processing considerations: examination of the visual systems shows that waveforms of light are discriminated and analysed along three different axes, and it is this three-dimensional information that is relevant to later processing. The three-dimensional structure of phenomenal colour space therefore corresponds directly to the three dimensional structure of visual awareness. This is precisely what we would expect. After all, every colour distinction corresponds to some reportable information, and therefore to a distinction that is represented in the structure of processing.

In a more straightforward way, the geometric structure of the visual field is directly reflected in a structure that can be recovered from visual processing. Every geometric relation corresponds to something that can be reported and is therefore cognitively represented. If we were given only the story about information-processing in an agent's visual and cognitive system, we could not *directly* observe that agent's visual experiences, but we could nevertheless infer those experiences' structural properties.

In general, any information that is consciously experienced will also be cognitively represented. The fine-grained structure of the visual field will correspond to some fine-grained structure in visual processing. The same goes for experiences in other modalities, and even for nonsensory experiences. Internal mental images have geometric properties that are represented in processing. Even emotions have structural properties, such as relative intensity, that correspond directly to a structural property of processing; where there is greater intensity, we find a greater effect on later processes. In general, precisely because the structural properties of experience are accessible and reportable, those properties will be directly represented in the structure of awareness.

It is this isomorphism between the structures of consciousness and awareness that constitutes the principle of structural coherence. This principle reflects the central fact that even though cognitive processes do not conceptually entail facts about conscious experience, consciousness and cognition do not float free of one another but cohere in an intimate way.

This principle has its limits. It allows us to recover structural properties of experience from information-processing properties, but not all properties of experience are structural properties. There are properties of experience, such as the intrinsic nature of a sensation of red, that cannot be fully captured in a structural description. The very intelligibility of inverted spectrum scenarios, where experiences of red and green are inverted but all structural properties remain the same, show that structural properties constrain experience without exhausting it. Nevertheless, the very fact that we feel compelled to leave structural properties unaltered when we imagine experiences inverted between functionally identical systems shows how central the principle of structural coherence is to our conception of our mental lives. It is not a *logically* necessary principle, as after all we can imagine all the information processing occurring without any experience at all, but it is nevertheless a strong and familiar constraint on the psychophysical connection.

The principle of structural coherence allows for a very useful kind of indirect explanation of experience in terms of physical processes. For example, we can use facts about neural processing of visual information to indirectly explain the structure of colour space. The facts about neural processing can entail and explain the structure of awareness; if we take the coherence principle for granted, the structure of experience will also be explained. Empirical investigation might even lead us to better understand the structure of awareness within animals, shedding indirect light on Nagel's vexing question of what it is like to be a bat. This principle provides a natural interpretation of much existing work on the explanation of consciousness (e.g. Clark 1992, Hardin 1992 on colours; Akins 1993 on bats), although it is often appealed to inexplicitly. It is so familiar that it is taken for granted by almost everybody, and is a central plank in the cognitive explanation of consciousness.

The coherence between consciousness and awareness also allows a natural interpretation of work in neuroscience directed at isolating the *substrate* (or the *neural correlate*) of consciousness. Various specific hypotheses have been put forward. For example, Crick and Koch (1990) suggest that 40-hertz oscillations may be the neural correlate of consciousness, whereas Libet (1993) suggests that temporally-extended neural activity is central. If we accept the principle of coherence, the most *direct* physical correlate of consciousness is awareness: the process whereby information is made directly available for global control. The different specific hypotheses can be interpreted as empirical suggestions about how awareness might be achieved. For example, Crick and Koch suggest that 40-Hz oscillations are the gateway by which information is integrated into working memory and thereby made available to later processes. Similarly, it is natural to suppose that Libet's temporally extended activity is relevant precisely because only that sort of activity achieves global availability. The same applies to other suggested correlates such as the 'global workspace' of Baars (1988), the 'high-quality representations' of Farah (1994), and the 'selector inputs to action systems' of Shallice (1972). All these can be seen as hypotheses about the *mechanisms of awareness*: the mechanisms that perform the function of making information directly available for global control.

Given the coherence between consciousness and awareness, it follows that a mechanism of awareness will itself be a correlate of conscious experience. The question of just *which* mechanisms in the brain govern global availability is an empirical one; perhaps there are many such mechanisms. But if we accept the coherence principle, we have reason to believe that the processes that *explain* awareness will at the same time be part of the *basis* of consciousness.

2. *The principle of organizational invariance*

This principle states that any two systems with the same fine-grained *functional organization* will have qualitatively identical experiences. If the causal patterns of neural organization were duplicated in silicon, for example, with a silicon chip for every neuron and the same patterns of interaction, then the same experiences would arise. According to this principle, what matters for the emergence of experience is not the specific physical makeup of a system, but the abstract pattern of causal interaction between its components. This principle is controversial, of course. Some (e.g. Searle 1980) have thought that consciousness is tied to a specific biology, so that a silicon isomorph of a human need not be conscious. I believe that the principle can be given significant support by the analysis of thought-experiments, however.

Very briefly: suppose (for the purposes of a *reductio ad absurdum*) that the principle is false, and that there could be two functionally isomorphic systems with different experiences. Perhaps only one of the systems is conscious, or perhaps both are conscious but they have different experiences. For the purposes of illustration, let us say that one system is made of neurons and the other of silicon, and that one experiences red where the other experiences blue. The two systems have the same organization, so we can imagine gradually transforming one into the other, perhaps replacing neurons one at a time by silicon chips with the same local function. We thus gain a spectrum of intermediate cases, each with the same organization, but with slightly different physical makeup and slightly different experiences. Along this spectrum, there must be two systems *A* and *B* between which we replace less than one tenth of the system, but whose experiences differ. These two systems are physically identical, except that a small neural circuit in *A* has been replaced by a silicon circuit in *B*.

The key step in the thought-experiment is to take the relevant neural circuit in *A*, and install alongside it a causally isomorphic silicon circuit, with a switch between the two. What happens when we flip the switch? By hypothesis, the system's conscious experiences will change; from red to blue, say, for the purposes of illustration. This follows from the fact that the system after the change is essentially a version of *B*, whereas before the change it is just *A*.

But given the assumptions, there is no way for the system to *notice* the changes! Its causal organization stays constant, so that all of its functional states and behavioural dispositions stay fixed. As far as the system is concerned, nothing unusual has happened. There is no room for the thought, 'Hmm! Something strange just happened!' In general, the structure of any such thought must be reflected in processing, but the structure of processing remains constant here. If there were to be such a thought it must float entirely free of the system and would be utterly impotent to affect later processing. (If it affected later processing, the systems would be functionally distinct, contrary to hypothesis.) We might even flip the switch a number of times, so that experiences of red and blue dance back and forth before the system's 'inner eye'. According to hypothesis, the system can never notice these 'dancing qualia'.

This I take to be a *reductio* of the original assumption. It is a central fact about experience, very familiar from our own case, that whenever experiences change significantly and we are paying attention, we can notice the change; if this were not to be the case, we would be led to the sceptical possibility that our experiences are dancing before our eyes all the time. This hypothesis has the same status as the possibility that the world was created five minutes ago: perhaps it is logically coherent, but it is not plausible. Given the extremely plausible assumption that changes in experience correspond to changes in processing, we are led to the conclusion that the original hypothesis is impossible, and that any two functionally isomorphic systems must have the same sort of experiences. To put it in technical terms, the philosophical hypotheses of 'absent qualia' and 'inverted qualia', while logically possible, are empirically and nomologically impossible.[4]

There is more to be said here, but this gives the basic flavour. Once again, this thought experiment draws on familiar facts about the coherence between consciousness and cognitive processing to yield a strong conclusion about the relation between physical structure and experience. If the argument goes through, we know that the only physical properties directly relevant to the emergence of experience are *organizational* properties. This acts as a further strong constraint on a theory of consciousness.

3. The double-aspect theory of information

The two preceding principles have been *nonbasic* principles. They involve high-level notions such as 'awareness' and 'organization', and therefore lie at the wrong level to constitute the fundamental laws in a theory of consciousness. Nevertheless, they act as strong constraints. What is further needed are *basic* principles that fit these constraints and that might ultimately explain them.

The basic principle that I suggest centrally involves the notion of *information*. I understand information in more or less the sense of Shannon (1948). Where there is information, there are *information states* embedded in an *information space*. An information space has a basic structure of *difference* relations between its elements, characterizing the ways in which different elements in a space are similar or different, possibly in complex ways. An information space is an abstract object, but following Shannon we can see information as *physically embodied* when there is a space of distinct physical states, the differences between which can be transmitted down some causal pathway. The states that are transmitted can be seen as themselves constituting an information space. To borrow a phrase from Bateson (1972), physical information is a *difference that makes a difference*.

The double-aspect principle stems from the observation that there is a direct isomorphism between certain physically embodied information spaces and certain *phenomenal* (or experiential) information spaces. From the same sort of observations that went into the principle of structural coherence, we can note that the differences between phenomenal states have a structure that corresponds directly to the differences embedded in physical processes; in particular, to those differences that make a difference down certain causal pathways implicated in global availability and control. That is, we can find the

---

[4] Some may worry that a silicon isomorph of a neural system might be impossible for technical reasons. That question is open. The invariance principle says only that *if* an isomorph is possible, then it will have the same sort of conscious experience.

same abstract information space embedded in physical processing and in conscious experience.

This leads to a natural hypothesis: that information (or at least some information) has two basic aspects, a physical aspect and a phenomenal aspect. This has the status of a basic principle that might underlie and explain the emergence of experience from the physical. Experience arises by virtue of its status as one aspect of information, when the other aspect is found embodied in physical processing.

This principle is lent support by a number of considerations, which I can only outline briefly here. First, consideration of the sort of physical changes that correspond to changes in conscious experience suggests that such changes are always relevant by virtue of their role in constituting *informational changes* — differences within an abstract space of states that are divided up precisely according to their causal differences along certain causal pathways. Second, if the principle of organizational invariance is to hold, then we need to find some fundamental *organizational* property for experience to be linked to, and information is an organizational property *par excellence*. Third, this principle offers some hope of explaining the principle of structural coherence in terms of the structure present within information spaces. Fourth, analysis of the cognitive explanation of our *judgments* and *claims* about conscious experience — judgments that are functionally explainable but nevertheless deeply tied to experience itself — suggests that explanation centrally involves the information states embedded in cognitive processing. It follows that a theory based on information allows a deep coherence between the explanation of experience and the explanation of our judgments and claims about it.

Wheeler (1990) has suggested that information is fundamental to the physics of the universe. According to this 'it from bit' doctrine, the laws of physics can be cast in terms of information, postulating different states that give rise to different effects without actually saying what those states *are*. It is only their position in an information space that counts. If so, then information is a natural candidate to also play a role in a fundamental theory of consciousness. We are led to a conception of the world on which information is truly fundamental, and on which it has two basic aspects, corresponding to the physical and the phenomenal features of the world.

Of course, the double-aspect principle is extremely speculative and is also underdetermined, leaving a number of key questions unanswered. An obvious question is whether *all* information has a phenomenal aspect. One possibility is that we need a further constraint on the fundamental theory, indicating just what *sort* of information has a phenomenal aspect. The other possibility is that there is no such constraint. If not, then experience is much more widespread than we might have believed, as information is everywhere. This is counterintuitive at first, but on reflection I think the position gains a certain plausibility and elegance. Where there is simple information processing, there is simple experience, and where there is complex information processing, there is complex experience. A mouse has a simpler information-processing structure than a human, and has correspondingly simpler experience; perhaps a thermostat, a maximally simple information processing structure, might have maximally simple experience? Indeed, if experience is truly a fundamental property, it would be surprising for it to arise only every now and then; most fundamental properties are more evenly spread. In any case, this is very much an open question, but I believe that the position is not as implausible as it is often thought to be.

Once a fundamental link between information and experience is on the table, the door is opened to some grander metaphysical speculation concerning the nature of the world. For example, it is often noted that physics characterizes its basic entities only *extrinsically*, in terms of their relations to other entities, which are themselves characterized extrinsically, and so on. The intrinsic nature of physical entities is left aside. Some argue that no such intrinsic properties exist, but then one is left with a world that is pure causal flux (a pure flow of information) with no properties for the causation to relate. If one allows that intrinsic properties exist, a natural speculation given the above is that the intrinsic properties of the physical — the properties that causation ultimately relates — are themselves phenomenal properties. We might say that phenomenal properties are the internal aspect of information. This could answer a concern about the causal relevance of experience — a natural worry, given a picture on which the physical domain is causally closed, and on which experience is supplementary to the physical. The informational view allows us to understand how experience might have a subtle kind of causal relevance in virtue of its status as the intrinsic aspect of the physical. This metaphysical speculation is probably best ignored for the purposes of developing a scientific theory, but in addressing some philosophical issues it is quite suggestive.

VIII: Conclusion

The theory I have presented is speculative, but it is a candidate theory. I suspect that the principles of structural coherence and organizational invariance will be planks in any satisfactory theory of consciousness; the status of the double-aspect theory of information is much less certain. Indeed, right now it is more of an idea than a theory. To have any hope of eventual explanatory success, it will have to be specified more fully and fleshed out into a more powerful form. Still, reflection on just what is plausible and implausible about it, on where it works and where it fails, can only lead to a better theory.

Most existing theories of consciousness either deny the phenomenon, explain something else, or elevate the problem to an eternal mystery. I hope to have shown that it is possible to make progress on the problem even while taking it seriously. To make further progress, we will need further investigation, more refined theories, and more careful analysis. The hard problem is a hard problem, but there is no reason to believe that it will remain permanently unsolved.

Further Reading

The problems of consciousness have been widely discussed in the recent philosophical literature. For some conceptual clarification of the various problems of consciousness, see Block 1995, Nelkin 1993 and Tye 1995. Those who have stressed the difficulties of explaining experience in physical terms include Hodgson 1988, Jackson 1982, Levine 1983, Lockwood 1989, McGinn 1989, Nagel 1974, Seager 1991, Searle 1992, Strawson 1994 and Velmans 1991, among others. Those who take a reductive approach include Churchland 1995, Clark 1992, Dennett 1991, Dretske 1995, Kirk 1994, Rosenthal 1996 and Tye 1995. There have not been many attempts to build detailed nonreductive theories in the literature, but see Hodgson 1988 and Lockwood 1989 for some thoughts in that direction. Two excellent collections of recent articles on consciousness are Block, Flanagan and Güzeldere 1996 and Metzinger 1995.

References

Akins, K. (1993), 'What is it like to be boring and myopic?' in *Dennett and his Critics*, ed. B. Dahlbom (Oxford: Blackwell).

Allport, A. (1988), 'What concept of consciousness?' in (eds.) *Consciousness in Contemporary Science*, ed. A. Marcel and E. Bisiach (Oxford: Oxford University Press).

Baars, B.J. (1988), *A Cognitive Theory of Consciousness* (Cambridge: Cambridge University Press).

Bateson, G. (1972), *Steps to an Ecology of Mind* (Chandler Publishing).

Block, N. (1995), 'On a confusion about the function of consciousness', *Behavioral and Brain Sciences*, in press.

Block, N, Flanagan, O. and Güzeldere, G. (eds. 1996), *The Nature of Consciousness: Philosophical and Scientific Debates* (Cambridge, MA: MIT Press).

Chalmers, D.J. (1996), *The Conscious Mind* (New York: Oxford University Press).

Churchland, P.M. (1995), *The Engine of Reason, The Seat of the Soul: A Philosophical Journey into the Brain* (Cambridge, MA: MIT Press).

Clark, A. (1992), *Sensory Qualities* (Oxford: Oxford University Press).

Crick, F. and Koch, C. (1990), 'Toward a neurobiological theory of consciousness', *Seminars in the Neurosciences*, **2**, pp. 263–75.

Crick, F. (1994), *The Astonishing Hypothesis: The Scientific Search for the Soul* (New York: Scribners).

Dennett, D.C. (1991), *Consciousness Explained* (Boston: Little, Brown).

Dretske, F.I. (1995), *Naturalizing the Mind* (Cambridge, MA: MIT Press).

Edelman, G. (1989), *The Remembered Present: A Biological Theory of Consciousness* (New York: Basic Books).

Farah, M.J. (1994), 'Visual perception and visual awareness after brain damage: a tutorial overview', in *Consciousness and Unconscious Information Processing: Attention and Performance 15*, ed. C. Umilta and M. Moscovitch (Cambridge, MA: MIT Press).

Flohr, H. (1992), 'Qualia and brain processes', in *Emergence or Reduction?: Prospects for Nonreductive Physicalism*, ed. A. Beckermann, H. Flohr, and J. Kim (Berlin: De Gruyter).

Hameroff, S.R. (1994), 'Quantum coherence in microtubules: a neural basis for emergent consciousness?', *Journal of Consciousness Studies*, **1**, pp. 91–118.

Hardin, C.L. (1992), 'Physiology, phenomenology, and Spinoza's true colors', in *Emergence or Reduction?: Prospects for Nonreductive Physicalism*, ed. A. Beckermann, H. Flohr, and J. Kim (Berlin: De Gruyter).

Hill, C.S. (1991), *Sensations: A Defense of Type Materialism* (Cambridge: Cambridge University Press).

Hodgson, D. (1988), *The Mind Matters: Consciousness and Choice in a Quantum World* (Oxford: Oxford University Press).

Humphrey, N. (1992), *A History of the Mind* (New York: Simon and Schuster).

Jackendoff, R. (1987), *Consciousness and the Computational Mind* (Cambridge, MA: MIT Press).

Jackson, F. (1982), 'Epiphenomenal qualia', *Philosophical Quarterly*, **32**, pp. 127–36.

Jackson, F. (1994), 'Finding the mind in the natural world', in *Philosophy and the Cognitive Sciences*, ed. R. Casati, B. Smith, and S. White (Vienna: Hölder-Pichler-Tempsky).

Kirk, R. (1994), *Raw Feeling: A Philosophical Account of the Essence of Consciousness* (Oxford: Oxford University Press).

Kripke, S. (1980), *Naming and Necessity* (Cambridge, MA: Harvard University Press).

Levine, J. (1983), 'Materialism and qualia: the explanatory gap', *Pacific Philosophical Quarterly*, **64**, pp. 354–61.

Lewis, D. (1994), 'Reduction of mind', in *A Companion to the Philosophy of Mind*, ed. S. Guttenplan (Oxford: Blackwell).

Libet, B. (1993), 'The neural time factor in conscious and unconscious events', in *Experimental and Theoretical Studies of Consciousness* (Ciba Foundation Symposium 174), ed. G.R. Block and J. Marsh (Chichester: John Wiley and Sons).

Loar, B. (1990), 'Phenomenal states', *Philosophical Perspectives*, **4**, pp. 81–108.

Lockwood, M. (1989), *Mind, Brai, and the Quantum* (Oxford: Blackwell).

McGinn, C. (1989), 'Can we solve the mind–body problem?', *Mind*, **98**, pp. 349–66.

Metzinger, T. (ed. 1995), *Conscious Experience* (Exeter: Imprint Academic).

Nagel, T. (1974), 'What is it like to be a bat?', *Philosophical Review*, **4**, pp. 435–50.

Nelkin, N. (1993), 'What is consciousness?', *Philosophy of Science*, **60**, pp. 419–34.

Newell, A. (1990), *Unified Theories of Cognition* (Cambridge, MA: Harvard University Press).

Penrose, R. (1989), *The Emperor's New Mind* (Oxford: Oxford University Press).

Penrose, R. (1994), *Shadows of the Mind* (Oxford: Oxford University Press).

Rosenthal, D.M. (1996), 'A theory of consciousness', in *The Nature of Consciousness*, ed. N. Block, O. Flanagan, and G. Güzeldere (Cambridge, MA: MIT Press).

Seager, W.E. (1991), *Metaphysics of Consciousness* (London: Routledge).

Searle, J.R. (1980), 'Minds, brains and programs', *Behavioral and Brain Sciences*, **3**, pp. 417–57.

Searle, J.R. (1992), *The Rediscovery of the Mind* (Cambridge, MA: MIT Press).

Shallice, T. (1972), 'Dual functions of consciousness', *Psychological Review*, **79**, pp. 383–93.

Shannon, C.E. (1948), 'A mathematical theory of communication', *Bell Systems Technical Journal*, **27**, pp. 379–423.

Strawson, G. (1994), *Mental Reality* (Cambridge, MA: MIT Press).

Tye, M. (1995), *Ten Problems of Consciousness* (Cambridge, MA: MIT Press).

Velmans, M. (1991), 'Is human information-processing conscious?' *Behavioral and Brain Sciences*, **14**, pp. 651–69.

Wheeler, J.A. (1990), 'Information, physics, quantum: the search for links', in *Complexity, Entropy, and the Physics of Information*, ed. W. Zurek (Redwood City, CA: Addison-Wesley).

Wilkes, K.V. (1988), '— , Yishi, Duh, Um and consciousness', in *Consciousness in Contemporary Science*, ed. A. Marcel and E. Bisiach (Oxford: Oxford University Press).

Deflationary
Perspectives

Daniel C. Dennett

Facing Backwards on the Problem of Consciousness

The strategy of divide and conquer is usually an excellent one, but it all depends on how you do the carving. Chalmers' attempt to sort the 'easy' problems of consciousness from the 'really hard' problem is not, I think, a useful contribution to research, but a major misdirector of attention, an illusion-generator. How could this be? Let me describe two somewhat similar strategic proposals, and compare them to Chalmers' recommendation.

1. The hard question for vitalism

Imagine some vitalist who says to the molecular biologists:

> The easy problems of life include those of explaining the following phenomena: reproduction, development, growth, metabolism, self-repair, immunological self-defence . . . These are not all *that* easy, of course, and it may take another century or so to work out the fine points, but they are easy compared to the really hard problem: life itself. We can imagine something that was capable of reproduction, development, growth, metabolism, self-repair and immunological self-defence, but that wasn't, you know, *alive*. The residual mystery of life would be untouched by solutions to all the easy problems. In fact, when I read your accounts of life, I am left feeling like the victim of a bait-and-switch.

This imaginary vitalist just doesn't see how the solution to all the easy problems amounts to a solution to the imagined hard problem. Somehow this vitalist has got under the impression that being alive is something over and above all these subsidiary component phenomena. I don't know what we can do about such a person beyond just patiently saying: your exercise in imagination has misfired; you can't imagine what you say you can, and just saying you can doesn't cut any ice. (Dennett, 1991, p. 281–2.)

2. The hard question for Crock

Francis Crick (1994) gives us an example of what happens when you adopt Chalmers' distinction, when he says, at the close of his book on consciousness. 'I have said almost nothing about qualia — the redness of red — except to brush it to one side and hope for

This paper was originally published in the *Journal of Consciousness Studies*, **3**, No.1 (1996), pp. 4–6.

the best.' (p. 256.) But consider what would be wrong with the following claim made by an imaginary neuroscientist (Crock) substituting 'perception' for 'qualia' in the quotation from Crick: 'I have said almost nothing about perception — the actual analysis and comprehension of the visual input — except to brush it to one side and hope for the best.' Today we can all recognize that whatever came before Crock's declaration would be forlorn, because not so many years ago this was a mistake that brain scientists actually made: they succumbed all too often to the temptation to treat vision as if it were television — as if it were simply a matter of getting 'the picture' from the eyes to the screen somewhere in the middle where it could be handsomely reproduced so that the phenomena of appreciation and analysis could then get underway. Today we realize that the analysis — the whatever you want to call it that composes, in the end, all the visual understanding — begins right away, on the retina; if you postpone consideration of it, you misdescribe how vision works. Crock has made a mistake: he has created an artifactual 'hard' problem of perception, not noticing that it evaporates when the piecemeal work on the easy problems is completed.

Is it similarly a mistake for Crick, following Chalmers, to think that he can make progress on the easy questions of consciousness *without in the process answering the hard question*? I think so (Dennett, 1991). I make the parallel claim about the purported 'subjective qualities' or 'qualia' of experience: if you don't begin breaking them down into their (functional) components from the outset, and distributing them throughout your model, you create a monster — an imaginary dazzle in the eye of a Cartesian homunculus (Dennett, 1995).

Chalmers has not yet fallen in either of these traps — not quite. He understands that he must show how his strategic proposal differs from these, which he recognizes as doomed. He attempts this by claiming that consciousness is strikingly unlike life, and unlike the features of perception misconstrued by Crock: when it comes to consciousness, the hard problem is 'almost unique' in that it 'goes *beyond* problems about the performance of functions.' *Almost* unique? He gives us no other phenomena with this special feature, but in any case, what he says in support of this claim simply repeats the claim in different words (p.12):

> To see this, note that when we have explained the performance of all the cognitive and behavioural functions in the vicinity of experience . . . there may still remain a further unanswered question: *Why is the performance of these functions accompanied by experience?* A simple explanation of the functions leaves this question open.

Our vitalist can surely ask the same dreary question: Why is the performance of these functions accompanied by life? Chalmers says that this would be a conceptual mistake on the part of the vitalist, and I agree, but he needs to defend his claim that his counterpart is not a conceptual mistake as well.

When he confronts the vitalist parallel head-on, he simply declares that whereas vitalist scepticism was driven by doubts about whether physical mechanisms could 'perform the many remarkable functions associated with life', it is otherwise with his scepticism:

> With experience, on the other hand, physical explanation of the functions is not in question. The key is instead the *conceptual* point that the explanation of functions does not suffice for the explanation of experience. (p. 18.)

I submit that he is flatly mistaken in this claim. Whether people realize it or not, it is precisely the 'remarkable functions associated with' consciousness that drive them to wonder about how consciousness could possible reside in a brain. In fact, if you carefully *dis*sociate all these remarkable functions from consciousness — *in your own, first-person case* — there is nothing left for you to wonder about.

What impresses *me* about my own consciousness, as I know it so intimately, is my delight in some features and dismay over others, my distraction and concentration, my unnamable sinking feelings of foreboding and my blithe disregard of some perceptual details, my obsessions and oversights, my ability to conjure up fantasies, my inability to hold more than a few items in consciousness at a time, my ability to be moved to tears by a vivid recollection of the death of a loved one, my inability to catch myself in the act of framing the words I sometimes say to myself, and so forth. These are *all* 'merely' the 'performance of functions' or the manifestation of various complex dispositions to perform functions. In the course of making an introspective catalogue of evidence, I wouldn't know what I was thinking about if I couldn't identify them for myself by these functional differentia. Subtract them away, and nothing is left beyond a weird conviction (in some people) that there is some ineffable residue of 'qualitative content' bereft of all powers to move us, delight us, annoy us, remind us of anything.

Chalmers recommends a parallel with physics, but it backfires. He suggests that a theory of consciousness should 'take experience itself as a fundamental feature of the world, alongside mass, charge, and space-time.' As he correctly notes, 'No attempt is made [by physicists] to explain these features in terms of anything simpler,' but they do cite the independent evidence that has driven them to *introduce* these fundamental categories. Chalmers needs a similar argument in support of his proposal, but

> when we ask what data are driving him to introduce this concept, the answer is disappointing: It is a belief in a fundamental phenomenon of 'experience'. The introduction of the concept does not do any explanatory work. The evidential argument is circular. (Roberts, 1995, fn 8.)

We can see this by comparing Chalmers' proposal with yet one more imaginary non-starter: *cutism*, the proposal that since some things are just plain cute, and other things aren't cute at all — you can just see it, however hard it is to describe or explain — we had better postulate *cuteness* as a fundamental property of physics alongside mass, charge and space–time. (Cuteness is *not* a functional property, of course; I can imagine somebody who wasn't actually cute at all but who nevertheless functioned exactly as if cute — trust me.) Cutism is in even worse shape than vitalism. Nobody would have taken vitalism seriously for a minute if the vitalists hadn't had a set of independently describable phenomena — of reproduction, metabolism, self-repair and the like — that their postulated fundamental life-element was hoped to account for. Once these phenomena were otherwise accounted for, vitalism fell flat, but at least it had a project. Until Chalmers gives us an *independent* ground for contemplating the drastic move of adding 'experience' to mass, charge, and space–time, his proposal is one that can be put on the back burner.

References

Chalmers, David (1995), 'Facing up to the problem of consciousness', *Journal of Consciousness Studies*, **2** (3), pp. 200–19 (reprinted in this volume).

Crick, Francis (1994), *The Astonishing Hypothesis: The Scientific Search for the Soul* (New York: Scribners).

Dennett, Daniel (1991), *Consciousness Explained* (Boston, MA: Little, Brown & Co.).

Dennett, Daniel (1995), 'Our vegetative soul' — review of Damasio, *Descartes' Error*, in *Times Literary Supplement*, August 25, 1995, pp. 3–4.

Roberts, John (1995), 'Qualia and animal consciousness', Center for Cognitive Studies working paper, 1995-#1, Tufts University (unpublished).

Patricia Smith Churchland

The Hornswoggle Problem

I: Introduction

Conceptualizing a problem so we can ask the right questions and design revealing experiments is crucial to discovering a satisfactory solution to the problem. Asking where animal spirits are concocted, for example, turns out not to be the right question to ask about the heart. When Harvey asked instead, 'How much blood does the heart pump in an hour?', he conceptualized the problem of heart function very differently. The reconceptualization was pivotal in coming to understand that the heart is really a pump for circulating blood; there are no animal spirits to concoct. My strategy here,[1] therefore, is to take the label, 'The Hard Problem' in a constructive spirit — as an attempt to provide a useful conceptualization concerning the very nature of consciousness that could help steer us in the direction of a solution. My remarks will focus mainly on whether in fact anything positive is to be gained from the 'hard problem' characterization, or whether that conceptualization is counterproductive.

I cannot hope to do full justice to the task in short compass, especially as this characterization of the problem of consciousness has a rather large literature surrounding it. The watershed articulation of this view of the problem is Thomas Nagel's classic paper 'What is it like to be a bat?' (1974) In his opening remarks, Nagel comes straight to the point: 'Consciousness is what makes the mind–body problem really intractable.' Delineating a contrast between the problem of consciousness and all other mind–body problems, Nagel asserts: 'While an account of the physical basis of mind must explain many things, this [conscious experience] appears to be the most difficult.' Following Nagel's lead, many other philosophers, including Frank Jackson, Saul Kripke, Colin McGinn, John Searle, and most recently, David Chalmers, have extended and developed Nagel's basic idea that consciousness is not tractable neuroscientifically.

Although I agree that consciousness is, certainly, *a* difficult problem, difficulty *per se* does not distinguish it from oodles of other neuroscientific problems. Such as how the brains of homeotherms keep a constant internal temperature despite varying external conditions. Such as the brain basis for schizophrenia and autism. Such as why we dream and sleep. Supposedly, something sets consciousness apart from *all* other macro-function

[1] This paper was originally published in the *Journal of Consciousness Studies*, **3**, No.5/6 (1996), pp. 402–8. It is based on a talk presented by the author at the 'Tuscon II' conference, 'Toward a Science of Consciousness' held at Tucson, Arizona, in April 1996. Many thanks are owed to the organizers of the meeting, and thanks also to Paul Churchland, David Rosenthal, Rodolfo Llinás, Michael Stack, Dan Dennett, Ilya Farber and Joe Ramsay for advice and ideas.

brain riddles such that it stands alone as The Hard Problem. As I have tried to probe precisely what that is, I find my reservations multiplying.

II: Carving Up the Problem Space

The-Hard-Problem label invites us to adopt a principled empirical division between consciousness (the hard problem) and problems on the 'easy' (or perhaps hard but not Hard?) side of the ledger. The latter presumably encompass problems such as the nature of short-term memory, long-term memory, autobiographical memory, the nature of representation, the nature of sensori-motor integration, top-down effects in perception — not to mention such capacities as attention, depth perception, intelligent eye movement, skill acquisition, planning, decision-making, and so forth. On the other side of the ledger, all on its own, stands consciousness — a uniquely hard problem.

My lead-off reservation arises from this question: what is the rationale for drawing the division exactly there? Dividing off consciousness from all of the so-called 'easy prob-lems' listed above implies that we could understand all those phenomena and still not know *what it was for* . . . what? The 'qualia-light' to go on? ? Is *that* an insightful conceptualization? What exactly is the evidence that we could explain all the 'easy' phenomena and still not understand the neural mechanisms for consciousness? (Call this the 'left-out' hypothesis.) That someone can *imagine* the possibility is not *evidence* for the real possibility. It is only evidence that somebody or other *believes* it to be a possibility. That, on its own, is not especially interesting. Imaginary evidence, needless to say, is not as interesting as real evidence, and what needs to be produced is some real evidence.[2]

The left-out hypothesis — that consciousness would still be a mystery, even if we could explain all the easy problems — is dubious on another count: it begs the question against those theories that are exploring the possibility that functions such as attention and short-term memory are crucial elements in the consciousness (see especially Crick, 1994; P.M. Churchland, 1995). The rationale sustaining this approach stems from observations such as that awake persons can be unaware of stimuli to which they are not paying attention, but can become aware those stimuli when attention shifts. There is a vast psychological literature, and a nontrivial neuroscientific literature, on this topic. Some of it powerfully suggests that attention and awareness are pretty closely connected. The approach might of course be wrong, for it is an empirical conjecture. But if it is wrong, it is wrong because of the *facts*, not because of an arm-chair definition. The trouble with

[2] As I lacked time in my talk at Tucson to address the 'Mary' problem, a problem first formulated by Frank Jackson in 1982, let me make several brief remarks about it here. In sum, Jackson's idea was that there could exist someone, call her Mary, who knew everything there was to know about how the brain works but still did not know what it was to see the colour green (suppose she lacked 'green cones' , to put it crudely). This possibility Jackson took to show that qualia are therefore not explainable by science. The main problem with the argument is that to experience green qualia, certain wiring has to be in place in Mary's brain, and certain patterns of activity have to obtain and since, by Jackson's own hypothesis, she does not have that wiring, then presumably the relevant activity patterns in visual cortex are not caused and she does not experience green. Who would expect her visual cortex — V4, say — would be set ahumming just by virtue of her *propositional* (linguistic) knowledge about activity patterns in V4? Not me, anyhow. She can have propositional knowledge via other channels, of course, including the knowledge of what her own brain lacks *vis à vis* green qualia. Nothing whatever follows about whether science can or cannot explain qualia.

the 'hard problem' characterization is that *on the strength of a proprietary definition*, it rejects them as wrong. I do find that unappealing, since the nature of consciousness is an empirical problem, not problem that can be untangled by semantic gerrymandering.

What drives the left-out hypothesis? Essentially, a thought-experiment, which roughly goes as follows: we can conceive of a person, like us in all the aforementioned easy-to-explain capacities (attention, short term memory, etc.), but lacking qualia. This person would be *exactly* like us, save that he would be a Zombie — an anaqualiac, one might say. Since the scenario is conceivable, it is possible, and since it is possible, then whatever consciousness is, it is explanatorily independent of those activities.[3]

I take this argument to be a demonstration of the feebleness of thought-experiments. *Saying* something is possible does not thereby guarantee it *is* a possibility, so how do we know the anaqualiac idea is really possible? To insist that it must be is simply to beg the question at issue. As Francis Crick has observed, it might be like saying that one can imagine a possible world where gases do not get hot, even though their constituent molecules are moving at high velocity. As an argument against the empirical identification of temperature with mean molecular KE, the thermodynamic thought-experiment is feebleness itself.

Is the problem on the 'hard' side of the ledger sufficiently well-defined to sustain the division as a fundamental empirical principle? Although it is easy enough to agree about the presence of qualia in certain prototypical cases, such as the pain felt after a brick has fallen on a bare foot, or the blueness of the sky on a sunny summer afternoon, things are less clear-cut once we move beyond the favoured prototypes. Some of our perceptual capacities are rather subtle, as, for example, positional sense is often claimed to be. Some philosophers, e.g. Elizabeth Anscombe, have actually opined that we can know the position of our limbs without any 'limb-position' qualia. As for me, I am inclined to say I do have qualitative experiences of where my limbs are — it feels different to have my fingers clenched than unclenched, even when they are not visible. The disagreement itself, however, betokens the lack of consensus once cases are at some remove from the central prototypes.

Vestibular system qualia are yet another non-prototypical case. Is there something 'vestibular-y' it feels like to have my head moving? To know which way is up? Whatever the answer here, at least the answer is not glaringly obvious. Do eye movements have eye-movement qualia? Some maybe do, and some maybe do not. Are there 'introspective qualia', or is introspection just paying attention to perceptual qualia and talking to yourself? Ditto, plus or minus a bit, for self-awareness. Thoughts are also a bit problematic in the qualia department. Some of my thoughts seem to me to be a bit like talking to myself and hence like auditory imagery but some just come out of my mouth as I am talking to someone or affect decisions without ever surfacing as a bit of inner dialogue. None of this is to deny the pizzazz of qualia in the prototypical cases. Rather, the point is just that prototypical cases give us only a *starting point* for further investigation, and nothing like a full characterization of the class to which they belong.

My suspicion with respect to The Hard Problem strategy is that it seems to take the class of conscious experiences to be much better defined than it is. The point is, if you

---

[3] Something akin to this was argued by Saul Kripke in the 1970's.

are careful to restrict your focus to the prototypical cases, you can easily be hornswoggled into assuming the class is well-defined. As soon as you broaden your horizons, troublesome questions about fuzzy boundaries, about the connections between attention, short term memory and awareness, are present in full, what-do-we-do-with-*that* glory.

Are the easy problems known to be easier than The Hard Problem? Is the hard/easy division grounded in fact? To begin with, it is important to acknowledge that for none of the so-called 'easy' problems, do we have an understanding of their solution (see the partial list on p. 38). It is just false that we have anything approximating a comprehensive theory of sensori-motor control or attention or short-term memory or long-term memory. Consider one example. A signature is recognizably the same whether signed with the dominant or non-dominant hand, with the foot, with the mouth or with the pen strapped to the shoulder. How is 'my signature' represented in the nervous system? How can completely different muscle sets be invoked to do the task, even when the skill was not acquired using those muscles? We do not understand the general nature of motor representation.

Notice that it is not merely that we are lacking details, albeit important details. The fact is, we are lacking important conceptual/theoretical ideas about how the nervous system performs fundamental functions — such as time management, such as motor control, such as learning, such as information retrieval. We do not understand the role of back projections, or the degree to which processing is organized hierarchically. These are genuine puzzles, and it is unwise to 'molehill' them in order to 'mountain' up the problem of consciousness. Although quite a lot is known at the cellular level, the fact remains that how real neural networks work and how their output properties depend on cellular properties still abounds with nontrivial mysteries. Naturally I do not wish to minimize the progress that has been made in neuroscience, but it is prudent to have a cautious assessment of what we really do not yet understand.

Carving the explanatory space of mind–brain phenomena along the hard and the easy line, as Chalmers proposes, poses the danger of inventing an explanatory chasm where there really exists just a broad field of ignorance. It reminds me of the division, deep to medieval physicists, between sublunary physics (motion of things below the level of the moon) and superlunary physics (motion of things above the level of the moon). The conviction was that sublunary physics was tractable, and it is essentially based on Aristotelian physics. Heavy things fall because they have gravity, and fall to their natural place, namely the earth, which is the centre of the universe. Things like smoke have levity, and consequently they rise, *up* being their natural place. Everything in the sublunary realm has a 'natural place', and that is the key to explaining the behaviour of sublunary objects. Superlunary events, by contrast, we can neither explain nor understand, but in any case, they have neither the gravity nor levity typical of sublunary things.

This old division was not without merit, and it did entail that events such as planetary motion and meteors were considered unexplainable in terrestrial terms, but probably were divinely governed. Although I do not know that Chalmers' easy/hard distinction will prove ultimately as misdirected as the sublunary/superlunary distinction, neither do I know it is any more sound. What I do suspect, however, is that it is much too early in the science of nervous systems to command much credence.

The danger inherent in embracing the distinction as a principled empirical distinction is that it provokes the intuition that only a real humdinger of a solution will suit The Hard

Problem. Thus the idea seems to go as follows: the answer, if it comes at all, is going to have to come from somewhere Really Deep — like quantum mechanics — or perhaps it requires a whole new physics. As the lone enigma, consciousness surely cannot be just a matter of a complex dynamical system doing its thing. Yes, there are emergent properties from nervous systems such as co-ordinated movement as when an owl catches a mouse, but consciousness (the hard problem) is an emergent property like unto no other. Consequently, it will require a very deep, very radical solution. That much is evident sheerly from the hardness of The Hard Problem.

I confess I cannot actually see that. I do not know anything like enough to see how to solve either the problem of sensori-motor control or the problem of consciousness. I certainly cannot see enough to know that one problem will, and the other will not, require a Humdinger solution.

III: Using Ignorance as a Premise

In general, what substantive conclusions can be drawn when science has not advanced very far on a problem? Not much. One of the basic skills we teach our philosophy students is how to recognize and diagnose the range of nonformal fallacies that can undermine an ostensibly appealing argument: what it is to beg the question, what a *non sequitur* is, and so on. A prominent item in the fallacy roster is *argumentum ad ignorantiam* — argument from ignorance. The canonical version of this fallacy uses ignorance as the key premise from which a substantive conclusion is drawn. The canonical version looks like this:

> We really do not understand much about a phenomenon *P*. (Science is largely ignorant about the nature of *P*.)

> Therefore: we *do* know that:

> (1) *P* can never be explained, or
> (2) Nothing science could ever discover would deepen our understanding of *P*, or
> (3) *P* can never be explained in terms of properties of kind *S*.

In its canonical version, the argument is obviously a fallacy: none of the tendered conclusions follow, not even a little bit. Surrounded with rhetorical flourish, much brow furrowing and hand-wringing, however, versions of this argument can hornswoggle the unwary.

From the fact that we do not know something, nothing very interesting follows — we just don't know. Nevertheless, the temptation to suspect that our ignorance is telling us something positive, something deep, something metaphysical or even radical, is ever-present. Perhaps we like to put our ignorance in a positive light, supposing that but for the Profundity of the phenomenon, we *would* have knowledge. But there are many reasons for not knowing, and the specialness of the phenomenon is, quite regularly, not the real reason. I am currently ignorant of what caused an unusual rapping noise in the woods last night. Can I conclude it must be something special, something unimaginable, something . . . alien . . . other-worldly? Evidently not. For all I can tell now, it might merely have been a raccoon gnawing on the compost bin. Lack of evidence for something is just that: lack of evidence. It is not positive evidence for something else, let alone something of a humdingerish sort. That conclusion is not very glamorous perhaps, but when ignorance is a premise, that is about all you can grind out of it.

Now if neuroscience had progressed as far on the problems of brain function as molecular biology has progressed on transmission of hereditary traits, then of course we would be in a different position. But it has not. The only thing you can conclude from the fact that attention is mysterious, or sensori-motor integration is mysterious, or that consciousness is mysterious, is that we do not understand the mechanisms.

Moreover, the mysteriousness of a problem is not a fact about the problem, it is not a metaphysical feature of the universe — it is an epistemological fact about *us*. It is about where we are in current science, it is about what we can and cannot understand, it is about what, given the rest of our understanding, we can and cannot imagine. It is not a property of the problem itself.

It is sometimes assumed that there can be a valid transition from 'we cannot now explain' to 'we can never explain' , so long as we have the help of a subsidiary premise, namely, 'I cannot *imagine* how we could ever explain . . .' But it does *not* help, and this transition remains a straight-up application of argument from ignorance. Adding 'I cannot imagine explaining *P*' merely adds a psychological fact about the speaker, from which again, nothing significant follows about the nature of the phenomenon in question. Whether we can or cannot imagine a phenomenon being explained in a certain way is a psychological fact about us, not an objective fact about the nature of the phenomenon itself. To repeat: it is an epistemological fact about what, given our current knowledge, we can and cannot understand. It is not a metaphysical fact about the nature of the reality of the universe.

Typical of vitalists generally, my high school biology teacher argued for vitalism thus: I cannot *imagine* how you could get living things out of dead molecules. Out of bits of proteins, fats, sugars — how could life itself emerge? He thought it was obvious from the sheer mysteriousness of the matter that it could have no solution in biology or chemistry. He assumed he could tell that it would require a Humdinger solution. Typical of lone survivors, a passenger of a crashed plane will say: I cannot imagine how I alone could have survived the crash, when all other passengers died instantly. Therefore God must have plucked me from the jaws of death.

Given that neuroscience is still very much in its early stages, it is actually not a very interesting fact that someone or other cannot imagine a certain kind of explanation of some brain phenomenon. Aristotle could not imagine how a complex organism could come from a fertilized egg. That of course was a fact about Aristotle, not a fact about embryogenesis. Given the early days of science (500 BC), it is no surprise that he could not imagine what it took many scientists hundreds of years to discover. I cannot imagine how ravens can solve a multi-step problem in one trial, or how temporal integration is achieved, or how thermoregulation is managed. But this is a (*not very interesting*) psychological fact about me. One could, of course, use various rhetorical devices to make it seem like an interesting fact about me, perhaps by emphasizing that it is a really really hard problem; but if we are going to be sensible about this, it is clear that my inability to imagine how thermoregulation works is *au fond*, pretty boring.

The 'I-cannot-imagine' gambit suffers in another way. Being able to imagine an explanation for *P* is a highly open-ended and under-specified business. Given the poverty of delimiting conditions of the operation, you can pretty much rig the conclusion to go whichever way your heart desires. Logically, however, that flexibility is the kiss of death.

Suppose someone claims that she *can* imagine the mechanisms for sensori-motor integration in the human brain but *cannot* imagine the mechanisms for consciousness. What exactly does this difference amount to? Can she imagine the former in *detail*? No, because the details are not known. What is it, precisely, that she can imagine? Suppose she answers that in a very general way she imagines that sensory neurons interact with interneurons that interact with motor neurons, and via these interactions, sensori-motor integration is achieved. Now if that is all 'being able to imagine' takes, one might as well say one can imagine the mechanisms underlying consciousness. Thus: 'The interneurons do it.' The point is this: if you want to contrast being able to imagine brain mechanisms for attention, short term memory, planning etc., with being unable to imagine mechanisms for consciousness, you have to do more that say you can imagine neurons doing one but cannot imagine neurons doing the other. Otherwise one simply begs the question.

To fill out the point, consider several telling examples from the history of science. Before the turn of the twentieth century, people thought that the problem of the precession of the perihelion of Mercury was essentially trivial. It was annoying, but ultimately, it would sort itself out as more data came in. With the advantage of hindsight, we can see that assessing this as an easy problem was quite wrong — it took the Einsteinian revolution in physics to solve the problem of the precession of the perihelion of Mercury. By contrast, a really hard problem was thought to be the composition of the stars. How could a sample ever be obtained? With the advent of spectral analysis, that turned out to be a readily solvable problem. When heated, the elements turn out to have a kind of fingerprint, easily seen when light emitted from a source is passed through a prism.

Consider now a biological example. Before 1953, many people believed, on rather good grounds actually, that in order to address the copying problem (transmission of traits from parents to offspring), you would first have to solve the problem of how proteins fold. The former was deemed a much harder problem than the latter, and many scientists believed it was foolhardy to attack the copying problem directly. As we all know now, the basic answer to the copying problem lay in the base-pairing of DNA, and it was solved first. Humbling it is to realize that the problem of protein folding (secondary and tertiary) is *still* not solved. *That*, given the lot we now know, does seem to be a hard problem.

What is the point of these stories? They reinforce the message of the argument from ignorance: from the vantage point of ignorance, it is often very difficult to tell which problem is harder, which will fall first, what problem will turn out to be more tractable than some other. Consequently our judgments about relative difficulty or ultimate tractability should be appropriately qualified and tentative. Guesswork has a useful place, of course, but let's distinguish between blind guesswork and educated guesswork, and between guesswork and confirmed fact. The philosophical lesson I learned from my biology teacher is this: when not much is known about a topic, don't take terribly seriously someone else's heartfelt conviction about what problems are scientifically tractable. Learn the science, do the science, and see what happens.

References

Chalmers, David (1995), 'Facing up to the problem of consciousness', *Journal of Consciousness Studies*, **2** (3), pp. 200–19 (reprinted in this volume).

Churchland, Paul M. (1995), *The Engine of Reason; The Seat of the Soul* (Cambridge, MA: MIT Press).

Crick, Francis (1994), *The Astonishing Hypothesis* (New York: Scribner and Sons).

Jackson, Frank (1982), 'Epiphenomenal qualia', *Philosophical Quarterly*, **32**, pp. 127–36.

Nagel, Thomas (1974), 'What is it like to be a bat?', *Philosophical Review*, **83**, pp.435–50.

Thomas W. Clark

Function and Phenomenology: Closing the Explanatory Gap

To truly explain consciousness, we must find a convincing place for it in the natural world and ultimately in the scientific description of that world as expressed in physical, biological, and information theory. The default assumption when undertaking an explanation of consciousness should be that there is nothing ontologically special about it, nothing which sets it apart from the rest of nature as we presently conceive it. In his keynote paper, 'Facing Up to the Problem of Consciousness', David Chalmers assumes much the opposite: subjectivity is something more than the naturally evolved neural processes which seem likely, given the available evidence, to instantiate it. Qualitative consciousness — qualia or phenomenal experience — is said to 'arise from' or 'accompany' or 'emerge from' these processes. This dualism of underlying process versus accompanying subjectivity creates the 'explanatory gap' that so worries Chalmers and other philosophers: why should subjectivity arise from some processes and not others? My claim is that the central mystery about qualitative consciousness supposedly in need of explanation is an artifact generated by this presupposition about its nature — that it is an 'effect' of an underlying process — and it is precisely this that we must question if we are to find the true place of consciousness in the world.

My strategy will be first to show that Chalmers' initial assumption about consciousness compromises widely held methodological canons of scientific theory construction that he himself avows. Next, I will suggest some reasons why this assumption has gained such currency, despite its serious shortcomings. In parts three and four, using the principles of Chalmers' theory of consciousness as discussion points, I will sketch an alternative picture, that subjectivity *is* certain sorts of physical, functional, informationally rich, and behaviour controlling (cybernetic) processes. Interestingly, Chalmers does much to support this picture in the latter part of his paper. Only the assumption that qualitative experience somehow *arises from* such functional processes prevents him from reaching the conclusion that I will defend here, that experience is identical to them. It is the elucidation of this (proposed) identity by the empirical investigation of what precisely these processes do — in contrast to unconscious processes — that will eventually constitute a robust explanation of consciousness. On this picture, there is no question needing an answer about why just these processes give rise to consciousness, since indeed it never 'arises' or 'emerges' at all. Consciousness is what we consist of as physically instantiated subjects, not something extra that our brains create.

I

The hard problem of consciousness, according to Chalmers, is that of experience. 'It is widely agreed that experience arises from a physical basis, but we have no good explanation of why and how it so arises. Why should physical processing give rise to a rich inner life at all? It seems objectively unreasonable that it should, and yet it does' (p. 11). Here, at the very outset, a specific conception of consciousness sets the stage for the rest of Chalmers' investigation. On this widely held view, experience emerges out of and accompanies certain neural functions, but is assumed not to be identical to these functions. The pressing question thus becomes, as Chalmers puts it, *'Why is the perform-ance of these functions accompanied by experience?'* (p. 12, original emphasis). If experience is taken to be something over and above neurally instantiated functions, something extra which accompanies them, the 'central mystery' of consciousness be-comes the 'explanatory gap . . . between function and experience.' (Levine 1993 takes more or less the same position, pp. 130–5.) This in turn leads Chalmers to suppose that 'To account for experience, we need an *extra ingredient* in the explanation' (p. 16–17, original emphasis). He despairs of finding an explanation of consciousness within existing scientific theory, since physicalist and functionalist accounts will forever omit this extra ingredient:

> For any physical process we specify there will be an unanswered question: Why should this process give rise to experience? Given any such process, it is conceptu-ally coherent that it could be instantiated in the absence of experience. It follows that no mere account of the physical process will tell us why experience arises. The emergence of experience goes beyond what can be derived from physical theory. (p. 18)

Of course, it is conceptually coherent that experience might be absent in the presence of certain physical, functional processes, *but only on the assumption that they may not be, and probably are not, identical.* But this is precisely the fundamental issue that must not be prejudged. As David Cole has pointed out recently,

> When a critic [of functionalism] supposes that there could be, 'ex hypothesi,' a system that instantiates the functional architecture yet fails to have the experience, the critic is 'ex hypothesis' supposing that any functionalist theory is false. To simply suppose that the theory is false is question begging, and cannot be the basis of an adequate *argument* against functionalism. (1994, p. 297, original emphasis.)

If we begin our investigation into the nature of consciousness with Chalmers' picture in mind – the picture of experience 'arising from' (hence not identical to) functional neural processes — naturally we will be led to doubt that functional explanations can fully account for experience. But the burden is on Chalmers to justify his starting point and its implicit dualism, the dualism that leads him to suppose that there must be an 'extra ingredient' in any explanation of qualitative consciousness which goes beyond descriptions of functions and physical processes. As Francis Crick observed recently, 'Whether there is something extra remains to be seen' (Crick, 1994 p. 12). Why, if we are conducting a more or less scientifically motivated investigation of a phenomenon, should we begin by assuming that this phenomenon is probably not of a piece with the rest of nature as we currently conceive it? The natural starting point, on the contrary, is to assume parsimoniously that we need *not* add experience, as Chalmers recommends we do, to our 'fundamental' ontological categories. Generally, we shouldn't posit as fundamental that which we are seeking to explain. Instead, we should start with what seems clearly a simpler and more straightforward hypothesis, namely that experience is identical to certain neurally instantiated cybernetic functions. The way is then open to understand consciousness by empirical investigation of whatever functions are found to correlate with experience. Such an explanation would best embody the virtues of 'simplicity, elegance, and even beauty' that Chalmers cites as hallmarks of good theory.

Chalmers says that it is 'a *conceptual* point that the explanation of functions does not suffice for the explanation of experience' (p. 18, original emphasis), but again this is a conceptual point only under the particular initial conception of experience that Chalmers adopts, a conception that in effect assumes a *conclusion* about the nature of consciousness that although widely accepted, can hardly serve as a methodologically sound starting point. After all, the basic explanatory motive in science and philosophy is to incorporate heretofore inexplicable phenomena into an existing theoretical framework, modifying the framework only as minimally necessary to effect the incorporation. This motive is defeated by assuming at the very start that consciousness is a phenomenon that transcends the explanatory reach of existing theory.

The debate about where to begin in explaining consciousness can thus be framed as a competition between powerful and widespread intuitions that there is something 'extra' about consciousness in need of explanation and commitments to standard scientific explanatory practice. I suggest that we are better off allied with the latter than the former, and that the history of successful science is on my side. It is not that the identity of phenomenal consciousness and cognitive function is obviously true, since if it were we'd all be functionalists. Upon further investigation it may turn out (although I doubt it) that experience does not correlate with any particular set of functions, or that in some essential respect it floats free of any physical or functional property. I am only arguing that it is methodologically more circumspect to start off with a simpler hypothesis, one which does not posit a special nature or essence of subjectivity to be explained.

For some, this may appear to prejudge the issue in the opposite direction, since it seems to deny the existence of the explanandum itself, at least in the form they are used to conceptualizing it. But my suggestion is only that we remain open about the nature of consciousness as the investigation gets underway, and that our starting hypothesis be shaped by methodological constraints, not by concepts or intuitions motivating the supposition, *at the start of the investigation*, that there likely exist fundamental properties or entities not already included in naturalistic theories.

II

What is so compelling about Chalmers' picture of subjectivity that it tends to override methodological considerations? That is, what leads many philosophers, scientists, and humanists to *strongly* doubt, at the outset, that qualitative consciousness might simply be identical to certain types of functional organization and hence suppose that it is some sort of contingent effect or accompaniment? This is a different question from asking why they might *merely* doubt that such an identity holds true. The answer to the latter, of course, is simply that the identity of phenomenal experience (qualia) and cognitive function is not obvious, and should be subject to the same legitimate methodological scepticism accorded any other hypothesis. But the answer to the former lies in appreciating the effect of several distinct trends in our philosophical tradition, some general and some specific, which bias our intuitions about the nature of consciousness against the possibility of identity.

First and perhaps foremost is the residual, and by now mostly subliminal, grip of Cartesianism on basic assumptions about mental life in general. This influence leads us to regard talk of the mental not just as a useful, predictive, 'intentional stance' (Dennett 1987) sort of discourse, but as talk that refers to an independent, or at least parallel realm which interacts with or accompanies physical processes. Pain, pleasure, perceptions, emotions, thoughts, beliefs, and other mental phenomena present themselves as a related set of states and events which for everyday predictive purposes seem virtually autonomous from the physical and functional (or, to use Dennett's typology, the physical and design stances). We need not ordinarily bring in physicalist or functionalist talk in order to get by in the interpersonal world, so it is unsurprising that the commonsense assumption about the autonomy — and hence the ontological separateness — of the mental still generates a philosophical bias despite the best efforts of many philosophers to uproot it.

I am not suggesting that dualism (of either substance or properties) is a priori untenable, although it has well-known difficulties, but only making the uncontroversial point that our philosophical tradition has been heavily influenced by Cartesian intuitions about the ontological divide between the mental and the physical, intuitions reinforced by ordinary mentalistic discourse. Thus when it comes to choosing a picture of consciousness to start our investigations (and we have to choose some picture, after all) we may well be biased in favour of one which puts consciousness in the autonomous realm of the mental, even if only in a rather subtle, sophisticated way. Chalmers' statements to the effect that certain neural processes 'give rise' to qualia constitute exactly such a picture, one which splits the mental from the physical/functional and which takes consciousness to be some sort of unextended, non-spatial property that likely eludes currently available scientific explanations. The resulting 'naturalistic dualism' Chalmers defends is Cartesian at its core, and despite his claim that such a position is 'entirely compatible with the scientific view of the world,' dualisms have fared badly as science proceeds to unify our conception of humankind in nature.

Another factor strengthening the intuition that qualia emerge from physical or functional processes is the supposition that there most likely exists a clear demarcation between those sorts of states likely to 'carry' phenomenal consciousness and those that don't. Qualia could well be absent in systems that are as smart as we are, but that are differently organized or instantiated, or so it is often supposed. (See, for instance, Flanagan, 1992, pp. 129–52 for a recent defence of this thesis.) Block's Chinese nation and Searle's Chinese room thought experiments trade on the intuition (although it begs the question against functionalism) that bizarre cognitive systems, however functional in real time, couldn't possibly constitute subjects (Block, 1978; Searle, 1980). Once the wedge is driven between function and qualia (or, as in Searle's paper, between function and intentionality) in the bizarre cases, the stage is then set to suppose that qualia are only a contingent accompaniment to cognition, even in systems functionally very similar to us. Likewise, it seems plausible to many that qualitative states are probably absent in systems that fall short of the functional *complexity* given to humans and (perhaps) the higher animals. Although the line of demarcation is obscure in both cases, the basic assumption is that if a system fails to be sufficiently like *us* in some respect — in its physical instantiation or functional design — then the chances are it's not a subject; it doesn't produce or give rise to qualitative states.

If only a certain class of cognitive or functional processes (those more or less like ours) are taken as plausible correlates of subjectivity, this reinforces the notion that something special about those processes produces subjectivity as an 'effect,' whether epiphenomenal or efficacious. Consciousness emerges only at a certain level of complexity, or only out of a certain type of functional design, or only as the product of a certain type of physical instantiation. Drawing a line in advance between systems which are thought to be likely candidates for consciousness and those that are not pushes us towards the picture of subjectivity as a contingent accompaniment to functional processes.

There is, of course, a good deal of anthropocentrism in drawing the line where those convinced by absent qualia thought experiments have placed it. But this may appear a reasonable prejudice, given that it seems we can only be certain of the existence of qualitative states from the single example of human experience. Surely it would be irresponsible as a starting assumption to grant qualia to just any old cognitive system, say a horsefly, a frog, or Hal of *2001*. Perhaps. But there is a difference, I suggest, between this sort of methodological conservatism (which in general I support) and the uncritical acceptance of the 'similarity to ourselves' criterion as a benchmark for assigning consciousness to a system. To turn the issue around, why should we assume, from the one example of human subjectivity, that qualia are *not* present in dissimilar cognitive systems, real or imaginary, that manage well in the world? It is initially at least as plausible, to paraphrase Paul Churchland, that any cognitive system operating at or near our level must contain a 'computational–executive organization' which would be a 'home for qualitative states' (Churchland, 1989, p. 38).[1] And more basically, why assume that consciousness 'accompanies' or is 'produced by' functional processes in the first place?

In response to the first question, I propose that we remain agnostic about the possible subjectivity of non-human and less complex systems, otherwise the anthropocentric bias

---

[1] Lycan makes somewhat the same point when considering systems that are functionally very much like us: 'Is it really possible to imagine something's sharing *my entire* many-leveled functional organization and still not being conscious in the way that I am?' (1987, p. 24 his emphasis). Of course one can *imagine* this, but the possibility of absent qualia in the face of functional near-equivalence need hardly be the default assumption. Despite intuitions to the contrary, there is no a priori conceptual barrier that separates experience from function.

may blind us to the true nature of consciousness. To the second, the focus of this paper, I propose likewise that we do our best to keep the issue open, not to assume at the outset the non-identity of function and qualia. Since the narrowing of candidates for qualitative subjectivity based on similarity to us suggests that (only a certain class of) cognitive functions *generate* qualia, it can be seen that staying agnostic about the subjectivity of other sorts of systems is a good way to keep this deeper issue open. Qualia may not be generated at all; they may simply *be* certain types of functional organization, the range of which may not be limited to what is familiarly human.

A third factor motivating the 'emergence' picture of qualitative consciousness is that only by having its own, independent existence could it possibly play the important causal role in our lives that it seems to. Involved here are fairly deep and emotional issues of human autonomy and specialness, especially the fear that if consciousness is nothing over and above physically instantiated function, then we lose our privileged status as rational agents riding above the flux of brute causality. As persons, we tend to identify ourselves with our conscious capacities, and moreover tend to believe that we are in some sense in control of these capacities. Consciousness, conceived of as a product of a very restricted class of functional, cognitive processes (ours), generated by a very restricted class of physical objects (human brains), is what crucially distinguishes us from the rest of insensate, mechanistic nature. If it turns out that subjectivity and the sense of self is 'merely' function, then it becomes terrifyingly (for some) clear that no principled distinction may exist between us and a very clever robot, at least on the question of who has 'inner states.' To the extent that we want, unconsciously or consciously, to preserve our special status *vis-à-vis* the robot we may opt for a picture of subjectivity, including qualia, that preserves for it a central causal role and restricts it to creatures very much like us. This picture of consciousness is just what the doctor ordered to keep 'creeping mechanism' at bay. (Dennett 1990 makes this point, pp. 523–4.)

But of course we must not let such fears prejudice our initial conception of consciousness or restrict our investigations. If it turns out (as I propose) that consciousness has no independent causal role over and above the functions which instantiate it, and if such functions could be realized in creatures (or artifacts) quite unlike us in some respects, then the implications of that for our personal and moral status must be dealt with as a separate issue.

I suspect that this same worry also works to make Chalmers' anti-reductionist approach to explaining consciousness an attractive alternative to standard scientific practice. After all, a reductive explanation of subjectivity, one which identifies it with a class of functional processes that are in principle realizable in a wide range of instantiations, obliterates having an inner life as the basis for a special human status. (Others remain, however.) There are good arguments against certain types of facile reductionism, of course, and I don't mean to imply that language referring to belief, intention, feeling, and thought is in any sense eliminable. But as a scientific strategy for unifying knowledge, the reductionist impulse is hardly to be eschewed but rather to be encouraged, one would suppose, and reductionism does not diminish us when we become the objects of knowledge. To 'reduce' mental phenomena to functional processes via some plausibly evidenced identification is, after all, not to eliminate them, but simply to redescribe them from a third person perspective. Why such a redescription might seem threatening is an interesting question for another time.

III

Having adduced some possible explanations (there are undoubtedly others) for why Chalmers' picture of consciousness has such currency, I wish now to defend an alternative, one which I believe is a better candidate for our attention this early in the game. I will argue for the identity of function and consciousness — what I will call the functional identity hypothesis — and as the argument develops, further reasons for doubting that qualia arise from or are produced by functional processes will come to light. (See Lloyd, 1992 for a recommendation to adopt such an identity hypothesis.)

As mentioned earlier, Chalmers has set out some of the preliminary argument for such a position in his paper, and he describes what in my view is the key characteristic of functions likely to instantiate consciousness: their role in representing informational content essential for the control of complex, adaptive behaviour.[2] The basic functional identity hypothesis is that qualitative experiences are what it is to *be* a set of multi-modal, discriminative, representational processes which deploy information for the control of behaviour. I use this extended form of identity expression ('what it is to be') quite deliberately in order to emphasize that we, as experiencing subjects, are *instantiated by* such processes.

To make this point clear, note the similarity, and dissimilarity, of this expression to Nagel's (1974) popular characterization of subjectivity as 'what it is *like* to be' a such-and-such. The difference between the two is not trivial. Nagel's formulation suggests the notion of an inner life which the subject somehow witnesses, or has direct epistemic 'access' to, so that for instance it (and only it) could say what it was *like* to have a particular quale. Nagel's central thesis about subjectivity is that this 'first person perspective' cannot be captured by science. By contrast, the formulation I wish to defend hinges crucially on the proposal that as subjects we are *constituted by* and *identical to* cognitive processes which themselves instantiate qualia, hence qualia are *what it is for us to be* these processes. Under this proposal we can't, finally, say what it's like to have qualia since we don't have a first person perspective on them: we don't 'have' them at all, neither do they 'appear' to us, nor are we 'directly acquainted' with them. We, as subjects, *exist as* them. The ineffability of qualia, among their other properties, is thus a consequence of and explained by the functional identity hypothesis, and qualia generally are not beyond the reach of science. (Part IV will return to these points.)

I believe Chalmers is very much on the right track in what he calls his two 'non-basic' psychophysical principles, although his commitment to the emergence picture of consciousness prevents him from realizing their full explanatory potential. He calls these the principles of 'structural coherence' and 'organizational invariance;' both concern the functional deployment of information in a cognitive system. Structural coherence amounts to the well-established, if not yet completely fleshed out, correspondence

---

[2] Several other philosophers have taken a similar tack, although they still by and large assume some version of the emergence picture. See for instance Flanagan, 1992, pp. 129–52; Van Gulick, 1993 pp. 152–3, and Van Gulick 1980 for discussions of the role of information in conscious processes.

between variable features within a sense modality and the empirically associated covariant neural structure and processing. For instance, the structure of our phenomenal experience of colour corresponds to the structure of the neural state space of our colour processing system (as described by Paul Churchland, 1989, pp. 102–10). There is at least a rough isomorphism between the sort of variability we report in our experience and the organization of neural events associated with this variability.

Chalmers theorizes (correctly, I think) that the *raison d'etre* of cognitive functional processes is to embody informational content which 'is brought to bear in a widespread way in the control of behaviour.' Consciousness, it seems, is usually involved with most, if not all, higher order cognition and behaviour, including memory, anticipation, speech, learning, planning, and complex motor activity. As Flanagan (1992) puts it 'What is consciously accessible is primarily just what we have the most need to know about: conditions in the sensory environment, and past facts, and events' (p. 134). Such knowledge, whether recognitional, propositional, or performative, requires some sort of representational system involving information about the world and the body. All in all, the connection between consciousness, information and behaviour, although not watertight and admitting of exceptions, seems a fruitful line of investigation.[3] The functional identity hypothesis makes a strong claim about this connection: that subjectivity is constituted by those central representational processes which transform and enhance sensory information to the point where it normally dominates in the control of behaviour. (See Van Gulick, 1993, pp. 147–50 for some interesting ideas on what sorts of processes these might be.)

If it is plausible that functional processes correlated with consciousness are primarily informational and behaviour controlling, and if the principle of structural coherence holds, (and so far it seems empirically the case that there exists isomorphism between experience and neural organization), it follows that the structure of qualitative experience mirrors the informational content essential to the control of complex behaviour. The burning question, however, is whether indeed qualia *mirror* the informational content of functional processes as some sort of separate, parallel entities in consciousness, or whether qualia *are* this informational content. Chalmers says, in support of the first position, that 'There are properties of experience, such as the intrinsic nature of a sensation . . . that cannot be captured in a structural description' (p. 23). So although the structure of experience might well be isomorphic to functionally derived informational content, experience itself cannot simply *be* this content, since (he believes) it has additional, non-functional mental properties, such as an intrinsic phenomenal nature. Such mental properties are irreducible to physical or functional properties, which is to say we can't explain them or redescribe them using only physical or functional predicates without leaving out something crucial. As Nagel (1986, p. 15) has expressed it, 'The subjective features of conscious mental processes — as opposed to their physical causes

---

[3] Blindsight experiments seem the obvious counterexamples, since the subject clearly has what Flanagan terms 'informational sensitivity' to objects in the blindfield without 'experiential sensitivity' (a reportable experience) of them (Flanagan, 1992, pp. 147–52). But the very limited sorts of behaviour possible with respect to blindfield objects actually highlights the centrality of consciousness in mediating most of our interaction with the world. These limitations, when compared with normal behaviour, suggest what the special informational functions that instantiate consciousness might be. See Van Gulick, 1993, pp. 147–50 for some speculations about candidate functions.

and effects — cannot be captured by the purified form of thought suitable for dealing with the physical world that underlies the appearances'. The truth of this claim is, of course, the central bone of contention between physicalism and functionalism on one side, and substance and property dualism and dual aspect theories on the other.

In introducing his second principle, that of 'organizational invariance', Chalmers says, 'This principle states that any two systems with the same fine-grained *functional organization* will have qualitatively identical experiences' (p. 25, original emphasis). This seems to contradict his earlier claim that the intrinsic nature of sensory experience is beyond the reach of structural distinctions, that is, beyond what the organizational structure of neural processes can account for. Indeed, organizational invariance comes perilously close, it seems, to *identifying* quality with function (same function, same quality) except that Chalmers continues to insist on the 'emergence of experience' as some sort of entity separate from functional organization.

Chalmers' passing observation that the principle of organizational invariance is 'controversial' is a bit of an understatement, since it is less a principle than a major thesis about the mind. Were it proved, then, as he puts it, 'the only physical properties directly relevant to the emergence of experience [would be] *organizational* properties' (p. 26, original emphasis). If one were to drop the notion of emergence then this would pretty much amount to the hypothesis I want to defend. Experience is up-and-running functional organization, not something emerging out of it; qualia just are *what it is to be* a subject instantiated by a set of informationally rich, discriminative, behaviour-controlling processes, not a separate ontology of intrinsic natures.

Note that in this purified form, such a hypothesis *explains* the principle of structural coherence. That is, the reason the structure of conscious experience so nicely mirrors the informational goings on of neural processes is because they are one and the same, under different descriptions, or very loosely speaking, from different perspectives, first and third person. (As the reader will have noted above, I question the literal accuracy of the expression 'first person perspective' as related to one's experience.) Once we discard the idea of emergence the full explanatory power of the functional identity hypothesis starts to become apparent. And working from the other direction (as I will in part IV below), appreciating the extent to which the identity thesis can account for various mental property ascriptions will make it easier to abandon the picture of emergence as explanatorily superfluous.

Chalmers' third, 'basic' and highly speculative principle sketches a deeper explanation for both structural coherence and organizational invariance, but in the end it seems less explanatory than ontologically inflationary. On this principle information 'is truly fundamental, and . . . has two basic aspects, corresponding to the physical and phenomenal features of the world' (p. 27). The parallel emergence of phenomenal *and* physical properties, then, is attributable to a yet deeper substratum of information. But, to return to an earlier point, it seems premature to hypothesize new fundamental entities (in this case universal 'bits') at the start of an investigation when simpler, less inflationary hypotheses might do as well. Positing an underlying basis of information with two aspects may explain the congruence of experience with informationally contentful neural organization, and may support the notion that similar, information-bearing functions might generate similar phenomenal qualities, but we are then left with the equally difficult task of explaining why information should possess two aspects to begin with. It doesn't help to 'solve' one explanatory problem by creating yet another at a more speculative level, at least not until more economical approaches have been thoroughly explored. It is also worth noting that with this proposal Chalmers has shifted from recommending that we accept *experience* as fundamental (p. 20) to speculating that *information* is fundamental (pp. 26–7). Either way, all the explanatory work still remains to be done.

<h1 style="text-align:center">IV</h1>

I have already suggested how the hypothesis that qualia are identical with higher level functional processes can explain structural coherence: the parallel structure of experience and neural organization is accounted for by supposing, parsimoniously, that experience is to exist as certain types of neural processes. Likewise, the principle of organizational invariance is simply a corollary of the identity hypothesis: two functionally equivalent systems will have the same sorts of qualitative experience because qualia *are* particular informational values within some sort of functional state space, however it may be realized. (Below I will amend this account of phenomenal quality by questioning the reality of the intrinsic, essential nature of qualia.) But these explications will likely seem beside the point for those whose primary intuition about consciousness is precisely that, as Chalmers insists, experience is something over and above functional processes.

To undercut this intuition, and thus make functional identity more appealing as an initial explanatory hypothesis, it will be helpful to consider some of the properties normally attributed to qualia: their privacy, ineffability, and intrinsic nature. The privacy of qualia, the fact that no one but myself can feel the pain that I feel, is relatively easy to explain as a matter of identity. Flanagan describes it thus: '. . . a particular realization [of an experience] will be an experience only for the agent who is causally connected to the realization in the right sort of way . . . [T]he biological integrity of the human body can account straightforwardly for the happy fact that we each have our *own,* and only our own experiences' (p. 94, original emphasis).

I would modify Flanagan's account somewhat: the reason no one else feels my pain, even though they might conceivably have a complete description of its neural instantia- tion, is that only I as a subject *consist* (partially) of that pain. There is no separate agent or subject apart from the sum total of my experience which could be causally connected to pain in the first place, so naturally no one else could stand in that relation to my experience either. That experience is private is thus explained not as a matter of direct epistemic access but as a matter of instantiation: subjectivity consists of a complex array of coordinated, information-bearing neural states, and as a subject I consist of those states, and no one else can so consist. That I can report being in pain is not, therefore, because I perceive pain (as I might perceive a tree or chair) by virtue of a special causal connection to it, but because I subjectively exist as pain — as stimulated C fibers and associated higher level processing — to some extent. (Under torture I might subjectively exist *mostly* as pain and the concomitant terror.)

Why, under the assumption of functional identity, might qualia be ineffable? Very much the same logic applies. The subject, since it consists of an ongoing stream of neurally instantiated experience, is not in a position to witness or observe the basic elements of that experience. We cannot, as it were, step back from and describe a quale as we might an external object; thus we can do no more than *name* basic qualitative experiences ('red', 'hot', 'sweet', etc.) and compare and contrast them to one another. We can't describe the redness of red or painfulness of pain precisely because we can't get a perspective on these qualities. (Again, it is a mistake to suppose that we have a first person point of view of our experience.) They are, so to speak, the counters in the game of perception and so cannot be made the object of play. External particulars, on the other hand, and complex internal states, *are* describable just because they are constituted by ensembles of qualitative elements. Chairs are (sometimes) brown, assume a given shape in my visual field, are hard to the touch, resonant when struck, etc. That the subject is identical to a set of representational processes can thus *explain* why the primitive components of that set, what we call qualia, are descriptively opaque and non-decomposable, that is, ineffable: we can't stand in an epistemic relation to those representational states which we consist of as knowers.

This brings us to the last, and perhaps most central (and controversial) of properties attributed to qualia, the notion that they have an intrinsic phenomenal nature. It is here, many suppose, that functionalist theories must founder, since the essential redness of red or painfulness of pain seem to float free of any functional role. We can imagine red objects looking blue (or imagine they look blue to someone else) without supposing that our (or the other person's) discriminative and behavioural capacities would be in any sense compromised. The essence of red, just because it is a non-decomposable, ineffable primitive, is thought not to be amenable to functional or structural explanation. As Van Gulick puts it: 'No matter how much structural organization we can find in the phenomenal realm and explain neurophysiologically, [the critic of functionalism] will insist that the distinct redness of phenomenal red will not have been captured or explained by our theory' (1993, p. 145). The purported intrinsic phenomenal nature of qualia creates the explanatory gap functionalism is supposed not to be able to fill.

The functional identity hypothesis can, however, meet this burden by supporting a challenge to the intuition that there are determinate phenomenal *facts* about the intrinsic nature of qualia in need of explanation. The challenge, simply put, is to specify what precisely is being claimed to be the case when we point to a patch of red and say our experience is like 'that.' Since there is nothing further we can *say* about the (purported) phenomenal essence of red, there is no way we can link such an essence with a property or state of affairs which specifies or fixes its occurrence, other than to gesture at red objects. Hence, referring to such an essence plays no explanatory or descriptive role in talk about our experiences, and this may begin to cast doubt on whether such an essence exists, even though it may strongly *seem* that it does. The ineffability of qualia, it turns out, could be a clue to their not having a determinate intrinsic nature after all.

The intuition that experiences do indeed have some sort of qualitative essence supports the possibility of inverted or 'alien' qualia, that the intrinsic character of an experience might differ across subjects. My red might be the same as your red, or perhaps not. A Martian's 'red' might even be a radically different sort of experience. But since experience is private, intersubjective comparisons of qualia are of course impossible. If we can never tell, finally, whether another subject's red is the same or different than mine, this might make us further doubt the validity of the notion of intrinsic phenomenal natures. Why, after all, should we take seriously a 'fact' — the 'fact' that my experience of red is possibly like or unlike yours — which is in principle impossible to ascertain? Both the ineffability *and* privacy of qualia, therefore, undermine the plausibility of first person phenomenological facts involving determinate qualitative essences which science cannot capture.

That we can reliably distinguish red from other colours isn't explained by there being an essence of red, a particular quality of redness that, for instance, we might suppose other perceivers of the same red object might or might not be experiencing. The ability to pick out red depends simply on the fact that there exists a range of contrasting colours against which red is distinguished as a *relationally defined* member of that range. This is borne out by the obvious point that every distinguishable bit of red we see is experienced against a background of non-red. If all the world were red, red would drop out as a discriminable property of experience. Imagine Mary, Jackson's colour-deprived neuroscientist, growing up in an environment where everything was red instead of (as originally conceived in the thought experiment) black and white (Jackson, 1982). Could she have a concept of 'first person' red? Not until, I suggest, other colours were introduced into her environment against which red could be reliably distinguished. A monochromatic world of whatever colour is a phenomenally colourless world, not a world in which the single colour could 'declare' itself by an intrinsic phenomenal nature.

A functionalist account of our sensory capacities makes plausible the relational, mutually defined nature of qualitative experience, hence supports the attack on the existence of intrinsic phenomenal essences. As the Churchlands have theorized, sensory state spaces, as realized in neural organization, instantiate a range of possible sensory-informational values within a given modality (vision, hearing, taste, etc.), values which correspond more or less to some range of stimulation from the external world and the body. What distinguishes different values of a given modality is variation along one or more of its component dimensions (three in the case of vision, four in the case of taste), a variation that defines each state of the modality *in relation to* its other states. These states gain their functional significance by virtue of mapping *differences* in stimulation originating from the external world or the body. Hence it is the difference between the neural instantiation of red and the neural instantiation of blue (among other colours) which defines them as distinct qualitative experiences, not that red is instantiated by a particular state that *by itself* defines it as red or that blue is instantiated by a particular state that *by itself* defines it as blue. If, as I hypothesize, we as subjects exist as such sensory modalities (along with other sorts of cognitive processes) the experience of a particular shade of red is just one in an array of possible states of the colour system that gets its qualitative value solely by having a particular *place* in the array. The 'way' red is, what it is 'like,' is simply to exist as a given colour state in contradistinction to other states. There is no need to posit an intrinsic nature of red as separate from its functional role as a placeholder in the neural processing that constitutes the experience of colour, and that, partially, constitutes us as subjects.[4]

---

[4] If one wishes to retain the notion of intrinsic qualitative nature but deny that this defeats functionalism, Paul Churchland offers a way out: admit that such natures exist but insist that 'such intrinsic natures are nevertheless not essential to the type-identity of a given mental state, and may

Conclusions

The foregoing analysis is meant to help undercut the intuition that there are phenomenal facts in need of explanation that cannot be captured by functional facts. The explanatory gap is closed by showing both that the privacy and ineffability of qualia are indeed explained by the functional identity hypothesis, and that their much vaunted intrinsic qualitative nature does not exist, hence needs no explaining. This helps to support the view that qualia are not phenomenal entities that emerge from or arise out of functional processes, but are instead best conceived of as being those processes. This is not to 'quine' qualia out of existence, but simply to identify them with certain sorts of neurally instantiated representational states. Of course, the *meaning* of the terms 'phenomenal consciousness' and 'qualia' is not (presently) identical to the meaning of the expression 'neurally instantiated representational states' and its functionalist and physicalist cousins. But talk about qualitative experience *refers to the same thing* as talk about particular neural processes, although precisely which processes we don't yet know.

I have tried to emphasize the explanatory virtues of the functional identity hypothesis, hoping to win converts to functionalism by showing that it can indeed account for subjectivity. Yet there still might seem a residual, fatal question left unaddressed (the frog grinning up at us from the bottom of Austin's beer mug): why should existing as functional processes of a particular kind be identical to qualitative experience? What is it *about* them that makes them phenomenally conscious, as opposed to unconscious? (This, it will be seen, is Chalmers' original, central question, but posed about identity instead of emergence.) Well, if by 'phenomenally conscious' we insist on meaning 'possessed of a first person, intrinsic, essential nature' then the question stands unanswered, since nothing in functionalism or science will ever show us how to get from physics, chemistry, biology, and cybernetics to consciousness thus defined. The causal and structural aspects of subjectivity might fall to functional explanation, but intrinsic natures will not, since after all, these are custom made to resist assimilation by science. Why? Because scientific explanation works, in part, by showing how the causal relations among elements of a system at one level can account for features at another level. The macroscopic properties of water, for instance, can be explained by the microstructure of water molecules. But since the property of having an intrinsic qualitative nature is defined (by its adherents) as independent of any causal role and as having no structure, no lower level explanation will ever reduce it. As Levine (1993, p. 134) puts it, '[T]o the extent that there is an element in our concept of qualitative character that is not captured by features of its causal role, to that extent it will escape the explanatory net of physicalist reduction.'

I have tried to cast doubt on the conviction that our concept of qualia need include the property of having a factually determinate intrinsic nature independent of function or

---

indeed vary from instance to instance of the same type of mental state'. (1988, p. 39) Of course some would object, for example, that Martian pain couldn't be radically different in its intrinsic nature from our pain and still count as pain. But, the reply comes back, if it played the same functional role why wouldn't we call it pain? My point to both sides, however, is that the impossibility of intersubjective qualia comparison renders this debate undecidable, hence irrelevant. See Shoemaker (1991) for a defence of intrinsic quality compatible with functionalism and Dennett (1990, pp. 538–44) for arguments against the existence of intrinsic properties of qualia.

physical instantiation. It is logically possible that qualia so exist, but there are no good empirical reasons, nor for that matter any good phenomenological reasons, for supposing they do. There are good reasons, on the other hand, for supposing that qualia are instead a matter of the contrast relations among functionally defined, neurally realized representational processes. If such is the case, then the conscious/unconscious distinction lies in whether or not such processes are instantiated. Discovering just which processes constitute phenomenal consciousness is an empirical matter that only neuroscience can answer, by correlating neural states with various conscious capacities.

There may or may not be a clear functional or physical line to be drawn between the conscious and the unconscious, but when we ask *why* a process is conscious we will no longer be wondering why qualitative essences accompany particular neural events. Rather, under the identity hypothesis, we will be asking why that process needs to involve the functions typically operational when we are conscious. The beating of my heart or the (mostly) silent operation of my digestive system obviously need not involve conscious processes, since neither requires the representation of a complex environment, or motivational economy, or set of future contingencies. Short-term memory, on the other hand, is a conscious process *because* it requires those representational capacities only normally available when we are conscious. Some sort of qualitative experience (whether of occurrent thought, feeling, or perception) is necessary as input to the short-term memory system, and such experience is likely to be empirically cashed out as a complex set of discriminative and integrative functions which manage information that serves to control moment-to-moment behaviour. The functional identity hypothesis thus explains why we have subjective experience: qualitative representations are what get the job done.

The functional identity hypothesis proposes no new fundamental classes of entities or properties or features to be added to naturalistic theory, and so has the virtues of simplicity, ontological parsimony, and methodological conservatism. If it turns out that consciousness depends fundamentally on a physical process, e.g., a phase locked 40 hertz neural oscillation, or if, as I suspect, it becomes identified with a rather sophisticated array of informational processes which could be realized by many different physical systems, in neither case will anything radically new be discovered to play an explanatory role (although figuring out the actual workings of the massively recursive networks embodied by the brain may reveal vast new realms of control theory). Of course it is remotely possible that a heretofore unknown fundamental property or entity, whether of experience or information or quantum coherence, may eventually be shown to exist. But asserting its probable existence in advance of strong empirical support and theoretical necessity would be to start off on the wrong foot.

If indeed qualia are identical to certain functional informational processes, then the hard problem of consciousness (what Chalmers more or less takes to be the easy problem) is the empirical one of discovering just what these processes are. Equally hard for many, perhaps, will be dropping the picture that consciousness is something ontologically special *produced by* these processes. Instead, we must get used to the idea that as much as our 'inner' lives seem a categorically different sort of thing than the external world (a world which includes our brains), they are, in fact, just more of that external, physical world which we as subjects happen to be. We must also get used to the idea that consciousness does not have a cognitive or functional role over and above the functions which constitute it, and that any system, artificial or natural, which instantiates such functions will be conscious.

In a sense there is nothing special about consciousness since, if I am right, nothing extra is produced by or emerges out of this set of functions. They just constitute a marvelously complex and adaptive representational system which keeps us out of trouble, more or less. Yet on the other hand, consciousness is indeed special in that these functions, as carried out in our day to day lives, have, as a historical fact, led most of us to suppose that an ontologically separate world of subjectivity exists. It may be that the sorts of higher level cognitive processes which are found to correlate with consciousness inevitably generate (among language users) a self/world model containing the strong intuition that the self and its experience cannot simply be the body, cannot simply be a bit of the world suitably organized. Explaining consciousness satisfactorily will consist in overcoming that intuition, and in placing experience fully within the natural, physical realm.[5]

References

Block, Ned (1978), 'Troubles with functionalism', *Minnesota Studies in the Philosophy of Science*, **IX**, ed. C. Wade Savage (Minneapolis: University of Minnesota Press). Reprinted in Rosenthal 1991, pp. 211–28.

Chalmers, David (1995), 'Facing up to the problem of consciousness', *Journal of Consciousness Studies*, **2** (3), pp. 200–19 (reprinted in this volume).

Churchland, Paul M. (1988), *Matter and Consciousness* (Cambridge, MA and London: MIT Press).

Churchland, Paul M. (1989), *A Neurocomputational Perspective* (Cambridge, MA and London: MIT Press).

Cole, David (1994), 'Thought and qualia', *Minds and Machines*, **4**, pp. 283–302.

Crick, Francis (1994), interview, *Journal of Consciousness Studies*, **I**, pp. 10–17.

Davies, M. and Humphreys, G.W. (eds.1993), *Consciousness* (Oxford and Cambridge, MA: Blackwell).

Dennett, Daniel (1987), *The Intentional Stance* (Cambridge, MA and London: MIT Press).

Dennett, Daniel (1990), 'Quining qualia', in *Consciousness and Contemporary Science*,ed. A. Marcel and E. Bisiach (Oxford: Oxford University Press). Reprinted in Lycan 1990 pp. 519–47.

Flanagan, Owen (1992), *Consciousness Reconsidered* (Cambridge, MA and London: MIT Press).

Jackson, Frank (1982), 'Epiphenomenal qualia', *Philosophical Quarterly*, **32**, pp. 127–36.

Levine, Joseph (1993), 'On leaving out what it's like', in Davies and Humphreys 1993, pp. 121–36.

Lloyd, Daniel (1992), 'Toward an identity theory of consciousness', *Behavioral and Brain Sciences*, **15**, pp. 215–16.

Lycan, William G. (1987), *Consciousness* (Cambridge, MA and London: MIT Press).

Lycan, William (ed. 1990), *Mind and Cognition* (Cambridge, MA: Blackwell).

Nagel, Thomas (1974), 'What is it like to be a bat?', *The Philosophical Review*, **LXXXIII**, 4, pp. 43–50.

Nagel, Thomas (1986), *The View From Nowhere* (New York and Oxford: Oxford University Press).

Rosenthal, David M. (ed. 1991), *The Nature of Mind* (New York: Oxford).

Searle, John (1980), 'Minds, Brains, and Programs', *Behavioral and Brain Sciences*, **3**, pp. 417–57.

Shoemaker, Sydney (1991), 'Qualia and consciousness', *Mind*, **C**, pp. 507–24.

Van Gulick, Robert (1980), 'Functionalism, information and content', *Nature and System*, **2**, Reprinted in Lycan 1990, pp.10–129.

Van Gulick, Robert (1993), 'Understanding the phenomenal mind: are we all just armadillos?', in Davies and Humphreys 1993, pp. 137–54.

[5] I am grateful to Mary Ellen Myhr for a close reading of an earlier draft of this paper, and to the referees for helpful criticisms from which the present version has benefitted. The paper was originally published in the *Journal of Consciousness Studies*, 2, No.3 (1995), pp. 241–54.

Valerie Gray Hardcastle

The Why of Consciousness:
A Non-Issue for Materialists

In my (albeit limited) experience of these matters, I have discovered that there are two sorts of people engaged in the study of consciousness. There are those who are committed naturalists; they believe that consciousness is part of the physical world, just as kings and queens and sealing wax are. It is completely nonmysterious (though it is poorly understood). They have total and absolute faith that science as it is construed today will someday explain this as it has explained the other so-called mysteries of our age.

Others are not as convinced. They might believe that consciousness is part of the natural world, but surely it is completely mysterious (and maybe not physical after all). Thus far, science has little to say about conscious experience because it has made absolutely no progress in explaining *why* we are conscious at all.

Different sceptics draw different morals from their observation. Some conclude that a scientific theory of consciousness is well-nigh impossible; others believe that it is possible, but do not expect anything of value to be immediately forthcoming; still others remain confused and are not sure what to think. (Perhaps unfairly, I put David Chalmers in the last category, as he remarks, 'Why should physical processing give rise to a rich inner life at all? It seems objectively unreasonable that it should, and yet it does.' (p. 11.) His intuition that consciousness is too bizarre to be real, yet still exists anyway illustrates the sentiments of the third category quite nicely. Further, as I discuss below, I think his tentative programme of redoing our basic scientific ontology reflects some basic confusions on his part.)

I have also noticed that these two camps have little to say to one another, for their differences are deep and deeply entrenched. I can't say that I expect to change that fact here. I fall into the former camp. I am a committed materialist and believe absolutely and certainly that empirical investigation is the proper approach in explaining consciousness. I also recognize that I have little convincing to say to those opposed to me. There are few useful conversations; there are even fewer converts.

In this brief essay, I hope to make clearer where the points of division lay. In the first section, I highlight the disagreements between Chalmers and me, arguing that consciousness is not a brute fact about the world. In section II, I point out the fundamental difference between the materialists and the sceptics, suggesting that this difference is not something that further discussion or argumentation can overcome. In the final section, I

This paper was originally published in the *Journal of Consciousness Studies*, **3**, No.1 (1996), pp. 7–13.

outline one view of scientific explanation and conclude that the source of conflict really turns on a difference in the rules each side has adopted in playing the game.

I

In large part, these divergent reactions turn on antecedent views about what counts as explanatory. There are those who are sold on the programme of science. They believe that the way to explain something is to build a model of it that captures at least some of its etiologic history and some of its causal powers. Their approach to explaining consciousness is the same as mine: isolate the causal influences with respect to consciousness and model them (cf. Churchland, 1984; Flanagan, 1992; Hardcastle, 1995; Hardin, 1988).

In contrast, others (e.g. Block, 1995; Chalmers, 1995; McGinn, 1991; Nagel, 1974; Searle, 1992) do not believe that science and its commitment to modelling causal interactions are necessarily the end-all and be-all of explanation. They believe that some things — many things — are explained in terms of physical causes, but qualia may not be. Isolating the causal relations associated with conscious phenomena would simply miss the boat, for there is no way that doing that ever captures the qualitative aspects of awareness. What the naturalists might do is illustrate *when* we are conscious, but that won't explain the *why* of consciousness. The naturalists would not have explained why it is neuronal oscillations (cf. Crick and Koch, 1990), or the activation of episodic memory (cf. Hardcastle, 1995), or an executive processor (cf. Baars, 1988), or whatever, should have a qualitative aspect, and until they do that, they cannot claim to have done anything particularly interesting with consciousness.

To them, I have little to say in defence of naturalism, for I think nothing that I as an already committed naturalist could say would suffice, for we don't agree on the terms of the argument in the first place. Nevertheless, I shall try to say something, if for no other reason than to make the points of disagreement clearer so that informed buyers can chose all the more wisely. Let me sketch in particular the point of conflict between Chalmers and me.

Let us assume a prior and fundamental commitment to materialism. I say that if we are materialists, then we have to believe that consciousness is something physical. Presumably it is something in the brain. If we believe this and we want to know what consciousness is exactly, then we need to isolate the components of the brain or of brain activity that are necessary and sufficient for consciousness. If I understand Chalmers' taxonomy of research programmes correctly, then I am advocating following option five: 'isolate the substrate of experience'. Indeed, it is my contention that pointing out the relevant brain activity conjoined with explaining the structure of experience (his option four) and some functional story about what being conscious buys us biologically (not one of Chalmers' options) would be a complete theory of consciousness. Let us pretend though that I have only completed the first step in this programme and have isolated the substrate of experience. Call this component of the brain C.

Chalmers would reply that though I might have been successful in isolating the causal etiology of consciousness, I have not explained why it is that C should be conscious. Why this? For that matter, why anything? Part of a good explanation, he maintains, is making the identity statement (or whatever) intelligible, plausible, reasonable. I have not done that. Hence, I have not explained the most basic, most puzzling, most difficult question of consciousness. I haven't removed the curiousness of the connection between mind and body. I haven't closed the explanatory gap.

How should I respond? He is, of course, exactly right: scientific theories of consciousness won't explain the weirdness of consciousness to those who find the identity weird. One possible move is to claim that consciousness just being C (or whatever theory you happen to believe) is just a brute fact about the world. That is just the way our universe works. At times, I am sure, it appears that this is what the naturalists are assuming, especially when they dismiss out of hand those overcome by the eeriness of consciousness. This, too, is what Chalmers wants to do with his dual aspect theory: phenomenal qualities are just part and parcel of information. No further explanation needed.

However, this response is too facile. It is true that we accept brute facts about our universe. We believe in things like gravitational attraction and the electromagnetic forces without question. We waste little energy wondering why our universe contains gravity. It just does, and we reason from there. On the other hand, there are other facts about the world that we do not accept as brute. We feel perfectly comfortable expecting an answer to why water is wet. That is not a brute fact. We explain the liquidity of water by appeal to other facts about the world, the molecular structure of water and its concomitant microphysical properties, for example. And these facts are explained in turn by other facts, such as the quantum mechanical structure of the world. Now *these* might be brute facts, but so it goes. (At least this is one popular and rosy view of scientific unity. I shan't defend that here.)

Notice two things. First, the facts we accept as brute are few and basic. Essentially, we accept the most fundamental elements and relations of the universe as given. The rest then depend upon these key ingredients in some fashion. Second, and following from the first observation, it seems highly unlikely that some relatively chauvinistic *biological* fact should ever be brute. For those facts turn on the more fundamental items in the universe. Hence, if one is to claim that consciousness being C is simply a brute fact about the universe, then one is *prima facie* operating with a perverse metaphysics.

Chalmers tries to overcome the latter difficulty by denying that consciousness is biological. However, he has no reason to claim this except that it saves his theory. Considerations of structural coherence and organizational invariance aren't telling because they are generally taken to support material identity. That is, if you find structural isomorphisms between our perceptions and twitches in the brain, then that is taken to be good reason to think that the mind is nothing more than activity in the brain. (What other sort of evidence could you use?) And if you hypothesize that the same 'fine-grained' functional organization supports the same phenomenal experiences, then you are advocating some sort of materialistic functional theory; otherwise the perceptions can diverge even though the functional organization remains the same (cf. Shoemaker, 1975; 1981; see also Lycan, 1987).[1]

The only consideration he brings to bear is the putative 'elegance' of a dual aspect theory. However, when we weigh a suggestion's simplicity and elegance against coun-

---

[1] I find it strange (though not inconsistent) that in the first portion of the paper, Chalmers uses the putative imaginability of inverted qualia as an argument against what he calls 'reductionism' (though to me it is simply a good old fashioned identity theory), yet in discussing constraints on possible theories he argues against the possibility of inverted qualia in support of his proto-theory. He should recognize that if the fine-grainedness of his functional organization is fine-grained enough, then we would be discussing the functional organization of neurons (or action potentials, IPSPs, EPSPs, or what have you), which is all one needs to muster a claim for mind–brain identity.

tervailing data, the data have to win. We already know that not all information has a phenomenal edge to it, insofar as we know quite a bit of our information processing is carried out *un*consciously. Documenting subliminal effects, implicit priming, and re-pressed but effective memories are all cottage industries in psychology, and have been since Freud.[2] Chalmers is either going to have to deny some of the most robust psycho-logical results we have and claim that no information processing is occurring in those cases, or do a 'bait-and-switch' and claim that, contrary to introspective verbal reports, we are conscious of all of those things (we just don't realize it). Neither option is plausible. Chalmers gives us no counter-examples to the mass of psychological evidence, and denying that first person viewpoints can tell us whether we are conscious denies exactly what Chalmers wants to defend. Hence, we are left with the *prima facie* plausible claim that for all cases of consciousness of which we are aware, consciousness is biological.

In any event, I don't want to make the claim consciousness is brute. So what do I say if I think that consciousness is a biological phenomenon?[3] How do I make my identifica-tion of consciousness with some neural activity intelligible to those who find it mysteri-ous? My answer is that I don't. The 'solution' to this vexing difficulty, such as it is, is all a matter of attitude. That is, the problem itself depends on the spirit in which we approach an examination of consciousness.

II

Let us return to the example of water being wet. Consider the following exchange. A water-mysterian wonders why water has this peculiar property. She inquires and you give an explanation of the molecular composition of water and a brief story about the connection between micro-chemical properties and macro-phenomena. Ah, she says, I am a materialist, so I am convinced that you have properly correlated water with its underlying molecular composition. I also have no reason to doubt that your story about the macro-effects of chemical properties to be wrong. But I still am not satisfied, for you have left off in your explanation what I find most puzzling. Why *is* water H_2O? Why couldn't it be XYZ? Why couldn't it have some other radically different chemical story behind it? I can imagine a possible world in which water has all the macro-properties that it has now, but is not composed of H_2O.

Of course, people like Kripke have a ready response to the water-mysterians. 'Water = H_2O' is an identity statement. Hence, you can't really imagine possible worlds in which water is not H_2O because you aren't imagining *water* in those cases (or, you aren't *imagining* properly). As Chalmers would claim, it is a *conceptual truth* about water that it is H_2O. But, to the sceptical and unconvinced, to those who insist that they can imagine honest-to-goodness water not being H_2O, what *can* one say? I think nothing. Water-mysterians are antecedently convinced of the mysteriousness of water and no amount of

---

[2] I take it that these facts are well known. I summarize quite a bit of this research in Hardcastle (1995). Aside from Freud, other important players include Endel Tulving, George Mandler, Anthony Marcel and Daniel Schacter.

[3] Note that claiming that consciousness is biological does not mean that we could not create consciousness artificially. Life is a biological phenomenon too, but that doesn't rule out creating life in test-tubes.

scientific data is going to change that perspective. Either you already believe that science is going to give you a correct identity statement, or you don't and you think that there is always going to be something left over, the wateriness of water.

I doubt there are any such mysterians, so perhaps this is a silly example. Let us now turn to life-mysterians. Consider the following exchange. A life-mysterian wonders why living things have the peculiar property of being alive. She inquires and you give a just-so story about the origin of replicating molecules in primordial soup and wave your hands in the direction of increasing complexity. Ah, she says, I am an evolutionist, so I am convinced that you have properly correlated the history of living things with their underlying molecular composition. I also have no reason to doubt that your story about increasing complexity to be wrong. But I still am not satisfied, for you have left off in your explanation what I find most puzzling, the *aliveness* of life. Why couldn't that be a soul? Why couldn't it have some other radically different evolutionary story behind it, namely, one with God in it? I can imagine a possible world in which living things have all the macro-properties that they have now, but are not comprised of DNA or RNA.

Of course, as Chalmers indicates, we too have a ready response to the life-mysterians. We presume that there is some sort of identity statement for biological life. (Of course, we don't actually have one yet, but for those of us who are not life-mysterians, we feel certain that one is in the offing.) Hence, they can't really imagine possible worlds in which life is not whatever we ultimately discover it to be because they aren't imagining *life* in those cases (or, they aren't *imagining* properly). But, that aside, what *can* we say to those who insist that they can imagine life as requiring an animator? I think nothing. Just getting on with the biological enterprise is perhaps appropriate. Life-mysterians are antecedently convinced of the mysteriousness of life and no amount of scientific data is going to change that perspective. Either you already believe that science is going to give you a correct identity statement, or you don't and you think that there is always going to be something left over, the aliveness of living things.

So what about Chalmers and other consciousness-mysterians? They are no different. They are antecedently convinced of the mysteriousness of consciousness and no amount of scientific data is going to change that perspective. Either you already believe that science is going to give you a correct identity statement, or you don't and you think that there is always going to be something left over, the phenomenal aspects of conscious experience. 'Experience . . . is not *entailed* by the physical.' Chalmers wants to know: 'Why is the performance of these [cognitive] functions *accompanied* by experience?' (p. 12; emphasis mine). Though he does believe that 'experience *arises* one way or another from brain processes,' he thinks that it is a 'conceptual point' that consciousness is not identical to C.

In some sense, of course, I have a ready response to the consciousness-mysterians. Like the water-mysterian and the life-mysterian, consciousness-mysterians need to alter their concepts. To put it bluntly: their failure to appreciate the world as it really is cuts no ice with science. Their ideas are at fault, not the scientific method. Materialists presume that there is some sort of identity statement for consciousness. (Of course, we don't actually have one yet, but for those of us who are not consciousness-mysterians, we feel certain that one is in the offing.) Hence, the sceptics can't really imagine possible worlds in which consciousness is not whatever we ultimately discover it to be because they aren't imagining *consciousness* in those cases (or, they aren't *imagining* properly). But nevertheless, what *can* I say to those who insist that they can imagine consciousness as beyond science's current explanatory capacities? I think nothing, for they can claim that I am conceptually confused as well. Agreeing to disagree is perhaps appropriate.

I suppose we have reached a stand-off of sorts. I say materialism and mechanism entail an identity statement for consciousness, just as we get one for water and we expect one for life. Consciousness is no more mysterious to me than the wetness of water or the aliveness of life. That is to say, I find all of the phenomena interestingly weird, and the identity statements that science produces marvelously curious. But all are on a par. The sceptics do not share my intuitions. So be it. However, I feel no more inclined to try to convince them otherwise than I do trying to convince the religious that souls don't exist. I recognize hopeless projects. Our antecedent intuitions simply diverge too much to engage in a productive dialogue.

III

But perhaps again I am not being fair. The reason water-mysterianism seems implausible is that we are able to embed our understanding of water and H_2O in the sophisticated larger framework of molecular chemistry and sub-atomic physics. We just know an awful lot about how atoms and molecules interact with one another and the corresponding micro- and macro-properties. Life-mysterianism seems implausible to those for whom it seems implausible for similar reasons. We don't know as much about biological history as we do about molecular chemistry, but we do know enough at least to gesture toward a suitable framework in which to embed a decomposition of life. But consciousness might be different. We have far, far to go before we can claim to understand either cognitive or brain processes with any surety. Perhaps there just isn't a suitable larger framework in which to embed an understanding of consciousness; hence, any scientific model we try to construct will appear strained and stilted at best. And perhaps this is what really drives the explanatory gap — we don't yet know what we are talking about when we claim that consciousness is a natural phenomenon.

Suppose this argument is correct (though I am not sure that it is, for reasons I explain below). What follows from it? It can't be that a theory of consciousness is not possible, nor even that consciousness is fundamentally odd. Rather, all we can say is that we have to wait and see what else we learn about the mind and brain before a decomposition and localization of consciousness can be intuitively satisfying. Consciousness might very well be C, but our informed intuitions lag behind.

(An aside: Can we *really* say what would happen if my neural circuits are replaced by silicon isomorphs? Maybe it is reasonable to think that your experiences would not be affected. But, in the same vein, it is reasonable to believe that the world is Euclidean — though it isn't, of course — and it used to be reasonable to burn witches at the stake — though it is no longer. What seems reasonable at first blush often isn't once the parameters of the problem are made sufficiently clear; moreover, our intuitions change as our perspective on the world changes. At present, we simply don't know enough about the explanatory currency of the brain to hypothesize *intelligently* about what will happen if we push on it in various ways. Intuition pumps only work if we have robust and well-founded intuitions in the first place.)

All we can say at this point is that an antecedent commitment to materialism means that an understanding of consciousness will someday be embedded in some larger mind–brain framework. We are just going to have to wait until that time before our intuitions concerning what counts as a satisfactory identification for phenomenal experience will be useful (or even usable).

Nevertheless, though there is a great deal we don't know about the mind and the brain, there is still a lot that we do. Indeed, within the broader framework of currently accepted psychological and neurophysiological theories, we have found striking parallels between our phenomenal experiences and activities in the brain. Chalmers points to some in his paper; others are more basic. E.g. removing area MT is correlated with phenomenal blindness; ablations in various regions of cortex are correlated with inabilities to perceive shapes, colours, motion, objects; lesions surrounding the hippocampus are correlated with the loss of episodic memory.[4] Or, for less invasive results, consider what happens when various chemicals are added to our brains. We decrease pain, increase sensitivity, induce hallucinations, alter moods, and so on. Data such as these should (someday) allow us to locate conscious experiences both within our information processing stream and within the head.

Perhaps more data, better constructed scientific models, and more agreement among the scientists themselves about the details, would alter the intuitions of the sceptics, but I doubt it. For the difference between someone like Chalmers and me is not in the details; it is in how we understand the project of explaining consciousness itself. It is a difference in how we think of scientific inquiry and what we think explanations of consciousness are supposed to do.

Explanations are social creatures. They are designed for particular audiences asking particular questions within a particular historically determined framework. (See van Fraassen, 1980, for more discussion of this point.) Materialists are trying to explain to each other what consciousness is within current scientific frameworks. Their explanations are designed for them. If you don't antecedently buy into this project, including its biases, history, context, central questions, possible answers, and relevant actors, then a naturalist's explanation probably won't satisfy you. It shouldn't. But that is not the fault of the explanation, nor is it the fault of the materialists. If you don't accept the rules, the game won't make any sense. If you do accept the rules, then the explanations will follow because they are designed for you as a member of the relevant community. (This is not to say that you will *agree* with explanations, just that they will seem to be of the right sort of thing required for an answer.) Who's in and who's out is a matter of antecedent self-selection. I opt in; the sceptics opt out. Because we don't agree on the rules, my explanations don't make sense to them, and their explanations don't make sense to me.

Explanation for the cognitive and biological sciences just *is* a matter of uncovering the appropriate parallels between the phenomena and the physical system. Huntington's

---

[4] I note that in each of these cases, there is evidence that such patients still process at least some of the information unconsciously. For example, prosopagnosics claim that they can no longer recognize faces upon visual inspection. However, their galvanic skin response changes in the presence of caretakers or loved ones in a manner consistent with their in fact knowing and recognizing the people. For a review of this literature, see Hardcastle (1995).

chorea is explained by a disruption in the GABA-ergic loop. Equilibrium in neurons is explained in terms of the influx and efflux of ions across the cell membrane. Perceptual binding is explained (maybe) in terms of 40 Hz neuronal oscillations. The withdrawal reflex in *Aplysia* is explained in terms of patterns of activation across the motor system. Echolocation is explained in terms of deformed tensor networks. So: find the parallels between brain activity and phenomenal experience and you will have found a naturalistic account of consciousness.

Denying the project and devising different criteria for explanation is a perfectly legitimate move to make, of course. There is always room for more. Winning converts though is something else. I wish Chalmers well in that enterprise, for how to do that truly is the gap that remains.

References

Baars, B.J. (1988), *A Cognitive Theory of Consciousness* (Cambridge: Cambridge University Press).
Block, N. (1995), 'On a confusion about a function of consciousness', *Behavioral and Brain Sciences*, **18** (2), pp. 227–47.
Chalmers, D.J. (1995), 'Facing up to the problem of consciousness', *Journal of Consciousness Studies*, **2** (3), pp. 200–19 (reprinted in this volume).
Churchland, P.M. (1984), *Matter and Consciousness* (Cambridge, MA: The MIT Press).
Crick, F. and Koch, C. (1990), 'Toward a Neurobiological Theory of Consciousness', *Seminars in the Neurosciences*, **2**, pp. 263–75.
Flanagan, O. (1992), *Consciousness Reconsidered* (Cambridge, MA: The MIT Press).
Hardcastle, V.G. (1995), *Locating Consciousness* (Amsterdam and Philadelphia: John Benjamins).
Hardin, C.L. (1988), *Color for Philosophers: Unweaving the Rainbow* (New York: Hackett).
Lycan, W.G. (1987), *Consciousness* (Cambridge, MA: The MIT Press).
McGinn, C. (1991), *The Problem of Consciousness* (Oxford: Blackwell).
Nagel, T. (1974), 'What is It Like to be a Bat?' *Philosophical Review*, **83**, pp. 435–50.
Searle, J. (1992), *The Rediscovery of Mind* (Cambridge, MA: The MIT Press).
Shoemaker, S. (1975), 'Functionalism and Qualia', *Philosophical Studies*, **27**, pp. 291–315.
Shoemaker, S. (1981), 'Absent qualia are not possible — A reply to Block,' *Philosophical Review*, **90**, pp. 581–99.
van Fraassen, B. (1980), *The Scientific Image* (Cambridge, MA: The MIT Press).

Kieron O'Hara and Tom Scutt

There Is No Hard Problem
of Consciousness

I: Introduction

Cognitive psychology has made many important advances over the past couple of decades. Conceived as a response to the hollow dogma of behaviourism, as a discipline it has clearly shown itself to possess greater explanatory power, and has been widely accepted as an important paradigm for the description and modelling of a number of psychological phenomena.

For example the work of Marr and Hildreth (1980), not only outlined the higher level functions (such as edge detection) that the visual system would need to be capable of, but also predicted many of the lower-level neural mechanisms for computing such functions, which have since been revealed by neurophysiological and psychophysical research.

One reason for the success of cognitive psychology is its technological aspect. Its methodology is distinctive for its concentration on computational and formal aspects of psychological phenomena. When confronted with some problematic behaviour, the typical response of a cognitive psychologist is to ask: *How is that done?* He or she typically lives in a world of simulations and models. This concentration on computation provides cognitive psychology with important links to the engineering discipline of artificial intelligence. In AI, the engineer asks: *How could that be done?* And we can see that the explanations in cognitive psychology will find a ready audience in AI, ready to test the psychological hypotheses to the limit.

Because of the important links between cognitive psychology and engineering, however, many thinkers find its theories unsatisfactory as *general* explanations of human psychological phenomena. The cognitive psychologist, by concentrating on computational aspects of such phenomena, will, according to these critics, miss out on precisely those aspects which are *not* computational. The cognitive psychologist's reply is that anything that is literally true about psychological phenomena will be fully accounted for by a concentration on their computational aspects, and his or her research programme will be an attempt to delve for satisfactory computational or formal explanations.

The result is a stand-off, with the critic emphasising the aspects of the phenomena which are *prima facie* independent of any possible computational account, and the cognitive psychologist standing by the record of the discipline in past investigations. In

This paper was originally published in the *Journal of Consciousness Studies*, **3**, No.4 (1996), pp. 290–302.

any particular area, the matter can only be resolved convincingly by the success or failure of the cognitive psychologist in providing successful theories.

One such area is that of consciousness. The question is how any straightforward physicalist account, such as would be provided by cognitive psychology, can show how such apparently non-physical phenomena as awareness are possible. The explananda of such an account are not often described as exactly as one might hope, as we shall discuss in section three, but there is a general consensus that, however they are described, they are problematic. In Nagel's formulation of the problem (1974), if something has consciousness, then it is *like* something to be that thing (it has a subjective aspect). But surely — the critic adds — it isn't like *anything* to be a computer program, or formal theory. How can the cognitive psychologist ever succeed in reducing the *sui generis* phenomenon of consciousness to a series of physical phenomena formally described?

This leads to the distinction drawn by the critic between the *easy problems* and the *hard problem* of consciousness. The easy problems are the problems that are clearly amenable to the methodology of cognitive science: Chalmers suggests as examples the ability to discriminate, categorize and react to environmental stimuli; the integration of information by a cognitive system; the reportability of mental states; the ability of a system to access its own internal states; the focus of attention; the deliberate control of behaviour; and the difference between wakefulness and sleep. All these phenomena — and doubtless others — will be susceptible to the methodology of cognitive psychology.

Contrasted with these problems is the hard problem, which is that of explaining consciousness itself, how consciousness is possible at all. Answers to the easy problems would fail to address the hard problem, which is the subjective aspect of consciousness, because the easy problems are clearly approachable using only objective terms. The sum of all the (objective) answers to all the easy problems would never be an explanation of subjectivity itself.

In this paper, we will defend the claims of cognitive psychology against the critic we have described, by arguing that the hard problem (or HP as we shall call it) is not a serious problem. For a problem to be a genuine problem, some sort of idea of a solution must be available (e.g. some way of recognizing a solution when one stumbles across one); whereas all discussion of HP seems to preclude any sort of answer being given. Our argument has two components. The first component is a pragmatic claim, to the effect that, since we know how to address the easy questions (at least in rough), and we haven't the foggiest idea of what to do about HP, we would be wasting our time if we didn't explore the easy problems first; we establish this in section two. The second component is a philosophical claim that we do not know what HP is as yet, and that the only possible way of approaching HP is via the easy problems; this is the business of section three. It may be thought that the existence of attempted answers to HP precludes the possibility that HP cannot sensibly be addressed; in section four we discuss some attempted answers to HP (the theories of Edelman, Crick and Chalmers), to show why they fail to address any actual problem. Finally, in section five, we will defend our position against charges that we have eliminated, or would like to eliminate, the notion of consciousness from scientific discourse.

II: Methodological Reasons to Ignore HP

In the venerable joke, little Johnny is peering hard at the lawn. 'Why Johnny,' says his mother, 'what are you doing?' Johnny points across the garden and says, 'I lost my pocket money over there.' 'If you lost your money over by the garage, why are you looking by the pond?' asks his mother; and little Johnny duly replies: 'Cos the grass is shorter over here.'

One should never analyse humour, but since this joke isn't actually very funny, we will, just this once. Why is it a joke that Johnny is looking where the grass is short, and not where the grass is long? Well, he thinks that he will save effort by looking where the grass is short, because such a search is easier in short grass than in long, but we know that he will expend greater effort, because the money is almost certainly concealed in the long grass, and furthermore, little Johnny has told us that himself. So, although a smaller amount of effort would be expended in the short grass per blade (or whatever unit is appropriate here), all that effort is guaranteed to be in vain, since the money is somewhere else entirely. And since he is aware of all that, and has simply failed to draw the obvious conclusion, little Johnny is just being stupid.

The analogy to consciousness is evident. The critic we discerned in the opening section argues that the answer to HP is to be found in the long grass over by the garage, and that cognitive psychologists who mess about with the easy questions by the pond will — to the extent that they see themselves as thereby addressing HP — be wasting their time.

However, approaching consciousness via the easy problems is only open to the same criticisms as little Johnny's approach to retrieving his money if two conditions hold, to render the analogy suitably watertight. In the first place, in the joke, we know that the money is in the long grass. For Johnny to be *really* stupid for the purposes of the joke, he must know that the money is in the long grass too, but the main point is that there is a laugh to be had as long as we in the audience know roughly where the money is. And in the second place, it must be the case that Johnny *could* look in the long grass, that he has a procedure for finding the money such that, if he employed it in the long grass, he would achieve his goal.

When we come to examine the extent to which the joke is analogous to the situation in the study of consciousness, we find that neither of these two conditions holds. We do not know where to look for the answer to HP, and in particular, we don't know that we are necessarily wrong to approach the question via the easy problems. The joke would not be funny if little Johnny knew only that he had lost his money *somewhere* in the garden; in that event, he would be rational, not stupid, to begin to look where least effort would be expended. For the second condition to hold, it would have to be the case that there was an alternative approach to consciousness to the one provided by the cognitive psychological investigation of the easy problems. But as it is, no-one really has any well-worked-out plan for approaching the problem any other way. If, in the joke, the long grass was completely and necessarily impenetrable, Johnny could not be blamed for not looking there.

We have, in the study of consciousness, an obvious problem which is that addressing the easy problems is the only game in town. We do not know that addressing the easy problems will automatically fail to provide insight into HP. We do not know any other way of addressing HP. We do know how to address the easy problems — indeed,

Chalmers seems to hold this as definitive of the easy problems. Pragmatically, it does look as if looking into the easy problems is as likely to be successful as any other way of approaching consciousness, and therefore it would seem to be as rational a way of proceeding as any.

Consider the alternative; the only alternative to the easy way is to develop a new paradigm of psychological investigation. For example — and this is an extreme, if genuine, example — take Penrose's (1994) suggestion that a new branch of physics is required to explain consciousness. Pragmatically, is there any reason at all why one should take the Penrose route to a solution to HP? Addressing the easy problems is hard enough, and work in those cognitive psychological fields is likely to produce interesting and important results (as no-one denies), even if the end result is not an answer to HP. The advantage of such an approach is that we know where to start, there is a body of work to build on, there are surrounding theories in which such work can be embedded and located. But developing a new branch of physics is the sort of paradigm-shifting, epoch-making task that, unless one was Nobel Prize material, one should probably avoid. Worse, one is not even guaranteed success with respect to the HP, since any such suggestion remains tentative, though the Nobel Prize ought to be consolation enough. It is difficult to see why anyone who is neither seriously irrational nor seriously clever, and who wishes to contribute to a solution to HP, would not take the pedestrian route and go for the easy problems.

We call this argument the *pragmatic argument*.

III: Philosophical Reasons to Ignore HP

Surprisingly, in this debate, pragmatic considerations carry little weight. Although the pragmatic argument seems to us to be sufficient to consign HP to the dustbin reserved for historical curiosities, the critic of cognitive psychological approaches to consciousness will certainly not agree. More *a priori* reasons are required here, since all the arguments to be met are firmly unencumbered with empirical detail.

Therefore, in addition to the pragmatic argument, we will now add two compelling *a priori* arguments to leave HP alone. Both are concerned with the lack of understanding of the nature of HP that precedes satisfactory answers to the easy problems.

The first *a priori* argument, which we shall refer to as the *context argument*, simply makes the obvious point that an understanding of a concept may be facilitated, at the very minimum, by the investigation of contexts in which that concept is important. Take the example of the concept of *life*. The analogy of HP in this context is the question of what life is (call this LHP). The analogy of the easy problems would be various biological questions to do with the processes that go on in things that are alive. Many major philosophers addressed the LHP, but very few addressed the easy problems. Indeed, between Aristotle and Harvey it is not obvious that *anyone* did. We can also agree that, remarkable as they were, Aristotle's discussions of the easy problems were inadequate. Yet as the discipline of biology grew up in the modern era, more and more easy problems fell to the advancing forces. Now, what happened to LHP? Since the vitalists, no-one has seriously attempted to answer the question; indeed, very few thinkers think the question is worth asking at all. Those who do still wonder about LHP are increasingly likely to assimilate it with one of the easy problems. The answers to the easy problems gradually undermined the air of mystery that underlay LHP, and suddenly LHP didn't really seem like a problem any more.

Consciousness may or may not be analogous to life in this way. It may be the case that answering all the easy problems completely and satisfactorily would still not get rid of HP. But that cannot be decided *a priori*. Clearly, answers to the easy problems are bound to lead to adjustments in the concept of consciousness. For example, there is no doubt that the research on epileptics who had had their corpus callosum severed (Gazzaniga, 1970; Nagel, 1971), so-called 'split-brain' patients, has led to a serious readjustment of the notion of the unity of consciousness, and no philosopher or psychologist investigating in this field can afford to ignore such results. But surely no-one would claim that the phenomena of consciousness thereby revealed would have been discovered *a priori*, without empirical research into this problem (presumably an 'easy' problem). Hence, had this easy problem been neglected in favour of HP, any putative solution to HP would quite simply have been wrong, because it would have failed to account for important properties of consciousness (in which case it couldn't have described consciousness fully). Furthermore, the only way to provide criticisms of the putative solutions to HP would be to perform the research into the easy problems to discover the properties of consciousness overlooked by HP-research.

So the very notion of consciousness we are dealing with will change as more answers to easy problems roll in (right *and* wrong answers). Older notions of consciousness will be seen to have been mistaken, or simply wither on the vine as their role in scientific research diminishes. Hence, addressing the easy problems will seriously affect any answers to HP that we get, via their effect on the notion of consciousness whose nature is the topic of HP. The lesson is clear: we cannot be confident of any putative solution to HP until we have a reliable picture of the topography of the ground via the less ambitious research into the easy problems. Not all easy problems would have to be solved, but a well-supported psychological consensus will, without a shadow of a doubt, precede any serious assault on HP. That consensus is not yet with us, and will only follow a long period of dedicated research into the easy problems.

The second *a priori* argument, which we shall call the *epistemological argument*, is an adaptation of a recent argument from Colin McGinn (1989). McGinn's argument has been widely criticized, and with good reason. But we feel that there is a kernel of truth in it, which is highly germane to the issue at hand. McGinn argues that we will never understand consciousness (i.e. we will never solve HP), and argues innovatively on epistemological grounds.

His argument goes as follows. We are all good physicalists, so any explanation of consciousness (solution to HP) will consist of some physical predicate, P, satisfaction of which by an entity will entail that that entity has consciousness. But, argues McGinn, it is inconceivable that we would ever recognize that a mere physical predicate confers consciousness in this way; we just do not understand consciousness in the right terms. So even if we discovered P, we would never recognize that it was the solution to HP.

There are many dubious points in McGinn's argument (which in addition we have necessarily caricatured). It is not obvious to us which side of our particular fence McGinn sits; he would probably advocate the pursuit of the easy problems on the ground that HP will be forever out of our reach, and therefore would probably see the point of our methodological argument in section two. But he would also discount the possibility of HP fading away, or changing rapidly, as a result of the investigation of the easy problems, and in this he agrees with the critic of cognitive psychology we discerned in section one.

What McGinn has done is highlighted the importance of our recognition that a solution to HP *is* a solution to HP. We do not agree that it is necessarily the case that we will never make such a recognition. But clearly some prerequisites for such a recognition must obtain before McGinn can be shown to be wrong. One such prerequisite is that we must know what we are talking about; until the nature of consciousness is more or less well-understood, we will never recognize that a theory solves HP. Note that this is independent of whether or not the theory actually *does* solve HP. Hence until HP is well-understood, it won't be rational to address HP.

As a parallel, consider the work of ancient philosophers about the nature of matter. Their version of HP was MHP, what the nature of matter is. The easy problems in this realm are the way that matter reacts in various circumstances (in effect, the problems of chemistry). Now it turned out that Democritus, and later Lucretius, hit the nail on the head with their solution to MHP, which was an atomic theory. Although their theories weren't particularly detailed in the way in which modern atomic theories are detailed, they were more nearly right than Anaxagoras or Empedocles.

But, because these authors were addressing MHP before the easy problems had been elucidated to any significant degree, it is fair to say that — from the point of view of chemistry at least — their answers to MHP are effectively worthless. However wonderful *De Rerum Natura* is as a piece of philosophical poetry, it is clear that its value is quite independent of the discovery that the right answer to MHP is that matter is atomic, as evinced by the poem's high reputation during periods when it was thought that the answer to MHP was that matter is *not* atomic. And it is also clear that Democritus and Lucretius weren't right for the right reasons. They were neither cleverer, nor more rational, nor more well-informed than their rivals; it is simply that their shot in the dark happened to hit the target, while their rivals' didn't.

It is our contention that the thinkers who approach the notion of consciousness via HP are going to be subject to the same problems. It may indeed be the case that a new branch of physics is required to solve HP, as Penrose claims. It may be the case that information has an irreducible phenomenal aspect, as Chalmers suggests. But since neither of these authors has any idea of the detailed consequences of their solutions to HP, then neither of their answers can be considered as authoritative. And the reason that neither author is able to be authoritative is that work on the easy problems has barely commenced. A research programme, the programme of cognitive psychology, is underway to address the easy problems. That programme may fail completely, or may gain partial success, or may claim to provide complete solutions to the easy problems. When the programme has been carried through sufficiently to make an estimate of the extent of the success of the research, anyone who makes a stab at HP will be on much more solid ground. And even if one of the currently competing claims — all shots in the dark, as we claim — *does* hit the target, that will be coincidence, and will be rejected as such.

IV: Edelman, Crick and Chalmers' Attempts to Address HP

The obvious reply to the arguments adduced in sections two and three above is that, although we have claimed that addressing HP will be at best very difficult and at worst impossible, there has been quite a number of serious attempts at solving HP. In turn, the obvious rejoinder to *that* would be that these attempts fail in the ways that we have suggested that they will fail.

We have already discussed Penrose's (1994) claim that a new branch of physics is required. This does not even look like an approach to HP, at least until the putative branch of physics is exhibited. Similarly, McGinn's (1989) idea that a physical predicate P, true of the brain, will explain 'the mind', is hardly of use in the context of HP, given that he doesn't suggest what this predicate may be (because he thinks that we can never understand how the predicate will explain the mind), which makes his argument more like a testament to his faith in materialism than anything else. Any solution to HP must give us a handle on the problem. Other attempts simply do not have the right form. Eccles' theory (Popper and Eccles, 1977) that random quantum effects will undermine physical determinism and 'let in' the mind will ultimately fail, because the effects of the mind are specifically *not* random.

Our aim in this section will be to take a number of influential attempts on HP, and show that they succumb to the three arguments given above. Our aim is to criticize theories that are plausible, in the sense that Penrose's, McGinn's and Eccles' are not, and furthermore which have gathered attention and support from the community. We hope they are sufficiently representative. Of course, criticizing existing theories can never be *decisive* — since another, better, theory may always come along later — but we expect that the exercise will demonstrate the plausibility of our arguments. To that end we consider the theories of consciousness of Gerald Edelman (1992), Francis Crick (Crick, 1994; Crick and Koch, 1990) and David Chalmers.

1. Edelman and the pragmatic argument

Edelman distinguishes between Primary and Higher-Order Consciousness. Animals with primary consciousness have phenomenal experience, but are not aware that they have it. They have no notion of self, and therefore nothing to 'attach' the experience to. Primary consciousness consists of a re-entrant loop connecting value-category memory to current perceptual categorization (1992, p. 120). There would be a fleeting phenomenal aspect, but

> Creatures with primary consciousness, while possessing mental images, have no capacity to view those images from the vantage point of a socially constructed self (Edelman, 1992, p. 124).

Edelman is very concerned — rightly, of course — to make sure that this notion of consciousness has a place in neuropsychology, and is not merely a metaphysical conceit.

> What is the evolutionary value of such a system? Obviously, primary consciousness must be efficacious if this biological account is correct. Consciousness is not merely an epiphenomenon (Edelman, 1992, p. 121).

The question then is how this promise can be cashed out. And this is where what Chalmers terms the bait-and-switch takes place. Edelman lists the properties that make consciousness useful (such as relating the creature's present inputs to previous dangers or rewards as experienced). But what actually happens is that Edelman lists the benefits of the re-entrant loop, the connection between value-category memory and current perceptual categorization, *i.e. the thing he attached the consciousness label to in the first place*. This is a common tactic: take some neuro-architectural item that seems to be doing the sort of thing we want consciousness to do; attach the consciousness label to it; and then show the benefits of consciousness by pointing to the assets of our newly labelled neuronal structure.

We can see that Edelman has fallen foul of the pragmatic considerations we discerned in section two. The only way we can make progress is to tackle the easy problems; concentration on HP will always fail to provide a lead. Hence, when attempting to tackle HP, the temptation will always be to move covertly towards the easy problems. In Edelman's case, the re-entrant loop is a phenomenon that is eminently open to study, and he applies his considerable expertise to that end, with interesting results. But the methodological difficulties involved in gaining a vantage point for HP will always lead the researcher to move via the easy problems, and we see why a common class of theories emerges, of which Edelman's is an exemplar, in which a neuronal phenomenon is assimilated to the phenomena of consciousness. Chalmers is correct to say that such a strategy will always be unsatisfying for someone interested in HP.

Incidentally, Edelman also exemplifies another methodological pitfall in assaulting HP. As Dennett puts it, Edelman's theory is

> . . . an instructive failure. It shows in great detail just how many different sorts of question must be answered before we can claim to have secured a complete theory of consciousness, but it also shows that no one theorist can appreciate all the subtleties of the problems addressed by the different fields (Dennett, 1991, p. 268, n.1).

There are so many easy problems to be understood, in so many fields, that the researcher who would take a crack at HP will be hard pressed to find (and argue for) a point of view that transcends them all. But such a point of view is vital if HP is to be regarded as a problem essentially distinct from the (sum of the) easy problems. Again, pragmatically, there are few who can move so easily between all the various disciplines that they can sift through the evidence provided by the various answers to the various easy problems and make correct judgments about them.

2. Crick and the context argument

Francis Crick, rather than give an exact *location* for consciousness (he does give locations for certain phenomena, for example, free will, in his (1994), but these speculations are probably better overlooked; indeed, perhaps his tongue is in his cheek), points instead to an observable phenomenon — certain 35–75 hertz neural oscillations in the cerebral cortex (Crick and Koch, 1990). These oscillations appear to be correlated with the binding of information from various sense modalities, but it remains unclear whether Crick and Koch think that these oscillations form the basis for consciousness, are merely correlated with consciousness, or form an observable aspect of consciousness. Chalmers is right to criticize Crick and Koch on the grounds that suggesting a correlation between two phenomena in no way explains how one gives rise to the other (or indeed, which gives rise to which).

Of course, concentration on particular observables amounts yet again to an assault on an easy problem. Once more, HP has been sidestepped, as Chalmers points out. But Crick and Koch are prepared to get excited over the properties of the easy problem they have concentrated on.

> We have suggested that one of the functions of consciousness is to present the result of various underlying computations and that this involves an attentional mechanism that temporarily binds the relevant neurons together by synchronizing their spikes in 40 hz oscillations (Crick and Koch, 1990, p. 272).

Let us assume that they are right, for the sake of argument. Now, consciousness as we presently understand it is not like this at all. If Crick and Koch have got it right, then our view of consciousness will have to change, to conform to their results. But note that it is their concentration on a particular *easy* problem that has given them this perspective on HP. In that event, the form that HP has finally taken would have depended on the results of some investigation into an easy problem.

On the other hand, if Crick and Koch have not provided us with any sort of handle on HP, as Chalmers says, then it is clear that they have uncovered some interesting results concerning the easy problems. No view of HP could *fail* to take these results into account. Good work on the easy problems will always have to be incorporated into HP. And such results are unlikely to be predictable in advance; recall our remarks concerning brain bisection and the unity of consciousness.

In other words, as we claimed in section three, the easy problems, when solved, alter HP; hence HP could not be considered as reaching any sort of 'final form' until the easy problems were beginning to be cracked. They don't all have to be solved, but we need to be comfortable enough in this area so that we do not expect to be surprised by any new discoveries. 'Comfortable enough' is a vague term, but its application seems clear. We are pretty familiar with the functions of the lungs, for example, and do not really expect to have our understanding of them turned upside-down (though of course that under-standing is always liable to be adjusted in the light of new discoveries). On the other hand, Big Bang theory is so new and untested that any speculation on the basis of its current form is probably going to be made redundant by massive changes in the theory itself. Our claim is that consciousness theory is more like Big Bang theory than lung theory, and that we are not yet comfortable enough with consciousness theory for it to be worth the risk in wasted resources to start speculating.

3. Edelman, Crick, Chalmers and the epistemological argument

The theories we have so far considered also provide evidence for our epistemological argument. Both Edelman and Crick are distinguished neurobiologists who have claimed to have located consciousness in the brain. In neither case is this fully explained, although in both cases it is work on the 'easy' problems which has led to a suggested solution of HP. We do not share Chalmers' pessimism that work on the former can never help with our search for the latter. However, at present it is too early (indeed, it often looks plain ridiculous) to point to a part of the brain and say 'this is where consciousness lies'. Diagrams of cognitive architecture in modern texts on the nature of mind often look like

medieval maps with labels saying 'Here be Dragons'. Until we have a much clearer idea
of what we are looking for, it is far too early to say where we have found it.

Chalmers, on the other hand, takes a very different route, but will still fall foul of the
epistemological argument. His position is founded on an *a priori* assumption that there
can be no scientific account of consciousness (at least in physical terms as currently
understood). He claims that there needs to be a non-reductive explanation of the hard
problem of consciousness. Reductive explanation, according to Chalmers, won't get us
anywhere. He gives an example of where such examples succeed and fail:

> If someone says, 'I can see that you have explained how DNA stores and transmits
> hereditary information from one generation to the next, but you have not explained
> how it is a *gene*,' then they are making a conceptual mistake . . . But if someone
> says, 'I can see that you have explained how information is discriminated, integrated,
> and reported, but you have not explained how it is *experienced*,' they are not making
> a conceptual mistake. This is a nontrivial further question (p. 13).

Indeed. But that is because at the moment it is impossible to see how experience *could*
be explained in terms of mere (sic) information processing — we lack the necessary
bridging concepts to see one in terms of the other. In fact we are in much the same
position as a geneticist would have been if such a term existed two hundred years ago.

From our present viewpoint, a statement such as 'I see how you have explained the
nature and transmission of electromagnetic radiation in the range 400–700 nanometres,
but you have not explained how it is light', seems somewhat naïve. But before these
scientific facts about the electromagnetic nature of light were carefully laid out by that
painstaking and haphazard endeavour we call science, the validity or otherwise of this
sentence would have been open to debate (and a very ill-informed debate at that). At the
end of the next millennium, a statement that consciousness can be explained in terms of
X, Y and Z may be widely accepted as being beyond doubt. The same statement from our
present viewpoint would be viewed with some scepticism, because we haven't yet done
the work (on the easy problems) which would justify this statement. Chalmers himself
admits that 'there is a direct correspondence between consciousness and awareness'
(p. 22). Wouldn't it make sense, this being the case, to research awareness (the easy
problem) to better understand consciousness? Is Chalmers *really* saying that understanding the former doesn't help us *at all* in understanding the latter? The naïve question
which began this paragraph is naïve only so long as it is understood in a particular way
(e.g. from the standpoint of the twentieth century). Before, in Kuhnian terms, the
paradigm shifted, it is a perfectly good question. For the paradigm with respect to
consciousness to shift, however, a good deal of evidence has to be built up with no
obvious home in any general theory — this is what provides the impetus for a paradigm
shift. And this evidence will only be built up by addressing the easy problems.

So what are we to make of Chalmers' alternative to a physical account of consciousness? In the 'dual-aspect theory of information', it appears to us that 'Information Space'
— the place where 'experience might have a subtle kind of causal relevance in virtue of
its status as the intrinsic nature of the physical' (p. 28) — is the pineal gland of Chalmers'
account. However overstated some may have been in their heralding of Crick and Koch's
neural oscillations as an aspect of consciousness, at least such work on the easy problems

may get us nearer to a solution of HP (or nearer to a *reasoned* rejection of a physical account). It is not so clear that the non-reductive account of Chalmers offers any such reward. It is, in our current epistemological state, impossible to understand how information can have a phenomenal aspect. It may turn out to be true, but we, in the twentieth century, have no idea what the implications of such a claim are. It is as unexplanatory to us as atomism was to the Ancient Greeks.

V: Eliminativism with Respect to Consciousness and HP

There is one final point that we would like to make, and that is to rebut the charge that our insistence that concentration on the easy problems and consequent neglect of HP amounts to eliminativism with respect to consciousness. HP, such a charge would maintain, is *the* fundamental, definitive problem of consciousness. Anything else, such as the ability to discriminate environmental stimuli, is mere effect. Hence to avoid or reject HP amounts to rejecting the scientific investigation of consciousness. Such a strategy results either in the elimination of consciousness from our discourse, or the cheerful acceptance of its irreducibly occult nature.

A sophisticated version of this charge would attempt to line us up with an eliminativist argument such as that of Kathy Wilkes (1988), where sceptical play is made with the notion that consciousness is not used to any great effect in natural science, is not rooted 'in observation or experiment' (1988, p. 38), cannot be seen as a natural kind, and has little or no explanatory power. The idea then is that, since the idea of consciousness fails to have any scientific *use* (although of course it may be the case that scientists have as a *goal* the elucidation of consciousness — i.e. the investigation of HP), nothing would be lost were consciousness removed from scientific discourse altogether.

First we note that this argument will not support the elimination of the notion of consciousness altogether, in a way that would effectively remove mental terms from discourse generally. Wilkes' argument will only apply to *scientific* discourse, as she herself is more than willing to concede (1991). Hence she is advocating treating the term 'consciousness' rather like the term 'dirt', admitting that it has a ready usage in ordinary everyday talk, while keeping it out of more technical scientific discourse.

Second, we note that if those who would support the investigation of HP are right in saying that HP is the only way of 'getting at' consciousness, then concentration on the easy problems and the removal of HP from the realm of scientific discourse *would* constitute an elimination of consciousness from science. As we argued in section three, we do not accept that they *are* right in so saying.

Our main reply to this charge, however, is to side-step it. We are quite happy to agree with Wilkes that her *conditional* premiss is correct (with a small modification). That is we accept that *if consciousness has no use in any practical context, then it should be eliminated from such contexts.* We have substituted the term 'practical' for 'scientific'. We do not want to define 'practical' here, but it certainly includes the scientific. Whether all practical contexts are scientific is a question we would like to leave open (many famous philosophers could be lined up both for and against that proposition).

It follows from this that we would accept the eliminativist charge if we accepted Wilkes' non-conditional premiss that *consciousness has no use in any practical context.*

However, we don't. There are a number of areas where some aspects of the notion of consciousness are used ineliminably. We think that the easy problems are examples of these (although this begs the question against our pro-HP critic). Perhaps the clearest case of a scientific (and therefore practical) context in which the notion of consciousness is centrally involved is the discipline of anaesthesiology, which is the science of making people lose conscious awareness. This is not the place to go into detail on this matter, but see Nikolinakos (1994) for a recent discussion of scepticism about consciousness in the context of anaesthesiology.

We think that the elimination or otherwise of the notion of consciousness depends entirely on that notion being used practically, and would not wish our attachment to it to be merely sentimental. Fortunately, we can get serious work out of the concept, in a number of psychological and/or medical fields, and therefore, despite our rejection of HP, we are very happy to accept that the notion of consciousness has an important role to play in our scientific and practical discourse. Of course, the nature of that notion would depend on its use in those practical contexts — many aspects of the 'common-sense' or 'folk' notion of consciousness would turn out to be of little or no use in any practical context. But we think that this is a good discipline, and should help prevent metaphysical obscurities muddying the waters of practical discourse.

VI: Let's Take It Easy

Our aim in this paper has been to establish that the easy problems of consciousness, as addressed by cognitive psychology, remain the most promising route to success. We adduced three arguments against approaching HP directly:

- the *pragmatic* argument — we know how to address the easy problems, whereas we can only speculate with respect to HP;

- the *context* argument — the elucidation of the easy problems will probably change the nature of our understanding of HP, and so any attempt to solve HP currently would be premature;

- the *epistemological* argument — a solution to HP would only be of value if its success could be recognized because the problem was well-enough understood.

We illustrated our claim with discussions of three prominent attempts to solve HP. Edelman, trying to avoid vacuousness, ends up conflating his answer to the easy problems with his answer to HP, showing the perils of ignoring the pragmatic argument. Crick, like the researchers into the split brain phenomena before him, doesn't solve HP, but provides important input into HP, subtly changing its nature, as we would expect from the context argument. Because our understanding of HP is so limited, Edelman, Crick and Chalmers all fall foul of the epistemological argument. Our final point was to say that our preference for the easy problems and consequent neglect of HP does not amount to eliminativism with respect to consciousness.

In this concluding section, we would like to expand a little on the nature of the easy problems and the hard problem. Part of the difficulty here is caused by the names given to the two groupings. Chalmers says:

The easy problems of consciousness are those that seem directly susceptible to the standard methods of cognitive science, whereby a phenomenon is explained in terms of computational or neural mechanisms. The hard problems are those that seem to resist those methods (p. 9).

Of course, rhetorically, easy problems don't seem to be worthwhile, and an assault on the hard problem appears more heroic. No prominent player in the game, least of all Chalmers, would make the crass error of saying that the easy problems are actually *easy*. Equally, no-one would suppose that HP were not hard.

But it is interesting to explore the reasoning behind calling the easy problems easy and HP hard. The easy problems are not easy, but we do have a handle on how to approach them. We have no guarantee of success, but at least we have a rough idea of where to go from here. What sets HP apart is the fact that we haven't the foggiest idea of how to begin. Compare, for example, Penrose's solution with Chalmers' or Crick's. They are not even remotely in the same ball park. We have three answers by three leading thinkers in three central disciplines, and they point in three mutually exclusive directions.

Consider an analogy with bridge building. Easy bridge building involves constructing structures to cross small spans. Hard bridge building involves constructions over more challenging spans, in unfavourable conditions. These notions of 'easy' and 'hard' do not map onto the ones used in this debate. Suppose we termed bridge building 'easy' just in case we had a rough idea of how to start, no matter how problematic the project, and 'hard' just in case we did not know how to start. Then an easy project might be the construction of a bridge across the Atlantic, and a hard project might be the construction of a bridge into the fourteenth century. A hard bridge builder then might echo Penrose's solution, that a new branch of physics needs to be developed before hard bridge building might begin in earnest. But the obvious response would be to say that, at our current state of ignorance, hard bridge building ought be be shelved, in favour of the easy sort, at least for the time being.

Science is an incremental activity. For every Einstein there are thousands of Scutts and O'Haras, adding their two penn'orth to the current state of knowledge. Ambition plays a role in science, but ambition needs to be tempered by a firm grasp of the possibilities available at any point. In particular, our understanding of the large questions often crucially depends on our answers to all the small and relatively insignificant questions. When enough of the small questions have been answered, then an attempt to answer the hard questions becomes a possibility (unless the hard questions have been shown to be wrong-headed).

We all want to understand consciousness. But the way to achieve that understanding is not to divert intellectual resources toward HP. Because the small questions relating to consciousness remain unanswered, we simply do not understand HP sufficiently well to determine whether there is a serious question to answer (and if so, precisely what that question is), or whether the whole thing is some ghastly metaphysical error best avoided. We can have opinions on these questions, sure, but those opinions are fundamentally ill-informed, and will remain so until the lessons from the easy problems have been learned and absorbed.

References

Chalmers, David J. (1995) 'Facing up to the problem of consciousness', *Journal of Consciousness Studies*, **3** (2), pp. 200–19 (reprinted in this volume).

Crick, F. (1994), *The Astonishing Hypothesis: The Scientific Search for the Soul* (New York: Scribners).

Crick, F. and Koch, C. (1990) 'Towards a neurobiological theory of consciousness', *Seminars in the Neurosciences*, **2**, pp. 263–75.

Dennett, Daniel C. (1991), *Consciousness Explained* (Harmondsworth: Penguin).

Edelman, Gerald (1992), *Bright Air, Brilliant Fire* (Harmondsworth: Penguin).

Gazzaniga, Michael S. (1970), *The Bisected Brain* (New York: Appleton-Century-Crofts).

Marr, D. and Hildreth, E. (1980), 'Theory of edge detection', *Proceedings of the Royal Society of London, Series B*, **207**, pp. 187–216.

McGinn, Colin (1989), 'Can we solve the mind–body problem?', *Mind*, **98**, pp. 349–66.

Nagel, Thomas (1971), 'Brain bisection and the unity of consciousness', *Synthese*, **22**, pp. 396–413.

Nagel, Thomas (1974), 'What is it like to be a bat?', *Philosophical Review*, **83**, pp. 435–50.

Nikolinakos, Drakon (1994), 'General anesthesia, consciousness and the skeptical challenge', *Journal of Philosophy*, **91**, pp. 88–104.

Penrose, Roger (1994), *Shadows of the Mind* (Oxford: Oxford University Press).

Popper, Karl and Eccles, John (1977), *The Self and Its Brain* (Berlin: Springer International).

Wilkes, Kathleen V. (1988), '_____, yìshì, duh, um, and consciousness', in *Consciousness in Contemporary Science*, ed. A.J. Marcel and E. Bisiach (New York: Oxford University Press).

Wilkes, Kathleen V. (1991), 'The relationship between scientific psychology and common-sense psychology', *Synthese*, **89**, pp. 15–39.

Mark C. Price

Should We Expect to Feel as if We Understand Consciousness?

Introduction

We would desperately like to understand, as the philosopher Thomas Nagel has put it, how on earth a subjectively experienced first person viewpoint on the world can emerge from a few pounds of subatomic particles (Nagel, 1986). But despite having exercised many of the best minds of science, the 'hard question' of how consciousness *per se* arises in the universe sadly continues to evade an answer. At best, all that objective science seems able to throw up are correlations between neurophysiological or cognitive descriptions of brain processes on the one hand and the occurrence of conscious experience on the other. But as causal explanations of consciousness, such correlations appear fundamentally insufficient. Chalmers is correct to point out that in all theories of consciousness to date there exists what Levine (1983) has termed a blatant *explanatory gap* between our objective accounts of brains and the fact that reality seems to include the existence of first person subjective viewpoints. This situation is repeatedly stressed in discussions on consciousness. A typical example is provided by Gray (1995, p. 9) who complains that 'there is no hint of a theoretical understanding of [the link between conscious experience and brain and behaviour] that would take us beyond brute correlation towards a "transparent" theory of causal connection' (my insertion).

Opinion varies as to whether and how the explanatory gap may be bridged. Some argue there can be no bridge at all (McGinn, 1989). Some suggest that epistemological innovation may be needed and that the gap may somehow be a function of our whole framework of inquiry and explanation (e.g. Nagel, 1986). And some, like Chalmers suggest that the gap may require an ontological solution which involves admitting new fundamental properties of the universe. What many approaches nevertheless share is the assumption that the occurrence of an explanatory gap is in itself problematic, that what is special about the hard problem is this unbridged gap. I would like to explore a slightly different perspective. I would like to suggest (1) that explanatory gaps are in fact ubiquitous in our causal explanations of the world, (2) that we are just very good at covering up these gaps, and (3) that what is special about consciousness is not the presence of a gap, but the fact that the gap just happens to be particularly obvious and difficult to obscure.

In other words I want to turn the hard question on its head. Instead of asking why consciousness suffers from an explanatory gap, I want to take a step back and ask why other aspects of our world-view do not seem to suffer from gaps of this sort. This will require looking at the psychology of understanding, and in particular at our perception of causation, of how we come to see one thing (e.g. consciousness) as arising from another (e.g. brains); what is it that allows us to walk away from a problem, having banished any explanatory gaps, with a smile on our face and warm glow in our hearts, feeling, 'Yes, I understand that now'? Two proposals will emerge from this examination. First, we may be placing too much importance on the presence of explanatory gaps. Second, we may be placing too much expectation on an answer to the hard question; *even if a scientifically acceptable answer of some kind were staring us in the face, we still might not feel as if we had understood.*

Let me begin by emphasizing a crucial distinction between, on the one hand, psychological accounts of our perception of cause and, on the other, philosophical accounts of causation 'as it really is', causation as an extensional relationship between states of affairs, what Hume (1740) called causation 'in the objects'.

Psychological accounts of our perception of cause are concerned with what I shall refer to as our *everyday conception* of causality; i.e. with our intuitive lay-person's beliefs about the kind of beast that causes are. Psychological accounts are also concerned with whether we *perceive* explanatory gaps and with our *feelings* of understanding. In contrast, philosophical accounts of causation 'as it really is' are concerned with ontological statements about the world as we aim to describe it scientifically.

The gist of the argument I want to present, which is based heavily on a paper by Rosch (1994), is as follows. In order to subjectively feel as if we understand causally how a state of affairs in the world comes about, we need to think that we have located a cause of a type that corresponds to our everyday conception of causality. This concept of cause differs from causation 'as it really is', as described by philosophical accounts. In fact under some philosophical accounts causes themselves do not really exist. There may therefore be, in reality, an explanatory gap between a state of affairs that we are trying to explain causally (henceforth an 'outcome'), and the state of affairs from which it arose (henceforth a 'ground'). Such explanatory gaps may be ubiquitous. However we happen to be very good at hiding these gaps by deceiving ourselves into thinking we have located a cause of a type that corresponds to our everyday conception of causality. The conditions under which we can do this are described by psychological accounts of our perception of causality. If we examine these conditions then the relationship between brains and consciousness turns out to be of a type that does not easily lend itself to such deception. *Feeling* that we understand consciousness is therefore going to be difficult.

To illustrate the argument I shall employ one example of a psychological account of causal perception, and one example of a philosophical account of causation. The choices of example are designed to make the argument as clear and as extreme as possible. Obviously other choices would have been possible, but I shall postpone until later a discussion of whether the argument rests or falls on the particular framework I use to illustrate it.

As an example of a psychological account of causal perception, I shall use the recent account suggested by Rosch (1994), which is partly based on traditional Buddhist psychological texts. I choose this account because it seems especially relevant to the issue of when we should expect to perceive explanatory gaps. As an example of a philosophical approach, I shall use the regularity theory of causality which has its origins in Humean scepticism, and which challenges whether causes exist at all. This approach is certainly not universally accepted, but neither is it universally rejected and there are modern versions of it which have considerable mileage (e.g. Mackie, 1974). I choose this approach for two reasons, partly in the spirit of devil's advocate. First, it contrasts nicely with the claim that we need more than correlations. Second, it contrasts maximally with our everyday conception of causality and will therefore make the argument as clear as possible.

Our Everyday Conception of Causality

Under our everyday conception of causality, causes are themselves really thought to exist. When we seek to understand how one state of affairs (A) gives rise to another state of affairs (B), our natural tendency is to follow our folk psychological instincts in search of an 'A makes B happen' type of explanation (Rosch, 1994). The kernel of the explanation, or causal nexus, is believed to lie in some kind of necessary connecting link between A (the ground) and B (the outcome). Our *feeling* of understanding is a state of mind which depends on thinking we have located this causal nexus.

The Regularity Conception of Causality

In contrast there is at least one philosophical tradition, initiated by Hume (1740), that regards the causal nexus as a bankrupt concept (see for example Mackie, 1974; Rosch, 1994; Searle, 1983; Von Wright, 1974). It teaches that causes themselves do not exist. Like the pot of gold at the end of the rainbow, the causal nexus is a mythical creature that recedes as fast as it is approached. We cannot causally explain why certain states of affairs arise from certain other states of affairs in any necessary *a priori* sense.[1] In other words there is no hidden string between ground and outcome. The idea of a causal nexus is in principle non-sensical because ground A and outcome B cannot at the same time be different from one another *and* account for each other. We seek to link two different states of affairs, but, by virtue of the very fact that they are different, an explanatory gap must remain between them. Causation 'as it really is' consists just of regularities in the relationships between states of affairs in the world (Hume's 'constant union and conjunction of like objects').

Of course modern regularity-based accounts of causation are more sophisticated than this. The cock may regularly crow every sunrise but clearly does not cause the sun to rise. Accidental regularities must therefore be distinguished from regularities that are 'necessary' in the counterfactual sense[2] that outcome B would not have occurred *unless* ground A had occurred. In addition, one has to distinguish grounds that are merely necessary (in the counterfactual sense) from those that are sufficient for a particular outcome. 'Causes'

---

[1] In fairness to Hume, he did speculate that such necessity might still arise as qualities with which we are as yet unaquainted. For discussion of some of the subtleties of Hume's arguments, see Strawson (1989).

[2] Note that the counterfactual sense of necessity should not be confused with *a priori* necessity. Mackie (1974) provides a good discussion of these different senses of necessity.

are usually complex; i.e. if outcome B is to arise, many grounds (X,Y,Z) may be needed. In practice we are rarely interested in all of these grounds, but rather in what Mackie (1974) refers to as INUS conditions — insufficient but necessary parts of an unnecessary but sufficient condition.

Regularity theories do have their problems, especially in distinguishing accidental from non-accidental regularities, but I shall gloss over these and merely refer the interested reader to modern defences such as those of Mackie (1974) and Smart (1993). For present purposes the main point is that regularity theories are an extreme example of the idea that there is no real cause 'in the objects' and that all we really have are correlations between states of affairs, albeit of a complex kind.

But if there are no causes, what are we doing as scientists? What are our causal explanations? Popper (1980) is helpful in pointing out that we do not need causes as such to do science. He argues that to talk about causes as showing how one state of affairs follows necessarily from other, is to use 'necessary' as 'a mere word . . . a label useful for distinguishing the universality of laws from "accidental" universality' (p. 438). What is important is the search for universal laws and the 'principle of causality' can be regarded as the metaphysical version of 'the simple rule that we are not to abandon the search for universal laws and for a coherent theoretical system . . .' (p. 61). 'To give a *causal explanation* of an event means to deduce a statement which describes it, using as premises of the deduction one or more *universal laws*, together with certain statements, the *initial conditions*' (p. 59).

So what we think of as causal relationships are merely instantiations of some universal regularity. To ask what the cause of something is, turns out to be a shorthand for asking for an expansion of its lawful relationship to other things (eventually to everything in the universe although we don't usually get that far!). And at least according to regularity accounts, we can look for these universal laws without recourse to 'real causes'. Perhaps we should not therefore be preoccupied with trying to pinpoint what it is about brains that actually *causes* consciousness. To Chalmers, regularities are not enough. He demands 'an account of why and how' (p. 16). But good science need not imply that any causal explanation of consciousness be transparent. Perhaps we should after all be content with an empirical programme of research which gradually fills in the jigsaw of relationships between the physical brain and consciousness.

Chalmers argues that cognitive science is unable to bridge the explanatory gap between accounts of brain function and consciousness because cognitive science is geared to explaining functional properties, and consciousness is not (or is not just) a functional property. However from the preceding argument the problem is more fundamental than this. It is a basic problem to do with the unbridgeability of causal explanatory gaps in general. The real issue, which I turn to below, is why the particular explanatory gap surrounding consciousness is not hidden from us in the way that explanatory gaps often are. The solution that Chalmers adopts is to propose that consciousness be considered a new fundamental entity, in the same way that, for example, the electromagnetic force was introduced to account for the otherwise inexplicable behaviour of certain physical systems. Consciousness would be characterized by new basic principles which Chalmers says would 'ultimately carry the explanatory burden' (p. 20). But it is difficult to see how this approach bridges the gap. New fundamentals merely beg the question. Their origin still demands explanation. We still need to explain how, for example, the electromagnetic force comes about to start with. To a certain extent Chalmers recognizes this. He states, 'Of course, by taking experience as fundamental, there is a sense in which this approach does not tell us why there is experience in the first place' (p. 20). However, given his stated aim of bridging the explanatory gap surrounding consciousness, Chalmers does not seem to acknowledge the full extent to which this qualification undermines the whole force of his arguments.

Our Psychological Perception of Cause

If we accept the ubiquity of explanatory gaps, what prevents us from usually noticing these gaps? What makes us sometimes *feel* as if we have understood? How do we end up thinking we have found the kind of causal nexus that philosophical analysis considers problematic. To answer this we need to turn to theories of our psychological perception of cause, and in particular to the interesting analysis recently provided by Rosch (1994).

Rosch's main argument is that there are various ways in which we deceive ourselves into seeing outcomes as already contained in their grounds. If, when we focus on ground A, we find outcome B in some sense already present within A, the explanatory gap between A and B will seem to disappear. This is because A and B are no longer seen as different. Under these circumstances, getting from state of affairs A to state of affairs B will not seem to require an explicit connecting link; we do not need to look for a cause because a causal link is implicitly contained within the fact that B is already in A. The illusion that a causal link is somewhere present then supports a feeling of understanding. In general events will only be perceived as coherent if they are seen to arise from themselves in this fashion.

From a logical point of view Rosch's proposal may appear incoherent and circular. Explaining the occurrence of B by pretending it is the same thing as A in the first place is no explanation at all. A proper scientific account of how anything new arises is required to be non circular and show how a state of affairs arises from something that is not already itself. But we have to remember that this is a psychological account, not a logical one. What we are talking about here is an aspect of the way that nature or nurture has endowed us.

According to Rosch all explanations that derive events from something other than themselves only come to feel like explanations because somewhere along the line they surreptitiously accomplish the trick of introducing the outcome itself; i.e. the account is turned into one that suffers from the hidden circularity of the outcome being already contained in the ground. Rosch argues that there are four basic types of situation in which outcomes are seen in this way as contained in their grounds. These are: (1) when a property is transferred from ground to outcome; (2) when we perceive an object or intend an action; (3) when grounds and outcomes are seen as the same entity, but transformed in some way; (4) when an outcome appears to be a property of a category to which the ground belongs.

If we accept Rosch's account of where our subjective sense of causal understanding comes from, any emerging jigsaw of relationships between the brain and consciousness should only generate a *feeling* of understanding if consciousness is seen to arise from its ground in some way. Let us therefore consider whether any of Rosch's four ways of making outcomes arise from grounds could accommodate a brain-consciousness relation-ship. In the following discussion I make the assumption that the brain is the ground which gives rise to the outcome of consciousness.

(1) Transfer of a property from ground to outcome:

An example is provided by mechanical causal events such as one ball hitting another, where the property of motion is transferred from ball A to ball B. If the object of interest in the outcome is the motion of ball B, the aspect of the outcome to which we are attending can be said to be already present in the ground. It is of note that Hume himself said that the perception of a causal relationship in motion is due to the relation of resemblance between ground and outcome.

For the hard question of consciousness, the property that we are crucially interested in is the first-person subjective nature of consciousness. However this property, which is the very essence of consciousness, does not seem to be obviously present in what we are taking to be the ground, i.e. brains. The transfer of a property from ground to outcome will not therefore help us to hide the explanatory gap surrounding consciousness. Indeed the inapplicability of this particular method of making outcomes appear to arise from their grounds succinctly characterizes the fundamental mystery of the hard problem.[3]

(2) Perceiving an object or intending an action:

When we perceive something, we believe our perception (an outcome) to be similar to the object that gives rise to the perception (the ground). And our actions (an outcome) usually seem similar to our preceding intention to act (the ground). In both cases there is a natural tendency to perceive a causal relationship; we see objects as directly causing perceptions, and intentions as directly causing actions. To the lay person, the explanatory gap between an object and its perception, or between an intention and its resultant action, tends to be hidden. Because of this, commonsense explanations at a mentalistic level of description are often taken as a form of causal understanding and introductory psychology courses place much emphasis on pointing out that there *is* a problem of perception and action to be explained. However as psychologically educated scientists we are unlikely to have our inquisitiveness dampened by this particular lay instinct. In any case, the hard question of consciousness is not about how particular objects of perception or particular actions map onto particular *contents* of consciousness — it is about how our internal representations are conscious at all.

(3) Seeing grounds and outcomes as the same entity, but transformed in some way:

Typical examples include objects which change their location, age, form, etc. One sense in which consciousness and its ground, the brain, can be considered as the same entity, is perhaps captured by the mind–brain 'identity thesis'. The strongest version of the thesis, which is allied to eliminative materialism, states that subjective consciousness and the

---

[3] The method might nonetheless be applicable to explanations of the *contents* of consciousness: to the extent that there is any structural isomorphism between the contents of consciousness and the way information is physically (or functionally) represented in the brain, a causal relationship between the two may be perceived.

physical brain are entirely identical. To most people this position seems rather meaning-less and difficult to maintain. Leibniz's Law of the Identity of Indiscernables requires that all properties of identical entities are shared, whereas the crux of the mind–brain problem is exactly that the physically described brain (or the functionally described cognitive system) does *not* share the crucial property of first person subjectivity.

In its weaker and more interesting sense the identity thesis proposes that consciousness and the physical brain are two different perspectives, or levels of description — inner and outer — that derive from the same ontological base. Consciousness is what it is like to be a brain 'from the inside', but consciousness and the brain are not fundamentally different types of stuff. (For a good elaboration of this view see Globus (1976); Popper & Eccles (1984) give further examples.) This version of the identity thesis has been labelled variously as 'parallelist', 'correspondence', or 'dual-aspect' theory. Chalmers himself embraces what he refers to as a 'double-aspect theory of information' in which it is information rather than matter which has two perspectives. By locating the mind–brain divide within a difference of perspective, all these varieties of the weak identity thesis attempt to escape the potentially problematic metaphysical implications of mind–brain dualism. But as Wimsatt (1976) warned, taking the identity thesis seriously involves at least a moderate kind of dualism, 'in that no identity theory will involve a satisfactory 'fit' unless it explains . . . the substantial and absolutely central differences between first and third-person (or subjective and objective) perspectives' (p. 232). In other words it is all very well to think of consciousness and its ground as the same thing viewed from differing perspectives, but this merely begs the question of how such radically differing perspectives can come about. Accepting the ontological identity of a ground and its outcome seems insufficient to hide the explanatory gap between them when they are separated by so novel a transformation. (The importance of novelty is something I elaborate on below.) The identity thesis is more an attempt to avoid the problems of dualism than to explain how consciousness arises. It cannot in itself throw us off the scent of a causal nexus and lull us into a sense of understanding.

(4) Seeing an outcome as a property of a category to which the ground belongs:

An example would be to say that opium puts you to sleep because it belongs to the group of substances with dormative power. One way in which this type of manoeuvre can be used to apparently bridge the gap between physical brains and consciousness is provided by panpsychism — the view that consciousness is a property of all matter and that everything is in some sense conscious. According to panpsychism, the arising of con-sciousness in brains is not particularly problematic because (i) brains are a type of material object, (ii) material objects have the property of consciousness, and so (iii) brains have consciousness. No specific connecting link between brains and consciousness is required since consciousness (the outcome) is already found in the ground (brains). Of course panpsychists still need to explain why matter itself has consciousness. To most modern commentators this quandary seems as problematic, if not more so, than the problem of how brains could give rise to consciousness. In our contemporary culture panpsychism is therefore usually rejected as a serious candidate theory. However there are notable exceptions, such as Globus (1976) and Chalmers. Chalmers, in an albeit disguised form of panpsychism, is willing to consider that conscious experience may be 'much more widespread than we might have believed, as information [of which consciousness is a fundamental inner aspect] is everywhere' (p. 27; my insertion). For anyone who *is* happy to accept consciousness as a property of all things (and in animistic cultures this is the norm), it becomes easier to take the mind–body relationship for granted. Accepting consciousness as a property of a general category, to which the brain belongs, generates at least a temporary feeling of having dealt with how brains give rise to consciousness. The problem has been pushed back to the ground and as long as we can keep our limited attentional capacity engaged on the mind–body relationship, we fail to notice the explanatory gap.

Similarity and Familiarity

So far it does not seem that any of Rosch's four ways of making events *seem* to arise from themselves will, for the majority of us, easily succeed in hiding the explanatory gap between consciousness and brain. Of course the account could be (and is likely to be) incomplete. But we can do better than arguing just that Rosch's prescriptions for hiding explanatory gaps do not apply too well to consciousness. We can use her framework to predict that consciousness will be a *particularly* difficult customer.

Consider again Rosch's last way of hiding explanatory gaps, namely seeing an outcome as a property of a category to which the ground belongs. This has two particular sub-classes which Rosch does not mention. These occur very commonly, are capable of breeding the same impression of causal coherence, and are of particular relevance to the relationship between brain and consciousness. They are (1) situations which are in some way *similar* to other types of situation, and (2) situations which are in themselves just very *familiar*.

First take similarity. Suppose that the relationship between a ground A and its outcome B has a degree of structural isomorphism with another ground–outcome situation, say the relationship between X and Y. Ground A can then be seen as a member of a more general category of states of affairs which have B-like outcomes. If the causal link between X and Y is felt to be understood, then this sense of understanding may transfer. A good example is provided by the computational metaphor of cognitive psychology: we think we know how computers work, brains are like computers, so we think that we know broadly how brains work. What we are talking about is the power of analogy, not just to provide a structural template for the shape of an explanation, but to obscure explanatory gaps and promote a *feeling* of understanding. Lakoff (1988) has argued that understanding is generally based on a group of structural templates which derive from the structure of our experience of our own bodies and our experience of social interaction. If this is so, these fundamental templates may themselves be prone to hiding explanatory gaps in the way that, according to Rosch, characterizes our folk understanding of perception and intentional action. Therefore transfer of a feeling of understanding, via the process of analogy, could be very general.

Next consider familiarity. Even if a relationship between A and B is *dissimilar* to other relationships we know of, it may still be *familiar* — perhaps the occurrence of the relationship is a very common event. If so, there is a sense in which B is a property of the category which is just the 'category of instances of A leading to B'. To the extent that instances of this category are familiar, and the category therefore also highly familiar, we may tend to see outcome B as a property of the category, not of the particular instance. Again there is a sense in which outcome B is contained in ground A, and we may be less likely to notice the absence of an explicit connecting link between A and B. Familiarity may therefore be another important way of obscuring explanatory gaps. If I cycle over broken glass, I really feel as if I understand why I get a puncture. This is because I am happy to let my explanation rest at a certain level, characterized by relationships I accept because they are common regularities and fit snugly into my world picture of what goes with what (knowledge about air in tyres, sharp objects, holes, pressure release, etc.). In this way every-day explanations leave us with the impression of getting to the causal nexus of events.

If similarity and familiarity help to obscure explanatory gaps, then when we encounter *unfamiliar* relationships which are also *unlike* anything else in our experience, the opposite will hold true. Explanatory gaps will be particularly obvious. Modern physics provides an excellent example of an area where this is commonplace, and where feelings of locating a causal nexus and of 'transparent' understanding consequently break down. All we are left with are mathematical regularities which defy direct visualization and expose a reality that seems fundamentally alien to the human mind (Davies & Gribbin, 1991).

Consciousness may find itself in a similar boat. It seems not improbable that the relationships between a physical system and consciousness may turn out to be so unique and unlike other types of relationship we have so far encountered, that neither analogy nor familiarity wil be able to lull us away from the search for a causal nexus. The explanatory gap will therefore continue to be glaringly obvious. Perhaps in time, as we become used to the relationships we have mapped, familiarity may breed a certain sense of understanding. But we should *not*, at least initially, expect to *feel* as if we understand.

Conclusion

In conclusion, whether we see explanatory gaps is at least partly to do with psychology, with what goes on in our head, and not just with the way the world *is* objectively. We must not ignore the psychology of the hard problem. Our ability to gauge the success of our scientific attempts to understand consciousness will be clouded if we do not consider the factors that govern our psychological perception of causal relationships, and, especially, the question of whether these factors prescribe that the relationship between brain and consciousness is likely to be of the type that lends itself to a psychological perception of causality.

We should not necessarily expect that progress in answering the hard question of consciousness will be accompanied by a *feeling* of understanding. As we search for an answer, we would therefore be unwise to depend on any intuitive sense of understanding as a guiding heuristic. In particular, those of us who are concerned with an experimentally based exploration of the relationships between consciousness and brain processes (whether at a neurophysiological or cognitive level of description) should not worry whether we are getting nearer to a feeling of understanding. Rather, we should be content to get on with the job of mapping the terrain.

Discussions of consciousness are often apologetic that their theoretical contributions do not appear to make inroads on the hard question. While I would not want to suggest that some humility in the face of the hard question is amiss, I think that this particular apology is unnecessary. For the reasons I have discussed, we should not necessarily expect a moment of blinding insight when we suddenly manage to get our heads round the problem. As far as the hard question is concerned, there is nothing second best about just chipping away at the relationships between brain and consciousness, and we do not need to apologize for doing it.

In order to avoid confusion, let me stress that I am not trying to argue any of the following. First, I am not trying to say anything about what form scientific theories should take, or denying any of the usual criteria for their success such as predictive power, falsifiablity, coherence with other theories, parsimony, etc. Second, I do not wish to deny the existence of a hard question; even if we are 'only' looking for lawful regularities, our search must address the existence of conscious experience itself. Third, I am not denying that there is an answer to the hard question, or that we should be trying to find one. Finally, I do not want to belittle the very great problems presented by the hard question. It is one thing to plot the relationships between neurophysiology, cognition and consciousness experience, but for reasons that I discuss elsewhere (Price, in press), it is an empirically non-trivial task to discover which brain processes are *necessary and sufficient* for consciousness.

My central point has been that the apparent adequacy of our progress in answering the hard question depends partly on psychological processes which mediate our perception of causality. In presenting this argument I have used the particular framework of Rosch's account of our psychological perception of cause on the one hand, and a regularity account of causation on the other. However I believe that the argument transcends this framework. Rosch's account is likely to be at best incomplete, but it importantly illustrates that our psychological reaction to what scientific exploration offers us can vary. It therefore cautions us to be wary about how we judge the fruits and direction of our scientific endeavour, and warns us that the hard question is not just the science, but also our reaction to the science. Similarly, a regularity account of causation may be contentious but it provides a good illustration of the difference between our everyday conception of causality, and factual accounts of causality 'in the objects'. I have taken an extreme account in order to make the contrast as clear as possible, but I suspect that other accounts will still not be able to offer us anything that completely matches our everyday concept of causation. This is because our everyday concept is not really a coherent one: how *can* two things that are different lead to each other? Like the notion of free will it is something that we are endowed with rather than a logical concept. And as with free will it is rather difficult to leave our everyday concept of causation behind. To climb out of our heads and adapt our everyday concept to fit our scientific or philosophical concept is far from easy.[*]

---

[*] **Author's Note.** I would like to thank Henry Howlett and especially Peter Grossenbacher for their extremely helpful comments on early drafts of this paper. I am also very grateful to Jonathan Shear and to the two anonymous referees whose critical comments helped to clarify my arguments. This paper was originally published in the *Journal of Consciousness Studies*, **3**, No.4 (1996), pp. 303–12.

References

Davies, P.C.W. and Gribbin, J. (1991), *The Matter Myth: Towards 21st Century Science* (London:Viking Press).

Chalmers, D.J. (1995), 'Facing up to the problem of consciousness', *Journal of Consciousness Studies*, **2** (3), pp. 200–19 (reprinted in this volume).

Globus G.G. (1976), '**Mind, structure and contradiction**', in *Consciousness and the Brain*, ed. G.G. Globus, G. Maxwell & I. Savodnik (New York: Plenum Press).

Gray, J.A. (1995), 'Consciousness — What is the problem and how should it be addressed?' *Journal of Consciousness Studies,* **2** (1), pp. 5–9.

Hume, D. (1740/1964), *A Treatise on Human Nature,* ed. L.A. Selby-Bigge (Oxford: Clarendon Press).

Lakoff, G. (1988), 'Cognitive semantics', in *Meaning and Mental Representations*, ed. Umberto Eco *et al.* (Bloomington: Indiana University Press).

Levine, J. (1983), 'Materialism and qualia: the explanatory gap', *Pacific Philosophical Quarterly,* **64**, pp. 354–61.

Mackie, J.L. (1974), *The Cement of the Universe* (Oxford: Oxford University Press).

McGinn, C. (1989), 'Can we solve the mind–body problem?' *Mind,* **98**, pp. 349–66.

Nagel, T. (1986), *The View from Nowhere* (New York: Oxford University Press).

Popper, K.R. (1980), *The Logic of Scientific Discovery* (New York: Routledge).

Popper, K.R. and Eccles, J.C. (1984), *The Self and its Brain: An Argument for Interactionism* (London: Routledge & Kegan Paul).

Price, M.C. (in press), 'Now you see it, now you don't. Preventing consciousness with visual masking', in *Finding Consciousness in the Brain: A Neurocognitive Approach (Advances in Consciousness Research, 8),* ed. P.G. Grossenbacher (Amsterdam: John Benjamins).

Rosch, E. (1994), 'Is causality circular? Event structure in folk psychology, cognitive science and Buddhist logic', *Journal of Consciousness Studies*, **1** (1), pp. 50–65.

Searle, J.R. (1983), *Intentionality* (Cambridge: Cambridge University Press).

Smart, J.J.C. (1993), 'Laws of nature as a species of regularities', in *Ontology, Causality and Mind,* ed. J. Bacon, K. Campbell & L. Reinhardt (Cambridge: Cambridge University Press).

Strawson, G. (1989), *The Secret Connexion: Causation, Realism and David Hume* (Oxford: Clarendon Press).

Von Wright, G.H. (1974), *Causality and Determinism* (New York and London: Columbia University Press).

Wimsatt, C.W. (1976), 'Reductionism, levels of organisation, and the mind–body problem', in *Consciousness and the Brain,* ed. G.G. Globus, G. Maxwell & I. Savodnik (New York: Plenum Press).

The
Explanatory
Gap

Colin McGinn

Consciousness and Space

I: The Location of Consciousness

Descartes famously held that, while the essence of body is spatial extension, the essence of mind is thought. Thought is taken to be the defining attribute of incorporeal substance — substance that is non-spatial in nature. He writes: 'For if we . . . examine what we are, we see very clearly that neither extension nor shape nor local motion, nor anything of this kind which is attributable to a body, belongs to our nature, but that thought alone belongs to it.' (Cottingham, Stoothoff, Murdoch, 1985, p. 195.) The mental and the spatial are thus mutually exclusive categories.

It is hard to deny that Descartes was tapping into our ordinary understanding of the nature of mental phenomena when he formulated the distinction between mind and body in this way — our consciousness does indeed present itself as non-spatial in character. Consider a visual experience, E, as of a yellow flash. Associated with E in the cortex is a complex of neural structures and events, N, which does admit of spatial description. N occurs, say, an inch from the back of the head; it extends over some specific area of the cortex; it has some kind of configuration or contour; it is composed of spatial parts that aggregate into a structured whole; it exists in three spatial dimensions; it excludes other neural complexes from its spatial location. N is a regular denizen of space, as much as any other physical entity. But E seems not to have any of these spatial characteristics: it is not located at any specific place; it takes up no particular volume of space; it has no shape; it is not made up of spatially distributed parts; it has no spatial dimensionality; it is not solid. Even to ask for its spatial properties is to commit some sort of category mistake, analogous to asking for the spatial properties of numbers. E seems not to be the *kind of thing* that falls under spatial predicates. It falls under temporal predicates and it can obviously be described in other ways — by specifying its owner, its intentional content, its phenomenal character — but it resists being cast as a regular inhabitant of the space we see around us and within which the material world has its existence. Spatial occupancy is not (at least on the face of it) the mind's preferred mode of being.

No doubt this is connected with the fact that conscious states are not *perceived*. We perceive, by our various sense organs, a variety of material objects laid out in space, taking up certain volumes and separated by certain distances. We thus conceive of these perceptual objects as spatial entities; perception informs us directly of their spatiality. But conscious subjects and their mental states are not in this way perceptual objects. We do not see or hear or smell or touch them, and *a fortiori* do not perceive them as spatially

This paper was originally published in the *Journal of Consciousness Studies*, **2**, No.3 (1995), pp. 220–30.

individuated.[1] This holds both for the first- and third-person perspectives. Since we do not *observe* our own states of consciousness, nor those of others, we do not apprehend these states as spatial. So our modes of cognition of mental states do not bring them under the kinds of spatial concepts appropriate to perceptual acquaintance. Perceptual geometry gets no purchase on them. And this is not just a contingent fact about the mind.[2]

Nor do we think of conscious states as occupying an unperceived space, as we think of the unobservable entities of physics. We have no conception of what it would even *be* to perceive them as spatial entities. God may see the elementary particles as arrayed in space, but even He does not perceive our conscious states as spatially defined — no more than He sees numbers as spatially defined. It is not that experiences have location, shape and dimensionality for eyes that are sharper than ours. Since they are non-spatial they are in principle unperceivable.

This is I think what people have in mind when they aver that 'consciousness is not a thing'. The thought expressed here is not the trivial one that to refer to consciousness is to invoke a category of events or states or processes and not a category of objects or continuant particulars. Our intuition that conscious states are not spatial is not the intuition that no *state* is an *object*. For ordinary physical states and events are spatial entities in the intended sense: we apprehend events as occurring *in* space, and states are features *of* spatially constituted objects. So it would be wrong to offer a deflationary interpretation of our non-spatial conception of consciousness by insisting that it comes to nothing more than a recognition that talk of consciousness is talk of events and states — just like talk of explosions and motions and electric charge. The non-spatial nature of consciousness, as we conceive it, is much more radical than that diagnosis suggests. Descartes was not committing the simple howler of failing to notice that conscious phenomena are not objects at all and hence not spatial objects. In fact, even when we do speak of something that belongs to the category of continuant object, namely the *subject* of consciousness, we still insist upon its non-spatial character.[3] The self is not a 'thing' either, in the intended sense. The mental realm is just not bound up in the world of objects in space in the way that ordinary physical events are so bound up. So, at any rate, our pretheoretical view assures us.

That may seem exaggerated, at least under one interpretation of the idea of connectedness to the spatial world. For, it might be said, we do in point of fact locate conscious events in the spatial world — not very precisely perhaps, but at least in a fairly systematic way. Thus we take each subject of consciousness to be somewhere in the vicinity of a distinguished body, and we locate conscious events in the approximate neighbourhood of the physical object we call the brain. We certainly do not suppose that I am in some *other* place than my body, and we locate my thoughts nearer to my head than to my feet. So, perhaps we do grant spatial characteristics to consciousness, at least of a rudimentary sort.

[1] Obviously I am not denying that there is a sense in which we can perceive persons, by perceiving their bodies; my point is that we do not perceive the psychological subject *qua* psychological subject. If you like, we do not perceive the *I* of the Cogito.

[2] We see an echo of this in two doctrines of Wittgenstein's: that self-ascription is not based upon observation; and that the notion of inner ostension (pointing) is ill-defined. In this respect, at least, Wittgenstein and Descartes converge on the same fundamental insights. I think, in fact, that a good deal of Wittgenstein's philosophy of mind is based upon a repudiation of a spatial model of the mind.

[3] I am assuming that the conscious subject is not simply identical with the body. But my overall position does not depend upon this, since the point applies equally to conscious states themselves.

I think this point should be granted, at least so far as it goes: but it does not go very far in undermining the intrinsic non-spatiality of the mental. How do we actually make the locational judgements about consciousness that we do? Not, clearly, by perceiving that conscious events occupy particular places; rather, by trading upon certain *causal* considerations. Events in particular physical objects are directly causally involved in changes of mental state, and we locate the mental change roughly where those causally proximate physical objects are. I am where that body is whose physical states bear most directly on my mental state; and my states of consciousness are situated in the vicinity of that brain whose activity is most directly implicated in the causal relations controlling my mental life. For example, my visual states are in the whereabouts of the eyes and brain that produce them, and not somewhere in (say) the Grand Canyon (unless my eyes and brain happen to be there). But this kind of causally based location of the mental should be taken for what it is. First, it is parasitic on a prior location of physical objects; there is no independent route on to mental location, since that is based solely on bearing causal relations to things that *can* be nonderivatively located. If we imagine abrogating these causal relations, by considering a world in which there are no psychophysical causal connexions, but only intra-mental ones, then we see that in such a world no form of spatial location would be available for mental events. They would not be tied down to any location at all, no matter how vague. Locating mental events as we do in the actual world is merely 'theoretical' — a sort of courtesy location. Considered in themselves, intrinsically, we do not regard mental events as having location. The imprecision of our locational judgements here is a mark of this. Second, to allow that consciousness can be roughly located is not to grant it the full panoply of spatial predications. We still do not get predications of shape, size, dimensionality, etc. And this shows that such spatiality as we do allow to mental matters is of a second-class and derivative nature. Descartes himself might readily have allowed this kind of causally based location of the mental while still insisting that concepts of extension have no proper application to the mental.

It might be objected that there are some mental events that do permit precise location, and that this is based on something like immediate perception. Thus I feel a pain to be in my hand, and that is indeed exactly where it is. Isn't this just like seeing the physical injury to my hand that produces the pain? Well, it is true enough that the pain presents itself as being in my hand, but there are familiar reasons for not taking this at face value. Without my brain no such pain would be felt, and the same pain can be produced simply by stimulating my brain and leaving my hand alone (I might not even have a hand). Such facts incline us to say, reasonably enough, that the pain is really in my brain, if anywhere, and only appears to be in my hand (a sort of locational illusion takes place). That is, causal criteria yield a different location for the pain from phenomenal criteria. Anyway bodily pain is an unusual case and does not generalise to other mental phenomena (perhaps this is why we ordinarily speak of pain as a bodily state rather than a mental one).

It is instructive to consider the notion of spatial exclusion in relation to the mind. A well-known metaphysical principle has it that no two material objects (of the same kind) can occupy the same place at the same time. It is in the very nature of space and objects that there should be this kind of necessary exclusion. And analogous principles can be formulated for material events, states and processes. Now ask whether this principle applies also to mental items. Can two subjects of awareness occupy the same place at the same time? Can two thoughts be spatio-temporally coincident? Can two bodily sensations? The questions seem misconceived, since the issue does not really *arise* for mental things. We want to say: 'Well, *if* mental things had location and other spatial properties, *then* there might be such exclusion; but since they don't it is not clear what to say. Maybe, for all we know, they can be spatio-temporally coincident, since nothing in their intrinsic nature rules it out.' The fact is that the question is too much like asking whether two numbers can be at the same place at the same time. We just do not conceive of these things in ways that bring them within the scope of the principle of spatial exclusion. This is a way of saying that the notion of *solidity* has no application to mental phenomena. If the essential mark of the spatial is competiton for space, as the metaphysical principle records, then the mental lacks that essential feature.

In view of the above considerations there is something highly misleading about the popular suggestion that mental phenomena have the same sort of conceptual status as the posits of physical science: that is, that both are unobservables postulated to make the best sense of the data. Apart from the obvious point that we also know about our mental states 'from the inside', there is a crucial disanalogy here, which underscores the *sui generis* character of the mental case. While we think of the unobservables of physics as existing in space and hence in spatial relation to the things we do observe, we do not think of the mental states that explain behaviour in this way. Explanatory posits they may be, at least from the third-person perspective, but they are not the reassuring spatial entities that other explanatory posits are. It is thus far more puzzling how they relate to behaviour, especially causally, than is the relation of atomic events to the macroscopic behaviour of material bodies. In the physical case, we have notions of contact causation and gravitational force acting across space, but in the mental case it is quite unclear how these causal paradigms are supposed to apply. *How* do conscious events cause physical changes in the body? Not by proximate contact, apparently, on pain of over-spatialising consciousness, and presumably not by action-at-a-distance either. Recent philosophy has become accustomed to the idea of mental causation, but this is actually much more mysterious than is generally appreciated, once the non-spatial character of consciousness is acknowledged. To put it differently, we understand mental causation *only* if we deny the intuition of non-spatiality. The standard analogy with physical unobservables simply dodges these hard questions, lulling us into a false sense of intelligibility.[4]

I conclude, then, from this quick survey of somewhat familiar terrain that consciousness does not, on its face, slot smoothly into the ordinary spatial world. The Cartesian intuition of unextendedness is a firm part of our ordinary conception of the mental. In advance of theoretical reconstruction consciousness is not spatially well-behaved. We shall next look at some consequences of this, inquiring what theoretical response should be made to it.

II: The Origin of Consciousness

If consciousness is not constitutionally spatial, then how could it have had its origin in the spatial world? According to received cosmology, there was a time at which the

---

[4] Of course, it is a presupposed materialism that permits the usual insouciance over mental causation. I am simply pointing out that *without* materialism the claim of mental causation, though no doubt correct, is burdened with severe problems of intelligibility. Once materialism is questioned all the old problems about mental causation resurface.

universe contained no consciousness but only matter in space obeying the laws of physics. Then the evolution of life began and matter started clumping together in novel ways, driven by the mechanism of natural selection. Soon, in cosmic time, neural nuclei appeared, leading to brains of various sizes and structures — and along with that (as we think) came consciousness. Evidently, then, matter fell into ever more complex and ingenious arrangements and as a result consciousness came into the world. The only ingredients in the pot when consciousness was cooking were particles and fields laid out in space, yet something radically non-spatial got produced. On that fine spring morning when consciousness was first laid on nature's table there was nothing around but extended matter in space, yet now a non-spatial stuff simmered and bubbled. We seem compelled to conclude that something essentially non-spatial emerged from something purely spatial — that the non-spatial is somehow a construction out of the spatial. And this looks more like magic than a predictable unfolding of natural law. Let us call the problem of how this is possible the 'space problem' with respect to consciousness.[5]

Notice that this problem has no parallel in the evolution of life forms *per se*. These are indeed cosmic novelties, but they do not essentially transcend the mechanisms of spatial aggregation, and we have a good theory of how the novelty is generated. There is no space problem in explaining the emergence of organisms as such; that problem only begins to bite when conscious states enter the scene. To put it in Descartes' terms: how can something whose essence is to be non-spatial develop from something whose essence is to be spatial? How can you derive the unextended from the extended? Note too that this problem has no parallel in the relation between the abstract and the physical, since, though non-spatial, the abstract is not supposed to have *emerged* from the material. The problem arises from a specific clash between the essence of consciousness and its apparent origin.

We might be reminded at this point of the big bang. That notable occurrence can be regarded as presenting an inverse space problem. For, on received views, it was at the moment of the big bang that space itself came into existence, there being nothing spatial antecedently to that. But how does space come from non-space? What kind of 'explosion' could create space *ab initio*? And this problem offers an even closer structural parallel to the consciousness problem if we assume, as I would argue is plausible, that the big bang was not the beginning (temporally or explanatorily) of all existence.[6] Some prior independent state of things must have led to that early cataclysm, and this sequence of events

---

[5] There are some suggestive remarks on the spatiality of organisms and the non-combinatorial nature of the mental in Nagel (1986, pp. 49–51).

[6] Here I am raising highly controversial issues. Let me just say that all the arguments I have heard for supposing the big bang to be the beginning of everything take the form of inferring an ontological conclusion from epistemic premises — to the effect that since we can't *know* anything about any earlier state we should suppose there to *be* no such state. But that, I assert, is an idealist fallacy. Sometimes it is suggested that time began with the big bang, because of its supposed internal connexion with space. I find such arguments unconvincing. But, actually, my point is consistent with allowing time to start with the big bang, since we could always introduce a notion of explanation that did not require temporal priority. I myself see no good reason to rule out a picture of the universe in which radically new realities come into existence as a result of other realities. Just as it took gravity to convert the gaseous early state of the universe into the clumpy galaxies we now take for granted, so the big bang may have been just one episode in which the universe underwent a radical transformation. In general, I think people are too ready to suppose that nothing antecedent to the big bang could have existed, usually on shaky philosophical grounds — ultimately of an anthropocentric nature. (No doubt I shall get into trouble for poking my nose into cosmologists' business here!).

itself must have some intelligible explanation — just as there must be an explanation for the sequence that led from matter-in-space to consciousness. The brain puts into reverse, as it were, what the big bang initiated: it erases spatial dimensions rather than creating them. It undoes the work of creating space, swallowing down matter and spitting out consciousness. So, taking the very long view, the universe has gone through phases of space generation and (local) space annihilation; or at least, with respect to the latter, there have been operations on space that have generated a non-spatial being. This suggests the following heady speculation: that the origin of consciousness somehow draws upon those properties of the universe that antedate and explain the occurrence of the big bang. If we need a pre-spatial level of reality to account for the big bang, then it may be this very level that is exploited in the generation of consciousness. That is, assuming that remnants of the pre-big bang universe have persisted, it may be that these features of the universe are somehow involved in engineering the non-spatial phenomenon of consciousness. If so, consciousness turns out to be older than matter in space, at least as to its raw materials.[7]

However that may be, we are still faced with the space problem for consciousness. How might it be dealt with? There are, historically, two main lines of response to the problem, commonly supposed to be exclusive and exhaustive. One response denies a key premise of the problem, namely that mind sprang from matter. Instead, mind has an autonomous existence, as independent of matter as matter is of mind. Perhaps mind has always existed, or maybe came about in some analogue of the origin of matter, or owes its existence to a direct act of God. In any event, mind is no kind of out-growth of matter but an independent ontological category. Thus we have classical dualism, Descartes' own position. In effect, dualism takes the space problem to be a *reductio* of the emergence hypothesis. Mind and matter may causally interact (let us not inquire how!) but it is absurd, for dualism, to suppose that mind could owe its very *being* to matter. That is simply metaphysically impossible, according to dualism. You can no more derive the unextended from the extended than you can derive an ought from an is.[8]

A second response questions what we have been assuming so far, namely that consciousness is inherently non-spatial. We may grant that we ordinarily *conceive* of it in this way, but we should insist that that mode of conception be abandoned. Here we encounter, it may be said, yet another area in which common sense misconceives the true nature of reality. In fact, conscious states are just as spatially constituted as brain states, since they *are* brain states — neural configurations in all their spatial glory. Thus we have classical materialism, the thesis that consciousness is nothing over and above the cellular structures and processes we observe in the brain.[9] Since these admit of straightforward spatial characterization, so, by identity, do conscious states. The case is analogous to the

[7] Clearly, there are many large assumptions here: not merely that reality did not begin with the big bang, but also that the prior reality has somehow persisted into the post-big bang state of the universe, presumably by virtue of some sort of conservation principle. These seem to me pretty plausible assumptions, though how to establish them is another question. I should note also that the speculation in the text pertains only to the non-spatiality of consciousness; I am not suggesting that all the features of consciousness could be explained by pre-big bang properties. In this paper I am leaving on one side questions about the subjectivity of consciousness, qualia and so on.

[8] In McGinn (1993a) I give dualism the best defence I can, though it is not a position I subscribe to.

[9] Functionalism and allied doctrines should be included here, since they are broadly materialist. Computationalism is harder to classify because of tricky questions about the ontology of computer

following: to common sense physical objects appear solid, but science tells us that this is an illusion, since they are really made up of widely spaced particles in a lattice that is anything but solid. Somewhat so, the materialist insists that the appearance of non-spatiality that consciousness presents is a kind of illusion, and that in reality it is as spatial (even solid!) as the cell clusters that constitute the brain.[10] It is Descartes' assumption of unextendedness that is mistaken, according to materialism, not the emergence hypothesis.

Now it is not my intention here to rehearse any of the usual criticisms of these two venerable positions, beyond noting that both have deeply unattractive features, which I think we would be reluctant to countenance if it were not for the urgency of the problem. These are positions we feel driven to, rather than ones that save the phenomena in a theoretically satisfying way. My purpose is to identify a third option, and to explore some of its ramifications. The point of this third option is to preserve material emergence while not denying the ordinary non-spatial conception of consciousness. The heart of the view, put simply, is this: the brain cannot have merely the spatial properties recognised in current physical science, since these are insufficient to explain what it can achieve, namely the generation of consciousness. The brain must have aspects that are not represented in our current physical world-view, aspects we deeply do not understand, in addition to all those neurons and electro-chemical processes. There is, on this view, a radical incompleteness in our view of reality, including physical reality. In order to provide an explanation of the emergence of consciousness we would need a conceptual revolution, in which fundamentally new properties and principles are identified. This may involve merely supplementing our current theories with new elements, so that we need not abandon what we now believe; or it may be — as I think more likely — that some profound revisions are required, some repudiation of current theory. Consciousness is an anomaly in our present world-view and, like all anomalies, it calls for some more or less drastic rectification in that relative to which it is anomalous. Some ideal theory T contains the solution to the space problem, but arriving at T would require some major upheavals in our basic conception of reality.

I am now in a position to state the main thesis of this paper: in order to solve the mind–body problem we need, at a minimum, a new conception of space. We need a conceptual breakthrough in the way we think about the medium in which material objects exist, and hence in our conception of material objects themselves. That is the region in which our ignorance is focused: not in the details of neurophysiological activity but, more fundamentally, in how space is structured or constituted. That which we refer to when we use the word 'space' has a nature that is quite different from how we standardly conceive it to be; so different, indeed, that it is capable of 'containing' the non-spatial (as we now conceive it) phenomenon of consciousness. Things in space can generate consciousness only because those things are not, at some level, just how we conceive them to be; they harbour some hidden aspect or principle.

---

programs. On one natural interpretation computer programs are constituted by abstract objects, so they are non-spatial. This may or may not be a good way to capture the non-spatiality of consciousness (actually not), but the view is clearly no longer materialist.

[10] This is an unspoken assumption of large tracts of contemporary philosophy of mind. Even those who recognise that consciousness poses problems for materialism in virtue of its phenomenal character seldom acknowledge that its non-spatiality is also a major stumbling-block for materialism — despite the fact that Descartes took it (and not qualia) to be critical.

Before I try to motivate this hypothesis further, let me explain why I think the needed conceptual shift goes deeper than mere brain physiology, down to physics itself. For, if I am right, then it is not just the science of matter in the head that is deficient but the science of matter spread more widely.[11] A bad reason for insisting that the incompleteness reaches down as far as physics is the assumption that physiology *reduces* to physics, so that any incompleteness in the reduced theory must be reflected in the reducing theory. This is a bad reason because it is a mistake to think that the so-called special sciences — geology, biology, information science, psychology, etc. — reduce to physics. I will not rehearse the usual arguments for this, since they have been well marshalled elsewhere. (See, for instance, Fodor, 1974.) If that were the right way to look at the matter, then physics would be *highly* incomplete and defective on many fronts, since all the special sciences have outstanding unsolved problems. But it is surely grotesque to claim that the problem of how (say) the dinosaurs became extinct shows any inadequacy in the basic laws of physics! Rather, the intransitivity of problems down the heirarchy of the sciences is itself a reason to reject any reductionist view of their interrelations. So it is certainly an open question whether the problem of consciousness requires revisions in neurophysiology alone, or whether those revisions will upset broader reaches of physical theory. It depends entirely on what is the correct diagnosis of the essential core of the problem. And what I am suggesting is that the correct diagnosis involves a challenge to our general conception of space. Given the fact of emergence, matter in space has to have features that go beyond the usual conception, in order that something as spatially anomalous as consciousness could have thereby come into existence. Somehow the unextended can issue from matter in space, and this must depend upon properties of the basis that permit such a derivation. It therefore seems hard to avoid the conclusion that the requisite properties are instantiated by matter prior to its organisation into brain structure. The brain must draw upon aspects of nature that were already there. According to our earlier speculation, these aspects may be connected to features of the universe that played a part in the early creation of matter and space itself — those features, themselves pre-spatial, that characterised the universe before the big bang. Consciousness is so singular, ontologically, and such an affront to our standard spatial notions, that some pretty remarkable properties of matter will be needed in order to sustain the assumption that consciousness can come from matter. It is not likely that we need merely a local conceptual revolution.

III: The Nature of Space

Let us perform an induction over the history of science. There is what might be called a 'folk theory of space', a set of beliefs about the general nature of space that comes naturally to human beings in advance of doing any systematic science. It probably develops, in part, out of our perceptual systems and it serves to guide our behaviour; we might think of it as a visuo-motor space. No doubt it would be difficult to describe this mental representation of space in full detail, but I think it is fair to report that it encodes a broadly Euclidian geometry and that it regards motion as relative to the position of the earth. It also has some firm ideas about what it is for something to *be* somewhere. Now it is a platitude of the history of science that this folk theory has come under successive

---

[11] Penrose (1989) also takes consciousness to challenge the adequacy of current physics.

challenges, which have substantially undermined and reformed it. Indeed, most of the big advances in physics and astronomy have involved revising our folk theory of space. Let me mention, sketchily, a few of these, to give flavour to what I am building up to. First, of course, there was the replacement of the geocentric view of the universe with the heliocentric one, and then the replacement of that with an a-centric view. The Newtonian scheme takes the earth to be just one body in space among others, subject to the same laws of motion; our earthly position does not define some privileged coordinate with respect to which everything else must be measured. We must also recognise the existence of a new force, gravity, which acts across space without benefit of a mechanical medium. Thus space has a hitherto unsuspected power — which Newton himself regarded as dubiously 'occult'. Later, and just as famously, the developments surrounding relativity theory called for the abandonment of a Euclidian conception of physical space, to be replaced by geometries that are counter-intuitive to the folk theory of space. Curved space-time was the upshot, among other exotica. Quantum theory also prompts serious questions about the nature of space: particles have no unique location, and various 'nonlocality effects' upset our usual ideas about physical things and their causal depend-ence. What it is to be *in* space becomes obscure. Then we have such speculations as string theory and twistor theory and the many-worlds hypothesis, in which further 'hidden' dimensions are introduced. Our folk theory of space has been regularly hung out to dry. From the point of view of the divine physicist, space must look to be a very different creature from that presented to the visuo-motor system of human beings.

All this is suggestive of a certain diagnosis of the problem with respect to conscious-ness. For here too we have a phenomenon that puts pressure on our ordinary conception of space. Conscious phenomena are not located and extended in the usual way; but then again they are surely not somehow 'outside' of space, adjacent perhaps to the abstract realm. Rather, they bear an opaque and anomalous relation to space as currently conceived. They seem neither quite 'in' it nor quite 'out' of it. Presumably, however, this is merely an epistemological fact, not an ontological one. It is just that we lack the theory with which to make sense of the relation in question. In themselves consciousness and space must be related in some intelligible naturalistic fashion, though they may have to be con-ceived very differently from the way they now are for this to become apparent. My conjec-ture is that it is in this nexus that the solution to the space problem lies. Consciousness is the next big anomaly to call for a revision in how we conceive space — just as other revisions were called for by earlier anomalies. And the revision is likely to be large-scale, despite the confinement of consciousness to certain small pockets of the natural world. This is because space is such a fundamental feature of things that anything that produces disturbances in our conception of it must cut pretty deeply into our world-view.

No doubt this is all very mind-stretching and obscure; and it is of course not a theory but an indication of where the correct theory might lie. There is a rather Kantian ring to it, what with noumenal space containing all the answers that phenomenal space cannot provide. But I am not really distressed by the lack of transparency of the conjecture, because I think that it is quite *predictable* that our intellects should falter when trying to make sense of the place of consciousness in the natural order. (See McGinn 1991; 1993b.) And here the bitter pill beneath the sweet coating begins to seep through. For to suggest that we need a radically new conception of space is not to imply that we *can achieve* any such conception, even in principle. It may be merely to point to the place at which we are incurably ignorant. To explain what I mean let us back up for a while to consider the question of human epistemology — the question of what we can and cannot know.

IV: The Limits of Human Knowledge

It is easier not to know than to know. That truism has long had its philosophical counterpart in rueful admissions that there are nontrivial limits on what human beings can come to grasp. The human epistemic system has a specific structure and mode of operation, and there may well be realities that lie beyond its powers of coverage. Chomsky, in particular, regards our cognitive system as a collection of special-purpose modules that target specific areas of competence, and fail to target others. (See Chomsky 1976; 1988.) The language faculty is one of these, which itself breaks down into a number of sub-modules. It is targeted away from certain possible languages as a by-product of its positive targeting: human languages, yes; Martian languages, no. Chomsky adopts essentially the same conception of what he calls our 'science-forming' faculties: they too are just a collection of contingent cognitive structures, biologically based, that have arisen in us over the course of evolution. They have a phylogeny and an ontogeny, and they operate according to certain specific principles, these being realised by machinery in the brain. They are as natural as any organ of the body. Given this, there is absolutely no reason to believe that the faculties in question are capable, at this period in our evolution, of understanding everything there is about the natural world. Viewing the matter in a properly naturalistic spirit, with the human species counted as just one evolved species among others, the overwhelming probability is that we are subject to definite limits on our powers of understanding, just as every other species is. We hardly suppose that the bipedal species who preceded us, traces of which sometimes show up in the fossil record, were themselves as intellectually advanced as we are, with our massively protruding frontal lobes and impressive manual dexterity. We just need to project ourselves into the position of the species that might succeed us to see how contingent and limited our capacities are.

This general viewpoint makes one open to the possibility that some problems may simply exceed our cognitive competence. But I think something more specific is suggested by our discussion so far: namely, that our troubles over space and consciousness arise from certain deep-seated features of the way we represent space to ourselves. We are, cognitively speaking as well as physically, spatial beings *par excellence*: our entire conceptual scheme is shot through with spatial notions, these providing the skeleton of our thought in general. Experience itself, the underpinning of thought, is spatial to its core. The world as we find it — the human world — is a preeminently spatial world. This is a line of thinking powerfully advocated by P.F. Strawson, who focuses particularly on the role of space in our practices of identification. (See Strawson 1959; 1974.) The guiding Strawsonian thesis is that the distinction between particular and universal, and hence between subject and predicate, is founded on the idea, or experience, of spatial distinctness. We regard x and y as distinct particular instances of the same universal P just in so far as we acknowledge that x and y are *at distinct places*. That is what the non-identity of particulars fundamentally consists in for us. Without that spatial resource we should not be able to frame the conception of multiple instances of a single property. This implies that the very notion of a proposition presupposes the notion of spatial separation, and hence location. At root, then, our entire structure of thought is based upon a conception of space in which objects are severally arrayed; though once this structure is in place we can extend and refine it by means of analogy and relations of conceptual dependence.

Now consider thought about consciousness. The non-spatiality of consciousness presents a *prima facie* problem for our system of thought: how, if the Strawsonian thesis is right, do we contrive to think about consciousness at all? It ought to be impossible. The answer lies in those analogies and dependencies just mentioned. We go in for spatialising metaphors and, centrally, we exploit relations to the *body* in making sense of numerically distinct but similar conscious episodes. We embed the mental in the conceptual framework provided by matter in space. We don't *reduce* it to that framework; we appeal, rather, to systematic relations that the two realms manifest. But — and this is the crucial point for me — this is to impose upon conscious events a conceptual grid that is alien to their intrinsic nature. It is as if we must resort to a spatial scheme because nothing else is available to us, given our *de facto* reliance on spatial conceptions. It is not that this scheme is ideally fitted to embed the target subject-matter. Thus we get a kind of partial fit in which location is causally based and notions of extension find no purchase at all. Consciousness comes out looking queasily quasi-spatial, a deformed hybrid. Deep down we know it isn't just extended matter in space, but our modes of thought drag it in that direction, producing much philosophical confusion. We represent the mental by relying upon our folk theory of space because that theory lies at the root of our being able to represent at all — not because the mental itself has a nature that craves such a mode of representation.[12]

To represent consciousness as it is in itself — neat, as it were — we would need to let go of the spatial skeleton of our thought. But, according to the Strawsonian thesis, that would be to let go of the very notion of a proposition, leaving us nothing to think with. So there is no real prospect of our achieving a spatially nonderivative style of thought about consciousness. But then, there is no prospect of our developing a set of concepts that is truly adequate to the intrinsic nature of consciousness; we will always be haunted by the ill-fitting spatial scheme. No doubt this lies behind the sense of total theoretical blankness that attends our attempts to fathom the nature of consciousness; we stare agape in a vacuum of incomprehension. Our conceptual lens is optically out of focus, skewed and myopic, with too much space in the field of view. We can form thoughts *about* consciousness states, but we cannot articulate the natural constitution of what we are thinking about. It is the spatial bias of our thinking that stands in our way (along perhaps with other impediments). And without a more adequate articulation of consciousness we are not going to be in a position to come up with the unifying theory that must link consciousness to the world of matter in space. We are not going to discover what space must be like *such that* consciousness can have its origin in that sphere. Clearly, the space of perception and action is no place to find the roots of consciousness! In that sense of 'space' consciousness is not spatial; but we seem unable to develop a new conception of space that can overcome the impossibility of finding a place for consciousness in it.[13]

---

[12] The inadequacy of spatially-based identification of conscious particulars is my contention, not Strawson's; he seems far more sanguine that the spatial scheme is satisfactory for talk of the mental.

[13] Cf. cognitive beings who have mastered Euclidian geometry but who constitutionally lack the mathematical ability to develop non-Euclidian geometry. An instructive parable on cognitive limitation, with special reference to space and geometry, is Abbott (1884). I am saying that we too are Flat-landers of a sort: we tend to take the space of our experience as the only space there is or could be.

I am presupposing here a robust form of realism about the natural world. The constraint to form our concepts in a certain way does not entail that reality must match that way. Our knowledge constitutes a kind of 'best fit' between our cognitive structure and the objective world; and it fits better in some domains than others. The mind is an area of relatively poor fit. Consciousness occurs in objective reality in a perfectly naturalistic way; we just have no access to its real inner constitution. Perhaps surprisingly, consciousness is one of the more knowledge-transcendent constituents of reality. It must not be forgotten that knowledge is the product of a biological organ whose architecture is fashioned by evolution for brutely pragmatic purposes. Since our bodies are extended objects in space, and since the fate of these bodies is crucial to our reproductive prospects, we need a guidance system in our heads that will enable us to navigate the right trajectory through space, avoiding some objects (predators, poisons, precipices) while steering us close to others (friends, food, feather beds). Thus our space-representing faculties have a quite specific set of goals that by no means coincide with solving the deep ontological problems surrounding consciousness and space. Many animals are expert navigators without having the faintest idea about the true objective structure of space. (The eagle, for one, still awaits its sharp-beaked Newton.) There is no good reason to expect our basic forms of spatial representation to lead smoothly to the ideal theory of the universe. What we need from space, practically speaking, is by no means the same as how space is structured in itself.

I suspect that the very depth of embeddedness of space in our cognitive system produces in us the illusion that we understand it much better than we do. After all, we *see* it whenever we open our eyes and we *feel* it in our bodies as we move. (Time has a similar status.) Hence the large cognitive shocks brought about by the changes in our view of space required by systematic science. We are prone to think that we *can't* be all that wrong about space. I have been arguing that consciousness tests the adequacy of our spatial understanding. It marks the place of a deep lack of knowledge about space, which is hard even to get into focus. No doubt it is difficult to accept that two of the things with which we are most familiar might harbour such intractable obscurities. Irony being a mark of truth, however, we should take seriously the possibility that what we tend to think completely transparent should turn out to transcend altogether our powers of comprehension.

References

Abbott, E.A. (1884), *Flatland: A Romance of Many Dimensions* (New York: Signet Classic).
Chomsky, N. (1976), *Reflections on Language* (London: Fontana).
Chomsky, N. (1988), *Language and Problems of Knowledge* (Cambridge, MA: MIT Press).
Cottingham, J., Stoothoff, R. and Murdoch, D. (eds. 1985). *The Philosophical Writings of Descartes*, Volume I. (Cambridge: Cambridge University Press).
Fodor, J. (1974), 'Special sciences', *Synthese*, **28**, pp. 77–115.
McGinn, C. (1991), *The Problem of Consciousness* (Oxford: Basil Blackwell).
McGinn, C. (1993a), 'Consciousness and cosmology: hyperdualism ventilated', in *Consciousness*, ed. M. Davies and G.W. Humphreys (Oxford: Basil Blackwell).
McGinn, C. (1993b), *Problems in Philosophy* (Oxford: Basil Blackwell).
Nagel, T. (1986), *The View from Nowhere* (Oxford: Oxford University Press).
Penrose, R. (1989), *The Emperor's New Mind* (Oxford: Oxford University Press).
Strawson, P.F. (1959), *Individuals* (London: Methuen).
Strawson, P.F. (1974), *Subject and Predicate in Logic and Grammar* (London: Methuen).

Eugene O. Mills

Giving Up on the Hard Problem of Consciousness

Suppose that there be a machine, the structure of which produces thinking, feeling, and perceiving; imagine this machine enlarged but preserving the same proportions, so that you could enter it as if it were a mill. This being supposed, you might visit its inside; but what would you observe there? Nothing but parts which push and move each other, and never anything that could explain perception.

— Leibniz, *Monadology*, sect. 17 [1]

I: Introduction

Our skulls house machines of the sort Leibniz supposes. Although we nowadays liken the brain more often to a computer than to a mill, his point remains. If we could wander about in the brain (à la the movie *Fantastic Voyage*), we could measure electrical impulses rushing along axons and dendrites, ride neurotransmitters across synapses, and observe all the quotidian commerce of neurobiological life. We still would have no clue why those physical events should produce the experience of tasting chocolate, of hearing a minor chord, of seeing blue.[2]

David Chalmers calls the problem of explaining why physical processes give rise to conscious phenomenal experience the 'hard' problem of consciousness.[3] He argues convincingly that no purely physical, 'reductive' account of consciousness can solve it. He holds that a *non-reductive* theory of consciousness promises a solution, and offers a preliminary sketch of such a theory. I will argue here that no such theory even addresses the hard problem of consciousness.

---

[1] In Leibniz (1965), p. 150.

[2] 'Production' smacks of causation, and that is how I shall take it. But I do not presuppose that experiences are substantially distinct from brain-processes; all the claims about causation to follow may be interpreted either along event-causation or property-causation lines. Furthermore, my arguments could be successfully modified to avoid mention of causation altogether, though with some cost in accessibility. The hard problem of consciousness concerns why, when there is a process that is F, there is something which is G, where 'F' is a physical (or neurobiological) predicate and 'G' a phenomenal one. One need not think that being F *causes* being G to see this as a problem.

[3] I think Leibniz's point applies not only to phenomenal experience but to many of the things whose explanation poses, according to Chalmers, only 'easy' problems. I will confine my remarks in this paper to phenomenal experience, but if I am right, they apply (*mutatis mutandis*) to a much broader range of phenomena.

II: Ways Of Explaining Consciousness

The hard problem of consciousness is supposed to be that of explaining why physical processes give rise to conscious experience. I begin by distinguishing this sort of explanation from explaining in physical terms why a conscious experience occurs. What Chalmers ought to mean by 'the hard problem of consciousness' is, I shall argue, the problem of providing a *non-causal* explanation of the production of consciousness by physical processes.

Chalmers mentions the suggestion by Crick and Koch (1990) that 35–75 hertz oscillations in the cerebral cortex (hereafter, 'CK oscillations') are the basis of consciousness. Suppose Crick and Koch are right. Would it be incorrect, then, to say that particular experiences are explained by complex neural events which include, among other things, the occurrence of CK oscillations?

This depends on what we mean in supposing that CK oscillations are the 'basis' of consciousness. According to Chalmers, 'Crick and Koch suggest that these oscillations are the neural *correlates* of experience'; even if they are right, he says, 'the *explanatory* question remains: Why do the oscillations give rise to experience?' (p. 14). Quite right. But if CK oscillations are *merely* neural correlates of experience, then Chalmers has leapfrogged over a different explanatory question, namely: 'Why does experience occur?' If CK oscillations are merely correlated with experience, then obviously they do not explain why experience occurs. If, on the other hand, they form the basis of experience in the sense that they *cause* it, then it seems a perfectly good answer to the question, 'Why did such-and-such experience occur?' to cite the occurrence of CK oscillations. [4]

The question, 'Why does experience occur?', differs not only from the question, 'What are the neural correlates of experience?', but also from the question, 'Why does neural activity give rise to experience?' For the first question may be answered by giving the causes of experience, perhaps in terms of CK oscillations; the last requires an explanation of *why those causes have the effects they do*.

Consider the suggestion, then, that a satisfactory explanation for the occurrence of conscious experience consists in citing the neural causes of that experience. Chalmers would object: 'For a satisfactory theory, we need to know more than *which* processes give rise to experience; we need an account of why and how. A full theory of consciousness must build an explanatory bridge' (p. 16). That is, a satisfactory theory will explain why the causes of experience have the effects they do.

This sort of explanation can take two forms. One consists of deeper, or higher order, causal explanation. This is an empirically formidable task, but it poses no conceptual difficulties and we have known for centuries how to go about it: look for empirically testable law-like statements that could serve to explain particular causal sequences. Leibniz would surely have accepted the possibility of general laws to the effect that whenever a machine performs physical functions of certain kinds, it produces conscious experiences. Such laws could be more or less fundamental, and the less fundamental may themselves be explained by more fundamental ones. (Kepler's laws of planetary motion,

---

[4] Of course, the CK oscillations would not be the *complete* cause, since presumably they underlie all sorts of conscious experience, not just this particular occurrence. I assume background conditions that make the occurrence of CK oscillations the appropriately salient feature.

used to explain particular planetary motions, were themselves explained by Newton's more fundamental laws.) Similarly, supposing there is a law to the effect that phenomenal experience arises from CK oscillations, we may strive for a more general, comprehensive law which will subsume it.

No such law — no matter how fundamental — would dissolve Leibnizian perplexity. It still would not explain *why* mills (or brains, or information spaces) with the designated features should be connected via causal law with consciousness. Surely Chalmers should relegate causal explanations of consciousness, no matter how general in scope, to the realm of 'easy' problems — those that will need only a century or two of roughly foreseeable work to solve. He would say, quite rightly, that the such explanations do not get at the hard problem. The explanatory gap remains unbridged.

This suggests the second way of answering the question, 'Why do physical events produce conscious ones?' What is wanted is an explanation of the sort we have no idea how to achieve: one which would explain, in a non-causal way, why physical events of certain sorts should give rise to consciousness. We would be satisfied, as Chalmers says, if we could articulate a *mechanism* by which neural events produce consciousness. But the prospects for discovering such a mechanism are, as Chalmers rightly argues, dim: purely conceptual considerations foreclose the discovery of such a mechanism, and preclude bridging the 'explanatory gap' between physicality and consciousness.[5] So if the only possible solution to the hard problem is that of finding the relevant mechanism, the hard problem is insoluble.

III: Chalmers's 'Third Way'

To recap: one way to 'explain consciousness' would be to explain it causally, and this task is easy in principle even if formidable in practice. A second way, which would address the hard problem, would be to explain consciousness reductively. As Chalmers points out, however, conceptual difficulties block this path. Chalmers promises a third way, a nonreductive solution to the hard problem. In this section I will sketch the essentials of Chalmers's position and then argue that his promise is unkept.

Chalmers sketches an 'outline of a [nonreductive] theory of consciousness' which takes consciousness as 'fundamental' — something real but 'not explained in terms of anything simpler' (p. 19), much as contemporary physics takes mass and space–time to be fundamental. As Chalmers rightly points out, taking an entity to be fundamental does not preclude theorizing about it: fundamental entities can interact in lawful ways, and a theory which states these laws can be both true and useful.

A nonreductive theory of consciousness, he says, 'will consist in a number of *psychophysical principles*, principles connecting the properties of physical processes to the properties of experience' (p. 22). Chalmers offers three such principles. He is modestly tentative about their truth, insisting only that principles of their general *kind* are needed to solve the hard problem of consciousness. Two of these principles are 'nonbasic', says Chalmers (p. 22). I will focus on the third principle, which is supposed to be basic and

---

[5] Some philosophers would object that merely conceptual considerations cannot establish claims of metaphysical modality. I cannot go into this issue; suffice it to say that, on this question, I share Chalmers's view (see his fn.3, p. 21).

which Chalmers calls 'the double-aspect principle' (hereafter, 'DAP'). It is that 'information (or at least some information) has two basic aspects, a physical aspect and a phenomenal aspect' (p. 27). This sort of principle, then, underlies the sort of theory that, in Chalmers's view, offers the best hope of solving the hard problem of consciousness.

What are we to make of DAP's parenthetical and tentative restriction to 'at least some' information? It is immensely counter-intuitive to maintain that *in every information space*, every informational difference corresponds to a phenomenal difference. The Shannonian (1948) notion of an 'information space' which Chalmers employs presupposes nothing about mentality. Information spaces are abstract objects, but they are realized whenever there is a 'space of distinct . . . states, the differences between which can be transmitted down some causal pathway' (p. 26). Clearly, thermostats and fuel gauges qualify as realizations of information spaces on this reading. Hence if DAP is supposed to apply to all information spaces, thermostats have experience. This seems far-fetched.

In fact, though, Chalmers flirts with the idea that DAP has unrestricted applicability:

> A mouse has simpler information-processing structure than a human, and has correspondingly simpler experience; perhaps a thermostat, a maximally simple information processing structure, might have maximally simple experience? (p. 27).

Chalmers calls this an open question, but speaks rather warmly of a positive answer. If he is willing to countenance the unrestricted applicability of DAP, though, his suggestion fails to go far enough. For not only thermostats but *all* physical systems are (representable as) information spaces, given the highly general characterization of an information space. If DAP has unrestricted applicability, then experience is *everywhere*: not just thermostats but pencils, rocks, and atoms have phenomenal experience.[6]

Either we take this as a *reductio* of DAP's unrestricted applicability, or not. In either case, we are no closer to a solution of the hard problem. Suppose, first, that we take only some (physically realizations of) information spaces to give rise to conscious experience and we take DAP to apply only to such systems. DAP should be read as telling us that *in such a system* — say, for example, the normal human brain — every informational state corresponds to a phenomenal state. Suppose now that this is true (a highly concessive supposition!).[7]

DAP is supposed to offer a solution to the hard problem of consciousness: it is supposed to answer the question, 'Why do physical events of certain kinds give rise to consciousness?' But DAP bypasses this question entirely. It asserts *that* informational states — which are understandable in purely physical terms — correspond to phenomenal states, and it may be taken to assert *that* these correspondences are lawful rather than accidental. But it says nothing at all about *why* these correspondences hold: it does nothing whatsoever to bridge the explanatory gap between physical operation and conscious sensation.

---

[6] In fact, all sorts of things which don't count (intuitively) as either natural or artifactual kinds could count as information spaces: a system comprising, say, my left thumb, the Washington Monument, and a shoe could easily count as an information space. (Thanks to Jonathan Shear for pointing this out to me.) This makes DAP's unrestricted applicability even more far-fetched.

[7] It would be even more concessive to grant that distinct information states always correspond to distinct phenomenal states, as Chalmers seems to suggest (p. 26).

A look at our limiting supposition reinforces this point. We are assuming for now that we must limit DAP's application to give it any chance at plausibility. I said above that we should limit it to information spaces that give rise to conscious experience. But phrasing the limitation this way makes it transparent that DAP sidesteps the hard problem of consciousness, for DAP does not even come into play until we have determined that a given information space gives rise to consciousness; obviously DAP cannot then have any hope of explaining *why* a given sort of physical system should give rise to consciousness.

We could articulate DAP's field of applicability with no explicit mention of consciousness. We could list purely physical properties *F,G,H,* . . . that underlie consciousness — properties such that DAP applies (non-vacuously) to an informational space just in case it has properties *F,G,H,* . . . These are properties — no doubt involving complexity, adaptability and so on — that distinguish human brains from (e.g.) pencil sharpeners, but they would be purely physical properties. Now our principle is:

> **DAP′:** In any information space which has physical properties *F,G,H,* . . .
> all informational states correspond to phenomenal states.

DAP′ may well be true, but it is completely silent on the question, 'Why should a physical system with properties *F,G,H,* . . . produce consciousness?' The explanatory gap between physicality and consciousness yawns as wide as ever.

I turn now to the second horn of our dilemma. Suppose we endorse the unrestricted applicability of DAP, and so the ubiquity of consciousness. This changes nothing. DAP still merely asserts *that* informational states correspond to phenomenal ones. It still says nothing about *why* these correspondences hold.

It might be suggested that the pan-experientialism suggested by the unrestricted applicability of DAP does at least offer a modest explanation of why certain informational states — those of the brain, for example — yield phenomenal experience. We can explain why *these* states yield consciousness, on this suggestion, by pointing out that they are *informational* states and citing a universal law to the effect that all informational states yield consciousness — on our current interpretation, that is, DAP.

This is like saying that the question, 'Why is this thing black?' is satisfactorily answered by saying, 'Because it is a member of a class, all of whose members are black.' We do sometimes seem to find this sort of 'explanation' at least partially satisfying; whether we *should* is another matter. It suffices for present purposes, however, to point out that even if this sort of explanation is genuine and available in the case of consciousness, the problem it solves cannot plausibly be thought of as the *hard* problem. For that problem is precisely why any physical process whatsoever — or all of them, for that matter — should give rise to consciousness. In the present context, the hard problem concerns *why DAP should be true*. The sort of limited explanation of consciousness that DAP promises does not strain our conceptual resources at all, as the hard problem is supposed to do.

The problem obviously does not lie with the particular psychophysical principle Chalmers suggests. It is that no principle of its general character, asserting a systematic correspondence between physical states and conscious states, can hope to solve what Chalmers calls the 'hard problem of consciousness'. And we have no clue as to what might solve it, short of reduction.

IV: A Chalmersian Reply

I have argued that, contrary to what Chalmers suggests, he has shown no alternative to the easy-in-principle task of giving empirical causal explanations of consciousness, on the one hand, and the impossible-in-principle task of giving a reductive account of it on the other. Chalmers might respond that I have misconstrued the hard problem and so the adequacy of his solution to it. I have characterized the hard problem as that of explaining why physical processes of *any* sort give rise to consciousness. Chalmers occasionally suggests, however, that the hard problem arises because 'the *usual explanatory methods* of cognitive science and neuroscience do not suffice' to explain consciousness (p. 13, my italics), whereas these usual methods — involving functional explanation in terms of computational or informational processes — yield successful reductive explanations of other mental phenomena. The hard problem, then, might be thought of as that of finding novel — non-functional, non-computational — explanatory methods to explain consciousness. On this understanding of the problem, Chalmers might argue, his theory (or one of its general shape) promises a solution.

The problem with this response is two-fold.[8] The first difficulty concerns consistency. The suggested construal fits poorly with Chalmers's own suggestion that the hard problem is quite general: 'For *any* physical process we specify there will be an unanswered question: Why should this process give rise to experience?' (p. 18, my italics). An explanatory gap yawns between consciousness and *any* purely physical process, he points out, not just between consciousness and some particular sort of such process.

Suppose, however, that Chalmers really means by 'the hard problem' the problem of explaining consciousness non-functionally. The difficulty is then that 'the hard problem' is easy, while the truly hard problem — that identified in the preceding paragraph — remains. There is nothing hard-in-principle about explaining consciousness (merely) non-functionally, so long as the resulting explanation still fits the familiar causal mould. Descartes was happy to accept (non-functionalist) causal laws linking physical processes in the brain with conscious experience; while advancing knowledge has overrun the specifics of his account, no one since has found reason to dismiss the possibility of such causal laws.[9] As Chalmers says, ' "easy" is a relative term' (p. 10). Discovering detailed neuropsychological laws, if there are any, may take a long time. But the challenge is a relatively straightforward empirical one, posing no conceptual puzzle at all. If the fundamental laws of a theory assert without explaining a correlation between physical processes and consciousness, then — no matter how 'basic' those laws may be — the theory fails to explain why these processes should give rise to experience, and so it fails to bridge the explanatory gap between physicality and consciousness.

Chalmers complains about papers on consciousness which promise a solution to the hard problem but end up by explaining something else, leaving the reader to feel 'like the victim of a bait-and-switch' (p. 11). Ironically, Chalmers has unintentionally used the bait-and-switch technique himself.

---

[8] Three-fold, really: Chalmers's assumption that the phenomena of attention, reportability, and so on admit of reductive functional explanation is, I believe, mistaken. But I cannot address this issue here.

[9] Davidson's (1980) rejection of psychophysical law is controversial, but in any case it is restricted to those laws invoking propositional attitudes; it does not apply to phenomenal experience.

V: The Moral

I object neither to Chalmers's outline of a theory of consciousness nor to his (general) characterization of the hard problem of consciousness. I differ with him on how these are connected. Contrary to what Chalmers suggests, his theory answers at most some easy problems; it leaves the hard problem untouched. It is fundamental in the sense that it posits brute lawful connections between physical events of certain sorts and phenomenal experience, connections which have no further explanation. But we should not confuse the point that these laws have no further explanation with the claim that they *provide* an explanation of the regularities they assert. No theory of the sort Chalmers suggests can explain why physical events, of any sort, produce consciousness. The proper conclusion to draw, from the considerations that Chalmers adduces and the ones I add here, is that there simply is no solution to the truly hard problem of consciousness.

Should this trouble us? I think not. The Newtonian analogy is instructive. Newton's invocation of gravity, that 'mysterious force', was attacked by his contemporaries as a surrender to mysticism (Dijksterhuis, 1986, pp. 479 ff.). They disapproved of his failure to explain *why* bodies behaved in accordance with his laws, or *how* distant bodies could act on one another. Newton's famous refusal to 'frame hypotheses' in answer to these questions seems a surrender to what his contemporaries might well have called 'the hard problem of explaining the motions of bodies'.

This sort of worry no longer bothers us, but not because we have answered it. We inherit from Hume the view that once we have reached fundamental laws governing empirical phenomena, there is no further explaining why these laws should be true (a truism, since the lack of further explanation *constitutes* 'fundamentalness'). There is no reason why this point should not apply to the empirical phenomena of consciousness: the real solution to the hard problem lies in seeing that it is miscast. We can study the workings of our Leibnizian 'millwork of the mind' and the experiences that result, but we will never be able to explain *why* such millwork should produce such experiences. This view is no more mysterian, though, than Newtonian physics or its relativistic and quantum-mechanical descendants, which aspire to state fundamental laws governing the physical world but disclaim explanation of those laws themselves. Consciousness is an empirical phenomenon, and a good theory of it — perhaps along Chalmersian lines — will reveal the fundamental laws that govern it and its relations to physical processes. More than this we cannot deliver and should not miss.[10]

References

Chalmers, David J. (1995), 'Facing up to the problem of consciousness', *Journal of Consciousness Studies*, **2** (3), pp. 200–19 (reprinted in this volume).

Crick, F. and Koch, C. (1990), 'Toward a neurobiological theory of consciousness', *Seminars in the Neurosciences*, **2**, pp. 263–75.

Davidson, Donald (1980), 'Psychology as philosophy', with 'Comments and replies', in *Essays on Actions and Events*, pp. 229–44 (Oxford: Clarendon Press).

Dijksterhuis, E.J. (1986), *Mechanization of the World Picture* (Princeton: Princeton University Press).

Leibniz, G.W. (1965), *Monadology and Other Philosophical Essays*, trans. Paul Schrecker and Anne Martin Schrecker (Indianapolis: Bobbs-Merrill).

[10] This paper was originally published in the *Journal of Consciousness Studies*, **3**, No.1 (1996), pp. 26–32. Thanks to Jonathan Shear and David Chalmers for valuable discussion of the paper.

E.J. Lowe

There Are No Easy Problems of Consciousness

David Chalmers is to be commended for challenging the complacent assumptions of reductive physicalism regarding the tractability of the problems of consciousness, but he concedes too much to such physicalists in allowing that some, at least, of these problems — the 'easy' ones — will fall prey to their favoured methods. I do not consider that there are *any* 'easy' problems of consciousness, and consider that Chalmers' division of the problems into 'easy' ones and the 'hard' one betrays an inadequate conception of conscious thought and experience — a conception which plays into the hands of physicalists by suggesting that the only problem with functionalism is its apparent inability to say anything about 'qualia'.[1]

At the beginning of his paper, Chalmers lists some of the problems of consciousness which he considers to be 'easy', in the sense that these are the ones which, in his view, 'seem directly susceptible to the standard methods of cognitive science, whereby a phenomenon is explained in terms of computational or neural mechanisms' (p. 9). These problems include: the ability to discriminate, categorize and react to environmental stimuli; the integration of information by a cognitive system; the reportability of mental states; and the deliberate control of behaviour. Chalmers remarks that, 'All of these phenomena are associated with the notion of consciousness,' and confidently asserts that, 'All of them are straightforwardly vulnerable to explanation in terms of computational or neural mechanisms' (p. 10). But it needs to be pointed out at once that the terms employed in describing these problems — terms like 'discrimination', 'information', 'report' and 'control' — are extremely slippery, and that we use them both in a 'high level' way to describe the conscious, intelligent activity of genuinely thoughtful creatures like ourselves and also in a 'low level' way (which may in fact be no more than a metaphorical way) to describe the programmed behaviour of mindless machines and various lowly forms of life. For example, we may speak of a thermostat as 'discriminating' ambient temperatures and as 'controlling' a switch, or of a computer as storing 'information' and 'reporting' on the contents of its 'memory'. But there is no reason whatever to believe that the activities thus described really have much in common with those activities of thoughtful human beings which we would customarily describe in these same terms. To suppose otherwise is to fall victim to the so-called pathetic fallacy — the fallacy of

---

[1] This paper was originally published in the *Journal of Consciousness Studies*, **2**, No.3 (1995), pp. 266–71. Much of what I have to say about consciousness, thought and experience in this paper is developed at much greater length in Lowe (1996) and, in an earlier version, in Lowe (1992).

ascribing thought and feeling to mindless objects on account of superficial likenesses between their behaviour or appearance and our own. Now, it is true enough that the activities of thermostats and computers which we describe in such terms can indeed be explained in the ways Chalmers suggests, but it is far from evident that those of human beings can. Indeed, I shall try to make it evident in what follows that the latter activities can certainly *not* be explained in these ways, and that the reason for this has to do with the nature of human consciousness and its relation to our capacities for thought, understanding and concept-formation.

As a preliminary to tackling this task, I want to say something more about Chalmers' notions of experience and consciousness, which I find seriously inadequate. As regards the notion of *experience*, it seems to me that he distorts this notion by focusing exclusively upon the *sensuous*, or *phenomenal*, or *qualitative* character of experience (the 'what it is like' aspect of experience, to use Thomas Nagel's well-worn phrase). And this distortion serves, in my view, to obscure the intimate relation between experience and thought. *Some* experiences — pains provide a possible example — are indeed almost purely sensational in character, but the sort of experiences which are central to our *cognitive* capacities — namely, *perceptual* experiences — are certainly not. Perceptual experiences — such as, for example, a visual experience of seeing a red book lying on top of a brown table — possess not only qualitative or phenomenal characteristics but *also*, most importantly, *intentional* or *representational* content. Not only is it 'like something' to enjoy such an experience, in which the phenomenal character of sensed colours impresses itself upon our awareness, but also such an experience represents — or, better, *presents* — our immediate physical environment as *being some way* (in this case, as containing a red book on top of a brown table). Moreover, and quite crucially, the intentional content of such an experience stands in an especially intimate relation to its qualitative or phenomenal character: the two aspects of the experience are not simply independent of one another.

I want to say that the intentional content of a perceptual experience is, in a certain sense, *grounded* in its phenomenal character, but that the grounding relation here is a complicated one, which arises at least in part through the subject's individual history of perceptual learning. One of the most important things we learn through perception is what various sorts of physical object *look like* (or otherwise 'appear' to other sense modalities — what they *sound like*, and *feel like*, for instance). And how objects *look* to us is, at least in part, a matter of how they affect the phenomenal or qualitative character of our visual experience. (The same applies, *mutatis mutandis*, with regard to the other sense modalities.) The importance of all this lies in the fact that how we *conceive* of physical objects is inextricably bound up with how they *appear* to us in perception — how they *look*, *sound*, *feel* and so forth. Thus, although conscious thought is not, of course, the same thing as perceptual experience, the *conceptual content* of thought is intimately related to the content, both phenomenal and intentional, of perceptual experience. Thoughts differ from perceptual experiences in possessing only *intentional*, and not *sensuous* content; yet, even so, the intentional content of our thought depends inescapably, by way of its conceptual structure, upon our capacity to enjoy perceptual experiences with sensuous or phenomenal characteristics. And, at the same time, our perceptual experiences possess intentional content — often, the very same content as may be possessed by our thoughts

— because we are able to bring concepts to bear upon the deliverances of our sense organs and so clothe our perceptual sensations with representational properties.

All this has been said before, of course — and no doubt much better than I have been able to — by Immanuel Kant, and is encapsulated in his famous dictum that 'Thoughts without [sensible] content are empty, [sensible] intuitions without concepts are blind' (1933, p. 93). But the upshot is that it is quite erroneous to suppose that we can ascribe genuine thoughts, with conceptually articulated structure, to creatures or machines lacking altogether the capacity to enjoy conscious experiences with phenomenal or qualitative character. Whatever a computer can do by way of information processing, storage and retrieval is not by any means to be confused with what a thinking human being does who reasons, remembers and recalls. And here I note a particularly serious inadequacy in the (essentially Shannonian) notion of *information* which Chalmers deploys in attempting to characterize aspects of human cognition. This notion of information is appropriate enough for describing the activities of computing machines, but is wholly *in*appropriate for characterizing the cognitive states — beliefs, thoughts and judgements — of human beings. And the reason, once again, has to do with *conceptual content*. An informational state in Chalmers' sense is not, essentially, a state possessing conceptually articulated content; but the beliefs, thoughts and judgements of human beings most certainly do possess such content essentially. A simple, if somewhat time-worn, example will serve to bring out this distinction. Consider the pattern of rings exposed by a horizontal cut through a tree's trunk: such a ring pattern is, in the sense of 'information' deployed by Chalmers, an *informational state* of the tree — it carries 'information' about the tree's age, amongst other things. Clearly, though, it is *not* a state with *conceptual* content: it would be ludicrous to suggest that the ring pattern somehow embodies the concepts of *number* and *time* (concepts which are themselves involved in the analysis of the concept of a tree's age). By contrast, one cannot properly ascribe to a person a *belief* that a certain tree is so-and-so many years old without simultaneously ascribing to that person *concepts* of number and time. And, once again, I would appeal to the Kantian principle that our conceptual capacities — even those relating to such relatively abstract concepts as those of number and time — are intimately related to our capacities for perceptual experience, in order to explain what the relevant difference between a human being and a tree is in this regard. That a tree can merely carry (Shannonian) 'information' about its age, whereas a human being can *believe* that, or *think* that, it has a certain age is intimately related to the fact that human beings can, whereas trees cannot, enjoy conscious perceptual experiences with phenomenal character.

So far I have criticized Chalmers' notions of *experience* and *information*, but there is a related criticism I have to make which goes to the heart of his attempted distinction between the 'easy' problems of consciousness and the 'hard' problem. This concerns his terminological proposal regarding the use of the words 'consciousness' and 'awareness'. Chalmers suggests that we 'reserve the term "consciousness" for the phenomena of experience, using the less loaded term "awareness" for the more straightforward phenomena described earlier' (p. 11). But given that I dispute Chalmers' claim that the latter phenomena are indeed 'more straightforward' (in the sense of being amenable to computational or neural explanation), I cannot acquiesce in his terminological proposal. To do so would be, implicitly, to concede far too much to reductive physicalism and at the same time would be to gainsay all I have just said concerning the intimate relationship between phenomenal consciousness and the intelligent thought and activity of human beings. In *Chalmers'* proposed sense of 'awareness', it seems fair to say, there could be nothing in principle wrong in speaking of a computer, or even a thermostat, as being 'aware' — but then to suggest that *human beings* are only 'aware' in this attenuated sense is completely to misrepresent the capacities involved in our being 'aware' of our selves and of our own thoughts and experiences.

My foregoing criticisms of Chalmers bear directly upon section III of his paper, in which he attempts to explain why the 'easy' problems are easy and the 'hard' problem hard. Here he asserts that 'The easy problems are easy precisely because they concern the explanation of cognitive *abilities* and *functions* [and] to explain a cognitive function, we need only specify a mechanism that can perform the function' (p. 11). He gives the following example, amongst others: 'To explain reportability . . . is just to explain how a system could perform the function of producing reports on internal states' (*ibid.*). But, of course, I must immediately protest that if by 'producing a report on an internal state' Chalmers just means generating a second-order informational state (in the Shannonian sense of 'information'), then although this is something which can indeed be perfectly well explained in a mechanistic way, it is *not* the sort of thing that *needs* to be explained when we are talking about the ability of human subjects to express in words their knowledge of the contents of their own thoughts and experiences — for such an ability demands the possession of genuine concepts, not only concepts of the things those thoughts and experiences are about but also the very concepts of *thought* and *experience* themselves. And the truth is that we have not the slightest reason to believe that a 'mechanistic' explanation is available, even in principle, for the capacity of creatures like ourselves to deploy the concepts of thought and experience and to ascribe the possession of such concepts to ourselves. Only by trading upon a thoroughly jejune sense of 'reportability' can Chalmers make out even the appearance of a case for saying that such a capacity, as exercised by human beings, is 'easy' to explain as being a 'function' performed by a computational or neural mechanism.

The key point here is that a 'function', in Chalmers's sense, is specified in terms of certain *behaviour* which a system subserving that function produces. (As Chalmers himself puts it, 'Here "function" is . . . used . . . in the . . . sense of any causal role in the production of behavior that a system might perform' (p. 11 f.).) But then everything turns on how we characterize the 'behaviour' in question. In the example just discussed, the 'behaviour' in question was described by Chalmers as that of 'producing reports on internal states'. But only if such 'behaviour' is interpreted in a narrowly physicalistic way — for example, in terms of the generation of a second-order (Shannonian) informational state — is a 'mechanistic' explanation of the corresponding 'function' going to be straightforwardly available. If, by contrast, we understand 'producing reports on internal states' to embrace such genuinely intelligent, thoughtful activities as a human being's using language to express its knowledge of the contents of its own thoughts and experiences, then there is not the slightest reason to suppose that a mechanistic explanation for this capacity is possible. *Mechanistically characterized* 'behaviour' is, quite unsurprizingly, amenable to mechanistic explanation, and this is what underlies Chalmers' own perception that 'In a way, the point is trivial' (p. 12) — the 'point' being that you can always explain the performance of a function by 'specifying a *mechanism* that performs the function' (*ibid.*). Chalmers' problem is that he entirely begs the real question at issue in supposing that the sort of *performance* we have to do with in cases of thoughtful human activity is something that can be characterized in a mechanistic way and which, consequently, a 'mechanism' can uncontroversially be supposed capable of engaging in.

Because Chalmers misconstrues what he sees as being the 'easy' problems of consciousness, he also misrepresents what he calls the 'hard' problem. According to Chalmers, the 'hard' problem is this: 'Why doesn't all this information-processing go on "in the dark", free of any inner feel?' (p. 13). Believing as he does that human thought and cognition in general are just a matter of 'information-processing', of a sort which could in principle go on in a mindless computer, he is left with the idea that all that is really distinctive about consciousness is its qualitative or phenomenal aspects (the 'what it is like', or 'inner feel'). And then it begins to look like a strange mystery or quirk of evolution that creatures like us should possess this sort of consciousness *in addition* to all our capacities for thought and understanding — these capacities being, for Chalmers, simply capacities for certain sorts of information-processing and storage. My response is that consciousness has only been put in this queer position by Chalmers (and, to be fair, by many others) *because* he has mistakenly denied it any role in his account of the nature of human thought and understanding. In short, it is the reductive, and wholly inadequate, *information-processing* conception of human cognition which is responsible for the misperception that 'consciousness' (in the form of 'qualia' and the like) occupies what threatens to be a merely epiphenomenal role as a peculiar additional feature of human mentation that is in no way essential to our basic intellectual capacities. Once we appreciate the Kantian point that genuine thought, with real conceptual content, is only available to creatures with a capacity for perceptual experiences bearing not only intentional but also phenomenal content, we see that the sort of phenomenal consciousness which we humans enjoy but which computers and trees do not, far from being an epiphenomenon of 'information-processing' in our brains, is an absolutely indispensable element in our cognitive make-up, without which we could not properly be described as thinking beings at all. In a curious way, it is perhaps a rationalistic, quasi-Cartesian bias which is responsible this side-lining of phenomenal consciousness as an epiphenomenon of cognition: a failure to recognize that human cognition is not a matter of abstract computation but is, on the contrary, thoroughly integrated with our sensitive nature as embodied creatures acted upon by and ourselves acting upon our physical environment. There is irony, then, in Chalmers' concessive remark, towards the end of section III of his paper, that 'Perhaps [experience] will turn out to play an important cognitive role' (p. 13). Perhaps! If Kant is right, no one who is in any doubt about this has even begun to achieve an adequate grasp of the notions of experience and cognition.

If what I have said so far is correct and our capacity for genuine thought and understanding is quite inseparable from our capacity for phenomenal consciousness, then, to the extent that Chalmers himself is correct in contending that reductive physicalism offers no prospect for an explanation of phenomenal consciousness, the conclusion ought to be that reductive physicalism, far from being equipped to solve the so-called 'easy' problems of consciousness, has in fact nothing very useful to say about *any* aspect of consciousness. This indeed is my own conclusion. (I hasten to add, though, that I am very far from considering disciplines such as cognitive neuropsychology as being utterly worthless and uninformative: such disciplines take the notion of conscious thought and experience *for granted*, and attempt to correlate features of such mental states with structures and processes in the brain — an enterprise with which I have no argument — but they do not and cannot pretend to explain what thought and experience *are* and how their existence is possible in physically embodied creatures like ourselves.) But Chalmers, by contrast, occupies an unstable position, precisely because he has already conceded *so much* to reductive physicalism. Effectively, he subscribes to a position which we might call 'functionalism plus qualia'. According to this view, everything about human mentation *except* for the fact of 'qualia' can be explained in reductive (computational or neural) terms. But how, then, can 'qualia' be anything but epiphenomenal — and in that case, why should they exist at all? The position is unstable because there is intense pressure on it *either* to give qualia some more substantive causal role — and this would be to challenge the reductive physicalist account of the rest of human mentation — *or else* to squeeze qualia out altogether, as Dennett and others have tried to do. The awkwardness of Chalmers' position is, I think, clearly brought out by his allegiance to what he calls the 'principle of organizational invariance' (p. 25). According to this principle, 'any two systems with the same fine-grained *functional organization* will have qualitatively identical experiences' (*ibid.*). As he himself points out, this means that the 'philosophical hypotheses of "absent qualia" and "inverted qualia", while logically possible, are empirically and nomologically impossible' (p. 26). But this is, in effect, finally to concede the whole game to functionalism. For once one has adopted what I just now called the position of 'functionalism plus qualia', the *only* reason for holding on to a special, physicalistically irreducible notion of phenomenal consciousness is that possibilities like those of absent and inverted qualia escape any attempt at functionalist explanation. But now that these 'possibilities' are denied to be anything more than merely *logical* possibilities, there is nothing substantive left which functionalism is allegedly incapable of explaining about human mentation. One can perfectly well see *why* Chalmers is attracted to his 'principle of organizational invariance', given how much ground he has already conceded to functionalism and given the correspondingly nugatory role he accords to phenomenal consciousness in an account of the nature of human cognition. What he doesn't seem to appreciate is that, having conceded this much, to adopt this principle as well is effectively to sell out completely to functionalism.

At the end of his paper, Chalmers becomes more speculative, suggesting that the most fundamental notion of all, both as regards the physical world and as regards conscious experience, is that of *information* (again, quite explicitly in Shannon's sense of this term). And he offers a 'double-aspect' hypothesis, whereby one and the same 'information space' is both physically and phenomenally embodied. Noting that physics only characterizes its basic entities 'extrinsically', he even goes so far as to speculate, in what seems to be a quasi-idealistic vein, that 'the intrinsic properties of the physical . . . are themselves phenomenal properties' (p. 28). This is heady stuff, and to some extent offsets the earlier concessions Chalmers has made to physicalism. But this sort of challenge to physicalism comes too late, operating as it does only at a level of speculative metaphysics. By this account, physicalism is still left unchallenged as a *scientific* doctrine. My own view, as I hope I have made plain, is that the challenge to a physicalist account of the human mind has to be mounted much earlier than this, and in mounting that challenge one of the first things to appreciate is that the (Shannonian) notion of information is too impoverished to be of use in characterizing the conceptually articulated structure of human thought and its intimate relation to our capacity for phenomenal consciousness (our 'sensibility', as Kant calls it). We humans beings are creatures capable of both thought and perceptual experience, but these capacities are inextricably interrelated. Thought is more than just information-processing and perceptual experience is more than just the having of 'qualia': *both* are states which are conceptually articulated and each depends for its possibility upon the other. Kant was right!

References

Chalmers, D.J. (1995), 'Facing up to the problem of consciousness', *Journal of Consciousness Studies*, **2** (3), pp. 200–19 (reprinted in this volume).

Kant, I. (1933), *Critique of Pure Reason* [1787], trans. N. Kemp Smith (London: Macmillan).

Lowe, E. J. (1992), 'Experience and its objects', in *The Contents of Experience*, ed. T. Crane (Cambridge: Cambridge University Press).

Lowe, E. J. (1996), *Subjects of Experience* (Cambridge: Cambridge University Press).

David Hodgson

The Easy Problems
Ain't So Easy

Reports of the April 1994 conference on science and consciousness in Tucson, Arizona, suggest that David Chalmers made a significant contribution by persuasively suggesting that much scientific work on consciousness is directed at problems that do not have a lot to do with the central fact of the mind — that we have subjective experiences — or with its central mystery — why should a physical system give rise to experiences at all? Chalmers identifies this mystery as the *hard problem* of consciousness — and he contrasts what he calls the *easy problems*, with which mainstream scientific work on consciousness has been concerned; such as how cognitive systems (including human brains) (i) discriminate, categorize, and react to environmental stimuli, (ii) produce verbal reports of mental states, (iii) scan their own internal states, and (iv) integrate information and exploit it in the control of behaviour.

However, while I applaud Chalmers' emphasis on the centrality of the problem of conscious experience, and on the indirect relevance to this problem of much scientific work which purports to be about consciousness, I want to suggest that, in drawing as he does this distinction between the hard problem and the easy problems, he is already making a move which is prejudicial not only to resolution of the hard problem he identifies, but also to any satisfactory resolution of some of the so-called easy problems. And this is because, in my opinion, both Chalmers and mainstream scientists are wrong in assuming that all the so-called easy problems can be answered fully without at the same time answering Chalmers' hard problem. Now I don't contend that systems without consciousness could never perform the functions with which the easy problems are concerned; and I accept that research into how such systems could do so is *relevant* to how human beings perform these functions. But I do contend that we will not *fully* understand how human beings *in fact* do such things as (i) discriminate, categorize, and react to environmental stimuli, (ii) produce verbal reports of mental states, (iii) scan their own internal states, and (iv) integrate information and exploit it in the control of behaviour, unless and until we understand the role of subjective experience in these processes; and David Chalmers is at one with mainstream scientists in assuming the contrary.

Where does he go wrong? His contention is that the 'easy problems' are easy because they concern the explanation of cognitive *functions*; and that we explain the performance

This paper was originally published in the *Journal of Consciousness Studies*, 3, No.1 (1996), pp. 69–75.

of any function by specifying a mechanism — either neural or computational — that performs the function. This might seem reasonable: indeed, Chalmers suggests it is trivial, or merely conceptual (p. 12). He does go on (p. 13) to allow for the possibility that experience itself may have a functional role — but contends that if so, the explanation (presumably, by specifying a mechanism) will not fully explain the experience.

The problem with all this is that it assumes that any function or causal role, which conscious experiences could have, could be fully realised by a mechanism — the sort of thing which the objective sciences are ideally suited to deal with. But a (perhaps *the*) central question about the mind is whether or not conscious experiences have causal roles or functions, which *cannot* be performed or realised or even simulated by mechanisms of the type studied by the objective sciences. My own opinion is that they probably do; so that a full explanation of the functional role of conscious experience will require, not just specification of mechanisms, but also explanation of the conscious experience itself.

To make good this criticism of Chalmers, I need to (1) show how it could be that conscious experiences might possibly have such roles or functions; and (2) give reasons for thinking that they really do so.

I: Roles beyond Mechanisms

As a first step towards showing that there can be roles for experiences beyond mechanisms, it is necessary to look at some features of the mechanisms studied by the objective sciences.

Since repeatable experimentation is at the heart of all scientific work, the mechanisms with which the objective sciences are concerned must operate in accordance with universal laws — which need not be fully deterministic, but must at least give objective probabilities of outcomes. When a hypothesis to be tested involves such laws, then it can be disproved by experiment — perhaps even by a single experiment, if the relevant laws are fully deterministic, but requiring a number of experiments giving statistically significant results, if some relevant laws give only probabilities. What could not be dealt with in this way are choices or decisions of a person or agent, if it be the case that each outcome is neither pre-determined nor random within pre-determined probability parameters; but rather is selected by the person or agent for non-conclusive reasons. Yet that is precisely our pre-scientific commonsense view of human choice, a view which I say should not be dismissed unless and until there are solid reasons for doing so.

Of course, psychological experiments may give consistent statistics concerning choices made by people in various circumstances; but that does not mean that each individual case is not a genuine choice of the person concerned, the result of a decision by that person which resolves non-conclusive reasons supporting the alternatives between which the choice is made — a choice which, consistently with all applicable objective universal laws of nature, could have been different.

Our commonsense view is that, in each case of choice, our conscious experiences have a role which is not merely the working out of the operation of universal objective laws, so that the outcome is not pre-determined, or purely random within pre-determined probability parameters; that each choice is a unique efficacious event, in which non-conclusive reasons are resolved by a decision. And if that is right, then conscious experiences have a role which can't be fully replicated or simulated by mechanisms which simply operate in accordance with universal laws, with or without randomness.

It may turn out that our commonsense view is a misconception, and that what common-sense sees as a choice, made by a conscious subject or agent for non-conclusive reasons which irreducibly involve conscious experiences, is in fact no more than the working out (with or without randomness) of objective universal laws operating on objective imper-sonal events. But nothing so far established by science or philosophy demonstrates that this is so.

II: Which View Is Presently Preferable?

I have argued at length elsewhere for the view that conscious experiences do have a role in human choices which can't be replicated or simulated by mechanisms without such experiences (Hodgson 1991; 1994a; 1994b; 1995; 1996); and I can only hint at the arguments here. There are many ways in which the arguments can be organised and presented: the following summary is just one, which I adopt in the context of the hard problem debate.

1. First, there is the very existence of the hard problem. If, as assumed by mainstream scientists and Chalmers alike, all *functions* of the brain/mind can be explained by specifying mechanisms operating in accordance with impersonal universal laws, there is no possibility of a functional explanation of consciousness: the development over time of any system will occur in accordance with the impersonal laws (with or without randomness), so that choice between available alternatives is excluded, and with it any efficacious subjectivity.
2. Some kinds of information we have in conscious experiences, such as sensations of colour and of pain, are available only to conscious entities; and it seems unlikely that what our brains/minds do with that information could equally be done without it — or with only an unconscious coded version of it (Hodgson 1991, Ch. 4).
3. In fact, careful consideration of human plausible reasoning, both theoretical and practical, suggests that it proceeds, using this consciousness-dependent information, in ways not available to non-conscious systems (Hodgson 1991, Ch. 5; 1995).
4. All this is supported by the circumstance that evolution has selected for conscious-ness; and also for the use of our very fallible consciousness, whenever new exigen-cies are encountered, in preference to the prodigious unconscious computing capacity of our brains (Hodgson 1991, Ch. 6; 1995).
5. Our commonsense conception of ourselves is deeply embedded in our language and attitudes: rejection of it would, for consistency, require thoroughgoing revision of our language and attitudes, including abandonment of widely-held ideas about justice and human rights — so there is a heavy onus of proof on those claiming to refute this conception (Hodgson 1991, Ch. 7; 1994b).
6. Conscious experiences correspond with myriad spatially extended and separated neural events, suggesting that some kind of non-local causality or efficacy is in-volved; and this in turn points towards some local indeterminism, which is not mere randomness, in brain processes (Hodgson 1991, Ch. 16; 1996).
7. The measurement problem of quantum physics suggests that physical processes may be interdependent with consciousness — not (I suggest) simply in triggering the

'collapse of the wave function', but rather in the deep and subtle ways examined in d'Espagnat (1989) (and see also Hodgson 1991, Chs. 14–15).

There are of course substantial arguments the other way. For example:

1. To suggest that systems develop otherwise than in accordance with universal laws of nature (with or without randomness) is to appeal to superstition and the supernatural.
2. The cognitive and neurological sciences are continually discovering more about the brain, and there is no good reason to suggest in advance a limit to what these sciences can explain: they require no appeal to non-physical causation, and leave no room for it.
3. The brain is so hot and wet, and its working parts so massive, that it is unlikely in the extreme that quantum indeterminism has anything to do with any supposed efficacy of conscious experiences.
4. Psychological experiments show that our commonsense view of ourselves is in many respects misconceived, due in part to a faculty we have for (unconsciously) fabricating and accepting plausible but untrue stories to explain our experiences and actions; so our commonsense view of choice is likewise suspect.

However, I believe that there is nothing supernatural about our ordinary conception of human action and choice; and that the suggestion that there is arises because of the difficulty of reconciling this conception with the operation of universal laws. As David Chalmers shows, the successes of the orthodox cognitive and neurological sciences give no grounds for confidence that they will explain consciousness. Post-classical science (in particular, quantum theory and chaos theory) suggests there may be room for the efficacy of consciousness; and although the hotness and wetness of the brain make it difficult to show how quantum indeterminism is relevant to the brain's functioning, I say the onus of proof is on those saying it cannot be relevant. It is true that commonsense is fallible, and that psychological experiments have disclosed misconceptions; but commonsense is the basis and the substance of our whole understanding of the world and the language which reflects that understanding; and we cannot jettison it — rather, we should modify it when and to the extent actually required by science and philosophy. (We are on a ramshackle boat in the middle of the ocean, and we can patch leaks and sometimes make substantial improvements, but we can't abandon it and start from scratch.)

III: Pain and Music

I will illustrate with two examples.

1. Pain

We accept that pain has useful functions which explain why evolution has selected in its favour: namely, it draws our attention to possible damage to ourselves and gives us a strong motive to take steps to remedy it and to avoid damage in the future.

But if in fact we did (i) discriminate, categorize, and react to environmental stimuli, and (iv) integrate information and exploit it in the control of behaviour, in ways which could be fully explained by specifying mechanisms, then the pain itself would be a superfluity. As we saw, the mechanisms with which the objective sciences are concerned develop in accordance with universal laws of nature, with or without randomness. Such laws may, of course, govern the development of the neural correlates of pain — and if pain accompanied those correlates wholly in accordance with psycho-physical bridging laws, the universal laws of nature could be given descriptions such that the pain itself had a place in the causal order. But the neural mechanisms would still work in the same way if the neural correlates happened to be associated, not with *subjective* feelings of pain, but rather with some *objective* global property, which would then play the same role in the mechanisms. The mechanisms would still 'run' in accordance with the universal laws, and no 'motive' would be required. Similarly, if the mechanisms were specified in computational terms, the program would just run, without the need of any motive.

My contention is that pain, as such, in giving us notice of possible damage and a motive to remedy it and avoid future damage, has an *irreducible* role; because it leaves us with a *choice* to do something else if we decide other reasons should prevail. This only makes sense if choices are not just the working out of mechanisms obeying universal laws or computational rules, but really do require a conscious agent who can treat both the pain and the opposing considerations as non-conclusive, and reach a decision which then, for the first time, determines which considerations are to prevail on that unique occasion. If, as I believe, there are advantages which a faculty for (fallible) qualitative judgment has over purely quantitative computation, then the role and usefulness of pain can be understood.

2. Music

A composer completes one section of a piece of music, and wants to continue. Two possibilities occur to her. She plays them on the piano, and/or imagines how they would sound. She notices her emotional reactions to them. She chooses one. Do we believe that the way the alternatives *sound*, and the way the composer *feels* upon hearing or imagining these sounds, are dispensible?

If human beings did (i) discriminate, categorize, and react, (ii) scan their own internal states, and (iv) integrate information and exploit it in the control of behaviour, by mechanisms operating wholly in accordance with universal laws, then the sounds and the feelings would be superfluities. The neural and/or computational mechanisms would simply run in accordance with the relevant universal laws and, while these developments might involve the hearing of sounds and the feeling of emotions, the mechanisms would run just as well if they happened to be correlated not with those subjective experiences, but with wholly objective global events.

Hofstadter (1980, Ch. 6; 1981) has put forward arguments for the dispensibility of the sounds of music, but they are unconvincing (see Hodgson 1991, pp. 107–10). I feel sure that the sounds of the music and the feelings of the composer have an irreducible and indispensible role in compositional decisions — because the composer as a conscious agent can treat the sounds and the feelings associated with each alternative as non-conclusive reasons, and can make a qualitative judgment that determines which reasons prevail.

Also, suppose a great pianist has acquired a prodigious technique, and has thoroughly learned a sonata. In a concert performance, he does not perform the sonata in the automatic way in which we often (say) drive a car, although the technique and the order of the notes may be pure habit: he *concentrates* intensely, and shapes the performance in ways dependent on the sounds he hears and the emotions he feels. I do not believe that the shape of the performance is entirely due to mechanisms, in which the sounds and the emotions are superfluous and dispensible.

IV: Chalmers' Proposals

What then is to be made of Chalmers' suggestions for a theory? Not surprisingly in the light of what I have written above, there are some things I like and some I dislike.

1. Experience as fundamental

Chalmers suggests that we should take experience as a fundamental feature of the world, as fundamental as physical features such as mass and electronic charge. I agree, but I say Chalmers does not go far enough here. An experience presupposes an experiencer, a bearer of the experience, a subject — so if experience is fundamental, so is the subject. And I would argue that equally fundamental is an associated feature of the world which I identify as *choice* (others may identify it as purpose); so that what I say is fundamental is the mental amalgam of experience, subject, and choice. (I am not suggesting there is a subject or self which is separate from the brain, or that subjects are fully aware of all factors influencing choice; rather that experience involves a broadly integrated subject, which can through choice make an input into what happens which is neither random nor pre-determined by universal laws.) If one concentrates just on experience, as Chalmers does, and disregards subject and choice, one immediately loses sight of what I say is the irreducible functional role of consciousness.

2. The need for bridging laws

Chalmers proposes that we look for bridging laws which link physical states and events with mental states and events. This is by no means a new idea. Much orthodox science and philosophy concerning the brain/mind has been directed towards just this: the linking of physical types and mental types, for example identifying the location and nature of brain processes which are associated with various experiences and the performance of various mental tasks. I accept that part of the explanation of consciousness will lie in establishing such laws; but if I am right about the irreducible role of experience and choice, these bridging laws will never be wholly complete and determinative. Since in my view choice cannot be wholly reduced to the development of physical systems in accordance with universal laws, there will be aspects of the mental which cannot be fully accounted for by laws linking the physical and the mental.

3. Structural coherence

One nonbasic psychophysical principle suggested by Chalmers is that there is isomorphism between the structures of conscious experience and those of the cognitive processes with which they are associated. Chalmers of course assumes that the cognitive processes can be explained by specifying mechanisms, an assumption I have attacked; but in any event, he does not suggest that this isomorphism is complete in every detail — and I see no reason to question that there is likely to be a broad isomorphism between structural properties of those experiences which have such properties, and structural properties of associated cognitive processes.

4. Organizational invariance

Chalmers' second nonbasic principle is substantially that of the functionalist approach to the mental, namely that any two systems with the same fine-grained *functional organiza-*

tion will have qualitatively identical experiences, irrespective of the kind of material in which the systems are realised — irrespective, for example, of whether they consist of neurons or silicon chips. Chalmers allows that a silicon isomorph of a neural system may be impossible for technical reasons: I think he should also allow that a neural isomorph of another neural system may likewise be impossible (see Hodgson 1991, pp. 429–30). And even if *neural* isomorphs are possible, they could develop differently, not just because of possible randomness but also, if my approach is correct, because they may *choose* differently between alternatives left open by the systems and applicable universal laws. This would be an important qualification to any principle of organizational invariance; and I question whether, in any event, identity of fine-grained functional organization could be demonstrated, even if it were possible.

5. Double-aspect theory of information

Chalmers suggests, as a basic psychophysical principle, that *information* (perhaps all information) has both a physical aspect and an experiential aspect; and points to this as a way experience might have a subtle kind of causal relevance. My comment on this is similar to that on his proposal that experience is fundamental: if 'information' realized in relevant physical structures and events has an 'internal aspect', this aspect is not just experiential information, but rather the amalgam of experience, subject, and capacity to choose. And this in turn links with my own dual-aspect proposal: that the brain/mind is a physical/mental whole, whose causal properties are not wholly captured by either the physical or the mental aspect on its own (Hodgson 1994a).

It is apparent that I don't regard the shape of the theory suggested by Chalmers as being altogether along the right lines. I would suggest rather a theory in which experience/subject/choice is fundamental, and in which one looks for physical explanations of the development in parallel of alternatives between which choices can be made — in combination with broad but not exact psychophysical bridging laws. In such a theory, some at least of Chalmers' 'easy problems' will not be fully solved in advance of the solution to his hard problem.

References

Chalmers, D.J. (1995), 'Facing up to the problem of consciousness', *Journal of Consciousness Studies*, **2** (3), pp. 200–19 (reprinted in this volume).
d'Espagnat, B. (1989), *Reality and the Physicist* (Cambridge: Cambridge University Press).
Hodgson, D. H. (1991), *The Mind Matters* (Oxford: Oxford University Press).
Hodgson, D. H. (1994a), 'Neuroscience and folk psychology — an overview', *Journal of Consciousness Studies*, **1** (2), pp. 205–16.
Hodgson, D. H. (1994b), 'Why Searle hasn't rediscovered the mind', *Journal of Consciousness Studies*, **1** (2), pp. 264–74.
Hodgson, D. H. (1995), 'Probability: the logic of the law — a response', *Oxford Journal of Legal Studies*, **14**, pp. 51–68.
Hodgson, D. H. (1996), 'Nonlocality, local indeterminism, and consciousness', Ratio (forthcoming).
Hofstadter, D. R. (1980), *Godel, Escher, Bach* (Harmondsworth: Penguin).
Hofstadter, D. R. (1981), 'A conversation with Einstein's brain', in *The Mind's I*, D.R. Hofstadter and D.C. Dennett (Brighton: Harvester Press).

Richard Warner

Facing Ourselves: Incorrigibility and the Mind–Body Problem

Exactly how the neurons in the opiate and benzodiazepine pathways function and how they might cooperate is unclear. But one plausible scenario goes like this: When a young monkey is separated from its mother, opiate-releasing and, consequently opiate-sensitive, neurons become inhibited. Such inhibition gives rise to a yearning for the mother and a generalized sense of vulnerability.

(Kalin, 1993)

This speculation about pathways provides no explanation of how 'such inhibition' produces the *feeling* of a yearning for the mother, or the *feeling* of a generalized sense of vulnerability. We learn only that the inhibition correlates with the feeling, and mere correlation is not explanation. In general, present-day psychology and neuroscience yield only physical–mental correlations and no explanatory account of how physical events give rise to mental phenomena.[1] Nonetheless, many remain confident that the physical sciences will ultimately *explain* the mind.

Such confidence is misplaced. Incorrigibility is the reason. Our beliefs about (certain kinds of) mental states exhibit a qualified incorrigibility — a conditional immunity to error[2] — that places the mental beyond the reach of explanation by physical science; or,

---

I am indebted to Taduesz Szubka for helpful discussions of the mind–body problem.

[1] I take this to be a clear empirical fact. It is no objection to this claim to note that empirical speculations abound. Penrose, for example, suggests that consciousness might be linked to the collapse of the quantum wave function. But this suggestion provides no explanatory model and yields no testable predictions. Speculation can play an important role in the development of science, but we should not confuse speculation with explanation.

[2] Some may wish to call this infallibility, instead of incorrigibility, for some may want to reserve 'incorrigibility' as a label for *uncorrectability by others*, as distinct from immunity to error. The issue is in part merely terminological. My concern is with conditional immunity to error — label it what you will. I have two reasons for using 'incorrigibility'. First, I do think that a standard use of 'incorrigibility' is to denote immunity to error, but it matters little here whether that is true. My second reason for using the term is precisely its connotation of uncorrectability by others. I will explain conditional immunity to error by appeal to *unimpaired* recognitional abilities, and, while I will not do so here, I would explain the relevant notion of *unimpairment* in terms of shared epistemological practices that determine when one's knowledge claims are and are not open to challenges from others. So correctability by others does indirectly come into play in understanding immunity to error. I have pursued these ideas, to a limited extent, in Warner (1992).

to be crucially more precise, beyond the reach of physical science *of the sort we now accept*. We will return to this qualification shortly. Subject to this qualification, I concur with David Chalmers' contention in the keynote essay that arriving at physical explanations of mental phenomena will require a significant extension of physical science; and I also concur that the extension that takes the form of 'add[ing] new principles to the furniture of the basic laws of nature' (p. 20). My concurrence, however, is partial. I also dissent. I dissent on the ground that accounting for incorrigibility requires a far more radical revision of contemporary science than Chalmers, and indeed the majority of philosophers, is willing to countenance. Further, in my emphasis on incorrigibility — an aspect of the reportability of mental states — I dissent from Chalmers' contention (p. 10) that reportability belongs with the 'easy problems of consciousness', and that the experiential character of consciousness — as distinct from incorrigibility — constitutes the true barrier to assimilating consciousness into the explanatory engine of current science.

To so dissent is to swim against the powerful tide of a large majority, and, before embarking on such a course, it is only reasonable to consider why the tide is flowing so strongly against one's chosen direction. We should see why so many are so convinced that the physical sciences will explain the mind. Doing so provides the background against which incorrigibility and experiential character stand out in revealing relief. Chalmers' excellent essay is particularly useful in developing this background; and, as I will criticize Chalmers' position, let me express my admiration for his clear, straightforward, and insightful essay that makes — hopefully fruitful — criticism possible.

I: The Explanatory Adequacy of Physics

The ultimate basis of the conviction that the physical sciences will explain the mind is (some version of) the *explanatory adequacy of physics*. This is, in David Lewis' lucid words,

> the plausible hypothesis that there is some unified body of scientific theories, of the sort we now accept, which together provide a true and exhaustive account of all physical phenomena (i.e. all phenomena describable in physical terms). They are unified in the sense that they are cumulative: the theory governing any physical phenomenon is explained by theories governing phenomena out of which that phenomenon is composed and by the way it is composed out of them. The same is true of the latter phenomena, and so on down to the fundamental particles or fields governed by a few simple laws, more or less as conceived of in present-day theoretical physics (Lewis, 1971, p. 169).

Two clarificatory points are in order. First, note that Lewis contends that 'there is some unified body of scientific theories, *of the sort we now accept,* which together provide a true and exhaustive account of all physical phenomena'. The reason for the 'of the sort we now accept' qualification that it is an almost entirely empty thesis to assert that physical science — *either* of the sort we now accept, *or* of a radically different sort — will ultimately explain the mind.[3] Very few deny that the present-day physical sciences will evolve into something that explains the mental and that we still *call* 'physical

---

[3] I discuss this point more fully in Warner (1994).

science'.[4] I shall, in what follows, mean by 'physical science' and related expressions, physical science of the sort we now accept.

The second point is that there are weaker and stronger forms of the requirement that 'the theory governing any physical phenomenon [the macro-theory] is explained by theories governing phenomena out of which that phenomenon is composed [the micro-theories] and by the way it is composed out of them'. Philosophers have advanced a variety of views about explanatory relations between macro- and micro-theories. The mind–body problem in particular has proven fertile ground for the proliferation of such views; suggestions include type-identity theories, token-identity theories, functionalism, supervenience, anomalous monism and eliminativism. Controversy abounds of course about which view is correct, but this debate need not detain us.

The point to emphasize is that the explanatory adequacy of physics leads to the conclusion all mental phenomena are fully describable and explainable in physical terms. Take pain. Pain has physical effects: it can cause you to take aspirin, or hold your hand to your head, for example. Now, according to the explanatory adequacy of physics, *all* physical phenomena are in principle ultimately explainable in terms of 'fundamental particles or fields governed by a few simple laws, more or less as conceived of in present-day theoretical physics.' In short: *physical* effects have *physical* explanations. Thus, the physical effects of pain must have such an explanation. Of course, *pain* is what explains these effects; consequently, pain itself is ultimately and in principle completely describable and explainable in terms of fundamental physics.[5]

Clearing the way for the inclusion of the mental in the explanatory scope of the physical sciences has been one major motive behind materialist theories of the mind. For roughly forty years, materialist-minded philosophers have labored to remove conceptual and theoretical barriers to holding that the mental can be completely described and explained in physical terms. In recent years, however, many philosophers — even many solidly in the materialist camp — have had a divided reaction to these materialist endeavors. They see them as successful for some kinds of mental states but much less so for other kinds. Chalmers is representative.

He contends (p. 10) that a variety of mental phenomena are 'straightforwardly vulnerable to explanation in terms of computational or neural mechanisms'; his examples include 'the reportability of mental states; the ability of a system to access its own internal states; the focus of attention; the deliberate control of behaviour; [and] the difference between wakefulness and sleep'. Chalmers — like many — has a much different attitude toward the ability of physical science to explain *experience*. 'The really hard problem,' he contends, 'is the problem of *experience*.' Chalmers rightly notes the clear failure of various attempts to show, in any convincing fashion, how experience can be described and explained in physical terms, and he claims that, to account for experience, we need

> a nonreductive theory of experience [that] will add new principles to the furniture of the basic laws of nature. These basic principles will carry the explanatory burden in a theory of consciousness. Just as we explain familiar high-level phenomena

---

[4] Colin McGinn (1994) denies this.

[5] Strictly speaking, this does not follow. What follows is that pain is physical, or it does not really explain the behaviour we currently think it causes. Lewis (1971) considers and rejects the latter possibility.

involving mass in terms of more basic principles involving mass and other entities, we might explain familiar phenomena involving experience in terms of more basic principles involving experience and other entities.

In particular, a nonreductive theory of experience will specify basic principles telling us how experience depends on physical features of the world. The *psycho-physical* principles will not interfere with physical laws, as it seems that physical laws already form a closed system. Rather, they will be a supplement to a physical theory. A physical theory gives us a theory of the physical processes, and psycho-physical theory tells us how those processes give rise to experience. We know that experience depends on physical processes, but we also know that this dependence cannot be derived from physical laws alone. The new basic principles postulated by a nonreductive theory give us the extra ingredient that we need to build an explanatory bridge (p. 20).

It is important to distinguish Chalmers' non-reductive theory from supervenience theories that may also claim to be 'non-reductive'.[6] Supervenience theories attempt to explain a relation — the supervenience relation — that can obtain between the principles and entities in, for example, psychology or neurobiology and the principles and entities in the physical sciences. The supervenience relation is (typically) to be such that: (1) the principles and entities of the supervening theory have a legitimate explanatory and causal role; (2) the supervening theory is not *reduced* to the physical theory on which it supervenes; the explanatory adequacy of physics is preserved (everything is completely describable and explainable in physical terms).[7]

Chalmers' non-reductive theory is *not* a supervenience theory. He does not assert a supervenience relation between some present or future psychological theory and some appropriate physical theory; rather he proposes we extend physical science by adding new, basic terms for experience. We are to 'add new principles to the furniture of the basic laws of nature [where] [t]hese basic principles . . . carry the explanatory burden in a theory of consciousness.' Part of the point of the characterizations 'new' and 'basic' is, I take it, precisely that the terms designating experiences are *not* understood in light of a supervenience relation, nor — *a fortiori* — in light of any explicit definition, nor through any of the sorts of accounts proposed by proponents of functionalism. This is why Chalmers characterizes his proposed extension of science as 'a variety of dualism' (p. 20). I shall mean by 'non-reductive' a non-reductive theory of the sort Chalmers envisions.

Suggesting such a theory may appear simply as sensible science. Extending current science by adding new fundamental terms is one, sometimes successful, response to phenomena that repeatedly defeat the explanatory powers of the unextended theories, and, as Chalmers rightly emphasizes, experience has indeed so far defied explanation in physical terms. So, should we accept Chalmers' suggestion? I think we should — in part. We should accept the non-reductive theory while rejecting Chalmers' suggestion that the theory — while a 'variety of dualism' — is 'an innocent version of dualism, entirely compatible with the scientific world view' (p. 20). The proposed non-reductive theory is far from 'innocent'. Chalmers thinks it is because he thinks that '[t]he *psycho-physical*

[6] See, for example, Horgan (1993), pp. 295–320.

[7] On some appropriate account of what counts as physical description and explanation.

principles will not interfere with physical laws, as it seems that physical laws already form a closed system. They will be a supplement to a physical theory.' This is a mistake. Psycho-physical principles in a non-reductive theory of experience *must* interfere with physical laws, for they necessarily yield violations of physical conservation laws.

To see why, assume — *arguendo* and along with Chalmers — that physical laws by themselves define a closed system; and assume that we will explain experience via 'a nonreductive theory of experience [that adds] new principles to the furniture of the basic laws of nature'. *Given these assumptions*, it follows that experience cannot have any role in producing physical effects. Such effects would violate various conservation laws that hold in 'closed system' defined by physical laws. The conservation of momentum, for example, asserts that the total amount of momentum in a physical system remains constant.[8] Now, suppose that an experience E increases a physical particle's momentum. If the *combined* psycho-physical *and* physical laws defined a closed system, a decrease in E's momentum could balance the increase in the physical particle's momentum. But Chalmers' view is that momentum is conserved in the system defined by the physical laws alone (I take this to be part of what he means by saying that the physical laws *alone* define a closed system), so the decrease in E's momentum lies outside the system, and there is no corresponding decrease *within* the system. This violates the conservation of momentum. Of course, experience might have physical effects without altering momentum, but, to have such effects, it has to change *something* physical — momentum, direction, charge, energy, or something.[9] It is difficult to see how such alterations would not violate one or another conservation law.

This means that, given our assumptions, there can be no psycho-physical laws of the form 'If experience E, then physical event P'. It also follows that there can be no psycho-physical laws of the form, 'If physical event P, then experience E'. Suppose there were such a law. One would expect that the production of E to involve a decrease in some physical quantity, a decrease counterbalanced by a corresponding increase in one or more 'mental quantities' when E occurs. We of course do not know now *what* 'mental quantities' since we lack any explanatory account of how the physical produces the mental, but it would seem that we must postulate such 'mental quantities' to have any

[8] To understand the conservation of momentum, we need to note two points. First, the momentum of a particle is the product of its mass and velocity; therefore the rate of change of a particle's momentum is its mass times its acceleration (acceleration being the rate of change of its velocity) — where mass times acceleration is, according to Newton's Second Law, just the force acting on the particle. Second, momentum is a directed quantity that can be specified by giving its components along three directions. Now, Newton's Third Law of Motion says that the force a particle P exerts on another particle P' is equal in magnitude and opposite in direction to the force P' exerts on P. This is true for the rate of change of momentum. Over any suitably short interval of time, any increase in any component of either particle's momentum is balanced by a decrease in that component of the other particle's momentum, so the total amount of momentum remains constant.

[9] Of course, one might suggest *either* that the occurrence of P is not associated with any increase in a physical quantity, *or* that the relevant increase is counterbalanced by a decrease, not in E, but in some other *physical* quantity. The first option is hardly coherent. How could P's occurrence *not* be associated with a change in some physical quantity? But, for the sake of argument, suppose not. Then how would we explain P's coming into existence? What would the causal link be between E and P? A link that could operate without changing physical quantities? The second option faces the same difficulty. If the decrease in the physical quantity is counterbalanced by an increase in some other physical quantity, what is the physical explanation of P's occurrence? What is the causal connection between P and E?

intelligible picture of how changes in physical quantities yield Chalmers' non-reducible mental events. But Chalmers cannot countenance such correlations between physical and mental quantities, for they would violate current conservation laws. We would have a change in a physical quantity balanced only by a change in a mental quantity lying outside closed system defined by physical laws.[10]

The impossibility of psycho-physical laws is an unacceptable result.[11] The point of Chalmers' non-reductive theory is to show how we could have viable psycho-physical laws. Moreover, we certainly currently think that mental experiences do have physical effects and the physical events can cause experience. Two simple examples: I miss my daughter, so I dial her phone number to call her long-distance from Chicago; smashing my thumb with the hammer causes me to experience pain.

We have two options at this point. First, we could abandon the idea that we should account for experience via a non-reductive theory that contains fundamental terms for experiences. If we assumed, for example, that experiences could be identified with some aspect of the physical, or that experiences supervened on the physical, we could not use the foregoing argument to derive the conclusion that there can be no psycho-physical laws.[12] The second option is to abandon the assumption that '*psycho-physical* principles will not interfere with physical laws, as it seems that physical laws already form a closed system'. As we have just seen, if physical laws do form a closed system, then psycho-physical interactions violate physical conservation laws. We can retain the non-reductive psycho-physiological theory if we are willing to hold that it is *not* true that 'physical laws . . . form a closed system'. We would hold that physical conservation laws are valid only in domains where psycho-physical interactions are excluded, and, to find conservation laws of unrestricted validity, we would look for laws that hold of the system defined by the physical *and* psycho-physical laws.

Faced with holding that physical conservation laws have only limited validity, many will find the choice clear. How could the reasonable option be anything but giving up on the non-reductive theory? My view is precisely the opposite. The reasonable course is to retain the non-reductive theory and look for new conservation laws. There is, of course, no point in trying to imagine such laws now. Lacking any explanation at all of how the

---

[10] Variations of the options considered in note 9 are possible here. One might suggest either that the occurrence of E is not associated with any decrease in a physical quantity, or that the relevant decrease is counterbalanced by an increase, not in 'mental quantities', but in some other physical quantity. These suggestions face essentially the same difficulties as before. If the occurrence of E is not associated with a decrease in a physical quantity, what is the physical explanation of its coming into existence? What is the causal connection between P and E? Similarly, if the decrease in the physical quantity is counterbalanced by an increase in some other physical quantity, what is the physical explanation of E's occurrence? What is the causal connection between P and E?

[11] Chalmers worries that this may be true. He remarks that 'the causal relevance of experience' is a 'natural worry, given a picture on which the physical domain is causally closed and on which experience is supplementary to the physical' (p. 28).

[12] If experiences were identical with some aspect of the physical, then experiences could cause physical events and physical events could cause experiences without violating conservation laws since experiences themselves would be physical items obeying the conservation laws of the physical system. The situation is less clear in the case of supervenience. There are a variety of supervenience theories, and they all face serious problems (see Kim, 1994). However, one typical goal of supervenience theorists is to provide an explanation of how mental causation is consistent with the picture of the world our physics provides. See, for example, Horgan (1993).

physical gives rise to the mental, any speculation about possible future conservation laws is arm-chair science (science fiction) having entertainment value only. The question to focus on instead is simply, why adopt this second, seemingly radical, option? Why adhere to the non-reductive theory now that the price of doing so is evident?

Chalmers' essay is a helpful starting point. According to Chalmers, the subjectivity of experience is the reason experience has failed to fall comfortably within the ambit of the physical sciences. As Chalmers explains (p. 10), experience is 'the subjective aspect' of consciousness. Experience involves 'felt qualities'; examples include visual sensations, sounds, smells, and bodily sensations, where 'what unites all of these states is that there is something it is like to be in them.' All this is correct, but, for our purposes insufficiently informative. This is not a criticism of Chalmers. He is simply summarizing the standard, Nagel-inspired characterization of the subjectivity of experience; and, while this is entirely adequate for his purposes, these characterizations of experience as 'subjective' and as states where 'there is something it is like to be in them' are, for our purposes, insufficiently informative. We need a characterization of experience, or some aspect of experience, that shows us why we should seek new conservation laws.

An adequate understanding of incorrigibility is the key to finding such a characterization. To see why, we first need to set present-day physical science in the relevant historical context.

II: Science and Objectivity

The relevant history is the rise of science.[13] We begin with the seventeenth century 'moderns' who rebelled against the Aristotelian view of the universe as a meaningful order of final causes. The Aristotelian vision yielded to a Pythagorean vision — of Bruno, Kepler, Galileo, and others — of a mathematically ordered world, and finally to the contemporary vision of the world as a complex of contingent correlations delineated by empirical observation. From our current point of view, Aristotelian science projected on nature what people wanted to find there — a meaningful order of final causes. Our scientific conviction, however, is that nature reveals its truths only to those who avoid such projection: the discovery of truth requires a constant struggle against what Bacon called the 'idols of the human mind'. This is why we must guard against various distorting influences — not just wish fulfillment and prejudice, but even a particular location in time and space, and our own innate sensory constitution. We must correct for the influence of *any* factor that makes the world appear different than it really is. In doing so, we achieve (we hope) a view of the world as it is in itself, not as it merely appears to this or that observer, or kind of observer. Science so conceived involves a practice of adjudication that corrects for the illusions of mere appearance and leads to a conception of the world as it really is. Israel Scheffler nicely captures the conception in his comments on scientific objectivity:

> A fundamental feature of science is its ideal of objectivity, an ideal that subjects all scientific statements to the test of independent and impartial criteria, recognizing no authority of persons in the realm of cognition. The claimant to scientific knowledge is responsible for what he says, acknowledging the relevance of consid-

---

[13] What follows is adapted from Taylor (1985).

erations beyond his wish or advocacy to the judgment of his assertions. In assertion
... he is trying to meet independent standards, to satisfy factual requirements whose
fulfillment cannot be guaranteed in advance. (Scheffler, 1967, p. 1.)

We can conveniently summarize these remarks by introducing the notion of *mind-independence*. An item is mind-independent just in case its being the way it is does not,
in any essential way, depend either on our beliefs about it, or on the way in which we
form those beliefs. For example, redness as a micro-structural property of surfaces is a
mind-independent feature of objects; objects with that property *appear* red to beings with
a certain sensory constitution, and appear in others ways to beings with other sensory
constitutions. Simply to assume — merely on the basis of our visual experience — that
red things are in themselves the way they appear to us would be to *assume* that the way
nature *appears* to us for the way it *is*. This would be to lose the Baconian struggle against
'idols of the human mind' by projecting onto nature the ways that it *merely seems to us*.
To see the world as it is in itself, we must correct all distorting influences that make the
world appear to be different than it really is. In correcting in this way for distortions in
our view of the world, independent and impartial criteria yield a picture of the world as
a complex of *mind-independent* items. These points apply to the mental. Pain, for
example, *feels* a certain way; indeed, it is natural to think that, for example, pain *just is*
an experience with a certain characteristic feel. But *if* everything has a mind-independent
nature, we cannot assume that the way pain feels to us reveals the way it is *in itself*;
scientific investigation, not introspective experience, reveals pain as it is in itself —
assuming that pain is a mind-independent phenomenon. Incorrigibility shows that this
assumption is wrong. Pain is not completely describable and explainable in mind-independent terms.

Let us turn then to incorrigibility, and let me begin by saying what my aim is *not*. My
aim is not to make a compelling case for incorrigibility; I have done — or at least tried
to do — that elsewhere.[14] My aim here is to explain what incorrigibility is and make it
plausible that it exists.

III: Incorrigibility

The received opinion is that incorrigibility does not exist and hence poses no threat to the
project of explaining the mind in terms of physical science. I concede that this is correct
for *the traditional conception* of incorrigibility. The traditional conception: for at least
some mental states, *necessarily*, if one believes that one is in that state, then one really is.
For example, necessarily, if one believes that one is in pain, then one is. The traditional
claim falls foul of the fact that, in taking something to be of a certain kind, one commits
oneself to the claim that the thing is relevantly similar to other things of that kind. The
relevant similarity may not really hold but merely appear to. This can happen even in the
case of pain. An example: you are at the dentist but, consumed with worry about whether
you will be on time for the important appointment you have afterwards, you are paying
no attention to what the dentist is doing. Suddenly, a particularly hard probe makes you
complain, 'That hurt!' Since you should be completely anesthetized, the dentist is
perplexed and asks if you will submit to the same probe again. This time, attending

---

[14] See Warner (1986; 1989; 1992; 1993 and 1994).

carefully to the sensation, you recognize it as qualitatively identical to the sensation you felt before; and, you also realize that the present sensation is not painful at all. It is just a sharp sensation of pressure — as was, you now realize, the previous, qualitatively identical sensation. You thought the previous sensation painful because the suddenness of the sensation so startled you that immediately, without attending at all carefully to the sensation, you took it for a pain. You did so because, for you, dentistry is an ordeal of anxiety and fear, and your agitation and apprehensiveness predispose you to take almost any sudden sensation to be a pain. To have managed to lose yourself in worry about the appointment was a blissful, if easily shattered, release.

To see how to formulate a defensible incorrigibility claim, we should first note that the cases in which one can falsely believe that one is in pain are all cases in which one's ability to recognize pain is *impaired*: to falsely believe that one is in pain one must be anxiety-ridden, or drugged, or hypnotized, or inattentive, or careless, or in some other state that impairs one's recognitional ability.[15] To see the way to a defensible incorrigibility claim, contrast the dentist case with a case in which your ability to recognize pain is completely *un*impaired. Imagine that you have, or at least that it seems you have, a pounding headache. It seems as if someone were relentlessly pounding with a hammer on the inside of your skull. Your ability to recognize pain is *completely* unimpaired; you are not drugged, hypnotized, over-anxious, or any such thing; quite the contrary — your attention is riveted remorselessly on the sensation. You complain about your pounding headache — manifesting your belief that you are in pain. I claim your belief could not be false.

To generalize, the incorrigibility I claim exists is a qualified incorrigibility. More precisely, I claim that a *certain kind* of mistake, possible in the recognition of physical things, is *not* possible in the case of — certain — mental items. I will focus exclusively on the example of pain. To illustrate the relevant kind of mistake in question, suppose your ability to recognize foxes is completely unimpaired, and that, as a result of using this ability, you believe a particular item to be a fox. You might be mistaken — the 'animal' might be a hologram, for example. Mistakes of this sort are impossible in the case of pain. Suppose your ability to recognize pain is completely *unimpaired*, and, as a result of using that ability, you believe you are in pain. Then, roughly and approximately:

(*) *Necessarily*, if your belief results from your unimpaired ability to recognize pain, your belief is true.

This is rough and approximate because the notion of impairment needs considerable explanation; I have offered the explanation elsewhere, where I have also argued at length that (*) really is *necessarily* true.[16] I will put these issues aside here — with the exception of four further points.

---

[15] By a recognitional ability I mean merely a capacity to reliably form true beliefs. Thus, in general, the ability to recognize F's is the capacity reliably to form true beliefs as to whether a given item is an F. I will, because it is natural and convenient, talk of the exercise of a recognitional ability; however, I do not mean to imply that the activation of the ability is always or even usually under one's voluntary control. An ability, e.g. to recognize foxes by sight may be causally and nonvoluntarily activated by a fox's coming in to view. Such nonvoluntary activation counts as an exercise.

[16] See note 14.

First, some may be puzzled the fact that (*) talks only about belief, not about feeling. After all, pain is something one *feels*. What is the link between the feeling and the belief? The answer is that the question presupposes too sharp a distinction between feeling and believing. Typically, when you feel pain, the sensory and the cognitive are mixed together in the state of 'feeling pain'. The belief and the feeling arise together in a single state of 'feeling pain', a state with both sensory and cognitive content. 'The feeling' and 'the belief' occur simultaneously; one does not arrive at the belief by first having the feeling and then inspecting it for appropriate features. It is a mistake to distinguish sharply between the sensory and cognitive aspects of experience.

Second, the ability mentioned in (*) has to be a *non-inferential* ability. Strictly speaking, (*) should read:

(*) Necessarily, if your belief results from your unimpaired *non-inferential* ability to recognize pain, your belief is true.

This ability is the capacity reliably to form beliefs as to whether or not one is in pain — *where the belief is not the result of an inference*. You typically do not arrive at your belief that you are in pain non-inferentially. You do not, for example, observe yourself taking aspirin while feeling a certain sensation in one's head, and then conclude that you must be in pain. Typically, the belief that one is in pain simply arises simultaneously with the feeling; it is neither the result of, nor justified by, any inference. To avoid counter-examples, it is essential that (*) involve the non-inferential ability. To see why, suppose the people from Alpha Centauri arrive. They never feel certain sensations — among them pain and nausea. However, an Alpha Centaurian neurophysiologist discovers a way to modify the Alpha Centaurian nervous system so that Alpha Centaurians can feel pain, and she finds a volunteer who wants to feel the sensation that humans call 'pain'. The experimenter tells the volunteer that she will produce pain in his stomach. This is sufficient to give the volunteer a limited *inferential* ability to recognize pain. If, in the context of the experiment, the volunteer feels a previously unfelt sensation in his stomach, he can infer it is pain. To make the inference reliable, suppose the experimenter has successfully, as the volunteer knows, produced pain in an unbroken series of a hundred prior experiments. The outcome of this experiment, however, is that the volunteer experiences nausea instead of pain. But, the volunteer, not realizing that the experiment has failed, believes that he is in pain; he infers that the feeling must be pain since he has never felt it before, and since it is the sensation produced by the experimenter. So the unimpaired use of the *inferential* ability leads to a false belief.[17]

Third, the necessity in (*) is *not* causal or nomological necessity. I have argued at length elsewhere that the necessity in (*) is a logical necessity — in the sense that the denial of (*) leads to an outright contradiction.[18] I will not repeat that argument; instead I offer the following briefer considerations. Suppose the necessity were causal or nomological. What evidence would we have that this was so? The evidence must be

[17] Some may object that the volunteer will recognize the sensation of nausea on the ground that he could recognize another instance of nausea as the same kind of sensation. He simply misconceptualizes (or mislabels, if one prefers) nausea as pain (or, as 'pain'). We may concede this. The point of the example is that the inferential ability to recognize pain leads to the volunteer's false belief that he is in pain (in a state called 'pain').

[18] In Warner (1992). The argument which follows is adapted from Warner (1986).

evidence we possess *now* — that is, prior to any psycho-physiological investigation — for we know *now* that (*) is true. But don't we have such evidence? Couldn't observation of oneself and others establish (*)? But exactly what 'observations' are we talking about here? Are we supposed to imagine that I check on myself to make sure, in those cases in which my ability is unimpaired, that I believe I am in pain only when I in fact am? The problem is that there is no such check. Once I establish that my non-inferential ability to recognize pain is unimpaired, *there is nothing more to do* to ensure that my belief is true.[19] The same point holds for others. Once we establish that the other's non-inferential ability to recognize pain is unimpaired, the other's sincere assertion that he or she feels pain settles the matter. *There is nothing more to do* to check on the assertion. It misses the point here to suppose *future* psycho-physiological knowledge and apparatus that would allow us to check the assertion. If we have *no* present evidence that (*) is causally or nomologically necessary, we do not *now* know (*) to be necessary. Therefore the necessity (*) refers to cannot be causal or nomological.[20]

Fourth, some remarks about unconscious motivation are in order. Do examples involving unconscious motivation raise problems for (*)? Suppose, for example, I think I am angry. A few months later, I realize that I was really feeling sorrow at what I perceived to a betrayal by an intimate other. Unable to acknowledge the betrayal, or deal with its pain, I remained unconscious of the betrayal and its sorrow. There are two situations to distinguish here. In the first, *I really do feel anger*, and my belief that I do results from my unimpaired non-inferential ability to recognize anger. Let us suppose that my anger results, at least in part, from my unconscious perception that I have been betrayed. When questioned, I deny that a perception of betrayal causes my anger. Nothing here raises any problem for (*). (*) does not claim that we have any non-inferential ability to recognize the *causes* of our feelings. In the second situation, I do *not* really feel angry at all. What I feel is sorrow that I misinterpret as anger. I do so because my unconscious perception of and reaction to the betrayal impairs my non-inferential ability to recognize both sorrow and anger. Again, this is entirely consistent with thinking that our *un*impaired non-inferential recognitional abilities necessarily yield correct results. The general issue these examples raise is the extent to which unconscious factors impair our non- inferential recognitional abilities. This is an empirical question. My own view is that, at least in the area of the emotions, unconscious impairment can be fairly pervasive and that truthful self-consciousness can be an achievement greatly to be prized.

Let us assume from now on the qualified incorrigibility exists and consider the consequence that follows.

IV: The Consequence

The consequence is that physical science as we currently conceive of it cannot explain the mind. Current physical science does not countenance necessary connections between

---

[19] I discuss this claim in detail in Warner (1992 and 1994).

[20] Unless one wishes to adopt a view of knowledge on which one can have empirical knowledge of something for which one has no present evidence or justification. Reliability theories of knowledge can be of this sort. I offer reasons for rejecting reliability theories of knowledge in the context of (*) in Warner (1989 and 1992).

the exercise of the ability to recognize F's and the truth of the resulting belief that a given item is (an) F, and one major motive behind current materialist theories of the mind is to show how the mental phenomena are *not* mind-dependent. The goal is to show how we can account for mental phenomena entirely in terms acceptable within a scientific practice that countenances only mind-*in*dependent entities. To acknowledge incorrigibility is to reject *all* such theories. To acknowledge incorrigibility is to acknowledge that we are *guaranteed* that something is (an) F when our unimpaired *human* recognitional ability leads us to believe that it is, and this is to recognize the authority of persons in the realm of cognition — with a vengeance. We are saying that the world *has to be* the way it appears to unimpaired humans. This is precisely what we do when we acknowledge qualified incorrigibility. This is a profound departure from *current s*cientific practice. Physical science has had the centuries-long *raison d'être* of giving a completely mind-*in*dependent account of nature. We are now contemplating including within such science an account of mind-*de*pendent items, items that necessarily are they way they appear.

No term of any current physical science designates such entities. Nor does any materialist, philosophical account show us how to incorporate such terms into physical theories. The motive behind materialist theories — whether type identity theories, token identity theories, functionalism, supervenience, anomalous monism, or eliminativism — is to show how the mental (insofar as the theory acknowledges its existence) can be incorporated within a scientific account that recognizes only mind-independent entities. To account for mind-dependent entities, we need a future psycho-physiological theory that contains undefined terms that designate mind-*de*pendent experiences. To use Chalmers words, a 'nonreductive theory of experience [that adds] new principles to the furniture of the basic laws of nature'. What other alternative is there?[21]

Two further points are in order. First, to endorse a non-reductive theory is to abandon the explanatory adequacy of physics. The explanatory adequacy of physics is 'the plausible hypothesis that there is some unified body of scientific theories, *of the sort we now accept*, which together provide a true and exhaustive account of all physical phenomena'. Our contemplated psycho-physiology departs from a central past and present *raison d'être* of scientific explanation — giving a mind-independent account of nature. In this way, it fails to qualify as a theory 'of the sort we now accept' — i. e. a theory countenancing only mind-independent entities.

Second, while it is a relatively minor point, it is worth noting that, in arguing via incorrigibility for a non-reductive theory, we have rejected another widely share conviction. Chalmers' is representative of the prevailing opinion. Chalmers distinguishes between hard and easy problems in the area of mind and body, and he allocates incorri-

---

[21] What about functionalism? Couldn't functionalists simply incorporate a version of (*) in the functional definition of kinds of mental states? Grant that this is possible, and consider the schema 'Necessarily, if the belief that one is in state S results from one's unimpaired non-inferential ability to recognize S, then one's belief is true'? If this schema were included in the functional definition of a mental state, what sorts of states would satisy the definition? No *mind-independent* state could, so a functionalism that incorporates (*) would be a functionalism whose definitions are *not* realizable by physical — i. e. mind-independent — states. A functionalism that incorporated (*) would not serve the materialist end of showing how a mind-independent account of the mind is possible. Of course, materialism aside, if functionalism did not face so many other devastating difficulties, one could regard a functionalism that incorporated a version of (*) as a competitor to a Chalmers'-like non-reductive theory.

gibility ('reportability' as he calls it) to the 'easy problems of consciousness' (p. 10). He contends that reportability is

> straightforwardly vulnerable to explanation in terms of computational or neural mechanisms . . . [W]e need only specify the mechanism by which information about internal states is retrieved and made available for verbal report (p. 10).

He asserts that the experiential character of consciousness — not incorrigibility — is the hard problem that scientific accounts of the mind must solve.

Given that incorrigibility — 'reportability' — is the aspect of experience that motivates a non-reductive theory, Chalmers is clearly mistaken. It is incorrigibility that captures the 'subjectivity' — the mind-dependence — of experience.[22] And, it is worth noting that there is really nothing special about experience here as distinct from other kinds of mental states. Many kinds of mental states enjoy qualified incorrigibility — including beliefs, desires, emotions. For example, your belief that you are now reading this sentence enjoys such incorrigible status (assuming your recognitional ability is unimpaired). Experience simply happens to be the domain of the most convincing examples of incorrigibility, for an adequate account of incorrigibility for the mental generally requires distinctions and qualifications that an account confined to experience does not demand.

V: Incorrigibility and Necessity

Some may accept everything we have said so far and still hold that incorrigibility presents no barrier to explaining the mind in terms of the physical sciences. Incorrigibility causes problems only if it involves a necessary connection between the exercise of a recognitional ability and truth. Some will deny the necessity. This denial does not require a complete rejection of (*). One can grant that — *in our current conceptual scheme* — we do accept the necessary truth (*) formulates. But — so the objection goes — we could change our conceptual scheme. Isn't this more palatable than incorporating incorrigibility into physical science?

One reply is that (*) does not express a conceptual-scheme-relative necessity; rather — so the reply goes — it expresses a truth that *any* acceptable conceptual scheme must acknowledge. This would be the position of one who thought (*) expressed an *a priori* truth in the traditional Kantian sense of 'a priori'. Such truths were absolute constraints on any acceptable scheme of empirical thought. I will not try to resolve the question of whether (*) expresses an absolute or merely relative necessity (were we do so we would be well advised to sceptically examine the absolute/relative necessity distinction); instead, I will — very briefly — sketch out a reason for retaining (*) even if it expresses a mere relative (and hence abandonable) necessity.

The argument is that denying incorrigibility is self-defeating (in a quite literal sense of *self*-defeating): to attempt to construct a picture of the mind in mind-independent terms is to erase the mental from the picture altogether. The proponents of physicalistic

---

[22] Of course, to put the point this way is to use a distinction we rejected earlier. Earlier we noted that we should not distinguish sharply between the experiential and cognitive aspects of experience. A better way to put the point would be to say that the mixed sensory-cognitive states of experience typically exhibit the qualified incorrigibility that (*) describes, and that this qualified incorrigibility is a barrier to accommodate experiential states within current physical science.

explanation in the name of painting a picture of themselves as they genuinely are in themselves, assiduously eliminate themselves from of that very picture. The irony might be amusing if it were not such a clear symptom of the misguided passion for objectivity that sadly pervades contemporary philosophy. Since these issues lie well outside the scope of this essay, I will simply state what I take to be the case. I begin with some observations about what it is to be a person; point out links between being a person and the notions of intention and reason; and then return to incorrigibility.

To be a person is, in part, to employ one's ability to act freely to control and direct one's actions.[23] The self-control and self-direction characteristic of persons as free beings intimately involves intending and reasoning. A simple example: I arrive at my intention to drive home at 4:00 p.m. by the following reasoning: 'I need to drive home at some point; if I drive home too late, I will get delayed in a traffic jam; I hate such delays, so I should be sure not to drive home too late, but I also need to stay at my office as long as is feasible. Any later than 4:00 is too late, so I shall drive home at 4:00.' Such reasoning-generated intentions are an essential locus of the self-control and self-direction characteristic of human freedom. Now grant for the moment that *incorrigible* knowledge of one's reasons and intentions is essential to such self-direction.[24] The standard counterexamples to the claim that we can sometimes have incorrigible knowledge of our intentions can all be handled as cases of an impaired recognitional ability. Of course, the extent to which we have incorrigible knowledge of our intentions depends in part on the extent to which unconscious factors impair the relevant recognitional ability. But we may put this issue aside. Grant *arguendo* that it is. Then, to eliminate incorrigibility from our theory of the mental is to erase ourselves from the — purported — picture of our own minds. But is qualified incorrigible knowledge of reasons and intentions really essential to the free self-direction that is definitive of persons? Yes; I do not, when acting freely, figure out my intentions and the significance of my bodily movements as if I were observing another; rather, I know 'directly' what I intend and what I am doing — that is, the mere unimpaired exercise of the relevant recognitional abilities is sufficient to give me knowledge.[25]

These brief considerations will not convert any sceptics, of course; nor are they intended to do so. They are, however, sufficient to suggest the broader issues that arise when considering the interface between incorrigibility and physical science. This interface is one of the most fundamental and important scientific and philosophical issues of our day.*

---

[23] This is a widely held view. I defend a particular version of it in Warner (1987).

[24] I assume we have the ability to non-inferentially recognize that we intend this or that; I also assume that if as result of exercising one's unimpaired ability non-inferentially to recognize one's intentions, one believes that one intends so-and-so, then one does intend so-and-so.

[25] The *locus classicus* for such a picture of free action is Hampshire (1983).

* This paper was originally published in the *Journal of Consciousness Studies*, **3**, No.3 (1996), pp. 217–30.

References

Chalmers, David (1995), 'Facing up to the problem of consciousness', *Journal of Consciousness Studies*, **2** (3), pp. 200–19 (reprinted in this volume).

Hampshire, Stuart (1983), *Thought and Action* (Notre Dame, Indiana : Notre Dame).

Horgan, Terrence (1993), 'Nonreductive materialism and the explanatory autonomy of psychology', in Wagner and Warner (1993).

Kalin, Ned (1993) 'The neurobiology of fear', *Scientific American*, **268** (5), pp. 54–60.

Kim, Jaegwon (1994), 'The myth of non-reductive materialism', in Warner and Szubka (1994).

Lewis, David (1971), 'An argument for the identity theory', in *Materialism and the Mind–Body Problem*, ed. David Rosenthal (New Jersey: Prentice-Hall).

McGinn, Colin (1994), 'Can we solve the mind–body problem?', in Warner and Szubka (1994).

Robinson, Howard (ed. 1992), *Objections to Physicalism* (Oxford: Oxford University Press).

Scheffler, Israel (1967), *Science and Subjectivity* (Indiana: Bobbs-Merrill).

Taylor, Charles (1985), *Philosophical Papers*, Introduction to Vol. 1 (Cambridge: Cambridge University Press).

Wagner, Steven and Warner, Richard (1993), *Naturalism: A Critical Appraisal* (Notre Dame, Indiana: Notre Dame).

Warner, Richard (1986), 'A challenge to physicalism', *Australasian Journal of Philosophy*, **64**, pp. 249–65.

Warner, Richard (1987), *Freedom, Enjoyment, and Happiness* (New York: Cornell).

Warner, Richard (1989), 'Why is logic a priori?,' *The Monist*, **79**, pp. 40–51.

Warner, Richard (1992), 'Incorrigibility,' in Robinson (1992).

Warner, Richard (1993), 'Is the body a physical object,' in Wagner and Warner (1993).

Warner, Richard (1994a), 'The mind–body debate', in Warner and Szubka (1994).

Warner, Richard (1994b), 'In defense of a dualism', in Warner and Szubka (1994).

Warner, Richard and Szubka, Tadeusz (eds. 1994), *The Mind–Body Problem* (Oxford: Blackwell).

William S. Robinson

The Hardness of the Hard Problem

The primary aim of this paper is to offer an explanation of why the Hard Problem is so hard. The broader purpose in doing this is to try to take a step toward reducing the dissatisfaction that we experience whenever the Hard Problem is forced upon our attention. This broader purpose can at best be partially achieved here, because my explanation of the hardness of the Hard Problem will depend on a considerable number of assumptions, and not all of them can be adequately explained and defended here. However, despite the dependence of this paper on work that lies outside it, I believe it will provide a way of looking at the Hard Problem that will recommend itself for further consideration.

I

We shall need to have a working statement of the Hard Problem. I shall phrase it as a question, and I shall clarify the question, and the scope of this paper, by reviewing a range of types of response to it. The question that I shall take to present the Hard Problem is this.

(HP) *Why should a subject S have a conscious experience of type F whenever S has a neural event of type G?*

My leading examples of conscious experiences will be pains and after-images. Although these examples form only a small subset of conscious experiences, they will prove sufficient to enable us to raise the key questions, and focusing upon them allows us to avoid a somewhat lengthy discussion of the range of qualities to be found in conscious experiences.

We should note that (HP) does *not* presuppose that *only* G neural events stand in a regular connection to F conscious experiences. Even with this point made explicit, however, some readers may regard our formulation of the Hard Problem as lamentably nonspecific about the relation between F conscious experiences and G neural events. They may, that is, hanker for the relation to be identified as causation, identity, or some kind of supervenience. However, the arguments of this paper do not depend on distinctions among these cases and it would be unfortunate to give the appearance that they apply to a less general class of cases than they do. This point will be easy to understand if we consider that we can be equally puzzled by the questions, 'Why should G neural

This paper was originally published in the *Journal of Consciousness Studies*, **3**, No.1 (1996), pp. 14–25.

events cause F conscious experiences? (or, *how* do they do so?)', 'Why are F conscious experiences identical with G neural events — how *can* they be, when they do not appear to be so?' and 'Why should F conscious experiences supervene upon G neural events?' From the point of view of this paper, these are merely specifications of the Hard Problem that arise when one has made some assumptions additional to recognizing conscious experiences and the generic regularity used to formulate (HP). To preserve this generic outlook I shall sometimes say that G neural events *yield* F conscious experiences, where 'yield' is neutral among causation, identity and supervenience.

Let us further clarify our question, (HP), by considering some reactions to it.

(*a*) Reject the question by denying one of its presuppositions, namely, that there are conscious experiences.

Although Dennett (1991) uses a different phrase, namely 'real seemings', I take him to be denying that there are conscious experiences. Thus, presupposing them must be counted as controversial. However, although Dennett deserves a reply,[1] this is not the place to give it. Thus, the remainder of this paper is addressed only to those who agree that there are conscious experiences of the kinds mentioned.

(*b*) Bypass the question by substituting a problem that is hard, but is not the Hard Problem, namely answering the correlational question:

(**CQ**) *Which kinds of neural events, exactly, yield which kinds of conscious experiences?*

Confusion between this question and (HP) can be found in Churchland (1994) and is endemic in Crick (1994). Further examples and discussion can be found in section IV of David Chalmers' keynote paper. In the present paper we shall presuppose that Crick (and others) are correct in their belief that (CQ) can be approached and ultimately answered by scientific means; but we shall remain clear that knowing *that* F conscious experiences occur when G neural events occur does not tell us *why* this regularity obtains, or *how* G neural events yield F conscious experiences rather than H conscious experiences or, indeed, how or why G neural events yield any conscious experiences at all.

There is, of course, no objection to saying that the occurrence of a *particular case* of an F conscious experience is fully explained by combining (i) the regularity that G neural events yield F conscious experiences with (ii) the fact that some particular G neural event has occurred. This fits the familiar deductive-nomological pattern. What the Hard Problem is about, however, is not explaining particular cases, but explaining why there should be regularities of the kind in (i). Scientific discovery of *which* regularities obtain must not be confused with the kind of theoretical unification that would *explain why* there are any such regularities.

(*c*) Answer (HP) directly by providing a derivation of the connection between G neural events and F conscious experiences.

If we could actually do this, the Hard Problem would have been solved and there would be no need for this paper or, I dare say, a goodly number of others. However, if we say that we 'cannot' answer (HP), we must be careful. That we cannot *now* give a direct answer, I shall take as granted in what follows — I am not arguing *that* there is a Hard

---

[1] I have replied to one aspect of Dennett's argument for his view in Robinson (1994a).

Problem, but trying to explain *why* it occurs, given that it does occur. It would be more controversial to say that we 'cannot answer (HP)' meaning, with McGinn (1991), that humans can never be in a position to answer it. This view is certainly not a *presupposition* of this paper. I will, however, argue for the view that we cannot answer (HP) within our present framework of concepts, theories, and basic principles. The grounds are different from McGinn's, and I will return at the end of the paper to explain how our conclusions differ.

(*d*) Concede that we cannot answer (HP) now, but affirm a faith that science will eventually provide an answer.

There are two difficulties in this common response. First, some triumphs of science have involved deep conceptual shifts, e.g. in quantum mechanics and relativity theory. So, if we speculate about future scientific results, we have to remain open to the possibility that they will involve conceptual shifts so large that our Hard Problem question can hardly be framed and that only some question that can be recognized as a successor to it may be answered. This possibility is congenial to the argument of this paper, which aims to explain why we cannot answer (HP) within our present conceptual framework. The second difficulty is that the argument behind (*d*) is apparently based on a history of progress in science. But if we so take it, we must also recognize that there has been no scientific progress on (HP) in three hundred years. So, an historical argument in the opposite direction is also available, namely, that scientific views and methods as we now understand them will *not* provide an answer to (HP). This is compatible with the view that some set of beliefs expressed in concepts that we cannot now comprehend may provide an answer to a successor question to (HP) that we do not now know how to ask; but so is the view that will be argued for below.

(*e*) Concede that we cannot answer (HP) but try to remove the sting of this fact through providing an understanding of *why* it is a fact.

This paper is one example of this approach. Before proceeding, however, I should mention that Searle (1992) provides another example of it. I have criticized Searle's view in Robinson (1994b). So, I want to make it clear here (as it is in the paper referred to) that the criticism applies only to Searle's particular execution of the strategy, and not to the strategy itself.

II

Two facts will lead us directly to the conclusion that we cannot answer the question why neural events yield corresponding conscious experiences within our present conceptual framework. Unfortunately, neither of these facts is easy to identify unambiguously. Thus, most of this section will be taken up with explanations designed to focus our attention on the right two facts.

The first fact that we need is this.

(F1) *Explanations of regularities between occurrences of two kinds proceed by deriving a matching between the structures of those occurrences.*[2]

[2] This principle is in close agreement with Chalmers' remarks about functions and structure in sections III–V of the keynote paper. The present discussion provides a detailed account of the

Some examples will illustrate what I mean, and I will begin with one that is very familiar in discussions of the present issue. Searle (1992) and Churchland (1994) disagree about many things, but they both think that pain is to neural events as liquidity is to collections of H_2O molecules.[3] Let us therefore focus on explaining liquidity from the assumption of composition out of H_2O molecules. It is safe to assume, in this case, that the desired explanation could be cast in the form of an argument that shows why something composed of H_2O molecules *must* be liquid at temperature T. Such an argument must have premises describing the properties of H_2O molecules and their relations at temperature T. However, if these premises are *all* we have, the argument will be invalid, because 'liquid' will be a term in the conclusion that fails to occur in the premises. To have validity we must, at least tacitly, have a premise that expresses liquidity as some kind of complex or structure — e.g. as the property of flowing if unconstrained, or as the property of conforming to shapes, but not volumes, of containers. If we can then show that H_2O molecules at temperature T behave in such ways, we will have constructed the complex properties out of H_2O molecules and we will have produced the desired explanation. The key part of all this, for our purposes, is that the kind of success we have just described rests on having a structural description of liquidity that our explanation can then match.

This example also illustrates a corollary of (F1), namely,

> **(F2)** *If a regularity involving a given kind is to be explained, the kind must be expressible as a structure.*

A second illustration of (F1) and (F2) will also support the following stronger claim.

> **(F3)** *Wherever we can find a structure in a kind of occurrence, there is hope of finding an explanation of it.*

(F3) is not part of the main argument of this section, nor do I have a proof of it. But the idea behind it will be clear from consideration of the fact that some pains throb. Can we derive this fact from other facts? Not so long as we have only the statement that some pains throb. But we can redescribe our target for explanation as rhythmic increase and decrease of intensity. Now we have a bit of structure, and we can look for another structure that matches it. For example, we might hold that activity in certain types of neurons is proportional to pain, that increase of activity in those neurons depends on pressure, and that pressure in a certain region rhythmically increases and decreases with heartbeat. These assumptions enable us to match the structure we identified in our explanatory target, and if they are all true they constitute an explanation of why certain pains throb.

Functionalist explanations typically involve functions that are sets of relations among two or more predicates, and so they fit the pattern I have been describing. An important kind of example is furnished by lightning. To get going, we have to turn occurrences of lightning into occurrences with some structure. In this case, the structure is a causal one: Lightning is typically caused by atmospheric conditions found in storms, it causes

---

relation between function or structure, on the one hand, and explanation on the other. We shall see that this account is rich in consequences of a sort that are not developed very far in the keynote paper, and that we will need to defend against two very serious challenges.

[3] I hasten to add that Searle denies that one can *explain* why or how pain stands to neural events as liquidity stands to H_2O molecules.

appearance of flashes, and it sometimes causes damage to objects that protrude from the surrounding landscape. We can discover that electrical discharges stand in exactly this structure of causal relations, and it is on that basis that we can explain lightning by electrical discharge.

The second fact we need in order to explain the hardness of the Hard Problem should now be evident. It is

(F4) *Among the properties of conscious experiences, there is always at least one that has no structural expression.*

(F4) and (F2) together clearly imply the inability to resolve the Hard Problem. For the Hard Problem is to explain a regularity, and (F2) tells us that doing this requires structure where (F4) tells us there is none.

But why should we believe (F4)? Our example of the throbbing of pain shows that *some* aspects of conscious experiences can indeed be explained. This example, however, contains a property, namely, pain, that rhythmically increases and decreases. This property, i.e. pain, has no necessary internal structure. Pains are, it is true, typically variegated, differing in intensity or other quality from place to place in the body. But there seems to be nothing necessary about this, i.e. the intensity and other qualities of pain *could* be uniform over some bodily region. Moreover, the variability that is typical of pains is not what constitutes the feeling *as* painful. These remarks hold of conscious experiences in general. After-images, for example, *may* be of uniform colour, auditory experiences may have a temporal stretch of constant pitch, a taste may last for a while unchanged, and so on. In none of these cases is a particular kind of variability what constitutes the quality. Indeed, this would not make sense: the qualities mentioned are the contents that vary when we have variable conscious experiences.

One may object that the colour of after-images does have a kind of structure, namely, the division into hue and saturation. I agree, and affirm that, as with the throbbing of pain, once we recognize this structure, we can hope for explanation. That is, it is a perfectly understandable project (although not one whose success is *a priori* guaranteed) to look for some neural property that would yield low saturation across different hues, and some other neural property that would yield a given hue across various degrees of saturation. If we could find such properties, we could appeal to their presence to explain why, on a particular occasion, a subject has an after-image of a certain hue and degree of saturation. It is of crucial importance, however, to note that this kind of explanation *presupposes* a regularity between, for example, some neural property and the hue of an after-image. Explaining why there should be any such regularity returns us to the Hard Problem. That is, we now have (some particular) *hue* as our explanatory target, and no way of expressing it as a structure.[4]

---

[4] This paragraph explains why I do not share Van Gulick's (1993, p. 145) optimism to the effect that 'the more we can explain relationally about the phenomenal realm, the more the leftover [unexplained] residue shrinks towards zero.' I certainly agree that 'without structure we have no place to attach our explanatory 'hooks'.' But in all the examples of which I am aware, in which we find structure within the phenomenal realm and then explain it, terms are required for the explanatory relations that are themselves properties of phenomenal (= conscious) experiences. Thus, each case provides no net shrinkage of the amount that needs to be explained, and therefore there is no reason to suppose there will be convergence to zero.

We can regard many functionalist accounts as, in effect, attempting to solve our explanatory problem by providing an (alleged) expression of properties of conscious experiences in structural form, i.e. as structures of causal relations. It is clearly impossible to include a full discussion of functionalism here, but it seems useful to distinguish two versions of the view and respond briefly to them.

Version 1 *Pains are those conscious experiences that are normally caused in certain ways (e.g. by bodily damage) and that normally have certain effects (withdrawal, groaning, pill taking, etc.).*

This version hides many complexities that lead to difficulties (Wall, 1992). But the main point that should be made in the present context is this. *Version 1* proposes a way of identifying which one among various possible conscious experiences are to be called *painful*, but it does not provide a structural expression of the experiences themselves. It thus presupposes a regularity (between circumstances and properties of conscious experiences) that it provides no help in explaining. Because of this limitation, we should consider a stronger version of functionalism, as follows.

Version 2 *A pain is whatever event is normally caused in certain ways (e.g. by bodily damage) and normally has certain effects (withdrawal, groaning, pill taking, etc.).*[5]

In order not to fall back into *Version 1*, *Version 2* must be taken strictly, that is, as compatible with what we get if we add to it the words, '. . . whether or not the event feels like anything.' (We certainly cannot see that there being any feeling *follows* from the occurrence of an event with the indicated causal relations by any formal argument — if we could, we would have already solved the Hard Problem.)

Functionalism in *Version 2* may appear to be helpful, because it does provide a relational structure that is relevant to pain. This structure, however, is not a structure of the property F (in this case, painfulness) of a conscious experience. It is, instead, a structure of relations into which the experience enters. We can, in principle, identify a neural event that has the causal relations mentioned in *Version 2*; and this event may have a structure (e.g. an order of action potentials in various neurons or a ratio of rates of action potentials). But, once again, *this* structure is not the structure of the property of being painful, and so explanations of this structure will not be explanations of painfulness. That is, explanations of this structure will not be explanations of the kind needed to solve the Hard Problem. Proponents of *Version 2* may deny that there is any property of painfulness to be accounted for, which amounts to simply rejecting the Hard Problem. Or, they may accept the property and try to account for it in some other way. But in neither case does *Version 2* offer a *solution* to the Hard Problem.

A while ago, I asked why we should accept (F4). Since then, I have looked for ways of enforcing exceptions to it. The result of this investigation can be summarized as follows. Neither version of functionalism can be accepted as providing the kind of structure that (F4) says is excluded. The other two cases we considered have this character: They

---

[5] One can add that the pain behaviour must be caused by various mechanisms, which may also be implicated in other experiences. Or, one can add that the causes operate within the same time constraints that hold for causes of our pains. These additions would complicate the statements of the views and criticisms considered here, but all of the arguments concerning the simpler statement of *Version 2* that I have used would apply to more complex statements of it.

provide some structure, which by (F3) gives us hope of giving some explanation; but they also imply that there are elements in this structure. These elements re-introduce the Hard Problem. Therefore, unless some other kind of explanation can be identified, the fact that each explanation of one property re-introduces the Hard Problem for another property ought to convince us that (F4) is indeed correct.

We are now at last in a position to affirm the conclusion of this section. The reason that the Hard Problem is so hard is that explanations of regularities can get a grip only on properties that are expressed as having some structure, but all conscious experiences have properties that have no structural expression.

Besides being able to draw our main conclusion, we can now evaluate the depth of the restriction on it, namely, that we cannot solve the Hard Problem *within our present conceptual framework*. The difficulty we have identified arises from just two sources, the nature of conscious experiences and the requirements of explanation. I assume that the nature of conscious experiences will not change. The difficulty will remain, therefore, so long as our conceptual framework maintains its present requirements for explanation. In other words, we will not be able to solve the Hard Problem unless we can come to accept something other than our present modes of explanation as providing something like the kind of intellectual satisfaction, or relief from the sting of curiosity, that we now get from explanations. Because I believe that the conditions for finding intellectual satisfaction are contingent, I take it that they are in principle changeable. However, I also believe that these conditions are extremely deeply embedded in our conceptual framework, and are therefore unlikely to undergo much change in any short period of time.

III

In part IV I shall suggest that we need not find our situation, as I have described it, altogether dismal. Before doing that, however, it is important to develop our understanding of *consciousness* in conscious experiences. It will be convenient to do this by stating and answering two objections. These objections focus attention precisely on the places where further development is needed. They are also important because they emerge from the most important alternatives to the conception of consciousness that lies at the heart of this paper.

Objection 1: Your account is just too simple. It does not invoke the *subjectivity* of conscious experiences, or indeed, the *consciousness* of experiences at all (despite the fact that the *word* 'conscious' has been used repeatedly). But surely, the hardness of the Hard Problem depends intimately on consciousness, or on features specific to it. The explanation of this hardness cannot lie simply in the *properties* of conscious experiences, or the properties of these properties, however interesting they may otherwise be.

This is a natural objection to what I have said so far, but, as we shall see, it depends upon adopting a relational view of consciousness. In Robinson (1988) and Robinson (forthcoming) I have argued that certain specific versions of the relational view are false. Although I cannot argue exhaustively here for a general refutation of relational theories, I believe that they are indeed false. Rejection of relational theories of consciousness, however, gives us most of what we need to see that the structureless properties of conscious experiences discussed in section II are *species* of consciousness, which entails that they cannot exist without consciousness. If all this is accepted, the tight, and not merely verbal, connection of the discussion of part II with consciousness will be clear, and the lack of any talk of a 'subject' to which conscious experiences are 'related' should be understandable. (Of course, I do not deny that particular conscious experiences belong to a person; see Robinson (1988) for explanation.) In the remainder of this reply to Objection 1, I shall spell out what I have just summarized. While we must bear in mind that a full dress defence of the views expressed would require another paper, I believe the present discussion will establish them as at least tentatively acceptable and worthy of further consideration.

Relational theories hold that for X to be a *conscious* X is for it to stand in some relation, R, to some *other* thing, Y. Such theories vary in candidates for R, and in characterization of what kind of thing Y must be. Rosenthal (1986; 1990) and Carruthers (1989; 1992a,b) are recent articulate defenders of relational views; see also Moore (1965/1922) and Armstrong (1968). Despite the ingenuity and thoroughness of these defences, the relational view seems to me to founder on the implausibility of the idea that something that is *not* a case of suffering (for example) can be made into a case of suffering by standing in a relation to something else. In Rosenthal's view, which I believe is the strongest candidate, the relation is being thought of, and the Y is a thought. His view is that there is some kind of thing, X, such that (i) by itself it is a pain, but not a conscious pain, where only conscious pains are cases of suffering, i.e. cases that we might have any moral concern about preventing; but (ii) if I have a nonobservational and noninferential thought of X, then it is a conscious pain and something for which moral solicitude is appropriate. My objection to this view is that the presence of a thought that is true and directed upon something that is not already, by itself, a case of suffering can provide no explanation of why there should be a case of suffering. Let the thought be represented as having the content that X has property H. Since the thought is (by hypothesis) true, and since X (by itself) is not a case of suffering, 'X has H' must not imply that X is a case of suffering. But a nonsuffering and a thought about it whose content does not imply that there is suffering do not form a plausible candidate for composing a case of suffering. A false thought fares no better. A mistaken thought about something that is not a case of suffering is not a plausible candidate for a case of suffering. The only further possibility is that in requiring that Y (i.e. the other constituent besides X that is allegedly required to make X conscious) be a thought, i.e. a mental event of some sort, one is really making Y by itself do all the work of being a case of suffering. But in that case Y is misdescribed as a mere thought: it is the feeling of pain itself, and the relational account has been abandoned in all but name.[6]

We can, of course, become concerned by recognizing an object of concern, that is, by coming to have thoughts about such things as an injury or a friend's illness. In such cases, however, the property of the object that warrants the concern is already present in the object. This feature is the one that, crucially, is missing in the case of pain. When I suffer, I am not concerned about the fact that I have neural events that link injury to pain behaviour; to the contrary, I am glad I have such neural events, because they are part of a protective mechanism. On relational accounts, the property I *am* concerned about — my suffering — is *not* already present in the object that is thought about, but comes into existence only with the thought. It is this feature of the view that seems implausible, even paradoxical, to me.

[6] For a different argument against relational theories, see Dretske (1993).

If we agree in rejecting relational theories, then we must hold that conscious experiences are not *made* to be conscious by being related to anything. This is to say that they are *intrinsically* conscious. This puts us well on the way to the view that conscious experiences are *essentially* conscious, i.e. that they cannot exist without being conscious events. To reach this conclusion, however, we need also to reject one further possibility, which can best be introduced by analogy with a piece of paper. When the opposite edges of a piece of paper have been brought together, the paper has the property of being cylindrical. This property is *intrinsic* — i.e. it does not depend on relations to anything outside the paper. But it is *not essential* — i.e. nothing else about the paper would have to change if it lost its property of cylindricality by being unrolled.

I have no proof to offer that consciousness does not stand to pain in the way that cylindricality stands to a (rolled up) piece of paper. However, I also have no idea how to make such a possibility plausible; I have no idea of what might be subtracted from a pain that leaves it just as much a *pain* as before, yet nothing to worry about, because nothing is conscious of it.[7] Moreover, it seems to me that any property whose absence clearly results in absence of consciousness will also be a property whose absence suggests that no suffering is occurring, and this is a reason for thinking that painfulness is also absent.[8] In absence of plausible alternatives, our best theory ought to hold that conscious experiences are not only intrinsically, but also essentially conscious, i.e. that they cannot exist without being conscious, or that there cannot be anything that is exactly like a conscious experience in every respect except that it is not conscious. If this is right, then we may regard conscious experiences as having properties that exist *only* in conscious events.[9]

In part II, we have seen that *some* properties, e.g. throbbing, are not essentially conscious — hearts, as well as pains, can throb. But we also saw that structural properties require properties that are elements of the structure. The properties that play the role of such elements in conscious experiences are the ones I am suggesting are essentially conscious properties. If this theory is accepted, the connection between the account of the hardness of the Hard Problem in part II, and consciousness, is extremely intimate. Thus, the point of Objection 1 has been answered.

---

[7] Some readers will think here of certain recipients of morphine, who report having pain but not minding it. This is not the place to go into the difficult issue of how best to analyse such cases. I will note only that no one has claimed that the morphine recipients are *not conscious* of the pains they are supposed to have but not to mind; and so, whatever it is that they lack, in comparison with normal subjects, is not a likely candidate for *consciousness*.

[8] Perhaps surprisingly, even *Version 2* functionalists ought to agree with this, because no state that is plausibly unconscious has all or even most of the effects that pains are supposed to have. Internal states caused by battlefield injuries, for example, may have *some* of the standard effects of pain (e.g. rubbing, favouring) while (perhaps) causing no conscious states while the battle remains intense; but those (unconscious) internal states do not cause complaining or seeking treatment.

[9] I am unable to rule out one further possibility, namely, that it is only some *combinations* of properties that can be found only in conscious events, while each property taken singly can be found both in conscious events and nonconscious events. However, I can see no reason that would make such a proposal plausible in the least. This, of course, is not the same as saying that Rosenthal's proposal has no plausibility, for higher order thoughts are supposed to be *external* to pains. The view I am saying has no motivation is one that would hold, for example, that pain by itself can exist in an unconscious event, but pain-with-throbbing, or pain-with-acuteness, or at any rate, pain-with-*some* further property could not exist in an unconscious event.

Objection 2: Part II, together with your reply to Objection 1, commit you to the view that colours (or, at least, hues) are intrinsically and essentially conscious. But that is a false account of colours, which in fact are sets of reflectance properties of surfaces of ordinary physical objects.[10] Therefore, your account is false. Moreover, pine trees and grass are green, but not conscious experiences. Therefore, again, your account is false.

It is not possible to include here a thorough discussion of the recent literature on colour properties.[11] We can, however, distinguish three kinds of properties that any full account of colour should recognize. It will be convenient to make the required distinctions for a particular colour, with the understanding that the discussion can be generalized to all colours and then, with suitable adjustments, to all sensory properties.

We may begin with the *word* 'green', which normal humans can learn to apply to a certain class of surfaces. There is no single *molecular* property of all the surfaces that would cause normal English speakers to apply, or accept applications of, this predicate. Nor is there a single such combination of light wave frequencies. We can, however, refer to the disjunctive property of having surface molecular structure $MS_1, \ldots or \ldots, MS_n$, where surfaces of each of the kinds MS_i would cause normal English speakers in normal conditions to apply or accept applications of the term 'green'. Let us call this disjunctive surface molecular property 'object-green' or 'greenO'. Analogously, we can refer to redO, blueO, etc., and to the whole range of these properties as colourO.

If we look at (HP), it will be evident that the Hard Problem presupposes that there are kinds of neural events and kinds of conscious experiences that neural events yield. What we must do here is to introduce a way of thinking, and writing, that preserves both the difference between these properties, and their difference from greenO, while maintaining their connection with greenO things and with the ordinary English word 'green'. To this end, let us note that experiences themselves can be compared in respect of their intrinsic properties.[12] Judgments regarding similarities and differences among these properties can be made, and these are found to parallel, for the most part, judgments of similarity and difference among colouredO objects. For example, in most cases, the qualities of my experiences are very similar when I am confronted with things to which I apply the word 'green', and different from the qualities of the experiences I have when I would apply 'red' or 'blue'. Because of this parallelism, normal English-speakers can learn a secondary use of 'green' in which the term indicates the quality of some of their conscious experiences.[13] As a first approximation, we may introduce 'greenC' for the intrinsic property of a conscious experience that goes with greenO things.[14] However, we must

---

[10] Dennett (1991, p. 373) appears to commit himself to this view. But see discussion in text, below.

[11] See Boghossian & Velleman (1991) for a penetrating discussion of many of the issues concerning this topic.

[12] Once again, this is a disputed claim — see, e.g. Harman (1990). However, denying it is a way of rejecting (rather than solving) the Hard Problem, so I leave its defence for another occasion.

[13] In contexts other than the present one it becomes crucially important to note that the parallelism is not perfect. There can be illusions that result in my judging my experiences to differ in their visual properties even though I judge the objects to be the same colourO, or vice versa.

[14] Words for bodily sensation properties, like 'pain' and 'itch', have no application to nonconscious things, and so need no 'C' suffix. Everything to which the ordinary word 'pain' or 'itch' applies is an experience that is intrinsically and essentially conscious.

respect the fact that interpersonal comparisons of intrinsic properties of conscious experiences are not possible. Let us, therefore, index these properties by subject and use 'greenC(S)' for the quality of the conscious experiences that S has when attending to greenO objects in normal conditions, where S is assumed to be able to learn the normal use of the English word 'green'.[15]

Between greenO objects and greenC(S) experiences there are two roles that must be satisfied by neural events. On the one hand, (HP) presupposes that neural events of certain kinds yield what we have just now learned to refer to as, e.g., greenC(S) events. On the other hand, the ability of normal people to learn to apply 'green' to greenO objects could hardly be explained unless we supposed that there are neural events that stand as intermediate events in a causal chain leading from greenO objects to predications of 'green'. The view I am proposing holds that it is the same neural events that perform both of these causal roles. This view also recognizes that the neural properties of such events may vary among subjects, and that therefore our words for these neural properties must be indexed to subjects. Further, it is possible that, even within one subject, there are several neural properties that perform the same causal roles. With these understandings in mind, we may introduce 'greenN(S)' for the (perhaps disjunctive) neural property that is normally caused in S by S's attending to greenO things and that yields greenC(S) experiences.

These distinctions among properties that are involved with colour enable us to find many points of contact with the views of others. For example, except for the inclusion of coloursC, the structure of the view I have been describing is entirely consistent with Dennett's (1991) presentation of Akins' (1989) view of why there are colours. The view I have been describing also connects with the intuition that experiences are important in our knowledge of colour. We can express this point by saying that we do know *some* colour properties that are not disjunctions of properties to which we have only theoretical access; and coloursC(S), alone among the colour-relevant properties, fit this description. Finally, and most importantly for the strategy of this paper, we can give a simple answer to Objection 2. GreenO is indeed a disjunction of reflectance properties of surfaces of ordinary things. This is what is right about reflectance theory, and it is not in conflict with the account of this paper. ColourC(S) properties are properties of conscious experiences, not ordinary objects. It is these properties, and neither colourO nor colourN(S), that are being claimed to be intrinsically and essentially properties of conscious experiences.

IV

In the previous section, I have explained the relation of conscious experiences to consciousness and shown how to avoid what might have seemed obvious difficulties for my account in part II. In the present section, I shall assume that that account is correct. I want briefly to draw some consequences regarding two views that also recognize the Hard Problem.

---

[15] There are, of course, deep issues in this paragraph, of which space does not permit discussion. Many of these were raised by Wittgenstein (1953). Although I do not agree with all of Nelkin's (1987) conclusions, he has brought these issues into clear focus, and related them to empirical material.

The first view is that of Colin McGinn (1991). McGinn suggests that the Hard Problem really does have a solution: there really is an explanation of how neural events give rise to conscious experiences. Unfortunately, this explanation is one that human beings are incapable of understanding. Cognitive ability comes in degrees, and the Hard Problem may require a degree that lies beyond our limits, just as chess lies beyond the cognitive ability of dogs.

This picture is certainly pessimistic, not to say offensive to our vanity. The view taken in this paper is less so. It has no place for a genuine explanation that we are forever condemned to be unable to understand. It proposes instead that we can understand why there can be no explanation of the kind we may desire. Namely, structureless properties cannot receive an explanation of a certain familiar kind, because that familiar kind of explanation *requires* that the targets of the explanation have structure.

The way I have argued for this view does leave it open that some alternative conceptual framework would result in less intellectual discomfort than the one we currently have. It is logically possible that there is such a framework that is usable by Martians but, perhaps due to complexity, is not usable by us. So, I have not proved that a scenario similar to that suggested by McGinn is impossible. The fact that we have not solved the Hard Problem, however, is, according to my account, no reason to suppose that such a scenario actually applies to us.

These remarks lead directly to a reflection on the positive suggestions made by David Chalmers in the keynote paper to this issue. In brief, I take Chalmers to propose our accepting conscious experiences as items about which we are to theorize, without imagining that they can be decomposed. We are then to look for laws that describe their relations to other things (i.e. bridge laws), and also for very general principles of explanatory coherence. The view of part II of this paper leads to both supportive and limiting comments on this proposal.

Let us have the limitation first. Chalmers' proposal is a move well within our current conceptual framework. This is not a criticism: it is impossible that a shift of conceptual framework of the depth that would be necessary for progress on the Hard Problem can occur in just one proposal. Nonetheless, there is a consequence. The result of my argument in part II is that there can be no solution to the Hard Problem within our current conceptual framework. Thus, Chalmers' theory, which remains within that framework, cannot provide a solution. We can, of course, accept Chalmers' bridge laws; but, as I believe Chalmers would agree, we can also ask why they should hold. It seems to me that this question is another one among the many ways in which the Hard Problem forces itself upon us.[16]

Chalmers' direction is, however, a promising one for the eventual generation of changes in our conceptual framework. It is not possible to foresee where this development may take us, and consequently it is not possible to be certain whether it will provide ultimate satisfaction. It seems likely, however, that progress in this line will require revision in what counts for us as a satisfying account. To make a change of this sort, we

---

[16] The historical view that appears to me as most similar to Chalmers' is that of Spinoza (1677). Spinoza's attributes are irreducible to one another, yet ideas and things correspond, and this correspondence is set in a wide theoretical framework. It is thus instructive to consider how the Hard Problem applies to Spinoza's view.

must pursue kinds of account that diverge from the general type with which we are familiar in significant ways. Chalmers' efforts seem to me to be a move of this kind.

I have said that the broader purpose of a discussion like the present one is reduction of the sense of discomfort or puzzlement that one has when one faces the Hard Problem. It should be clear that the remarks I have made do not reduce my puzzlement to zero. It does seem to me, however, that they go as far in this direction as any view of which I am aware.

References

Akins, Kathleen (1989), *On Piranhas, Narcissism and Mental Representation: An Essay on Intentionality and Naturalism* (Ph.D. Dissertation, Dept. of Philosophy, University of Michigan, Ann Arbor).

Armstrong, David (1968), *A Materialist Theory of the Mind* (London: Routledge).

Boghossian, Paul & Velleman, David (1991), 'Physicalist theories of color', *The Philosophical Review*, **C**, pp. 67–106.

Carruthers, Peter (1989), 'Brute experience', *The Journal of Philosophy*, **LXXXVI**, pp. 258–69.

Carruthers, Peter (1992a), *The Animals Issue: Moral Theory in Practice* (Cambridge: Cambridge University Press).

Carruthers, Peter (1992b), 'Consciousness and concepts', Part II (reply to Kirk), *Aristotelian Society Proceedings*, Suppl. Vol. **LXVI**, pp. 41–59.

Chalmers, David (1995), 'Facing up to the problem of consciousness', *Journal of Consciousness Studies*, **2** (3), pp. 200–19 (reprinted in this volume).

Churchland, Patricia (1994), 'Can neurobiology teach us anything about consciousness?', *Proceedings and Addresses of the American Philosophical Association*, **LXVII**, pp. 23–40.

Crick, Francis (1994), *The Astonishing Hypothesis* (New York: Charles Scribner's Sons).

Dennett, Daniel (1991), *Consciousness Explained* (Boston: Little, Brown & Co.).

Dretske, Fred (1993), 'Conscious experience', *Mind*, **CII**, pp. 263–83.

Harman, Gilbert (1990), 'The intrinsic quality of experience', *Philosophical Perspectives*, **IV**, pp. 31–51.

McGinn, Colin (1991), *The Problem of Consciousness* (Oxford: Blackwell).

Moore, G.E. (1965/1922), 'The refutation of idealism', in *Philosophical Studies* (Totowa, NJ: Littlefield, Adams & Co.).

Nelkin, Norton (1987), 'How sensations get their names', *Philosophical Studies*, **LI**, pp. 325–39.

Robinson, William (1988), *Brains and People* (Philadelphia: Temple University Press).

Robinson, William (1994a), 'Orwell, Stalin and determinate qualia', *Pacific Philosophical Quarterly*, **LXXV**, pp. 151–64.

Robinson, William (1994b), 'Searle and subjectivity'. Paper read to Eastern Division, American Philosophical Association, 12/30/94. Available from author on request.

Robinson, William (forthcoming), 'Some nonhuman animals can have pains in a morally relevant sense', *Biology and Philosophy*.

Rosenthal, David (1986), 'Two concepts of consciousness', *Philosophical Studies*, **XLIX**, pp. 329–59.

Rosenthal, David (1990), *A Theory of Consciousness* (Report No. 40 of the Research Group on Mind and Brain, Zentrum Für Interdisziplinäre Forschung, University of Bielefeld, Bielefeld, Germany).

Searle, John (1992), *The Rediscovery of the Mind* (Cambridge, MA: MIT Press).

Spinoza, Benedict (1677), *Ethics*.

Van Gulick, Robert (1993), 'Understanding the phenomenal mind: Are we all just armadillos?', in *Consciousness*, ed. M. Davies and G.W. Humphreys (Oxford: Blackwell).

Wall, Patrick (1992), 'Defining "pain in animals"', in *Animal Pain*, ed. C.E. Short & Alan Van Poznak (New York: Churchill Livingstone, 1992).

Wittgenstein, Ludwig (1953), *Philosophical Investigations* (New York: Macmillan).

Physics

C.J.S. Clarke

The Nonlocality of Mind

I want to explore the thesis that mind is non-local.[1] Although it is a dangerous practice to allude to what one is not saying — since there will always be a reader who fails to notice the word 'not' — it is important to understand the difference between this thesis and many other proposals about mind. In particular there is such a prevalence of authors arguing that mind is located in some higher dimensional space that I need to make a sharp distinction between these authors' and my own views. To begin with let me stress that I am *not* arguing that mind is extended; rather I am saying that it is not located in space at all. Next I want to go even further, claiming not only that mind is not located in ordinary 3-D physical space but that it is not located in a higher dimensional space, and it is not located *in* a generalized space, for most of the generalized concepts of space that I shall describe shortly. These more general structures are certainly implicated in the study of mind and we cannot understand mind without them, but in most cases they do not provide a location for mind.

Generalized Spaces

In order to ellucidate these points I need to explain the meaning of some of the concepts involved. The primary meaning of 'space' is that of the flat, Euclidean, three-dimensional space of our everyday actions. Mathematicians have then got hold of this idea and made use of it for their own purposes, generalizing the meaning in a number of different ways, altering or weakening some aspects of the basic Euclidean idea.

The simplest generalization is to *many-dimensional space*. This involves keeping the same geometric properties (except where these refer explicitly to the number of dimensions) and in particular the same concept of *symmetries*: the principle that all directions in the space are absolutely equivalent. The only thing that is altered is the number of mutually perpendicular lines that can be drawn through any given point, which is increased from three to some greater number *n*. Mathematicians refer to this as *n*-dimensional Euclidean space; not thereby claiming that Euclid would recognize it, but signalling that little has been altered from the Euclidean picture, beyond the dimension. Saying that mind is located in such a space is to assert something very specific about the existence of a higher-dimensional geometry that mimics Euclidean geometry. There has never been any evidence for such a geometry, and there are practically no physical theories that postulate it. The many higher-dimensional physical theories that are in vogue all involve spaces that are *not* Euclidean.

[1] This paper was delivered at the 5th Mind and Brain Symposium, Institute of Psychiatry, London, October 1994.

There is a different sort of generalization, known as *curved space* (in which I include curved space-time). This involves altering the basic geometry of the space: it is supposed to be of an approximately Euclidean form over very small regions, but over large regions all geometrical properties (rules about the existence of lines, planes and so on) break down. One can combine curvature with increased dimensions. The simplest higher-dimensional physical theories are of this form. We would only be entitled to assert that mind occupied a space such as this if we had evidence of a small-scale Euclidean structure and of its non-Euclidean breakdown on larger scales.

There are a number of other more extreme generalizations that drop the Euclidean structure even at small length scales. These include metric spaces, where there exists a concept of distance, as well as topological and fuzzy spaces where there is only a concept of nearness. To make matters more confusing, metric spaces carry with them a definition of dimension which is different from the geometrical sense of dimension examined earlier.

One might well ask, since these generalizations are so very different from the space of our awareness, is it not confusing to call them 'spaces' at all? The mathematician might defend the name by saying that all these generalizations involve their own particular sorts of laws which generalize the laws of geometry that hold in ordinary space, and thereby entitle one to call the result a space. Without such quasi-geometrical laws one would have not a space but a *set*. A marginal position, between set and space, is occupied by fuzzy set theory (which I shall refer to later) where the word 'space' is occasionally used.

All these generalizations are useful both in physics and psychology. Curved space-time is used to study gravity, tolerance geometry has been used to study the colour space that encodes our visual perception of extended areas of colour (Zeeman, 1962). It will probably turn out that all these concepts are needed for different aspects of mind. Yet mind itself, I want to argue, is not located in any of them.

The Phenomenology of Mind

The starting point for the study of mind has to be experiential. This is where our primary data comes from. Moreover, while I disagree radically with most of Descartes' conclusions, I shall accept his position that the *existence* of mind is axiomatic: it is logically inconsistent for *me* to postulate the non-existence of mind because without mind there is no me (see Cottingham, 1992). But we can, and usually are, deluded about the *nature* of mind — indeed this is one of the first realizations that come from the practice of meditation.

Concerning the nature of mind, then, it is entirely possible that mind is a derivative concept, reducible to some sort of physical mechanism. If, however, I acknowledge that the existence of mind is the primary aspect of our experience, then it seems unnatural to derive mind from physics, because this would be to try to explain something obvious and immediate (mind) from something (physics) that is an indirect construction of mind. So for me it seems a more fruitful method not to derive mind from physics but to reconcile the experience of mind with the world description of physics.

In trying to reconcile mind with physics I start from the fact that, in one sense, I actually know a lot about mind. This knowledge is, however, fundamentally different in its nature from the knowledge that I have of the objects investigated by physics. To use the terminology of Alexander (to which I will turn shortly) my knowledge of mind is the knowledge of 'enjoying', whereas my knowledge of physical objects is that of 'contemplating'. One could characterize these as knowledge from within and from without. The philosophical problems of mind stem from this fundamental difference.

By the phenomenology of mind I mean the exploration of mind from within. (The term 'phenomenology', from psychology, is perhaps unfortunate since it means something quite opposite to the physicist.) I want to ask, from this point of view, what is the phenomenology of 'position in space': in particular, what items in our mental world have such position?

This mental world, the world of our awareness, comprises a mass of different thoughts which can be segregated into various categories — percepts, feelings, judgments, volitions etc. I want to suggest that the majority of these have little to do with Euclidean space. Certainly Euclidean space has a role in visual and proprio-motor percepts, and to some extent in hearing. (One of the triumphs of modern psychology is the unravelling of the contributions of these different senses to our spatial perception.) In addition, many of our feelings — of anger, fear and so on — have important links with parts of the body and hence indirectly with space; but it would be hard to claim that this was the aspect of them that was uppermost in normal awareness. Other thoughts in our mental world, I would claim, have no direct link with Euclidean space at all.

Neither, however, are these thoughts linked to any generalized space; because there are no spatial concepts at all that apply to most of them. Except in a purely poetic way, would it make sense, for example, to say that my realization that $\sqrt{2}$ is irrational is 'between' my feeling annoyed with my secretary and my hearing an indistinct roaring noise from the central heating? All that can be said is that these various thoughts are buzzing around with some kind of togetherness, but without any sort of betweenness, nearness, or any other spatial relation to each other.

Another way of appreciating this is through the practice of meditation. In normal awareness we are dominated by visual percepts — and these are precisely the ones that do happen to be linked to space. But even in the very first exercises of (some forms of) meditation, one quickly strips away these visual components by shutting the eyes and turning inwards, and one can then pay attention to a world that is entirely non-spatial.

One counter-argument comes from the fact that there is a spatial component to many non-waking states of consciousness. Dreaming and shamanic travel certainly manifest some sort of spatial organization which suggests that there might be some kind of fundamental generalized mental space manifesting itself here. But to argue in this way is to treat the dream or shamanic reality in too simplistic a way. Theirs is usually a non-standard, fluid space with quite different properties to Euclidean space. Just as the visual forms of dream objects are the superficial manifestations of archetypal realities, so too is the space in which these objects are located: it is a temporary presentational device, not a basic structural aspect of the underlying reality.

The situation is confused by the way in which in our awareness the spatial is entangled with the non-spatial, sometimes giving the impression that everything is located in space. We need to make an effort to segregate the spatial from the non-spatial. In ordinary states of consciousness the spatial thoughts are essentially all *percepts* — impressions on me of something that is not me. All other thoughts, I would argue, are intrinsically non-spatial, though they may derive some spatiality through being associated with percepts. This distinction is not clear-cut: there is no such thing as a pure percept, but every percept is bound to some concept (the percept of a chair is bound to the concept of 'chair') and that bound concept is given a secondary spatial location.

All our conscious thoughts, both spatial and non-spatial, are as noted earlier in some sense *compresent*. They have a degree of togetherness, though this may often be qualified: we should not assume that the content of consciousness is completely well defined, with an unambiguous dividing line between conscious and non-conscious, and with everything that is conscious clearly experienced as together. It is in describing this qualified togetherness that there may be a role for the most degenerate sense of 'space', namely in fuzzy set theory. A fuzzy set (there are various possible formal definitions) is marked by a criterion that can be satisfied to varying degrees: a standard example is 'the set of long streets', where we would agree that a 10m street with one house is out, and a 10km street with 1000 houses is in, with some sort of gradation in between. It could then plausibly be argued that the togetherness of thoughts is a fuzzy relation, and that the set of conscious thoughts is a fuzzy subset of the 'space' of all thoughts furnished with this relation. (See Zadeh, 1975, for a survey of different aspects of fuzziness.)

This is, however, so far from the sort of thing envisaged by most people who think of mind as being in some kind of many-dimensional space that the term 'space' is misleading. A further argument for disallowing, as confusing, the term 'space' for this sort of mental togetherness relation is the fact that it operates independently of space in the Euclidean sense. My consciousness of a distant star is mentally together (compresent) with my consciousness of the nearby trees even though they are Euclideanly far apart.

Even though we may qualify the 'togetherness' aspect of consciousness by some stucture distantly related to spatial ideas, and even though spatial and non-spatial aspects of thoughts are tangled together, this should not obscure the primary distinction between the Euclideanly spatial aspect of (at least visual) percepts, and the non-spatial togetherness of all thoughts considered as parts of the contents of my mind, whether or not those thoughts are linked to a Euclidean spatial position. Except for percepts, or thoughts that in dreams or trance clothe themselves with the form of percepts, neither space in the Euclidean sense nor space in almost any of the derived senses is present in our awareness.

This suggests that the spatial aspect of percepts derives entirely from outside the mind, from the physical world, and that mind is in its nature non-spatial but in perception can become compresent with spatial things.

To conclude this section I should return to the seminal work of S. Alexander (1920). He argued that all experience is spatial, even if only vaguely so. There was thus a mental space, as well as a physical space. The distinction between the two was the distinction of subject and object already referred to: mental space is enjoyed while physical space is contemplated. Yet enjoyed space and contemplated space, he claimed, match. There is a precise correspondence between the space of experience and the space of the physicist.

Reading Alexander, one observes that all his examples of thoughts are visual ones. Here is a writer who is dominated by visual images and who therefore ignores the pre-eminence of non-spatial thoughts in our awareness. As a result he is led to postulate two spaces with a correspondence between them. A fuller appreciation of the range of our thoughts shows that space only comes from percepts. If we take this into account the alternative picture arises in which enjoyed space is actually derivative from contemplated space.

This formulation raises one interesting philosophical footnote. If enjoyed space, in which we place things, is derived from percepts and from contemplated space, then percepts are not only percepts of things in space but are at the same time *percepts of space*. Thus we reach a view that is opposed to that of Kant, who held that space was mental in origin, being the *a priori* form under which external objects were perceived.

Physical Perspective

We must now look at the task of reconciling mind and physics, shifting from psychological to physical, from enjoyed to contemplated. In this area we are presented with physical systems, namely brains, whose operations clearly have a great deal to do with mind and which are, under the more conventional ways of thinking about physics, located in space. Can this line of thought lead us to conclude that, despite the contrary appearance from introspection, minds are in fact really located in space?

To begin with I want to clear out of the way the two arguments for the localization of mind presented by Lockwood (1991), though these do not depend on any particular view of the relation of mind to brain.

The first argument is as follows. Suppose we are given two mental events A and B for which it can be said that A comes before B. It is a tenet of special relativity that whenever two events are related by 'before' there exists a frame of reference in which they are in the same place. So 'place' must be a property of mental events. This argument clearly begs most of the question by assuming that special relativity is applicable to mental events. Indeed the argument does not even hold for physical events, because it involves a confusion between 'event' in the general sense and 'event' in the technical sense in relativity of a point event. The tenet quoted above is only true for point events.

The second argument is more serious, however. Whatever we may think about mind, most of us hold that our decisions have physical consequences — so a given decision affects a particular region of space-time. Let us call P the region that is capable in principle of being affected by a given decision. If we believe that causality is a universal physical principle, then P will be what is called a *future set*, with the property that if x is in P and if y is after x (in the causal sense) then y is also in P. Similarly, our decision depends on (is affected by) a particular region Q of space time which is a past set (defined by replacing 'after' by 'before'). Moreover — again by appealing to widely believed causal principles — P and Q will have no overlap, because if they did there would be a causal 'vicious circle' with an event that was influenced by the decision but which also influenced the decision.

Lockwood now wishes to argue that this situation will itself define a region in space-time within which the decision is located, thus establishing the principle that mental events do have a location in space-time. That is, he claims that given the two sets P and Q as described, there is some region R with the property that every point in R lies to the past of the whole of P and to the future of the whole of Q. The trouble is that there is no reason whatever why this should be so, unless we beg the question by assuming in the first place that mental events are indeed located in space-time. Without such a question-begging assumption it is entirely possible to construct examples of sets P and Q for which there is no such R. The argument therefore fails.

There is a further problem with this argument. Even if a set R did exist, that would only indicate that the *action* of the mental event was spatially restricted. The mental event itself could be non-located — provided, of course, that one does not assume at the outset that the only sort of action possible is an action between located entities that are in contact, which would again beg the question.

Having, I hope, buried this red herring, we must return to the problems posed by the physical description, and address the different ways in which the connection between mind and brain can be formulated. I will sketch some of these in turn.

Cartesian dualism

This view takes as absolutely fundamental the idea that Soul is non-spatial. In the form originally proposed by Descartes it is then (rather unconvincingly) argued that the soul acts on the body through a single point. The essence of the argument seems to be that Soul is *simple*, in the sense of not having parts, and so the soul can only be present to a region of space without parts, that is to a single point. Matter, by contrast, is entirely bound by spatial location and it only has local interactions with adjacent pieces of matter.

While probably no one today would hold to this original Cartesian form, it is worth examining because it reveals many misunderstandings that beset other dualistic approaches. First, there is no reason to suppose that since Soul is non-spatial it is without parts. The analogy of a computer program shows that it may be appropriate to analyse a system into functional parts without these parts being spatially located. Second, it ignores the possibility of causal influences that act on a physical material system in a distributed way, such as occurs with superconductivity in which the charge carriers are distributed over a large region and the mechanisms governing their behaviour are global in nature.

The overriding objection, however — which undermines most dualistic theories — is that in fact it fails to offer any explanation. In an attempt to explain what is happening when we see a tree it describes how a neural image of the tree is conveyed to the visual cortex (to modernize Descartes a little), but then calls in a separate soul to observe the neural image. To the question, how does the soul observe the image, no answer can be given, because the soul is assumed totally simple and so incapable of being further analysed. The theory is thus not an explanation but a means of avoiding explanation.

Epiphenomenalism

This is a sort of one-way dualism, in which consciousness is a product of brain processes but is itself without any causal effect on those processes. As far as perception is concerned it therefore suffers from exactly the same problem as dualism, in being a denial of the possibility of giving an explanation.

Both of these approaches are impaled on the dilemma of reconciling a physics that is purely spatial and quantitative with a total world of experience that is fundamentally non-spatial and qualitative. Their only recourse is largely to ignore the latter, relegating it to an area where explanation is ruled out.

It would seem, at this point, that all that is left is explanations that identify mind with some aspect of the brain (various types of identity theories). Since the brain is apparently spatial, so are its processes and aspects, and hence so, it would seem, is mind. If we follow this route, then we appear to be led to the position that, though mind may be non-spatial from a phenomenological point of view, it is spatial from a physical point of view. Those who place physics above phenomenology would add that this meant that it was *really* spatial.

Quantum theoretic approach

There is an important assumption in this, however, that must be challenged; namely that the brain is entirely spatial. There is a whole complex of assumptions bound up in the vocabulary being used, which still incorporates dualistic ways of thinking. 'Brain' means something entirely 'physical' (as opposed to 'mental') and the 'physical' is 'material', and 'matter' is located in space. Cartesian dualism is still rampant in the assumptions underlying all the language being used. I want now to suggest that there is a perfectly good place for the non-spatial in physics, and hence in the physics of the brain, so that there need be no contradiction — despite their very different methodologies — between the view of physics and the view of introspection. In fact, the only way of reconciling the physical and phenomenological views lies in a change of emphasis in our understanding of the physical world which makes the non-spatial primary.

Such a change is natural if one takes a quantum theoretic view, so I need to say more about what that implies. There are three basic approaches to quantum theory.

1. Qualified Newtonian

This holds that the universe is composed of independent particles moving in an absolute space-time. On the very small scale they are governed by quantum theory, which occasionally results in large-scale (non-local) correlations. But because the particles are independent, in virtually all cases of interest the quantum aspect of particles gets averaged out when one passes to the large scale. This view is challenged by the effect proposed by Einstein, Podolsky and Rosen (called the EPR effect) in which an atom emits spinning particles, where the directions of the spins, even when the particles have separated to a large distance, exhibit a correspondence of behaviour that points to an underlying unity. The qualified-Newtonian has to regard this as a sort of freak, in which the averaging out, which is the norm in the universe, is somehow avoided.

2. Crypto-Newtonian

By this I refer to views that start from a basically quantum-mechanical position (usually with a rather traditional interpretation of quantum mechanics) but then impose modifications of the quantum formalism so as to ensure that the net result is basically Newtonian. Examples are hidden variable theories and the primary state diffusion theories (e.g. Percival, 1994). These give a similar picture to (1) but with the concession that there may rather often be special cases where the averaging-out doesn't happen and non-local behaviour appears on a large scale.

(In both the preceeding two views a strong emphasis is placed on the wave function as the fundamental object of quantum theory, and a 'collapse' is invoked to pass to a Newtonian picture. As a result they are very firmly bound to a spatial picture.)

3. Non-Newtonian

These views adopt a quantum description from the start. The classical world is a special case of the quantum world. We live in a quantum universe so that everything should be described by quantum mechanics, although in special cases it may reduce to the more easily handled classical mechanics. Rather than using a wave-function formulation of quantum theory with a collapse mechanism (as in (2)), this viewpoint starts from a quantum logic formulation of quantum mechanics (Mackey, 1963). In this formulation one explicitly recognizes not only that various incompatible possibilities are combined in the wave function, but also that there are different incompatible ways of analysing the wave function into incompatible possibilities! These different ways of analysing things are thought of as different schemes of questions that could in principle be asked of the wave function. (A question, to which the answer can only be 'yes' or 'no', is a special case of that central quantum concept the observable, which admits a range of answers. Observables can be built up out of sets of questions.) In each situation within the universe one such scheme of questions is singled out. The ways in which the collections of questions that can be asked in different situations mesh together is determined by a local operator algebra formalism. The consistency between different chains of questions is determined in a way that we do not yet fully understand by decoherence conditions, as explored by Gell-Mann and Hartle (1993). Decoherence between chains of questions (or histories, as they are called) is a mathematical condition that ensures that the answers to questions will obey the classical logic of probability theory, rather than quantum logic. The general idea is illustrated by the EPR effect referred to earlier. Here the positions of the emitted particles are affected by minute interactions with the rest of the universe, so that they become essentially classical observables with no holistic connection between them: they decohere. Their spins, however, because of their essentially non-classical nature, are very little affected by external interactions and so exhibit a holism: they cohere. On the quantum logic approach, the questions (or observables) come first and the state (which ultimately is the state of the universe) then becomes a global determinant of the probabilities of various answers to these questions.

The consequence of this is that physics becomes fundamentally non-local. We do not start off assuming that the universe is composed of independent atoms. So global effects do not require special mechanisms to make them happen; rather, special mechanisms are required to break things down to the point where physics becomes local.

There is, alas, one basic problem with this approach: we can't do it! Current decoherence schemes of describing quantum theory have clarified a great deal, but they are still ultimately unsatisfactory in that they prescribe a God-given collection of decohering histories. As Gell-Mann and Hartle explicitly stress, however, the universe is not observed from the outside. Rather, the questions that consitute the physically realized decohering histories after any point in time are determined by the past history up to that point. The universe, in other words, observes itself, and we don't know how to handle the fact. (Is it an accident that this is the characteristic feature of mind?) What is needed is a method for formulating the way in which the collections of meaningful quantum questions in each situation are engendered not from the outside but from within.

In order to explain how this non-Newtonian view can shed light on the nature of mind it will be useful to refer to the 'hard problem' of Chalmers: the problem of explaining why, apparently, brain processes give rise to an *experience*; why there is such a thing as the *view from inside* such processes (what it is like to experience them) as well as the scientific observation from outside. For the dualist there is no problem at this point, because the dualist can postulate a separate soul that observes the brain processes from the inside and thereby generates the experience. The problem for the dualist comes later, in making sense of a dual world.

For the nondualist, things are not so simple. It might be thought that one could resort to supposing that some special part of the brain, the mebrain, observes other parts of the brain and thereby experiences what is going on there. But if one postulates this, then one must ask the same question as before of the mebrain and thereby fall into an infinite regress. This sort of explanation is still rooted in dualistic thinking, in that it separates the experiencing entity from the information processing entity, even though these are now at the same level of brain function.

With Chalmers, I would hold that the basic experiential aspects of consciousness cannot be explained in terms of existing physical categories, but require the addition of a fundamentally new area of science, associated with but not reducible to existing physics, corresponding to experience. Chalmers uses the analogy of electric charge, which is associated with mass in being located on massive particles, but which is none the less a quite distinct quality. If one has a cloud of electrons, the total mass and the total charge are (almost) exactly proportional to each other quantitatively, but they remain qualitatively distinct. I am claiming that consciousness is a quality that is carried by brain processes, as charge is carried by massive particles, and which therefore inherits some of the structure of the brain processes, but which is distinct from them. Because this experiencing is carried by some brain processes we can deduce logical, structural things about experience from observations of brain processes; but the fundamental nature of experience remains separate from the brain processes.

It is here that nonlocality enters. Since the structure of experience has to reflect the structure of the processes that carry it, and since mind is nonlocal, the structure that carries mind has to be nonlocal. That means, straight away, that it is futile to look for mind in generalisations of charge at the particle level, as has been attempted in many speculative writings that try to identify consciousness with fundamental particle properties such as muonness. The carriers have to be global entities, and at present the only candidates for these are the quantum states that can be defined in the quantum logic (that is, the non-Newtonian) approach to physics. Note that if we restrict ourselves to a narrow wavemechanics view of quantum theory then the quantum states are still so closely tied to space and time that it is hard to see their nonlocality. The quantum logic approach, on the other hand, takes this nonlocality as its starting point.

The first step in the direction of making a global quantum state the carrier of consciousness was taken by Ian Marshall in proposing that global Bose condensations might underlie consciousness. But such a move assumes that the only quantum states that are of relevance to consciousness are those characterized by largescale *physical* order. These are the only ones that might manifest interesting physical properties analogous to superconductivity. On the other hand, there is no reason why we need be bound by these physical considerations. Since we do not yet know what the new science of consciousness is going to be like, in our present state of ignorance there is no obvious limit to the sort of quantum states that might be significant to experience.

A key aspect of the sort of non-Newtonian approach that I have been referring to is that there is a whole range of possible quantum states that could potentially have a role in the universe but which in our present theory have no interpretation. The total quantum state of the human brain, in all its complexity, is potentially the ground within which mind can operate, is potentially the carrier of mind. On the crypto-Newtonian view of current physics, however, most such states would simply be regarded as arrays of apparently meaningless patterns of phases distributed across the particles of the brain, and any possible information that they contain would be dismissed as meaningless. Yet any discrimination of such states that can be formulated mathematically (provided that it is reasonably stable: technically, provided that it is represented by an global operator that almost commutes with the Hamiltonian) can define a possible quantum question (observable).

I suggest that things would be different if we were to *turn round* our whole pattern of description. First we need to turn round physics, so that we could see the local Newtonian picture as a specially disintegrated case of the fundamentally global reality. Within this more general non-Newtonian view there would be a natural place for mind at the point where the current effective state of the person, and the universe, as it is given by our past history, determines which chains of future questions are to make up reality. This will involve both those states that are now regarded as meaningful, including those considered by Marshall and Penrose, and also those others, dismissed as meaningless by Newtonian physics but having an internal meaning to consciousness. Second we need to turn round our whole approach by putting mind first. We would be in a position to understand how it was that mind could actually do something in the cosmos; not by acting as a separate force in addition to the Hamiltonian, nor by determining directly the answers that are obtained to quantum questions (though that may happen indirectly) but by determining which decohering histories of questions are realized in the process of self-observation that is embodied in consciousness.

Our much prized capacity for free will is not exhibited at all when we make a choice among totally defined alternatives with all the available information clearly specified. This is something that a well-constructed adaptive learning programme on a computer could do. Real human creativity is rather exercised in our ability upset the board; to redefine the alternatives; to set up new and unforseen connections. It is this that is the essence of quantum logic, where the range of possibilities is not fixed in advance. What I call 'choosing' whether to eat quiche or nut roast for dinner is in reality only my post hoc emotional reaction to a largely non-conscious decision process. A true exercise of free will would be to respond by cooking a nut quiche.

In this picture the action of mind is not restricted to the brain but extends to the whole system: a 'system' meaning everything that is in interaction at a given moment. Mind breaks out of the skull.*

* This paper was originally published in the *Journal of Consciousness Studies*, **2**, No.3 (1995), pp. 231–40.

Summary

On one hand Mind is inherently non-local. On the other the world is governed by a quantum physics that is inherently non-local. This is no accident but a precise correspondence: mind and the quantum operator algebras are the enjoyed and contemplated aspects of the same thing. This fundamental non-locality of the universe has, however, broken down in various ways. Space and time are themselves manifestations of this breakdown, and with them the incoherent array of atomic particles that dominate large areas of the universe. Consciousness as we know it arises from the interplay of mind — developing within the non-local aspect of the universe — and matter — which is the localized aspect of this same universe.

On this view mind is not extended, because the fundamental quantum world from which mind emerges is prior to space and time.

The way ahead, I believe, is to place mind first as *the* key aspect of the universe. It is what determines the operator-histories without which the universe does not exist. We have to start exploring how we can talk about mind in terms of a quantum picture which takes seriously the fundamental place of self-observation; of the quantum logic of actual observables being itself determined by the current situation. Only then will we be able to make a genuine bridge between physics and psychology.

References

Alexander, S. (1920), *Space, Time, Deity* (London: Macmillan).
Cottingham, J. (1992), *The Cambridge Companion to Descartes* (Cambridge: CUP).
Chalmers, D.J. (1995), 'Facing up to the problem of consciousness', *Journal of Consciousness Studies*, **2** (3), pp. 200–19 (reprinted in this volume).
Gell-Mann, M. and Hartle, J.B. (1993), 'Classical equations for quantum systems', *Physical Review D*, **47**, pp. 3345–82.
Lockwood, M. (1991), *Mind, Brain and the Quantum* (Oxford: Blackwell).
Mackey, G.W. (1963), *Mathematical Foundations of Quantum Mechanics* (New York: Benjamin).
Percival, I.C. (1994), *Proc. Roy. Soc. Lond.*, A **447**, pp. 189–209.
Zadeh, L.A. *et al.* (eds. 1975), *Fuzzy Sets and their Applications to Cognitive and Decision Processes* (New York: Academic Press).
Zeeman, E.C. (1962), 'The topology of the brain and visual perception', in *Topology of 3-manifolds*, ed. M.K. Fort (Englewood Cliffs, NJ: Prentice-Hall), pp. 240–56.

Stuart R. Hameroff and Roger Penrose

Conscious Events as Orchestrated Space–Time Selections

Introduction: Self-Selection in an Experiential Medium?

The 'hard problem' of incorporating the phenomenon of consciousness into a scientific world-view involves finding scientific explanations of qualia, or the subjective experience of mental states (Chalmers, keynote paper and 1996). On this, reductionist science is still at sea. Why do we have an inner life, and what exactly is it?

One set of philosophical positions, addressing the hard problem, views consciousness as a fundamental component of physical reality. For example an extreme view — 'panpsychism' — is that consciousness is a quality of all matter: atoms and their subatomic components having elements of consciousness (e.g. Spinoza, 1677; Rensch, 1960). 'Mentalists' such as Leibniz and Whitehead (e.g. 1929) contended that systems ordinarily considered to be physical are constructed in some sense from mental entities. Bertrand Russell (1954) described 'neutral monism' in which a common underlying entity, neither physical nor mental, gave rise to both. Recently Stubenberg (1996) has claimed that qualia are that common entity. In monistic idealism, matter and mind arise from consciousness — the fundamental constituent of reality (e.g. Goswami, 1993). Wheeler (1990) has suggested that information is fundamental to the physics of the universe. From this, Chalmers (keynote paper and 1996) proposes a double-aspect theory in which information has both physical and experiential aspects.

Among these positions, the philosophy of Alfred North Whitehead (1929; 1933) may be most directly applicable. Whitehead describes the ultimate concrete entities in the cosmos as being actual 'occasions of experience', each bearing a quality akin to 'feeling'. Whitehead construes 'experience' broadly — in a manner consistent with panpsychism — so that even 'temporal events in the career of an electron have a kind of 'protomentality'. Whitehead's view may be considered to differ from panpsychism, however, in that his discrete 'occasions of experience' can be taken to be related to 'quantum events' (Shimony, 1993). In the standard descriptions of quantum mechanics, randomness occurs in the events described as quantum state reductions — these being events which appear to take place when a quantum-level process gets magnified to a macroscopic scale.

This paper was originally published in the *Journal of Consciousness Studies*, **3**, No.1 (1996), pp. 36–53.

Quantum state reduction (here denoted by the letter **R**; cf. Penrose 1989, 1994) is the random procedure that is adopted by physicists in their descriptions of the quantum measurement process. It is still a highly controversial matter whether **R** is to be taken as a 'real' physical process, or whether it is some kind of illusion and not to be regarded as a fundamental ingredient of the behaviour of Nature. Our position is to take **R** to be indeed real — or, rather to regard it as a close approximation to an objectively real process **OR** (objective reduction), which is to be a non-computable process instead of merely a random one (see Penrose 1989; 1994). In almost all physical situations, **OR** would come about in situations in which the random effects of the environment dominate, so **OR** would be virtually indistinguishable from the random **R** procedure that is normally adopted by quantum theorists. However, when the quantum system under consideration remains coherent and well isolated from its environment, then it becomes possible for its state to collapse spontaneously, in accordance with the **OR** scheme we adopt, and to behave in non-computable rather than random ways. Moreover, this **OR** scheme intimately involves the geometry of the physical universe at its deepest levels.

Our viewpoint is to regard experiential phenomena as also inseparable from the physical universe, and in fact to be deeply connected with the very laws which govern the physical universe. The connection is so deep, however, that we perceive only glimmerings of it in our present day physics. One of these glimmerings, we contend, is a necessary non-computability in conscious thought processes; and we argue that this non-computability must also be inherent in the phenomenon of quantum state *self*-reduction — the 'objective reduction' (**OR**) referred to above. This is the main thread of argument in *Shadows of the Mind* (Penrose, 1994). The argument that conscious thought, whatever other attributes it may also have, is non-computable (as follows most powerfully from certain deductions from Gödel's incompleteness theorem) grabs hold of one tiny but extremely valuable point. This means that at least some conscious states cannot be derived from previous states by an algorithmic process — a property which distinguishes human (and other animal) minds from computers. Noncomputability *per se* does not directly address the 'hard problem' of the nature of experience, but it is a clue to the kind of physical activity that lies behind it. This points to **OR**, an underlying physical action of a completely different character from that which would appear to underlie nonconscious activity. Following this clue with sensitivity and patience should ultimately lead to real progress towards understanding mental phenomena in their inward manifestations as well as outward.

In the **OR** description, consciousness takes place if an organized quantum system is able to isolate and sustain coherent superpositions until its quantum gravity threshold for space–time separation is met; it then *self*-reduces (non-computably). For consciousness to occur, *self*-reduction is essential, as opposed to the reduction being triggered by the system's random environment. (In the latter case, the reduction would itself be effectively random and would lack useful non-computability, being unsuitable for direct involvement in consciousness.) We take the *self*-reduction to be an instantaneous event — the climax of a *self*-organizing process fundamental to the structuring of space–time — and apparently consistent with a Whitehead 'occasion of experience'.

As **OR** could, in principle, occur ubiquitously within many types of inanimate media, it may seem to imply a form of 'panpsychism' (in which individual electrons, for example, possess an experiential quality). However according to the principles of **OR** (as expounded in Penrose, 1994; 1996), a single superposed electron would spontaneously reduce its state (assuming it could maintain isolation) only once in a period longer than the present age of the universe. Only large collections of particles acting coherently in a single macroscopic quantum state could possibly sustain isolation and support coherent superposition in a timeframe brief enough to be relevant to our consciousness. Thus, only very special circumstances could support consciousness:

1) High degree of coherence of a quantum state — a collective mass of particles in superposition for a time period long enough to reach threshold, and brief enough to be useful in thought processes.

2) Ability for the **OR** process to be at least transiently isolated from a 'noisy' environment until the spontaneous state reduction takes place. This isolation is required so that reduction is not simply random. Mass movement in the environment which entangles with the quantum state would effect a random (not non-computable) reduction.

3) Cascades of **OR**s to give a 'stream' of consciousness, huge numbers of **OR** events taking place during the course of a lifetime.

By reaching the quantum gravity threshold, each **OR** event has a fundamental bearing on space–time geometry. One could say that a cascade of **OR** events charts an actual course of physical space–time geometry selections.

It may seem surprising that quantum gravity effects could plausibly have relevance at the physical scales relevant to brain processes. For quantum gravity is normally viewed as having only absurdly tiny influences at ordinary dimensions. However, we shall show later that this is not the case, and the scales determined by basic quantum gravity principles are indeed those that are relevant for conscious brain processes.

We must ask how such an **OR** process could actually occur in the brain? How could it be coupled to neural activities at a high rate of information exchange; how could it account for preconscious to conscious transitions, have spatial and temporal binding, and both simultaneity and time flow?

We here nominate an **OR** process with the requisite characteristics to be occurring in cytoskeletal microtubules within the brain's neurons. In our model, microtubule-associated proteins 'tune' the quantum oscillations leading to **OR**; we thus term the process 'orchestrated objective reduction' (**Orch OR**).

Space–Time: Quantum Theory and Einstein's Gravity

Quantum theory describes the extraordinary behaviour of the matter and energy which comprise our universe at a fundamental level. At the root of quantum theory is the wave/particle duality of atoms, molecules, and their constituent particles. A quantum system such as an atom or subatomic particle which remains isolated from its environment behaves as a 'wave of possibilities' and exists in a coherent complex-number valued 'superposition' of many possible states. The behaviour of such wave-like, quantum-level objects can be satisfactorily described in terms of a state vector which evolves determin-istically according to the Schrödinger equation (unitary evolution), denoted by **U**.

Somehow, quantum microlevel superpositions lead to unsuperposed stable structures in our macro-world. In a transition known as wave function collapse, or state reduction (**R**), the quantum wave of alternative possibilities reduces to a single macroscopic reality — an 'eigenstate' of some appropriate operator. (This would be just one out of many possible alternative eigenstates relevant to the quantum operator.) This process is invoked in the description of a macroscopic measurement, when effects are magnified from the small, quantum scale to the large, classical scale.

According to conventional quantum theory (as part of the standard 'Copenhagen interpretation'), each choice of eigenstate is entirely random, weighted according to a probability value that can be calculated from the previous state according to the precise procedures of the quantum formalism. This probabilistic ingredient was a feature with which Einstein, among others, expressed displeasure: 'You believe in a God who plays dice, and I in complete law and order.'[1] Penrose (1989; 1994) has contended that, at a deeper level of description, the choices may more accurately arise as the result of some presently unknown 'non-computational' mathematical/physical (i.e. 'Platonic realm') theory, that is they cannot be deduced algorithmically. Penrose argues that such non-computability is essential to consciousness, because (at least some) conscious mental activity is unattainable by computers.

It can be argued that present-day physics has no clear explanation for the cause and occurrence of wave function collapse **R**. Experimental and theoretical evidence through the 1930's led quantum physicists (such as Schrödinger, Heisenberg, Dirac, von Neumann, and others) to postulate that quantum-coherent superpositions persist indefinitely in time, and would, in principle be maintained from the micro to macro levels. Or perhaps they would persist until conscious observation collapses, or reduces, the wave function (subjective reduction, or '**SR**'). Accordingly, even macroscopic objects, if unobserved, could remain superposed. To illustrate the apparent absurdity of this notion, Erwin Schrödinger (e.g. 1935) described his now-famous 'cat in a box' being simultaneously *both* dead and alive until the box was opened and the cat observed.

As a counter to this unsettling prospect, various new physical schemes for collapse according to objective criteria (objective reduction — '**OR**') have recently been proposed. According to such a scheme, the growth and persistence of superposed states could reach a critical threshold, at which collapse, or **OR** rapidly occurs (e.g. Pearle, 1989; Ghirardi *et al.*, 1986). Some of these schemes are based specifically on gravitational effects mediating **OR** (e.g. Károlyházy, 1966; Károlyházy *et al.*, 1986; Diósi, 1989; Ghirardi *et al.*, 1990; Penrose, 1989; 1994; Pearle and Squires, 1995; Percival, 1995). Table 1 categorizes types of reduction.

The physical phenomenon of gravity, described to a high degree of accuracy by Isaac Newton's mathematics in 1687, has played a key role in scientific understanding. However, in 1915, Einstein created a major revolution in our scientific world-view. According to Einstein's theory, gravity plays a unique role in physics for several reasons (cf. Penrose, 1994). Most particularly, these are:

1) Gravity is the only physical quality which influences causal relationships between space–time events.

---

[1] From a letter to Max Born.

2) Gravitational force has no local reality, as it can be eliminated by a change in space–time coordinates; instead, gravitational tidal effects provide a *curvature* for the very *space–time* in which all other particles and forces are contained.

Context	Cause of Collapse (Reduction)	Description	Acronym
Quantum coherent superposition	No collapse	Evolution of wave function (Schrödinger equation)	U
Conventional quantum theory (Copenhagen interpretation)	Environmental entanglement, Measurement, Conscious observation	Reduction; Subjective reduction	R SR
New physics (Penrose,1994)	Self-collapse — quantum gravity induced (Penrose, Diosi, etc.)	Objective reduction	OR
Consciousness (present paper)	Self-collapse, quantum gravity threshold in microtubules orchestrated by MAPs etc.	Orchestrated objective reduction	Orch OR

Table 1: Description of wave function collapse

It follows from this that gravity cannot be regarded as some kind of 'emergent phenomenon', secondary to other physical effects, but must be a 'fundamental component' of physical reality.

There are strong arguments (e.g. Penrose, 1987; 1996) to suggest that the appropriate union of general relativity (Einstein's theory of gravity) with quantum mechanics — a union often referred to as 'quantum gravity' — will lead to a significant change in *both* quantum theory and general relativity, and, when the correct theory is found, will yield a profoundly *new* understanding of physical reality. And although gravitational *forces* between objects are exceedingly weak (feebler than, for example, electrical forces by some 40 orders of magnitude), there are significant reasons for believing that gravity has a fundamental influence on the behaviour of quantum systems as they evolve from the micro to the macrolevels. The appropriate union of quantum gravity with biology, or at least with advanced biological nervous systems, may yield a profoundly new understanding of consciousness.

Curved Space–Time Superpositions and Objective Reduction ('OR')

According to modern accepted physical pictures, reality is rooted in 3-dimensional space and a 1-dimensional time, combined together into a 4-dimensional space–time. This space–time is slightly curved, in accordance with Einstein's general theory of relativity, in a way which encodes the gravitational fields of all distributions of mass density. Each mass density effects a space–time curvature, albeit tiny.

This is the standard picture according to *classical* physics. On the other hand, when *quantum* systems have been considered by physicists, this mass-induced tiny curvature in the structure of space–time has been almost invariably ignored, gravitational effects having been assumed to be totally insignificant for normal problems in which quantum theory is important. Surprising as it may seem, however, such tiny differences in space–time structure *can* have large effects: for they entail subtle but fundamental influences on the very rules of quantum mechanics.

Superposed quantum states for which the respective mass distributions differ significantly from one another will have space–time geometries which correspondingly differ. Thus, according to standard quantum theory, the superposed state would have to involve a quantum superposition of these differing space–times. In the absence of a coherent theory of quantum gravity there is no accepted way of handling such a superposition. Indeed, the basic principles of Einstein's general relativity begin to come into profound conflict with those of quantum mechanics (cf. Penrose, 1996). Nevertheless, various tentative procedures have been put forward in attempts to describe such a superposition. Of particular relevance to our present proposals are the suggestions of certain authors (e.g. Károlyházy, 1966; 1974; Károlyházy *et al.*, 1986; Kibble, 1981; Diósi, 1989; Ghirardi *et al.*, 1990; Pearle and Squires, 1995; Percival, 1995; Penrose, 1993; 1994; 1996) that it is at this point that an objective quantum state reduction (**OR**) ought to occur, and the rate or timescale of this process can be calculated from basic quantum gravity considerations. These particular proposals differ in certain detailed respects, and for definiteness we shall follow the specific suggestions made in Penrose (1994; 1996). Accordingly, the quantum superposition of significantly differing space–times is unstable, with a life-time given by that timescale. Such a superposed state will decay — or 'reduce' — into a single universe state, which is one or the other of the space–time geometries involved in that superposition.

Whereas such an **OR** action is not a generally recognized part of the normal quantum-mechanical procedures, there is no plausible or clearcut alternative that standard quantum theory has to offer. This **OR** procedure avoids the need for 'multiple universes' (cf. Everett, 1957; Wheeler, 1957, for example). There is no agreement, among quantum gravity experts, about how else to address this problem. For the purposes of the present article, it will be assumed that a gravitationally induced **OR** action is indeed the correct resolution of this fundamental conundrum.

Figure 1 (adapted from Penrose, 1994, p. 338) schematically illustrates the way in which space time structure can be affected when two macroscopically different mass distributions take part in a quantum superposition. Each mass distribution gives rise to a separate space–time, the two differing slightly in their curvatures. So long as the two distributions remain in quantum superposition, we must consider that the two space–times remain in superposition. Since, according to the principles of general relativity, there is no natural way to identify the points of one space–time with corresponding points of the other, we have to consider the two as separated from one another in some sense, resulting in a kind of 'blister' where the space–time bifurcates.

A bifurcating space–time is depicted in the lowest of the three diagrams, this being the union ('glued together version') of the two alternative space–time histories that are depicted at the top of Figure 1. The initial part of each space–time is at the lower end of

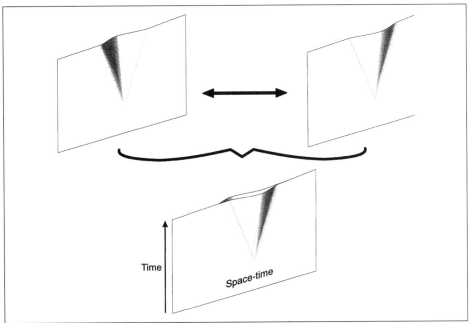

Figure 1. Quantum coherent superposition represented as a separation of space–time. In the lowest of the three diagrams, a bifurcating space–time is depicted as the union ('glued together version'), of the two alternative space–time histories that are depicted at the top of the Figure. The bifurcating space–time diagram illustrates two alternative mass distributions actually in quantum superposition, whereas the top two diagrams illustrate the two individual alternatives which take part in the superposition (adapted from Penrose, 1994, p. 338).

each individual space–time diagram. The bottom space–time diagram (the bifurcating one) illustrates two alternative mass distributions actually in quantum superposition, whereas the top two illustrate the two individual alternatives which take part in the superposition. The combined space–time describes a superposition in which the alterna-tive locations of a mass move gradually away from each other as we proceed in the upward direction in the diagram. Quantum mechanically (i.e. so long as **OR** has not taken place), we must think of the 'physical reality' of this situation as being illustrated as an actual superposition of these two slightly differing space–time manifolds, as indicated in the bottom diagram. As soon as **OR** has occurred, one of the two individual space–times takes over, as depicted as one of the two sheets of the bifurcation. For clarity only, the bifurcating parts of these two sheets are illustrated as being one convex and the other concave. Of course there is additional artistic licence involved in drawing the space–time sheets as 2-dimensional, whereas the actual space–time constituents are 4-dimensional. Moreover, there is no significance to be attached to the imagined '3-dimensional space' within which the space–time sheets seem to be residing. There is no 'actual' higher dimensional space there, the 'intrinsic geometry' of the bifurcating space–time being all that has physical significance. When the 'separation' of the two space–time sheets reaches a critical amount, one of the two sheets 'dies' — in accordance with the **OR** criterion — the other being the one that persists in physical reality. The quantum state thus reduces (**OR**), by choosing between either the 'concave' or 'convex' space–time of Figure 1.

It should be made clear that this measure of separation is only very schematically illustrated as the 'distance' between the two sheets in the lower diagram in Figure 1. As remarked above, there is no physically existing 'ambient higher-dimensional space' inside which the two sheets reside. The degree of separation between the space–time sheets is a more abstract mathematical thing; it would be more appropriately described in terms of a *symplectic measure* on the space of 4-dimensional metrics (cf. Penrose, 1993) — but the details (and difficulties) of this will not be important for us here. It may be noted, however, that this separation is a space–time separation, not just a spatial one. Thus the *time* of separation contributes as well as the spatial displacement. Roughly speaking, it is the product of the temporal separation T with the spatial separation S that measures the overall degree of separation, and **OR** takes place when this overall separation reaches the critical amount. [This critical amount would be of the order of unity, in absolute units, for which the Planck-Dirac constant $\hbar$ ($= h/2\pi$), the gravitational constant G, and the velocity of light c, all take the value unity; cf. Penrose, 1994, pp. 337–9.] Thus for small S, the lifetime T of the superposed state will be large; on the other hand, if S is large, then T will be small. To calculate S, we compute (in the Newtonian limit of weak gravitational fields) the gravitational self-energy E of the difference between the mass distributions of the two superposed states. (That is, one mass distribution counts positively and the other, negatively; see Penrose, 1994; 1996.) The quantity S is then given, in absolute units, by:

$$S = E$$

Thus, restoring standard units,

$$T = \hbar \, E^{-1}$$

Schematically, since S represents three dimensions of displacement rather than the one dimension involved in T, we can imagine that this displacement is shared equally between each of these three dimensions of space — and this is what has been depicted in Figure 3 (below). However, it should be emphasized that this is for pictorial purposes only, the appropriate rule being the one given above. These two equations relate the mass distribution, time of coherence, and space–time separation for a given **OR** event. If, as some philosophers contend, experience is contained in space–time, **OR** events are *self-organizing* processes in that experiential medium, and a candidate for consciousness.

But where in the brain, and how, could coherent superposition and **OR** occur? A number of sites and various types of quantum interactions have been proposed. We strongly favour microtubules as an important ingredient; however various organelles and biomolecular structures including clathrins, myelin (glial cells), presynaptic vesicular grids (Beck and Eccles, 1992) and neural membrane proteins (Marshall, 1989) might also participate.

Microtubules

Properties of brain structures suitable for quantum coherent superposition, **OR** and relevant to consciousness might include: 1) high prevalence, 2) functional importance (for example regulating neural connectivity and synaptic function), 3) periodic, crystal-like lattice dipole structure with longrange order, 4) ability to be transiently isolated from external interaction/observation, 5) functionally coupled to quantum-level events, 6)

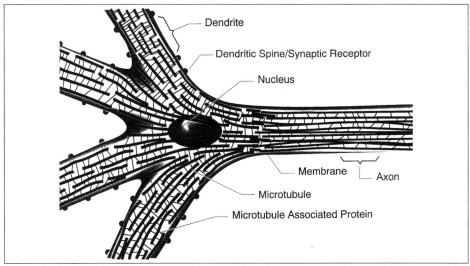

Figure 2. Schematic of central region of neuron (distal axon and dendrites not shown), showing parallel arrayed microtubules interconnected by MAPs. Microtubules in axons are lengthy and continuous, whereas in dendrites they are interrupted and of mixed polarity. Linking proteins connect microtubules to membrane proteins including receptors on dendritic spines.

hollow, cylindrical (possible wave-guide), and 7) suitable for information processing. Membranes, membrane proteins, synapses, DNA and other types of structures have some, but not all, of these characteristics. Cytoskeletal microtubules appear to qualify in all respects.

Interiors of living cells, including the brain's neurons, are spatially and dynamically organized by *self*-assembling protein networks: the cytoskeleton. Within neurons, the cytoskeleton establishes neuronal form, and maintains and regulates synaptic connections. Its major components are microtubules, hollow cylindrical polymers of individual proteins known as tubulin. Microtubules ('MTs') are interconnected by linking proteins (microtubule-associated proteins: 'MAPs') to other microtubules and cell structures to form cytoskeletal lattice networks (Figure 2).

MTs are hollow cylinders 25 nanometers (nm) in diameter whose lengths vary and may be quite long within some nerve axons. MT cylinder walls are comprised of 13 longitudinal protofilaments which are each a series of subunit proteins known as tubulin (Figure 3). Each tubulin subunit is a polar, 8 nm dimer which consists of two slightly different 4 nm monomers (α and β tubulin — Figure 4). Tubulin dimers are dipoles, with surplus negative charges localized toward monomers (DeBrabander, 1982), and within

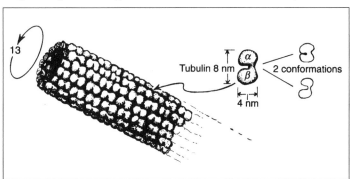

Figure 3.

Microtubule structure: a hollow tube of 25 nanometers diameter, consisting of 13 columns of tubulin dimers. Each tubulin molecule is capable of (at least), two conformations. (Reprinted with permission from Penrose, 1994, p. 359.)

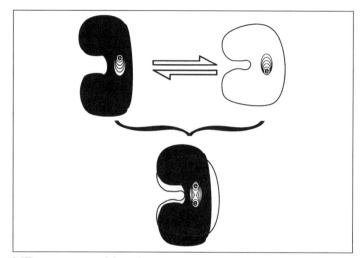

Figure 4.

Top:
Two states of tubulin in which a *single* quantum event (electron localization), within a central hydrophobic pocket is coupled to a *global* protein conformation. Switching between the two states can occur on the order of nanoseconds to picoseconds.

Bottom:
Tubulin in quantum coherent superposition.

MTs are arranged in a hexagonal lattice which is slightly twisted, resulting in helical pathways which repeat every 3, 5, 8 and other numbers of rows. Traditionally viewed as the cell's 'bonelike' scaffolding, microtubules and other cytoskeletal structures also appear to fill communicative and information processing roles. Numerous types of studies link the cytoskeleton to cognitive processes (for review, cf. Hameroff and Penrose, 1996). Theoretical models and simulations suggest how conformational states of tubulins within microtubule lattices can interact with neighbouring tubulins to represent, propagate and process information as in molecular-level 'cellular automata', or 'spinglass' type computing systems (Figure 5; e.g. Hameroff and Watt, 1982; Rasmussen *et al.*, 1990; Tuszyński *et al.*, 1995). In Hameroff and Penrose (1996, and in summary form Penrose and Hameroff, 1995), we present a model linking microtubules to consciousness, using quantum theory as viewed in the particular 'realistic' way referred to above, and as described in *Shadows of the Mind* (Penrose, 1994). In our model, quantum coherence emerges, and is isolated, in brain microtubules until the differences in mass–energy distribution among superposed tubulin states reach the above threshold of insta-

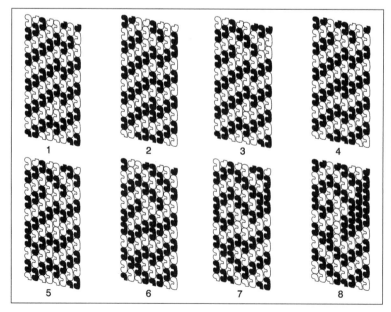

Figure 5. Microtubule automaton simulation (from Rasmussen *et al.*, 1990). Black and white tubulins correspond to states shown in Figure 2. Eight nanosecond time steps of a segment of one microtubule are shown in 'classical computing' mode in which patterns move, evolve, interact and lead to emergence of new patterns.

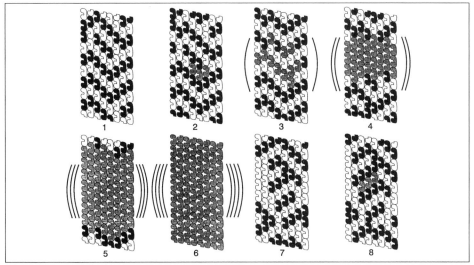

Figure 6. Microtubule automaton sequence simulation in which classical computing (step 1), leads to emergence of quantum coherent superposition (steps 2–6), in certain (grey) tubulins due to pattern resonance. Step 6 (in coherence with other microtubule tubulins) meets critical threshold related to quantum gravity for self–collapse (**Orch OR**). Consciousness (**Orch OR**) occurs in the step 6 to 7 transition. Step 7 represents the eigenstate of mass distribution of the collapse which evolves by classical computing automata to regulate neural function. Quantum coherence begins to re–emerge in step 8.

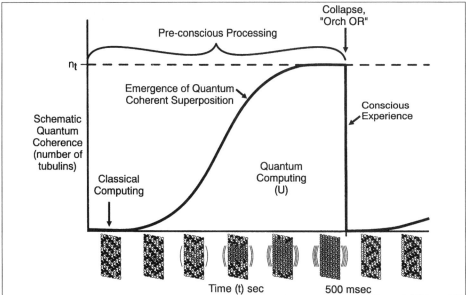

Figure 7. Schematic graph of proposed quantum coherence (number of tubulins), emerging vs time in microtubules. 500 milliseconds is time for pre–conscious processing (e.g. Libet *et al.*, 1979). Area under curve connects mass–energy differences with collapse time in accordance with gravitational **OR**. This degree of coherent superposition of differing space–time geometries leads to abrupt quantum → classical reduction ('self–collapse' or 'orchestrated objective reduction: **Orch OR**').

bility, related to quantum gravity (Figure 6). The resultant *self*-collapse (**OR**), considered to be a time-irreversible process, creates an instantaneous 'now' event in our model. Sequences of such events create a flow of time and consciousness (Figures 7 and 8).

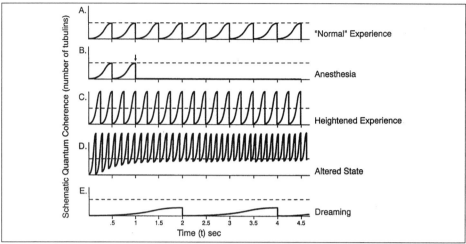

Figure 8. Quantum coherence in microtubules schematically graphed on longer time scale for five different states related to consciousness. Area under each curve equivalent in all cases. A. Normal experience: as in Figure 8. B. Anaesthesia: anaesthetics bind in hydrophobic pockets and prevent quantum delocalizability and coherent superposition (e.g. Louria and Hameroff, 1996). C. Heightened Experience: increased sensory experience input (for example), increases rate of emergence of quantum coherent superposition. **Orch Or** threshold is reached faster (e.g. 250 msec), and **Orch Or** frequency is doubled. D. Altered State: even greater rate of emergence of quantum coherence due to sensory input and other factors promoting quantum state (e.g. meditation, psychedelic drug, etc.). Predisposition to quantum state results in baseline shift and only partial collapse so that conscious experience merges with normally sub–conscious quantum computing mode. E. Dreaming: prolonged quantum coherence time. (Highly schematic.)

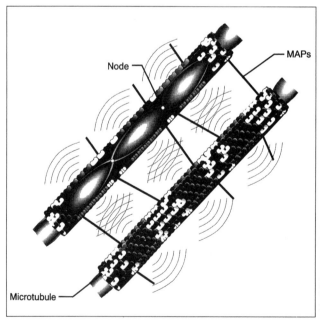

Figure 9. Quantum coherence in microtubules. Having emerged from resonance in classical automaton patterns, quantum coherence non–locally links superpositioned tubulins (grey), within and among microtubules. Upper microtubule: cutaway view shows coherent photons generated by quantum ordering of water on tubulin surfaces, propagating in microtubule waveguide. MAP (microtubule-associated protein), attachments breach isolation and prevent quantum coherence; MAP attachment sites thus act as 'nodes' which tune and orchestrate quantum oscillations and set possibilities and probabilities for collapse outcomes ('orchestrated objective reduction': **Orch OR**).

We envisage that attachments of MAPs on microtubules 'tune' quantum oscillations, and 'orchestrate' possible collapse outcomes (Figure 9). Thus we term the particular *self*-organizing **OR** occurring in MAP-connected microtubules, and relevant to consciousness, orchestrated objective reduction ('**Orch OR**'). **Orch OR** events are thus *self*-selecting processes in fundamental space–time geometry. If experience is truly a component of fundamental space–time, **Orch OR** may indeed begin to to address the 'hard problem' of consciousness.

Summary of the 'Orch OR' Model for Consciousness

The full details of this model are given in Hameroff and Penrose (1996). The picture we are putting forth involves the following ingredients:

(1) Aspects of quantum theory (e.g. quantum coherence) and of the suggested physical phenomenon of quantum wave function '*self*-collapse' (objective reduction: **OR** — Penrose, 1994; 1996) are essential for consciousness, and occur in cytoskeletal microtubules (MTs) and other structures within each of the brain's neurons.

(2) Conformational states of MT subunits (tubulins) are coupled to internal quantum events, and cooperatively interact with other tubulins in both classical and quantum computation (Hameroff *et al.*, 1992; Rasmussen *et al.*, 1990 — Figures 4, 5 and 6).

(3) Quantum coherence occurs among tubulins in MTs, pumped by thermal and biochemical energies (perhaps in the manner proposed by Fröhlich, 1968; 1970; 1975). Evidence for some kind of coherent excitation in proteins has recently been reported by Vos *et al.* (1993).

It is also considered that water at MT surfaces is 'ordered' — dynamically coupled to the protein surface. Water ordering within the hollow MT core (acting something like a quantum waveguide) may result in quantum coherent photons (as suggested by the phenomena of 'super-radiance'and '*self*-induced transparency' — Jibu *et al.*, 1994; 1995). We require that coherence be sustained (protected from environmental interaction) for up to hundreds of milliseconds by isolation (a) within hollow MT cores, (b) within tubulin hydrophobic pockets, (c) by coherently ordered water, (d) sol-gel layering (Hameroff and Penrose, 1996). Feasibility of quantum coherence in the seemingly noisy, chaotic cell environment is supported by the observation that quantum spins from biochemical radical pairs which become separated retain their correlation in cytoplasm (Walleczek, 1995).

(4) During preconscious processing, quantum coherent superposition/computation occurs in MT tubulins and continues until the mass-distribution difference among the separated states of tubulins reaches a threshold related to quantum gravity. Self-collapse (**OR**) then occurs (Figures 6 & 7).

(5) The **OR** *self*-collapse process results in classical 'outcome states' of MT tubulins which then implement neurophysiological functions. According to certain ideas for **OR** (Penrose, 1994), the outcome states are 'non-computable'; that is they cannot be determined algorithmically from the tubulin states at the beginning of the quantum computation.

(6) Possibilities and probabilities for post**OR** tubulin states are influenced by factors including initial tubulin states, and attachments of microtubule-associated proteins (MAPs) acting as 'nodes' which tune and 'orchestrate' the quantum oscillations (Figure 9). We thus term the *self*-tuning **OR** process in microtubules 'orchestrated objective reduction' — **Orch OR**.

(7) According to the arguments for **OR** put forth in Penrose (1994), superposed states each have their own space–time geometries. When the degree of coherent mass–energy difference leads to sufficient separation of space–time geometry, the system must choose

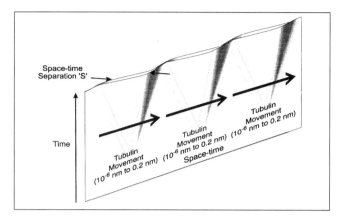

Figure 10.

Schematic space–time separation illustration of three superposed tubulins. The space–time differences are very tiny in ordinary terms (10^{-40} nm), but relatively large mass movements (e.g. hundreds of tubulin conformations, each moving from 10^{-6} nm to 0.2 nm), indeed have precisely such very tiny effects on the space–time curvature.

Figure 11.

Centre:
Three superposed tubulins (e.g. Figure 4), with corresponding schematic space–time separation illustrations (Figures 1 and 10). Surrounding the superposed tubulins are the eight possible post–reduction 'eigen–states' for tubulin conformation, and corresponding space–time geometry.

and decay (reduce, collapse) to a single universe state. Thus **Orch OR** involves *self*-selections in fundamental space–time geometry (Figures 10 & 11).

(8) To quantify the **Orch OR** process, in the case of a pair of roughly equally superposed states, each of which has a reasonably well-defined mass distribution, we calculate the gravitational *self*-energy E of the difference between these two mass distributions, and then obtain the approximate lifetime T for the superposition to decay into one state or the other by the formula $T = \hbar / E$. Here, $\hbar$ is Planck's constant over 2π. We call T the coherence time for the superposition (how long the coherence is sustained). If we assume a coherence time $T = 500$ msec (shown by Libet *et al.*, 1979, and others to be a relevant time for preconscious processing), we calculate E, and determine the number of MT tubulins whose coherent superposition for 500 msec will elicit **Orch OR**. This turns out to be about 10^9 tubulins.

(9) A typical brain neuron has roughly 10^7 tubulins (Yu and Baas, 1994). If, say, 10 % of tubulins within each neuron are involved in the quantum coherent state, then roughly 10^3 (one thousand) neurons would be required to sustain coherence for 500 msec, at which time the quantum gravity threshold is reached and **Orch OR** then occurs.

(10) We consider each *self*-organized **Orch OR** as a single conscious event; cascades of such events would constitute a 'stream' of consciousness. If we assume some form of excitatory input (e.g. you are threatened, or enchanted) in which quantum coherence emerges faster, then, for example, 10^{10} coherent tubulins could **Orch OR** after 50 msec,

or 10^{11} after 5 msec (e.g. Figure 8c). Turning to see a bengal tiger in your face might perhaps elicit 10^{12} in 0.5 msec, or more tubulins, faster. A slow emergence of coherence (your forgotten phone bill) may require longer times. A single electron would require more than the age of the universe.

(11) Quantum states are non-local (because of quantum entanglement — or 'Einstein-Podolsky-Rosen' (EPR) effects), so that the entire non-localized state reduces all at once. This can happen if the mass movement that induces collapse takes place in a small region encompassed by the state, or if it takes place uniformly over a large region. Thus, each instantaneous **Orch OR** could 'bind' various superpositions which may have evolved in separated spatial distributions and even over different time scales, but whose net displacement *self*-energy reaches threshold at a particular moment. Information is bound into an instantaneous event (a 'conscious now'). Cascades of **Orch OR**s could then represent our familiar 'stream of consciousness', and create a 'forward' flow of time (Aharonov and Vaidman, 1990; Elitzur, 1996; Tollaksen, 1996).

It may be interesting to compare our considerations with subjective viewpoints that have been expressed with regard to the nature of the progression of conscious experience. For example, support for consciousness consisting of sequences of individual, discrete events is found in Buddhism; trained meditators describe distinct 'flickerings' in their experience of reality (Tart, 1995). Buddhist texts portray consciousness as 'momentary collections of mental phenomena', and as 'distinct, unconnected and impermanent moments which perish as soon as they arise'. Each conscious moment successively becomes, exists, and disappears — its existence is instantaneous, with no duration in time, as a point has no length. Our normal perceptions, of course, are seemingly continuous, presumably as we perceive 'movies' as continuous despite their actual makeup being a series of frames. Some Buddhist writings even quantify the frequency of conscious moments. For example the Sarvaastivaadins (von Rospatt, 1995) described 6,480,000 'moments' in 24 hours (an average of one 'moment' per 13.3 msec), while other Buddhist writings describe one moment per 0.13 msec (Conze, 1988), and some Chinese Buddhism as one 'thought' per 20 msec. These accounts, including variations in frequency, seem to be consistent with our proposed **Orch OR** events. For example a 13.3 msec preconscious interval would correspond with an **Orch OR** involving 4×10^{10} coherent tubulins, a 0.13 msec interval would correspond with 4×10^{12} coherent tubulins, and a 20 msec interval with 2.5×10^{10} coherent tubulins. Thus Buddhist 'moments of experience', Whitehead 'occasions of experience', and our proposed **Orch OR** events seem to correspond tolerably well with one another.

The **Orch OR** model thus appears to accommodate some important features of consciousness:

1) control/regulation of neural action
2) pre-conscious to conscious transition
3) non-computability
4) causality
5) binding of various (time scale and spatial) superpositions into instantaneous 'now'
6) a 'flow' of time, and
7) a connection to fundamental space–time geometry in which experience may be based.

Conclusion: What Is It Like to Be a Worm?

The **Orch OR** model has the implication that an organism able to sustain quantum coherence among, for example, 10^9 tubulins for 500 msec might be capable of having conscious experience. More tubulins coherent for a briefer period, or fewer for a longer period ($E = \hbar / T$) will also have conscious events. Human brains appear capable of, for example, 10^{12} tubulin, 0.5 msec 'bengal tiger experiences', but what about simpler organisms?

From an evolutionary standpoint, introduction of a dynamically functional cytoskeleton (perhaps symbiotically from spirochetes, e.g. Margulis, 1975) greatly enhanced eukaryotic cells by providing cell movement, internal organization, separation of chromosomes and numerous other functions. As cells became more specialized with extensions like axopods and eventually neural processes, increasingly larger cytoskeletal arrays providing transport and motility may have developed quantum coherence via the Fröhlich mechanism as a by-product of their functional coordination.

Another possible scenario for emergence of quantum coherence leading to **Orch OR** and conscious events is 'cellular vision'. Albrecht-Buehler (1992) has observed that single cells utilize their cytoskeletons in 'cellular vision' — detection, orientation and directional response to beams of red/infrared light. Jibu *et al.* (1995) argue that this process requires quantum coherence in microtubules and ordered water, and Hagan (1995) suggests the quantum effects/cellular vision provided an evolutionary advantage for cytoskeletal arrays capable of quantum coherence. For whatever reason quantum coherence emerged, one could then suppose that, one day, an organism achieved sufficient microtubule quantum coherence to elicit **Orch OR**, and had a 'conscious' experience.

At what level of evolutionary development might this primitive consciousness have emerged? A single cell organism like *Paramecium* is extremely clever, and utilizes its cytoskeleton extensively. Could a paramecium be conscious? Assuming a single paramecium contains, like each neuronal cell, 10^7 tubulins, then for a paramecium to elicit **Orch OR**, 100% of its tubulins would need to remain in quantum coherent superposition for nearly a minute. This seems unlikely.

Consider the nematode worm *C elegans*. It's 302 neuron nervous system is completely mapped. Could *C elegans* support **Orch OR**? With 3×10^9 tubulins, *C elegans* would require roughly one third of its tubulins to sustain quantum coherent superposition for 500 msec. This seems unlikely, but not altogether impossible. If not *C elegans*, then perhaps *Aplysia* with a thousand neurons, or some higher organism. **Orch OR** provides a theoretical framework to entertain such possibilities.

Would a primitive **Orch OR** experience be anything like ours? If *C elegans* were able to *self*-collapse, what would it be like to be a worm? (cf. Nagel, 1974). A single, 10^9 tubulin, 500 msec **Orch OR** in *C elegans* should be equal in gravitational *self*-energy terms (and thus perhaps, experiential intensity) to one of our 'everyday experiences'. A major difference is that we would have many **Orch OR** events sequentially (up to, say, 50 per second) whereas *C elegans* could generate, at most, 2 per second. *C elegans* would also presumably lack extensive memory and associations, and have poor sensory data, but nonetheless, by our criteria a 10^9 tubulin, 500 msec **Orch OR** in *C elegans* could be a conscious experience: a mere smudge of known reality, the next space–time move.

Consciousness has an important place in the universe. **Orch OR** in microtubules is a model depicting consciousness as sequences of non-computable *self*-selections in fundamental space time geometry. If experience is a quality of space–time, then **Orch OR** indeed begins to address the 'hard problem' of consciousness in a serious way.

References

Aharonov, Y. and Vaidman, L. (1990), 'Properties of a quantum system during the time interval between two measurements', *Phys. Rev. A*, **41**, p. 11.

Albrecht–Buehler, G. (1992), 'Rudimentary form of ''cellular vision'' ', *Cell. Biol.* **89**, pp. 8288–92.

Beck, F. and Eccles, J.C. (1992), 'Quantum aspects of brain activity and the role of consciousness', *Proc. Natl. Acad. Sci. USA,* **89** (23), pp. 11357–61.

Chalmers, D. (1995), 'Facing up to the problem of consiousness', *Journal of Consciousness Studies*, **2** (3), pp. 200–19 (reprinted in this volume).

Chalmers, D. (1996), *The Conscious Mind (New York:* Oxford University Press).

Conze, E. (1988), *Buddhist Thought in India*, Louis de La Vallee Poussin (trans.), Abhidharmako'sabhaa.syam: English translation by Leo M. Pruden, 4 vols (Berkeley), pp. 85–90.

DeBrabander, M. (1982), 'A model for the microtubule organizing activity of the centrosomes and kinetochores in mammalian cells', *Cell Biol. Intern. Rep.*, **6**, pp. 901–15.

Diósi, L. (1989), 'Models for universal reduction of macroscopic quantum fluctuations', *Phys. Rev. A*, **40**, 1165–74.

Elitzur, A. (1996), 'Time and consciousness: The uneasy bearing of relativity theory on the mind–body problem', in Hameroff *et al.* (1996).

Everett, H. (1957), 'Relative state formulation of quantum mechanics', *Rev. Mod. Physics,* **29**, pp. 454–62. Reprinted in *Quantum Theory and Measurement*, ed. J.A. Wheeler and W.H. Zurek (Princeton: Princeton University Press, 1983).

Fröhlich, H. (1968), 'Long–range coherence and energy storage in biological systems', *Int. J. Quantum Chem.,* **2**, pp. 641–9.

Fröhlich, H. (1970), 'Long range coherence and the actions of enzymes', *Nature,* **228**, p. 1093.

Fröhlich, H. (1975), 'The extraordinary dielectric properties of biological materials and the action of enzymes', *Proc. Natl. Acad. Sci.,* **72**, pp. 4211–15.

Ghirardi, G.C., Grassi, R. and Rimini, A. (1990), 'Continuous–spontaneous reduction model involving gravity', *Phys. Rev. A*, **42**, pp. 1057–64.

Ghirardi, G.C., Rimini, A. and Weber, T. (1986), Unified dynamics for microscopic and macroscopic systems', *Phys. Rev. D*, **34**, p. 470.

Goswami, A. (1993), *The Self-Aware Universe: How Consciousness Creates the Material World* (New York: Tarcher/Putnam).

Hagan, S. (1995), Personal communication.

Hameroff, S.R., Dayhoff, J.E., Lahoz–Beltra, R., Samsonovich, A. and Rasmussen, S. (1992), 'Conformational automata in the cytoskeleton: models for molecular computation' *IEEE Computer* (October Special Issue on Molecular Computing), pp. 30–9.

Hameroff, S.R., Kaszniak, A. and Scott, A.C. (eds. 1996), *Toward a Science of Consciousness – The First Tucson Discussions and Debates* (Cambridge, MA: MIT Press).

Hameroff, S.R. and Penrose, R. (1995), 'Orchestrated reduction of quantum coherence in brain microtubules: A model for consciousness', *Neural Network World*, **5** (5), 793–804.

Hameroff, S.R. and Penrose, R. (1996), 'Orchestrated reduction of quantum coherence in brain microtubules: A model for consciousness', in Hameroff *et al.* (1996).

Hameroff, S.R. and Watt, R.C. (1982), 'Information processing in microtubules', *J. Theor. Biol.*, **98**, pp. 549–61.

Jibu, M., Hagan, S., Hameroff, S.R., Pribram, K.H. and Yasue, K. (1994), 'Quantum optical coherence in cytoskeletal microtubules: implications for brain function', *BioSystems*, **32**, pp. 195–209.

Jibu, M., Yasue, K. and Hagan, S. (1995), 'Water laser as cellular ''vision'' ', submitted.

Károlyházy, F., Frenkel, A., and Lukacs, B. (1986), 'On the possible role of gravity on the reduction of the wave function', in *Quantum Concepts in Space and Time,* ed. R. Penrose and C.J. Isham (Oxford: Oxford University Press).

Károlyházy, F. (1966), 'Gravitation and quantum mechanics of macroscopic bodies', *Nuovo Cim.* A, **42**, p. 390.

Károlyházy, F. (1974), 'Gravitation and quantum mechanics of macroscopic bodies', *Magyar Fizikai Polyoirat*, **12**, p. 24.

Kibble, T.W.B.(1981), 'Is a semi–classical theory of gravity viable?' in *'Quantum Gravity 2: A Second Oxford Symposium'*, ed. C.J. Isham, R. Penrose and D.W. Sciama (Oxford: Oxford University Press).

Libet, B., Wright, E.W. Jr., Feinstein, B. and Pearl, D.K. (1979), 'Subjective referral of the timing for a conscious sensory experience', *Brain*, **102**, pp. 193–224.

Louria, D. and Hameroff, S. (1996),' Computer simulation of anesthetic binding in protein hydrophobic pockets', in Hameroff *et al.* (1996).

Marshall, I.N. (1989), 'Consciousness and Bose–Einstein condensates', *New Ideas in Psychology*, **7**, 73–83.

Margulis, L. (1975), *Origin of Eukaryotic Cells* (New Haven: Yale University Press).

Nagel, T. (1974), 'What is it like to be a bat?' *The Philosophical Review*, **83**, pp. 435–50. Reprinted in *The Mind's I. Fantasies and Reflections on Self and Soul,* ed. D.R. Hofstadter and D.C. Dennett (New York: Basic Books, 1981).

Pearle, P. (1989), 'Combining stochastic dynamical state vector reduction with spontaneous localization', *Phys. Rev. D*, **13**, 857–68.

Pearle, P. and Squires, E. (1995), 'Gravity, energy conservation and parameter values in collapse models', *Durham University preprint*, DTP/95/13.

Penrose, R. (1987), 'Newton, quantum theory and reality', in *300 Years of Gravity*, ed. S.W. Hawking and W. Israel (Cambridge: Cambridge University Press).

Penrose, R. (1989), *The Emperor's New Mind* (Oxford: Oxford University Press).

Penrose, R. (1993), 'Gravity and quantum mechanics', in *General Relativity and Gravitation. Proceedings of the Thirteenth International Conference on General Relativity and Gravitation held at Cordoba, Argentina 28 June–4 July 1992. Part 1: Plenary Lectures*, ed. R.J. Gleiser, C.N. Kozameh and O.M. Moreschi (Bristol: Institute of Physics Publications).

Penrose, R. (1994), *Shadows of the Mind* (Oxford: Oxford University Press).

Penrose, R. and Hameroff, S.R., 'What gaps? Reply to Grush and Churchland', *Journal of Consciousness Studies*, **2** (2), pp. 99–112.

Penrose, R. (1996), 'On gravity's role in quantum state reduction', *Gen.Rel.Grav.*, to appear May 1996.

Percival, I.C. (1995), 'Quantum space–time fluctuations and primary state diffusion', *Proc. Roy. Soc. Lond.* A, **451**, pp. 503–13.

Rasmussen, S., Karampurwala, H., Vaidyanath, R., Jensen, K.S. and Hameroff, S. (1990), 'Computational connectionism within neurons: A model of cytoskeletal automata subserving neural networks', *Physica D*, **42**, pp. 428–49.

Rensch, B. (1960), *Evolution Above the Species Level* (New York: Columbia University Press).

Russell, B. (1954), *The Analysis of Matter* (New York: Dover).

Schrödinger, E (1935), Die gegenwarten situation in der quantenmechanik. *Naturwissenschaften*, **23**, pp. 807–12, 823–8, 844–9. (Translation by J. T. Trimmer, 1980, in *Proc. Amer. Phil. Soc.,* **124**, pp. 323–38.) In *Quantum Theory and Measurement*, ed. J.A. Wheeler and W.H. Zurek (Princeton: Princeton University Press, 1983).

Shimony, A. (1993), *Search for a Naturalistic World View – Volume II. Natural Science and Metaphysics* (Cambridge: Cambridge University Press).

Spinoza, B. (1677), *Ethica in Opera quotque reperta sunt,* 3rd edition, ed. J. van Vloten and J.P.N. Land (Netherlands: Den Haag)

Stubenberg, L. (1996), 'The place of qualia in the world of science', in Hameroff *et al.* (1996).

Tart, C.T. (1995), Personal communication and information gathered from 'Buddha–1 newsnet'.

Tollaksen, J. (1996), 'New insights from quantum theory on time, consciousness, and reality', in Hameroff *et al.* (1996).

Tusz&yski, J., Hameroff, S.R., Sataric, M.V., Trpisová, B. and Nip, M.L.A. (1995), 'Ferroelectric behavior in microtubule dipole lattices: implications for information processing, signalling and assembly/ disassembly', *J. Theor. Biol.*, **174**, pp. 371–80.

von Rospatt, A. (1995), *The Buddhist Doctrine of Momentariness: A survey of the origins and early phase of this doctrine up to Vasubandhu* (Stuttgart: Franz Steiner Verlag).

Vos, M.H., Rappaport, J., Lambry, J. Ch., Breton, J. and Martin, J.L. (1993), 'Visualization of coherent nuclear motion in a membrane protein by femtosecond laser spectroscopy', *Nature*, **363**, pp. 320–5.

Walleczek, J. (1995), 'Magnetokinetic effects on radical pairs: a possible paradigm for understanding sub–kT magnetic field interactions with biological systems', in *Biological Effects of Environmental Electromagnetic Fields* (Advances in Chemistry, No. 250), ed. M. Blank (Washington, DC: American Chemical Society Books, in press).

Wheeler, J.A. (1957), 'Assessment of Everett's ''relative state'' formulation of quantum theory', *Revs. Mod. Phys.,* **29**, pp. 463–5.

Wheeler, J.A. (1990), 'Information, physics, quantum: The search for links', in *Complexity, Entropy, and the Physics of Information*, ed. W. Zurek (Addison–Wesley).

Whitehead, A.N. (1929), *Science and the Modern World* (New York: Macmillan).

Whitehead, A.N. (1933), *Process and Reality* (New York: Macmillan).

Yu, W. and Baas, P.W. (1994), 'Changes in microtubule number and length during axon differentiation', *J. Neuroscience*, **14** (5), pp. 2818–29.

Henry P. Stapp

The Hard Problem: A Quantum Approach

I: Introduction: Philosophical Setting

In his keynote paper David Chalmers defines 'the hard problem' by posing certain 'Why?' questions about consciousness. Such questions must be posed within an appropriate setting. The way of science is to try to deduce the answer to many such questions from a few well defined assumptions.

Much about nature can be explained in terms of the principles of classical mechanics. The assumptions, in this explanatory scheme, are that the world is composed exclusively of particles and fields governed by specified mathematical laws that refer neither to any individual person, nor to anyone's experiences. These physical laws are supposed to be such that particles and fields, acting in concert, can form causally efficacious real functional entities such as driveshafts and propellers. Similarly, surges of electrical and mechanical activity in appropriately designed material substrates, composed of particles and fields acting in concert, could implement, in the world of matter, complex functional structures and long sequences of logical operations. Thus it is conceivable that all of our behaviour, and all of the internal processing that occurs in our bodies and brains could be *deduced*, at least in principle, from the principles of classical mechanics and appropriate boundary conditions.

There is, however, a problem in principle with 'experience', i.e. with the streams of consciousness that constitute our psychological selves. Although, according to the principles of classical mechanics, all of our internal processing, and functionally described body/brain activity, should in principle be deducible from the principles of classical physics, and appropriate boundary conditions — namely the presence of a living body/brain in a certain state of readiness — and although we scientists may therefore one day be able to identify a particular functional activity F as the unambiguous sign of the presence of all of the causal and functional properties needed to identify F as the brain correlate of a certain feeling F' that the person calls 'a searing pain in my left index finger', nevertheless, it is impossible to *deduce* simply from the principles of classical mechanics that F *must* be accompanied by the felt *feeling* F'. This is because the principles of classical mechanics never mention 'feels', and hence these principles alone

This paper was originally published in the *Journal of Consciousness Studies*, **3**, No.3 (1996), pp. 194–210. This work was supported by the Director, Office of Energy Research, Office of High Energy and Nuclear Physics, Division of High Energy Physics of the U.S. Department of Energy under Contract DE-AC03-76SF00098.

cannot entail that certain implementations of functional or logical structures *must neces-sarily* be accompanied by 'experiences'.

Since the principles of classical mechanics do not include any notion that some new sort of ontological entities come into being at some level of functional complexity, one seems to be led either to the notion that there just IS an extra kind of beingness, conscious experience, that is not mentioned in classical mechanics, but that is part of the full description of nature, yet plays no efficacious role in classical dynamics; or to the notion that certain implemented functional (or logical) structures ARE conscious experiences. The first of these possibilities, namely that some new kind of beingness just arises, but makes no physical difference, seems too capricious and unnatural to be true. But what about the second possibility: *functionalism*?

The difficulty with functionalism, within the explanatory framework provided by the principles of classical mechanics, is that the two things that are claimed to be the very same thing are, as initially characterized, described differently, and these differently described things are moreover incapable of being causally connected within the frame-work of classical mechanics, which never mentions one of them. 'Pains' are known to us from childhood, and it therefore does not resolve the problem of explaining their connection to brains either to deny their existence, or say that they are something different from the very feelings that they are defined to be. On the other hand, as one passes from simple thermostats to more and more complex servo-mechanisms with more and more complex self-monitorings, and memories, and decision-making capacities, etc., etc., all implemented ultimately in a material structure assumed to be exactly represented in terms of the primitives of classical mechanics — namely space, time, particles, fields, and local laws of motion — one can never arrive at the point of being able to deduce from the principles of classical mechanics the necessary presence of a 'feeling of pain'. The classical principles are therefore simply too impoverished to serve as a basis for a description for all of nature, including the felt experiences that constitute for each of us an immediately present reality.

The principles of classical mechanics are, of course, unable to explain the properties of the materials from which living brains are made, or the complex chemical reactions that are the basis of brain dynamics. Quantum mechanics is needed for that. But quantum mechanics, according to the the orthodox (Copenhagen) interpretation, involves a huge conceptual shift away from the classical ideal: it brings experiences of observers into the physical theory. The theory is constructed to be fundamentally 'about' our experiences, which thereby become the basic elements of the theory. Thus one need not go beyond the elements of the basic physical theory to accommodate consciousness. Conscious experi-ence is already there, and it is there in a mathematically specified way that is perfectly suited to give it a central and causally efficacious role in mind/brain dynamics. Let me elaborate.

The key idea of the Copenhagen interpretation is encapsulated in two quotations:

> In our description of nature the purpose is not to disclose the real essence of phenomena but only to track down as far as possible relations between the multifold aspects of our experience (Bohr, 1934, p. 18).

> Strictly speaking, the mathematical formalism of quantum theory and electro-dynamics merely offers rules of calculation for the deduction of expectations pertaining to observations obtained under well-defined conditions specified by classical physical concepts (Bohr, 1958/1963, p. 60; see also Stapp, 1993).

Bohr is emphasizing here that science, in the end, has to do with correlations among our experiences: that our experiences are the ultimate data that science must explain. Hence one can renounce the classical ideal of giving a mathematical description of the objective world itself in favour of constructing a set of mathematical rules that allow us to compute expectations pertaining to certain kinds of experiences. Thus, in contrast to classical mechanics, human experiences occupy a basic primitive place in quantum mechanics: the theory is basically 'about' experiences, even though the mathematical formulation of the 'rules of calculation' pertaining to these experiences is based on a quantum mechanical generalization of certain of the 'matter-like' properties that occur in classical mechanics. The crucial point here is that quantum theory has a larger base of primitives than classical mechanics, and this base includes experiences (cf. Stapp, 1972). The Copenhagen approach is essentially dualistic because the two things that it deals with are, on the one hand, our *experiences* (of a certain special type, namely classically describable perceptions) and, on the other hand, a set of mathematical rules that allow us to compute expectations pertaining to these experiences. These rules are expressed in terms of a generalization of the mathematical structure that occurred in classical mechanics, and which represented, in that idealization, the 'objective world of particles and fields'.

Bohr's pragmatic approach was revolutionary in its day, and was opposed by some of the most prestigious scientists of that time. In Einstein's opinion: 'Physics is an attempt conceptually to grasp reality as it is thought independently of its being observed' (Einstein, 1951, p. 81).

This attitude of Einstein, and of many other scientists, seems so reasonable that one must ask why top scientists interested in atomic physics, which seems so far removed from psychology, should bring 'our experiences' into atomic physics, and why that move should be accepted by the scientific community as the correct way of comprehending atomic phenomena, and why physical theory did not thereby become devoid of objective content.

The answers rest on two points. The first is that the Copenhagen claim is not that physical theory is about *all* of our experiences: it was claimed that physical theory is about what can be called, for purposes of easy identification, our 'classically describable' perceptions of the world about us. The phrase 'world about us' is meant to describe only how we refer to these experiences, not to specify any particular ontological commitment. The phrase 'classically describable' is connected to the fact that visible objects normally appear to us to have a reasonably well defined location: a billiard ball does not appear to us to be, simultaneosly, both at one end of a billiards table and also at the other end. The second point is that the basic equation of quantum mechanics, the Schrödinger equation, applied universally, necessarily leads, in some easily arranged situations, to states in which the state of the billiard ball has one part that is localized at one end of the table and another part that is localized at the other end of the table.

The founders of quantum theory resolved this contradiction between the form of the quantum state and the form of our experience by postulating that the quantum state represents not the full reality itself, but rather the probabilities for, or tendencies for, our perceptions to be various possible specified perceptions. In this formulation, the experience of the observer becomes what the theory is 'about', and this experience enters in a fundamental way, because it is only by bringing these experiences, and their *de facto* classicality, explicitly into the overall theory that the theory is able to account for the classicality that we always observe, but which the quantum mechanical equation of motion neither entails nor (generally) allows.

The key point, in the context of the mind–brain problem, is that this most orthodox interpretation of quantum theory brings the experiences of the human observers into the basic physical theory on at least a co-equal basis with the 'physical' or 'matter-like' aspects of the description: the matter-like aspects give only half of the dynamical and ontological story.

Under the pressure of diverse goals (e.g. to expand the scope of the theory to include cosmological systems) a number of 'ontological formulations' of quantum theory have been created. They attempt to give a rationally coherent description of (what at least could be) the world itself, not just a set of rules that allow us to form expectations about our future experiences. An underlying aim of most of these alternative interpretations is to avoid the explicit occurrence in the theory of the experiences of observers. But all of these interpretation are dualistic in that they have two kinds of entities that obey different, though intertwined, dynamical laws. One of these two parts is the 'wave funtion'. This part is the quantum analogue of the 'matter' of classical mechanics, in the sense that it normally evolves in accordance with a local deterministic equation of motion that is the quantum analogue of the corresponding classical equation of motion. The other part is associated with mind, in the sense that it 'picks out' from an amorphous mass of potentialities, represented by the first part, a sequence of particular actual experiences of the kind we actually experience.

It will be useful to give a brief description of these alternative formulations, emphasizing these two aspects. This will pave the way to an understanding of a quantum theory of the mind–brain proposed in Stapp (1993) and elaborated upon here. I shall spend what may seem like a inordinate amount of time on the model of David Bohm: this is because I shall treat all the other proposals by contrasting them with Bohm's.

The simplest quantum ontology is that of David Bohm (1952; Bohm &Hiley, 1993). In the orthodox (Bohr) theory one spoke of the complementary 'particlelike' and 'wavelike' aspects of a quantum system. That was confusing because particles stay confined to tiny regions while waves spread out: the two concepts contradict each other, physically. This is what forced Bohr into his epistemological stance, and his idea of 'complementarity'.

For a world consisting of a single quantum entity Bohm's model would have both *a particle* and *a wave*: the particle rides like a surfer on the wave. One easily sees how the puzzling double-slit experiment is explained by this model: the wave goes through both slits and influences the motion of the particle, which goes through just one slit. This model is dualistic in the sense of having both a particle and a wave. But this dualism is basically a mind–matter dualism, because the function of the 'particle', or more specifically its generalization to the many-particle universe, is basically to specify what *our experiences* will be. There is a huge gap in quantum theory between the information contained in the 'wave' and the information contained in our experience. The purpose of, and need for, the particle, and its generalization to the many-particle universe, is basically to supply the information — not contained in the wave (function) — that specifies *which one* of the many mutually incompatible experiences allowed by quantum theory the observer actually has. If there were no need to describe the *experiential* aspects of reality, which are very different in character from what the deterministically evolving wave (function) describes, there would be no need for the 'particle-part' of Bohm's ontology. The critical assumption in Bohm's model is precisely the assumption that even though the 'wave' (i.e. wave function of the universe) might describe a superposition of many different brains of some one particular scientist, say Joe Smith, and although each these different superposed 'brains' would correspond to Joe's perceiving a different result of some experiment that he is performing, nevertheless, only one of these brains will actually be illuminated by the light of consciousness, and this particular brain — the one that possesses consciousness — is picked out from the host of possibilities by the 'particle' aspect of the theory: in Bohm's theory the contents of our consciousness is determined by what the 'particle' part of the universe is doing, not the wave part, and, in fact, the only reason to bring in this particle part is, first, to account for the empirical fact that we 'experience' only one of the branches of the wave, and, second, to determine which branch this is.

To explain how this (and also the other models) work, I shall often use the term 'branches of the wave (function)'. To visualize these branches, imagine a large pond with an initially smooth surface (no waves). A source of waves is placed at the center, but is surrounded by a barrier that has some gaps. These gaps allow ripples to spread out only along certain beam-like regions, with most of the surface of the pond remaining smooth. These well separated beam-like regions of propagating ripples I call 'branches', or 'branches of the wave (function)'.

The surface of a pond is only two dimensional. But the quantum-mechanical wave that corresponds to a universe consisting of **N** particles would be a wave in a **3N**-dimensional space. The 'branches of the wave (function)' will typically be relatively narrow beams of waves in this **3N**-dimensional space, and each beam will correspond, in a typical measurement situation, to some particular 'classically describable' result of the measurement. For example, one beam may describe, at some late stage, a particle detector having detected a particle; *and* a corresponding pointer having swung to the right as a consequence of the detector's having detected the particle; *and* the eye and the low-level processing parts of the brain responding to the light signal from the pointer in the swung-to-the-right position; *and* the top-level neural activity that corresponds to the observer's perceiving the pointer in the swung-to-the-right position: the other branch would describe the particle detector's having failed to detect the particle; *and* the pointer remaining in the centre position; *and* the eye and low-level processing parts of the brain responding to the light signals coming from the pointer in the centre position; *and* the top-level neural activity corresponding to the observer's perceiving the pointer in the center position. The fact that *both* branches of the wave are present simultaneously is not surprising once one recognizes that the wave represents essentially only a *probability for an experience to occur*: there is, in a typical measurement, a possibility for each of several possible experiential results to occur, and the probability function (or wave function) must therefore have a 'branch' corresponding to each possibility.

Of course, the observer, Joe Smith, will see only one of the two possibilities: he will see *either* the pointer swung-to-the-right *or* the or the pointer remaining at the centre position. To accommodate this empirical fact Bohm introduces his 'surfer' in the **3N**-dimensional space. The surfer is merely a point in the **3N**-dimensional space that move always in a direction defined by the shape of the **3N**-dimensional wave at the place where this point is, and this rule of motion for the surfer ensures that the surfer will end up in one branch or another, not in the intervening 'still' part of the **3N**-dimensional space. Each branch corresponds to one of the possible experiences. If the 'surfer' (which is just the moving point in the **3N**-dimensional space) ends up in the branch that corresponds to the experience 'I see the pointer in the swung-right position' then, according to Bohm's theory, this perception of the pointer 'swung-to-the-right' is the experience that actually occurs: only the single branch in which the surfer ends up will be 'illuminated'; all others 'remains dark'. Bohm's rules for the motion of the surfer ensure that if the various possible initial conditions for the surfer are assigned appropriate 'statistical weights' then the statistical predictions of his theory about what observers will experiences will agree with the those given by the orthodox (Bohr) rules. In this way Bohm's causal model reproduces the quantum statistical predictions about what our experiences will be.

The two parts of Bohm's ontology, namely the wave in the **3N**-dimensional space and the 'surfer', can both be considered 'material', yet they are essentially different because the waves describe all the possibilities for what our actual experiences might be, and therefore has a beingness that is essentially 'potential', whereas the trajectory of the surfer specifies the actual choice from among the various alternative possibilities, and therefore has a beingness that represents 'actuality' rather than mere 'potentiality': the wave generates all the *possible* experiences, whereas the trajectory defined by the surfer specifies which one of these possible experiences actually occurs.

Bohm's model is very useful, but as a model of reality it has several unattractive features. The first is the 'empty branches': once two branches separate they generally move further and further apart in the **3N**-dimensional space, and hence if the 'surfer' gets in one branch then all of the alternative ones become completely irrelevant to the evolution of experience: the huge set of empty branches continues to evolve for all of eternity, but has no effect upon anyone's experience.

A more parsimonious ontological theory, not having these superfluous empty branches, was described by Heisenberg (1958, ch. 3). It also involves a reality consisting of two kinds of things. His two kinds of things are 'actual events', and 'objective tendencies for those events to occur'. The objective tendencies can be taken to be represented by the wave on the **3N**-dimensional pond, and the actual events can be represented by sudden or abrupt changes in this wave. Each such change 'collapses the wave' to one of its branches. Thus Bohm's 'surfer', which specifies a *choice* between branches, is replaced by an 'actual event', which also specifies a choice between branches. But whereas Bohm's surfer has no back-reaction on the wave, each of Heisenberg's actual events obliterates all branches but one. The big problem with Heisenberg's theory is to find a reasonable criterion for the occurrence of these actual events.

Wigner (1961) and von Neumann (1932/1955, ch. 6), noting that there is nothing in the purely material aspect of nature that singles out where the actual events occur, suggest that these events should occur at the points where consciousness enters: i.e. in conjunction with conscious events. This theory can be regarded as the 'ontologicalization' of the Copenhagen interpretation, in the sense that the change of the state that occurs when a perception generates new knowledge is basically subjective in the Copenhagen interpretation, but is interpreted as an objective change in the Wigner–von Neumann interpretation used here. This ontology is the most parsimonious possibility: all of the verified predictions of quantum theory can be reproduced by limiting the actual events to brain events that correspond to experiential events.

An argument based on survival of the species (Stapp, 1995) provides support for the idea that actual events occurring in human brains will tend to occur at the brain-wide level of activity that corresponds to conscious events, rather than at some microscopic (e.g. molecular, or individual-neuron) level. This Wigner–von Neumann version of Heisenberg's theory will be discussed presently in some detail. But first a few remarks about the final major interpretation are needed.

In the Everett many-minds theory the basic quantum mechanical equation of motion, the Schrödinger equation, holds uniformly: there are no sudden collapses of the wave function; all branches continue to exist. Moreover, it is assumed that, because all of the branches exist, all of the corresponding streams of conscious must also occur.

Since the various branches propagate into different parts of the $3N$-dimensional space they will evolve independently of each other: the physical 'memory banks', associated with one branch will not affect, or be affected by, the brain activities specified by another branch. Hence each different branches can be considered to define a different 'self', or 'psyche', with each of these selves continually dividing into different extentions of itself into the future.

At first sight this idea seems to allow the whole theory to be reduced to just one entity, the evolving wave, with the different psychological persons being just 'aspects' of corresponding brain activities on different branches. But that is not correct. The branches of the wave function appear as parts of a *conjunction* of branches: all branches on the 'pond' exist simultaneously, even though they evolve independently. But the predictions of quantum theory are an essential part of the theory, and these statistical predictions pertain to experiences that are 'this experience' *or* 'that experience', not 'this experience' *and* 'that experience'. To speak of probabilities one needs something with an *or* character: something that can become associated with *either* this branch *or* that branch, not both simultaneously. Just as the different branches of a wave on a pond are conjunctively present and hence do not, by themselves, provide any ontological basis for assigning different probabilities to these simultaneously present things, so also is the quantum wave, by itself, insufficient for this task.

In Bohm's theory this extra element of the theory was the 'surfer', which determined the experiences of the observers; in Heisenberg's theory the extra things were the actual events, which also determined the experiences of the observers. In the Everett interpretation the only existing things besides the waves are our experiences, and there is supposed to be a separate experience associated with each branch. Thus we end up again with a dualistic theory; with a world that is composed of the one 'material' universe represented by the wave function, which evolves always according to the the Schrödinger equation, plus, for each named person, an great profusion of many minds, or streams of consciousness: the stream of consciousness of Joe Smith must be continually splitting into different separate branches, with at least one for each of the perceptibly different results of any experiment that he performs. Consequently, the proponents of the theory need to develop, in order to complete this interpretation, some coherent dualistic ontology involving, for each of us, a profusion of branching minds, each known only to itself, and a theory that assigns to each of these 'independent' (but generally overlapping) branches a well defined 'subjective probability to occur', even though these branches all occur together in the full 'objective' description of reality. In summary, all the major ontological interpretations of quantum theory are dualistic, in the sense that they have one aspect or component that can be naturally identified as the quantum analogue of the *matter* of classical mechanics, and a second aspect that is associated with *choices* from among the possible *experiences*. All interpretations are, in this sense, basically similar to the Wigner–von Neumann interpretation to be explored here, but are less parsimonious, in that they involve either existing but unobserved branches (Bohm), or existing but unobserved actual events (Heisenberg), or existing but inaccessible and unverifiable other branches of reality (Everett, 1957).

II: A Quantum Model of the Mind–Brain

The main features of the mind–brain theory proposed in Stapp (1993) are briefly described in the following fourteen points:

1. Facilitation
The pattern of neurological activity associated with any occurring conscious thought is 'facilitated', in the sense that the activation of this pattern causes certain physical changes in the brain structure, and these changes *facilitate* subsequent activations of this pattern.

2. Associative recall
The facilitation of patterns mentioned above is such that the excitation of a part of a facilitated pattern has a tendency to excite the whole. Thus the sight of an ear tends to activate the pattern of brain activity associated with a previously seen face of which this ear was a part.

3. Body–world schema
The physical body of the person in its environment is represented within the brain by certain patterns of neural and other brain activity. Each such pattern has *components*, which are sub-patterns that represent various parts or aspects of the body and its environment, and these components are normally patterns of brain activity that have been facilitated in conjunction with earlier experiences.

4. Executive-level template for action
A main task of the alert brain at each moment is to construct a template for the impending action of the organism. This template is formed from patterns of neural and brain activity that, taken together, represent a coordinated plan of action for the organism. This representation is implemented in the brain by means of an automatic causal spreading of neural excitations from the executive level to the rest of the nervous system. This subsequent activity of the nervous system causes both motor responses and lower-level neural responses.

The executive-level templates are based on the body–world schema, in the following sense. There are two kinds of templated actions: attentions and intentions. Attentions *up date* the body–world schema: they bring the brain's representation of the body in its environment up to date. Intentions are formulated in terms of a *projected* (into the future) body–world schema: they are expressed in terms of an image of how the body in its environment is intended to be at a slightly future time. (Thus, for example, the tennis player imagines how he will strike the ball, or where the ball he is about to hit will land in his opponent's court).

5. Beliefs and other generalizations

The simple body–world schema, with attentional and intentional templated actions, is the primitive level of brain action: it gives the general format. However 'beliefs' can be added to the landscape. Also, each templated action has both intentional and attentional aspects.

6. Quantum theory

The features mentioned above are key elements of this theory. But they are aspects that hold at the level corresponding to a particular classically described 'branch'. But classical mechanics cannot account for the essential properties of the materials (such as tissues and membranes) from which the brain is made. Hence, an adequate basic theory of nature must show how the classically describable aspects of nature that seem important, and that we seem to experience, arise in rational way from the quantum underpinning.

7. Superposition of templates

An analysis (Stapp, 1993, 1996) of processes occurring in synapses shows that if there were no quantum collapses occurring in brains then a brain evolving according to the quantum laws *must* evolve, in general, into a state that contains a superposition of different 'branches', with each of these branches specifying the template for a different macroscopic action. Each of these different templates for action will evolve into a different response of the nervous system, and consequently into a difference macroscopic response of the organism. Thus without collapses the body/brain would evolve into a superposition of macroscopically distinguishable possibilities, just as a measuring device normally does.

8. The reduction postulate

Following the Wigner-von-Neumann approach, I postulate that the quantum collapse of the brain state occurs at the high level of the template for action. The (Heisenberg-picture) state (of the universe) undergoes the collapse

$$\Psi_i \rightarrow \Psi_{i+1} = P_i \Psi_i$$

where P_i is a projection operator that acts on appropriate macroscopic variables associated with the brain. It picks out and saves, or 'actualizes', *one* of the alternative possible templates for action, and eradicates all others. The organism will then proceed to evolve automatically in accordance with this one particular plan of action, rather than evolving (à la Everett) into a superposition of states corresponding to *all* of the different possible macroscopically distinguishable courses of action that were formerly available to it. Thus the 'quantum event', or 'collapse of the wave function', *selects* or *chooses* one of the alternative possible coherent plans of action — previously generated by the purely mechanical functioning of the brain — by actualizing the executive-level pattern of brain activity that constitutes *one* of the alternative possible templates for action.

This collapse of the wave function is to be understood not as some anomalous failure of the laws of nature, but rather as a natural consequence of the fact that wave function does not represent actuality itself, but rather, in line with the ideas of Heisenberg, merely 'objective tendencies' for the next actual event.

Each such event is represented, within the Hilbert space description, as a sudden shift in the wave function, or state Ψ_i, to a new form that incorporates the conditions or requirements imposed by the new actual event.

These 'collapse' events in the Hilbert space are not introduced willy-nilly: they are needed to block what will otherwise automatically occur, namely the evolution of the wave function to a form that directly contradicts collective human experience: all of us who see the pointer agree that the pointer does not both swing to the right *and* also remain motionless. Under the conditions of the measurement it does one thing *or* the other, and all of us who witness what it does, and are able communicate our findings to each other, agree about which one of these two possible things actually occurs.

9. The psycho-physical postulate

Adhering to the Wigner–von Neumann approach, I postulate that the physical brain event, namely the collapse of the wave function to the branch that specifies one particular template for action, is the brain correlate of a corresponding psychological or experiential event. Thus the occurrence or emergence of the psychological command 'raise the arm' is represented in the physical description of nature by the occurrence or emergence of the physical command 'raise the arm'. The causal relationship is discussed in point 15.

Attending is a special kind intending: the intention, in the case of attending, is to up-date the body–world schema.

Notice an important difference between the context in which the Wigner–von Neumann idea is applied here, and the context in which they themselves applied it. They were considering a large system consisting of some atomic system plus a device that measures some property of that system plus the human observer's body and, finally, his brain. In that context the collapse at the level of the observer's consciousness determined the outcome of the earlier distant experiment on the atomic system. I am focussing, however, on the mind–brain system itself, and the role of the collapse event in determining principally the internal dynamics of this system. This role is more in line with what seems, intuitively, to be the role of conscious. For the present purpose one may assume that collapses occur already at the level of all quantum devices, so that the principal effect of the conscious event is then to determine only the internal dynamics of the brain, not the results of any measurements performed externally to the brain.

10. The efficacy of consciousness

In this model the choices associated with conscious events are dynamically efficacious: each such event *effects* a decision between different templates for action, and these different templates for action lead on to different distingushable responses of the organism.

11. Consciousness and survival

It is often thought that consciousness emerges because it aids survival. For this to be so consciousness must be efficacious. Yet in the Bohm and Everett models (just as in classical physics) consciousness is not efficacious: all behaviour is completely determined with no mention of any causal role for consciousness. Consciousness would be nonefficacious also in the Heisenberg model if we did not follow Wigner–von Neumann in associating actualizing events with conscious events. (The survival issue is addressed in Stapp, 1996.)

12. Conscious events and unconscious processing

The general temporal development in the brain proceeds by periods of unconscious processing punctuated by conscious events. A conscious event actualizes a template for action that, by the automatic spreading of top-level neural activity to the rest of the nervous system, controls:

1) motor action,
2) the collection of new information (including the monitoring of ongoing processes), and
3) the formation of the next template for action.

13. Overall picture

Classically only a single 'next template' would be formed. This could be achieved either by the formation of a resonant state that sucks energy from competing possibilities, or by inhibitory signals, or by dropping into the well of an attractor. But in any of these cases the quantum uncertainties entail that the quantum brain will, if no collapse occurs, necessarily evolve into a superposition of branches corresponding to the different alternative possible classical templates for action. One of these virtual templates for action will then emerge as the actual one, and the automatic (unconscious) neural processes will proceed to carry out the instructions encoded in the template. Thus there is an alternation between discrete conscious events and periods of unconscious activity controlled by the local deterministic laws. Each of the discrete events chooses from among the alternative possible allowed templates for action generated by the automatic action of the local deterministic laws of quantum mecanics, and hence between the different associated macroscopic responses of the organism.

14. The generality of psycho-physical connection

My focus above has been on the human mind–brain system, and on the interplay between the experiential and physical aspects of nature in this particular system, for which we have both verbal reports and personal knowledge pertaining to the form and content of the experiential aspect. These special characteristics make the human mind–brain unique as a subject of scientific study by human scientists. However, it is unreasonable to suppose that events of this kind are confined to human beings. This suggests, therefore, that there is in nature a general 'second process' that includes as a special case the one that is needed, according to (Wigner–von Neumann) ontologicalization of the Copenhagen interpretation, to bring the quantum process into accord with human experience. In line with the ideas of Wigner and von Neumann, each such event in nature is assumed to be an 'experiential reality' with physical ramifications. But the specific qualities of the experiences associated with different systems can be vastly different from human conscious experiences, although all are considered to belong to the same ontological category.

To support this suggestion of a universal connection of collapse events to experience I note, first of all, that, as Arthur Eddington observed, the quantum world is more like a 'giant mind' than like the 'giant machine' described by classical mechanics. For, the evolving state vector represents not 'substance', but rather a 'probability' for something to happen, and probability is normally considered to be a subjective or mental sort of thing, not a material reality. The second part of the quantum reality is the 'actual' event, which Heisenberg contrasts with the 'potentia' from which the event arises. The 'actual' specifies what is able to be experienced: only the actualized branches can be experienced. This connection of the actual to experience is tightened by the Wigner–von Neumann proposal, which is essentially to *identify* the actual with experience. This proposal is the quantum analogue of the dictum *esse est percipi*: to be is to be perceived.

Technically there is a specific need for a tie-in of the actualization event with features characteristic of experience. This tie-in has two aspects. The first is that the actualization singles out a 'classically describable' structure. This is a feature of experience that is not inherently present in the physical aspect of nature represented by the (Schrödinger-directed) evolving wave (function). The great and essential move of the Copenhagen interpretation was precisely to realize that although no classical aspect naturally pops out from the quantum physical reality, represented by the normally evolving wave, (certain of) our experiences are, in fact, classically describable, and hence the empirically observed classical aspect of nature can be brought consistently into physical theory by introducing our (classically describable) experiences, per se, directly into the theory as the very thing that the theory is about. The whole history of efforts to go beyond the Copenhagen interpretation is essentially the history of attempts to find some *other* rationally coherent way of explaining why our perceptions of the quantum universe are classically describable. The present suggestion is essentially to accept, following the Copenhagen approach, that this classical aspect does not come from the physical side of nature, but comes instead from the experiential side. This makes the experiential aspect of the actualization events the *cause* of the classical character of the collapse events, which otherwise appears to have no natural explanation.

15. Causation

This reference to 'cause' raises the general question of the cause of both the occurrence of the actualizations and of the form (e.g. the classical form) of the actualizations. Much can be said without delving into the question of the cause of the event. Indeed, all of contemporary quantum mechanics is covered without delving into that question, by just accepting the statistical rules as 'given': then the cause of the events is effectively 'pure chance'.

This occurrence of pure chance is quite acceptable in an admittedly pragmatic interpretation of quantum theory, such as the Copenhagen interpretation. But it is not acceptable, I think, in an account that represents itself as ontological, i.e. as a putative description of reality itself. Thus if one wishes, in an ontological context, to discuss the 'cause' of the occurrence of an actual event then *something* is needed to replace the 'irrational' — that's

Pauli's word for it — element of pure chance: to embark upon an ontological discussion of the 'cause' of the actualizations entails assuming that the element of 'pure chance' that occurs in contemporary quantum theory is merely a mask for our ignorance of the true cause, which must necessarily be highly nonlocal (Mermin, 1994; Stapp, 1993, pp. 5–9; 1994).

The part of the dynamics that is matter-like is represented by the Schrödinger (directed) evolution, which is the contrary of the collapses. This fact, together with the general mind-like quality of the quantum world mentioned above, suggests that the cause of the actualizations must come from the experiential aspect of things.

The orthodox (Copenhagen) interpretation is based on the fact that certain features of the quantum state can be regarded as a superposition of states that represent different possible experiences. This connection becomes more direct when the quantum system in question is the brain itself. The process of selection of the actual experiential state from the superposition of possible ones must, of course, depend upon this decomposition into the possible experiential states. So the decomposition of the Hilbert space state vector into the possible experiential components must play a central role in the dynamical processes, at least if one accepts the naturalistic hypothesis that the possible experiences are represented in the same mathematical structure that represents the matter-like aspects of nature. This suggests that the selection process is essentially a competition among the experiential possibilities, with the winner becoming the actual experience, which is the reality whose coming into being is represented by the transition to the new quantum state.

This conception of the process of selecting the actualized state entails that the experiential aspect of the actualization event is, effectively, the cause of this event, in the sense that this experience, in its potential form, has raised itself above its competitors to become the actual experience: each actualization is a self-actualization.

In this conception, the experienced reality is the coming into being of a psychologically felt command: 'Do X!' This experiential reality, in its potential form, is represented (or embodied) in Hilbert space, and the coming into actual being of this representation (or embodiment) constitutes a coming into actual being of both the psychologically felt command 'Do X!' and the physically implemented command: 'Do X!'. This connection is somewhat like a dual-aspect theory, but now in the context of a physical theory that properly accounts for *all* brain processes, and that, following the ideas of the quantum physicists Bohr, Heisenberg, von Neumann, Wigner, and others, incorporates human experience into the basic fabric of physical theory in order fulfill the scientific demand for a closed rational account of physical phenomena.

III: Person and Self

According to William James:

> Such a discrete composition is what actually obtains in our perceptual experience. We either perceive nothing, or something that is already there in a sensible amount. This fact is what is known in psychology as the law of the 'threshold'. Either your experience is of no content, of no change, or it is of a perceptible amount of content or change. Your acquaintance with reality grows literally by buds or drops of perception. Intellectually and on reflection you can divide these into components, but as immediately given they come totally or not at all (James, 1910/1987, p. 1062).

... however complex the object may be the thought of it is one undivided state of
consciousness (James, 1890/1950, p. 276).

The consciousness of Self involves a stream of thought, each part of which as 'I'
can (1) remember those that went before, and know the things they knew; and (2)
emphasize and care paramountly for certain ones among them as *'me'*, and *appropriate* to these the rest . . . This *me* is an empirical aggregate of things objectively
known. The *I* that knows them cannot itself be an aggregate. Neither for psychological purposes need it be considered to be an unchanging metaphysical entity like
the Soul, or a principle like the pure Ego, viewed as 'out of time'. It is a *Thought*,
at each moment different from that of the last moment, but *appropriative of the
latter*, together with all that the latter called its own . . . *thought is itself the thinker*,
and psychology need not look beyond . . . (James, 1890/1950, p. 401).

In line with these ideas of James, and those of the preceding section, the conception of
a 'person' that emerges here is that of a sequence of discrete psychological (i.e. experiential or conscious) events bound together by a matter-like structure, namely the
brain/body, which evolves in accordance with the local deterministic laws of quantum
mechanics. Each conscious event is a new entity that rises from the 'ashes' of the old,
which consists of the propensities for its occurrence carried by the brain/body.

A felt sense of an enduring 'self' is experienced, and hence it must, within this theory,
be explained as an aspect of the structure of the *individual* discrete conscious events. The
explanation is this: each conscious event has a 'fringe' that surrounds the central image,
and provides the background in which the central image is placed. The slowly changing
fringe contains the consciousness of the situation within which the immediate action is
taking place; the historical setting including purposes (e.g. getting some food to eat). The
sense of feeling of self is in this fringe. It is not an illusion, because the physical
brain/body is providing continuity and a reservoir of memories that can be called upon,
even though each thought is, according to this model, a separate entity. As explained by
James — see also Stapp (1993) — each thought, though itself a single entity, has
components that are sequentially ordered in a psychological time, and hence each thought
has within its own structure an aspect that corresponds to the flow of physical time.

IV: Free-Will

Our experience includes the feeling that we are 'free'. That feeling is, in some sense,
accurate. The whole organism is free to make high-level choices in which the various
perceived possible consequences enter as whole experiential units. One's fate is not
controlled exclusively by mechanical local deterministic laws, or by an avalanche of
microscopically entering chance elements that would make a mockery of the idea of
personal choice.

It might be objected that we are not free because, according to quantum theory, our
choices are determined by blind chance. That misses the point. In the first place the
choices are not blind. If the quantum events in the brain occurred at the level of the
neurons then the choices would be blind, for the consequences of each individual choice
would be screened from view by the inscrutable outcomes of billions of similar independent random choices. But the choices being made by the organism, acting as a unit,

are choices between plans for actions that have clear and distinctive consequences for the organism as a whole, in terms of its future behavior. The choice is made at the level of the organism as a whole, and the event has a distinctive 'feel' that accurately portrays its consequences for the organism as a whole. The conditioning for this event is an expression of the values and goals of the whole organism, and the choice is implemented by a unified action of the whole organism that is normally meaningful in the life of the organism. And this meaning is felt as an essential aspect of the act of choosing. The final 'random' decision between the alternative possible distinctive actions of the organism is not some wild haphazard stab in the dark, unrelated to the needs or goals of the organism. It is a choice that is governed essentially by the number of ways in which the mechanistic aspect of the organism, which has been honed to construct templates for action concordant with the needs of the organism within its environment, can come up with that particular template. Thus the choice is not like the throw of an unconditioned die. It is a carefully crafted choice that tends to be the 'optimally reasonable' choice under the conditions defined by the external inputs, and the needs and goals of the organism. Each of the alternative possible templates for a coherent and well-coordinated action of the organism emerges from the quantum soup, and is given, by the quantum mechanism, a weighting that reflects the interests of the organism as a whole, within the context in which he finds himself. The choice is conditioned by these personally moulded weights, and therefore tends to be a decision that is optimally reasonable from the point of view of the organism. This arrangement avoids both the Scylla of a fate sealed at the birth of the universe by a microscopically controlled blind mechanism, and also the Charybdis of a haphazard wild chance that operates at a microscopic level, and is therefore blind as regards likely consequences. The intricate interplay of chance and determinism instituted by quantum mechanics effectively frees the organism to pursue, in an optimal way, its own goals based on its own values, which have themselves been created, from a wealth of open possibilities, by its own earlier actions. Each human being, though never in full control of the situation in which he finds himself, does create both himself and his actions, through a process of a microscopically controlled deterministic evolution punctuated by organic meaningful choices that are top-down in the sense that each one is instituted by an actualization event that selects as a unit, and feels as a unit, an entire top-level plan of action.

Within the contemporary framework of quantum theory that I have been adhering to in the above three paragraphs there remains, in the end, an element of 'pure chance' that selects one of the templates for action 'randomly'. Whether this occurrence of pure chance is a permanent feature of basic physical theory, or merely a temporary excursion, no one knows. In my own opinion this occurrence of pure chance is a reflection of our state of ignorance regarding the true cause, which must in any case be nonlocal, and hence both difficult to study and quite unlike the local causes that science has dealt with up until now. In another place (Stapp, 1996) I have described in more detail the technicalities of the actualization process, and also the possibility of replacing the element of pure chance by a nonlocal causal process that makes the felt psychological subjective 'I', as it is represented within the quantum-theoretic description, rather than pure chance, the source of the decisions between one's alternative possible courses of action.

V: The Hard Problem

'The Hard Problem' is the problem of *conscious experience*: What is it? Why is it present at all? Why is it so different from the other part of Nature, namely the objective aspect of reality? Why is it personal, or subjective? Why is it so fleeting, whereas matter is permanent and conserved? Can it be 'reduced' to matter? Can any purely physical account explain it? Is the material of which the brain is made crucial, or is it only the functional aspect that is critical? Why is it so closely connected to function? How do functional aspects become ontological aspects, i.e. how does function become being? How can anything, and in particular consciousness, be added to the already closed laws of physics? Is experience a fundamental element of nature, or derivative, or emergent? What are the *bridging laws* that connect mind to matter?

Chalmers asks these questions, and says that right now we have no candidate theory that answers these questions. But we do!

Chalmers suggests that perhaps there is a small loop-hole in quantum theory that might provide an opening for consciousness. But there is not just a small loop-hole: there is a gigantic gap, which consists of *fully half of the theory*, and this hole provides an ideal home for consciousness. For, quantum dynamics consists not only of the mechanical process that is governed by the Schrödinger equation, which controls the matter-like aspect of nature, but also an entirely different 'second process', which involves a beingness of an entirely different kind. This second process is needed to bring the experiential aspect of nature into concordance with the physical part of the theory, and to specify or determine what our experiences will actually be.

The core idea of Bohr was to recognize that physics is basically about our experiences, and to introduce our experiences directly into the physical theory in order to resolve a deep problem with the theory that otherwise arose. Bohr's stance was cautious and pragmatic, and avoided ontological commitment. But von Neumann, and more unambiguously Wigner, went the next step and brought consciousness into the theory as a causal agent that actively did what needed to be done to make the theory work at the ontological level in the same way that it worked at the practical level. The ontology then included conscious experience as the co-equal partner of a more shadowy world of 'possibilities', or, in Heisenberg's terminogy, of 'objective tendencies' for transitions from the possible to the actual.

The new ontology is fundamentally different from the classical-mechanics ontology in many ways. The first is that the physical 'possibilities' acquire an ontological reality that is mathematically represented or embodied. The second is that possible conceptual/experiential realities are represented or embodied in this same structure. Thus the actualization of a conceptual/experiential possibility is simultaneously an actualization of a corresponding physical reality. In this way concept evolves into implementing functional structure in a mathematically described way.

Each actualization event has its physical side, which is just the 'collapse' of the wave function itself, and also its experiential side. In a rational causal theory the collapse must have a cause. This cause is not to be found in that physical part of the quantum ontology: considered from the purely physical standpoint the collapse seems to come from nowhere, as an unpredictable and undetermined 'bolt from the blue'. And the collapse represents merely a sudden 'change in tendencies' for a 'change in tendencies' for a 'change in tendencies' for . . . etc., etc.: there is no closure, no basic reality. For the technical reasons mentioned earlier the theory needs something that will bring 'classicality' into the dynamics, and it needs a 'cause' for the collapse, and it needs a reality to complement the 'potentia'. This missing element is not present in the physical part of the theory. It must be something that exists, and the only thing that we know exists, besides the physical part of reality, (which perhaps we do not really 'know' at all, directly) is the experiential part. This part fills the various needs perfectly, and, of course, needs to be included in a complete description of nature. So we put the two parts of nature together in the natural way that fits all these needs simultaneously.

How does this theory answer the questions, listed above, that Chalmers raised about consciousness? *What is consciousness?* It is the part of nature that: 1) complements the the background 'physical' aspect by being the reality that the quantum potentiality is the potentiality for; 2) specifies the classical character of reality that is not determined by the background physical aspect of the quantum, which represents only an amorphous potentiality, with no inherent preference for a unique and specifically classical reality; and 3) causes the physical state to collapse to a new form that incorporates the conditions specified by the new experiential new reality.

Why is consciousness present at all? Because the local-reductionistic laws of physics, regarded as a causal description of nature, are incomplete: something else is needed to cause the collapse events to occur, to inject 'classicality' into nature, and to provide the reality that the quantum state is the potentiality for.

Why is consciousness so different from the other part of Nature, namely the physical aspect of reality? The physical part of reality represents merely the possibilities for an actual experience, not the actually experienced reality itself.

Why is consciousness subjective? An actualization event has many components, all of which are integral parts of the whole. The totality contains the slowly changing fringe of the experience that constitutes the 'I', or 'psyche', which is felt as the experiencing subject and actualizer. The experiencing subject is *part of the thought*, not an outside observer of the thought: if the 'I' were not *part of the thought* then there could be in the thought no awareness of 'I' as the background relative to which the focus of the thought is the foreground. Thus it is not that the thought belongs to an 'I', but rather that an 'I' belongs to the thought.

Why is a thought so fleeting, whereas matter (energy) is conserved? Because a thought is an element in a discrete sequence of events, whereas 'matter' is the continuously evolving 'potentia' for such an event to occur.

Can consciousness be 'reduced' to matter? 'Matter' is the ground from which the experiential event springs: the whole process is represented in the Hilbert space in which the quantum analogue of matter is represented. But rising out of the matter-like aspects of nature lies another dynamics governed by the experiential aspects of nature.

Can any purely physical account explain it? That depends on what 'physical' means. The account given here is physical in that it is rooted in quantum mechanical description of nature. But there is something decidedly unphysical about the idea of 'pure chance'. The present account allows the orthodox (?) idea that pure chance is an essential part of nature's process to be replaced by the more 'physical' idea that the collapse process, which is needed to bring the quantum mechanical representation of the physical world into concordance with our experience of it, is a causal process that is representable in the Hilbert space of quantum theory. This proposal is based on the fact (which is the key element upon which the orthodox Copenhagen interpretation is based) that certain aspects of the quantum mechanical superposition of the physical possibilities can be interpreted also as a superposition of experiential possibilities. The dynamics that controls the emergence of one experienced reality from the superposed comglomerate must, of course, depend upon the set possible experiential realities.

Is the material of which the brain is made crucial, or is it only the functional aspect that is critical? Neither! What is important is the presence in the physical substrate of potentialities for quantum actualizations of experiential structures.

Why is consciousness so closely connected to function? Because the event is an actualization of a template for action. The biological reason for this link of actualization to function is undoubtedly the survival advantage it confers (Stapp, 1996).

How do functional aspects become ontological aspects? The actualization events actualize functional structures.

How can consciousness be added to the already closed laws of physics? Nothing efficacious could be added if the laws were already complete! But the quantum laws are grossly incomplete before consciousness, or some stand-in for consciousness, is added.

Is experience a fundamental element of nature, or is it derivative, or emergent? It is fundamental because the fundamental realities are experiential. On the other hand, the particular sort of consciousness that we human beings experience is emergent, because it represents a highly evolved form of the general ontological type. The complexity of a human experience is a consequence of the complexity of the body/brain that supports the physical activity. The complexity of the physical carrier has undoubtedly co-evolved with the complexity of the associated experiential reality.

What are the bridging laws that connect mind to matter? They have been described here.[*]

References

Bohm, David (1952), 'A suggested interpretation of the quantum theory in terms of hidden variables' I and II, *Phys. Rev.*, **85**, pp. 166–93.
Bohm, David and Hiley, Basil (1993), *The Undivided Universe: An Ontological Interpretation of Quantum Theory* (London: Routledge).
Bohr, Niels (1934), *Atomic Physics and Human Knowledge* (Cambridge: CUP).
Bohr, Niels (1958/1963), *Essays 1958/1962 on Atomic Physics and Human Knowledge* (New York: Wiley).
Einstein, Albert (1951), *Albert Einstein: Philosopher-Scientist*, ed. P.A. Schilpp (New York: Tudor).
Everett III, Hugh (1957), 'Relative state formulation of quantum mechanics', *Rev. of Mod. Phys.*, **29**, pp. 454–62.
Heisenberg, Werner (1958), *Physics and Philosophy* (New York: Harper and Row).
James, William (1890/1950), *The Principles of Psychology*, Vol. 1 (New York: Dover).
James, William (1910), *William James: Writings 1902-1910* (New York: The Library of America, Viking, 1987).

[*] **Acknowledgements:** This paper has greatly benefited from useful correspondences with David Chalmers, Gordon Globus, Jonathan Shear and Aaron Sloman.

Mermin, N. David (1994), 'Quantum mysteries refined', *American Journal of Physics*, **62**, pp. 880–7.

Stapp, Henry P. (1972), 'The Copenhagen Interpretation', *Amer. J. Phys.*, **40**, pp. 1089–116; reprinted in Stapp (1993).

Stapp, Henry P. (1993), *Mind, Matter, and Quantum Mechanics*, (Springer-Verlag, Heidelberg, Berlin, New York). Chapter 6: A Quantum Theory of the Mind-Brain Interface LBL-28574 (1990)\\ http://www-physics.lbl.gov/~stapp/stappfiles.html

Stapp, Henry P. (1994), 'Strong versions of Bell's Theorem', *Phys. Rev.*, **A49**, 3182–7.

Stapp, Henry P. (1995), 'Quantum mechanical coherence, resonance, and mind', To appear in the Proceedings of the Norbert Wiener Centenary Congress (ed. V. Mandrekar and P.R. Masini) to be published in the American Mathematical Society series *Proceedings of Symposia in Applied Mathematics* (PSAPM). Lawrence Berkeley Laboratory Report LBL-36915mod. http://www-physics.lbl.gov/~stapp/stappfiles.html

Stapp, Henry P. (1996), 'Chance, choice, and consciousness: A causal quantum theory of the mind/brain', LBL-39744mod, (Tucson II) http://www-physics.lbl.gov/~stapp/stappfiles.html

von Neumann, John (1932/1955), *Mathematical Foundations of Quantum Mechanics*, (Princeton: Princeton University Press).

Wigner, Eugene (1961), 'Remarks on the mind–body problem', in *The Scientist Speculates*, ed. I.J. Good (London: Heineman).

Douglas J. Bilodeau

Physics, Machines and the Hard Problem

I: The Physical Substrate

In his paper 'Facing up to the problem of consciousness', David Chalmers presents compelling arguments for the logical independence of the phenomenal mind from purely physical concepts. However, I think his arguments are weakened and deeper truths obscured by an oversimplified concept of the physical, which is even more apparent in the fuller discussion given in his book *The Conscious Mind*, (Chalmers, 1996). He appeals constantly to 'the rock-bottom microphysical facts and laws, which have to be taken as fundamental' (1996, p. 88). It is taken for granted that there is a set of all physical facts which is unproblematic and accessible in principle — at least until the last chapter on quantum mechanics (all interpretations of which, he admits, are a little 'crazy').

If the foundations of physics are so controversial that no agreement can be reached on the meaning of physical concepts, then physics is hardly suitable as a basis for a discussion of the ontology of mind at all. I will be bold enough to claim, however, that much of the controversy is based on a misconception, and that if we take as our guide quantum physics as it is practised along with some interpretive principles which at one time were considered normative and proceed with a little courage, we will arrive at a richer conception of reality in which mental and physical properties coexist in a more natural way. To this end, I will have to develop some basic physical concepts in depth. I believe it is especially appropriate to do so in the context of a discussion of the hard problem. Within the scope of physics proper, the problems are generally straightforward enough that deeper questions can be neglected. Even in quantum theory, there are many ways to accommodate oneself to the paradoxes for practical purposes. But the question of how phenomenal consciousness could 'arise from' a physical object demands the greatest rigour in our conceptions of both mind and matter.

II: The Crisis of Objectivity

The modern idea that the world is made of 'inanimate' matter (the presumption which makes the hard problem hard) arose from a convenient distinction which solidified into an axiom. Descartes' famous dualism is now notorious for having grafted a dubious ghost onto the machine we think we know the world to be. But, of course, his aim was not to

This paper was originally published in the *Journal of Consciousness Studies*, **3**, No.5/6 (1996), pp. 386–401.

join the objective with the subjective, but to separate them as far as was reasonably possible. He did this by affirming the physical world to be purely geometric. All its components were characterized completely by properties of extension and nothing else. Physical analysis could then proceed with the familiar and powerful methods of geometry, unimpeded by consideration of possible occult (i.e. non-geometrical) properties.

The passion for physics is intimately tied to a love of geometry. Geometric reasoning seems to flower naturally in the human mind (as Plato thought). Its methods are powerful and its truths convincing and satisfying, so that ancient philosophers thought the highest bliss was to contemplate them for eternity. Perhaps to most people the prestige of science is based on the power of technology, but to most physicists, I think, it is the exhilaration of that time in the seventeenth century when the concept of the world as geometric was established and it appeared that the fundamental order of the world was laid open to reason. It is important to appreciate that exhilaration at the root of physics, because this paper is largely about the limitations of the geometric concept of the physical and how the natural (and partly unconscious) resistance to accepting those limitations has clouded our understanding of the picture of reality conveyed by modern science.

As physics has developed, it has been necessary to include concepts which are non-geometric in the Cartesian sense. A well-known example is the difficulty of formulating a mechanical description of the electromagnetic field (i.e. describing the 'aether' in terms of the motions of particles), and the eventual abandonment of mechanical models and reliance on field concepts as fundamental. Maxwell's equations (in the compact form made familiar by Heaviside) along with the Lorentz force law both defined the fields and expressed their properties.

When quantum mechanics (henceforth QM) appeared in the 1920's, the theory was defended and explained in terms borrowed from that earlier controversy: the atom could not be understood in terms of 'models' or 'mental pictures'. Only the abstract mathematical description could give a rigorous account of atomic events free from paradox and contradiction.

The parallel drawn between these two developments in physics obscured the real novelty of QM. Even though Maxwell's theory may have parted with the strictly Cartesian programme of attributing all physical properties to spatial extension, the most crucial aspect of the Cartesian view of physics was preserved. Physics was still a realm populated entirely by mathematical abstractions which could be defined and described axiomatically (at least in principle, it was thought) without explicit reference to experience. Since the field could stand on its own as a mathematical entity, there was no threat in electromagnetic theory to the Cartesian split between objective and subjective.

QM does pose such a threat, as Bohr was entirely aware:

> It has been my desire to emphasize as strongly as possible how profoundly the new knowledge has shaken the foundations underlying the building up of concepts, on which not only the classical description of physics rests but also all our ordinary mode of thinking. ('Physical science and the problem of life', first published 1957, reprinted in Bohr, 1958.)

While in the mechanical conception of nature, the subject–object distinction was fixed, room is provided for a wider description through the recognition that the consequent use of our concepts requires different placings of such a separation. ('Atoms and human knowledge', first published 1955, reprinted in Bohr, 1958.)

A close connection exists between the failure of our forms of perception, which is founded on the impossibility of a strict separation of phenomena and means of observation, and the general limits of man's capacity to create concepts, which have their roots in our differentiation between subject and object. . . . For describing our mental activity, we require, on the one hand, an objectively given content to be placed in opposition to a perceiving subject, while, on the other hand, as is already implied in such an assertion, no sharp separation between subject and object can be maintained, since the perceiving subject also belongs to our mental content. From these circumstances follows not only the relative meaning of every concept, or rather of every word, the meaning depending upon our arbitrary choice of view point, but also that we must, in general, be prepared to accept the fact that a complete elucidation of one and the same object may require diverse points of view which defy a unique description. Indeed, strictly speaking, the conscious analysis of any concept stands in a relation of exclusion to its immediate application.[1] ('The quantum of action and the description of nature', first published 1929, reprinted in Bohr, 1961.)

The physics community happily adopted Bohr's language as a pragmatic convention for containing the conceptual difficulties, while applied QM was proving enormously successful in atomic and nuclear physics, astrophysics, and the theory of solids. Text-books gave at least a deferential nod to 'the role of the observer' and 'the distinction between the quantum system and the measuring apparatus'. But, though this much of Bohr's thought became canonical, unfortunately his deeper insights made little impact, perhaps partly because the world crisis of the thirties and forties put a premium on practicality. In any case, the 'standard' account of QM made mention of Bohr, but when technical questions arose, the authorities were Dirac (1930) and von Neumann (1955). It is clear why this happened. Bohr's writings were difficult and perhaps more obscure than they had to be, in spite of the great pains he took in composing them. Dirac, on the other hand, summarized quantum principles in a formalism of great mathematical elegance and simplicity. Some of his concepts appeared dubious at first, but von Neumann's book put the whole system on a sound mathematical foundation. Now quantum states were described as vectors in a Hilbert space. This is geometrical language, which is as soothing to the ears of physicists as talk of subjectivity and arbitrarily shifting concepts is anxiety-producing. Von Neumann even went so far as to violate Bohr's taboo and apply the quantum formalism to the measuring apparatus. He wished to show that the results of a quantum measurement were independent of the location of the boundary between system and apparatus. In that he succeeded. But by introducing the idea of 'the state of the apparatus', and also by portraying the 'collapse' or projection of the state vector as a physical event, he opened the door to the measurement problem and all its offspring — Schrödinger's cat, Wigner's friend, and even the 'many worlds' hypothesis. The new formalism appeared to give the state an objective meaning, but not quite. If the measure-ment problem could be 'solved', so that an objective state was assignable in principle to every physical object, including measuring devices, then physical reality would be

---

[1] This last quotation is an explanation of the basis of Bohr's principle of 'complementarity'.

describable after all as a purely abstract system with a definite structure independent of any reference to experience, and the Cartesian dyke holding back the sea of subjectivity would still stand. Almost the entire discussion of the interpretation of QM in recent decades has been based on the approach of Dirac and von Neumann, the measurement problem, and the quest for the objective quantum state. Any defence of Bohr's warnings to the contrary is likely to be seen by enthusiasts as defeatism and superstition. Those who desire to maintain a purely objective, abstract, and mechanical physics often seem unaware of the essential conservatism motivating their position. For example, the 'many world' or 'relative state' interpretation has been put forward and defended as daring and radical.[2] Its purpose, however, is to maintain the objectivity of a formally describable state of the universe as a whole. It does this by attributing the ambiguity that arises from the 'relative' nature of the states of subsystems to the perceptions of the observer. In other words, the 'objective nature of physical reality' (that is, the formal independently-defined quality of the systems described by physics, which are taken to be the ontological basis of all reality) is maintained by shifting everything we think of as objective physical fact (in the common intuitive sense of the specific details of the world as we experience it) over to the subjective side of the Cartesian split — that is, over to oblivion (as a materialist understands subjectivity). This manoeuvre is certainly desperate, but not radical. Its purpose is to protect a certain view of the physical world from radical change.

III: The Nature of Physical Analysis

It is tempting to think of the brain, like any physical object, as a collection of component parts. We understand nature by dissecting. We subdue nature by constructing components and assembling them into machines. We see an aggregation of neurons and think of them also as components we might have designed and assembled. Our analytical habits — our passions for division and recombination — have more to do with the way the human mind works than with the way nature really is. The idea of a physical 'substrate' arises from an oversimplified view of how we observe and analyse the physical world. There is a continuum of precision from naive common sense notions to strict laboratory standards which makes it difficult to keep in mind the limited validity of some physical concepts.

The ideas of physical observation and measurement arise from the most fundamental acts of everyday life. We observe objects, note their detailed structure, note their location, how they move, how they change, and when these events occur. This kind of knowledge is essential for any purposeful human action. The concepts of geometry and analysis allow us to refine and quantify our notions of space and time, which then become an arena for the occurrence of physical objects and their motions and transformations.

The Cartesian geometric view of the world held that all our observations are in fact discoveries of structural details in an overall geometric edifice which constitutes the physical universe. The progress of classical physics gave credibility, even a sense of inevitability, to this view. If we can in principle observe any corner of space and time, and if all we find there is ruled by Newton's laws, and if any object can be analysed and resolved into a structure of mechanical components (and in fact into a ground-level

---

[2] Though first proposed in 1957 (Everett, 1957), it is perhaps no coincidence that it was first popularized among physicists in 1970 (De Witt, 1970) in the era of cultural revolution.

structure of interchangeable atoms with simple mechanical properties, as increasingly appeared to be the case) then what could remain when physical/geometric analysis had completed its task?

When the observer himself, however, was viewed in this light, conceptual difficulties abounded. Descartes had created the geometric world by removing the subjective self from it entirely (except for a tenuous influence on the pineal gland). Others found his solution unconvincing, and an account of the alternatives proposed might constitute a survey of modern philosophy. Today, those who are committed to the ontological primacy of the physical must show the physical world to exist completely independently of the subjective by showing how subjectivity itself can arise from a purely objective physical world. Hence the hard problem.

Even apart from the limits to measurement revealed by QM, there have been good reasons to doubt the power of physical observation to penetrate to ontological foundations. I will focus on one of these, which is fundamental but not widely understood — the idea of dynamics.

The geometric idea of the physical seems simpler than it really is — there are simple geometrical entities (perhaps Newtonian particles) which inhabit physical space, which move and interact according to simple physical laws and form larger structures which are the objects of our ordinary experience. It might seem at first that, with the tools of modern science, the structure and nature of such a world would be open to observation with no conceptual difficulties. But, of course, actual observations require that we *use* this world in order to observe it. We must manipulate and modify certain parts of it in order to create situations (experiments) in which information about the structure of other parts can be conveyed to us. Some measurements necessarily preclude others. We cannot dissect a microscope at the same time we are using it to study a sample of brain tissue (much less use the same brain tissue to think about the microscope, etc.). In pure geometry, the intellect can wander over every detail of a geometric structure, as one can gaze over a blueprint or electronic schematic diagram, going here and there and back again at will. But the physical observer has no such freedom. It is impossible to examine every point in space and time. We will never be able to obtain more than an exceedingly tiny fraction of the total information contained in the structure of the universe (to the extent that it can be considered a structure).

The goal of physics, however, is not to describe every detail of the universe. The interesting questions are 'What kinds of things exist or can exist?', 'What kinds of things happen or can happen?', and 'Why are things the way they are?' And so physics turns from geometric description to dynamics. If the universe were simply a geometric structure, there could hardly arise the concept of cause or of law. A detached intellect moving over the structure of the world might detect recurring patterns, which could be considered laws of a sort. But genuine dynamics is a more robust enterprise. A physical experiment sets up *typical* situations which can be repeated and modified as desired. By typical I mean conforming to a given set of conditions which are considered to be physically relevant and differing in many other details which are considered irrelevant. What I think I may call the Art of Physical Understanding consists of awareness of what factors are likely to constitute a typical situation and when they are likely to be relevant or irrelevant and what sort of situation will yield desirable knowledge.

The physicist *acts* and intervenes in nature. Typical situations are limited and determined in part by what the experimenter can manage to contrive. The idea of causality in physics depends on the freedom of the experimentalist to alter the conditions of the experiments. I first gained an appreciation of the importance of this idea from an argument by Roger Newton (1970):

> The most practical and the only foolproof method of scientifically testing a causal connection between A and B is 'wiggling' one of them and watching the response of the other. We are not interested here in what might be called 'historical causality' (establishing a causal connection in a single chain of events) but in 'scientific causality' (establishing such a connection in repeatable events) . . . It is the external control of A together with the correlation with B that establishes, in a good Humean sense, the causal connection between them, as well as the fact that A is the cause and B, the effect.

This observation contains a great profundity. The laws of physics are dynamical — they are not laws of being but laws of action. They are human constructions based on our experience of nature and in form and concept derive from our role as creative agents.[3] The importance of action can be seen in the advance of celestial mechanics from Kepler to Newton. Kepler observed the patterns of the motion of the planets and distilled them into three laws which described the elliptical shape of orbits and the speed with which the planets move along them at each point. These are purely geometrical and kinematical ideas. Newton took Galileo's work on the motion of physical objects developed in experiments and refined it and extrapolated the concepts of gravitational force and mass (both dynamical rather than purely geometrical notions) out into the solar system and so was able to derive Kepler's laws from his own dynamical laws of inertia and gravitation.

The dynamical description of cause, force, and law stands in contrast to the 'historical' denoting of particular things and events in the course of time. These are two 'modes of description' which are equally essential to any account of the physical world.

Historical description always makes reference to particular physical experience. We point out objects and events by comparing their location in space and time with other familiar objects and events. Description of an object can identify it up to a point — I might refer to a copy of War and Peace, a 1958 translation with a grey cover, but to identify it uniquely I generally must say something like 'the one you bought in Boston last year' or 'the one now sitting on the kitchen table'. Even if a description is unique *de facto*, it is not unique logically — the description does not provide a basis for deriving or computing all properties of the object (the results of all possible observations of it). The object is instead indicated or pointed out by the description, and its properties beyond that are implicit. Its nature is whatever-you-see-when-you-go-look-at-it. The object is defined not as something in itself but only according to its role in the larger world of experience. The concepts of space and time used here are means of ordering our thoughts about experience. Historical description specifies objects by pointing to them in the realm of experience. Their properties are determined by observation.

---

[3] When I write of the physicist's 'freedom' of action in setting up experiments and controlling parameters, I am not taking a position on the philosophical question of 'freedom of the will'. I mean here only a pragmatic freedom which is independent of the physical entities being observed.

Dynamical description focusses not on the particular but on the typical. An object or situation is abstracted and represented as a 'system' which takes into account only the relevant conditions. A system is a mathematical construct which can be completely defined and described independently of experience. Dynamics is the art of representing processes in the world in terms of these abstract systems in a consistent way — i.e. so that the evolution of the system as required by general physical laws corresponds to relevant observed features of experience and so that the same set of general laws applies to all systems. In a dynamical description, space and time become simply the geometric basis for the mathematical description of the system. Dynamical description specifies objects by definition and axiom. Their properties are determined by deduction.

By historical description I do *not* mean phenomenological, in the sense of derivable from 'sense-data'. Rather, it is based on a common objective language (perhaps inter-subjectively objective — cf. Margenau and Park, 1967) referring to facts which could in principle have been ascertained and verified by any set of observers in the right place and time. The metaphysical status of this mode may be up for debate, but I think it is clear that there is such a thing and that it plays a fundamental role in physics. It is, I believe, what Bohr meant when he spoke of 'classical concepts' which were necessary for the unambiguous communication of experimental results. This does not mean that the apparatus must be thought of as classical in the sense of being governed only by Newtonian laws, but rather that the apparatus necessarily belongs to the facet of the experiment approached in the historical mode, as opposed to the 'system', which is the abstract causal facet of the experiment as it is described dynamically. This is why Bohr said there was a complementary relationship between a space-time (i.e. historical) description of events and dynamical concepts. Neither historical nor dynamical descrip-tion is primitive or *a priori*. Each has developed its appropriate language and conceptual structure based on the long accumulation of experience and knowledge, and, of course, each has influenced the other.

The mechanical world view (in its most general form) is essentially the expectation that the physical universe as a whole is representable as a dynamic system, so that the typical and particular become equivalent and no aspect of reality is excluded from the abstract representation. There is no distinction between an historical object and its dynamical model — except perhaps to say that the object we encounter in experience is an instantiation or realization of the model (and nothing more). For some time, this belief was taken for granted as a necessary feature of the scientific attitude, and indeed it is difficult for some to imagine any alternative. One of the great benefits of the rise of quantum theory has been to emphasize the logical distinction between the two modes of description and to provide an example of a physical theory in which the two are not identified.

In the light of this distinction, consider again Descartes' physical world of pure geometry. What makes this world physical — that is, how is it different from the same geometrical structure as merely imagined or hypothesized by a mathematician which, if it could exist independently at all, could do so only in some Platonic sense? It appears that the only difference is that this particular geometry is the one our minds or souls are linked to. It is the subjective which makes the objective physical. This consideration led some empiricists to claim that to be is to be observed. When scientific and philosophical fashion decapitated Descartes' world by eliminating the soul, what then could give physical reality to abstract form? We are fortunate that contemporary physics does *not* present us with a model of the world as abstract form. The convoluted paradoxes of QM are really a road map out of our ontological impasse. The world described by physics is not an independently-existing structure. It is, I think, an empirical manifestation of a non-mechanical mode of existence, a concept which I will try to elucidate as best I can below.

IV: Abandoning the Geometrical Paradigm

Inward Bound (Pais, 1986) is the title of an excellent history of the progress of twentieth century physics towards the analysis of matter at ever smaller scales. QM grew out of this process, but paradoxically the success of this program of explaining larger structures in terms of component parts (an ostensibly mechanical procedure) has contributed to obscuring the nonmechanical nature of quantum physics. It is still common even for particle physicists to think of quarks and leptons as 'building blocks' of nature, though Heisenberg (1976) warned against the naïveté of this view near the end of his life. In the first chapter of his *Lectures on Physics*, (Feynman *et al.*, 1963), Feynman describes the atomic hypothesis as the most useful single piece of information about the physical world. Certainly nature seems to be partitionable into individual parts in nearly all macroscopic cases. But this property of the physical world is in effect a 'broken symmetry' — it fails in quantum phenomena. The breaking of a symmetry is generally highly significant for deep understanding. An effect which may appear to be almost negligible can lead to a fundamental revision of concepts. The most famous example is the nonconservation of parity which was discovered in particle physics in the 1950s. Before that time, it was taken for granted that all physical laws had a mirror symmetry. If a physical process was permitted by the laws, then so was its mirror image. The discovery that this was not the case was a great shock to physicists. In the decay of certain particles involving the weak nuclear force, a particular 'handedness' is preferred. The effect may not appear at all in most processes, but the fact that it could occur at all was an important clue in the development of modern quantum field theory and the standard model of elementary particles. Parity or reflection symmetry holds nearly all the time but is broken in weak interactions. Strictly speaking, the term symmetry breaking refers to a mathematical property of formal descriptions of particle interactions. I use it here somewhat metaphorically when I apply it to the empirical divisibility of the physical into distinct objects.

The dynamics of the solar system can be described in terms of the positions and momenta of the sun, planets, and moons, with mostly small corrections for the finite size of the bodies and their rotations and tidal forces. The position vectors which enter into the equations of motion have an obvious and trivial relation to the attributes of these bodies as objects of our experience. The same vectors which determine the relative forces on the planets also tell us what direction to look to see them. Each object has its own individual state given by its position and momentum. To complete the picture, we need only an account of the gravitational field, which has a well-defined value at every point in the dynamical space and time, which we think of as exactly identical to the historical space and time in which the phenomena of our experience occur.

No such description can be found for the atom. The state of the atom is a function in which the positions of the nucleus and electrons are arguments. The state generally does not define an unambiguous value for any of these. Furthermore, the electrons are taken to be identical to each other in a radical sense, so that the wave function must be antisymmetrized with respect to an exchange of any two of them. In this description, the electrons appear less as independent objects and more as tokens representing the degrees of freedom of the atom.

Even when a free electron is studied individually, the state is a function which does not appear to have the properties necessary to describe a particle. In fact, we discover, the state is a representation not so much of the 'state of being' of a particle as of the procedure or typical situation which brought it into being. The electron is particle-like mainly in the local and discreet way it interacts with other objects. The paradigm for understanding quantum dynamics is as follows: The empirical relevant conditions of an experiment constitute a 'state preparation'. The state embodies the causal propensities of the experimental situation. The measurement is a registration of some empirical outcome. From the state can be derived the probability of each possible outcome. The causal propensity of the experimental situation is conceptualized as a 'quantum system', generally composed of one or more particles. The particles are perhaps best thought of as units of causal influence.[4] The nature of the quantum state is lucidly explained by Peres (1984 and 1993) and Hartle (1968). It is especially important to resist the temptation to think of the system as an object in the empirical sense and the state as an attribute of that object. What happens to the system after the measurement? It is sometimes convenient to think of the system as persisting with a new 'reduced' state, but this substitution of one state for another is not a physical process (referred to as the collapse of the wavefunction) but simply a shift to a new dynamical situation which is defined in part by the outcome of the previous measurement. The state represents the causal propensities of an empirical stuation, not the structure of reality itself. Reality cannot be reduced to a mathematical structure.

Bohr's purpose was to make sense of this unfamiliar and counterintuitive form of physical analysis. He showed that the mechanical nature of classical physics depended on the phenomena studied, which could be described in terms of objects having well-defined properties independent of observation. Bohr hastened to emphasize that quantum phenomena were also objective in the sense which makes physics possible. That is, the results of experiments can be unambiguously described and communicated in a way which is consistent with the experience of all observers. He referred to the 'classical' nature of the apparatus, a phrase which has caused much confusion. It does not mean that two separate dynamical theories are required, one for small objects like the quantum system and another for the macroscopic apparatus. Rather, Bohr is simply emphasizing that the experiment, like all physical phenomena, is first defined empirically in the realm of experience and that even though the abstract dynamical models may have changed, the apparatus is still described historically in much the same terms it has always been. In classical physics, there was a sort of isomorphism between the two modes of description, which we now know is not true of physical theories in general. Our empirical mode of describing laboratory phenomena is based on a refinement of common-sense concepts, which in turn are based heavily on the 'broken symmetry' of the divisibility of the physical world into independent objects. Without that fortuitous near-divisibility, physi-

---

[4] The old phrase 'quantum of action' carries the right connotation.

cal analysis might not be possible at all. Classical mechanics mirrored the structure of our empirical concepts. Classical dynamics is superseded, but the empirical conceptual structure remains. In that sense, the apparatus is still 'classical'.

The distinction between quantum system and apparatus has nothing to do with size. They play different logical roles in the description of phenomena. The apparatus is simply the experiment approached from the historical empirical point of view. The microsystem is the experiment approached from the abstract dynamical point of view. These are two aspects of the same thing, a duality as inescapable as left and right, and — as Bohr said — related to the subject–object duality.

It is fine to attempt a quantum dynamical description for the apparatus as long as we realize that the object so described no longer plays the logical role of apparatus. Often, we are not even really referring to the same thing. The historical and dynamical modes partition the world in subtly different ways. In physics, the concept of object is not really fundamental. It is the dynamical process which is central. It is noteworthy that when Feynman (1961) published a volume of lecture notes on elementary particles and their interactions, he called it *The Theory of Fundamental Processes*.

Chalmers dismisses Bohr's views as incomprehensible or else vacuous. This is unfortunate, because, in a real sense, Bohr's account is not an 'interpretation' at all but an integral part of quantum physics as it is actually practised (see Rosenfeld, 1957, and also similar remarks of his quoted in Stapp, 1973). But Chalmers' attitude is a common one and it will be useful here to quote him at length and deal with his objections specifically. His discussion of quantum concepts in this chapter includes an account of the famous thought experiment referred to as 'Schrödinger's cat'. Schrödinger imagined a cat in a box with a bottle of poison gas set up so that when an unstable nucleus decays, it emits a particle which is registered by a detector which triggers a mechanism which smashes the bottle, releasing the poison and killing the cat. A quantum dynamical description of the whole apparatus from nucleus to cat as a single system would be presumably described by a state which evolves according to the Schrödinger equation. Once the system is activated and isolated, then after an interval equal to the half-life of the nucleus, there is a 50% chance that the nucleus has decayed and the cat is dead. The final state would be a bizarre mixture (or more correctly 'superposition') of live cat and dead cat. The state description and its evolution in time make no provision for a selection of one possibility or the other, unless we introduce von Neumann's suggested projection or collapse of the state vector. If this projection is thought of as a physical event, then it is usually said to occur during measurement. However, measurement seems to be an unacceptably vague or unphysical concept. Does the measurement occur when a physicist — or animal rights activist — looks into the box to see if the cat is alive or dead? Was the cat in biological limbo until that happened? Or is the cat itself, as a conscious organic being, capable of 'measuring' the toxicity of its air supply? Or does the particle detector, as a macroscopic object, qualify as an observer and perform a measurement? These questions point out the conceptual inadequacy of common textbook accounts of quantum theory. On the other hand, if the state is not thought of as an ontological description of the 'state of being' of physical objects so that projection is not invoked as a physical event, then there is no difficulty — except the lack of a 'complete' formal description of the event. Here are Chalmers' (1996) objections to the Copenhagen view:

Perhaps the dominant view among working physicists is that one simply should not ask what is going on in the real world, behind the quantum mechanical calculus. The calculus works, and that is that. There are two versions of this view. According to the first version, maybe something is going on in the world, but we can never know what it is. The calculus gives us all the empirical information that we will ever have, so that anything further is pure speculation. We might as well stop worrying and continue to calculate. This view makes sense for practical purposes, but it is unsatisfying for anyone who wants physics to tell us about the basic level of reality. Given that the calculus works, we want to have at least some idea of how it could possibly work. Perhaps we can never know for sure, but it makes sense to ask.

The second version takes a harder line, and says that there is no fact of the matter about what is going on in the world. According to this view, the facts are exhausted by the fact that the calculus works. This view is often not put forward quite as explicitly as this, perhaps because put so straightforwardly the view is almost impossible to believe. It offers us a picture of reality that leaves out the world! It leads to a version of idealism, on which all that exists are our perceptions, or to something very close to this. Before we open the cabinet containing Schrödinger's cat, it is not in a dead state, it is not in an alive state, and it is not in a superposed state; it is simply in no state at all. By giving up on a fact of the matter about what lies behind our measurements, this view gives up on an independently existing reality (p. 342).

He goes on to say that Bohr's view, if accurately represented by the second paragraph above, 'offers a picture of the basic level of reality that is no picture at all.' Chalmers' dissatisfaction with standard QM is clearly based on a longing for the geometrical paradigm — a 'picture of the basic level of reality'. It is assumed that an independently existing reality must take the form of a mathematical structure which the structure of our experience reflects and from which all physical truth may be derived. If physics is not working to bring that structure to light, then it is not doing its job. It is not necessary, however, that reality take such a form. In fact, I expect realities of this type (if we can speak in this way of possible realities) constitute a restricted and ontologically impoverished class. One purpose of this paper is to invite the reader to open her or his mind to other possibilities.

First, it is not necessary to think of the physical as a 'basic level of reality.' Nor is the only alternative an incoherent idealism of rootless sense data. The physical world of empirical objects remains as solid and dependable as it ever was. Consider the basic concept of reality as that-which-is, not as a set of all particular things (events, objects, ideas, feelings, etc.), nor as a structure, but rather as simply the ultimate referent of all we say about any of those things. If today is rainy, then that-which-is is of such a nature that I experience a rainy day and that the ground is wet. Any such statement involves applying analytical concepts to reality. We might think of the applying of concepts as asking questions of reality. Intelligence requires the formulation of appropriate concepts to apply to reality and of methods to answer the resulting questions. Physical questions (is it raining?) are a subset of general analytical questions (is democracy viable in post-industrial society?). The truths we discover about reality are not required *a priori* to have any particular propositional structure. Any such structure is created by the process or act of understanding with which we approach reality. Such a structure is not so much an attribute of reality as a tool to facilitate our understanding of it. Physical concepts develop along with the means of asking and answering the questions they suggest. Physics is strongly instrument-driven. The coherence of physical concepts does not depend on their attainment of a special fundamental status nor on recasting reality as a purely physical structure. Physics is coherent as long as each interrogation of nature gives a definite result. Such an interrogation is an active intervention in the universe which in a sense creates the result. There is no set of all physical facts independent of what we do. Not every question is answered by a formal structure. The formalism answers only dynamical questions (what sort of thing can happen in a situation of this type?). Questions about what actually has happened must be answered empirically.

What about Schrödinger's cat in the cabinet? I open the door and see it is alive. Was it alive before I opened the door? Yes, we can say it was as an inference from empirical facts. Of course, such a statement has the contingency and 'fuzziness' of all empirical truth.[5] It may be frustrating to Chalmers that physical facts have this fuzzy quality, but they must because any mathematical description is only a simplified map of reality, not reality itself. We can claim as a fact that the cat was alive, but we are not required to assign a *state* to the cat. The state description has no significance apart from dynamical analysis. We may seem to lose something in no longer having a complete mathematical picture of the physical world, but what we have gained is much greater. We have come up against the limits of the applicability of mechanical concepts to the world — and that is a profound kind of knowledge in itself. To say that quantum theory has given up on a complete description of nature is a little like complaining that Darwinian evolutionary theory has given up on taxonomy, because species are no longer so well defined and blend into each other in a disconcerting way. That is not a flaw but a revelation.

Similarly, to protest that the quantum 'calculus' gives right answers but tells us nothing about the world shows, I think, a failure to appreciate what physics is all about. One could also have complained that Newton's laws allow us to calculate the effects of gravity but tell us nothing about gravity itself. On the contrary, Newtonian mechanics was an enormous advance in understanding nature. Physical understanding is not simply the adoption of a formalism or geometrical picture (together with the mathematical knowledge required to understand the formalism). It is a mental discipline involving action, observation, and contemplation. It is the cultivation of faculties of judgement necessary for interrogating the physical aspects of reality. Bohr's counterintuitive language of complementarity is not a restriction on knowledge or a manifesto of resignation or failure. It is an attempt to describe the profound new modes of understanding which physics has developed in the twentieth century and the awesome vision of the deep workings of causal processes opened up to us by these developments. Alternative 'interpretations' seem absurdly contrived, frail, and ramshackle by comparison.

Reality is not invalid or incomprehensible because we cannot know or model everything about it. Even in Chalmers' view, not all truths are accessible or describable — e.g. what it is like to be a bat. But apparently he takes comfort in a belief that all these things are determined (naturally, if not logically) by a physical substrate which is accessible. This is typical of the way his account trivializes the distinctiveness of the phenomenal realm whose nonsupervenience on the physical he took such pains to establish. One might

---

[5] 'What is the exact height of Mt. Everest?' is not a meaningful physical question. Exact magnitudes have mathematical but not physical significance.

also question his sweeping claim about the supervenience on the physical of all higher order concepts other than phenomenal experience. The supervenience of, say, prosperity depends on criteria for judging the state of the economy from physical evidence. By what faculty of the mind are such criteria discovered? In chapter two, Chalmers pleads the weakness of the supervenience relation (p. 71), but he begins the next chapter with the startling claim, 'Almost everything in the world can be explained in physical terms.' It seems trivial to say that something is 'explained in physical terms' simply because physical evidence allows us to make judgements about it. I suspect most judgements depend also on modes of understanding which have nothing to do with the physical. Chalmers' use of the idea of the physical seems to shift meanings in this way at several points in his argument, becoming weaker or stronger as might be convenient.

I have discussed the concepts of QM at length here, not because they are likely to provide us with a physical basis for the generation of consciousness but because they help to dispel the tyranny of mechanical and geometrical models over the imagination. Once we are freed from these prejudices, the hard problem dissolves. It does not disappear, but is now manifested as a collection of smaller problems which we may hope to answer. I will touch on these briefly in the final section.

V: Machines and Brains

A machine is an abstract configuration imposed on matter. It consists of a number of components whose properties are sufficiently close to a certain required ideal which the conception of the machine depends upon. As long as the components behave in the expected way, the whole configuration will also behave properly; furthermore, its operation is 'sealed off' from any lower level phenomena in the components — only the ideal aspect of their behaviour has any effect on the operation of the machine (the design engineer has seen to that). When a component fails (e.g. when a watch spring breaks or a transistor develops high leakage currents), then an understanding of the behaviour of the whole requires a deeper knowledge of the actual physical nature of the components.

The brain is not a machine. It is an organ which has evolved from the action of natural processes. It is sometimes useful to use machine analogies in discussing biological systems, but such thinking can also be misleading. Organic systems originate spontaneously and are self-maintaining. The term 'function' is used in both engineering and biology, and to think in terms of functions can also aggravate the confusion between the two types of entities if one is not careful. The function of a machine is determined by the purposes of the designer or user. The function of an organ or structure in the body of an organism is understood in terms of the biological imperatives attributed to the organism itself.

A machine is a tool, an instrumentality. A bodily structure can also be thought of as an instrumentality (the heart as a pump, a combination of joint and muscle as a lever). As long as a part of the body fulfils a simple unambiguous function — transmitting force, digesting food, relaying information — the machine analogy is a useful one. In general, however, a naturally occurring object does not have much in common with a machine. It will not have a limited set of recurring states and a predictable pattern of moving from one state to another.[6] From an evolutionary point of view, the brain might be thought of as

---

[6] Chalmers was quite right to stress the artificiality of computing machines. Nothing like that is likely to occur in nature.

an instrument used by the body to enhance its chances of survival, but here things get tricky. The mind often disregards the needs of the body and even the reproductive imperatives of the species. (You might say that the mind has a mind of its own.) The mind must be treated differently from ordinary biological functions.

The concept of the brain as machine has been favoured both by neuroscientists, who want a paradigm to organize our rapidly increasing knowledge of brain physiology and psychology, and by cognitive scientists as a model to guide them in their quest for machine consciousness. I think, however, that such a concept will not serve the purposes of either group. There is a vast difference between the structure of a machine, whose components have been formed with difficulty from contrary matter (which often asserts its less than ideal behaviour in unexpected ways at inconvenient times), and a complex organ like the brain, whose structure has not been imposed on matter but seems to arise as an expression of the potentialities of the organic molecules themselves. A machine is constrained by design to behave in accordance with rules imposed from without. The brain follows its own nature. It is hardly conceivable to me that this distinction is not relevant to understanding the relation of consciousness to the brain.

A mechanical concept of the brain (and matter generally) has been reinforced, I think, by textbook graphics which picture atoms as brightly coloured spheres stuck together in regular patterns to form molecules. Of course, everyone knows that molecular reality is far more complex than that. But it is tempting to think that, for the purposes of biology, it is often sufficient to regard cellular processes as the sorting and shifting around of little spheres into various arrangements. If I glue plastic balls together in the form of an amino acid to what extent am I doing the same thing organic molecules are doing? If I were to build an enormous machine which builds up and tears down these molecular models and takes in models of nutrients and emits models of waste molecules, to what extent is my creation performing some of the functions of a cell in a different material manifestation? It seems clear to me that the 'functioning' of a cell is not a mechanical operation which can be carried over to another context without essential loss of significance. A cell is a complex and spontaneous molecular process which can be understood only in the context of its particular physical embodiment (the quantum nature of molecular dynamics) and the overall evolutionary process of which it is a part. A description of matter as the motion of little spherical components is a crude abstraction of the reality and one which emphasizes only the features we can most easily imagine rather than what is most essential. Just as we cannot abstract 'cellness' or 'organicness' from a cell and build it into a machine, neither can we abstract consciousness from a brain. These qualities are not patterns but relationships to the underlying physical processes and to the world process.

A neuron may be said to have a 'function' in some cases (as in the transmission of sensory information from sense organ to brain), but generally its most essential function is to be a neuron. Its behaviour is far more complex than any electronic component. Any model we devise of neuron firing and the causal relationships among neurons will be a simplified picture of certain features of neuron behaviour which are most obvious to us. Such models are certainly important for understanding the nervous system, but they do not constitute a recipe for 'doing just what a neuron does'. The behaviour of a neuron in a conscious brain may involve processes and interactions far too subtle for us to detect and model or large scale collective behaviour not readily understood in terms of the properties we can discover about individual neurons. I would not volunteer for Chalmers' neuron replacement experiments — I would fully expect both fading qualia and functional deterioration. In saying this, am I betting the farm against probable future knowledge? Perhaps, but I'm willing to wager past and present advances in the sophistication of physical concepts against the *presumed* future results of cognitive science and neuroscience.

If the day comes when we can observe the physiological functioning of the brain in great detail and correlate it with behaviour and thought, I expect what we will find is not a mechanically deterministic process but what will appear to us to be the spontaneous formation of large scale patterns in neural activity, and that these will not be random but follow recognizable sequences which will be intelligible in terms of high level mental and behavioural concepts. It might be thought that spontaneity necessarily implies a randomness or unpredictability which would detract from brain performance. These things are generally undesirable in machines. The brain, however, need not function as a machine. Its imperatives are internal, not external. Its causal patterns need not be analysable by external observers. But then wouldn't the brain exhibit strange correlations which contradict the dynamical laws of physics? Perhaps. We have been able to test the behaviour of matter only in simple systems or else in crude statistical representations of large systems. The possibility exists that processes associated with consciousness may exhibit regularities not predicted by today's physics. Chalmers claims that in such a case the new-found regularities would then be subsumed under a new physics. Not necessarily. An anomalous correlation in brain function might not be detectable at all, and if it were, it might depend only on some higher level mental quality (say virtue or irony) for which no physical correlate could be found, in which case the correlation (such as it is) would not be suitable as a basis for physical law.

The idea of consciousness as an attribute of information flow is an appealing one (and now reinforced by our digital culture and a long tradition in science fiction) but difficult to maintain. Chalmers refers to a thermostat with three states as an example of a minimal information processing device. But how does the thermostat know it is only supposed to have three states and which ones they are? A great deal else is going on inside among the vast number of atoms. The thermostat as a three state device (the machine *as* machine) exists only in the mind of the beholder. It is simply the aspect of the device which happens to interest us. If functional organization implies consciousness only naturally and not logically, as Chalmers maintains, then consciousness cannot be a machine property. The properties of a machine *do* follow logically from the organization of its components and their relevant idealized properties. Information is too flimsy and abstract a concept on which to base the link between consciousness and physical processes. I would suggest an alternative principle. To the extent that a brain process can be described mechanically or is 'sealed off' from the molecular level, it corresponds to routine functioning having little to do with consciousness itself. Likewise for computer consciousness, to the extent that a cognitive process is contrived and mechanical, it is something we are doing; to the extent it is autonomous and nonmechanical, it is something the world process is doing, and consciousness may result. If artificial consciousness is ever created, it will not be machine but organic consciousness.

VI: The Real Problems

The hard problem of phenomenal consciousness is really the inconsistency with our own experience of a complex of beliefs about the physical world: matter is 'inanimate' and mechanical, its ontology is mathematical so that all its properties are properties of form or structure, it is divisible into components so that the properties of the whole are implied by the properties of the parts plus their spatial relationships. Phenomenal experience has no place in such a world. A mechanical brain cannot generate a sentient mind. Fortunately, as we have seen above, modern physics has revealed that those beliefs, which once appeared inevitable, are in fact naïve and simplistic. Having driven experience out of our world picture, one's first impulse (desiring to make amends) is to graft it back on, without disturbing the independence of the physical. Any such graft is bound to be rejected by the host. The next step is to transcend the hard problem by accepting a richer nonmechanical ontology. This is not physicalism nor idealism nor dualism, but a view of reality as a unified process in which we are participants and which we conceptualize in many ways in accordance with the many kinds of knowledge we can have about the world.

Consider the following myth as an alternative to the familiar myth of God the Clock Maker. The words are chosen carefully to be suggestive, but are not meant to convey any technical (much less literal) meaning.

> There is Being. Being is aware. Being acts. The action of Being (from our perspective as participants) represents itself (in part) as the physical universe in historical space and time. The universe enacts a pattern of evolution in which accumulating action propagates as continuing process. Evolution results in a nucleation of processes into complex process-structures which are the physical representation of the nucleation of Being into individual centers of awareness and action.

What could be meant by 'nucleation of Being'? I don't have the slightest idea. But it expresses my intuition that consciousness must be closely related to existence itself, that it is vastly nearer to the 'basic level of reality' than anything signified by physical concepts. The fate of the individual ego-consciousness is obviously linked in some way to its physical expression in the body, but consciousness itself as a category and as a possibility is something more basic. We make machines and we analyse natural objects in terms of machine analogies because it is natural for us to think in that way. But we can hardly expect that that which the mind readily produces is the same as that which produces the mind. Mind is surely not epiphenomenally superimposed on a pattern of information-processing the brain happens to enact. It is far more plausible that brain and mind are both manifestations of an underlying process, and that our own ego-awarenesses are merely the tip of an ontological iceberg as yet unknown to us. If so, the concept of 'information' is not likely to be a useful guide. Information is an enormously useful idea, but it is an abstraction of an abstraction. The immediacy of consciousness lies in the opposite direction.

There are still plenty of problems facing us, and some of these are linked especially to the slippery qualities of phenomenal consciousness associated with the hard problem. We may not worry anymore how experience as a category can be explained in terms of the physical (no more than we would wonder how to explain triangles in terms of emotions) but the following questions remain, among others:

- What neural processes are associated with various identifiable states of consciousness? In particular, what conditions are necessary for consciousness to function at all. Even if we do not expect a mechanism of mind there is obviously much to learn about the relationship between consciousness and brain physiology. Neuroscience will certainly be the primary source of new insights and new concepts in the field of consciousness. Neither reason nor imagination can compete with the example provided to us by nature.

- Is there a natural generalization of the concept of consciousness? The nature of the universe is such that consciousness can occur in organisms, but we see no evidence of it anywhere else. Are there other manifestations of a general property which allows for consciousness? Can we come to understand the spectrum of consciousness in animals and at what level of neural development phenomenal experience becomes possible? Are there varieties of mind or subjectivity which transcend the human?

- Do quantum processes have a direct identifiable relationship to consciousness? It seems unlikely to me that models involving ideas of collapse of the quantum state vector or coherence will have any practical value in understanding consciousness and the brain, but I could be wrong. Quantum features of the physical world are important in a general way — they are consistent with an experiential aspect of reality in a way that mechanical paradigms are not and quantum laws are also essential for the stability and interchangability of atoms and molecules without which life would not be possible. Perhaps a more direct connection will become evident. Even erroneous concepts (such as, in my opinion, state collapse as a physical event) have been known to lead to correct results, so these ideas are worth pursuing.

The rapid advance of neuroscience makes it especially important to approach the phenomena with an open mind. If we view the enormous amount of new information with old ideas and inadequate concepts, then our theories will merely reflect back to us our own prejudices. If we try to force our knowledge into an arid and constricted paradigm not suited to the task, we will be blind to much that would otherwise be apparent and fail in the purpose behind our seeking. Inevitably, at some point, the goal of our investigations into the nature of Being ceases to be knowledge and becomes wisdom.

References

Bohr, N. (1958), *Atomic Physics and Human Knowledge* (New York: John Wiley and Sons).
Bohr, N. (1961), *Atomic Theory and the Description of Nature* (Oxford: Clarendon Press).
Chalmers, D.J. (1995), 'Facing up to the problem of consciousness', *Journal of Consciousness Studies*, **2** (3), pp. 200–19 (reprinted in this volume).
Chalmers, D.J. (1996), *The Conscious Mind* (New York: Oxford University Press).
De Witt, B.S. (1970), 'Quantum mechanics and reality', *Physics Today* **23** (9), pp. 30–5.
Dirac, P.A.M. (1930), *The Principles of Quantum Mechanics* (Oxford: Clarendon Press).
Everett, H. (1957), ' ''Relative state'' formulation of quantum mechanics', *Rev. Mod. Phys.* **29** (3), pp. 454–62.
Feynman, R.P. (1961), *The Theory of Fundamental Processes* (New York: W.A. Benjamin).
Feynman, R.P., Leighton, R.B., and Sands, M. (1963), *The Feynman Lectures in Physics, Vol. I* (Reading, MA: Addison-Wesley).
Hartle, J.B. (1968), 'Quantum mechanics of individual systems', *Am. J. Phys.* **36** (8), pp. 704–12.
Heisenberg, W. (1976), 'The nature of elementary particles', *Physics Today* **29** (3), pp. 32–40.

Margenau, H. and Park, J.L. (1967), 'Objectivity in quantum mechanics', in *Delaware Seminar in the Foundations of Physics*, ed. M. Bunge (New York: Springer Verlag).

Newton, R. (1970), 'Particles that travel faster than light?', *Science* **167** (3925), pp. 1569–74.

Pais, A. (1986), *Inward Bound* (New York: Oxford University Press).

Peres, A. (1984), 'What is a state vector?', *Am. J. Phys.* **52** (7), pp. 644–50.

Peres, A. (1993), *Quantum Theory: Concepts and Methods* (Dordrecht: Kluwer Academic Publishers).

Rosenfeld, L. (1957), 'Misunderstandings about the foundations of quantum theory', in *Observation and Interpretation,* ed. S. Korner (New York: Academic Press).

Stapp, H.P. (1973), 'The Copenhagen Interpretation', *Am. J. Phys.* **40**, pp. 1098–116, reprinted in *Mind, Matter, and Quantum Mechanics* (Berlin: Springer Verlag).

von Neumann, J. (1955), *Mathematical Foundations of Quantum Mechanics* [translation of 1932 German edition] (Princeton: Princeton University Press).

Neuroscience
and
Cognitive Science

Francis Crick and Christof Koch

Why Neuroscience May Be Able to Explain Consciousness

We believe that at the moment the best approach to the problem of explaining conscious-ness is to concentrate on finding what is known as the neural correlates of consciousness — the processes in the brain that are most directly responsible for consciousness. By locating the neurons in the cerebral cortex that correlate best with consciousness, and figuring out how they link to neurons elsewhere in the brain, we may come across key insights into what David J. Chalmers calls the hard problem: a full accounting of the manner in which subjective experience arises from these cerebral processes.

We commend Chalmers for boldly recognizing and focusing on the hard problem at this early stage, although we are not as enthusiastic about some of his thought experi-ments. As we see it, the hard problem can be broken down into several questions: Why do we experience anything at all? What leads to a particular conscious experience (such as the blueness of blue)? Why are some aspects of subjective experience impossible to convey to other people (in other words, why are they private)? We believe we have an answer to the last problem and a suggestion about the first two, revolving around a phenomenon known as explicit neuronal representation.

What does 'explicit' mean in this context? Perhaps the best way to define it is with an example. In response to the image of a face, say, ganglion cells fire all over the retina, much like the pixels on a television screen, to generate an implicit representation of the face. At the same time, they can also respond to a great many other features in the image, such as shadows, lines, uneven lighting and so on. In contrast, some neurons high in the hierarchy of the visual cortex respond mainly to the face or even to the face viewed at a particular angle. Such neurons help the brain represent the face in an explicit manner. Their loss, resulting from a stroke or some other brain injury, leads to prosopagnosia, an individual's inability to recognize familiar faces consciously — even his or her own, although the person can still identify a face as a face. Similarly, damage to other parts of the visual cortex can cause someone to lose the ability to experience colour, while still seeing in shades of black and white, even though there is no defect in the colour receptors in the eye.

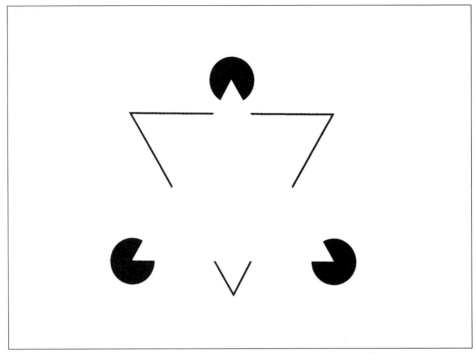

Figure 1: Kanizsa Triangle stimulates neurons that code explicitly for such illusory contours.

At each stage, visual information is reencoded, typically in a semihierarchical manner. Retinal ganglion cells respond to a spot of light. Neurons in the primary visual cortex are most adept at responding to lines or edges; neurons higher up might prefer a moving contour. Still higher are those that respond to faces and other familiar objects. On top are those that project to pre-motor and motor structures in the brain, where they fire the neurons that initiate such actions as speaking or avoiding an oncoming automobile.

Chalmers believes, as we do, that the subjective aspects of an experience must relate closely to the firing of the neurons corresponding to those aspects (the neural correlates). He describes a well-known thought experiment, constructed around a hypothetical neuroscientist, Mary, who specializes in colour perception but has never seen a colour. We believe the reason Mary does not know what it is like to see a colour, however, is that she has never had an explicit neural representation of a colour in her brain, only of the words and ideas associated with colours.

In order to describe a subjective visual experience, the information has to be transmitted to the motor output stage of the brain, where it becomes available for verbalization or other actions. This transmission always involves reencoding the information, so that the explicit information expressed by the motor neurons is related, but not identical, to the explicit information expressed by the firing of the neurons associated with colour experience, at some level in the visual hierarchy.

It is not possible, then, to convey with words and ideas the exact nature of a subjective experience. It is possible, however, to convey a difference between subjective experiences — to distinguish between red and orange, for example. This is possible because a difference in a high-level visual cortical area will still be associated with a difference in the motor stages. The implication is that we can never explain to other people the nature of any conscious experience, only its relation to other ones.

* * *

The other two questions, concerning why we have conscious experiences and what leads to specific ones, appear more difficult. Chalmers proposes that they require the introduction of 'experience' as a fundamental new feature of the world, relating to the ability of an organism to process information. But which types of neuronal information produce consciousness? And what makes a certain type of information correspond to the blueness of blue, rather than the greenness of green? Such problems seem as difficult as any in the study of consciousness.

We prefer an alternative approach, involving the concept of 'meaning.' In what sense can neurons that explicitly code for face be said to convey the meaning of a face to the rest of the brain? Such a property must relate to the cell's projective field — its pattern of synaptic connections to neurons that code explicitly for related concepts. Ultimately, these connections extend to the motor output. For example, neurons responding to a certain face might be connected to ones expressing the name of the person whose face it is and to others for her voice, memories involving her and so on. Such associations among neurons must be behaviourally useful — in other words, consistent with feedback from the body and the external world.

Meaning derives from the linkages among these representations with others spread throughout the cortical system in a vast associational network, similar to a dictionary or a relational database. The more diverse these connections, the richer the meaning. If, as in our previous example of prosopagnosia, the synaptic output of such face neurons were blocked, the cells would still respond to the person's face, but there would be no associated meaning and, therefore, much less experience. A face would be seen but not recognized as such.

Of course, groups of neurons can take on new functions, allowing brains to learn new categories (including faces) and associate new categories with existing ones. Certain primitive associations, such as pain, are to some extent inborn but subsequently refined in life.

Information may indeed be the key concept, as Chalmers suspects. Greater certainty will require consideration of highly parallel streams of information, linked — as are neurons — in complex networks. It would be useful to try to determine what features a neural network (or some other such computational embodiment) must have to generate meaning. It is possible that such exercises will suggest the neural basis of meaning. The hard problem of consciousness may then appear in an entirely new light. It might even disappear.

Bernard J. Baars

Understanding Subjectivity: Global Workspace Theory and the Resurrection of the Observing Self

The world of our experience consists at all times of two parts, an objective and a subjective part . . . The objective part is the sum total of whatsoever at any given time we may be thinking of, the subjective part is the inner 'state' in which the thinking comes to pass.

William James, *Varieties of Religious Experience: A Study in Human Nature.* p. 499

Introduction

Can human beings learn to understand conscious experience, even in its subjective aspect? Many analytic philosophers in this century have said no. David Chalmers is more optimistic, believing that human consciousness is understandable but that subjectivity presents a particularly hard problem. Chalmers takes Global Workspace theory as a prototype of a cognitive theory of consciousness, but raises the question whether such a theory can deal with subjectivity (see Baars, 1983; 1988; and 1996a). GW theory gives the most complete account to date of the interplay of conscious and unconscious processes in perception, imagery, action control, learning, attention, problem-solving and language. These topics can all be usefully treated as types of information processing, and today we are discovering many of their brain correlates as well. Indeed, GW theory shows many striking points of convergence between brain, behavioural and experiential evidence.

David Chalmers endorses a central hypothesis from GW theory, namely that conscious contents become 'globally available' to many unconscious systems. The reader's consciousness of *this phrase,* for example, makes *this phrase* available to interpretive systems that analyse its syntax and meaning, its emotional and motivational import, and its implications for thought and action. It appears therefore that even single conscious experiences have global consequences. Global availability is an information-processing

This paper was originally published in the *Journal of Consciousness Studies*, **3**, No.3 (1996), pp. 211–16.

claim about consciousness — what Chalmers considers to be part of the 'easy' problem. Whether a scientific theory like this can deal with subjectivity is the central point at issue.

I would suggest that GW theory has a number of plausible implications for understanding subjectivity. The really significant distinction is not between inherently hard vs. easy problems, but between *the contents of consciousness* and *what we intuitively think of as an observing self.* 'Subjectivity' from this point of view corresponds to the sense of an observing self.

In the last ten years I have presented evidence for the proposition that we need a concept of self to fully understand consciousness (e.g. Baars, 1988; 1996a). The notion of self has been criticized mercilessly in analytic philosophy, yet a great body of evidence from brain and behaviour speaks in its favour. I believe that we must deal with the self in an intellectually rigorous fashion if we are ever to understand the meaning of such humanly vital terms as subjectivity. This quest for understanding can be seen as a deeply humanizing enterprise, promising to bring us far beyond the mechanistic tendencies that have so vitiated life in this century (Baars, unpublished).

What makes the hard problem so hard, I suggest, is the criterion we adopt for subjectivity. By shifting criteria we can make the problem either easy or hard.

The Hard Problem Is Hard Because It Involves an Implausible Criterion

In traditional philosophy 'subjectivity' was a fairly well-understood idea. One can imagine a conversation between Immanuel Kant, William James and Aristotle, for example, with a good deal of mutual agreement. Traditionally, subjectivity concerns the experiencing self. Thus Kant (1985) writes that 'It must be possible for the "I think" to accompany all of my (conscious) representations, for otherwise . . . (they) *would be nothing to me.*' (italics added). And James (1985), in the epigraph to this paper, tells us that 'the subjective part (of consciousness) is the inner "state" in which the thinking comes to pass.' That state, he writes, is what we generally mean by self. From Kant to James, subjectivity was not viewed as impossible to understand.

It is only in this century that subjectivity was first expelled from Anglo-American philosophy and then, decades later, reintroduced as a hard or even impossible problem. For that reason we need first to untangle the current philosophical sense of subjectivity and show that at bottom it has not changed. In recent years 'subjectivity' has come to be identified with Thomas Nagel's question, 'What is it like to be a bat?' In Nagel's view, the key to understanding whether bats or humans are conscious is to know what it is like to *be* a bat or a human. To know whether you, the reader, are conscious, I must know what it is like to be you. In more traditional language the Nagel criterion demands proof of 'observer empathy' as the criterion for consciousness. Chalmers writes, 'As Nagel (1974) has put it, there is *something it is like to be* a conscious organism. This subjective aspect is experience.' (p. 10)

For empirical studies of consciousness, however, the empathy criterion is not helpful. In practice we use a much simpler standard. Neurologists who routinely evaluate patients with head injuries define consciousness in terms of waking EEG, the ability to answer questions, report perceptual events, show alertness to sudden changes in the environment, exercise normal voluntary control over speech and action, use memory, and maintain orientation to time, place, and self. These practical criteria are used all over the world to evaluate mental status in head injury cases. Physicians make life-or-death decision on the basis of these observable events, and in practice this works very well. Very similar criteria are used in psychological and brain research. Thus medicine and science seem to agree with traditional philosophy that consciousness and subjectivity can be identified in practical ways.

The empathy criterion is far more demanding. It requires something that has never so far been a scientific aim, namely that one observer should somehow share the experience of another. That may be a commendable ethical goal, but it does not help us decide in practice today whether a person looking at a chair, who can describe it in great detail, is actually conscious of that chair. It therefore fails to tell us what we need to know in practice, and insists instead that we cannot meaningfully talk about subjectivity until, in some indefinite future, we learn what it is like to be a bat or another human. This is not the mark of a useful criterion. The empathy criterion constitutes a rhetorical blocking position instead, one that tends to keep us from thinking about subjectivity at all. It is much like the demand made by vitalists about 1900 that biologists adopt the criterion of an *élan vital,* an unspecified vital essence, as the standard for living organisms. Doing so would have blocked progress on the molecular basis of life for an indefinite time. If we are honestly interested in understanding consciousness it is not the right way to go.

The traditional philosophical concept of subjectivity is much more plausible, as shown by the words of William James and Immanuel Kant quoted above. The Oxford English Dictionary points out that 'subjectivity' originated in the concept of being a subject, including being the subject of a reigning king. Over time it evolved into a more general sense of being a person with certain traits. In psychological terms, subjectivity in this sense has to do with a sense of self. This meaning, I would suggest, is a theoretically deep yet workable sense of the term. It has a long and distinguished history in philosophy and psychology. And as usual, once we find a workable criterion, the way toward genuine insight becomes much clearer.

For example, there seems to be a close connection between the sense of subjectivity and what Michael Gazzaniga has called the 'left-brain interpreter,' the part of the brain that maintains a running commentary about our experience. In split-brain patients, where transfer of information between the two hemispheres is blocked, the left side can be shown to maintain a narrative account of its reality that can be quite different from the right side's story. But the left-hemisphere system is clearly not the only 'self-system' in the brain. There is good evidence for a sensorimotor self, an emotional and motivational self probably represented in the right hemisphere, a social self-system, and perhaps an appetitive self. All these self-systems ordinarily work in reasonable coordination with each other, though they can be in conflict at times.

Notice that we need not know 'what it is like to be a split-brain patient' in order to come to reasonable conclusions about the left-side self system. We can simply ask the patient's left cortex, and it seems to give sensible answers. Given practical criteria for consciousness and subjectivity therefore, we can increase our understanding significantly.

The following points can be made on the evidence we have to date.

Consciousness is generally accompanied by a subjective sense of self

You are the perceiver, the actor and narrator of your experience. Every statement of personal experience in English refers to a personal pronoun, an *I*, as in 'I saw a pussycat,' 'She believes murder is wrong,' and 'He smelled a rat.' Unconscious and involuntary activities do not mandate such a connection with a self. 'We' do not acknowledge permanently unconscious knowledge as our own, and 'we' disavow responsibility for slips and unintended errors. They are not ours. Conscious events are invariably attributed to yourself. People routinely report having some definite but hard-to-specify sense of themselves in connection with conscious experiences. All this suggests that *consciousness is generally accompanied by subjectivity.*

The interpenetration of 'easy' and 'hard' aspects of psychological reality

Let us take an 'easy' claim about consciousness, one that is understandable in information-processing terms. For example, we know that if you can experience the letter 'p' you will be able to *discriminate,* to distinguish 'p' from 'q', 'b' and 'd'. The ability to discriminate is taken by David Chalmers to be an easy problem, because we can easily imagine a robot that can do the task. The fact that robots can do it, evidently without consciousness, leads many philosophers to conclude that *consciousness is not a necessary condition for discrimination between perceptual events.* However, scientifically this is an odd argument indeed, because *empirically* we know that many things we do to decrease conscious access to the letter 'p' will also change the ability to discriminate between it and other letters. We can decrease your conscious access to 'p' by means of distraction, overloading immediate memory, boredom, fatigue and a dozen other factors. As you become less clearly conscious of 'p', your ability to discriminate between it and other letters tends to decline precipitously. *Empirically, therefore, consciousness appears to be a necessary condition for discrimination, at least in creatures we believe to be conscious.*

But as we pointed out above, consciousness is always accompanied by subjectivity. It appears therefore that far from being separate from information-processing functions, the 'hard' problem interpenetrates what are said to be easy problems!

Causal interaction between 'hard' and 'easy' aspects of consciousness

Take the phenomena of limited conscious capacity, the fact that we can only be conscious of one consistent percept or concept at any given moment. To go back to the ambiguous word 'focus' mentioned above, try for example to be aware of two separate meanings of that word at the same time. The evidence is strong that humans cannot keep two inconsistent ideas in mind at the same time, though we can often find metaphors and images that unify the two meanings. Nor can I see two perceptual interpretations of an ambiguous figure, nor can I hear two streams of conversation at a cocktail party.

Limited conscious capacity implies that different conscious contents will interfere with each other. Try, for example, to read the following few sentences while keeping in mind three numbers such as 92, 14 and 6. Interference is understandable in Global Workspace theory as competition for a small working memory, the stage of the theatre of the mind, called the global workspace. It is rather well understood in modern information-processing theories. But it also happens to correspond with your personal experience! That is, as soon as you try to keep the numbers listed above in immediate memory while reading, you also lose conscious access to the meaning of any sentence you try to read at the same time. There is clearly some sort of causal interaction between your personal experience and our information-processing account of limited-capacity interference. Further, the self-systems described above, like the left-brain narrative interpreter, clearly respond to conscious information. It seems therefore that there must causal interactions between the 'hard' and the 'easy' problems. But how can that be, if the hard problem is so different from the information-processing account?

Independent variation of a sense of self and the contents of consciousness

While conscious contents and a sense of self generally go together, that does not mean that they are identical. We can maintain what seems to be a pretty stable sense of self while shopping in the supermarket or reading this sentence, even though those are different conscious experiences. But we can also keep conscious contents stable and change our sense of self. That is what seems to happen when we become *absorbed* in a fairy tale as children, actually identifying with the characters. Years later we may read the same story again without such identification, though the conscious stimulus is the same. There are numerous other examples of such changes in self, independent of conscious contents (Baars, 1988; 1996b). In technical jargon, conscious contents and self may be orthogonal constructs, which always coexist but do not necessarily covary. In this same sense all objects have size and shape, but size and shape do not necessarily covary.

Consciousness creates access for self

Daniel Dennett (1978) has phrased our common intuition about self and consciousness as follows:

> That of which I am conscious is that to which I have *access*, or (to put the emphasis where it belongs), that to which *I* have access . . .

'I' have *access* to perception, thought, memory, and body control. Each of us would be mightily surprised if we were unable to gain conscious access to some vivid recent memory, some sight, smell or taste in the immediate world, or some well-known fact about our own lives such as our own name. The 'self' involved in conscious access is sometimes referred to as the self as observer. William James called it the knower, the 'I'.

One way to think of 'self' is as a framework that remains largely stable across many different life situations (Baars, 1988; 1996b). The evidence for 'self as stable context' comes from many sources, but especially from the effects of deep disruptions of life goals. Contextual frameworks are after all largely unconscious intentions and expectations that have been stable so long that they have faded into the background of our lives. We take them for granted, just as we take our health and limbs for granted. It is only when those assumptive entitlements are lost, even for a moment, that the structure of the self seems to come into question. Losing a loved friend may be experienced as a great gap in oneself. 'A part of me seems to be gone,' is a common way of expressing such a gap. It helps to take this common tragedy seriously as a basic statement about the self in human psychology. Thus 'consciousness' and 'self' always seem to coexist, though they can vary independently of each other.

Is the subjective self an illusion?

Oxford philosopher Gilbert Ryle famously pointed out an apparent contradiction in the everyday notion of 'the self as observer.' He thought it made no sense to postulate an observing self because it does not *explain* anything at all, it merely moves the job of explanation to another level. If we had an observing self contemplating the contents of consciousness, he argued, how would we explain the self itself? By another observer inside the inner self? That would lead to a infinite regress of observing selves, each looking into the mind of the preceding one, little imaginary men sitting inside our heads observing each other's observations. The observing self — the homunculus or little human — was said to be a fallacy of common sense. Ryle's arguments against the 'ghost in the machine' persuaded countless scientists and philosophers that 'the self' is a snare and a delusion.

The only trouble with Ryle's impossibility proof is that some notion of self is indispensable and not noticeably problematic in daily life, and indeed in much contemporary psychology and brain science. Ryle's impossibility proof applies only if the concept of self is not decomposed into cognitive or brain entities that are better understood than the word 'self'. As Daniel Dennett has written, 'Homunculi are bogeymen only if they duplicate entire the talents they are rung in to explain. If one can get a team or committee of relatively ignorant, narrow-minded, blind homunculi to produce the intelligent behaviour of the whole, this is progress.' (Dennett, 1978, p. 123.)

Consider William James' 'self as observer'. It is hard to see anything impossible about it if we think of observers as *pattern recognizers.* Many brain systems 'observe' the output of another, and we now know a great deal about pattern recognizers in the brain. There seems to be plentiful brain and psychological evidence regarding self-systems.

All that is not to deny the existence of genuine mysteries about self. But there seem to be aspects of self that are not beyond human understanding. If they were, we would have an awfully difficult time dealing with ourselves or other people. As we understand more of the details of the cortical self system, Rylean doubts may begin to sound more and more dated.

Oddly enough, in the sensorimotor area on top of the cortex there are four maps of a little upside-down person, distorted in shape, with every bit of skin and muscle represented in detail. This upside-down map is called the *sensorimotor homunculus,* the little human. The nervous system abounds in such maps, some of which appear to serve as 'self systems', organizing and integrating vast amounts of local bits of information. The anatomy of the brain looks like a physical refutation of Ryle's position.

Summary and Conclusions

Contrary to widespread belief, many aspects of consciousness are quite knowable, witness productive research in selective attention, perception, psychophysics, protocol analysis, spontaneous thought monitoring, imagery, neuropathology of coma and stupor, and so on. All these efforts meet the most widely used operational criterion of conscious experience, namely verifiable voluntary report of some event described as conscious by a human observer: Statements like 'Mommy, airplane!' 'She smelled a rat' or 'My stomach hurts' fit the bill, but also more abstract sentences like 'I was conscious of her painful dilemma' and 'I just realized how to prove Fermat's last theorem'.

The reader can consult his or her own experience to see whether these conscious events are accompanied by a sense of subjectivity, of selfhood. But is it *real* consciousness, with real subjectivity ? What else would it be? A clever imitation? Nature is not in the habit of creating two mirror-image phenomena, one for real functioning, the other just for a private show. The 'easy' and 'hard' parts of mental functioning are merely two different aspects of the same thing.

References

Baars, B.J. (1983), 'Consciousness presents the nervous system with coherent global information', in *Consciousness and Self-Regulation*, ed. I.N.R. Davidson, G. Schwartz and D. Schapiro (New York: Plenum Press).

Baars, B.J. (1988), *A Cognitive Theory of Consciousness* (New York: Cambridge University Press).

Baars, B.J. (1996a), *In the Theater of Consciousness: The Workspace of the Mind* (New York: Oxford University Press).

Baars, B.J. (1996b), 'A thoroughly empirical approach to consciousness: contrastive analysis', in *Consciousness in Science and Philosophy*, ed. N. Block, O. Flanagan, and G. Guzeldere, (Cambridge, MA: MIT Press).

Baars, B.J. (unpublished), 'Consciousness is humanizing: A scientific program for the new millenium'.

Chalmers, D. (1995), 'Facing up to the problem of consciousness', *Journal of Consciousness Studies,* **2** (3), pp. 200–19 (reprinted in this volume).

Dennett, D. C. (1978), *Brainstorms* (NY: Bradford Books).

James, W. (1985), *Varieties of Religious Experience* (New York: Macmillan).

Kant, I. (1985), *Prolegomena to Any Future Metaphysics*, trans. P. Carus (New York: Open Court).

Nagel, T. (1974), 'What is it like to be a bat?' *Philosophical Review,* **4**, pp. 435–50.

Bruce MacLennan

The Elements of Consciousness and Their Neurodynamical Correlates

Why the 'Hard Problem' Is Hard

Special epistemological status of consciousness

I take the 'hard problem' of consciousness to be to understand the relation between our subjective experience and the brain processes that cause it; that is, to reconcile our everyday feeling of consciousness with the scientific worldview (MacLennan, 1995). This problem is hard because consciousness has unique epistemological characteristics, which must be accommodated by any attempted solution. I will summarize these characteristics; more detail can be found in Searle (1992, chs. 4, 5) and Chalmers (keynote paper; 1996), whose positions, if I have understood them correctly, are consistent with mine.[1]

First, science is a public enterprise; it attains knowledge that is independent of the individual investigator by limiting itself to public phenomena. Ultimately it is grounded in shared experiences, for example, when we both look at a thermometer and read the same temperature. Traditionally science has accomplished its ends by focusing on the more public, objective aspects of phenomena (e.g. temperature as measured by a thermometer), and by ignoring the more private, subjective aspects (how warm it feels to me). In other words, science has restricted itself to facts about which it is easy to reach agreement among a consensus of trained observers. Although this restriction has aided scientific progress, it prevents the scientific study of consciousness, which is essentially private and subjective.[2]

Second, science's neglect of the subjective is also apparent in its reductive methods. For example, once the experiential phenomenon of temperature has been separated into

* This paper was originally published in the *Journal of Consciousness Studies*, **3**, No.5/6 (1996), pp. 409–24. I am grateful to David Chalmers, Jonathan Shear and two anonymous referees for many helpful criticisms and suggestions on two previous drafts.

[1] A more detailed comparison will be found at the end of this paper.

[2] It should be apparent that I am using 'subjective' and 'objective' to distinguish private, 'first person' phenomena from public, 'third person' phenomena. As Searle (1992) observes, progress on the mind–body problem has been impeded by the connotations acquired by these terms, viz., the objective is unbiased and factual, whereas the subjective is biased or distorted. Indeed, I will argue for the possibility of unbiased, factual statements about subjective (private, first person) phenomena.

its subjective and objective parts (felt *vs.* measured temperature), the objective part can be reduced to other objective phenomena (mean kinetic energy of molecules), but the subjective components of the original phenomenon remain unreduced. Although this approach has been very fruitful for the development of physical theory, it fails when the topic of the investigation is precisely that subjectivity that it ignores.

In summary, the standard reduction pattern in science, which reduces the objective to the objective, cannot solve the hard problem, which deals with the relation between the subjective and the objective. If reduction is to play a role at all, it must take a different form.

Finally, science traditionally seeks facts — observations — that are independent of the observer; this supposes that the observer can be separated from the observed (another aspect of the subject–object distinction). However, in confronting the hard problem we cannot separate the observer and the observed, for consciousness is observation, the subject experiencing the object. That is, experience comprises both observer and observed, the termini of the vector of consciousness. Separating the two breaks the very connection that we aim to study.

Scientific investigation of consciousness

The preceding observations might suggest that the hard problem is invulnerable to scientific methods, but I believe that progress may be made by loosening a few of science's self-imposed restrictions, many of which are relics of long discredited philosophies of science, such as naive empiricism and logical positivism. Consciousness is our opening to the world; it is the vehicle by which we experience anything. Therefore we cannot *observe* consciousness *per se*, since we observe *through* consciousness. Nevertheless, with practice we can identify characteristics of consciousness that are relatively independent of its content, and in this way separate them from its content.

An analogy may make this clear. The aperture of a camera is its 'window to the world', since any image in the camera must come through the aperture. (For the sake of the analogy we suppose the camera cannot be opened in any way.) From within the camera the aperture *per se* is not visible; all we can see is the image it transmits, the scene at which it is aimed. Although the aperture is visible only by virtue of the images it transmits, observation nevertheless shows that certain characteristics of the image (focus, brightness, depth of field) are more a consequence of the aperture than of its content. Thus the aperture may be investigated indirectly. So also we may investigate the structure of consciousness independently of its content.

It may seem that by advocating such private 'observation' of consciousness, we have abandoned all hope of publicly validatible science, but it is worth remembering that all observation is ultimately private. Science has developed methods (such as measurement) that, in a context of shared training and experience, lead to general agreement among qualified observers (with varying theoretical commitments), and thus provide a reasonably stable body of public facts, which may be used for the support or critique of theories.[3] To bring consciousness into the scope of science will require a body of

---

[3] One cannot ignore the importance of training, shared experience and institutions in the creation of 'facts'. Even something so simple as accurately reading a thermometer requires training and skill (e.g. reading the top or bottom of the meniscus). Training is all the more necessary for reading bubble-chamber images and gas chromatographs. The histories of N-rays and polywater show how

appropriately trained observers; the public facts necessary for a scientific theory of consciousness will emerge from their consensus.

The camera analogy shows the importance of training, for the relevant phenomena, e.g. depth of field, might not be apparent to untutored observers. The difficulties with 'split-brain' and 'blindsight' patients as informants also illustrate the need for trained observers. I believe that the best example of the kind of training required comes from phenomenological philosophy and psychology (cf. Ihde, 1986).

In summary, although consciousness cannot be reduced to physical phenomena by the standard reductive methods of the sciences, it can be investigated to yield publicly validatible facts about the structure of consciousness, which can be related, in turn, to the observations of neuroscience.

Phenomenology

Phenomenology studies the structure of *phenomenal worlds*, that is, the worlds actually experienced by individuals. Henceforth 'phenomenon' will be used in a technical sense: a *phenomenon* is anything that appears in consciousness, anything we experience, no matter what its origin. For example, perceptions, recollections, dreams, pains (whether real or phantom), mental images, mental dialogues, moods, anticipations, desires and hallucinations are some of the kinds of phenomena. Further, your phenomenal world determines the structure of possible phenomena, and the *state* of your phenomenal world at a time is equivalent to the content of your consciousness at that time. That is, your phenomenal world is a structure of *potential* experiences; at any given time one of these is actualized as your conscious experience at that time.

The phenomena are the starting point of all science, for they are what is given to us (cf. Latin *data* = given things).[4] However, this is easily misunderstood for, at least since the appearance of logical positivism in the philosophy of science, there has been a tendency to suppose that the phenomena are simple things, such as sense data. 'Red-here-now', that is, the current experiencing of a patch of red at a particular location in the visual field, is a well-known example. The phenomenologists, especially Husserl and Heidegger, have demonstrated the incorrectness of this view, for rarely, if ever, do we actually experience red-here-now; they have revealed some of the complexity of real phenomena.

Suppose, for example, you rotate an ordinary die in front of me and ask for a phenomenological account of what I see.[5] I would be incorrect to describe a certain arrangement of black ellipses in white parallelograms, both of systematically changing shape. That does not accurately describe the phenomenon as I experience it, for I recognize the object and so it is seen as a die, and I see it rotating in space, not changing shape in some mysterious way. Even if I were unfamiliar with dice, I would see the rotation of a white cube marked with spots. Indeed, it would take very unusual conditions

---

competent observers can disagree over even the existence of a phenomenon (let alone its measurement); 'cold fusion' is a more recent example. See Fleck (1979) for an informative case study.

[4] This is true of the empirical sciences, but also of the so-called *a priori* sciences, such as mathematics, which start from the apparently invariable structure of the phenomenal world.

[5] The die example derives from Husserl's *Cartesian Meditations*, §§ 17–19, where it is developed at length.

to make me see the die as parallelograms and ellipses changing shape. (Such a situation, a consequence of a brain tumor, is described by Oliver Sacks (1985) in the title essay of his *The Man who Mistook his Wife for a Hat*.)

An additional complexity of phenomena is that they are not entirely in the here-and-now; for example, my current experience of the die includes some foreshadowing of future possible experiences. Thus we have expectations — some vague and others precise in accord with our familiarity with dice — about what we will see as the die is rotated. These expectations go beyond the visual; for example, we also have expectations about the hardness and weight of dice, and if we see two dice in an open palm, we have the expectation of some kind of dice game. All these and more are part of 'phenomenal field' surrounding the visual perception of the die. Further, we see that much of the phenomenon is a construct, both of the culture and of individual experience.

We must include expectation as part of our current conscious experience because, for example, we are in a different conscious state if we come to the pantry door expecting the shelves to be bare or come expecting them to be full. To the extent that the expectations contained in a phenomenon are met, we experience normality and familiarity; to the extent they are not, we experience dissonance and novelty. Phenomena appear gradually over the horizon of consciousness, and as they do so they actualize some, but not all, of the possibilities that may have been foreshadowed in the current state. This gradual actualization of foreshadowed phenomena creates the continuity of subjective time.[6]

In summary, phenomena are not simple; they are highly complex and strongly coupled to the rest of the phenomenal world in which they appear. Therefore some training is necessary to be able to observe phenomena accurately and to analyse the structure of the phenomenal world. Nevertheless I believe that phenomenological training of this kind provides a basis for making the characteristics (though not the experience) of consciousness public.[7]

Protophenomena

Decomposition of phenomenal worlds

I have argued that the subjective is not reducible to the objective according to the usual pattern in science. Nevertheless it is important to strive for some kind of reduction of the more complex to the simpler or better understood. This can be accomplished by an analysis of the structure of consciousness, which allows a phenomenological subjective-to-subjective reduction that parallels a neurological objective-to-objective reduction. It is to be expected that progress in each reduction will facilitate the other, in turn. In this section I'll outline the results of such a process, which suggests a theoretical entity that may be useful in constructing a scientific theory of consciousness.

At the highest level the phenomenal world can be analysed along modal and functional lines (appearance, sound, smell, memory, intention, etc.), but the rotating-die example shows that these components are far from independent (the rotating die phenomenon is not visual alone, but includes kinesthetic and other aspects). Fortunately we can expect

---

[6] Pribram (1991, pp. 214–20) argues that the alternations of familiarity and novelty parse experience into episodes.

[7] Despite the importance of phenomenology, in this essay I have avoided its technical terminology, which would be more confusing than helpful.

neuroscientific investigations of functional areas and pathways will correct erroneous preconceived ideas about the structure of the phenomenal world. The resulting analysis of consciousness into components of different kinds can be called a *qualitative* reduction.

A different kind of reduction, which analyses some aspect of consciousness into constituents of a like kind, may be called *quantitative*. This analysis is suggested by *topographic maps*, which are ubiquitous in the brain. A familiar example is the *somato-topic map* in the somatosensory cortex: nearby parts of the body are mapped to nearby parts of the cortex, so that the arrangement of neurons mimics the arrangement of the body. Similarly, in the early vision areas we find *retinotopic maps*, where neurons are arranged in a pattern mimicking the arrangement of their receptive fields in the retina.

The *receptive field* of a neuron in a topographic map refers to the stimuli to which it responds; for example, a neuron in a somatosensory map might respond to pressure on a particular patch of skin, or a neuron in the visual cortex to light on a particular patch of the retina. In such a case we can identify the subjective experience corresponding to activity in this neuron, namely, the feeling of pressure in that patch of skin, or the sensation of light on that patch of retina. I call such an element of experience a *phenomeniscon* or *protophenomenon*.[8] Further, we can see how, to a first approximation, the objective neurological processes corresponding to tactile or visual sensation can be reduced to a large number of receptive fields of this kind. This suggests phenomeno-logical subjective-to-subjective reductions (phenomena to protophenomena) paralleling neurological objective-to-objective reductions (e.g. topographic maps to their neurons, and sensory surfaces of skin to receptive fields).

This may seem to be a return to the red-here-now model of phenomena, but there are important differences. First, neurons have *functional receptive fields* that are more abstract than simple spatial patches. For example, primary visual cortex contains neurons whose receptive fields are four-dimensional combinations of retinal location, spatial orientation and spatial frequency (see MacLennan, 1991, for a survey). Indeed, Pribram (1991, pp. 79–83) has stressed that they are not limited to these four dimensions, but respond to many additional dimensions of the stimulus.

Next, as shown by the rotating-die example, there is much more to ordinary phenomena than the sense data, so we will have to take account of nonsensory protophenomena that represent the constituents of expectations, interpretations, intentions and many more abstract properties. Third, few neurons have simple fixed receptive fields, since even sensory neurons receive inputs from higher brain areas; therefore, virtually all protophe-nomena depend on other protophenomena. Finally, although I have used a simple sensation as an example, because its protophenomena are easy to visualize, sensation is only one aspect of most phenomena (many of which involve no sensation).

The preceding model can be extended to nonsensory neurons as follows. The activity of a sensory neuron reflects the presence of a stimulus in its receptive field, which is a region of some (possibly abstract) physical space (pressure, light, sound, heat, space, frequency, orientation, etc.); it responds maximally to stimuli in that region. Similarly, the activity of a nonsensory neuron reflects the activities of other neurons, and so it has

---

[8] This is an approximate definition; protophenomena are described more precisely in the following sections. 'Phenomeniscon' (accent on penult), a diminutive of 'phenomenon', is used in MacLennan (1995). I am grateful to David Chalmers for suggesting the alternative 'protophenomenon'.

a *functional receptive field*, comprising certain patterns of activities of its input neurons, to which it responds. That is, as sensory neurons respond to combinations of physical energy, so nonsensory neurons respond to combinations of neural activity. Turning to the subjective side, we see that, as a sensory protophenomenon corresponds to the experience of the physical phenomena in a sensory neuron's receptive field, so a nonsensory protophenomenon corresponds to the experience of combinations of other protophenomenal intensities, those intensities corresponding to activity in the nonsensory neuron's functional receptive field.[9]

Definition of protophenomena

Chalmers has argued in the keynote paper that 'a theory of consciousness requires the addition of *something* fundamental to our ontology' and that 'where there is a fundamental property, there are fundamental laws'. In this section I will propose protophenomena as a candidate for this 'something' and describe fundamental laws governing them (analysed mathematically in MacLennan, 1996, Appendix).

We have seen that activity in a neuron reflects the extent to which its functional receptive field is occupied at that point in time. Subjectively, this activity corresponds to the intensity in consciousness of a protophenomenon corresponding to the site of that activity. Therefore I hypothesize a one-to-one relationship between protophenomena and certain *activity sites* in the brain, and further hypothesize that the intensity of a protophenomenon varies directly with the neurological activity at that site. What are these activity sites?

Following Sherrington, who said, 'Reflex action and mind seem almost mutually exclusive — the more reflex the reflex, the less does mind accompany it', Pribram has argued that consciousness is associated with graded dendritic processes rather than all-or-nothing axonal spiking (Miller *et al.*, 1960, pp. 23–4; Pribram, 1971, pp. 104–5; Pribram, 1991, pp. 7–8). For concreteness I will accept this hypothesis and take synapses to be the activity sites (though the identification is not crucial to most of the following).[10] Candidates for the activity of the synapse include presynaptic membrane potential, postsynaptic membrane potential and neurotransmitter flux across the synaptic cleft. Since for the most part each is proportional to the others, it doesn't matter much which we pick; for concreteness, I'll hypothesize postsynaptic membrane potential.

The easiest way to understand protophenomena is to think of them as the atoms (indivisible constituents) of consciousness. As atoms make up macroscopic objects (trees, tables, etc.), so protophenomena make up phenomena. In both cases, the effect of each individual element on the whole is usually minute. Indeed, our phenomenal world comprises perhaps 10^{14} to 10^{15} protophenomena (i.e. the number of synapses in a human brain). Normally a change in the intensity of a single protophenomenon will not be perceived since it will not usually lead to a macroscopic change in conscious state, such as a judgement. Normally the intensity of a large number of protophenomena must

---

[9] This description is simplified for the sake of exposition, since sensory neurons also respond to other neurons, and so their complete receptive field includes the activities of other neurons. Correspondingly, the subjective intensity of a sensory protophenomenon depends on the subjective intensities of other protophenomena as well as on the experience of objective physical processes.

[10] In particular, my proposal does not exclude the possibility that microtubules, as proposed by Hameroff (1994), are among the activity sites.

change in a coherent way for a phenomenon to appear in consciousness, that is, for there to be a macroscopic change in conscious state.

On this view, the state of the phenomenal world, that is, the content of consciousness, is identical with the intensities of all the protophenomena. The appearance of coherent or stable phenomena can be identified with cohesive or coherent patterns of intensity among the protophenomena (just as macroscopic objects and events can be identified with cohesive and coherent patterns of activity among atoms).[11]

Ontological status of protophenomena

Are protophenomena real? At this time I believe it is best to treat protophenomena as *theoretical entities* (Hempel, 1965, pp. 177–9; Maxwell, 1980), that is, hypothetical constructs that are postulated for the sake of the theory, and are validated by their explanatory value and fruitfulness for scientific progress. (Quarks are examples of theoretical entities in contemporary physics.)

Here again the atomic analogy is helpful. When atoms were first postulated, they were theoretical entities; indeed it is only in recent years that they have become observable (still, of course, through instruments). At first many respected scientists denied their existence, while admitting their convenience for theory. In time, their explanatory value became so great that they were accepted as real. Now we accept atoms (or more elementary particles) as the ultimate constituents of matter, which cause the properties of macroscopic objects, and in this sense, in physical theory, atoms are prior to trees. Nevertheless, in experience, trees are prior to atoms. Similarly, in theoretical phenomenology, protophenomena are prior to phenomena, for they are the causes of phenomena, but in experience phenomena are prior to protophenomena; we experience trees, and by analysis break the phenomena down into protophenomena.

Another ontological issue is whether an isolated synapse (in a petri dish or simple organism, for example) has an associated protophenomenon. One answer is that protophenomena, as components of the phenomenal world, make sense ('exist') only in the context of a sufficiently complex nervous system. ('Sufficiently complex' is of course a matter of degree.) Such 'emergent existence' is not uncommon in scientific theories. For example, sound is a compression wave in air or another medium. The theory assigns a pressure to every point in the medium, yet it makes little sense to talk about the pressure

---

[11] An interesting question is just how the intensities of protophenomena combine to form a conscious state. A recent analysis by Sanger (submitted) of activity in populations of neurons suggests an answer. The functional receptive field of a neuron is proportional to a *conditional probability density field* (CPDF), defined over possible stimuli, which determines the probability a given stimulus will cause the neuron to fire. (More precisely, it determines the rate of a Poisson firing process). Collectively, a population responding to a common set of inputs has a CPDF that is proportional to the (pointwise) product of the fields of the neurons firing at a given time.

This analysis can be transferred to the phenomenal realm as follows. Each protophenomenon has an associated CPDF defined over the protophenomena upon which it depends (its 'inputs'). (In fact, the conditional probability density of an input signal is proportional to the temporal convolution of that signal with the protophenomenon's characteristic pattern, defined below, pp. 257–8) A population of protophenomena dependent on the same input protophenomena has a CPDF that is the product of the CPDFs of all the high-intensity input protophenomena, that is, of all the input protophenomena present in the current conscious state.The CPDFs of individual protophenomena can be quite broad, but in the joint response to the same input of a large number, the product can be very narrow, so that they define a phenomenal state quite precisely.

(or sound) of an isolated air molecule. The compression wave, which comprises elementary units of pressure assigned to individual molecules, makes sense only in the context of a large number of molecules. Similarly, I think it may make sense to assign protophenomena to activity sites only in the context of a large number of activity sites. This emergence does not make the protophenomena any less real; they are as real as the elementary units of pressure which constitute the sound wave.[12]

I have said that conscious states are the totality of protophenomenal intensities, so phenomena, as aspects of the phenomenal world, are cohesive and coherent patterns of protophenomenal intensity. I see no reason to hypostasize these patterns by postulating (subjective) entities corresponding to phenomena (images, ideas, perceptions, etc.). The coherence of the intensity patterns constitutes the appearance of macroscopic phenomena in experience (as will be explained in more detail later). By analogy, to explain the coherent physical effect of a baseball on a window it is not necessary to postulate the existence of anything beyond the baseball's constituent atoms, such as a 'ball entity', to represent the ball's coherence. So also, the collective action of protophenomena are sufficient to explain the experience of a coherent phenomenon.

Protophenomena correspond one-to-one with activity sites

Next I must explain why I have claimed that protophenomena correspond one to one with activity sites. First, I take it as given that phenomenal differences imply neural differences, that is, that a difference in conscious state is dependent on an underlying difference in neural (or physiological) state. Denying this would permit conscious states unsupported by physical states, which would, it seems to me, undermine the whole project of reconciling conscious experience with the scientific world view, the *raison d'être* of the 'hard problem'.

Second, I hypothesize that differences in activity at activity sites imply differences in conscious experience. Here the reason is Occam's Law, for we would otherwise have to suppose that some activity sites (e.g. synapses) have associated protophenomena while others don't. Although this may be the case, I see no evidence supporting it.[13] In any case, this hypothesis is not necessary for the overall theory of protophenomena.

Structure of phenomenal worlds

So far I have discussed protophenomena as elementary units of experience, but I have had little so say about how they are assembled into a phenomenal world and the phenomena it reveals. Clearly, the phenomenal world is spread out in space; although it is generated predominantly in the brain, it is projected 'out there': I feel indigestion in my stomach,

---

[12] By again transferring Sanger's (submitted) analysis to protophenomena, we may say that a small number of protophenomena so weakly delimit the inputs to which they might be responding that we can hardly say there *is* a definite conscious state. Conversely, a large number of protophenomena can define the possible inputs quite precisely, so that it is useful to talk of a definite conscious state.

[13] Note, that the claim is only that differences of activity lead to differences of protophenomenal intensity and hence (microscopic) changes in conscious state, not necessarily that the difference will have a significant effect on future (macroscopic) conscious states, or that it will change behaviour, judgements, verbal reports or stored memory. Analogously, changing a pixel changes the picture, but such a change would not make a difference normally. The issue of the unconscious is treated below, p. 262 f; suffice it to say that it does not contradict the hypothesized one-to-one relation.

not in my brain; I see the approaching cars in front of me, not in my visual cortex. How are neural events in the brain projected into the body and surrounding space? For example, what makes me experience activity in a certain neuron as pain in my finger and not pain in my toe?

Our discussion of topographic maps suggests that they have an important role to play, but how, precisely, do the spatial relations among neurons lead to phenomenal relations (such as perceived spatial and more abstract relations) among protophenomena? Although there may be some diffuse electrical and chemical effects on the activity of neurons, it seems that in general the spatial arrangement of neurons is significant only because it correlates with connectivity: nearer neurons are more likely to be connected than are more distant ones, and connections create dependencies between neurons.

Specifically, connections between neurons create dependencies between their activities.Thus, if one neuron synapses on another, then the activity of the first will tend to increase or decrease the activity of the second (depending on whether the synapse is excitatory or inhibitory). Also, if one neuron synapses on two others, it will indirectly establish a (positive or negative) correlation between the activities of the two post synaptic neurons.

We have corresponding dependencies in the phenomenal realm. Increased intensity of one protophenomenon can tend to increase or decrease the intensities of other protophenomena that depend on it. In this way protophenomenal dependencies constrain the possible conscious states and their evolution through time, and thus they define the necessary structure of the phenomenal world ('necessary' in the sense that this structure is invariable so long as the connections in the nervous system remain the same).

It is these dependencies between protophenomena that gives them their meaning. By analogy, a set of pixels constitutes a picture only when combined in a certain arrangement (relations of nearness or adjacency); with a different arrangement they would be a different picture; so also, with different dependencies, a set of protophenomenal intensities would constitute a different conscious state.

Protophenomenal dependencies

Let's consider protophenomenal relations in more detail. Neurologically, the activity at a synapse is a complex spatiotemporal integration of the activities of the synapses which connect to it. To a first approximation this process is linear, and can be described by the methods of linear system analysis (MacLennan, 1993b), which shows there is a certain spatiotemporal pattern to which the synapse shows the maximum response. Indeed, this pattern can be used to characterize the temporal response of the synapse to any spatiotemporal signal, in so far as the synapse behaves linearly. For this reason I will call this maximum-response spatiotemporal pattern the *characteristic pattern* of the synapse.[14] (Technically, the response of a synapse is a temporal convolution of its characteristic pattern with the input signal.)

This account may be transferred directly to the phenomenal realm. Each protophenomenon has a characteristic pattern, which is the spatiotemporal pattern of intensities of

---

[14] In physics and engineering it is commonly called the *impulse response* of the system; it corresponds (via the Laplace transform) to the *transfer function*, which describes the system dynamics in terms of its transparency to different frequencies of activity.

its input protophenomena that will maximize its intensity. Further, its characteristic pattern determines (by convolution) the protophenomenon's time-varying intensity in response to any spatiotemporal pattern in the intensities of the protophenomena on which it depends. As a consequence we can give a mathematical theory of the dynamical relations among protophenomena (see MacLennan, 1996, Appendix). The characteristic patterns may be simple, as when a protophenomenon corresponds to a conjunction or disjunction of protophenomena, or more complex, as when they respond to appearance or disappearance of protophenomena, rhythmic or other temporal patterns in protophenomena, priming or inhibition of future occurrences of protophenomena, etc.

Each protophenomenon contributes its characteristic pattern to conscious experience, with its intensity at a given moment determining the degree of the pattern's presence in that moment's experience. That is, conscious experience is given by a dynamic superposition of the characteristic patterns of the protophenomena.

Overall, the dynamical relations among protophenomena are nondeterministic. First consider a synapse formed by a sensory neuron, the activity of which depends on physical stimuli as well as on the activities of other synapses. Corresponding to this activity site in the phenomenal realm we have a protophenomenon whose intensity depends on physical processes as well as on other protophenomena. But physical processes are not part of the phenomenal world, so such a protophenomenon is phenomenologically undetermined (i.e. not fully determined by other protophenomena); the physical inputs act as independent variables in the phenomenal world. In terms of the ontology of the phenomenal world, they are causal primaries, which does not imply, however, that there are not corresponding phenomenal expectations (as the rotating-die example shows). Thus sensory protophenomena are inherently nondeterministic (i.e. undetermined in the phenomenal world).

Since nonsensory protophenomena depend only on other protophenomena, to a first approximation they can be considered deterministic; indeed their responses are defined by their characteristic patterns. This is only an approximation because even nonsensory neurons depend on non-neural processes, such as the physiology of the brain, and the physical environment of the body. Although these effects can sometimes be treated as extra, hidden inputs to the synapses, they are often nonlinear and comparatively nonspecific in their effects, so it is usually better to treat them as phenomenologically undetermined alterations of the characteristic patterns of the affected protophenomena.[15]

I have described the protophenomenal dependencies from a mechanistic perspective; now it is worthwhile to say a few words from a functional perspective. Topographic maps show us how receptive fields are ordered in space, frequency, speed, colour and many other dimensions, and hence how their protophenomena are ordered in corresponding

---

[15] Thus there may be phenomenologically causeless change to the phenomenal world; an extreme example is a stroke. The view advocated here might be seen as either epiphenomenalism or parallelism, but it is not; rather, it is dual-aspect monism. That is, causal relations in the phenomenal world parallel causal relations in the physical world, but, just as the phenomenal and physical worlds are alternative perspectives on one reality, so also phenomenal causation and physical causation are two alternative and equally valid descriptions of the constraints on the evolution of events in this reality. We can switch between the two kinds of causation as convenient for the problem at hand. There can be no contradiction between the phenomenological and physical accounts because they are both bound to conform to the same reality.

subjective domains. Thus dependencies among protophenomena correspond to order in a variety of dimensions. This order means that objects extended in space or other dimensions will lead to high intensities among closely dependent protophenomena (which will therefore cohere as full-fledged phenomena).

Furthermore, since change is generally continuous, or if discontinuous in some dimensions, then continuous in others, it follows that changing objects tend to move from the receptive fields they occupy to others that overlap along one or more dimensions. Think of a visual image of a moving object: it moves between overlapping spatial receptive fields; further, its edges change orientation continuously, and the light it reflects changes continuously, and so it also moves gradually from receptive field to receptive field in these dimensions. Phenomenologically, we can say that change tends to be between protophenomena that are strongly connected. Conversely, the presence (high intensity) of a protophenomenon is correlated with the future presence of the other protophenomena that depend on it. In approximate terms, the dependencies among protophenomena correspond to the likelihood (or unlikelihood) of change between protophenomena. More accurately, the characteristic pattern of a protophenomenon represents likely (excitatory) or unlikely (inhibitory) antecedent spatiotemporal patterns of protophenomena.

Phenomenological plasticity

I have treated the phenomenal world, the structure of possible conscious states, as fixed, but it is now time to say a few words about plasticity.[16] One type of plasticity is short- or long-term change in synaptic efficacy as a result of learning or habituation, which changes the strength of the dependencies between protophenomena, or, more accurately, changes the characteristic patterns that define their time-varying intensity. These changes affect the topology (the abstract relations of near and far) and the protophenomenal dependencies of the phenomenal world. These changes, in turn, affect coherence and cohesion among protophenomena, and thus the emergence of coherent, high-level phenomena.

Second, although the adult brain does not generate new neurons, it does generate new synapses for a number of reasons, including injury and learning (Shepherd, 1994, pp. 222–3). Since I have hypothesized that protophenomena correspond one-to-one with synapses, the generation of new synapses implies the generation of new protophenomena, that is, new degrees of freedom in the phenomenal world — literally, 'expanded consciousness'. Thus we see that the phenomenal world has a flexible ontology at both the macroscopic (phenomenal) and microscopic (protophenomenal) levels.

Implications

I will consider briefly the implications of this theory for several issues pertaining to consciousness.

Degrees of consciousness

By hypothesis the degrees of freedom of a phenomenal world correspond to the protophenomena it comprises, which are equal in number to the activity sites in the nervous system; further, the structural relations of the phenomenal world correspond to the con-

---

[16] My concern here is not so much plasticity in the developing animal as plasticity in the adult.

nections between activity sites. Therefore, with decreasing nervous system complexity we expect a proportional decrease in both the dimension and structure of the corresponding phenomenal world. The conclusion to be drawn is that consciousness is a matter of degree; in general terms we can say that the consciousness of simpler animals is less than ours in both dimension and structure.[17]

Nonbiological consciousness

I'll consider briefly whether the theory of protophenomena sheds any light on the perennial question of computer consciousness. From the perspective of the theory, the central question is: what sorts of physical processes have associated protophenomena, and how could we tell? For example, liquidity follows from certain physical properties of H_2O molecules, but other substances besides water may be liquid because they share these properties. Analogously, consciousness follows from certain physical properties of synapses, but other things besides brains may be conscious if their parts share these properties. Thus we need to determine sufficient conditions for the existence of protophenomena, that is, the properties of synapses (or whatever the activity sites may be) that cause them to have protophenomena.

It is possible, at least in principle, to attack this problem empirically. We would have to identify some observable protophenomenon, the presence or absence (high or low intensity) of which can be reported reliably by a trained observer, and for which the corresponding synapse (or other activity site) can be identified and made accessible (e.g. through brain surgery). With care we may control some of the variables (e.g. postsynaptic potential) independently of the others (e.g. presynaptic potential), and thus determine which affect protophenomenal intensity. Indeed, one could replace the synapse by devices that are functionally equivalent in one way or another (e.g. electrically or chemically), to determine which are necessary or sufficient for the existence of the protophenomenon.

It will be objected that the investigation depends on subject report, which is a form of behaviour, and therefore need not reflect subjective experience. That is correct. Since subjectivity is private, the only way such doubts can be eliminated is for the doubter to be the subject of the experiment.[18] Practically, though, the observations would become public through a consensus of trained observers of differing commitments.

From such a demonstration of protophenomena associated with nonsynaptic or even nonbiological objects we could reasonably conclude that a phenomenal world, and therefore consciousness, would emerge from sufficiently complex interconnections of those objects. Indeed, my guess is that we will find that the representational and information processing properties of synapses are all that matters, and that other physical

---

[17] Chalmers tentatively reaches the same conclusion on the basis of his 'double-aspect principle'. Also, from the probabilistic perspective, for a given sensory bandwidth, the conditional probability density fields associated with the protophenomena of a simpler nervous system less sharply delimit the input phenomena; thus, for simpler nervous systems, perceptual experience is less definite.

[18] If this seems far-fetched, it is worth noting that William McDougall requested, if he should become incurably ill, that Sherrington would perform a cerebral commissurotomy (split-brain operation) on him, so that he might directly experience its effect on his consciousness (Gregory, 1987, p. 741).

systems with the same capabilities (such as appropriately structured massively parallel analogue computers) will have protophenomena and be conscious.[19]

Origin of sensory qualities

A traditional conundrum in discussions of consciousness is the problem of sensory inversions (e.g. Dennett, 1991, pp. 389–98), which goes back at least to Locke: Could you tell, for example, if you experienced the colour spectrum oppositely from me? I believe that an improved understanding of protophenomenal dependencies will show that these inversions are in fact impossible, and so there is no problem to solve.[20] This is because the topology of a phenomenal space (its relations of distance and nearness) is determined by the interdependencies of its constituent protophenomena. I will use hearing to illustrate the method.

Consider a pitch inversion, in which the sensations of high and low are reversed.[21] This is impossible, because of the unique characteristics of low pitches: for if we listen to a sine wave of decreasing frequency, our perception of it will change gradually from a tone, to a buzz, to a rhythm. Neurologically, a pitch, which is mapped spatially in the auditory cortex, changes to an amplitude variation, which is mapped temporally. As the pitch decreases below about 1000 Hz., the nerve impulses begin to synchronize with the sound vibrations; below about 20 Hz., they are not perceived as pitch, but as periodic loudness variations (rhythm). In other words, at low frequencies the pitch and loudness axes are not independent; this does not happen at high frequencies, so the low end is differently structured topologically from the high end. The proposed inversion is impossible.

What may we conclude from the impossibility of pitch inversions? First, that subjective experience of sound must be just the way it is. For example the hearing of a low pitch is identical to intensification of certain pitch protophenomena that are connected in a certain way with loudness protophenomena. This view may seem tautologous, and therefore useless, but it is not. For example, if we discovered an organism with sense organs sensitive to vibrations of another kind (electrical, say), but of similar frequency, so that similar interrelations hold among the frequency and amplitude protophenomena, we could reasonably conclude that its experience of those sensations would be like sound. (Sensory qualities are explored in more detail in MacLennan, 1995.)

Unity of consciousness

A phenomenal world derives its structure from the dependencies between proto-phenomena, which correspond to connections between activity sites; thus the unity of a phenomenal world is a consequence of this connectivity. We see this in split-brain operations (cerebral commissurotomy), wherein severing the corpus collosum causes a

---

[19] It will be apparent from this that I do not accept Searle's reply to the Virtual Minds version of the System Reply to the Chinese Room Argument (MacLennan, 1993a, 1994). See also the thought experiment in the keynote paper.

[20] Thus I disagree with Chalmers when he asserts, 'There are properties of experience, such as the intrinsic nature of the sensation of red, that cannot be fully captured in a structural description' (p. 23). I will argue that the experience is exhausted by its structure.

[21] The analysis here addresses pitch inversions rather than colour inversions, since colour vision is considerably more complex than hearing. Nevertheless, I am confident that a similar analysis will show the impossibility of a colour inversion.

split in consciousness: each hemisphere is unconscious of what the other is experiencing (Gregory, 1987, pp. 740–7). However, it is significant that these operations do not completely separate the hemispheres; at very least the brainstem is left intact. Therefore the protophenomena corresponding to the two hemispheres are not completely independent, and so the phenomenal world has separated into two loosely-coupled subworlds.

An analogy may clarify this. A picture is an emergent effect of its individual pixels and their relative positions. If we cut a picture in half, it becomes two pictures, because there is no longer a fixed relations between pixels in one half and those in the other. However, instead of cutting the picture, we may gradually separate it into two parts, pixel by pixel, by stretching and eventually breaking the connections between them. The gradual uncoupling of the pixels in the two halves causes the picture to change gradually from one to two. So also, consciousness is emergent from the individual protophenomena and the dependencies between them. As the neural connections are weakened or broken, the protophenomena in the two subworlds decouple from each other, and the one mind becomes two.

This thought experiment demonstrates that the unity of consciousness is a matter of degree. Indeed, in principle we can measure the unity of consciousness by the tightness of the coupling between its protophenomena, for it is this coupling that gives the phenomenal world its coherence. (The tightness of coupling can, in principle, be calculated from the characteristic patterns; it can be quantified in terms of mutual information.)

One may wonder what sort of coupling is sufficient to unify consciousness. For example, in split-brain patients it has been observed that one hemisphere may communicate with the other through transactions with the external world, for example, twitching the skin on one side of the face so that it can be felt on the other. (The patient is unconscious of doing this.) Can 'external transactions' such as these effect the coupling of protophenomena? If so, then our individual phenomenal worlds may not be so independent as we commonly suppose, for any sort of communication couples protophenomena in one mind to those in another. I think the answer is, again, a matter of degree. There is an enormous difference between the bandwidth of the corpus collosum (approximately 800 million nerve fibres) and the narrow bandwidth of most external media. Nevertheless, the interconnection of phenomenal worlds by non-neural physical processes is a thought-provoking possibility.

The unconscious mind

The present view, which associates protophenomena — elementary units of consciousness — with all synapses, would seem to leave no room for the unconscious mind.[22] There are several possible resolutions.

(1) Unconscious processes may correspond to low-intensity, loosely-coupled protophenomena. By becoming coherent they come into consciousness (i.e. cohere into phenomena). That is, unconscious processes are incoherent patterns in protophenomenal

---

[22] There are a number of definitions of the unconscious; for my purposes Jung's is as good as any: 'Everything of which I know, but of which I am not at the moment thinking; everything of which I was once conscious but have now forgotten; everything perceived by my senses, but not noted by my conscious mind; everything which, involuntarily and without paying attention to it, I feel, think, remember, want, and do; all future things that are taking shape in me and will sometime come into consciousness: all this is the content of the unconscious.' (CW 8, ¶ 382; Storr (1983), p. 425.)

intensity. Therefore, unconscious processes are not literally unconscious; they are present in consciousness as a kind of background noise until and unless they cohere into macroscopic phenomena.

An analogy may clarify this. Project a slide on a screen, and defocus the lens. All of the same information is being projected on the screen as before, but now it is incoherent and the pattern is not salient; this is analogous to unconscious patterns in the protophenomena: they are there but not manifest. Focusing the lens makes the image manifest, which is analogous to the emergence of the unconscious content into conscious experience.

(2) The split-brain operations suggest another solution: in many cases the right hemisphere is unable to respond verbally to problems, and so it cannot easily manifest its consciousness to observers. Further, since the consciousness of the right hemisphere is largely disjoint from that of the left, the right forms a kind of unconscious mind for the left. Of course, the right hemisphere is as conscious as the left, and can manifest its consciousness in other ways, but its experience is not part of the left hemisphere's experience (or vice versa). The analogy becomes more striking when we recall that in these patients the hemispheres are not completely disconnected, so the right hemisphere can inject ideas into the left via the brainstem or via external transactions. Indeed, split-brain patients experience these communications as inexplicable 'hunches' — just like those from the unconscious (Gregory, 1987, p. 743). In summary, what the perceiving-acting-speaking ego experiences as the 'unconscious mind' may be an equally conscious but loosely coupled part of the phenomenal world, which manifests itself only through hunches, dreams, urges, etc. More precisely, my phenomenal world may comprise two (or more) loosely coupled populations of tightly coupled protophenomena. One of these subworlds, which includes the motor protophenomena, is identified with the conscious ego because it can manifest its consciousness in behaviour. However, other populations may be just as conscious, but unable to declare or demonstrate their consciousness to observers.

(3) Finally, according to the hypothesis of Sherrington and Pribram discussed earlier, consciousness is associated with graded dendritic microprocesses but not with all-or-none impulses in the axon. Therefore the unconscious mind may reside in the axons, which would make it comprise the more reflexive or instinctive aspects of the psyche. In fact, such a model fits well with Jung's description of the unconscious, for he stressed that the 'archetypes of the collective unconscious' are contentless behavioural patterns grounded in our shared biological — or even physical — nature.[23] Thus they correspond to the axonal pathways, which are for the most part genetically determined. On the other hand, when an archetype emerges into consciousness, it does so with some individual

---

[23] 'Again and again I encounter the mistaken notion that an archetype is determined in regard to its content, in other words, that it is a kind of unconscious idea (if such an expression be admissible). It is necessary to point out once more that archetypes are not determined as regards their content, but only as regards their form and then only to a very limited degree. A primordial image is determined as to its content only when it has become conscious and is therefore filled out with the material of conscious experience . . . The archetype in itself is empty and purely formal, nothing but a *facultas praeformandi*, a possibility of representation which is given *a priori*. The representations themselves are not inherited, only the forms, and in that respect they correspond in every way to the instincts, which are also determined in form only.' (Jung, CW 9 i, ¶ 155; Storr (1983), p. 415–6.)

content, which determines its particular appearance. The conscious manifestation of the archetypes corresponds to the dendritic microprocesses triggered by the axonal processes.

In fact, it is reasonable to suppose that all three of these explanations apply to the unconscious mind (which is primarily, it must be noted, a negative concept).

Comparison to Other Work

The philosophical view advocated here is consistent with that proposed independently by Chalmers (keynote paper; 1996). First, it acknowledges his distinction between consciousness, the phenomenal world as experienced, and what he calls 'awareness', the neurological correlates of consciousness as an emergent physical phenomenon. Next, it is consistent with his 'principle of coherence', which postulates a direct correspondence between the structure of consciousness and the structure of awareness, since the phenomenological dependencies between protophenomena directly parallel the neurological dependencies between synapses, even to the extent of obeying the same mathematical laws, so the emergence of higher level structures is also parallel. Third, my theory is consistent with his 'principle of organizational invariance', which postulates that identity of microscopic functional organization implies qualitative identity of experience, since it is the dynamical interdependencies among protophenomena that create the phenomenal world. Finally, my view is compatible with his 'double-aspect principle', which hypothesizes that information has two aspects, one phenomenal and one physical. In the present theory, the basic units of information have a phenomenal aspect as protophenomena in consciousness and a physical aspect as activity sites in the brain. Beyond that, the theory of protophenomena is a step toward the sort of fundamental theory for which Chalmers has called, for it postulates a simple theoretical entity governed by mathematical laws, which provides a foundation for understanding the structure and dynamics of consciousness.

There are some superficial similarities between protophenomena and the psychons proposed by Sir John Eccles (1990; 1993); they are both elementary units of consciousness associated with synaptic activity in dendrites. The first difference is one of scale: Eccles associates psychons with dendrons, bundles of the apical dendrites of approximately one hundred pyramidal cells. Therefore, a dendron contains approximately 100,000 synapses, and so we could say that a psychon corresponds to approximately 100,000 protophenomena. The second difference is ontological, for Eccles' theory is explicitly dualistic. He takes a psychon to be a causal primary, which can influence synaptic processes by momentarily altering the quantum mechanical probability of an exocytosis of neurotransmitter into the synaptic cleft. In contrast, my theory is essentially monistic, for it views the phenomenal and the physical as two aspects of the same reality.

The theory presented in this paper has both philosophical and scientific aspects. As Searle (1992, pp. 54–5) and others have noted, distinctions such as monism/dualism and mentalism/physicalism have outlived their usefulness, and their use to classify views such as ours are more likely to be misleading than helpful. Nevertheless, it is worthwhile to explain the philosophical aspects in these terms.

The present theory is dualistic in the sense that certain objects in certain situations (namely, activity sites in a functioning brain) have fundamental properties (protophenomena and their intensities), which are not reducible to physical properties. It is also dualistic in that the inherently private fact of experience is not reducible to the phenomena experienced, which are all potentially public (through a consensus of trained observers). Nevertheless, it is a kind of monism in postulating one 'stuff', which happens to have two fundamental, mutually irreducible aspects (phenomenal and physical).

Irreducibility enters in another way, for emergent causation operates in both the phenomenological (mental) and neurological (physical) realms: macroscopic consciousness governs microscopic protophenomenal dynamics (without violating the microscopic protophenomenal laws), as macroscopic awareness governs microscopic neurodynamics (without violating microscopic neurophysiology). Once the philosophical arguments for irreducibility are granted, scientific investigation can proceed by parallel analyses in the phenomenological and neurological realms, each supplying the other with hypotheses, theories and empirical data. However, phenomenologically trained observers will be needed to obtain repeatable observations of the characteristics of consciousness.

Summary

As a first step I have proposed a theoretical entity, the protophenomenon, as an elementary unit of consciousness associated with microscopic activity sites in the brain, tentatively identified with the synapses. Like other theoretical entities in science, protophenomena are validated by their explanatory value and their fruitfulness for further progress. According to this theory the phenomenal world is structured by dynamical dependencies among the protophenomena, which parallel the neurodynamical dependencies among the corresponding activity sites; indeed they are described by the same mathematical laws.

References

Chalmers, D.J. (1995), 'Facing up to the problem of consciousness', *Journal of Consciousness Studies*, **2** (3), pp. 200–19 (reprinted in this volume).
Chalmers, D.J. (1996), *The Conscious Mind* (New York: Oxford University Press).
Dennett, D.C. (1991), *Consciousness Explained* (Boston, MA: Little, Brown and Company).
Eccles, J.C. (1990), 'A unitary hypothesis of mind-brain-interaction in the cerebral cortex', *Proceedings Royal Society London B*, **240**, pp. 433–51.
Eccles, J.C. (1993), 'Evolution of complexity of the brain with the emergence of consciousness', in *Rethink- ing Neural Networks: Quantum Fields and Biological Data*, ed. K.H. Pribram (Hillsdale: L. Erlbaum).
Fleck, L. (1979), *Genesis and Development of a Scientific Fact*, trans. F. Bradley & T.J. Trenn (Chicago and London: University of Chicago Press).
Gregory, R.L. (ed. 1987), *The Oxford Companion to the Mind* (Oxford and New York: Oxford Univ. Press).
Hameroff, S.R. (1994), 'Quantum coherence in microtubules: a neural basis for emergent consciousness?', *Journal of Consciousness Studies*, **1** (1), pp. 91–118.
Hempel, C.G. (1965), *Aspects of Scientific Explanation and Other Essays in the Philosophy of Science* (New York: The Free Press).
Ihde, D. (1986), *Experimental Phenomenology: An Introduction* (Albany: State Univ. of New York Press).
MacLennan, B.J. (1991), 'Gabor representations of spatiotemporal visual images', Technical Report CS-91-144 (Knoxville: University of Tennessee Computer Science Department); accessible via URL http://www.cs.utk.edu/~mclennan.
MacLennan, B J. (1993a), 'Grounding analog computers', *Think*, **2**, pp. 48–51.

MacLennan, B.J. (1993b), 'Information processing in the dendritic net', in *Rethinking Neural Networks: Quantum Fields and Biological Data*, ed. K.H. Pribram (Hillsdale: Lawrence Erlbaum).

MacLennan, B.J. (1994), ' "Words lie in our way" ', *Minds and Machines*, **2** (4), pp. 421–37.

MacLennan, B.J. (1995), 'The investigation of consciousness through phenomenology and neuroscience', in *Scale and Conscious Experience: Is the Brain Too Important to be Left to Specialists to Study?*, ed. J. King & K.H. Pribram (Hillsdale: Lawrence Erlbaum).

MacLennan, B.J. (1996), 'Protophenomena and their neurodynamical correlates', Techical Report CS-96-331 (Knoxville: University of Tennessee Computer Science Department); accessible via URL
  http://www.cs.utk.edu/~mclennan.

Maxwell, G. (1980), 'The ontological status of theoretical entities', in *Introductory Readings in the Philosophy of Science*, ed. E.D. Klemke, Robert Hollinger & A. David Kline (Buffalo: Prometheus Books).

Miller, G.A., Galanter, E. & Pribram, K.H. (1960), *Plans and the Structure of Behavior* (New York: Adams-Bannister-Cox).

Pribram, K.H. (1971), *Languages of the Brain: Experimental Paradoxes and Principles in Neuropsychology* (Englewood Cliffs: Prentice-Hall).

Pribram, K.H. (1991), *Brain and Perception: Holonomy and Structure in Figural Processing* (Hillsdale: Lawrence Erlbaum).

Sacks, O. (1985), *The Man who Mistook his Wife for a Hat* (London: Duckworth).

Sanger, T.D. (submitted), 'Probability density estimates for the interpretation of neural population codes', submitted to *Journal of Neurophysiology*.

Searle, J. (1992), *Rediscovery of the Mind* (Cambridge, MA: MIT Press).

Shepherd, G.M. (1994), *Neurobiology*, 3rd ed. (New York and Oxford: Oxford University Press).

Storr, A. (1983), *The Essential Jung* (Princeton: Princeton University Press).

Rethinking Nature

William Seager

Consciousness, Information and Panpsychism

I: The First Datum

The hard problem of consciousness, according to David Chalmers, is explaining why and how experience is generated by certain particular configurations of physical stuff. Let's call this the 'generation problem', bearing in mind that the term 'generates' might be misleadingly causal: the explanatory relation we seek might be identity, instantiation, realization or something else altogether.[1] While the generation problem has the outward appearance of a genuine scientific problem, one might dispute whether it is useful, mandatory or, even, intelligible. Suppose one divided the problems of statistical thermo-dynamics into the easy and the hard. The easy problems would be ones like 'how/why do gases expand when heated', 'why/how does pressure increase with increasing tempera-ture', etc. By contrast, the hard problem would be to account for the generation of thermodynamic properties by the 'thermodynamically blank' particles which form the subject of statistical mechanics. What a mystery! Not only does a collection of inde-pendent particles *act like* a gas with thermodynamic properties, the collection somehow *generates* these very properties.

It is easy to see through this sham mystery and many are the philosophers who would suggest that the case of consciousness is no different. Once you have explained the appropriate and, no doubt, exceedingly complex internal structures which, ultimately, generate behaviour there is simply nothing more to be explained. Don't mistake a task made impossible because it is utterly senseless for one that embodies a deep metaphysical mystery. Chalmers insists that because consciousness is not a functional property, someone asking for an explanation of how a 'behaviourally sufficient' functional organi-zation generates experience is 'not making a conceptual mistake' (p. 13). Certainly, this is not as obvious a mistake as that which demands an independent, additional explanation of how *heat* arises apart from the account provided by statistical mechanics of the functional isomorphism between statistical and macrothermodynamics. But how can one show that the case of consciousness is not fundamentally similar?

---

[1] The generation problem has been around for a long time; a very clear formulation is given by John Tyndall (as quoted by William James): 'The passage from the physics of the brain to the correspond-ing facts of consciousness is unthinkable. Granted that a definite thought and a definite molecular action in the brain occur simultaneously; we do not possess the intellectual organ, nor apparently any rudiment of the organ, which would enable us to pass, by a process of reasoning, from one to the other' (quoted in James, 1890, p. 147, from Tyndall, 1879).

A straightforward reply is simply to point out the intelligibility of the classical problem of other minds. There is no *a priori* argumentation that can eliminate this problem; everyone who thinks about it can see that each of us is, in a fundamental sense, *alone*. Perhaps against this, Wittgenstein said: 'if I see someone writhing in pain with evident cause I do not think: all the same, his feelings are hidden from me' (1953/1968, p. 223). A tendentious reply is: of course not, for we operate on the assumption that other people do indeed have experience and this is no time to question basic assumptions. But what if it is a beetle writhing about as it is impaled on the specimen seeker's pin or a lobster squirming as it's dropped into the boiling water? There is no easy answer, let alone a philosophically innocent *a priori* answer, to the question of where in the chain of biological development experience emerges, although even at the levels of the beetle and lobster one certainly sees behaviour similar (at least) to that caused by pain.

Daniel Dennett's theory of consciousness (1991) can be seen as fixated on debunking the generation problem. His discussion of philosophical zombies (i.e. creatures that act just like us but who are entirely unconscious, entirely without experience) is reminiscent of Wittgenstein's remark, and is similarly perplexing. At one point Dennett says (pp. 405–6) that if zombies were possible, you wouldn't really be able to tell whether something was a zombie or not (every coin has two sides) so it would be immoral to treat a putative zombie as an entirely unconscious being. This is no argument against the possibility of zombies and so even less an argument undermining the intelligibility of the generation problem. Elsewhere, Dennett allows that animals do have experiences even though they do not have the fully developed consciousness of human beings (pp. 442 ff.). He intimates that many distinct functional architectures could underwrite the ascription of (I avoid saying 'generate'[2]) experience and with regard to bats in particular remarks that we can know something of the range of bat experience by finding out what the bat nervous system can represent and which representations actually function in the modulation of behaviour (p. 444). But this only tells us what the bat *could be* conscious of, it does not tell us whether the bat *is* conscious of these things, for there can be no question of eliminating the distinction between conscious and unconscious representations which 'modulate behaviour'. So here we find a very stark form of the generation problem located in a theory that was supposed to banish it: given the viability of the conscious/unconscious representation distinction (endorsed by Dennett even as he asserts that this distinction is not absolutely clear cut) and given the undeniable fact that some unconscious representations modulate behaviour, what makes the difference between conscious and unconscious behaviour modulating representations in nonverbal animals? How come the states that represent bodily injury in bats are conscious experiences, if they are, whereas those representing the details of wing positioning during the hunt are not, if they aren't? (Here I am just imagining that bats are like me: I feel the pain in my ankle but am not usually aware of the complex foot work involved in running over an uneven surface,

---

[2] But I note that the reviewer for the New York Times, George Johnson (1991), takes Dennett to be providing a generation theory of consciousness: '. . . from the collective behaviour of all these neurological devices consciousness emerges — a qualitative leap no more magical than the one that occurs when wetness arises from the jostling of hydrogen and oxygen atoms.' I very much doubt that Dennett would accept this view of his theory, for he patently never attempts to solve anything like the generation problem in his book (Dennett 1991).

yet both involve behaviour modulating representations.) We have no recourse to the usual behavioural test of consciousness here — verbal behaviour — since, of course, bats can't *tell us* what they are aware of, but Dennett generously, if puzzlingly, admits that animals have experiences despite this.

Or again, in his discussion of splitbrain cases Dennett denies that 'commissurotomy leaves in its wake organizations both distinct and robust enough to support . . . a separate self' (p. 426). But the issue should be, does the right hemisphere have *experiences* (is it like a nonverbal animal) whether or not it is a fullfledged self. Obviously, the right hemisphere deploys various *representations* and some of these modulate behaviour (as the mass of splitbrain research amply reveals). So what makes them, or some of them, into experiences? If it is not simply the behaviour modulating powers of a representation, is it a representation's having behaviour modulating power above degree n (on some scale of efficacy)? Obviously, this is the generation problem all over again: what makes n (or a vaguely defined region around n) the right sort of thing to enable consciousness?

A theory of consciousness ought to tell us what consciousness is, what things in the world possess it, how to tell whether something possesses it and how it arises in the physical world (both synchronically from physical conditions and diachronically as an evolutionary development). The hard problem of consciousness is evidenced by the very real 'zombie problem' we have with animals. The honey bee, for one more example, acts like a creature that has experiences (visual, olfactory, as well as painful and pleasurable). Its behaviour, we have reason to suppose, is modulated by a complex system of internal representations generated, maintained and updated by a sophisticated neural parallel processor (rather like our own, if much less complex) — representations coordinated, for all I know, by the famous 40 hz oscillations. Now, on which side of the fuzzy line between sentience and nonsentience does the bee reside, or in the fuzzy zone itself?[3] More important, for whatever answer, *why*? Suppose we made a robot bee that fitted well into bee life (beginnings are being made, see Kirchner and Towne (1994)). Suppose also we were sure the robot could not have experiences (it was truly an 'apian zombie'). Would that show that *bees* do not have experiences? *Why*? On the other hand, suppose we think that bees most certainly do experience things. Would that show that the robot also experiences (it certainly passes a *bee-level* Turing Test)? *Why*?[4]

As Chalmers claims, no extant theory of consciousness really addresses this range of questions, even as they admit that questions about bees' experiences are perfectly intelligible. Forgive me for harping on this, but the existence of the generation problem is absolutely crucial. Without it, there is *no* hard problem of consciousness. With it, the problem looks very hard indeed.

So hard, in fact, that Chalmers looks to a radical solution to bridge the so-called explanatory gap between physical system and conscious system. He suggests that consciousness is a fundamental feature of the universe, which must be simply accepted as the First Datum in the study of the mind. This is a neat way to finesse the generation question

[3] For more on the mental lives of honey bees, see Griffin (1992).

[4] Imagine we try to answer by, to take a current example, noting that the bee brain deploys the 40 hz oscillation binding system whereas the robot's processor does not. Then: how come only the 40 hz BS generates consciousness? Aren't other binding systems possible? Of course, this worry holds for any putative purely physical correlate of consciousness.

since there can be, by definition, no explanation of why fundamental features of the world arise whenever they do arise. For example, there is no explanation of why fundamental particles come in their observed mass ratios.[5] Perhaps, once we accept the reality of the generation problem, there is no other way to proceed. And since I am strongly inclined to see the generation problem as a real problem, I am naturally attracted to Chalmers' solution. Yet I confess to find some disturbing elements in Chalmers' account, which I will argue suggest that a yet *more radical* view of the problem of consciousness might be dictated by his assumption that consciousness is a fundamental feature of the universe.

II: Organizational Invariance and Explanatory Exclusion

Begin with Chalmers' idea of the conditions under which consciousness arises, what he calls the principle of organizational invariance. Strictly speaking, this principle asserts only that 'any two systems with the same finegrained functional organization will have qualitatively identical experiences' (p. 25). But it follows from this that whether or not a system, S, is conscious depends upon its fulfilling some *functional* description. For suppose not: then there is some other, nonfunctional feature of S, call it Q, that generates consciousness. We could then build a system functionally isomorphic to S that lacks Q which will, by hypothesis, not be conscious, which is impossible by the organizational principle.[6] It is disturbing that consciousness can be an absolutely fundamental feature of nature while being dependent upon particular systems satisfying purely functional descriptions, with the relevant similarity among these description being *behavioural* capacities. No other fundamental feature of the world has this character, or a character even remotely like it. It is rather as if one declared that 'being a telephone' was a fundamental feature of the world, generated by a variety of physical systems agreeing only in fulfilling the relevant, highly abstract, behaviourally defined functional descriptions.

Also, since Chalmers is adamant that consciousness presents a hard problem because it is *not* itself a functional feature it is very odd that consciousness should depend solely upon whether a system meets a certain abstract functional description. Of course, seeing that consciousness is a truly fundamental feature we cannot ask *how it is* that all and only systems meeting certain functional descriptions are conscious, yet this idea does seem to deepen rather than mitigate the mystery of the generation problem.

We also face here a variant of the generation problem which grows out of the inherent vagueness in the phrase 'finegrained functional organization'. Chalmers provides the example of a brain suffering a gradual substitution of its neurons, one by one, by 'silicon isomorphs' as an instance of his principle of organizational invariance (*ibid.*). But how do we know that this is the appropriate level of specificity of functional description? The silicon isomorphs, we may suppose, are not *internally* functionally identical to the

---

[5] The set of 'brute facts' changes with the advance of science however. The velocity of light appeared to be a brute fact until Maxwell deduced it from independently measurable magnetic and electric parameters (and since 1983 the velocity of light has been a matter of *definition*). But there is little prospect of science altogether eliminating brute facts.

[6] Thus Chalmers' position is a generalization of a view expressed by Richard Boyd (1980, p. 96): 'there are certain configurations such that whenever they are realized by a physical system, whatever substances compose it, the qualitative feeling of pain is manifested'.

neurons they replace, yet the internal workings of a neuron certainly fulfils some functional description. Or, from the other direction, why couldn't we replace large groups of neurons with a single silicon device that mimics the input/output relations of the whole neural group it replaces? Here is a new generation problem: how come just a *particular* level of functional description generates consciousness, and exactly which level does it? The problem is that functional duplicates of a system on various levels could, in principle, duplicate the whole system's behaviour. Would any system that acts like a conscious system be judged conscious by the principle? If not, suppose we have two systems which are functionally isomorphic at level n but are not functionally isomorphic at level $n-1$ (as in Chalmers' own example as I take it). Whether they share the same states of consciousness apparently depends upon which level is the appropriate level of description, but who decides? What does the *universe* know about levels of functional description?

A pernicious problem of explanatory exclusion[7] arises from the aligning of consciousness with functional description. Any functionally described system must be actually instantiated by some assemblage of physical parts, if it is to take any part in the workings of the world. The causal efficacy of the system depends entirely upon the causal efficacy of its physical instantiation. Thus when we say such things as 'the thermostat turned on the furnace' the efficacy of the thermostat is entirely explained by the particular physical instantiation of *this* thermostat (say by the physical details of its thermocouple, or whatever else lets it serve its function). Perhaps a better example would the power of water to dissolve salt: this is entirely explained by the interactions of individual H_2O molecules with the NaCl molecules that constitute salt, and these interactions are in turn entirely explained by the ultimately quantum mechanical properties of hydrogen, oxygen, sodium and chlorine. There is no room for water to have any causal powers save those grounded in its constituents. The *principle of causal grounding* states that the causal efficacy of any complex, whether functionally or mereologically described, is entirely dependent upon the causal efficacy of the basic constituents of its physical instantiation. The problem is now worrisomely clear. Does consciousness have *any* causal power in the world? If the causal powers of conscious systems obey the principle of causal grounding so that the causal powers of any conscious system are entirely dependent upon the powers of its instantiation then, seeing as consciousness is a fundamental feature of the universe which cannot be *reduced* to its instantiations, consciousness has no efficacy in the world — consciousness turns out to be completely epiphenomenal. On the other hand, if this conclusion is resisted and some independent causal power is granted to consciousness, then some assemblages of physical parts have causal powers that don't depend entirely upon the causal powers of those parts. This is what philosophers call *radical emergentism*.[8] Only here we have an ultra radical form for it is not the mere assembling of physical parts into particular molar combinations that yields the emergent properties, but rather it's the assemblage managing to fulfil a certain abstract *functional* description that produces the miracle (we might call this the doctrine of radical functional emergentism). Neither horn of this dilemma is very attractive.

---

[7] I take this characterization and the general form of the problem from Jaegwon Kim (1994).

[8] A doctrine interesting in its own right and especially popular earlier in this century. See ch. 8 of Kim (1994) for more on emergentism and its connection with the problem of explanatory exclusion.

This problem of explanatory exclusion can also be seen to arise from another of Chalmers' principles: that equating the phenomenal character of conscious experience with 'information states'. Now, every physical state is an information state relative to some possible information receiver, and the causal differences which correspond to differences in the information encoded into any physical state are normally thought to obey the principle of causal grounding (this fact, of course, is what underlies our ability to exploit physical processes to transmit information). So again we have our dilemma: if conscious experience is isomorphic to information load then the causal powers of conscious experience are either (1) entirely dependent upon the physical properties of the information bearer or (2) some information bearers violate the principle of causal grounding. If (1) we have explanatory exclusion and conscious experience is epiphenomenal. If (2) we have another form of radical emergentism, now somehow dependent upon the information carried by the physical state in question. Again, neither horn is attractive.

It is also worth mentioning a familiar ambiguity in the notion of information, which may mean nothing more than the 'bit capacity' of a physical state or it can mean some *semantically* significant content carried by the transmitted bits. It is not clear to which sort of information Chalmers means to assign the phenomenal qualities of conscious experience, though what he says inclines me to the former interpretation. The bit capacity of the brain is no doubt gigantic, but it is obviously doubled by considering *two* brains as a single system, yet it is doubtful that there is a kind of *third* consciousness associated with the interaction of two human beings, even though these two brains then form a causally interacting system. So we have yet another generation problem: which information states actually yield consciousness, and why/how just those?

III: The Nature of Information

Chalmers conjectures that perhaps information is itself a fundamental feature of the world, which makes it a 'natural associate' of consciousness. But consciousness and information connect at the level of semantic significance, not at the level of bit capacity. Insofar as the classical theory of information is situated at the level of bit capacity it would seem unable to provide the proper (or *any*, for that matter) connection to consciousness. Furthermore, the classical theory treats information as a feature of certain causal processes (albeit very abstractly conceived) which is to say that information is a functional notion: information is embodied in causal processes that can be variously instantiated, and obeys the principle of causal grounding (so leading to the problems of explanatory exclusion discussed above).

We can begin to move towards a more radical view of the fundamental nature of consciousness with a move towards a more radical view of information. This view of information sees causal processes as one species of information transfer but does not expect that all information 'connections' will be restricted to such processes. The natural place to seek a notion of information like this is in Quantum Mechanics.

The role of 'pure information' can be illustrated by a simple discussion of the famous two-slit experiment. A beam of photons, electrons, atoms or whatever is directed towards an appropriately separated pair of slits in an otherwise opaque surface. A detector screen is set up behind the slits. QM predicts, and less ideal but more practical experiments amply verify, that the 'hits' on the screen will form an interference pattern, which results in some way from the interaction of the two possible paths an element of the test beam can take to the screen.

More particularly, the QM formalism demands that the state, Ψ, of the particles in the beam be represented as a superposition of the states associated with each spatial path:

(1) $\Psi = \Psi_1 + \Psi_2$

(for clarity here, I leave aside the nicety of normalization — for details see the appendix). Ψ_1 represents the particle taking the left slit — call this path 1. Ψ_2 represents the particle taking the right slit — path 2. Now it turns out that when we calculate the probability of a particle hitting a certain region of the detector screen *both* possible paths contribute to this probability in a complex way; there is no way to regard the particle as in reality taking just one of these paths (though we are ignorant of which one) so that our calculation could proceed simply by adding up the probabilities generated by each path independently. This is revealed by the 'interference pattern' found on the detector after a sufficient number of particles have traversed the apparatus, which is strikingly different from the pattern expected if the particles were passing, one by one, through just one of the slits.

This feature of the two-slit experiment is well known and, as is equally well known, the interference pattern disappears if we have some way of determining which path the particles are taking. This is sometimes explained in terms of the disturbance of the particle's state which such a measurement will involve, and sometimes it is said that such a disturbance is unavoidable and is the proper account of this aspect of the phenomenon. But this is not what the theory says. There is no need to posit disturbance in order to explain the loss of the interference pattern; mere *information* about which path the particles take will suffice. For suppose that there was a *perfect detector* that could determine which path a particle has taken without altering the particle's state. Such a detector would be capable of only two output states, let's say L, R (for left slit and right slit respectively), and the output of the detector would be perfectly correlated with the components of the state, Ψ_1 and Ψ_2. There is nothing mathematically wrong with the idea of a perfect detector and the effect of the detector's presence will be to eliminate the interference pattern despite having no effect on the state of the particles. This is of some interest to those who need to be reminded that complementarity is not the result of the clumsiness of measurement, but is rather an intrinsic and ineradicable feature of QM. The theory maintains that the mere fact that our detectors carry the relevant *information* is sufficient to destroy the interference effects, whether or not the detector in some way 'disturbs' the system under measurement.

The kind of information at issue here is not bit capacity but the semantically significant correlation of 'distinct' physical systems, where there is no requirement that the correlation be maintained by some causal process connecting the two systems. This remarkable feature of QM is made more apparent by a device hinted at by the notion of a perfect detector. What about the possibility of retrieving the original interference patterns simply by *erasing* the information within the detector? Since the particle states have not been altered by the initial operation of the detectors, this would appear to be at least theoretically feasible. To speak figuratively: the particles, now far along on their way towards the screen upon which their position will eventually be recorded, have no idea whether their paths have been registered or not. Such an interference retrieval device is called a *quantum eraser* (see Scully and Drühl, 1982; Scully *et al.*, 1991; also Englert *et al.*, 1994; Seager, forthcoming). Quantum erasers are somewhat delicate creatures, for they must obey the stricture that no 'bit channel' be established between the systems in question — in this case the operation of the detectors and the target screen (for this could violate a fundamental stricture of the theory of relativity that no information be transmitted faster than the velocity of light). Nonetheless, they can be, at least theoretically, realized. Let us imagine that we have added to our two-slit plus perfect detector apparatus some unspecified method of erasing the information in the detector (this is actually the delicate part of constructing an eraser).

The analysis of the quantum eraser does indeed reveal that the interference patterns can be retrieved by simply erasing the information in the detectors, and this without the establishment of a bit channel (again, see the appendix for details). The operation of the eraser strongly suggests that each particle is responsive to the state of the eraser. But there can be no question of any causal process between the particle and the eraser operation if we arrange our experiment properly (we could, for example, make the distance between detector screen and the eraser so great and delay the operation of the eraser so long that a light signal could not reach the particle from the eraser before it got to the screen).

The natural interpretation of both the quantum eraser and the simpler, basic two-slit experiment is that there is a noncausal, but *information laden* connection amongst the elements of a quantum system. And this connection is *not* a bit channel or any sort of causal process (which shows once again, incidentally, that we are dealing here with a semantic sense of information). Here, perhaps, we find a new, nontrivial and highly significant sense in which information is truly a fundamental feature of the world (maybe *the* fundamental feature).

IV: Panpsychism

It seems to me possible to use this more robust sense of the fundamental nature of information to mold a theory which takes consciousness to be itself a fundamental feature of the world, where I mean by fundamental something elemental, not dependent upon the satisfaction of any functional description by any physical system, and not subservient to the principle of causal grounding. Chalmers himself makes a gesture towards such a theory in his remarks on information and notes that such a theory is 'not as implausible as it is often thought to be' (p. 28). We might as well be blunt about it: the theory at issue is *panpsychism*, which is the doctrine that 'all matter, or all nature, is itself psychical, or has a psychical aspect' (this from the OED), and it is indeed thought to be implausible. I offer a defence of it only with great diffidence. The generation problem seems real to me and sufficiently difficult to warrant fairly untrammelled speculation. Several strands of thought, some in defence of and some attacking panpsychism also come together in a curiously satisfying way once we unite the ideas that consciousness is a foundational feature of the world with our new notion of information and its significance.

I said above that on Chalmers' account, consciousness is a radically emergent phenomenon and hence is fundamental only in the sense that it cannot be explained in terms of the properties of the relevant complex systems that exhibit it. Chalmers is also adamant that consciousness cannot be reduced to these subordinate properties. It was noted some time ago, by Thomas Nagel (1979), that the denial of radical emergentism coupled with nonreductionism seems to entail panpsychism. The argument is straightforward: if consciousness is not reducible then we cannot explain its appearance at a certain level of physical complexity merely in terms of that complexity and so, if it does not *emerge* at these levels of complexity, it must have been already present at the lower levels.[9] Thus, if we are to *reject* a radical emergentism and yet respect the generation problem we will be naturally driven to panpsychism.

Panpsychism has seen better times. Perhaps it was the favoured doctrine of our forebears, echoed in the animism of many prescientific cultures. The polymath philosopher Leibniz endorsed a form of panpsychism, essentially for the reasons given by Nagel. But panpsychism was always at the fringe of scientific/philosophical respectability and tended to lose whatever respectability it possessed as the scientific understanding of the world expanded. So it is somewhat ironic that the revolution in biology wrought by Darwin occasioned a rekindling of interest in panpsychism. In a paper which still retains interest W. K. Clifford (1874)[10] presented an argument that was evidently in the air: the theory of evolution's application to the mind requires that some element of consciousness be present in all matter. Clifford says of consciousness, in recognition of the generation problem, that

> we cannot suppose that so enormous a jump from one creature to another should have occurred at any point in the process of evolution as the introduction of a fact entirely different and absolutely separate from the physical fact. It is impossible for anybody to point out the particular place in the line of descent where that event can be supposed to have taken place. The only thing that we can come to, if we accept the doctrine of evolution at all, is that even in the very lowest organism, even in the Amoeba which swims about in our own blood, there is something or other, inconceivably simple to us, which is of the same nature with our own consciousness ... (1874, p. 266).

Is this not Nagel's argument in a nutshell? Emergence is impossible, reduction is absurd — so elements of consciousness must be found in the basic construction materials of the universe (in Clifford's restriction of his argument to organisms we see a vitalistic error,

---

[9] I think that Nagel's argument is invalid, as it stands, because of an equivocation on the notion of 'reduction', which can be taken in either an epistemic or an ontological sense. Chalmers is pretty clear that his notion of reduction is an ontological one (but see his remarks on p. 21) and this clarity rescues Nagel's argument (at the cost of making the 'no reduction' premise less secure). An alternative to panpsychism is, then, the view that while there is no *explanatory* relation between matter and consciousness — no solution to the generation problem that is — consciousness is, at the bottom of its being so to speak, a physical phenomenon. Such a view has been derisively labelled the New Mysterianism (by Owen Flanagan, 1992, whose attachment to neural correlates of consciousness I fear does not even begin to address the generation problem). In fact mysterianism is quite attractive if one accepts the seriousness of the generation problem while retaining an attachment to physicalism.

[10] This is the same Clifford whose early speculations about the curvature of space prefigured General Relativity and the more radical programme that reduces matter to 'knots' of tightly curved space–time.

for the generation problem will arise no less for the gap between organism and nonorganism than for any gap in the intraorganism hierarchy). The addition of the theory of evolution which gives, or at least, at the time of Clifford, postulates, a palpable mechanism by which the simple is differentially compounded into the complex adds impetus to the slide towards a true panpsychism.

On the other hand, one can raise potent objections against panpsychism. Perhaps the single most concentrated and insightful attack on panpsychism is found in William James's *Principles of Psychology* (1890). James vigorously scourges the view he derisively terms the 'minddust' theory and presents what I think is the most difficult problem facing any panpsychist theory of consciousness. I will label this (1) *the combination problem*, which is the problem of explaining how the myriad elements of 'atomic consciousness' can be combined into a new, complex and rich consciousness such as that we possess. Isn't this just the generation problem all over again? James is very good on this:

> Take a sentence of a dozen words, and take twelve men and tell to each one word. Then stand the men in a row or jam them in a bunch, and let each think of his word as intently as he will; nowhere will there be a consciousness of the whole sentence. We talk of the 'spirit of the age' . . . but we know this to be symbolic speech and never dream that the spirit . . . constitute[s] a consciousness other than, and additional to, that of the several individuals whom the word 'age' . . . denote[s] (p. 160)

Or again,

> Where the elemental units are supposed to be feelings, the case is in no wise altered. Take a hundred of them, shuffle them and pack them as close together as you can (whatever that might mean); still each remains the same feeling it always was, shut in its own skin, windowless, ignorant of what the other feelings are and mean. There would be a hundred-and-first feeling there, if, when a group or series of such feeling were set up, a consciousness *belonging to the group as such* should emerge. And this 101st feeling would be a totally new fact; the 100 original feelings might, by a curious physical law, be a signal for its *creation*, when they came together; but they would have no substantial identity with it, nor it with them, and one could never deduce the one from the others, or (in any intelligible sense) say that they *evolved* it (p. 160, original emphasis).

In sum, James thinks that the *second* fundamental posit of panpsychism — that units of experience can *merge* into higher forms of experience — without which panpsychism offers no escape to those enthralled by the generation problem is 'logically unintelligible' (p. 158).

If James is right then the combination problem points to a distinctive generation problem in panpsychism which is formally analogous to the problem of generating consciousness out of matter. Panpsychism will have no advantage over physicalism if essentially the same problem lurks at its heart, and of course, it faces the intrinsic implausibility of asserting that atoms are conscious (in whatever degree you like — it remains undeniably implausible). If James is right then nothing whatever is gained by the *first* postulate of panpsychism, and hence the utility of making it in the first place is entirely undercut.

Another objection flows from this one[11] which might be called (2) *the unconscious mentality problem*. One might be inclined to avoid the implausibility of the first posit by accepting the *mentality* of the elemental units of mind while denying that they are actually *conscious* experiences. But this would of course leave the generation problem unsolved and might even be thought to exacerbate it, for how are we to account for the generation of conscious experience from the combination of nonconscious entities, even if they are in some sense mental entities. In this case, panpsychism faces a problem which is *strictly* analogous to the generation problem facing physicalists.

Yet another serious problem arises upon considering the role of mentality in the workings of the world. One might expect that a fundamental feature as significant as consciousness should take some part in the world's causal commerce. But if it does play such a role, then we should expect it to turn up in our investigation of the physical world; we should expect, that is, to see physically indistinguishable systems at least occasionally diverge in their behaviour because of the lurking causal powers of their mental dimension. In that case, our physical picture of the world is radically incomplete and many would find this extremely implausible. I often have to worry about whether my car will start, but I thankfully don't have the additional worry about its failing to start even when there is absolutely nothing mechanically wrong with it but just because it 'feels like' staying in the garage today! Let's call this (3) *the completeness problem*. I will reserve my replies to these objections until later, but one unsatisfying reply to (3) should be discussed here. A panpsychist could urge that physically identical systems will have, in virtue of their physical identity, identical mental features and so physically identical systems will always behave in exactly similar ways even if the mental aspect is providing some of the driving force. This is unsatisfying because it immediately raises the explanatory exclusion problem: what ground for positing any mental influence at all if the physical properties of the system *can* account for all its behaviour? The mental then becomes, at the very least, *explanatorily* epiphenomenal and threatens to be a truly superfluous appendage. So the problem is that either panpsychism asserts that our physical picture of the world is incomplete or that mentality is explanatorily epiphenomenal. The first horn is implausible and the second undercuts much of the point of the panpsychist enterprise.

Finally, there are the two simplest objections. We have (4) *the no sign problem*: there is no evidence whatsoever of a nonphysical dimension to the elemental units of nature and, (5) *the not-mental problem*: if there was some feature of these units we chose to label as 'mental', what possible ground could one provide to justify this label. Surely we would like to see some 'sign' of mentality, as such, in the basic features of the world before we could think there was any real content to the doctrine of panpsychism.

---

[11] In these objections, I am indebted to Colin McGinn's critical remarks on David Griffin's manuscript (1994) defending a Whiteheadian style panpsychism as presented to a conference on *Consciousness in Humans and Animals* held at Claremont School of Theology last year. I would like to express my gratitude to Prof. Griffin for organizing this conference and inviting me, and to the other participants for their vigorous debate. I cannot deal with the intricacies of Process Philosophy panpsychism here but I thank Prof. Griffin for stimulating my interest in the doctrine.

V: The Quantum Panacea

There is a coherent view of panpsychism that can go some way towards answering *all* of these objections. I want to examine them back to front since it seems to me that by and large they were presented in order of decreasing difficulty. As to (5): if one takes consciousness to be a truly fundamental feature of the world then it will not seem odd that it might manifest itself in regions remote from our normal encounters with it. There is no apparent sign of any gravitation between subatomic particles but since we take gravitation to be fundamental we are willing to accept that the gravitation force between two electrons really does exist. But we must always remember that those philosophers who deny that there is any generation problem for consciousness will be likely to regard the ascription of consciousness to anything that gives no behavioural sign of consciousness as more than implausible but utterly unintelligible.[12] I have tried to argue above that the generation problem is a real problem and this means that one can postulate with at least bare intelligibility that consciousness is a fundamental feature of the universe.

And this provides something of a reply to (4) as well. For if the analogy with gravitation is acceptable, then we would expect that the effects of the 'degree' of consciousness associated with the elemental units of physical nature would be entirely undetectable. There is no requirement that fundamental features provide operationally observable effects at every possible scale. This reply may be sufficient, but it also may not be necessary for, significantly, it is not entirely clear that the elemental units present absolutely *no* evidence of their postulated nonphysical (and indeed mental) aspect.

To explain what I mean is to address (3). I think it is reasonable to expect that a truly fundamental feature of the world should take a distinctive causal role in the world. And so we would expect that a picture of the world that is expressed in purely physical terms, without making any reference to this fundamental feature, would be incomplete. Occasionally, that is, the world should act in ways that are inexplicable from the purely physical viewpoint. No one really knows whether human thoughts and actions are entirely determined by physical features, so no one really knows whether human behaviour is purely physically determined either. But let us regard the elemental units of physical nature and see if *they* ever act in a way that is inexplicable from a purely physical standpoint. Of course they do — the Quantum theory insists upon this. As a physical theory, QM asserts that there is no explanation of certain processes since these involve an entirely random 'choice' amongst alternative possibilities. The world's behaviour does leave room for an additional fundamental feature with its own distinctive role.

There are various proofs that QM cannot be extended into a fully deterministic physical theory.[13] As I understand it, these proofs all depend on disputable assumptions. But we

---

[12] As in Wittgenstein's example: 'You surely know what 'it is 5 o'clock here' means; so you also know what 'it's 5 o'clock on the sun' means. It means simply that it is just the same time there as it is here when it is 5 o'clock' (§ 350). If the *metric* of time was a really fundamental feature of the universe, as Newton seems to have believed, then there would actually be a sensible interpretation of '5 o'clock on the sun' even if we in fact did not have access to the universal temporal metric. But of course, the nature of time is such that it makes no sense to wonder when 5 o'clock on the sun *really* is. See Nagel's discussion of this point (1986, pp. 23 ff.).

[13] See Jammer (1974) or Hughes (1989) for discussion.

might nonetheless take them as at least a sign of the ineradicable incompleteness of a purely physical picture of the world.

It will be urged, along the lines of (5), that the incompleteness appealed to here has absolutely no relation to consciousness, but this is not entirely clear. If we ask what features of the world our elemental units seem to respond to, one major influence is *information*. In the two-slit experiment, we might say that the particles are *informed about* the results of the perfect detector; in the quantum eraser the particles are *informed whether* information has been erased or not, in the demonstrable absence of any causal connection between them and the eraser. Responsiveness to information is hardly foreign to the realm of mentality although here it applies in an admittedly very circumscribed and impoverished sense, but this is to be expected of a fundamental feature manifesting itself at an elemental level. It may be worth repeating here that the kind of information at issue is not just the bit capacity of classical information theory but something more like semantically significant information and this is a notion of information more akin to mentality.

On this view, the elemental units of physical nature possess a mental aspect which enjoys a distinctive causal role in the behaviour of those units. Thus it grasps the first horn of the dilemma: the physical viewpoint *is* incomplete. But, I urge, at the level of the elemental units, the physical picture of the world does indeed *look* incomplete. And it may be that this incompleteness extends upward through the complex hierarchy of physical composition.

Reflecting upon the composition of more complex physical entities brings us naturally to the most difficult problem facing panpsychism: the combination problem. For while it is manifest that the basic physical elements combine in a multitude of ways to produce molecules, proteins and people, it is far from clear that it even makes sense to speak of the combination of basic mental elements, even granting they are in some sense conscious,[14] into distinct and more complex conscious experiences.

I doubt that the difficulty of the combination problem can be completely overcome, but I think that a fairly natural response to it springs from a little deeper look at the metaphysical presuppositions underlying James's position. According to James, the combination problem stems from a very general consideration:

> no possible number of entities (call them as you like, whether forces, material particles, or mental elements) can sum *themselves* together. Each remains, in the sum, what it always was; and the sum itself exists only *for a bystander* who happens to overlook the units and to apprehend the sum as such; or else it exists in the shape of some other *effect* on an entity external to the sum itself. Let it not be objected that H_2 and O combine of themselves into 'water', and thenceforward exhibit new properties. They do not. The 'water' is just the old atoms in the new position H–O–H; the 'new properties' are just their combined *effects* . . . (pp. 158–9.)

Or again:

---

[14] This is the only answer to problem (2). The panpsychist must proclaim that it is consciousness itself that divides down to the elemental units. Otherwise the generation problem returns with its full force. But given the considerations adduced above which ameliorate its implausibility, there is no reason why the panpsychist cannot make this basic postulate.

Just so, in the parallelogram of forces, the 'forces' themselves do not combine into the diagonal resultant; a *body* is needed on which they may impinge, to exhibit their resultant effect. No more do musical sounds combine *per se* into concords or discords. Concord and discord are names for their combined effects on that external medium, the *ear*. (p. 159.)

I won't dispute that such a view has a certain attractiveness; it seems no more than a reasonable generalization of the mereological reductionism of which the world provides so much evidence. But we know it to be false. The most startling revelations of its error spring, as the reader knows or guesses, from QM. Consider again the two slit experiment. It is the most natural assumption in the world to regard the particles as they pass through the two slits to form a *mixture* which contains one-half the particles in state Ψ_1 (a state representing, recall, the particle as having passed through the left slit) and one-half the particles in state Ψ_2 (particle having passed through right slit). But they do not. They instead are in the *superposition* of the two possible states, $\Psi_1 + \Psi_2$, and the superposition is a 'combination' of states which itself forms a genuinely new state with properties observably different from the properties of the mixture. Quantum wholes are not just the sum of their parts.

Yet the ability to enter into superpositions like $\Psi_1 + \Psi_2$ is a reflection of the properties of the elements that enter into it, so the notion of mereological reductionism is not to be expunged from our philosophy altogether, which is surely a good thing for this sort of reductionism lies at the heart of our notion of scientific explanation itself. However, we cannot accept the principle of mereological composition espoused by James and thus there is no argument from general principles against the panpsychist's combinations of elemental mental units into distinctive mental wholes.

VI: Further Speculation

Thus can the philosophical objections against panpsychism be answered. The kind of panpsychism I have envisaged states that the physical world-view is incomplete, as evidenced by the fact that physically identical systems can nonetheless act in different ways. The 'hidden variable' is not physical but a form of elementary consciousness — but, as Clifford remarks, the kind of consciousness 'which goes along with the motion of every particle of matter is of such inconceivable simplicity, as compared with our own mental fact, with our consciousness, as the motion of a molecule of matter is of inconceivable simplicity when compared with the motion of the brain' (p. 267). This is the 'psychist' part of the picture. The 'pan' part of the picture comes to the assertion that consciousness is an utterly fundamental feature of the world: not one element of physical reality is lacking its associated mental aspect. These mental elements combine according to some principle by which the summing together of parts yields more than just the assemblage of parts in causal interaction, just as do the physical elements.

We might speculate that there is a connection between the summation principles, so that in cases of superposition of states of physical elements we have mental combination as well. If we extend this idea to the case of multiparticle systems immersed in a non-ideal environment, which in truth we must, we arrive at the notion that *quantum coherence* might underlie more complex states of consciousness, for only coherent multiparticle systems will preserve the peculiar quantum mechanical properties that underlie the appropriate 'summation rules'. However, just *how* large systems could maintain coherence in the face of a highly energetic environment is quite unclear. Still, this idea has been espoused by a surprisingly large number of authors (see Michael Lockwood's, 1989, discussion of this issue; more recently Roger Penrose, 1994, has adopted it) but they fail to see the rather natural connection between panpsychism and their views. I mean that quantum coherence *cannot* solve the generation problem satisfactorily, but it might solve the combination problem.

In any event, a series of yet more speculative ideas suggest themselves if we entertain this approach, which I would like to sketch here in conclusion. The first idea is that only systems that can maintain quantum coherence will permit 'psychic combination' so that complex states of consciousness will be associated only with such systems. Given that the brain supports animal and human consciousness, the brain (or some significant part of it) is such a quantum system (this is *almost* the hypothesis of Penrose in *Shadows of the Mind* (1994); it differs from Penrose in that it denies that there is any new physics behind the phenomena). On the other hand, we may suppose that envisagable computers will not sustain quantum coherence; let's say that they are devices that *deamplify* quantum effects, and so they will not support complex, unified states of consciousness. Of course, an intentionally designed quantum computer, if such can be constructed, would not necessarily suffer from this weakness.[15] Here we have a modern reincarnation of an old idea, which goes back at least to Leibniz, distinguishing unified entities, or what Leibniz called *organisms*, from mere aggregates.

It might be objected that most quantum coherent systems could hardly be thought to sustain any kind of complex life of consciousness, as for example a pot of liquid helium. This seems a cogent objection fostering further speculation: could we not imagine that the nature of the combinatory consciousness is connected to the informational structures of the physical system at issue? The essential simplicity of the structure of liquid helium is informationally impoverished as compared to the complex structures of the brain (even though, we are assuming, both maintain coherence). Thus while our speculative panpsychist ought to (in fact, has to) admit that the liquid helium does indeed have an associated unified state of consciousness, it would remain an extremely primitive state of consciousness, perhaps not so different from the state of consciousness associated with the single lowly helium atom.

Looking at this point from another direction, modern computers have an informationally rich internal structure, which is what permits the complex range of behaviour in which they can engage. Yet since they are quantum deamplifiers, panpsychism (at least of the stripe we are discussing here) denies that they have any conscious mental life. Thus the panpsychist might support Searle's contention that computers have no understanding, which he draws from his famous 'Chinese Room' thought experiment (Searle 1980), and at the same time *explain* it, in terms a little clearer than Searle's brute insistence that the brain 'secretes intentionality'.

I must reiterate my diffidence in presenting such speculations. To borrow a phrase from Nagel, they all too obviously reek of the 'faintly sickening odour of something put

---

[15] See Deutch (1985) and Lockwood (1991, pp. 246–52) for discussions of this remarkable device.

together in the metaphysical laboratory'. The panpsychism offered here is a purely philosophical theory; as it stands, it has no distinctive empirical consequences. Still, I find it remarkable that a number of issues involved in the question of consciousness get a surprisingly unified treatment under panpsychism. It does seem to me that the acceptance of the reality of the generation problem and the subsequent perception of its extreme difficulty leads quite naturally, as Chalmers notes, to the idea that consciousness is a *fundamental* feature of the world. I would like to urge that panpsychism is the most natural way to incorporate consciousness as *truly* fundamental. But I would actually expect the argument to lead many back towards the difficult task of denying the reality of the generation problem.

Appendix: The Two-Slit Experiment and the Quantum Eraser

The state of a particle after passing through the two-slit experiment is:

(1) $\Psi = 1/\sqrt{2}(\Psi_1 + \Psi_2)$

The probability of a region of the detector screen, r, being hit be a particle is given by the inner product:

(2) $\langle\Psi|P_r\Psi\rangle$,

where P_r is an operator which projects onto the subspace representing those states in which the particle is found in r. The full expansion of (2) reveals the interference terms:

(3) $1/2[\langle\Psi_1|P_r\Psi_1\rangle + \langle\Psi_2|P_r\Psi_2\rangle + \langle\Psi_1|P_r\Psi_2\rangle + \langle\Psi_2|P_r\Psi_1\rangle]$.

The first two terms respectively represent the probability of the particle being in region r if it takes path 1 or if it takes path 2. The final two terms are the unavoidable cross terms which account for the interference pattern.

Now we introduce our perfect detectors. The particle plus detector state, after passing through the apparatus and being detected, would be written as a superposition of tensor products so:

(4) $\Psi_d = 1/\sqrt{2}[(\Psi_1 \otimes L) + (\Psi_2 \otimes R)]$.

Now if we wish to compute the probability of finding a particle in region r, we require an operator that works on the tensor product space of the particle *plus* detector; this operator is $P_r \otimes I$, where I is the identity operator. The probability of finding the particle in region r is now:

(5) $\langle\Psi_d|(P_r \otimes I)\Psi_d\rangle$

Written out in full this gets rather messy:

(6) $\langle1/\sqrt{2}[(\Psi_1 \otimes L) + (\Psi_2 \otimes R)]|(P_r \otimes I)1/\sqrt{2}[(\Psi_1 \otimes L) + (\Psi_2 \otimes R)]\rangle$,

but if we abbreviate $(\Psi_1 \otimes L)$ to X, $(\Psi_2 \otimes R)$ to Y and the operator $(P_r \otimes I)$ to **O**, the fundamental form becomes apparent:

(7) $\langle1/\sqrt{2}(X + Y)|\mathbf{O}1/\sqrt{2}(X + Y)\rangle$

which is analogous to (2) above. However, when (7) is expanded the cross terms take on a distinct form; the first step gives us:

(8) $1/2[\langle X|\mathbf{O}X\rangle + \langle Y|\mathbf{O}Y\rangle + \langle X|\mathbf{O}Y\rangle + \langle Y|\mathbf{O}X\rangle]$.

The expansion of just the first and last term of (8) should be enough to reveal what will happen to the probabilities in this case. The noncross term case goes as follows:

$$(9) \quad <X|OX> = <(\Psi_1 \otimes L)|(P_r \otimes I)(\Psi_1 \otimes L)>$$
$$= <(\Psi_1 \otimes L)|(P_r\Psi_1 \otimes L)>$$
$$= <\Psi_1|P_r\Psi_1> \times <L|L>$$

Since all our state vectors are normalised, $<L|L> = 1$ and (9) is simply the probability of the particle being in region r if it took the first path. As we would expect, the detector state has no effect on this probability.

Consider now a cross term of (8), say $<Y|OX>$:

$$(10) \quad <Y|OX> = <(\Psi_2 \otimes R)|(P_r \otimes I)(\Psi_1 \otimes L)>$$
$$= <(\Psi_2 \otimes R)|(P_r\Psi_1 \otimes L)>$$
$$= <\Psi_2|P_r\Psi_1> \times <R|L>$$

This cross term is accompanied by the factor $<R|L>$ (the other cross term of (8) will of course be accompanied by $<L|R>$). But in a perfect detector, distinct indicator states are orthogonal, so these inner products have the value 0 and the interference terms thus disappear. The probability that the particle will be found in region r is now just the sum of the probability of its being in r if it takes the path 1 and the probability of its being in r if it takes path 2.

The introduction of the quantum eraser is somewhat complex and depends upon a 'mathematical trick' (see Scully, Engleret and Walther (1991)). Four new states are defined as follows:

$$\Psi_+ \equiv 1/\sqrt{2}(\Psi_1 + \Psi_2)$$
$$\Psi_- \equiv 1/\sqrt{2}(\Psi_1 - \Psi_2)$$
$$G_+ \equiv 1/\sqrt{2}(R + L)$$
$$G_- \equiv 1/\sqrt{2}(R - L)$$

The states G_+ and G_- are to be thought of as states the detector can enter through the operation of the eraser. The original state, Ψ_d, can be written in terms of our new states:

$$(11) \quad \Psi_d = 1/\sqrt{2}[(\Psi_+ \otimes G_+) + (\Psi_- \otimes G_-)],$$

as can be verified from the properties of the tensor product. So this state exhibits no interference since the cross terms contain the vanishing $<G_+|G_->$ and $<G_-|G_+>$.

The action of the eraser is revealed by considering the probability of the particle being in region r *given* that the detector is in the state G_+. On the assumption that the detector is in G_+ the second term of (11)'s left side must vanish and the probability will be calculated from the state $\Psi_+ \otimes G_+$. The probability of the particle being in region r given that the detector is in state G_+ is:

$$(12) \quad <\Psi_+ \otimes G_+|(P_r \otimes I)(\Psi_+ \otimes G_+)>,$$

which reduces to

$$(13) \quad <\Psi_+|P_r\Psi_+> \times <G_+|G_+>.$$

Since $<G_+|G_+> = 1$ the probability we seek is simply $<\Psi_+|P_r\Psi_+>$. But, given the definition of Ψ_+, this probability expression expands into (3) above. We have recovered the original two-slit configuration with its interference effects despite the operation of the detector and we have done so via the operation of the eraser!

But no bit channel is set up. For consider the probability on the alternative assumption that after the operation of the eraser the detector goes into state G_-, which will be equal to $<\Psi_-|P_r\Psi_->$. This state generates interference effects too, but they are precisely opposite to those of (13). So unless we know which of G_+ or G_- the detector system goes into we cannot 'see' any interference pattern, and there is no way to transmit information about the detectors save by ordinary means.*

References

Boyd, R. (1980), 'Materialism without reductionism: what physicalism does not entail', in *Readings in the Philosophy of Psychology*, vol. 1, ed. Ned Block (Cambridge, MA: Harvard University Press).

Chalmers, D.J. (1995), 'Facing up to the problem of consciousness', *Journal of Consciousness Studies*, **2** (3), pp. 200–19 (reprinted in this volume).

Clifford, W.K. (1874), 'Body and mind', *Fortnightly Review*. Reprinted in *Lectures and Essays*, ed. L. Stephen and F. Pollock (London: Macmillan, 1879), pp. 31–70.

Dennett, D.C. (1991), *Consciousness Explained* (Boston: Little, Brown and Co.).

Deutsch, D. (1985), 'Quantum theory, the Church-Turing principle and the universal quantum computer', in *Proceedings of the Royal Society of London*, A400, pp. 97–117.

Englert, B., Scully, M. and Walther, H. (1994), 'The duality in matter and light', *Scientific American*, **271**, pp. 86–92.

Flanagan, O. (1992), *Consciousness Reconsidered* (Cambridge, MA: MIT Press).

Griffin, David (1994), *Unsnarling the World Knot: Consciousness, Freedom and the MindBody Problem*, unpublished manuscript.

Griffin, Donald (1992) *Animal Minds* (Chicago: University of Chicago Press).

Hughes, R.I.G. (1989), *The Interpretation of Quantum Mechanics* (Cambridge, MA: Harvard University Press).

James, W. (1890), *The Principles of Psychology*, vol. 1, (New York: Henry Holt and Co. Reprinted by Dover Books, 1950).

Jammer, M. (1974), *The Philosophy of Quantum Mechanics* (New York: Wiley).

Johnson, George (1991), 'What really gores on in there?', *New York Times*, 10 November.

Kim, J. (1994), *Supervenience and Mind* (Cambridge: Cambridge University Press).

Kirchner, W. and Towne, W. (1994), 'The sensory basis of the honeybee's dance language', *Scientific American*, **270**, pp. 74–80.

Lockwood, M. (1989/91), *Mind, Brain and the Quantum* (Oxford: Blackwell).

Nagel, T. (1979), 'Panpsychism', in *Mortal Questions* (Cambridge: Cambridge University Press).

Nagel, T. (1986) *The View From Nowhere* (Oxford: Oxford University Press).

Penrose, R. (1994) *Shadows of the Mind* (Oxford: Oxford University Press).

Seager, W. (forthcoming). 'A note on the quantum eraser', in *Philosophy of Science*.

Searle, J.R. (1980), 'Minds, brains and programs', *Behavioral and Brain Sciences*, **3**, pp. 417–58.

Scully, M. and Drühl, K. (1982), 'Quantum eraser: a proposed photon correlation experiment concerning observation and 'delayed choice' in quantum mechanics', *Physical Review A*, **25**, pp. 2208–13.

Scully, M., Engleret, B. and Walther, H. (1991), 'Quantum optical tests of complementarity', *Nature*, **351**, pp. 111–16.

Tyndall, J. (1879), *Fragments of Science: A Series of Detached Essays, Addresses and Reviews* (London: Longmans).

Wittgenstein, L. (1953/1968), *Philosophical Investigations* (Oxford: Blackwell). My page reference is to the 3rd English edition, 1968.

* This paper was originally published in the *Journal of Consciousness Studies*, **2**, No.3 (1995), pp. 272–88.

Gregg H. Rosenberg

Rethinking Nature: A Hard Problem within the Hard Problem

I: Nature and the Problem of Consciousness[1]

In the keynote paper, David Chalmers has separated two sets of problems about the conscious mind. The first set of problems he calls the 'easy' problems of consciousness, and they are the problems of explaining our mental functions. In this paper, I will refer to this aspect of consciousness simply as its cognitive aspect; so, by 'cognition' I will always mean the functions properly associated with possession of a mind.[2] The second set of problems Chalmers collects under the label of the 'hard' problem, and these are the problems associated with giving an account of the intrinsic character of experience, its existence, structure, and evolution. The mystery of the hard problem is that experience seems to be a further fact about the mind over and above facts about cognitive function.

I accept Chalmers' basic framework, and I am going to argue that the hard problem of consciousness is also a hard problem about nature. The irreducible character of experience implies that fundamental natural laws are governing it, laws on the same level as those governing properties such as mass, motion, and gravity. As Chalmers points out, because these laws are fundamental, superempirical standards are relevant in evaluating candidate formulations of them. The argument in this essay is an extended, critical reflection on the form those laws would take if we attempt to explain the qualitative aspect of our mental lives in a way that ties it too closely to cognition. Ultimately, such reflection shows that we have good reason to believe our attempt to fit consciousness within an adequate naturalistic framework will force us to go beyond issues specific to psychology and the philosophy of the mind.

---

[1] I would like to thank Leslie Gabriele, David Chalmers, Tim O'Connor, two anonymous referees, and the audience of a March 1995 presentation at Indiana University for comments on early versions.

[2] I should point out that I am using 'cognition' to refer to *mental* phenomena of a kind assumed to subsist entirely in the *physical*. I am assuming cognition may subsist entirely in the proper functioning of a *purely* physical system. My terminology is unprejudiced in the following sense. It is compatible with each of the possibilities, (a) that a system possesses phenomenal feeling just in case it is cognitive, (b) that there can be phenomenal Zombies which we might still claim have minds due to their having the proper cognitive capacities, and (c) that feeling may exist in the absence of cognition, and therefore in the absence of mind. Note that my use of cognition is *not* meant to be compatible with the possibility (d) that minds, with feeling or without, may exist without a properly functioning physical substrate.

Among naturalists, those such as McGinn (1989) occupy one extreme. They are so impressed by the difficulty of the problem they have concluded that it is just not soluble. Their opponents on the other extreme have dubbed them, a bit derisively, 'The New Mysterians'. These opponents sometimes continue to hold out for more traditional science (Churchland & Churchland, 1990; Flanagan, 1992), and sometimes simply deny the phenomenon at issue (Dennett, 1988). We can call those on this other extreme 'The Gung-Ho Reductionists'.

A reasonable middle ground exists. Let us dub the people occupying this middle ground 'The Liberal Naturalists'. The Liberal Naturalists (like Chalmers) are naturalists in that they believe there is a single natural world, constructed from a relatively small set of fundamental properties, and unified by a single set of natural laws relating these properties. They are liberal because they are willing to suppose the existence of funda- mental properties and laws beyond the properties and laws invoked by physics. The Liberal Naturalists, like The New Mysterians, recognize with honesty the difficulties presented by consciousness, but they also recognize the possibility that physics, and what subsists in physics, may not circumscribe nature's limits. That allows them comfortably to step outside the standard physicalist ontology, while retaining a naturalist world view. From The Gung-Ho Reductionist and New Mysterian standpoints, this is something of an end-around.[3]

The emergence of the Liberal Naturalist is a sign that we are continuing to mature as naturalists. We are now beginning, just beginning, to realize that the natural world we actually live in encompasses the physical, but only as an aspect. Consciousness shows us that our world has another *fundamental* aspect that we must understand if we are to understand the qualitative character of our mental lives. Now we must do the dirty work of rolling up our sleeves, figuring out just what kind of thing this other aspect is, and how we must revise our understanding of the world to smoothly integrate it. Unfortunately, the price we will pay to understand this aspect will exceed first expectations. As Liberal Naturalists, we must do more than simply supplement our physical understanding of the world by postulating some other, qualitative *mental* properties. Instead, to understand consciousness we will have to treat human cognition as a special context which is manifesting a phenomenon far more general and basic than cognition (and, by implica- tion, than *mind*).

I am going to call this phenomenon the 'qualitative field'. 'Qualitative' is just meant to capture the close relation to qualia; perhaps it subserves them in some way. I use 'field' to denote a bounded collective. Our phenomenal lives contain many distinct qualia: itches, sounds, smells, emotional tones and tickles are examples. All these different qualia, however, are merged by nature into one subject of experience, individuated from other qualia not only by their type, but also by the *field* of experience to which they belong (e.g. mine and not yours). The boundaries of this field individuate *subjects* of experience by including and excluding feeling. We can think of the unified, bounded

---

[3] An 'end-around' is a misdirection play in American football. The offensive team makes the defen- sive team believe it is taking the ball in one direction, but then hands it to the split-end, who runs in the other direction around the startled defence. In this case, the Liberal Naturalist *rejects* any form of physicalism, but goes around traditional forms of defence against dualism by *retaining* naturalism. The end-around is a high risk/high reward play. If all goes well, it results in a large gain. If it develops poorly, usually a large loss results as the split-end gets tackled behind the line of scrimmage.

collection of qualia which constitutes the experience of an individual as the qualitative field associated with that individual. The Liberal Naturalist must face the problem of providing a basis in nature for the existence of such a thing.[4] If successful, we will be able to identify the set of individuals that a qualitative field is associated with. Below, I show why our best strategy is to first rethink nature, and then fit consciousness within our new, enlarged understanding of the natural world.

This required rethinking of nature is really what makes the hard problem *hard*.

II: Why We Must Go beyond the Mind

As evidence for how uncomfortable the problem makes us, we can observe how difficult it is to dislodge the physical from its accustomed place of primacy in our world view. Even Chalmers, in the keynote article, continues to pose the problem as one of how 'experience arises from physical processes.' (p. 20) Such language pushes us to think of the physical as primary, with whatever aspect of nature consciousness is a part of viewed as a mere add-on; it just 'arises.' Are we to think of experience as an artist's flourish? A more satisfying result would be a *deeper* view of nature, a view which somehow gets under physics. The fact that we need to get under physics is obscured by this 'arising' intuition, which in turn is lent crucial support by the intuition that experience exists only in cognitive systems. Therefore, shedding this blinder is an important first step in learning to properly appreciate the scope of the challenge.

Chalmers has made an important distinction, but has not quite put us in position to take this first step. He has teased apart various problems of consciousness, bringing the hard problem of experience into sharp focus, highlighted against the background of the easier problems concerning function and structure. I accept that classification, but believe it does not cut finely enough. Additionally, we must tease apart the problem of conscious experience from its cognitive entanglements, and learn to see in it the more general problem of finding the basis in nature for qualitative content. That is, even the hard problem of consciousness is really two problems superposed. It is a general problem about finding the basis for these qualitative fields, their place in nature, and the laws governing them. Also, it is a specific problem about how the influence of cognition can give a qualitative field the character of consciousness. I will argue both that *in principle* and *in fact* these are separable problems, and that the need to separate them is what forces us to rethink nature.

Many readers will resist this conclusion very strongly, so we should more clearly understand just what the natural objection is. The problem I have posed is to find a place in nature for qualitative fields. The position I am defending is that such fields must have a basis more fundamental and ubiquitous than cognition. Most people possess a natural and strong opposing intuition that these qualitative fields are quite special things peculiar to minds. Since systems are only mental when they support cognition, qualitative fields must 'arise' within cognitive systems alone. Intuitively, we make this stipulation because we want to avoid an unpalatable panpsychism. We do not want experiences popping up in unlikely places.

[4] Probably many readers will be helped here by being reminded that Liberal Naturalists are working within a non-reductive, dualistic framework. Therefore, the fact that the brain does not contain a single place where 'it all comes together,' does not imply that the appearance of a unified, bounded field of experience is an illusion. So any motivation to deny the existence of such a thing is severely diluted.

Things get a little tricky here, since the criterion for a system being cognitive is itself so unclear. To be fair to the objector, we cannot simply define cognition so loosely or behaviouristically that an unacceptably wide net is cast. We do not want to make nearly *everything* cognitive simply by definition. So we can either allow a narrow definition of cognition, or simply stipulate that the class of cognitive systems that support experience must be like humans in certain important respects. At least, the systems in question must possess some kind of awareness, memory, perceptual ability, and conceptual capacity. For the purposes of what follows, we do not have to be too specific about these capacities. But we do need to be clear that they must be relatively *high-level* cognitive capacities. That way, we can constrict instrumental or behaviouristic definitions of 'cognition' enough to save consciousness for some (ill-defined) class of intuitively acceptable systems. From this point on, I will just refer to cognitive and non-cognitive systems. For those attracted to wide definitions of cognition, the terms should be understood implicitly as specifying high-grade and low-grade cognitive systems, respectively.

These contrary intuitions are initially very compelling; I held to them myself for quite a while. Nevertheless, upon reflection they ultimately must be rejected. In what follows, I will first give reasons for rejecting them. Afterward, I will try to say something to undermine the intuitive pull they possess. Essentially, I will try to make more palatable the idea that our intuitions here are misguided, and they should topple under the weight of the good reasons we have for ignoring them.

So, just what *is* wrong with the idea that qualitative fields are associated only with cognitive systems? The trouble is that it is very difficult to see how an appropriate set of fundamental laws can meet the constraint. For example, what *class* of base properties would guarantee the existence of consciousness on such a theory? There seem to be only three possibilities: the level of complexity of the system, the kinds of functionality possessed by the system, or one of those plus biology. I will argue that each of these seems implausible as a feature in a fundamental law of nature. We can, even now, imagine the coarse grained forms such laws must take, and we can use three main criteria to evaluate those laws. We can judge whether the concepts employed are appropriate as features in a fundamental law of nature; we can speculate about the simplicity of the resulting laws; and we can speculate about possible empirical consequences with an eye toward judging the plausibility of such consequences. Below, I am going to apply each of these three criteria to each of the three possibilities, where applicable.

1. Complexity

The first possibility is that some fundamental law of nature guarantees that a qualitative field becomes associated with a system when it reaches a certain level of complexity. The coarse form of the fundamental law would have to be, *'If a system reaches level of complexity N, then a qualitative field must arise from and co-evolve with it.'* Of course, to meet the constraint, the level of complexity featuring in the law will have to be sufficiently high to exclude many very complex systems. Additionally, the specific laws would have to say much more: such things as the structure of the field, its character, and the timing of its evolution will have to be systematically related to properties of the physical system. Any theory of consciousness should explain these things, though, so they are not special problems for this option.

Concepts employed — The antecedent of this law has a very unlikely form for a fundamental law of nature. The concepts of 'system' and 'complexity' are both far too vague to govern phenomena as definite as the qualitative fields of our minds. Explicating them will not be easy, at least not in a way respectful of their hypothesized status as characteristics nature is sensitive to on a fundamental level. I am going to leave aside the difficult task of defining 'system', and concentrate instead on the problems associated with giving a definition of 'complexity'. To begin with, many different kinds of complexity exist: there are the structural complexities inherent in the spatial organization of a system's components, the functional complexities of a system's contribution to a larger system, the computational complexities associated with the range of internal states the system may evolve through, and the relational complexities exhibited between a system and its environment.

Complexity also varies in description-relative ways. For instance, is the activity of a cell, described in terms of the molecular and atomic interactions within it, more or less complex than the activity of a brain, described in terms of the interactions of cell-assemblies? Should we include the complexity of the cells in the account of brain functioning, or should cells be abstracted away from and treated as primitive functional units? Also, how these complexities themselves are measured can vary along different dimensions internal to the kind of complexity being considered.

Picking out these appropriate dimensions also presents problems. Consider the problem of quantifying the complexity of the Amazon rain forest. Which dimensions should we pick to measure it? How do we find the 'units of measurement' which would quantify it? The need to quantify complexity across radically different kinds of systems also presents a problem; economies, brains, weather systems and ecologies spring to mind as examples. Which is more complex and why: Einstein's brain or the system of global ocean currents?

Simplicity — The general moral here is that the terms occurring in the antecedents of fundamental laws of nature must be sharp, not vague. Furthermore, articulation of a law relating qualitative fields to complexity will require postulating a favoured kind (or kinds) of complexity (computational complexity, perhaps). Nature must be uniquely sensitive to this kind, as it alone gives rise to consciousness. Whatever specification we give will count as a new fundamental feature of nature because nothing like 'computational complexity' currently features in any fundamental laws. That means the whole analysis of complexity, added to nature as a fundamental feature, will figure into the complexity of the resulting law. In the end, we will postulate some kind of innate and basic causal sensitivity to 'complexity' in nature to provide a basis for our fundamental laws concerning consciousness. This almost guarantees that the fundamental laws governing consciousness will not be simple, and believing that the laws really are fundamental will be difficult.

Empirical questions — Even if we imagine biting the bullet and accepting this added messiness in nature, can we specify a dimension of complexity that will give intuitively satisfying results? I can see no reason for optimism. The first, and most obvious, problem is that an arbitrary cut-off point will exist. At some point, conscious experience will mysteriously disappear (or, alternatively, magically appear). Consciousness then becomes subject to Sorites-type[5] decision: some system will exist, say a typical mouse brain, which has level of complexity N and is conscious, but in which some relatively

---

[5] Sorites paradoxes are paradoxes of vagueness. For instance, which hair lost makes the difference between being bald and not being bald?

small change to its internal functioning could decrease this level of complexity and wipe consciousness cleanly away.

Here is why: we know enough about cognitive systems now to understand that their performance degrades gracefully with a decrease in computational or organizational complexity. When conjoined with the graceful degradation of cognition, a theory of consciousness based on complexity will yield paradoxical consequences. They would be similar to, although not quite as troubling as, dancing qualia[6] problems. The law would govern robots, for instance. Now imagine a situation with some artificial system just complex enough to be conscious. Let us imagine outfitting this system with artificial neurons, and attaching a device to the crucial neuron that allows us to enable and disable it with the flick of a switch. We could then get a case of 'blinking qualia' where the conscious experience of the system is rapidly appearing and disappearing. Nevertheless, the flickering of the conscious field does not affect the system's behaviour or its thoughts, or affects them just barely.

The problem gets its force from the dilemma created by the need to avoid panpsychism. If consciousness were to change character smoothly with complexity without limit, we would not be able to avoid panpsychism. So our law implies that there must be a sharp point of complexity where consciousness disappears. Here is the dilemma: either that point is something that can support a non-cognitive system, or some cognitive system can exist without supporting experience. We can reject the first horn, because once we allow consciousness to be associated with systems that are too simple, we might as well throw the constraint away completely. So, by hypothesis, *any* system which is conscious must be cognitive. Conversely, there must also be some cognitive system which does not support consciousness. That is because the graceful degradation of cognition will make it impossible to match the complexity condition perfectly with cognition. To avoid panpsychism, the law must err on the side of excess, not deficiency. Finally, there must be some cognitive system which is right on that line. Its consciousness, however dim, is still accompanied by complicated perception, some kind of memory, thought, and so forth.

Our robot is to be built to be that minimally conscious system, and that same robot with one neuron disabled must be the maximally cognitive non-conscious system. In *this* system, blinking qualia are possible even when it is exercising its (virtually) full cognitive capacity. An important point here is that the robot's *cognitive* system is more or less *fully* functional. Really, we should not expect the loss of one neuron from a sufficiently complex, fully functioning cognitive system to make it incoherent like a drunkard or a sleeper. Nevertheless, the magic complexity line gets crossed, so the creature's *conscious experience* is gone completely. The only way out is if we allow degradation to occur to a point where the system was supporting experience *without* being high-grade cognitive, thus opening the door to panpsychism and violating the original purpose of our laws.

We also need to settle the question of an upper bound on the complexity which can support conscious experience. If we do not posit a law that sets an upper bound on complexity then we will not be able to avoid the kind of panpsychism that tying consciousness to minds is supposed to avoid. The reason is that any system in which conscious components are involved likely will count as at least as complex as the

---

[6] 'Dancing qualia' is Chalmers' name for qualia whose character shift without change in the functioning of the system. See the keynote paper for more detail.

conscious systems themselves, and so would have to be conscious. Consider two people sitting on a train having a conversation. For the system corresponding to their disciplined interactions to function, it must encompass all the cognitive capacities of *both* partici-pants. Thus, it will be more complex than either of them alone. According to the no-upper-bound theory of complexity, theirs would be a super-consciousness having experiences distinct from either of them. Our prospects for specifying such an upper bound are extremely dim. We can foresee how a given proposal for an upper bound, moti-vated by considerations like those above, will always admit cases of single systems (e.g. a creature with a brain twice as complex as a typical human brain) which we would never want to exclude from the consciousness club. Eventually, tremendous problems will arise for those of us who wish to individuate all the consciousnesses that must exist, problems tied in with how we are going to define 'system' as it occurs in the fundamental law.

2. Functionality

Mere complexity possesses obvious shortcomings as the basis for consciousness. The natural reaction is to suggest supplementing it with something else, something that would allow us to bypass some of the problems above. The most promising strategy is to circumscribe some range of capabilities as relevant to the presence of a qualitative field. Perhaps we should explicitly include some paradigmatically 'cognitive' capacities such as awareness, the ability to believe, to plan, or to perceive as necessary for the existence of a qualitative field. This is the second option: perhaps qualitative fields are associated only with systems that possess certain kinds of 'cognitive functionality' suitably defined. The coarse grained form of the proposed law would be, '*If a system evidences paradig-matically cognitive capacities XYZ, then it will have an associated qualitative field co-evolving with it.*'

Concepts employed — After hearing this kind of suggestion, we should step back to remind ourselves that we are searching after a *fundamental law of nature*. The kinds of laws we are looking for are on the same level as those governing gravitation, motion, and mass. We must keep in mind that whatever concepts occur in the antecedent of such laws impute direct causal relevance to the things that fall under the concepts, causal relevance not derivable from any constituents. This is very different from the kind of causal relevance typically enjoyed by high-level phenomena. That relevance is typically deriva-tive on the causal natures of constituents. Finding precise criteria for the concepts used by this kind of proposal is a very problematic enterprise, as anyone familiar with twentieth century psychology and philosophy of mind is aware. Including any of them into the laws governing the qualitative field will make those laws very complex, and imputes a character to natural laws not at all in harmony with those we have already discovered.

What makes one kind of system cognitive, and not another? At least at the beginning, defining cognition requires an appeal to norms. Like complexity, this is a vague matter. Presumably a correct account will involve concepts such as '*appropriate* behaviour', 'capable of *veridical* perception', 'supports beliefs that can be *true or false*', 'is *rational*', and so forth. The basic obstacle here is that cognitive systems are the kind of systems which can make *mistakes*, and the possibility of error requires the specification of a *norm* (Millikan, 1984; Dretske, 1986). In contrast, we should expect a fundamental law of nature to appeal only to purely descriptive conditions attaining in the physical system.

Again, it would be quite a peculiar law of nature that took effect only when a system was capable of making mistakes. The resulting challenge is to turn our intuitive, norm-filled concept of cognition into some workable, descriptive characterization.

One promising strategy for meeting the challenge is the thesis that cognitive systems are just a subclass of computational systems. If this thesis is correct, then any system implementing one of a certain set of algorithms would necessarily be a cognitive system. Such implementations would meet the conditions for applying cognitive norms, but they would not, themselves, be described normatively. Unfortunately, this solution just pushes the problem backwards a level. We will still need an explanation of what makes a computational system cognitive so that we can specify the relevant subset. That will depend on our concept of cognition, and not the other way around. Furthermore, our concept of cognition does contain the norms, and it seems to be a vague matter when they can and cannot be applied. This vagueness will infect our decision about which computational systems to cover in our fundamental law, and which to exclude. On the surface it will seem that we have a descriptive account of the conditions necessary for generating a qualitative field. Yet at a deeper, implicit level it will still seem as if nature is mysteriously honouring a set of norms. We will need to invoke norms to explain the lines drawn through the space of possible computational systems. Also, that subspace of systems itself will seem arbitrary along its edges.

Simplicity — A worse problem arises for how we will formulate the fundamental law. Somehow we must pick out, in our fundamental law, precisely the subset of systems whose implementation produces associated qualitative fields. Obviously, an infinite disjunction will not do. The most coherent alternative is to be able to specify some precise set of rules embodying 'criteria for cognition'. Again, this leads us back to the problem of defining cognition. Even in the unlikely event that we can specify such rules, they will not be simple. Also, although every *specific* cognitive system will have some descriptive features which account for why it is cognitive, we cannot assume that they will all share a set of necessary and sufficient descriptive properties. So we cannot assume a *general* analysis of cognition will be able to eliminate reference to norms. Therefore, if we are to specify the class of functional systems via some precise analysis of what it means to be cognitive, then we do have to worry about including the norms of cognition in a fundamental law of nature.

If a law of nature were to rely on some normative considerations, it would not be at all clear what that implies about our world. How is it that nature could decide when the law should 'kick in' and a qualitative field pops into existence? Imagine the problem in the context of a developing foetus. It would seem to require nature to evaluate the system, as it is functioning in nature, against a Platonic conception of ways systems *should* function, and further determine if it is *rational* (or *appropriate*) to hold the system to the standard. At that point, it begins to look like we are attributing mentality to nature as a whole at the fundamental level. Therefore, our fundamental law is again expanding the character of our world far beyond just adding a primitive phenomenal component to our psychological ontology. It is adding, as a fundamental constituent of nature, a power of semantic divination. This is far from the character of the fundamental laws we have thus far discovered. Those laws have a certain mechanical elegance that is ingenious without forcing nature to continuously evidence ingenuity.

Empirical questions — We may succeed in specifying the class of cognitive systems in some non-normative way. Probably, the best we can hope for is a functional account, either a computational account or something broader. In such a case we likely will still need teleology (Lycan, 1987). Teleology is necessary because the functional character of a given state cannot be determined locally in space or time. The functional contribution of a state is relative only to a series of other states, to interconnections between them, and against the background of 'normal' environmental conditions. The factual existence of consciousness will always depend, then, on a vast number of counterfactual truths extending widely through space and time. These facts are of the form, 'If the system is in state-type X, and were it to encounter input-type Y, then it would transit to state-type Z.' Here, the state-types themselves are supposed to be functionally or teleologically defined, and thus *their* identity-determination requires reference to further counterfactuals, and onwards in a grandly holistic fashion.

We know now that nature does exhibit such counterfactual sensitivities on the quantum scale (Penrose, 1994), so it is not something entirely new. Yet the form of the law we are now considering will require such activity routinely and ubiquitously on unheard of scales, and in macro-systems not known to exhibit these quantum effects. A law of that kind cries out for further explanation. It shows the arbitrariness and ad hoc character we normally interpret as signs that something deeper in nature is being exhibited.

3. Biology

A third alternative ties consciousness to biology by specifying that only biological systems reaching a certain level of complexity (or capable of certain kinds of functionality) can be conscious. That would rule out (presumably) global weather patterns, economies, and ecologies. Searle (1992) and Block (1980) have recently defended positions something like this. Unfortunately, this proposal has all the same problems plaguing the first two proposals. A system's biological character cannot be taken as a sufficient condition for consciousness. Inevitably, it will need to incorporate one (or both) of the notions of complexity and cognitive functionality. We are asked to believe that there is a fundamental law of nature whose antecedent contains a clause to the effect, '. . . *the system is of complexity N and is carbon based . . .*' Or, worse, a disjunction of the form, '*the system functions cognitively and is carbon or silicon based, suspended in liquid, with a cellular construction . . .* ' Proponents of the 'wetware' position are likely hoping that we will discover something subtle about cellular mechanics or chemical reactivity as relevant to consciousness. Yet it is very hard to see at this point what they have in mind. The coarse grained forms given above are therefore caricatures, admittedly, but they are caricatures that capture the essence of their subject.

Concepts employed — To avoid panpsychism, the law tying consciousness to biology will incorporate either the complexity or functionality constraints previously discussed, or both. Additionally, it must specify just what about biology (or 'wetware') is important for consciousness. Making a satisfactory case for any kind of biological constraint will be difficult. Consider two recent lines of thought that have been popular in the philosophy of mind, the appeal to evolution and the appeal to 'wetware'.

Millikan (1984) has argued that evolutionary considerations are essential to understanding the intentional properties of systems. Since consciousness seems rife with intentional content, some people might want to suggest that evolutionary considerations are also important for understanding why consciousness arises. Some people might want to do this, but I hope not many. Millikan's main concern is accounting for the normative aspect of content, and we have already seen the implausibility that the kinds of laws we are searching for involve normative considerations. The difference between consciousness and intentionality (as Millikan conceives the latter) is that consciousness is undoubtedly intrinsic, 'in the head', and basic. Millikan argues at length that content does not meet any of these conditions. Therefore, the analogy between intentionality and consciousness breaks down.

A much more popular suggestion is that, somehow, the 'wetware' of the brain is responsible for producing consciousness. Here, though, it does not seem as if it is biology that is really the issue, but chemistry. What, though, could be so special about chemistry? Why can it produce consciousness if solid state interactions cannot? Finding a plausible answer to this question is difficult. One option is that chemistry might allow for certain kinds of causal relations that solid state physics might not allow for, and these causal relations support consciousness. However, this is just another way of stating the functionality requirement, adding to it the additional bet that only biology could meet the functional conditions (see Edelman, 1989, for suggestive observations along these lines). But then we have not made any advance over the functional criteria. Once we realize that the functional difference chemistry might make is what we are really interested in, then the addition of 'biology' to the requirement of functionality seems superfluous after all.

Empirical questions — One has to wonder how we are going to fill in the exact association between biological elements and the elements of experience. If the theory is going to have any bite to it, it should say specifically what about biology supports and drives the evolution of our conscious experience. I can see only two possibilities. We are going to tie elements of experience specifically either to biological events, or to biological objects. Furthermore, it seems to me that the first possibility reduces to the second.

As our example we can imagine an experience like the light-headed enjoyment of a surprising and funny joke. If the theory ties this feeling to the occurrence of some kind of biological event, the first question that will arise is why it is important that the relevant type of event be a *biological* event? Holding true to our constraint is going to require tying the raw feeling specifically to biological structures such as cells or cell assemblies, with their peculiar chemical components. That is why the first possibility reduces to the second.

The biological markers for given experiences likely will not support the events underlying a *unique* kind of experience. Much more plausibly, at different times the same biological objects will support different kinds of experiences by participating in different kinds of events. Our theory is likely to have the consequence that a cell assembly (for example) can support a little patch of phenomenal blue, and a little patch of pain, and a little patch of angst, and that its participation in different events attaches these patches to it. Yet the biological nature of these assemblies remains relatively constant from one event to another. A neuron's firing as part of a 'blue qualia' event should not be significantly, biologically different from its firing as part of a 'purple qualia' event.

The underlying nature of the biological objects is not changing, and the experiences are constantly changing. Clearly, the event types are going to be doing the real explanatory work. They will be differentiable from each other holistically, as playing a certain role in the continuing evolution of the system as a whole, and should be carrying information based on the history of the system. Furthermore, for the purposes of explaining experience these events will be functionally construable since adding 'and the neural firings were realized in a system using serotonin, glucose, and . . . ' will add nothing new to differentiate the experience being explained from many other experiences. We then have the unpalatable consequence that an explanatorily impotent X-factor, biology, is nevertheless presumed to be a necessary ingredient in conscious experience.

If it turns out that we cannot give an account of mental events which abstracts from the biological substrate, then the conclusion above would fail. Should that be the case, however, it will be because the biology is the only substrate capable of supporting the proper functioning of the system; perhaps we can give no description of the functional capacities necessary for being cognitive creatures like us that does not refer to biology. This is a real possibility, but if that is the reason why biology is relevant then the relevance of the biological conditions will be derivative upon the relevance of the functional conditions. In essence, biology will be important only because of its unique capacity for supporting certain kinds of functioning. In this case, the biological requirement becomes redundant since the functional requirement entails it.

III: Is Panpsychism Palatable?

The preceding discussion does not in any sense *prove* that the fundamental laws do not tie qualitative fields peculiarly to cognitive systems. The point rests, mainly, on convictions concerning the simplicity, clarity, objectivity, and elegance of fundamental laws. They are convincing only to the extent that one possesses this conviction about nature. These kinds of considerations can yield strong reasons for rejecting such a constraint. In rejecting it we should conclude that qualitative fields have a basis much more uniformly spread in nature. It follows that cognition is merely a specific context inside which this basis is being expressed.

I have offered reasons for rejecting our intuitions that qualitative fields are phenomena that simply 'arise' from certain physical systems, but I also promised to try to undermine the intuitive pull of the considerations that lead so many to insist on that constraint. Those intuitions seem to rest mainly on two points: 1) we have no evidence for qualitative fields outside of cognitive contexts, and 2) the mere supposition is incoherent since it requires experiences without experiencers.

We can answer (1) simply by noting that every theory goes beyond the direct evidence that we have, because we have direct evidence only in our own cases. From my own perspective, any theory that attributes consciousness to people other than myself is going beyond my evidence. More generally, we can note that what counts as evidence for attributing consciousness beyond one's own case *depends* on the theory one might have of it. Therefore, in the general case, the concept of 'going beyond the evidence' is not well-defined. For instance, if I believe consciousness is dependent on language ability then verbal reports of conscious states are the only 'evidence' that such a belief will allow. Under the influence of such a theory, I would deny consciousness to animals because we only have evidence for consciousness, via verbal reports, in people. Alternatively, if I believed that consciousness depends primarily upon biology then I would extend attributions of consciousness down the phylogenetic chain to other animals. The basis of the extension will be a claim that the common biology we share with them is evidence that they also are conscious. Similarly, if I adopted the stance that only cognitive functioning is relevant to the presence of consciousness then I would, based on the evidence, suppose competently functioning silicon robots to be conscious.

The moral is that what we will count as evidence for consciousness, and what our theory of consciousness is, are heavily intertwined. Thus no pre-theoretical bias about the evidential base that we should not 'go beyond' can carry an overriding veto power on the form of the final theory. Surely, the theory must *include* certain systems as conscious. Any theory that had the result that only Gregg Rosenberg was conscious should give us pause. In general, our theory should include people, and expecting it to include other mammals, fish and birds is reasonable also. Things get a bit fuzzy when we begin to consider insects, perhaps, and also artificial systems, but that is alright.

What should be important to us pre-theoretically is that our evidence makes its strongest demands concerning certain kinds of organisms our theory must *include*, and can make only much weaker demands concerning which kinds of systems our theory must *exclude*. It follows that we should concentrate primarily on finding the simplest, most coherent set of laws that include the systems which intuitively should be included. If an otherwise exceptional theory has the consequence of also associating qualitative fields with some surprising class of systems, then we should accept that consequence as a discovery about nature.

The second intuitive basis for wishing to tie qualitative fields to minds alone is the charge of incoherence for any attribution outside a cognitive context. For many readers this is probably the main reason for the constraint. Appropriately, this is also the most difficult hurdle to clear on the way to shedding the prejudices that can keep us from finding a simple and satisfying theory. I am not sure one can ever fully shake this intuition, but there are ways a person can come to lose confidence in it. The thesis I suggest to undermine this intuition is that only certain kinds of qualia force themselves on us as essentially the experience of a mind, and other kinds, with very different characters from those we know, might subsist outside of minds.

A first step toward undermining our confidence that such a thing is inconceivable is simply to notice that, for most qualia, learning to regard them as objects of awareness in and of themselves is possible. That is how speculation and puzzlement about consciousness gets off of the ground. For instance, after some effort I can consider a blue region of my visual field as an object in front of my mind, being experienced, and not just an experience itself. The change in attitude is not so much reflected in my visual field, as in the background feelings which my visual field contributes to my overall experience. What I mean by this is something analagous to how a transforming idea system, or a moving experience, can change one's perceptions of the world or oneself. In these situations there is a definite sense in which one's perceptual fields, say the visual field, stay largely the same. Nevertheless, the contributions they make to one's overall experience are distinctly different in a way that is clearly responsive to the overall conceptualization of the world currently active. In a difficult to articulate way, one's experiences are both the same and still very different than they were before. The sameness seems reflected at a lower, relatively concrete organizational level of perception, and the differences at a much more abstract level of conceptualization which is clearly tightly connected to one's perception, but not completely coupled to it.

Here is what I try to do. I force myself to regard the blue region as an *object* of awareness; here, I regard it as *being experienced* like a dog, or a rock, or a flower petal (it is much like putting the secondary qualities out into the world). This contrasts with regarding it as *being an experience*, and, as such, constituting part of my representational awareness of the world (it is much like putting the secondary qualities back into the mind). The feeling flips back and forth, and in that respect is a bit like when one is staring at a Necker cube. At a moment, it seems that the blue region is part of my awareness, and partly constitutes my experience of *the world*. Then, at the next moment, it is an *object* of my awareness, an object of something which constitutes my experience of *myself*. If dwelt upon, it comes to seem a very strange capability. That I can do it, however, is very clear to me. Most other qualia can be reconceived similarly; sounds in themselves, and even pleasures and pains. It is a very peculiar fact that my experiences, under the appropriate conceptualization, can come to seem objects of experience discovered by my awareness. The only feeling that escapes this illusion is the feeling associated with awareness[7] itself. The feeling of awareness seems conceptually, irreducibly cognitive.

The fact that I can regard some parts of my inner self in that funny way does not show that *my* experiences are, or could be, objects out *there*, existing independently of my mind. Of course my experiences are essentially dependent on my mind. It does, however, seem to undermine my confidence that such a hypothesis is incoherent. We can assign some sense to the proposition that a visual field could exist in itself, as something that enters awareness but is not dependent upon it. More tellingly, it reinforces some further considerations and, together with them, lends much more credibility to the underlying coherence of the position.

First among these other considerations is the simple fact that when we speak of the qualitative field of some other, non-cognitive system we are obviously not attributing to it the qualities of our own experiences. We are not attributing little pangs of pain, or experiences of tiny blue dots to non-cognitive systems. Whatever we are attributing, it is not any kind of experience that we can empathize into. Instead, we are attributing to it a qualitative field that has a character in some very *abstract* sense like that of our experiences, but *specifically* unimaginable to us and unlike our own qualia. The best attitude toward such attributions is to maintain that the properties in question must fill a place holder for the solution to an analogy problem, for example: 'X is to a thermostat as conscious experience is to the human mind,' where we know X must have a solution in nature, but we do not really know what that solution is. It is an existential claim whose instantiation is something that we cannot be acquainted with, and hence should not pretend to understand deeply. For these reasons, referring to the qualitative fields of non-cognitive systems as proto-experiential rather than experiential is probably best. The term suggests both an hypothesized kinship between the qualitative fields of such systems and our own qualitative fields, and also the alienation from its richness, variety, and, most importantly, its awareness.

---

[7] I am trying to stay within Chalmers' framework as much as possible, so awareness is here being construed as a functional notion. *Associated with it*, however, is a feeling of being aware.

The answers to the second intuitive objection are then (1) We seem able to reconceive our own qualia, in many cases, as objects of experience as well as experiences themselves. (2) The qualitative fields we might attribute to non-cognitive systems do not contain 'little pains' or 'little specks of blue,' but instead have some kind of qualitative character very alien to us. (3) The best way to conceive of those fields is via a mental place holder for the solution to the analogy problem, 'Y is to system X as experience is to the human mind,' which sets up Y as a qualitative object that we know must exist, but which we cannot concretely imagine. (4) The best term for the alien character of these fields is proto-experiential, a term meant to suggest that they are qualitative objects without, strictly speaking, being experienced by a mind. Of course, there is going to be a perfectly good *sense* in which each is the essential part of a subject of experience, but this is just to point out the panpsychist conclusion that not all subjects are cognitive (and hence *mental*) systems. Considerations 1–4 show us how to regard coherently the qualitative fields of non-cognitive systems, even if they do not give us concrete ways of conceiving them. Collectively, what 1–4 suggest is that the difficulty of imagining qualitative fields that are not associated with minds comes from a shortcoming in our empathy, and not from a fundamental conceptual incoherence.

IV: Conclusion

I have argued in the preceding pages that we have good reason to believe the problem of qualitative content is a general problem for our view of nature, and not just a problem for psychology. I have argued on positive grounds by considering the form of the fundamental laws that we would have to posit to tie qualitative fields to conscious minds; also, I have argued that the intuitions that lead us to want to do so are not so sturdy as they seem at first glance. Especially, considerations about the arbitrary seeming forms the fundamental laws would have to take under the proposed constraints should make us suspect that there is something very deep about the structure and character of nature that is missing from our current, purely physicalistic world view. If I am right, then we must look for clues to tell us how our view of nature must be revised.*

References

Block, Ned (1980),'Troubles with functionalism', in *Readings In The Philosophy of Psychology, Vol. 1*, ed. N. Block (Cambridge, MA: Harvard University Press).

Chalmers, David (1995),'Facing up to the problem of consciousness', *JCS*, **2** (3), pp. 200–19.

Churchland, Patricia & Churchland, Paul (1990),'Intertheoretic reduction: a neuroscientist's field guide', *Seminars in the neurosciences*, **2**, pp. 249–56.

Dennett, Daniel C. (1988),'Quining qualia', in *Consciousness in Contemporary Science*, ed. A. Marcel and E. Bisiach (New York: Oxford University Press).

Dretske, Fred (1986), 'Misrepresentation', in *Belief: Form, Content, and Function*, ed. R. Bogdan (New York: Oxford University Press).

Edelman, Gerald (1989), *The Remembered Present* (New York: Basic Books).

Flanagan, Owen (1992), *Consciousness Reconsidered* (Cambridge, MA: The MIT Press).

Lycan, William G. (1987), *Consciousness* (Cambridge, MA: The MIT Press).

McGinn, C. (1989), 'Can we solve the mind–body problem?', *Mind*, **98**, pp. 349–66.

Millikan, Ruth G. (1984), *Language, Thought, and Other Biological Categories* (Cambridge: MIT).

Penrose, Roger (1994), *Shadows of the Mind* (New York: Oxford University Press).

Searle, John (1992), *The Rediscovery of the Mind* (Cambridge, MA: The MIT Press).

* This paper was originally published in *Journal of Consciousness Studies*, **3**, No.1 (1996), pp. 76–88.

Benjamin Libet

Solutions to the Hard Problem of Consciousness

The 'hard problem' in dealing with consciousness, as presented by Chalmers, is that of subjective experience. It is agreed that experience arises from a physical basis but there is no good explanation of why or how it so arises.

At first glance the hard problem appears to be a metaphysical one, scientifically insoluble. Chalmers agrees to that aspect, pointing out that even for fundamental phenomena in physics, such as mass or electromagnetism, there is nothing to tell us why matter may have properties of mass or electromagnetism in the first place. That is, we simply accept such fundamental properties or phenomena as 'givens' and develop theories to explain various facts related to these fundamental properties.

The meaningful, workable crux of Chalmers' hard problem is then to deal with subjective experience as another fundamental property in nature, one that is not reducible to or explainable by any other known physical phenomena. Chalmers states this position well but it is not without precedent. I had myself explicitly stated it as a required basis for any valid study of conscious experience (Libet, 1987; 1989; 1992). And that view of conscious experience as an independent non-reductive phenomenon was an essential one in our own experimental investigations of brain processes that mediate conscious experience, starting in the late 1950s (Libet, 1965; 1973; 1993a,b).

So, what kinds of theories does Chalmers propose as possible gateways to the solution of the 'hard problem'? He presents three candidates for 'psychophysical principles, connecting the properties of physical processes to the properties of experience'. I suggest all three of his principles contain fundamental flaws.

1. The 'principle of coherence between the *structure of consciousness* and the *structure of awareness*' seems to be essentially meaningless, under the usual sense of the term 'awareness'. Chalmers begins by making a sharp distinction between awareness and experience. He wants to use the term 'awareness' for the 'straightforward phenomena' described in his listing of the 'easy problems of consciousness'. But most if not all of those straightforward phenomena can and often do occur without any awareness (e.g. Velmans, 1991). In any case, awareness is a *subjective* phenomenon; it is accessible only to the individual who has it and is thus indistinguishable from conscious experience. I have repeatedly insisted that the phenomenon of 'detection' (whether of weak signals, colour differences, etc.) must be distinguished from 'awareness'; that distinction is based not upon theory but upon a large variety of experimental evidence (e.g. Libet *et al.*, 1991). Chalmers completely blurs this distinction. Chalmers finally concludes that ' if we accept

this coherence principle, we have reason to believe that the processes that *explain* awareness will at the same time be part of the *basis* of consciousness'. Of course, since awareness and conscious subjective experience refer to the same phenomenon!

2. 'The principle of organizational invariance . . . states that any two systems with the same fine grained *functional organization* will have qualitatively identical experiences'. Chalmers then describes a thought-experiment designed to reduce an alternative hypothesis to absurdity. But thought-experiments are only as good as the *assumptions* that underlie them; only an actual experiment, properly designed, can firmly settle an issue.

Chalmers admits that it is logically possible that his principle is incorrect. However, acceptance of his principle is based on a behavioural criterion for conscious experience. That is, if two different systems like the human brain and a silicon chip computer/robot are both 'functionally isomorphic', the principle states they both also 'will have the same sort of conscious experience'. But we have evidence that such a behavioural (functional) criterion for conscious experience can be misleading (see Libet, 1987; 1993b; Libet *et al.*, 1991). There are numerous examples of functional behaviour that appear to be associated with conscious experience when in fact the human subject reports being completely unaware, non-conscious of the process (see also Velmans, 1991). The distinguishing feature for a conscious experience is an introspective report by the individual who alone has access to the subjective experience. That is what makes it so difficult to distinguish a conscious experience from a non-conscious behavioural event even in non-human primates. Acceptance of this Chalmers principle, therefore, requires by-passing the distinction between purely behavioural criteria and criteria that indicate subjective experience in a more convincing manner.

3. 'The double-aspect theory of information' proposes that 'we can find the *same* abstract information space embedded in physical processing and in conscious experience' (pp. 26–7). So Chalmers 'natural hypothesis is that information (or at least some information) has two basic aspects, a physical aspect and a phenomenal . . . Experience arises by virtue of its status as one aspect of information, when the other aspect is found embodied in physical processing'. Chalmers admits that this 'double-aspect principle is extremely speculative', but that does not prevent him from extending it to an inference that experience may be widespread, like information; that perhaps even a thermostat . . . might have maximally simple experience' (p. 27).

Chalmers' linkage between information and experience is in part based on his principle of organization invariance. But, as I indicated above, that principle may itself be subject to serious argument. The formal 'isomorphism between certain physically embodied information spaces and certain *phenomenal* (or experiential) spaces' is again a functional relationship, and it ignores much similar isomorphisms between physical information and non-experiential (i.e. non-conscious) phenomena (see also Velmans, 1991; 1995). To then propose that experience emerges as a phenomenal aspect of information is not convincing.

Are there, then, other theories or lines of evidence that meet the requirements of the 'hard problem', treating conscious experience as a fundamental property in nature? Chalmers accepts 'that the processes that *explain* awareness will at the same time be part of the *basis* of consciousness'. On that view, our own experimental discoveries, of time factors in cerebral processes involved in producing the independently measured conscious experience (Libet, 1993a, b) would qualify as providing some partial answers to the hard problems.

An even more direct theory was advanced by me, published in the first issue of this same journal (Libet, 1994). I proposed that a 'conscious mental field' (CMF) emerged from the appropriate neural activities or the brain. That hypothetical field would be a new fundamental phenomenon, not reducible to or explainable, by any known physical processes. (A somewhat related theory has been proposed by Popper; see Popper *et al.*, 1993). The field would have the attribute of integrated subjective conscious experience, and it could also act back on the brain so as to provide a basis for conscious modulation of some neural processes. This theory is certainly speculative. But, unlike Chalmers' double-aspect theory of information, my theory is testable; indeed, my paper included a detailed experimental design that could potentially confirm or falsify the theory. I was unable to arrange to carry out that difficult though feasible experiment; my hope is that a qualified neurosurgery group will perform that fundamentally important experiment. For investigational purposes, it should be noted that non-human animals are not excluded from having their own kinds of CMF; however, nothing precludes the possibility that only the human brain, or all vertebrate brains, produce a CMF, since these brains have unique structural and functional characteristics. If some convincing criteria of conscious experience can be developed for a non-human primate it would become possible and much more feasible to test the theory with such an animal.

In conclusion, my theory takes the 'hard problem' seriously; it does *not* 'deny the phenomenon, explain something else, or elevate the problem to an eternal mystery'. I believe Chalmers has eloquently drawn attention to a fundamentally important issue in the attempts to deal with conscious experience, even though I am critical of some of his proposed solutions. And I endorse his final statement, that 'The hard problem is a hard problem, but there is no reason to believe it will remain permanently unsolved.' (p. 28)*

References

Libet, B. (1965), 'Cortical activation in conscious and unconscious experience', *Perspectives in Biology and Medicine*, **9**, pp. 77–86.

Libet, B. (1973), 'Electrical stimulation of cortex in human subjects, and conscious sensory aspects', in *Handbook of sensory physiology, vol. 2: Somatosensory system*, ed. A. Iggo (New York: Springer-Verlag) pp. 743–90.

Libet, B. (1987), 'Consciousness: conscious subjective experience', in *Encyclopedia of Neuroscience, Vol. 1*, ed. G. Adelman (Boston, MA: Birkhäuser).

Libet, B. (1989), 'Conscious subjective experience vs. unconscious mental functions: a theory of the cerebral process involved', in Models of Brain Function: ed. R.M.J. Cotterill (NY: CUP) pp. 35–49.

Libet, B. (1992), 'The neural time-factor in perception, volition and free will', *Revue de Metaphysique et de Morale*, no. 2/1992, pp. 255–72.

Libet, B. (1993a), *Neurophysiology of Consciousness* (Boston: Birkhäuser)

Libet, B. (1993b), 'The neural time factor in conscious and unconscious events', in *Experimental and Theoretical Studies of Consciousness*, ed. G.R. Block and J. Marsh (Chichester: Wiley).

Libet, B. (1994), 'A testable field theory of mind-brain interaction', *Journal of Consciousness Studies*, **1** (1), pp. 119–26.

Libet, B., Pearl, D.K, Morledge, D.E., Gleason, C.A., Hosobuchi, Y. and Barbaro, N.M. (1991), 'Control of the transition from sensory detection to sensory awareness in man by the duration of a thalamic stimulus: the cerebral "time-on" factor', *Brain*, **114**, pp. 1731–57.

Popper, K.R., Lindahl, B.I.B. and Århem, P. (1993), 'A discussion of the mind-brain problem', *Theoretical Medicine*, **14**, pp. 167–80.

Velmans, M. (1991), 'Is human information processing conscious?', *Behavioral and Brain Sciences*, **14**, pp. 651–69.

Velmans, M. (1995), 'The relation of consciousness to the material world', in this volume.

* This paper was originally published in *Journal of Consciousness Studies*, **3**, No.1 (1996), pp. 33–5.

Piet Hut and Roger N. Shepard

Turning 'the Hard Problem' Upside Down and Sideways

I: Introduction

The two of us — an astrophysicist and a cognitive psychologist — struggling with questions concerning the relation between the mental and the physical, but starting from the two contrasting disciplines of the cognitive and the physical sciences, discovered that we had come to essentially the same conclusions about what is wrong with prevailing views of what are variously referred to as 'the mind–body problem', 'the problem of consciousness', or what Chalmers has termed 'the hard problem'. This paper represents our initial attempt to articulate the core of the view we have come to share.[*]

1. The hard problem concerning consciousness

The 'hard problem' is not the 'third-person' problem of providing a scientific account for how a physical system, such as a human brain, can come to carry out the information processing necessary for intelligent behaviour. The reason that this is not the 'hard problem' is that no physical limitation has so far been identified concerning what a sufficiently complex physical system might be capable of in the way of adaptive information processing (and, surely, the human brain is as complex a physical system as any so far known to science).

The 'hard problem' is, instead, the 'first-person' problem of understanding how the subjective quality of experience (including, the seemingly nonphysical 'qualia' of pains, colours, odours, etc.) can be explained or understood as arising from any physical system as described in the objective terms of present day physics — whether at the level of electro-chemical processes in neurons and their synapses, at the much smaller scales of interactions of elementary particles, relativistic quantum fields, or even more exotic objects postulated to underlie those fields. The reason we say this is the 'hard problem' is that (despite the contrary statements of many commentators on the problem of consciousness) no so far imagined advance in understanding the physical processes going on in a nervous system (at any level) seems capable of moving us one iota closer to bridging the chasm between physical description and subjective quality.

[*] This article is an extension of some of the points we put forward at the conference 'Toward a Science of Consciousness', Tucson, AZ, 8 April 1996 (Tucson II) under the title: 'My experience, your experience, and the world we experience: Turning the "hard problem" upside down'.

To set the stage for our discussion, we will list a handful of common assumptions, and then point out some of their defects.

2. Some widely shared notions

The standard scientific approach to the 'hard' problem of consciousness (among those who recognize that there is a hard problem), appears to be based (whether explicitly or implicitly) on the following widely shared notions:

1. Conscious experience is not itself adequately described or explained in the purely physical terms of electro-chemical processes, particles, waves, or the like.
2. Conscious experience is nevertheless supposed to arise as a manifestation of (and perhaps only of) physical systems of enormous complexity — most indubitably in that most complex of known systems, the human brain.
3. Yet, even in such a system, only some processes in some spatial regions and in some (e.g. waking) states are supposed to be accompanied by conscious experience; other processes within the same system (though indistinguishable in their local, physical properties and processes) remain unconscious.
4. Consciousness is, accordingly, posited to be an emergent, but evidently non-physical accompaniment of only certain, as yet uncharacterized, parts or phases of certain processes in certain highly complex physical systems.
5. Whether these nonphysical accompaniments of those particular physical processes have causal effects back in the physical system itself (psychophysical interactionism) or not (epiphenomenalism) remains a matter of dispute.

3. Some serious problems

Though seemingly taken for granted by many researchers, these notions underlying standard scientific approaches to the problem of consciousness face several difficulties:

1. There are no generally accepted criteria for deciding whether any externally observed physical process is or is not accompanied by conscious experience. The sciences, from fundamental physics up through neurophysiology, proceed on the assumption that verbal reports, being themselves physical processes, must be fully explainable as the physical effects of other, preceding purely physical processes. Hence, verbal reports even of conscious experiences cannot serve as guarantors of the occurrence of conscious experience. Conversely, when such reports fail to emerge from a mute physical system (whether the right cerebral hemisphere of a 'split-brain' patient, or from a chimpanzee, a rat, or a single atom), the absence of such a report does not preclude that physical events in the system under consideration have subjective accompaniments or 'qualia'.

2. Indeed, no fundamental physical property has been identified that might distinguish those physical events that are — from those that are not — accompanied by conscious experience. Speaking in the first person, I presume that measurement and analysis of the electrochemical processes in one or more neurons in my own brain whose firing is perfectly correlated with my own experience of a flash of red, say, would reveal no differences from the electrochemical processes in other neurons in my own brain whose firing has no conscious correlate. Even if I should discover that the firing of particular neurons in a particular location of my brain was necessary and sufficient for my own conscious experience of a flash of red, this would tell me nothing about why just this externally observed physical event had such a phenomenal accompaniment while another

event that, at the level of fundamental physics, was indistinguishable from the first did not.

3. If nonphysical conscious experience is taken to have a causal influence back on the physical process from which it arose (psychophysical interactionism), how is this to be reconciled with the fundamental assumption of science that every physical state of a system is strictly determined by a preceding physical state of the system and its environment (determinism) — except for possible quantum mechanical influences that are purely random (indeterminism)?

4. If conscious experience does not causally affect the course of those physical processes (epiphenomenalism), then: (a) Why does it seem that I can control my own actions (free will)? (b) What function does consciousness serve; and why would it have evolved? (c) What causes some physical bodies (namely, other persons) to make those physical acts (of speech, writing, or typing) that express the (hard) problem of consciousness (including the problems of 'solipsism', of the existence of 'other minds', of whether robots could feel pain, of whether your experiences of red and green are the same as mine or just the reverse, etc.)?

5. Finally, of course, there is the difficulty that the standard reductionistic approach of contemporary science simply makes no provision for a nonphysical, phenomenal experience that is not ultimately composed of physical constituents (such as atoms and molecules, or particles and waves).

II: Turning the Hard Problem Upside Down

In a nut shell, we can summarize the situation as follows. There is clearly room for physical objects within experience; it is not at all clear whether there is room for experience within physical objects. To try to see how what we understand to be physical objects produce experience is in fact the 'hard problem', a problem that may simply be wrongly posed. Let us try as an alternative to turn the hard problem upside down, starting from experience, in order to see how what we understand to be physical objects may arise out of it.

1. Motivation

Some of the difficulties reviewed in the previous section appear to us to be consequences of starting from the reductionistic and materialistic presuppositions of physical science. The standard approach builds upon an epistemologically weak foundation: what it takes for granted is a physical world containing physical brains composed of atoms, molecules, ions, electric fields, and so on. But what are directly given to any scientist are only the consciously experienced appearances (filled with 'qualia' and their relationships) that (on the basis of certain regularities and correlations) are interpreted as independently existing physical objects. The weakness of this starting point is evident to those of us who experience vivid dreams populated with what we take to be independently existing physical objects until we awake.

Indeed, the atoms, molecules, and fields that (on the standard scientific view) constitute the material basis of any object, including a brain, are in fact known only as abstractions, not themselves directly experienced. The hypothesized invisible constituents of material objects can only be referred to by words, diagrams, or equations that are themselves (from this objective standpoint) but meaningless arrangements of molecules or (from the subjective standpoint) but constellations of qualia in the scientist's own conscious experience that lead the scientist to expect other experiences to ensue upon the performance of particular operations.

2. Starting from experience

Suppose, then, that we set aside the presuppositions that have been foisted upon us by the standard scientific view and build, instead, upon the foundation of what is indubitably given in our own experience. This is not to abandon what has been gained by science; only to find a more certain basis for science.

The macroscopic objects of common sense and the microscopic objects posited by science then become, alike, hypotheses whose meaning cashes out in an individual's expectations about future experiences. Phrased, most naturally, in the first person, some of these expectations concern the behaviour of those 'objects' of the kind I call 'other persons'. Thus, from the experience of a colleague emitting the utterance, 'There is a package for you in the mail room,' I infer that if I were to enter the mail room, I would have particular kinds of visual and tactile experiences. And, from the experience of reading of Galileo's discovery of the moons of Jupiter, I infer that if I build and look through a telescope in a particular direction in the night sky, I will have other particular kinds of visual experiences. This type of analysis of intersubjectivity in science was long ago advocated by the Nobel laureate physicist Percy Bridgeman (1940) and, before him, by the philosopher Rudolf Carnap (1928). It has sometimes been referred to as 'methodological solipsism' (cf. Shepard, 1981).

It may seem that the 'hard problem', though inverted, is still with us. Before, we started with a physical world and found it difficult to understand:

- how nonphysical conscious experience could arise in this physical world,
- why it would arise only from some particular physical processes and not from others that from the outside appear to be entirely equivalent, or
- how it could act back on — or play a functional role in — the physical world.

Now, each of us starts only with what is directly given in our own conscious experience and must explain what we mean by, and why we believe in:

- the external world of common sense as well as that of modern physics, and
- the existence of other conscious experiences (or 'minds') beyond our own.

3. The hard problem softened

So far, we do not pretend to have given a solution to the 'hard problem', or anything like a detailed alternative to the usual picture of reality that physics presents. As we will stress at the end of this paper, our strategy is not aimed at adding yet another model of consciousness to the literature. Rather, we question the underlying methodology of almost all attempts currently pursued in consciousness research. Once our questioning is taken seriously, we can explore the new terrain that opens up with a shift in the way we pose the whole problem of consciousness. But already at this early stage, simply by turning the hard problem upside down, we feel that this hard problem has already been softened.

When we turn the hard problem upside down, everything is grounded in our indubitable immediate experience, not in the hypothesized 'noumenal' world of unexperienced atoms, particles, or waves. Far from making our knowledge more insecure, this turn shifts us to firmer ground, away from attempts to reduce our felt reality to ever-more chimerical constructs in mathematical physics, that are posited to underlie our physical reality. Fascinating as explorations of the properties of matter on ever-smaller scales are, the grounding they so far afford for the whole of reality strikes us as undesirably precarious. For one thing, several ingredients that physicists use to describe the world are intrinsically unobservable, which makes their ontological status unclear. In addition, quantum mechanics seems to preclude any meaningful interpretation in terms of a single objective reality that exists prior to any attempt at measuring it.

The problem of the existence of other minds is softened in that by starting with subjective experience (my own) instead of with an 'objective reality', I begin with something closer to other subjective experiences (such as yours). Intersubjectivity might be viewed as expressing properties that are inherent in subjective conscious experience, but in addition are mutually agreed upon by different subjects. Taken this way, intersubjectivity provides an antidote against solipsism that is not more mysterious or artificial than any other form of knowledge, based on experience, including the more abstract varieties.

An analogy with Euclidean geometry may be helpful: once we specify the lengths of two sides of a triangle, and the magnitude of the enclosed angle, the length of the third side is fixed, and so are the magnitudes of the remaining two angles. Why is this? Wherein resides this magical power of space? How can space enforce these 'laws' of geometry, laws that physical objects obey as well, to very high accuracy? Compared to material objects, space seems like a very flimsy something, or really a nothingness, or at least a no-thing-ness. How could anyone imagine space enforcing all these 'rules'?

The reason we don't worry about such questions is that we simply 'see' that triangles are fully specified with two sides and an angle. But if that is the case, why can't we start with consciousness, and say that we simply 'see' that the different consciousnesses of different observers are obeying various rules that leave room for differences in, say, the size of an imagined chair, but not for differences in making conclusions about the size of a chair that is actually present?

In brief, as long as we have no ultimate foundation for any of our forms of knowledge, be they geometry or physics, we will have to live our lives layered on top of a sea of unanswered questions. Invoking a lack of grounding therefore is not a valid argument against one philosophical attitude, in favour of another. Rather, we should be more empirical, accepting from the outset what we indubitably experience, without becoming entangled with anxious worries about foundations.

Thus the biggest mystery is no longer consciousness but the objective physical world, which is never directly experienced but is only inferred on the basis of order and correlations within subjective experience. It seems to us more natural and epistemologically more justifiable to leave as inference what is inferred and to take as given only what is given, than the other way around. As for regularities and correlations, that are often interpreted as pointing to the brain as the seat of consciousness, we can think of many other explanatory avenues. After all, effectively jamming a printer does not 'prove' that computer processing takes place in the printer heads; nor does switching channels on a TV 'prove' that the information in the channels is produced inside the TV set. This is not to suggest that the 'source' of experience is outside the brain, in some other physical location; rather, the whole notion of a source that is reducible to spatio–temporal–physical terms, is something we question.

4. Radical consequences

Inverting the usual view in this way does, however, call for some rather radical changes in the way we usually think and talk about mind and matter.

For one thing, we should no longer speak of conscious experience as taking place 'in the head' or 'in the brain'. (What, after all, would be different in our experience if it took place somewhere else?) Rather, we should speak of the head or the brain, alike, as something that appears in or is inferred from conscious experience. Nor should we point to our surrounding environment to indicate the objective physical world and to our head to indicate our subjective experience. Everything we experience (whether 'out there' or 'in here') is, alike, a part of our experience.

Spatial extension, too, is no exception. We should not follow Descartes in distinguishing the physical from the mental on the basis of whether it is spatially extended or not (i.e. contrasting res extensa and res cogitans). We directly experience the world and the things in it as spatially extended. Spatial extension, as known to us, is thus, by virtue of being known, a mental phenomenon. If the physical world, independent of our conscious experience possesses spatial extension, it can only be known in a more abstract, mathematical (as opposed to experiential) sense.

Temporal extension, too, takes on a whole different character, once we start from experience, rather than from an objective world view grounded in a physical description of reality. One of the most glaring aspects of time is the distinction between past, present and future. Only in the 'now' is anything directly given in experience. Past and future are also given in the now, as present memories and present anticipations. While their contents point to the past and the future, as experienced memories and anticipation they take place in the experienced now. In contrast to this plain fact of every-day (or, better, every-moment) experience, physics has never provided an explanation for the special status of the present moment.

Whereas a global 'moving now' could be introduced by fiat (although rather artificially) in a Newtonian picture of space and time, we do not even have that luxury any more. In special relativity, in which each enduring object is represented by a four-dimensional 'world line' and in which simultaneity is relative to the motion of the observer (i.e. to the orientation of that observer's world line), there is no single preferred basis for an objectively moving common 'now' within which all observers are simultaneously conscious. In general relativity, things are far worse: an observer falling into a black hole will reach the hole in a finite time according to his or her own clocks, but will be seen to 'hover' just outside the black hole's horizon for all eternity, as far as far-away observers are concerned.

Thus, in the third-person view of physics, there simply is no privileged position along the world line of any observer. The moving now has been filtered out, reduced to an arbitrary number, and as a result all times have acquired equal status. What could be farther from our experience, and what could point more blatantly to the process of reduction underlying the whole physicalistic approach?

Finally, we should resist the temptation to invoke the complexity of the brain as somehow providing an explanation of the quality of conscious experience. There is, after all, nothing complex about a momentary flash of red or twinge of pain. (Complexity may be a component of intelligent reasoning or thought, but even those who believe that all mental processes are concomitants of neural ones might not wish to exclude the possibility that the firing of a single neuron in a brain could be the sufficient condition for an experience of pain.)

5. Philosophical Company

Even those (if any) who find some cogency in our proposed inversion of the hard problem may conclude, at this point, that we have merely advocated a return to something very like the 1710 idealism of Bishop George Berkeley (*esse est percipi*: 'to be is to be perceived') — hardly much of an advance from the perspective of present day science! There are, however, a number of respects in which our line of thinking departs from that of traditional idealism and (as we shall try to argue in a subsequent section) can provide insights into the problem of consciousness.

Certainly, in proposing to start from what is given in experience, we do not propose to take the given to be exclusively, or even primarily, concrete pointillistic 'sense data'. In contrast with the British empiricists, and more in line with the more phenomenological approaches of Husserl (in Germany; 1913) and Nishida (in Japan; 1911) as well as with the radical empiricism of William James (in the U.S.; 1912), we find that what is given in experience is largely of a different character: rather than a two-dimensional array of coloured spots or patches (in the visual case), what we find to be given is a three-dimensional arrangement of objects that evoke expectations about what further experiences will follow upon various actions that (in the terminology of James Gibson, 1979) they appear to 'afford'. (From the experience of dreams, however, we also recognize that there is no guarantee that such expectations will be confirmed on any given occasion.) Likewise, what is given is not confined to the concrete colours, shapes, sounds, tastes, odours, feels, etc. presented by any particular sensory modality. Rather, we are directly aware of relations, affordances, meanings (with, again, the caveat that the associated expectations carry no guarantees) as well as the 'abstract ideas' that Berkeley was wont to reject.

Moreover, we do not deny (as Berkeley did) the possible existence of a world behind the phenomena we directly experience — such as Kant's world of noumena. But, rather than taking the physical world presumed to be known by common sense or (in a very different form) by modern physics, we treat any notions about such a world as hypotheses that are useful to the extent that they predict and explain the regularities in our experience.

Finally, as we shall note, our line of reasoning leads to some rather novel 'panpsychist' speculations about mind that the British empiricists (as well as many present day scientists) would probably find quite counterintuitive. In contrast, twentieth-century continental philosophers, most notably Husserl, would have been much more sympathetic to our views. For Husserl, an empirical approach to reality meant dealing with reality as it presents itself to us, in the form of conscious experience. Interpretations, in terms of atoms and molecules, are exactly that: interpretations.

As Husserl stressed, seemingly simple and fundamental notions, such as that of an electron, in fact carry an enormous amount of baggage with it, including the whole methodology of science, as well as the cultural setting that leads one into a scientific attitude in the first place. An interestingly parallel and much more modern attempt to show this has recently been made by Brian Smith (1996).

All this is not to deny the significance of the *products* of science, its deep insights as well as its powerful technological applications, for better or worse. Rather, we want to stress that the *interpretation* of modern science is far from cut-and-dried, even though methods, results, and interpretations are usually presented as a package deal, the connections between them unquestioned.

III: Turning the Hard Problem Sideways

Having tried our hands at turning the 'hard problem' upside down, let us now consider alternatives. Rather than making a switch from physical reality to experience as providing a grounding for reality, perhaps we can consider both on an equal footing, without trying to make the one into a foundation for the other.

1. A second-person point of view

Another way to approach the 'hard problem' is thus to acknowledge the third-person character (in the grammatical sense) of knowledge based on a physical description of reality. In the objective approach, there simply is no room for the 'moving now' as experienced by me, as an individual human being. In contrast, turning the hard problem upside down suggests that all knowledge starts with the subject, the first person, the 'I' who looks at the world, standing on the ground of 'my' experience. If this way of turning the problem 180 degrees around seems to be too much of a good thing, how about a more modest turn, by only 90 degrees?

Turning the hard problem sideways brings us to the remaining grammatical choice: that of the second person. Whereas an I-based attitude raises the spectre of solipsism, and an it-based attitude offers only a cold objectivism, an I-and-you based orientation may combine the best of both alternatives, while avoiding the unpalatable extremes. In other words, the notion of intersubjectivity cannot be seen as a simple superposition of subjective and objective properties. Rather, acknowledging consciousness in others as being on a par with our own, we see a world around us, filled with physical objects as well as conscious experience of humans and other animals. The fact that we can and do interact with others is an aspect of conscious experience that is at least as important as the possibility that we humans have of reflecting upon our own existence.

2. Self-reference

It may seem that the original 'hard problem' was not eliminated by simply turning it upside down. If the proposed inversion of the problem turned its daunting frown into a smile, that smile may now appear to be one that is more ironic than comforting. Again speaking in the first-person, each of us may well regard brains as things that arise within our experience (rather than regarding experience as something that arises within brains). We may even adopt the 'methodological solipsism' approach to science.

Nevertheless, one of the brains for which my own experience already provides good evidence is the brain I call my own. Moreover, everything I have experienced makes me confident that I could obtain even more detailed evidence about my own brain by seeking certain further experiences — such as those we would call functional magnetic resonance imaging (fMRI) or positron emission tomography (PET) of my own brain. In a manner reminiscent of the 'autocerebroscope' envisioned by Herbert Feigl (Feigl, 1958; Meehl, 1966; cf. Shepard, 1978), then, I might have a 'first-order' experience (whether of a flash of red, a twinge of pain, a beloved face, or a scientific insight) and, simultaneously, a 'second-order' experience of an (fMRI or PET) image of my own brain in which locations corresponding to the first-order experience were 'lighting up'.

Quotation marks surround 'first-order' and 'second-order' here, in recognition that, in a sense, all experiences are 'first-order' experiences; it is only one's interpretations of experience of the two kinds that might be said to be of 'second' order — and these interpretations, too, are parts of one's experience. Ultimately, we encounter this curious circle: part of the 'lighting up' in the brain image I experience may represent the very neuronal activity that corresponds to my experiencing the brain image of that same activation. This may lead to Gödelian paradoxes.

After all, mathematics and consciousness have in common that they can be described self-reflexively. This in contrast to, say, physics, where mathematics as the language of physics is different from physics, or chemistry, which is dependent on physics for providing its basic building blocks. Maths, however, can be directly modeled by maths, and consciousness can be directly studied by consciousness.

In other words, if we view (somewhat naively) the sciences as providing a tower, starting with maths on the ground floor, physics on top of that, then chemistry, biology, etc., and psychology on top, then we have to conclude that only the bottom and top layer are truly self-reflexive, and therefore provide the conditions of possibility for unique forms of paradox as exemplified by Gödel's incompleteness theorems.

3. Other-reference

Even within one's own experience, then, several puzzles remain:

- How is one to understand the relation between 'first-order' experiences and 'second-order' experiences of their corresponding brain activities?
- Why is it that only some activities of my own brain (as I might experience them through brain imaging) correspond to my 'first-order' experiences while other activities (apart from the just noted 'curious circularity') evidently have no conscious manifestation?
- Where, indeed, am I to draw the line between those things in my experience that (in the 'second-order' sense) are accompanied by some 'first-order' experiences — whether experienced by what I call 'me' or by some other, independent experiencing agent or entity?

Just as we may take certain kinds of experienced regularities — and also surprises — as manifestations of an invisible and intangible (i.e. a 'noumenal') world behind the phenomenal world of experience, so too we may take certain other kinds of experienced regularities — and also surprises — as manifestations of other minds.

For example, I may have the experience of another person presenting an extended argument that leads up to a particular, unexpected conclusion that I see to be valid only after I subsequently think through the argument (or, perhaps, after I verify the conclusion by performing an actual experiment or calculation). Such an experience seems to provide compelling evidence for the occurrence of mental processes independent of my own. Granted, given the distinction (mentioned at the outset) between adaptive behaviour and subjective experience, this does not in itself provide a definitive answer for the 'hard problem' of other minds experiencing the same qualia I do or, indeed, experiencing any qualia at all (cf. Shepard, 1995).

It would, however, seem a strange and inexplicable violation of symmetry if the other bodies that I experience as being so much like my own in structure and behaviour differed so radically as to have no conscious experience. Nor does there seem to be any basis for drawing a sharp dividing line between humans and other animals — including such diverse species as apes, dogs, dolphins, and birds, which have more or less similarly structured brains and which exhibit behaviours similar to those that in ourselves are the outward manifestations of felt joy, lust, love, affection, caring, anger, fear, or pain (Shepard, 1993). It would seem more reasonable to grant reality the necessary structure to take care of the occurrence of consciousness, just as space seems to somehow take care of providing the correct angles and sides for a triangle, as we saw in section *II.3*. This aspect of reality, then, must be a different aspect from the more familiar notions of space and time. We will consider this possibility further in section *IV. 2*.

IV: Upside Down and Sideways May Be Compatible

Having described both of the turns we have given to the hard problem of consciousness, we have reached a point where we can begin to speculate about the relationship between the 90 degree and 180 degree rotations. We think both may turn out to be valid.

For example, we could consider matter and consciousness both as emergent properties of underlying and more fundamental aspects of reality. Just as matter might ultimately be explained as a property of space and time (as is already the case for the mass and energy of a black hole), so consciousness might be a property of another aspect of reality, X for short.

We realize that such a proposal immediately faces two serious problems. If we stop at this point, merely mentioning the notion of an unspecified aspect X, the reader may consider us glib and/or superficial, deriding us for not providing more detail. However, if we follow the temptation to construct an ad hoc model, we might be able to make our point more clearly, but with the penalty attached of almost certainly being wrong, in more than just the details of the model.

In this paper, we will try to avoid both horns of this dilemma. We will resolutely avoid any premature form of model building. Our goal here is not to provide a solution, let alone 'the' solution, to the hard problem of consciousness. At present, most specific models of consciousness strike us as naive. Instead, we see a greater need for new questions, rather than new attempts at answers, and we hope that the present paper will provide a step in that direction. At the same time, we do want to illustrate our thinking as clearly as possible. To that end, we start with an analogy from physics, in section *IV. 1*, and apply that in *IV. 2* to our view of the role of consciousness as a derived aspect of a more fundamental property of reality, X, on a par with space and time.

1. Space and time

How reasonable is it, to view matter and mind on the same level, as complementary? Starting with matter, let us imagine that a future form of physics will have succeeded in describing matter and energy as forms of excitations of space–time (in analogy with the case of a black hole, say, where space–time curvature directly provides a definite mass, with no need for any specific 'matter' ingredient). Is it, then, reasonable to turn the hard problem sideways, viewing conscious experience to be complementary to space–time, neither of the two being reducible to the other?

We will address that question in the next section. As a warm-up exercise, and in order to provide a helpful analogy (Hut, 1996, p. 149), we first remain on the physics side, in order to have a closer look at space and time. They, too, cannot be reduced, one to the other, even though they can be *partly* transformed into each other, according to relativity theory. But let us keep things simple, and start with everyday experience.

What is space? If we should meet somebody from another culture in which there were no word for space, how would we be able to describe our concept of space? Each specific description would even strike ourselves as being too crude. We could try to point to space as something that is present everywhere, as what remains behind after taking away all objects. But we would immediately realize how such an attempt would be almost certainly misunderstood. It would invite a view of space as a type of all-pervading substance, like air or ether. And while both can be used to some extent as metaphors, neither captures the notion of space.

What is time? This is an even more difficult question. Let us imagine that we meet someone who has a working knowledge of space, and shares the way we talk about space, but for some reason is not familiar with the notion of time. Perhaps that person has had a stroke or car accident, resulting in a form of selective amnesia. How might we begin to teach such a person what it means for us, to live in a world of space and time, rather than just in a world of space?

As in the case of space, we would be hard put to capture the notion of time in a purely verbal description. It would seem to make more sense to try to use a more action-based approach. We could take a series of snapshots of a street scene, say. We could put those pictures on a table, and point out that each picture shows the same space, but at different times.

Our 'space man', who had somehow lost the notion of time, might nevertheless recognize a house in each of the snapshots. We then tell him that it is the same house in each picture, that he has to identify all these houses with each other. And what about that cloud, which has slightly different positions in each picture? These, too, all have to be identified with each other, as all pertaining to one and the same cloud.

In short, each object is really a summary notion for a whole series of objects, as seen through the stack of pictures. And where does time come in? Can our space man get a clue from the fact that the cloud is occupying slightly different positions in each photograph? 'Yes indeed,' we tell him, 'there is a significant difference between the house and the cloud. The house does not move; it has no motion. The cloud has some motion.'

The conversation with the space man could then continue according to the following dialogue. Puzzled by the notion of motion, he would ask:

'So time is the same as motion?'

'No. Time is what makes motion possible.'

'But clearly, the cloud has more "time" than the house. The house is the same in all pictures. I can understand that from a purely space-based picture. No need to introduce this mysterious notion of "time".'

'No, there is as much time in the house as in the cloud. In fact, time is not located anywhere. It is equally present everywhere.'

'Like space! So, after all, space and time are exactly the same.'

'No, not at all. I understand that it is hard to imagine, and indeed space and time could both be said to be everywhere, in some sense. Still, they are completely different.'

'Hmm. Hard to imagine indeed. And what about that middle picture? It contains a car, one that is not present in any of the other pictures. Surely, there must be an error of some sort.'

'No, it simply means that the car went by so fast that it did not register in the other "nearby" snapshots. It had a greater amount of motion, but that does not make it more or less real.'

Clearly, even with a stack of snapshots, it would not be easy to get the idea of time across. And of course, this whole process of explanation would unroll in time. It could never happen in the first place if we were dealing with a purely 'spacey' being, one that did not partake in time at all. It is this observation that connects our example to the hard problem of consciousness.

2. Space, time and X

In the world described by physics, there is room for space and time (or at least for space–time), but there is no room for conscious experience (cf. McGinn, 1995). Of course, in any laboratory experiment, and in any derivation of a piece of theoretical physics, consciousness of the physicists is necessary, if nothing else, to comprehend the final results. But let us imagine that someone did not understand the notion of consciousness, just as in our previous example someone did not understand the notions of time and motion.

The analogy here would be between consciousness and motion. A car seems to have more motion than a house (in the rest frame of the house at least), and a human brain seems to have more consciousness than a rock (from a human perspective at least). In the previous section, the 'space man' had to learn two things, in turn: motion, which was visible, and time, which was inferred, invisible, but considered a more fundamental aspect of reality. So in this section, we find our work cut out for us: the space–time person (the physicist) has to be shown, first, the presence of conscious experiences, and then the more fundamental aspect of reality that provides the condition of possibility for experience. Let us call the latter X, for lack of a better designation at this point. X then stands to consciousness as time stands to motion.

Since the notion of some aspect of reality, X, is rather abstract, we can try to use a more familiar label, one that at least points in the direction we are contemplating. One possibility would be to use the label 'sense' to stand for X (Hut, 1996; Hut and van Fraassen, 1996; cf. Rota, 1989). Like space, like time, sense[1] is for us what water is for a fish. Our lives are embedded in it, given by it, irremovably linked to and through it. If we would lack any understanding of the world around us, in other words if nothing would make sense, we would not have any understanding of either space or time. But since the world does make sense to us, we can explore what it means, this notion of sense. Like space and time, sense it not something that can be directly experienced as such. We can form an impression of space through separations between particular objects. Similarly we can form an impression of time through observing specific changes taking place in time. And we can look at the same object or situation with a different 'depth' of sense, possibly looking at it 'from a different angle' (figuratively speaking).

Sure, we can interpret our world as a world of things. But what is a thing? When we look carefully, then we find that what we considered to be an object appears in our consciousness as a bundle of meanings, draped around sense impressions that are far, far less complete and filled in and filled up than the 'real thing' we feel to be present, three-dimensionally, continuous in time. What then remains of the solidity of the object? It is recognized in its givenness for us through the sense of solidity we have. Its continuity? This follows from our sense of continuity and identity. Its reality? Nothing but a sense of reality. The indubitability of its reality? The only thing we have a real handle on is our sense of indubitability of its reality. And this brings us back to sense as X, not so much a form of 'background field', but rather even more fundamentally, a primordial aspect of reality. Sense is seen then as a dimension of reality, on a par with space and time (cf. Tarthang Tulku, 1977).

No more can we walk out of sense than we can walk out of space or out of time. Still, we have to learn to see this, to see what such a statement may mean, experientially. In that respect we are initially in a situation very much like the space man trying to find time. Using this analogy, we could conjecture that sense is 'everywhere' just as space and time are.

More accurately, space is 'everywhere', time is 'everywhen', and sense is 'in every which sense'. Space is also there where there are no objects present. Time is also there where there are no specific events to be located. And sense, then, could be postulated to exist also there where no specific information would be at hand.

This idea, that we live in a world of sense, and that we can move around in sense, may sound strange. But it is clear that sense pervades our lived world. It seems hard to escape the conclusion that everything we know, as we know it, is what we know it to be through the way it makes sense to us. In this light, even nonsense is yet another form of sense.

---

[1] The word 'sense' is used here in its aspect of 'meaning', *not* in connection with 'sense experience' — the word sense seems to convey more directly a grasp of something than the more abstract word meaning.

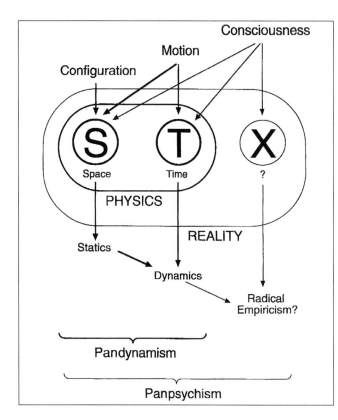

Figure 1

A schematic summary of our view of the role of consciousness, in analogy with that of motion.

Motion is a phenomenon that cannot be captured in the study of statics. Rather, it points to the presence of time as an aspect of reality equally fundamental as space. Similarly, it seems that consciousness cannot be captured in a study of purely physical phenomena, unless we extend our notion of physics to include at least one new element, on a par with space and time, indicated here by 'X'. We offer this suggestion as an sharpening of the notion of panpsychism, just like the notion of time would be a sharpening of the concept of 'pandynamism' that someone could introduce as a condition of possibility for motion.

Physics, then, describes a simplification of the real world, by projecting it down along the X axis. There is an analogy within physics itself. Projecting physics down along the time axis, we are left with space only, and we can then study statics. Of course, statics is nothing more than a limiting case of kinematics, in which all motions have been reduced to zero, or ignored. Similarly, physics studies only a limiting case of our reality in which the presence of the X 'dimension' of reality has been ignored, with the consequence that those aspects we call value and beauty have been reduced to zero as well. This is not to say that a physicist cannot find beauty or sense in physics; after all, we need to apply motion in order to set up an equilibrium situation that can be studied with statics alone. It is just that beauty and value *as such* do not appear as part of the formalism of physics.

3. Beyond pandynamism and panpsychism

A graphic way to illustrate the role of consciousness in our view of reality as woven out of space, time and X is presented in Figure 1. Confronted with the hard problem of the relation between conscious experience and the physical world, our first move is to postulate the presence of a third aspect of reality, besides the dimensions of space and time that underlie our description of the world in terms of physics. We have used the term 'X' here, for lack of a specific model, or even a specific set of notions as to what might be the structure of this extra 'dimension' of reality (Hut and van Fraassen, 1996).

Our second move is to make an analogy between motion and physics, on the one hand, and consciousness and reality including X, on the other. As we argued in section *IV. 1*, if we would have limited a study of physics to the field of statics, we would by definition have had no way of dealing with motion. Any attempt to introduce the notion of motion in purely spatial terms would then have led to confusion and puzzlement. A first attempt to broaden a description of reality, beyond statics, could have postulated a new and as yet unknown 'field of potential motion', pervading all of space — since, after all, motion is possible in any position in space. Such a mysterious field could then be considered to somehow 'carry' motion, and such a theory could properly be called a form of 'pandynamism'.

Similarly, attempts to postulate the pervasive presence of (proto-) consciousness under the banner of panpsychism, may seem puzzling, if not downright obscure, when starting with physics on its natural stage of space and time. Our conclusion is that attempts to *embed* consciousness in space and time are doomed to failure, just as equivalent attempts to *embed* motion in space only. Yes, motion does take place in space, but it also partakes in time. Similarly, consciousness certainly takes place in space and time, but in addition seems to require an additional aspect of reality, namely X, in order for us to give a proper description of its relation with the world as described in physics.

At this point, we can only guess what the third term will be, following the succession of statics and dynamics. In our figure, we have used the term 'radical empiricism', coined by William James (1912), since the ideas expressed by James are sufficiently simple and general as well as close enough to our views to serve as a place holder in the figure.

4. Taking turns

The 180 degree turn we started out with, when we turned the hard problem upside-down, is natural when we analyse the world from within our own experience, individually and collectively. In such a move, the first thing to notice is that our own sense of self and individuality is given with (and as part of) experience. Experience has a self, not the other way around. However, once we have accepted conscious experience as fundamental, the question arises of the ontological status of experience. Can experience itself provide the foundation of all of reality, as a basic sort of substratum (and what would that even mean?), or would it be more accurate to view experience as something that points to a more basic aspect of reality, an aspect X that provides the condition of possibility for experience? The latter seems to us more plausible, in light of the intersubjectivity we encounter in our world (cf. section *II. 3*).

When starting with space and time as the conditions of possibility for our physical reality, and some form of X as the condition of possibility for our conscious experience, we naturally find ourselves having made something that might be more aptly described as a 90 degree turn. The hard problem has been turned sideways, as we saw with the use of a few analogies. A bullet has more motion than a mountain, but not more time;[2] the whole world is drenched in time; it may be drenched in a form of pre-experience (X) as well. In fact, you can't say which is drenched in which: space in time, time in space, time and space in pre-experience, pre-experience and space in time, etc. We suggest that all

---

[2] Slightly less, in fact, according to special relativity.

three are equiprimordial, co-eval aspects of reality, intimately interwoven, and only together making up reality, 'as we know it'.

This change of perspective has implications that go beyond questions of epistemology or ontology. In the usual interpretation, we grant that different bodies, and their respective brains, share the same space and time, while we assume their associated experiences to be wholly separated. In our view, however, the experiences of different individuals are more intimately connected, in sharing the pre-experience aspect of reality, as well as the space and time aspects. It is here that intersubjectivity, dealing with different subjects in the second person, on an I-and-you basis, acquires its 'inter'.

Differences between turning the hard problem upside down and turning it sideways may lose their meaning. How we may describe such a reinterpretation may reflect more our predeliction for interpretation. We can illustrate this with another example from physics. Do we consider matter and energy on the same level? Is it equally reasonable to call energy a rarefied form of matter, as it is to call matter a solidified form of energy? Intuitively, the latter may seem more accurate. Once matter is seen to be no longer bound to a fixed mass or form of representation, matter partakes in the greater degree of mobility and fluidity of energy, at least potentially. Considering both forms, matter and energy, to have more 'energy-like' properties might seem like the natural conclusion. But ultimately, it is more a matter of convention, of defining what one means exactly with the word 'energy', which determines whether matter is seen as a form of energy, or whether matter and energy are considered to be on a par.

Somewhat similarly, we could allow the hard problem of consciousness also to be turned sideways *as well as* upside-down, depending on the view we would take. On a more practical level of describing how human minds interact with material objects, for example, an effective dualism may carry us quite far, in a sideways approach. But as soon as we reflect on the lack of consistency of a dualistic view, and the unsatisfactory nature of splitting up the world into parallel and seemingly incommensurable aspects, we can take the more fundamental view in which the hard problem is turned upside down. The question then is: what is the nature of the 'conscious mind' that is seen as more fundamental than 'matter'? And how does consciousness 'arise' in a mind, or vice versa? As long as all these terms — consciousness and mind and arising — are used as vaguely and variously as they are today, the above question is not even well-posed. If the word 'mind' is used for what we have designated as X, the hard problem can be considered to be turned upside down. If the word 'mind' is associated with conscious experience, a turn sideways may form a better description.

In either case, however, we may question whether it still makes sense to use the labels consciousness or experience. Maybe a label such as 'appearance' is more appropriate. Something appears. That's a given. From moment to moment we find ourselves in an ongoing flux of appearing. Everything else, events, experience, consciousness, let alone material objects, are late-comers, results from taking interpretive stances. Even though we may have been trained in accepting such interpretive stances, to the exclusion of everything else, at pre-kindergarten age, still this by itself is no reason not to question such stances. When approaching the hard problem of consciousness, let us try to remain as open-minded as we possibly can.

Aren't these statements rather rough and qualitative forms of speculation? Yes indeed, and that is all we feel ready for, now. Is there no hope to flesh these ideas out, make them perhaps more quantitative? Yes, there is. Physics and maths were not created overnight, so it is unreasonable to expect — let alone demand — miracles the day we abandon the overly rigid 'straight-up' view of nature that has been with us for the last few centuries. Instead, let us try to flesh out some of our speculations a bit further, using yet other analogies. One appropriate analogy is found in the fact that we all are accomplished experimenters in dealing with reality transformations, in the process called dreaming.

Within a dream, we identify ourselves with our own bodily presence, and consider other people and things to be independent of us, and to reside 'outside' ourselves. But after we wake up, we switch perspective: we view each and every element of the dream as being part of us, something constructed in our consciousness. Not only can we then consider ourselves as having scripted the role of each person we have met in the dream, but the role of each animal, plant, or inert object as well.

What is more, we must conclude that we have provided the supporting background notions of the dream-time and the dream-space that have formed the stage for all (seemingly) material objects to appear. Yet, somehow our usual identification with our body seems to prevent us from more than rarely dreaming ourselves to be an animal or a plant — or a rock, a piece of trash, or a patch of empty space that generously allows each and any object to pass through without being modified by it in the least.

Granted, in dreams we may also believe in the independent existence both of the physical world we seem to perceive around us and of the minds of the other persons with whom we interact in the dream. Yet, on awakening, that 'physical world' and the 'other minds' that expressed themselves in it vanish. Their evanescence does not, however, preclude a dependence of such directly experienced phantasms on a (noumenal) something beyond themselves. The prevailing scientific view is, in fact, that both the order and the surprises within the dream arose from something external to the experienced dream — namely, the restless activity of our own physical brain.

In short, there may be some justification — in waking and dreaming consciousness alike — for hypothesizing the existence of something behind what we experience as an explanation for both its predictable or conservative aspect and its unanticipated or creative aspect. But whatever that something may be, it would be a category mistake to take particular elements from *within* experience, whether based on dreaming or waking, as fundamental. However abstract our notions of atoms, quantum fields, or more exotic constructs may be, all of these notions are ultimately grounded *in* experience. As such, they cannot even be considered as candidates for whatever it might be, if anything, that could be considered to underlie conscious experience. Such a candidate had better be far more pervasive. We view our attempt to label such a candidate with 'sense' or better 'X' as no more than a shot in the dark — but, we hope, a shot in the right direction.

Acknowledgments. We thank Sean Murphy and Jonathan Shear, as well as an anonymous referee,[3] for comments on the manuscript. This work was supported in part by a

---

[3] This referee also alerted us to some parallels between our notion of 'turning the hard problem upside down' and several papers by Velmans, most recently his 'What and where are conscious experiences?', in *The Science of Consciousness: Psychological, Neuropsychological and Clinical Reviews*, ed. M. Velmans (Routledge, 1996).

grant to the authors from the Alfred P. Sloan Foundation, for research on limits to scientific knowledge. We thank John Casti and Joseph Traub, organizers of the workshop on 'Limits to Scientific Knowledge', held at the Santa Fe Institute in May 1994, for providing a natural opportunity for the two of us to meet each other. We also thank SFI for their hospitality, and the Sloan Organization for sponsoring that workshop.*

References

Bridgeman, P.W. (1940), 'Science: public or private?', *Philosophy of Science*, **7**, 36–48.

Carnap, R. (1928), *Der Logische Aufbau der Welt* . English translation by Rolf A. George (1967), *The Logical Structure of the World* (Berkeley: University of California Press).

Chalmers, D.J. (1995), 'Facing up to the problem of consciousness', *Journal of Consciousness Studies*, **2** (3), pp. 200–19 (reprinted in this volume).

Feigl, H. (1958), 'The "mental" and the "physical" ', in *Minnesota Studies in the Philosophy of Science, Vol. II*, ed. G. Maxwell and M. Scriven (Minneapolis: University of Minnesota Press).

Gibson, J.J. (1979), *The Ecological Approach to Visual Perception* (Boston: Houghton-Mifflin).

Husserl, E. (1913), *Ideen zu einer reinen Phänomenologie and phänomenologischen Philosophie I, Erstes Buch*, translated as *Ideas Pertaining to a Pure Phenomenology and to a Phenomenological Philosophy, first book,* 1982 (Dordrecht: Kluwer).

Hut, P. (1996), 'Structuring reality: the role of limits', in *Boundaries and Barriers*, ed. J. Casti and A. Karlqvist (Reading, MA: Addison-Wesley).

Hut, P. and van Fraassen, B. (1996), 'Elements of reality: A dialogue', submitted to *Journal of Consciousness Studies*.

James, W. (1912), *Essays in Radical Empiricism*, reprinted in *Essays in Radical Empiricism — A Pluralistic Universe*, 1967, by W. James (Gloucester, MA: Peter Smith).

McGinn, C., 1995, 'Consciousness and space', in this volume

Meehl, P. E. (1966), 'The compleat autocerebroscopist', in *Mind, Matter, Method: Essays in Philosophy and Science in Honor of Herbert Feigl*, ed. P.K. Feyerabend and G. Maxwell (Minneapolis: University. of Minnesota Press).

Nishida, K. (1911), *Zen no Kenkyuu*, translated as *An Inquiry into the Good*, 1990 (Yale University Press).

Rota, G-C. (1989), 'Fundierung as a logical concept,' *The Monist*, **72**, pp. 70–7.

Shepard, R.N. (1978), 'The mental image', *American Psychologist*, **33**, Figs. 1, 2 & 4.

Shepard, R.N. (1981), 'Psychophysical complementarity', in *Perceptual Organization*, ed. M. Kubovy and J. Pomerantz (Hillsdale, NJ: Erlbaum).

Shepard, R.N. (1993), 'On the physical basis, linguistic representation, and conscious experience of colors', in *Conceptions of the Mind*, ed. G. Harman (Hillsdale, NJ: Erlbaum).

Shepard, R.N. (1995), 'What is an agent that it experiences P-consciousness? And what is P-consciousness that it moves an agent?', *Behavioral and Brain Sciences*, **18**, pp. 267–8.

Smith, B.C. (1996), *On the Origin of Objects* (Cambridge, MA: The MIT Press).

Tarthang Tulku (1977), *Time, Space, and Knowledge* (Berkeley: Dharma Publications).

This paper was originally published in the *Journal of Consciousness Studies*, **3**, No.4 (1996), pp. 313–29.

First-Person Perspectives

Max Velmans

The Relation of Consciousness to the Material World

I: Why Consciousness Is Puzzling

The relation of consciousness to the material world is a puzzle, which has its origin in dualism, a philosophy of mind which posits their fundamental separation. Dualism, in turn, has its roots in folk wisdom. The belief that humans are more than bodies and that there is something in human nature that survives bodily death has its origins in prehistory; it becomes explicit in the mythology of Ancient Egypt and Assyria and was formulated into a philosophical position in the Platonic thought of Ancient Greece. But the contemporary view that the interaction of consciousness with matter poses a problem which *may be beyond scientific understanding* can be traced to a clearer formulation of dualism proposed by Descartes.

According to Descartes (1644) the Universe is composed of two fundamentally different substances, *res cogitans*, a substance which thinks, and *res extensa*, a substance which extends in space. *Res extensa* is the stuff of which the material world is made, including living bodies and brains; *res cogitans* is the stuff of consciousness. Descartes maintained that, in humans, *res cogitans* and *res extensa* interact via the pineal gland, located in the centre of the brain. However, even in the seventeenth century, the causal interaction of substances as different as these was thought by some to pose an insuperable problem.

Leibniz (1686), for example, argued that only physical events could cause physical events and only mental events could cause mental events. Fortunately, he thought, God has arranged physical events and mental events into a pre-established harmony so that given sequences of mental and physical events unfailingly accompany each other ('parallelism'). Consequently, there is an *apparent* causal interaction of mind with body rather than an actual one. This view resurfaces in the contemporary assumption that for every conscious experience there is a distinct neural 'correlate'. However, attribution of such correspondences to the workings of a munificent Deity has little appeal to the modern scientific mind.

Within twentieth century philosophy and science it is far more fashionable to reduce dualism to a form of materialism, for example to assume or attempt to show that consciousness is nothing more than a state or function of the brain (physicalism or functionalism). If either form of reduction is successful the explanatory gap left by dualism disappears, for the reason that all that needs to be explained can then be explained within the domain of natural science. Fashion, however, is beginning to change (see, for example, the debates between Dennett, Fenwick, Gray, Harnad, Humphrey, Libet, Lockwood, Marcel, Nagel, Searle, Shoemaker, Singer, Van Gulick, Velmans and Williams in Ciba Foundation Symposium 174, 1993). The reasons for this are many — but in essence they have to do with the realization that once one has explained everything that there is to explain about the material structure and functioning of brains, one will still be left with the problems of consciousness. To put matters crudely, one cannot find consciousness by any conceivable histological examination of the brain. Nor, as Nagel (1974) puts it, can one know what it is like to *be* something from a physical description alone. In Velmans (1991a) I have considered functional explanations of consciousness, tracing functional models of the mind through from input to output and concluded that consciousness cannot be found within any information processing 'box' within the brain. Consciousness accompanies or results from certain forms of processing but can be dissociated conceptually, and in most cases empirically from the processes with which it is commonly identified in the cognitive literature (perception, learning, memory, language, creativity and so on). The same can be said of models of functioning couched in other terms, such as parallel distributed processing or the language of neurophysiology (Gray, 1995; Velmans, 1995a).

In short, while it is likely that consciousness will eventually be found to be *associated* with given forms of processing, it looks increasingly likely that consciousness cannot be *reduced* to such processing. Or, to put matters another way, 'first-person perspective facts' cannot be fully reduced to 'third-person perspective facts' (cf. Goldman, 1993; Velmans, 1991a;b; 1993a). In his 'keynote' article in this issue, Chalmers comes to the same conclusion.

But if consciousness cannot be reduced to a state or function of the brain, how might one fill the explanatory gap left by dualism? Logically, it might be possible to reduce matter to forms of existence in the mind, for example to argue along with Berkeley (1710) that material events only exist in so far as they are *perceived* to exist (idealism). Idealism has its modern defenders, for example in some interpretations of the observer effect in quantum mechanics (the view that the Schrödinger wave equation only collapses into an actuality once an observation is made). In the macroworld it may also be true that the world *as-perceived* only exists if there are perceivers (Velmans 1990). However, as a general theory of the ontology of macroevents this position has its own well-known problems. It might be that the material world cannot have an *appearance* without perceivers, but it seems counterintuitive that its very *existence* is similarly vulnerable. Closing one's eyes does not seem to be enough to make unpleasant events go away.

Given the implausibilities of both materialist and mentalist reductionism, it is important to consider nonreductionist forms of monism (ways of healing the split induced by dualism, without reducing either consciousness or the material world to something other than they appear to be). An early version of this is the 'dual-aspect theory' of Spinoza (1677) — the view that mind and matter are manifest aspects of something deeper in 'nature', which appear to interact by virtue of some unfolding, grounding process within nature itself. This view may be thought of as a precursor of the contemporary proposal that consciousness and its correlated brain states may be thought of as dual aspects of a particular kind of 'information', which is in turn, a fundamental property of nature (Velmans 1991b; 1993a; Chalmers, keynote paper).

II: The Interface of Consciousness and Brain

We do not yet have precise knowledge of the events which form the interface of consciousness with the brain. However, in Velmans (1991a; b; 1993a) I considered what the general character of such events might be. Conscious experiences are representational (they are about something); consequently it seems likely that the neural or other physical correlates of conscious experiences will also be representational (i.e. that they will be representational states). It seems plausible to assume that for every distinct conscious experience there will be a distinct neural or other physical correlate. If so, any information (about something) manifest in experience will also be encoded in the correlates in a neural or other physical form. It follows from these assumptions that *given conscious experiences and their physical correlates encode identical information that is formatted in different ways.*

For human beings, of course, the physical correlates of consciousness are formed within living brains with multiple functions, and there has been much research and theory about where, in this complex system, consciousness 'fits in' (cf. Velmans 1991a). Information at the focus of attention usually enters consciousness (like this sentence). Conversely, information which is not attended to does not enter consciousness (like the pressure of your tongue against your upper teeth). So the relation of consciousness to focal-attention is close. But once information at the focus of attention enters consciousness it *has already been analysed.* For example, the processes involved in reading and comprehending this text are extremely complex — involving visual pattern recognition, syntactic analysis, semantic analysis, relating of input information to global knowledge in long-term memory, judgements about plausibility, conversion into some consciously experienced visual form and, if it is accompanied by inner speech (verbal thoughts), into phonemic imagery. But all that enters consciousness is the *result* of such processing (in the form of seen words, phonemic imagery, feelings of comprehension and so on).

Given this, I have argued that consciousness relates closely to a *late-arising product* of focal-attentive processing. Clues about the nature of this late-arising product come from those rare situations where focal attention is devoted to input analysis *without* accompanying consciousness. One striking example is blindsight, a condition in which subjects are rendered blind in one half of their visual field as a result of unilateral striate cortex damage. If stimuli are projected to their blind hemifield, subjects cannot see them in spite of the fact that their full attention is devoted to the task. As they cannot see the stimulus they maintain that they have no knowledge about it. However, if they are persuaded to make a guess about the nature of the stimulus in a forced choice task, their performance may be very accurate. For example, one subject investigated by Weiskrantz *et al.* (1974) was able to discriminate horizontal from vertical stripes on 30 out of 30 occasions although he could not see them. In short, the subject *has* the necessary knowledge but *does not know that he knows.* In information processing terms, it is as if one (modular) part of his system has information which is not generally available throughout the system. On the basis of this and other evidence I have argued that consciousness relates closely to *information dissemination* (Velmans 1991a). Chalmers makes the same suggestion. (A similar suggestion regarding information dissemination has also been made by Baars, 1988 and Navon, 1991.)

III: A New, Nonreductionist Consensus?
Points of Agreement with Chalmers

It might be premature to speak of a new, 'nonreductionist consensus', but the resemblance of some of Chalmers' elegantly argued proposals to my own (in Velmans, 1991a; b; 1993a) is encouraging. I will not quote from my earlier papers in detail, however points of agreement include:

1. that the mind/body problem is not one problem but many (see also Velmans, 1995b; 1996a);
2. that exploration of the physical and functional causes of consciousness can be undertaken by conventional scientific procedures, but that consciousness as such cannot be captured by such procedures;
3. that the proper route through this is to adopt a *nonreductive* approach, which relates first-person accounts of experience to third-person accounts of physical structure and functioning without seeking to reduce consciousness to brain or vice-versa;
4. that at the interface of consciousness with the brain, the structure of conscious representations can be related to the structure of physical representations in the brain through the notion of *information* and, in particular, to information dissemination;
5. that this amounts to a form of dual-aspect theory in which conscious experiences and their physical correlates may be thought of as dual manifestations of something more fundamental than either — the information structure of some thing-itself (there are also some differences between us on this point, but more of this in section IV.4 below).

IV: Points of Disagreement with Chalmers

1. Definitions
Within his keynote article Chalmers suggests that it would be useful to distinguish 'consciousness' from 'awareness'. The term 'consciousness' refers to 'experience', 'qualia', or 'phenomenal experience'. 'Awareness', he suggests, should refer to phenomena associated with consciousness, such as the ability to discriminate, categorize, and react to environmental stimuli, the integration of information by a cognitive system, and so on (pp. 10–11). Contributors to this issue have been urged to follow this usage — and, if there is consensus, this might become standard within the field as a whole. Given this, it is important to examine Chalmers' usage with care.

As noted earlier, I have also argued that consciousness in the sense of 'experience' should be clearly distinguished from the information processing functions with which it is commonly associated (Velmans, 1991a); however Chalmers' choice of the term 'awareness' for such functions is unfortunate. In common usage, the terms 'consciousness', 'awareness', and 'experience' are often interchangeable as are the terms 'conscious awareness' and 'conscious experience'. More seriously, the use of the term 'awareness' for information processing *functions* is not theoretically neutral. It suggests (subtly) that information processes associated with consciousness are themselves in some sense 'sentient'. Indeed, Chalmers goes on to argue that information processing of certain kinds is inevitably associated with consciousness of certain kinds, whether or not such processes are embodied in the brain (p. 25). This might, or might not be so (we return to this below). But the matter cannot be decided by defining information processing functions in such a way that they already have something of the quality of consciousness (in the form of 'awareness').

Blurring of the functioning/sentience distinction also leads to confusion about what scientific or conceptual advances might illuminate our understanding of consciousness. For example, many of the 'easy' problems of consciousness listed by Chalmers (p. 10) are, strictly speaking, not problems of consciousness at all. The ability to discriminate, categorize and react to environmental stimuli, the integration of information in a cognitive system, and the ability of a system to access its own internal states, can be accounted for (in principle) in information processing terms which make no reference to consciousness or awareness. For example, personal computers which print error messages on a screen have access, of a kind, to their own internal states. But this rudimentary form of meta-representation reveals nothing about PC consciousness or awareness.

For reasons such as this a number of other recent reviewers of the field have tended to use the terms 'consciousness', 'awareness' and 'experience' interchangeably, and to express information processing functions in neutral information processing terms (see Farthing, 1992; readings in Velmans, 1996b). This retains the convention within cognitive psychology that human information processing can be investigated without making any presumptions about the extent to which it enters consciousness or awareness. It allows the possibility that various forms of information processing can take place in humans *without* 'conscious awareness' (in blindsight, visual masking experiments, etc.). It also remains open to the possibility that machines can perform many of the functions performed by humans without any awareness of what they do.

Chalmers notes that, 'The ambiguity of the term "consciousness" is often exploited by both philosophers and scientists writing on the subject' enabling them to present theories of functioning as if they are theories of consciousness (p. 11). His suggestion that the term 'awareness' should be reserved for such information processing functions perpetuates this exploitation for theoretical reasons of his own.

2. *Do all systems with the same functional organization have qualitatively identical experiences?*

According to Chalmers, systems with the same fine-grained functional organization have identical experiences and, if the functional organization associated with consciousness is defined to be the system's 'awareness', this controversial claim becomes more plausible. But Chalmers' case is not simply a matter of definition. His principal argument is a thought experiment which demonstrates that systems which are functionally isomorphic could not themselves distinguish between having experiences of different kinds. He implies that if functionally isomorphic systems cannot notice differences in what they experience, then such differences do not exist. Conversely, if the systems could make such distinctions (and noticed or reported different experiences) they would not be functionally isomorphic.

However, whether functionally isomorphic systems could *notice* experiential differences must be distinguished from whether experiential differences in such systems *exist*. A totally nonconscious machine, for example, would have no way of noticing that it was totally nonconscious — as the conscious/nonconscious distinction would have no meaning for it. It could nevertheless be made to respond as if it were conscious — for example, it could be programmed to report only on information at the focus of attention being disseminated throughout its system (assuming that in humans only such information is conscious). If the machine could be made functionally isomorphic to a conscious human being there would be no way of distinguishing the machine from a human by its behaviour alone. Nor would the machine have any way of distinguishing its own simulation of consciousness from *actual* consciousness. But that would not alter the fact that in the machine there is 'nobody at home'.

According to Chalmers there is *no* empirical way to distinguish differences in sentience in functionally isomorphic systems. Perhaps for *completely* isomorphic systems he is right. However, experiments with humans which investigate the relationship of sentience to functioning do not, in general, compare completely isomorphic systems.

A cortical implant for blindsight

In typical psychology experiments on consciousness, one requires subjective reports, for example about whether a subject has experienced a stimulus or not. One has to accept that these two potential outcomes are associated with functional differences, if only for the reason that they are associated with different verbal reports. Usually, there are additional functional differences in these two situations. Suppose, however, that we are able to eliminate these additional differences so that the *only* functional difference between the two situations is that in one case there is a conscious experience (of the stimulus) with a corresponding verbal report, and in the other case there is not.

Suppose also that consciousness is most closely associated with information dissemination (as suggested above). Recall that in blindsight, subjects can identify stimuli projected to their blind hemifields without conscious experience, but information about the stimuli does not appear to be disseminated throughout the brain. Consequently, subjects do not 'know that they know' what the stimuli are and have to be forced to guess.

Imagine that we could implant a cortical network constructed out of silicon chips which restores information dissemination (of stimuli in the blind hemifield) so that in terms of all functions *other than the appearance of consciousness and its associated verbal report* blindsighted patients can no longer be distinguished from normals. Equipped with their new implants blindsighted patients now identify stimuli presented to their blind hemifields with confidence, learn from them, behave appropriately towards them and so on. But suppose that they *still* report that only stimuli presented to their nonaffected hemifields are consciously experienced. If so, information dissemination is dissociable from consciousness.

Of course, this experiment might have a different outcome. Fitted with their implants, blindsighted subjects might not only function like normals but also have visual experiences like normals. If so, one might conclude that there is nothing exclusive about the relation of consciousness to neurophysiological hardware — at least one other functionally equivalent system (embodied in silicon) would now be associated with phenomenally equivalent experience.[1]

In short, we cannot second-guess the outcome of the implant experiment. But the experiment is not unthinkable. And if it is not unthinkable, then Chalmers is wrong to argue that functional equivalence (in this case, in terms of information dissemination) *cannot* be empirically extricated from phenomenal equivalence *in principle*.

3. Is all information associated with consciousness?

Chalmers is open to the possibility that not all information has a phenomenal aspect but argues that it is both plausible and elegant to suggest that it does so. If so, not just mice, but even thermostats might have some maximally simple experience (p. 27). If his argument that functional equivalence entails phenomenal equivalence were correct, it would follow that machines that function like humans would also have the experiences of humans.

While I have also argued that consciousness may be related to certain forms of information in a fundamental way, there are very good empirical grounds for supposing that this does not apply in every case. In the human brain, for example, there is massive information, but at any given moment only a small proportion of this has any manifestation in conscious experience. There is, for example, a vast store of knowledge in long-term memory which at any given moment remains unconscious. Of the currently processed information, only that which is at the focus of attention ultimately reaches consciousness (like this sentence); the details of current information processing do not themselves enter consciousness (like the processing required to read this sentence). In fact, very few information processing details ever enter consciousness (Velmans, 1991a). Given that *human* information processing operates in largely nonconscious fashion it is plausible to assume that it operates in a similarly nonconscious fashion in machines.

It follows from this that we need to *constrain* the theory that information (always) has phenomenal aspects. This leaves open the possibility that information of *certain kinds* has phenomenal aspects. But what characterizes such information?

This is an empirical question to which there are no confident answers (as yet). It could be that information only has a phenomenal aspect if it is embodied in a neurochemical form. But this would not be a sufficient constraint as most neural representations have no manifestation in consciousness. An additional constraint might be that neural representations only become conscious when they have been activated above a given threshold. Another common hypothesis is that information only becomes conscious when it is passed to a particular region or circuit in the brain. A third possibility is that information only becomes conscious when it is subjected to a certain kind of processing (such as information dissemination, as suggested above). A fourth possibility is that information in the brain becomes conscious only when the conditions above combine in some way —

---

[1] Note that this conclusion would be warranted *only* if one had replaced the neuronal systems *most closely associated* with conscious experience (the C-systems) with functionally equivalent silicon circuitry. Replacing the peripheral or central systems which feed information to the C-systems would not establish anything about the ability of silicon to support consciousness as such. Cochlear implants, for example, stimulate the auditory nerve to produce a form of auditory experience, but the C-systems remain entirely neurophysiological.

for example, if information activated above some threshold is disseminated throughout the brain.

These suggestions share the assumption that for information to become conscious something *added* has to happen. There is, however, another intriguing possibility. It could be that information has a phenomenal aspect *unless it is prevented from doing so.* In the human brain, for example, it could be that information and accompanying consciousness is massively inhibited, to prevent information (and consciousness) overload. Much of neural activity is known to be inhibitory. To enable coherent, adaptive response it might be that only the information at the focus of attention which is disseminated throughout the system, is *released from inhibition.*

Release from inhibition has been hypothesised to explain certain psychological effects, for example, the sudden improvement in short-term memory performance, if after a series of trials with similar stimuli, one changes the features of the to-be-remembered stimuli (Wickens, 1972). There is also evidence that selective attention operates, in part, by the inhibition of nonattended stimuli (cf. Arbuthnott, 1995). This is consistent with the view that the brain may act as a filter (as well as an organizer) of information (e.g. Broadbent, 1958). If consciousness *is* a naturally occurring accompaniment of neurally encoded information (which is massively inhibited) Chalmers' suggestion that information *generally* has a phenomenal aspect could not be so easily dismissed.

One would still, of course, have to establish whether consciousness can be decoupled from neurochemistry — for example, by experiments such as the cortical implant for blindsight suggested above. And, even if it were found that consciousness accompanies information embodied in silicon and other physical substances, one would still have to be cautious about the *forms* of consciousness that might accompany different forms of information.

Chalmers, for example, suggests that thermostats have some minimal experience. But, of what? For *human* purposes, thermostats convey information about temperature. Feelings of hot and cold also convey information about temperature. Given this, it is possible (in principle) to devise a thermostat which controls temperature in a way that would be indistinguishable from a human responding to feelings of hot and cold. So for these purposes one could create a form of man/machine functional equivalence. But it would be facile to assume that thermostats (in this situation) *feel* hot and cold in the way that humans do.

In humans, feelings of hot and cold are mediated by free nerve endings embedded in the skin which pass their information to complex circuitry in the thalamus and cerebral cortex. A simple thermostat might be constructed out of a bimetal strip. Because the expansion coefficient of one metal is greater than the other, the strip bends as temperature increases. If the metal bends enough it opens (or closes) a circuit which controls a source of heat. In short, differential expansion in metals is used by human beings for the purposes of human beings — to convey information about and control temperature. But the bimetal strip simply expands and bends. If it does experience something that relates to how it expands and bends, there is no reason to suppose that this will relate in any way to the feelings of hot and cold experienced by human beings. As I have argued above, functional equivalence does *not* guarantee phenomenal equivalence.

4. Dual-aspect theory or naturalistic dualism?

One can only speculate about thermostat consciousness, but few would deny the existence of human consciousness, or its close association with activities in brains. As noted above, it is also plausible to link different *forms* of consciousness to different forms of neural or other physical encoding (via the notion of information). But this does not explain how, in an otherwise physical system, consciousness comes to *exist*. We have seen that the neural conditions for the appearance of consciousness can in principle be determined empirically. For example, it might turn out that given combinations of activation, brain location and information processing are involved. Isolation of the necessary and sufficient conditions for the appearance of consciousness in the brain would provide a form of causal explanation. But that would not provide an understanding of why these neural activities are accompanied by something *so unlike* neural activities.

It is worth bearing in mind that nature does not always bother to arrange things so that they are immediately obvious to humans. Sometimes, for example, apparently dissimilar phenomena (to our eyes) are fundamentally linked. For example, electric current passing through a wire produces a surrounding, spatially distributed magnetic field. Conversely, moving a wire through an existing magnetic field produces current in the wire. In Velmans (1991b; 1993a) I have suggested that there is some similarly fundamental process taking place in the brain that unifies certain forms of neural functioning with conscious experience.

As noted in section 1 above, there are different ways in which one can construe the nature of this consciousness/ brain relationship, for example in dualist or reductionist terms. However, the simplest nonreductionist way to capture the *intimate linkage of consciousness to its neural correlates* is to suppose that they are *two aspects* of *one representational process* (dual-aspect theory). As noted in section II above, it is plausible to think of conscious experiences and their neural correlates as representational states, and to assume that the information encoded in a given conscious experience and its physical correlates is identical. Given this underlying identity, why does the information embodied in conscious experiences and accompanying neural states appear so different? In Velmans (1991b; 1993a) I have argued that the appearance of this information depends entirely on the perspective from which it is viewed — i.e., it depends on whether the information in question is being viewed from an external observer's third-person perspective or from the first-person perspective of the subject.

Suppose a subject S is asked to focus his attention on a cat, while an experimenter E tries to determine what is going on in the subject's brain. Using his visual system and aided by sophisticated physical equipment E might, in principle, be able to view the information about the cat being formed in S's brain. Given our current knowledge of brains, it is reasonable to assume that this information will be embodied in a neurophysiological or other physical form. We also know that for S, the same information will be displayed in the form of a phenomenal cat out in the world. We do not know how representations in S's brain are translated into a conscious experience, but we can safely assume that the biological arrangements whereby information (about the cat) in S's brain is translated into S's experience are very different to the experimental arrangements used by E for accessing the same information in S's brain. Consequently, it is not surprising that for S and E the same information appears to be formatted in very different ways. Note that there is nothing unusual about identical information appearing in very different formats. This happens, for example, to the information encoded in the form of magnetic variations on videotape, once it is displayed as a moving picture on a TV screen.

But this is only an analogy. The manner in which different arrangements for observing the information in S's brain produce such dramatically different phenomenal consequences, is more closely reminiscent of wave/particle duality in quantum mechanics. In Velmans (1991b; 1993a) I have sketched out the beginnings of a 'psychological complementarity' principle (operating at the interface of consciousness with the brain). This resembles complementarity in physics in its stress on the dependence of the observation on the entire observation arrangements. Psychological and physical complementarity are also similar in requiring *both* (complementary) descriptions for completeness. Both a wave and a particle description are required for a complete understanding of photons. Likewise, both a (third-person) neural/physical and a (first-person) phenomenal description are required for a complete psychological understanding of subjects' representations.

But there the similarities end. I do not suggest for example that consciousness is wavelike, or that neural correlates are like particles. And crucially, wave/particle manifestations are both accessible to an external observer, whereas it is a unique feature of the consciousness/brain relationship that the complementarity obtains between what is accessible to an external observer versus an experiencing subject.

This account of psychological complementarity is only a first sketch, but attempts to grapple with *how* a fundamental representational process might have such different manifestations. While Chalmers also argues that experience is a fundamental feature of the world, his analysis of how it relates to physical features is quite different. According to Chalmers, experience is a fundamental feature *alongside* mass, charge, and space–time. Consequently he suggests that the relationship of experience to physical processes may be thought of as a kind of *'naturalistic dualism'* (p. 20). Although elsewhere (p. 26) Chalmers considers his theory to be a form of 'double-aspect' theory, and he refers to the intrinsic versus the extrinsic nature of information, the relation of this double-aspect theory to naturalistic dualism is not made clear.

V: How to Bridge a Nonexistent Gap

There can be little doubt that some of the questions about consciousness are hard — and that not all the questions are just the result of conceptual confusion. For example, there really are conscious experiences and we have every reason to suppose that there really are neural or other physical accompaniments of these. Working out the details of the brain/consciousness interface is consequently important.

But I believe that there are some 'hard' questions that *are* the result of conceptual confusion. It must be remembered that the 'mind/body problem' has resulted, in part, from the splitting of mind from body implicit in dualism. Consciousness, in Descartes' formulation, is nonmaterial and has no location or extension in space. Conscious states are commonly thought to be private and subjective in contrast to physical states which are public and objective. Given this, it is hardly surprising that consciousness has been thought to pose an insuperable problem for science — with a consequent shift towards materialist reductionism within twentieth-century philosophy of mind.

In Velmans (1990; 1993b; 1996c) I have reviewed evidence that Descartes' way of describing consciousness and its relation to the brain accords neither with science (the nature of perception) nor with the everyday experiences of human beings. That is to say, the mind/body problem results in part from a description of everyday experience that does *not correspond* to everyday experience. I have also taken issue with the private vs. public and subjective vs. objective distinctions in the forms that they usually appear.

It is not possible to enter into the detailed analysis relating to these basic points in the limited space available here. But, to put matters very briefly, *very few* aspects of consciousness have the nonextended character suggested by Descartes (thoughts, some feelings, some images and so on). Classical 'mental' events such as pains nearly always have a location and distribution in one's body, and the same applies to other tactile sensations. Auditory and visual phenomena are generally perceived to be outside the body and distributed in three-dimensional space. In short, the contents of consciousness include not just 'inner events' such as thoughts, but body events, and events perceived to be in the external phenomenal world. This external phenomenal world is what we normally think of as the 'physical world'. In short, what we normally think of as the 'physical world' is *part-of* the contents of consciousness (part-of what we experience). Consequently, there is no unbridgeable divide separating 'physical phenomena' from the 'phenomena we experience'.

Consider how this description applies to the situation described in IV.4 above, in which an experimenter observes the brain of a subject. While the experimenter focuses on the subject, his phenomenal world includes the subject, and if his experimental arrangement is successful, the representational states in the brain of the subject. While the subject focuses on the cat his phenomenal world includes the cat. It is fashionable (at present) to think of E's 'observations' (of the subject's brain) as public and objective. S's 'experiences' of the cat, by contrast, are private and subjective. Indeed, this radical difference in the status of E and S is enshrined in the different terminology applied to what they perceive; that is, E makes 'observations', whereas S merely has 'subjective experiences'.

But suppose they turn their heads, so that E switches his attention to the cat, while S switches his attention to what is going on in E's brain. Now E is the 'subject' and S is the 'experimenter'. Following the same convention, S would now be entitled to think of his observations (of E's brain) as public and objective and to regard E's observations of the cat as private and subjective. But this would be absurd — as nothing has changed in the character of the observations of E and S other than the focus of their attention.

I cannot do more in a few lines than to sow a few seeds of doubt. A full pursuit of such simple points requires a re-analysis of idealism vs. realism, of private vs. public, of subjectivity, intersubjectivity and objectivity, of the relation of psychology to physics, and of the proper nature of a science of consciousness (Velmans, 1990; 1993b; 1996c; Harman, 1994).

Suffice it to say that, in the new analysis, the problem of how to incorporate conscious 'qualia' into empirical science disappears. All phenomena in science are seen to be aspects of the phenomenal worlds of observers, and therefore *part-of* the world that they experience. 'Qualia' are in there from the beginning. Indeed, the *whole* of science may be seen as an attempt to make sense of the phenomena that we observe or experience.*

* This paper was originally published in *Journal of Consciousness Studies*, **2**, No.3 (1995), pp. 255–65

References

Arbuthnott, K.D. (1995), 'Inhibitory mechanisms in cognition: phenomena and models', *Cahiers de Psychologie Cognitive*, **14**(1), pp. 3–45.

Baars, B.J. (1988), *A Cognitive Theory of Consciousness* (Cambridge: Cambridge University Press).

Berkeley, G. (1710), *The Principles of Human Knowledge*. Reissued 1942 (London: T. Nelson & Sons).

Broadbent, D.E. (1958), *Perception and Communication* (Pergamon Press).

Chalmers, D. (1995), 'Facing up to the problem of consciousness', *Journal of Consciousness Studies*, **2** (3), pp.210–19 (reprinted in this volume).

Ciba Foundation Symposium 174 (1993), *Theoretical and Experimental Studies of Consciousness* (Chichester: Wiley).

Descartes, R. (1644), *Treatise on Man*, trans. T.S.Hall. (Harvard University Press, 1972).

Farthing, W. (1992), *The Psychology of Consciousness* (Prentice-Hall).

Goldman, A.J. (1993), 'Consciousness, folk psychology, and cognitive science', *Consciousness and Cognition*, **2**, pp. 364–82.

Gray, J. (1995), 'The contents of consciousness: a neuropsychological conjecture', *Behavioral and Brain Sciences* (in press).

Harman, W. (1994), 'The scientific exploration of consciousness: towards an adequate epistemology', *Journal of Consciousness Studies*, **1** (1), pp. 140–8.

Leibniz, G.W. (1686), *Discourse of Metaphysics, Correspondence with Arnauld, and Monadology*, trans. M. Ginsberg (London: Allen & Unwin, 1923).

Nagel, T. (1974), 'What is it like to be a bat?', *Philosophical Review*, **83**, pp. 435–51.

Navon, D. (1991), 'The function of consciousness or of information?', *Behavioral and Brain Sciences*, **14**, pp. 690–1.

Spinoza, B. (1677), *The Ethics*. Reprinted in *The Ethics of Benedict Spinoza* (New York: Van Nostrand, 1876).

Velmans, M. (1990), 'Consciousness, brain, and the physical world', *Philosophical Psychology*, **3** (1), pp. 77–99.

Velmans, M. (1991a), 'Is human information processing conscious?', *Behavioral and Brain Sciences*, **14** (4), pp. 651–69.

Velmans, M. (1991b), 'Consciousness from a first-person perspective', *Behavioral and Brain Sciences*, **14** (4), pp. 702–26.

Velmans, M. (1993a), 'Consciousness, causality, and complementarity', *Behavioral and Brain Sciences*, **16** (2), pp. 404–16.

Velmans, M. (1993b), 'A reflexive science of consciousness', in *Experimental and Theoretical Studies of Consciousness*: Ciba Foundation Symposium No.174 (Chichester: Wiley).

Velmans, M. (1995a), 'The limits of neurophysiological models of consciousness', *Behavioral and Brain Sciences* (in press).

Velmans, M. (1995b), 'Theories of consciousness', in *The Handbook of Brain Theory and Neural Networks*, ed. M. Arbib (Cambridge, MA: Bradford Books / The MIT Press).

Velmans, M. (1996a), 'An introduction to the science of consciousness', in M. Velmans (1996b).

Velmans, M. (ed. 1996b), *The Science of Consciousness: Psychological, Neuropsychological and Clinical Reviews* (London: Routledge).

Velmans, M. (1996c), 'What and where are conscious experiences?' in M. Velmans (1996b).

Weiskrantz, L., Warrington, E.K., Sanders, M.D. & Marshall,J. (1974), 'Visual capacity in the hemianopic field, following a restricted occipital ablation', *Brain*, **97**, pp. 709–28.

Wickens, D.D. (1972), 'Characteristics of word encoding', in *Coding Processes in Human Memory*, ed. A.W. Melton & E. Martin (Washington, DC: V.H. Winston & Sons. Distributed by John Wiley, New York).

Francisco J. Varela

Neurophenomenology: A Methodological Remedy for the Hard Problem

This paper responds to the issues raised by D.J. Chalmers by offering a *research direction* which is quite radical in the way in which some basic methodological principles are linked to the scientific studies of consciousness. Neuro-phenomenology is the name I am using here to designate a quest to marry modern cognitive science and a *disciplined approach* to human experience, thus placing myself in the lineage of the continental tradition of phenomenology.[1] My claim is that the so-called hard problem that animates these Special Issues of the *Journal of Consciousness Studies* can only be addressed productively by gathering a research community armed with new pragmatic tools enabling them to develop a science of consciousness. I will claim that no piecemeal empirical correlates, nor purely theoretical principles, will really help us at this stage. We need to turn to a systematic exploration of the only link between mind and consciousness that seems both obvious and natural: the *structure of human experience itself.*

In what follows I open my proposal by briefly examining the current debate about consciousness in the light of Chalmers' hard problem. Next, I outline the (neuro)phenomenological strategy. I conclude by discussing some of the main difficulties and consequences of this strategy.

I: A Cartography of Approaches

The riddle of experience

Chalmers opens up the discussion of the 'hard problem' by focusing on *the* problem that seems central: the *experience* associated with cognitive or mental events.

> Sometimes terms such as 'phenomenal consciousness' and 'qualia' are also used here, but I find it more natural to speak of 'conscious experience' or simple 'experience' (p. 11).

---

[1] The use of 'neuro' should be taken here as a *nom de guerre*. It is chosen in explicit contrast to the current usage of 'neurophilosophy', which identifies philosophy with anglo-american philosophy of mind. Further, 'neuro' refers here to the entire array of scientific correlates which are relevant in cognitive science. But to speak of a neuro-psycho-evolutionary-phenomenology would be unduly cumbersome. This paper was originally published in the *Journal of Consciousness Studies*, **3**, No.4 (1996), pp. 330–49.

After describing case studies of some popular functionalist explanations, Chalmers moves to qualify the remaining challenge as some necessary 'extra ingredient'. The choice of the term is already revealing, for Chalmers seems to assume from the outset that the only avenue is to find theoretical principles that will bridge the gap between cognition and experience. As I will detail below, it seems that another fundamental alternative is to change the entire framework within which the issue is discussed. In any case '[t]he moral of all this is that *you can't explain conscious experience on the cheap*' (p. 18; his italics). I entirely agree but hasten to add that the price we need to pay is heavier than most people are willing to concede. Again the central difficulty is that experience is 'not an explanatory posit, but an explanandum in its own right, and so it is not a candidate for [reductive] elimination' (pp. 18–19). What is needed, he concludes, is a form of non-reductive explanation. Here again, I concur with Chalmers, but one of my tasks will be to detail how different our options are from this point onwards.

Let me begin my re-focusing the question of experience in the current boom in the scientific study of consciousness. As we all know, the number of books, articles and meetings on the subject has increased exponentially over the last few years. Why this current outburst after all the years of silence, during which consciousness was an impolite topic even within cognitive science?

To be sure, after the peak of dominance of behaviourism there had to be a conservative phase before cognitive science felt that it had some ground under its feet. More important perhaps was the style of the dominant philosophy of mind in the USA (with numerous followers in Europe), which is intrinsically suspicious of subjective experience. Within this framework, significant developments in cognitive science have been accomplished almost exclusively within a cognitivist-computationalist or a connectionist perspective. Connectionism in particular made possible a revolutionary idea of transitions and bridges between levels of explanation, better understood as a philosophy of emergence: how local rules can give rise to global properties or objects in a reciprocal causality. This gave new meaning to the traditional mind/body interface, which in the form of cognitive processes as computationalist or connectionists schemes, made an array of specific cognitive phenomena (vision, motion and associative memory are prime examples) solvable (if not solved) in principle. These developments, at the same time, created the very background for the 'hard problem', since they made consciousness appear as devoid of any causal relevance. This is well illustrated in Ray Jackendoff's pioneering book, in which the 'phenomenological mind' (i.e. consciousness *qua* experience) is seen as projection from a 'computational mind' (i.e. cognitive mechanisms) where all causality takes place. Thus the only conclusion he can come to is that consciousness 'is not good for anything' (1987, p. 26).

Further, in parallel developments, new techniques for large-scale analysis of brain activity and neuropsychology have for the first time allowed us to ask direct experimental questions concerning complex cognition correlates in action, such as mental imagery and emotions (see for example Posner and Raichle, 1992; Mazoyer, Roland and Fox, 1995). The experiments involving such non-invasive on-line measurements are particularly interesting since they have led researchers to confront such questions as: Can a subject's report be taken at face value? What are verbal reports expressions of? These are basically experiential questions that already imply a significant revision of the manner in which accounts of human experience have to be approached in empirical research.

One day the intellectual history of the peculiar twists and turns of this problem space will be reviewed thoroughly. But it has a *déjà-vu* aura to it, reminding us of many swings of the pendulum, between rejecting and total fascination with the scientific discussions of conscious experience. This can hardly be otherwise, since any science of cognition and mind must, sooner or later, come to grips with the basic condition that we have no idea what the mental or the cognitive could possibly be apart from our own experience of it. As John Searle has aptly remarked in his own contribution to the boom, if there is a research phase favouring strictly materialist theories of mind:

> [the philosopher] encounters difficulties. It always seems that he is leaving some-thing out . . . [and] underlying the technical objections is a much deeper objection . . . [that] can be put quite simply: The theory in question has left out the mind; it has left out some essential feature of the mind, such as 'consciousness' or 'qualia' or semantic content . . . [Thus] if we were to think of the philosophy of mind as a single individual we would say of that person that he is a compulsive neurotic, and his neurosis takes the form of repeating the same pattern of behavior over and over (Searle, 1992, pp. 30–1).

I agree with the diagnosis as much as I disagree with Searle's proposed cure (more on that later). Clearly we need some radical measures to compensate for this compulsive behaviour. That is precisely what I intend to do here, with a proposal that will probably seem radical for some; but nothing short of it will break the vicious circle and bypass the attempts to fix it with yet another abstract, theoretical model.

A four-way sketch

In order to appreciate my position the reader should now turn to the sketch in Figure 1 outlining four axes that seem to capture the essential orientations in the current boom of discussion on consciousness. It is not intended to be an all-encompassing chart of the various viewpoints, but an occasion to place myself in context with modern authors that have published extensive arguments (generally in book form) over the past few years.[2]

In the far right orientation, I have put the very vocal trend best represented by P.S. Churchland, but including F. Crick and C. Koch, and close to the spontaneous philosophy of many other of my colleagues in neuroscience, and appropriately labelled as neuro-reductionism or eliminativism. As is well-known, this view seeks to solve the hard problem by eliminating the pole of experience in favour of some form of neurobi-ological account which will do the job of generating it (Churchland and Sejnowski, 1992). Or as Crick puts it with characteristic bluntness: 'You're nothing but a pack of neurons' (1994, p. 2).

---

[2] Note that this is a chart of naturalistic approaches, that is, positions that each in their own way provide a workable link to current research on cognitive science. This excludes at least two streams of popular discussion: on the one hand views that take a traditional dualistic stance (à *la* J.C. Eccles); on the other hand calls for new foundations from the quantum mechanics proponents. I find both these views extreme and unnecessary, and concentrate on those that are based on current neuro-science and cognitive science in some explicit manner.

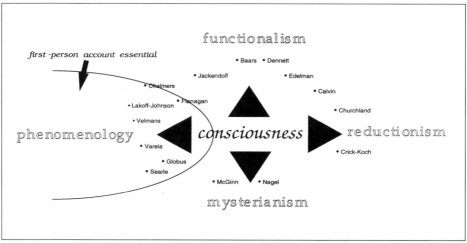

Figure 1

At the centre north I have collected a variety of positions that can be labelled as functionalist, and identified by Chalmers as being the most popular ecology of ideas active today (pp. 11–13). Functionalism has been drastically preferred in cognitive science over the last 20 years, followed by the strategy to replace the link between cognition and consciousness (the most immediate one in western philosophical tradition) by the link between cognition and its corresponding functional or intentional states. In the best of cases the problem of consciousness is assimilated with that of 'qualia' for some particular features of mental states. Thus the notion of experience becomes forcefully assimilated with that of cognitive behaviour, propositional attitude, or functional role.

These views include a number of well-developed proposals including, R. Jackendoff's (1987) 'Projective Mechanism', B. Baars' (1988) 'Global Workspace', D. Dennett's (1991) 'Multiple Drafts', W. Calvin's (1990) 'Darwinian Machines', or G. Edelman's (1989) 'Neural Darwinism'. The basic move in these proposals is quite similar. First start from the modular items of cognitive capacities (i.e. the 'soft' problems). Second, construct a theoretical framework to put them together so that their unity amounts to an account of experience. The strategy to bridge this emergent unity and experience itself varies, but it is left typically vague since the entire approach relies almost entirely on a third-person or externalist approach to obtain data and to validate the theory. This position seems the most popular one in the current boom literature, and it represents an important segment of researchers in cognitive science. This popularity rests on the acceptance of the reality of experience and mental life while keeping the methods and ideas within the known framework of empirical science .

At the centre south we have the mirror image of functionalism. Mysterians such as T. Nagel (1986) and C. McGinn (1991) seek to conclude by principled arguments that the hard problem is unsolvable, based on intrinsic limitations of the means through which our knowledge of the mental is acquired.

Finally, to the left, I have put the sector that interests me the most, and which can be roughly described as giving an *explicit* and central role to first-person accounts and to the irreducible nature of experience, while at the same time refusing either a dualistic concession or a pessimistic surrender to the question, as is the case for the mysterians.

This is in line with Chalmers' identification of where the hard problem lies. As are the other orientations in my sketch, the group gathered here is a motley one, with odd bedfellows such as G. Lakoff and M. Johnson's (1987) approach to cognitive semantics, J. Searle's (1992) ideas on ontological irreducibility, G. Globus' (1995) 'post-modern' brain, and at the edge, O. Flanagan's (1992) 'reflective equilibrium', and Chalmers' (1996) own proposal as fully developed in his recent book.

What is interesting about this diverse group, within which I place myself, is that even though we share a concern for first-hand experience as basic fact to incorporate in the future of the discipline, the differences are patent in the manner in which experience is taken into account. The phenomenological approach is grounded on a peculiar move to explore experience which is at the centre of my proposal. This sufficiently clarifies, I hope , the context for my ideas within the current scene. Now we may move to the heart of the matter, the nature of the circulation between a first person and an external account of human experience, which describes the phenomenological position in fertile dialogue with cognitive science.

II: A Phenomenological Approach

Irreducibility: the basic ground

The phenomenological approach starts from the *irreducible* nature of conscious experience. Lived experience is where we start from and where all must link back to, like a guiding thread. Most modern authors are disinclined to focus on the distinction between mental life in some general sense and experience, or manifest some suspicion about its status.

From a phenomenological standpoint conscious experience is quite at variance with that of mental content as it figures in the anglo-american philosophy of mind. The tension between these two orientations appears in a rather dramatic fashion in Dennett's (1991) book, where he concludes with little effort (15 lines in a 550 page book) that phenomenology has failed. He remarks:

> Like other attempts to strip away interpretation and reveal the basic facts of consciousness to rigorous observation, such as the Impressionistic movements in the arts [*sic*] and the Introspectionist psychologists of Wundt, Titchener and others, Phenomenology has failed to find a single settled method that everyone could agree upon (p. 44).

This passage is revealing: Dennett mixes apples and oranges by putting impressionism and introspectionism in the same bag; he confuses introspectionism with phenomenology which it is most definitely not (*vide infra*); and he finally draws his conclusion from the absence of some idyllic universal agreement that would validate the whole. Well, we do not demand 'that everyone could agree' upon, say, Darwinism, to make it a remarkably useful research programme. And certainly *some* people do agree on the established possibility of disciplined examination of human experience. In a book that is in many other respects so *savant* and insightful, this display of ignorance concerning phenomenology is a symptom that says a lot about what's amiss in this field.

The main point that must be brought to the fore is clearly made by Searle:

> . . . much of the bankruptcy of most work in the philosophy of mind . . . over the past fifty years . . . has come from a persistent failure to recognize and come to terms

with the fact that the ontology of the mental is an irreducibly first-person ontology
. . . There is, in short, no way for us to picture subjectivity as part of our world view
because, so to speak, the subjectivity in question is the picturing (Searle, 1992,
pp. 95, 98).

But in Searle's defence of the irreducibility of consciousness there is an inability to come
to any conclusion about how to solve the epistemological issue concerning the study of
consciousness. Searle wants us to accept that 'the irreducibility of consciousness is
merely a consequence of the pragmatics of our definitional practices' (p. 122), and
therefore, although the irreducibility of consciousness is a 'straightforward argument' it
'has no deep consequences' (p. 118). In fact,

> The very fact of subjectivity, which we were trying to observe, makes such an
> observation impossible. Why? Because where conscious subjectivity is concerned,
> there is no distinction between the observer and the thing observed . . . Any
> introspection I have of my own conscious state is itself that conscious state' (p. 97).

The mental does not have any obvious manner to investigate itself, and we are left with
a clear logical conclusion, but in a pragmatic and methodological limbo.

This is not unlike the limbo in Jackendoff's views, who in his own way also claims the
irreducibility of consciousness but is tellingly silent when it comes to method. He does
claim that insights into experience act as constraints for a computational theory of mind,
but follows with no methodological recommendations except 'the hope that the disagreements about phenomenology can be settled in an atmosphere of mutual trust' (Jackendoff,
1987, p. 275). Mutual trust indeed! What is needed is a strict *method* and that is where
both the difficulty and the revolutionary potential of the topic lie.

Method: moving ahead

We need to examine, beyond the spook of subjectivity, the concrete possibilities of a
disciplined examination of experience that is at the very core of the phenomenological
inspiration. To repeat: it is the re-discovery of the primacy of human experience and its
direct, lived quality that is phenomenology's foundational project. This is the sense in
which Edmund Husserl inaugurated this thinking in the West, and established a long
tradition that is well and alive today not only in Europe but world-wide. In fact, between
1910 and 1912, while Husserl was at the peak of his creative formulation of phenomenology, in the United States William James was following very parallel lines in his
pragmatic approach to cognitive life. And to complete the planetary 'synchronicity' of
this turn, a very innovative philosophical renewal appeared in Japan, the so-called Kyoto
School, initiated by Nishida Kitaro and then followed by Nishitani Keiji and others.
Husserl and James knew and read each other, and the members of the Kyoto school read
widely in western phenomenology and spent extensive periods of training in Germany.
Thus I believe we should consider these *anni mirabiles* for phenomenology, akin to the
years 1848–52 for the birth of modern evolutionary biology.

It is fair to say that phenomenology is, more than anything else, a *style of thinking*,
which Husserl started in the West, but it is not exhausted by his personal options and style
(Lyotard, 1954). I do not want to engage in an account of the diversity and complexity of
western phenomenology (see e.g. Spiegelberg, 1962). The contributions of individuals

such as Eugen Fink, Edith Stein, Roman Ingarten, and Maurice Merleau-Ponty to cite only a few have attested to a continuing development of phenomenology. More recently various links with modern cognitive science have been explored (see for instance Dreyfus, 1982; Varela *et al.*, 1991; Klein and Wescott, 1994; Petitot, 1995; Petitot *et al.*, 1996; Thompson and Varela, 1996). I mention this explicitly because it has been my observation that most people not familiar with the phenomenological movement automatically assume that phenomenology is some sort of Husserlian scholasticism, a trade better left to dusty continental philosophers who can read German.

At best cognitive scientists might have read the collection edited by Dreyfus (1982), which presents Husserl as some form of proto-computationalist, and they assume that this bit of history is all there is to know about phenomenology. This has become an oft-quoted interpretation, but critics have made clear that Dreyfus' cognitive reading of Husserl is seriously flawed. This is not the occasion to expand on this issue, but it is essential to flag a caveat here lest the reader with a scientific background thinks it has been settled once and for all.[3]

My position cannot be ascribed to any particular school or sub-lineage but represents my own synthesis of phenomenology in the light of modern cognitive science and other traditions focusing on human experience. Phenomenology can also be described as a *special type of reflection* or attitude about our capacity for being conscious. All reflection reveals a variety of mental contents (mental acts) and their correlated orientation or intended contents. Natural or naive attitude assumes a number of received claims about both the nature of the experiencer and its intended objects. The Archimedean point of phenomenology is to suspend such habitual claims and to catalyse a fresh examination. Whence Husserl's famous dictum: 'Back to the things themselves!',[4] which for him meant — the opposite of a third-person objectification — a return to the world as it is experienced in its felt immediacy. It was Husserl's hope, and still the basic inspiration behind phenomenological research, that a true science of experience would be gradually established which could not only stand on equal footing to the natural sciences, but in fact would give them a needed ground, for all knowledge necessarily emerges from our lived experience.

On the one hand experience is suffused with spontaneous pre-understanding, so that it might seem that all 'theory' about it is quite superfluous. But on the other hand this pre-understanding must itself be examined since it is not clear what kind of a knowledge it stands for. Experience demands a specific examination in order to free it from its status as habitual belief. As Merleau-Ponty puts it:

> To return to the things themselves is to return to that world which precedes knowledge, of which knowledge always *speaks* and in relation to which every scientific schematization is an abstract and derivative sign language, as the discipline of geography would be in relation to a forest, a prairie, a river in the countryside we new beforehand (M. Merleau-Ponty, 1945, p. ix).

---

[3] For a critique of Dreyfus' take on Husserl see Langsdorf (1985) and also the objections of R. McIntyre (1986). For a recent account of this controversy through a contrast between Fodor and Husserl see J.M. Roy (1995).

[4] 'Zurück zu den Sachen selbst!', *Logische Untersuchungen*, Vol. II, Part 1, p. 6.

I insist on bringing to the fore this basic principle of the phenomenological approach since it if often quickly translated into an empirical quest for mental correlates. We need to return repeatedly to this issue since it is only by appreciating its depth that phenomenological bridges can claim to keep a meaningful link to lived experience and to be a remedy for the hard problem.

Phenomenology grounds its movement towards a fresh look at experience in a specific gesture of reflection or *phenomenological reduction* (PhR).[5] I need now to unfold the bare bones of this attitude or gesture through which is the habitual way we have to relate to our lived-world changes. This does not require us to consider a different world but rather to consider this present one *otherwise*. As we said before this gesture changes a naive or unexamined experience into a reflexive or second-order one. Phenomenology correctly insists in this shift from the natural to the phenomenological attitude, since only then the world and my experience appears as open and in need of exploration. The meaning and pragmatics of PhR have taken several variants from this common trunk. It is not my intention to recapitulate them here.[6]

The conscious gesture that is at the base of PhR can be analysed into four intertwined moments or aspects:

(1) Attitude: reduction

The attitude of reduction is the necessary starting point. It can also be defined by its similarities to doubt: a sudden, transient suspension of beliefs about what is being examined, a putting in abeyance our habitual discourse about something, a bracketing of the pre-set structuring that constitutes the ubiquitous background of everyday life. Reduction is self-induced (it is an active gesture), and it does seek to be resolved (dissipating our doubts) since it is here as a source of experience. It is a common mistake to assume that suspending our habitual thinking means stopping the stream of thoughts, which is not possible. The point is to turn the direction of the movement of thinking from its habitual content-oriented direction backwards towards the arising of thoughts themselves. This is no more nor less than the very human capacity for *reflexivity*, and the life-blood of reduction. To engage in reduction is to cultivate a systematic capacity for reflection on the spot thus opening new possibilities within our habitual mind stream. For instance, right now the reader is very likely making some internal remarks concerning what reduction is, what it reminds her of, and so on. To mobilize an attitude of reduction would begin by noticing those automatic thought-patterns, let them flow away, and turn reflection towards their source.

(2) Intimacy: intuition

The result of reduction is that a field of experience appears both less encumbered and more vividly present as if without the habitual fog separating experiencer and world. As

---

[5] The reader should resist the temptation to assimilate this usage of the word 'reduction' to that of 'theoretical reduction' as it appears for instance in the neuroreductionist framework and well articulated in the writings of P.S. Churchland. The two meanings run completely counter to one another; it is therefore convenient to append a qualifier.

[6] For a recent discussion about the varieties of reduction see: R. Bernet (1994), pp. 5–36. Husserl's own first articulation can be found in his breakthrough lectures of 1907 (Husserl, 1962).

William James saw, the immediacy of experience thus appears surrounded by a diversity of horizons to which we can turn our interest. This gain in intimacy with the phenomenon is crucial, for it is the basis of the criteria of truth in phenomenological analysis, the nature of its evidence. If intimacy or immediacy is the beginning of this process, it continues by a cultivation of imaginary *variations*, considering in the virtual space of mind multiple possibilities of the phenomenon as it appears. These ideal variations are familiar to us from mathematics, but here they are put into the service of whatever becomes the focus of our analysis: perception of three-dimensional form, the structure of 'nowness', the manifestations of empathy, and so on. It is through these multiple variations that a new stage of understanding arises, an 'Aha!' experience which adds new evidence that carries a force of conviction. This moving intimacy with our experience corresponds well to what is traditionally referred to as intuition, and represents, along with reflection, the two main human capacities that are mobilized and cultivated in PhR.

(3) Description: invariants

To stop at reduction followed by imaginary variations would be to condemn this method to private ascertainment. The next component is as crucial as the preceding ones: the gain in intuitive evidence must be inscribed or translated into communicable items, usually through language or other symbolic inscriptions (think of sketches or formulae). The materialities of these descriptions however are also a constitutive part of the PhR and shape our experience as much as the intuition that forms them. In other words we are not merely talking about an 'encoding' into a public record, but rather of an 'embodiment' that incarnates and shapes what we experience. I like to refer to these public descriptions as *invariants*, since it is through 'variations' that one finds broad conditions under which an observation can be communicable. This is not so different from what mathematicians have done for centuries: the novelty is to apply it to the contents of consciousness.

(4) Training: stability

As with any discipline, sustained training and steady learning are key. A casual inspection of consciousness is a far cry from the disciplined cultivation of PhR. This point is particularly relevant here, for the attitude of reduction is notoriously fragile. If one does not cultivate the *skill* to stabilize and deepen one's capacity for attentive bracketing and intuition, as well as the skill for illuminating descriptions, no systematic study can mature. This last aspect of the PhR is perhaps the greatest obstacle for the constitution of a research programme since it implies a disciplined commitment from a community of researchers (more on this below).

Phenomenological Reduction	
aspects of method	*characteristics of resulting examination*
Attitude	bracketing, suspending beliefs
Intuition	intimacy, immediate evidence
Invariants	inscriptions, intersubjectivity
Training	stability, pragmatics

Avoiding some standard traps

In previous presentations of these ideas I have found a number of misunderstandings and misleading conclusions recurring. Let me anticipate a few of these common traps and address them immediately.

- *Phenomenological analysis is not just introspectionism.*

As many have remarked, introspection presupposes that we have access to our experience in the same manner that we have access to an 'inner' visual field, as the etymology of the word suggests, by inspection. Such an internal examination is a normal cognitive ability of reflective doubling, a gesture in which we engage regularly. It assumes a certain referential 'I' who does the self-observation, a narrative network that shapes what we identify as a subject.

In pre-phenomenology days (i.e. without reduction) introspection elicited a wave of interest in psychology starting with the work of W.Wundt, followed by others such as E.Titchener in USA and the Würzburg school. Despite an initial enthusiasm the research programme advanced by introspectionism did not take root. Among other problems, reports from different laboratories could not reach a common ground of validation. A classic case was the issue of whether visual imagery played a role in problem solving or not. The method employed began with reflection but gave explicit direction as to what to look for or what kind of distinctions to make, much as we are used to seeing done in modern experimental psychology. Inevitably the reports became more and more influenced by the theoretical underpinnings of the studies, and in fact rapidly degenerated into arguments about authority. The historical account of Lyons (1986) is written as an obituary for introspection. But this would be a premature conclusion, as Howe (1991) reminds us.

This manner of mobilizing reflexive capacities still falls into the natural attitude for a phenomenologist, for it rides on the wave of previous elaborations and assumptions. Phenomenology does share with introspectionism an interest in the reflective doubling as a key move of its approach to phenomena. But the two attitudes part company. In PhR the skill to be mobilized is called bracketing for good reasons, since it seeks precisely the opposite effect of an uncritical introspection: it cuts short our quick and fast elaborations and beliefs, in particular locating and putting in abeyance what we think we 'should' find, or some 'expected' description. Thus PhR is not a 'seeing inside', but a tolerance concerning the suspension of conclusions that allows a new aspect or insight into the phenomenon to unfold. In consequence this move does not sustain the basic subject–object duality but opens into a field of phenomena where it becomes less and less obvious how to distinguish between subject and object (this is what Husserl called the 'fundamental correlation').

It is important to re-open the debate concerning the key differences between introspectionism (which did not lead to a fruitful succession), and phenomenology (with its uninterrupted history). Searle, for instance, who claims that first-person experiences are irreducible, makes no reference to this complex intellectual and historical issue, and rapidly concludes that introspection is merely another mental state. Hence it cannot claim to have a privileged access to experience, and the irreducibility of experience 'has no deep consequences' (1992, p. 118). This dismissal of introspectionism and (by default) of phenomenology does not take Searle very far. Despite his disclaimer about introspection, that is precisely what he does in the chapter called 'The structure of consciousness: An introduction', containing twelve attributes that appear to him as fundamental. On what basis? By doing a suddenly valid introspection? How does he validate these observations? Why not an alternative list of attributes?

- *Intuition is not some fluffy stuff*

Many people react to the mention of intuition with suspicion. In this context, intuitive capacity does not refer to some elusive, will-o'-the-wisp inspiration. It is, on the contrary a basic human ability which operates constantly in daily life, and that has been widely discussed in studies of creativity. Think about mathematics: ultimately the weight of a proof is its convincing nature, the immediacy of the evidence which is imposed on us, beyond the logical chains of symbolic reasoning. This is the nature of intuitive evidence: born not of argument but from the establishment of a clarity that is fully convincing. We take this capacity for granted but do little to cultivate it in a systematic manner. Obviously there is no contradiction here between reasoning and inference: intuition without reasoning is blind, but ideas without intuition are empty.

- *There is life beyond the objective/subjective duality*

One of the originalities of the phenomenological attitude is that it does not seek to oppose the subjective to the objective, but to move beyond the split into their fundamental correlation. PhR takes us quickly into the evidence that consciousness is inseparably linked to what goes beyond itself (it is 'transcendental' in the Husserlian language). Consciousness is not some private, internal event having, in the end, an existence of the same kind as the external, non-conscious world.

To begin with, phenomenological investigation is not my 'private trip' since is destined for others through intersubjective validation. In this sense what one is up to in phenomenological attitude is not radically different from other modes of inquiry. As Hut and Shepard point out in their contribution here:

> An analogy with Euclidean geometry may be helpful: once we specify the lengths of the two sides of the triangle, and the magnitude of the enclosed angle, the lengths of the third side is fixed and so are the magnitudes of the remaining two angles. Why is this? Wherein reside the magical power of space? How can space enforce the 'laws' of geometry, laws that physical objects obey as well, to a very high accuracy? (Hut and Shepard, p. 309, in this volume)

We are similarly convinced by empirical and intuitive evidence that our human experience, mine as well as yours, follow some fundamental structural principle which, like space, enforces the nature of what is given to us as contents of that experience.

Through PhR, consciousness appears as a foundation which sheds light on how derived notions such as objective and subjective can arise in the first place. Hence consciousness in this style of examination is drastically different from that of anglo-american empiricism. We are not concerned with a private inspection but with a realm of phenomena where subjective and objective, as well as subject and others emerge naturally from the method applied and its context. This is a point that reductionists and functionalist often miss. Experience is clearly a personal event, but that does not mean it is *private*, in the sense of some kind of isolated subject that is parachuted down onto a pre-given objective world. It is one of the most impressive discoveries of the phenomenological movement to have quickly realized that an investigation of the structure of human experience inevitably induces a shift to considering the several levels on which my consciousness is inextricably linked to those of others and the phenomenal world in an empathic mesh.[7]

Consequently, the usual opposition of first-person vs. third-person accounts is misleading. It makes us forget that so-called third-person, objective accounts are done by a community of concrete people who are embodied in their social and natural world as much as first-person accounts. As B.C. Smith aptly asks: 'Who's on third?' (Smith, 1996). The line of separation — between rigour and lack of it — is not to be drawn between first and third person accounts, but determined rather by whether there is a clear methodological ground leading to a communal validation and shared knowledge.

- *Better pragmatics are needed*

On the whole, my claim is that neurophenomenology is a natural solution that can allow us to move beyond the hard problem in the study of consciousness. It has little to do with some theoretical or conceptual 'extra ingredient', to use Chalmers' expression. Instead, it acknowledges a realm of *practical* ignorance that can be remedied. It is also clear that — like all solutions in science which radically reframe an outstanding problem rather than trying to solve it within its original setting — it has a revolutionary potential, a point to which I shall turn at the end of this article. In other words, instead of finding 'extra ingredients' to account for how consciousness emerges from matter and brain, my proposal reframes the question to that of finding meaningful bridges between two irreducible phenomenal domains. In this specific sense neurophenomenology is a potential solution to the hard problem by casting in an entirely different light on what 'hard' means.

I am painfully aware that what I have said here and what is available in published form about reduction is limited.[8] This is both a symptom and a cause of the relative paucity of recent work on phenomenological approaches to mind. The reader cannot be blamed for not having more than a passing whiff of what I mean by emphasizing the gesture of reduction, the core of the methodological remedy I am offering here. It is remarkable that this capacity for becoming aware has been paid so little attention as a human pragmatics. It is as if the ability for rhythmic movement had led to no development of dance training. A phenomenologicallly-inspired reflection requires strategies for its development as

---

[7] E. Stein and A. Schutz were two of the most active explorers of empathy (*Einfhlung*) in the early days of phenomenology. For an excellent recent discussion on the development on transcendence, empathy , and intersubjectivity in Husserlian phenomenology see Depraz (1996). Abrams (1996) offers a poetic evocation of the same issues with an environmentalist eye. This phenomenological discovery of empathy can be illustrated for our purposes here with various parallel empirical studies, that is, some of its natural correlates from scientific studies rather than PhR itself. As studies on the natural history of mind continue to progress, it is becoming clear that like many other supposedly higher human functions, solidarity and empathy are present in all higher mammals and certainly in primates. As de Waal (1996) convincingly argues in his recent essay, monkeys display the whole spectrum of moral inclinations, and from an early age they can put themselves in the place of another individual even unrelated by blood. Thus from our early evolutionary roots the sense of self is more adequately seen as a holographic point which cannot be separated from the distributed, multiple others which are our inescapable human ecology.

[8] But see the early attempts of Don Ihde (1977) to remedy this situation.

cognitive practicians have known for some time (Vermersch, 1994), and as attested in the mindfulness tradition of various Buddhist schools (Varela *et al.*, 1991). My only comment when faced with this relative poverty of pragmatical elaboration is that it represents an urgent call for research to fill up this gaping hole. My own contribution concerning the practice of reduction and its training will be presented in a forthcoming joint work (Depraz *et al.*, 1996).

In the West we have not had a rich pantheon of individuals gifted for phenomenological expertise (with notable exceptions, such as Husserl or James) rendering their investigations public to an attentive community. In consequence this avenue of inquiry may appear foreign to many readers. But my contention is precisely that this absence is at the root of the opacity of consciousness for science today. What is needed are precisely the *connecting structures* provided by PhR since they are both immediately pertinent for experience (by their very nature) and at the same time sufficiently intersubjective to serve as constructive counterparts for external analysis.

III: A Neurophenomenological Circulation

Case studies

In this Section I wish to sketch a few domains of experience and mental life in order to illustrate more concretely what a neurophenomenological circulation might mean in practice. Needless to say, these case studies do not constitute a proof of what I am proposing, nor do they preclude the detailed examination of other examples more interesting to the reader. Moreover, in recent years there has been a number of different studies where, while remaining well-grounded in the scientific tradition of cognitive neuroscience, the part played by the lived experience is progressively more important to the extent that it begins to enter inescapably into the picture apart from any interest in first-person accounts (Picton and Stuss, 1994). Clearly, as more sophisticated methods of brain imaging are becoming available, we shall need subjects whose competence in making phenomenological discriminations and descriptions is accrued. This is an important philosophical issue but it is also a pragmatic, empirical need. The following are illustrative cases touching both on large and more local issues.

1. Large issues

Attention can be understood as one of the basic mechanisms for consciousness (Posner, 1994). In recent years studies of electrical recordings and more specifically of functional brain imaging have led to the identification of networks and pathways that provide a useful background for distinguishing conscious from non-conscious cognitive events. Three such attentional networks can be distinguished involving orienting to sensory stimulation, activating patterns from memory, and maintaining an alert state. These results indicate that attentional mechanisms are a distinct set of processes in the brain which are neither located in a few neurons, nor merely the ensemble of the brain in operation. At the same time it is clear that the experiential distinctions between these forms of attention require detailed structural investigation of the varieties of ways in which attention is manifest in experience. A systematic study of the structures and strategies of attention is still a largely unfulfilled task. But how is one to investigate the neural mechanisms relevant to consciousness unless such experiential counterparts can be sufficiently discriminated, recognized and trained?

Present-time consciousness. Temporality is inseparable from all experience, and at various horizons of duration from present nowness to an entire life-span. One level of study is precisely the experience of immediate time, the structure of nowness as such or in James' (1912) happy phrase 'the specious present'. This has been a traditional theme in phenomenological studies, describing a basic three part structure of the present with its constitutive threads into past and future horizons, the so-called pretentions and retentions (Husserl, 1966; MacInerny, 1991). In fact, these structural invariants are not compatible with the point-continuum representation of linear time we have inherited from physics. But they do link naturally to a body of conclusions in cognitive neuroscience that there is a minimal time required for the emergence of neural events that correlate to a cognitive event (Dennett and Kinsbourne, 1992). This non-compressible time framework can be analysed as a manifestation of the long-range neuronal integration in the brain linked to a widespread synchrony (Singer, 1993; Varela, 1995). This link illuminates the nature of phenomenological invariants via a dynamical reconstruction which underlies them, as well as giving to the process of synchrony a tangible experiential content. I have developed this case of neuro-phenomenological circulation more in detail elsewhere (Varela, 1996).

Body image and voluntary motion. The nature of will as expressed in the initiation of a voluntary action is inseparable from consciousness and its examination. Recent studies give an important role to neural correlates which precede and prepare voluntary action, and the role of imagination in the constitution of a voluntary act (Libet, 1985; Jeannerod, 1994). Yet voluntary action is preeminently a lived experience which has been well discussed in the phenomenology literature — most specifically in the role of embodiment as lived body (*corps propre*, Merleau-Ponty, 1945), and further in the close relation between lived body and its world (*Leibhaftigkeit*). Pain, for instance, is an interesting 'qualia' which reveals this dimension of embodiment most vividly, and its phenomenological study yields surprising insights both in body-image and its relation to neurophysiological correlates (Leder, 1991). Here again, a phenomenological analysis of voluntary action and embodiment is essential but only partially developed so far.

2. Local issues

Perceptual filling-in as used in visual science involves the spontaneous completing of a percept so that the appearance (i.e. a visual contour) is distinct from the physical correlate (i.e. discontinuous borders, as in the case of the popular illusory contours). These questions can be studied even at the cellular level, and raise more questions concerning experiential distinction of the appearances. In fact the neuronal data on filling-in seem to correlate well with what PhR had concluded some time ago: there is an important difference between 'seeing as', visual appearance, and 'seeing what', a visual judgment (Pessoa *et al.*, 1996). This is the opposite conclusion from Dennett (1991) for whom consciousness is 'all tell and no show'. These are issues that can only be solved with the concerted convergence of external and first hand accounts.

Fringe and centre. Interestingly for us here a number of studies have gone back to consider some traditional phenomenological issues such as the two-part structure of the field of consciousness between a centre and a fringe. This mostly has come from the influence of William James, but carried into modern laboratory protocols. In these studies the crucial experience to explore and target for refinement is the feeling of 'rightness', here standing as a summary of cognitive integration representing the degree of harmony between conscious content and its parallel unconscious background (Mangan, 1993).

Emotion. Recent years have seen significant advances in the understanding of the brain correlates of emotions; the separation between reasoning and emotions is rapidly disappearing (Damasio, 1994; Davidson and Sutton, 1994). Evidence points to the importance of specific structures such as the amygdala, the lateralization of the process, and on the role of arousal in emotional memory. Yet these studies are entirely based on verbal protocols, and the questions of the competence for emotional distinction and the patterns of relations between mood, emotion and reasons need to be addressed explicitly at this stage of research.

The evocation of these study cases tries to provide a concrete background to discuss further the central concern of the neurophenomenological programme I am presenting here. On the one hand we have a process of emergence with well defined neurobiological attributes. On the other, a phenomenological description which links directly to our lived experience. To make further progress we need cutting edge techniques and analyses from the scientific side, and very consistent development of phenomenological investigation for the purposes of the research itself.

Do I expect the list of structural invariants relevant to human experience to grow *ad infinitum*? Certainly not. I surmise that the horizon of fundamental topics can be expected to converge towards a corpus of well-integrated knowledge. When and how fast this happens will of course depend on the pace at which a community of researchers committed to this mode of inquiry is constituted and creates further standards of evidence.

The working hypothesis

This brings me back to my initial point: only a balanced and disciplined account of both the external and experiential side of an issue can make us move one step closer to bridging the biological mind–experiential mind gap. Let me now be more explicit about my basic working hypothesis for a 'circulation' between external and phenomenological analysis:

The Working Hypothesis of Neurophenomenology

Phenomenological accounts of the structure of experience
and their counterparts in cognitive science
relate to each other through reciprocal constraints.

The key point here is that by emphasizing a co-determination of both accounts one can explore the bridges, challenges, insights and contradictions between them. This means that both domains of phenomena have equal status in demanding a full attention and respect for their specificity. It is quite easy to see how scientific accounts illuminate mental experience, but the reciprocal direction, from experience towards science, is what is typically ignored. What do phenomenological accounts provide? At least two main aspects of the larger picture. First, without them the firsthand quality of experience vanishes, or it becomes a mysterious riddle. Second, structural accounts provide constraints on empirical observations.

The study of experience is not a convenient stop on our way to a real explanation, but an active participant in its own right. Clearly in this research programme, like in all others worthy of their name, a certain body of evidence is slowly accumulated, while other aspects are more obscure and difficult to seize. The case studies mentioned above obviously need substantially more development, but I hope it is clear how they begin to provide a 'stereoscopic' perspective on the various large and local issues where experience and cognitive science become active partners.

This demand for a disciplined circulation is both a more precise and a more demanding standard than the 'reflective equilibrium' proposed by Flanagan (1992) or the 'conscious projection' put forth by Velmans (1996). Although there is a similarity in intention to what I am proposing here, they propose no explicit or new methodological grounds for carrying out these intentions. It is surely an improvement on Searle, who insists on the fact that he takes a naturalistic attitude and that 'obviously' consciousness is an emergence. And yet this naturalism does no work in his book: there is not a single line about explicit mechanisms, and thus his naturalism remains barren. At the very least, the hypothesis presented here provides an explicit avenue to conduct research in cognitive science as if both brain physiology and mental experience mattered. Thus, for example, a large-scale integration mechanism in the brain such as neural synchrony in the gamma band should be validated *also* on the basis of its ability to provide insight into first-person accounts of mental contents such as duration. The empirical questions must be guided by first-person evidence. This double constraint would not apply to descriptions that are not directly relevant to the level of experience, for instance for cellular responses or neurotransmitter diffusion.

The claim about appropriate levels of description between brain events and behaviour is, of course, not new and rather uncontroversial except for those who are extreme reductionists. The novelty of my proposal is that *disciplined first-person* accounts should be an integral element of the validation of a neurobiological proposal, and not merely coincidental or heuristic information. This is why I choose to describe the situation by the hypothesis that both accounts be mutual *constraints* on each other.

Still, is this not just a fleshed-up version of the well-known identity theory (or at least a homomorphism) between experience and cognitive neuroscientific accounts? Not really, since I am claiming that the correlates are to be established, not just as a matter of philosophical commitment or physicalist assumption, but from a methodologically sound examination of experiential invariants. Again, this is a question of pragmatics and learning of a method, not of *a priori* argumentation or theoretical completeness.

In contrast, a more conventional psycho-identity thesis works on the form of a reasoning that Pessoa *et al.* (1996) call linking propositions (following D. Teller). These are propositions of the form:

$$\Phi \text{ looks like } \Psi \implies \Phi \text{ explains } \Psi$$

where Φ are neural–psychological terms and Ψ are phenomenal terms, and the implication operator has a conditional sense: if the empirical events 'look like' the phenomenal events, then these are explained. An excellent example is Crick's enthusiasm when discussing single neuron correlates associated with the sudden shift in experience in binocular rivalrous visual figures (Leopold and Logothetis, 1996), which he assimilates to an explanation of that form of visual consciousness. These kinds of bridges are unsatisfactory because they leave the problem untouched. We still have to contend with the nature of the arrow: how are these neural units related to the rest of the brain's activity, how do they acquire their sense, and specially what in them makes them into an experiential event. We are back to square one with the hard problem intact. What is different in the research strategy proposed by neurophenomenology is that these bridges are not of the 'looks like' kind but they are built by mutual constraint and validated from both phenomenal domains where the phenomenal terms stands as explicit terms *directly* linked to experience by a rigorous examination (e.g. reduction, inavariance and intersubjective communication).

This working hypothesis does have some points of similarity with the notion of 'structural coherence' as put forth by Chalmers, amongst his three basic principles for the structure of consciousness. Indeed 'precisely because the structural properties of experience are accessible and reportable, those properties will be directly represented in the structure of awareness' (p. 23). This is quite correct from my viewpoint but it is fatally incomplete as stated at least in regards to two key issues raised here. First, this structure of experience needs a method for exploration and validation, and it is not enough to simply claim that we can work with the structure of awareness. Second, there is no ontological value on Chalmers' principle since he assumes consciousness is an added ontological term. In our case, phenomenal experience does represent an irreducible ontological level, but it retains its quality of immediacy because it plays a role in structural coherence via its intuitive contents, and thus keeps alive its direct connection to human experience, rather than pushing it into abstraction.

This makes the whole difference: one obtains an intellectually coherent account of mind and consciousness where the experiential pole enters directly into the formulation of the complete account, making direct reference to the nature of our lived experience. The 'hardness' and riddle become a research programme open for its exploration in an open-ended manner with the structure of human experience playing a central role in our scientific explanation. In all functionalistic accounts what is missing is not the coherent nature of the explanation but its alienation from human life. Only putting human life back in will erase that absence; not some 'extra ingredient' or profound 'theoretical fix'.[9]

By the same token it would be missing the point to expect from the neurophenomenological approach some completely new insights into empirical mechanisms. ('So what *do* you add to cognitive science with your method that we don't know already?') Surely, the PhR approach does provide interesting ideas concerning the structure of mental life (cf. the cases of temporality or filling in), but its main force is that it does so in a way that makes our experience recognizable. I am quite sure that this second order

---

[9] Incidentally, Chalmers' own theoretical fix (or extra ingredient) is his notion of 'double information' derived from the old Shannonian theory of signs, incorrectly known as a 'theory of information'. In a book which displays such clear intellectual acuity, I was dumbfounded to see that in the end Chalmers argues that the best choice is to revive a cybernetic tradition, largely transformed after its inception into truly informational tools by the work done in computationalist, connectionist or embodiment approaches to cognition, not once discussed by Chalmers in this context. Even assuming the position that an 'extra ingredient' is needed, I simply do not see what could possibly be derived from this move, and neither do some of the scientists that have commented on it. See for instance Koch's otherwise rather positive review (Koch, 1996).

twist will be the most difficult for those researchers of a persistent functionalist inclination to appreciate.

IV: In Conclusion

Consciousness: hard problem or time bomb?

Practically since its inception cognitive science has been committed to a very explicit set of key ideas and metaphors which can be called *representationalism*, for which the inside–outside distinction is the centre piece: an outside (a feature-full world) represented inside through the action of complex perceptual devices. In recent years there has been a slow but sure change towards an alternative orientation, one that I have contributed to and defended for many years (see Varela, 1979; Varela *et al.*, 1991). This orientation differs from representationalism by treating mind and world as mutually overlapping, hence the qualifying terms *embodied*, situated or *enactive* cognitive science.

I cannot elaborate here the current state of embodied cognitive science, but my present proposal concerning the study of consciousness aligns itself with those larger concerns. It seems inescapable to take the trend towards embodiment one step further in the direction of a principled consideration of *embodiment as lived experience*. In our book (Varela *et al.*, 1991) we first highlighted the intrinsic circularity in cognitive science wherein the study of mental phenomena is always that of an experiencing person. We claimed that cognitive science cannot escape this circulation, and must cultivate it instead. We explicitly draw from Asian traditions, Buddhism in particular, as living manifestations of an active, disciplined phenomenology. It was not the intention of that book to dwell on Asian traditions *per se* but to use them as a distant mirror of what we needed to cultivate in our science and the western tradition.

The present proposal takes what was started in that book one step further by concentrating on the key issue of methodology. I hope I have seduced the reader into considering that we have in front of us the possibility of an open-ended quest for resonant passages between human experience and cognitive science. The price however is to take first-person accounts seriously as valid domain of phenomena. And beyond that, to build a sustained *tradition* of phenomenological examination that is almost entirely nonexistent today in our western science and culture at large.

One must take seriously the double challenge my proposal represents. First, it demands a re-learning and a mastery of the skill of phenomenological description. There is no reason why this should be any different from the acquisition of any know-how, like learning to play an instrument or to speak a new language. Anyone who engages in learning, be it in music, language or thinking, will be bringing forth a change of everyday life. This is what is listed as the fourth item in PhR: sustained, disciplined learning *does* entail transformation, and so does anything else we do in a sustained mode. This is fine if we reject the assumption (as I do) that there is some kind of well-defined standard for what should count as real or normal experience: experience appears to be inherently open-ended and pliable, and hence there is no contradiction in saying that sustained training in a method can make available aspects of experience that were not available before. The point of PhR is to overcome the habit of automatic introspection among others, and we need not carry with us a mourning for what may be lost, but an interest in what can be learned.[10]

The second challenge that my proposal represents is that of a call for transforming the style and values of the research community itself. Unless we accept that at this point in intellectual and scientific history some radical re-learning is necessary, we cannot hope to move forward and break the historic cycle rejection–fascination with consciousness in philosophy of mind and cognitive science. My proposal implies that every good student of cognitive science who is *also* interested in issues at the level of mental experience, must inescapably attain a level of mastery in phenomenological examination in order to work seriously with first-person accounts. But this can only happen when the entire community adjusts itself — with a corresponding change of attitude in relation to acceptable forms of argument, refereeing standards and editorial policies in major scientific journals — so that this added competence becomes an important dimension for a young researcher. To the long-standing tradition of objectivist science this sounds anathema, and it is. But this is not a betrayal of science: it is a necessary extension and complement. Science and experience constrain and modify each other as in a dance. This is where the potential for transformation lies. It is also the key for the difficulties this position has found within the scientific community. It requires us to leave behind a certain image of how science is done, and to question a style of training in science which is part of the very fabric of our cultural identity.

In brief: what's the story?

Let me conclude by summarizing the main points I have raised in this reaction to the 'hard' problem of consciousness based on an explicit proposal for its remedy.

The argument:

- In line with Chalmers' basic point, I take lived, first-hand experience is a proper *field of phenomena*, irreducible to anything else. My claim there is no theoretical fix or 'extra' ingredient in nature can possibly bridge this gap.
- Instead, this field of phenomena requires a proper, rigorous *method* and pragmatics for its exploration and analysis.
- The orientation for such method is inspired from the style of inquiry of *phenomenology* in order to constitute a widening *research community* and a research programme.
- This research programme seeks *articulations by mutual constraints* between the field of phenomena revealed by experience and the correlative field of phenomena established by the cognitive sciences. I have called this point of view *neurophenomenology*.

---

[10] H. Dreyfus (1993) in a critical review of our book chided us for emphasizing the transformation that accompanies the learning of phenomenological observation since this itself interferes with 'everyday experience'. This would be a mistake if one believes that one exposes a 'deeper layer' by acquiring some skill such as stable reduction or engaging in a practice such as mindfulness/awareness, which was not at all our claim. Even Dreyfus would have to conclude that there is no privileged vantage point to tell us what counts as 'real' experience. He has plainly misunderstood the main point: phenomenological reduction does not 'uncover' some objective ground, but it does bring forth new phenomena within the experiential realm, in an unfolding of multiple possibilities.

The consequences:

- With no radical expansion of the style of work in the scientific tradition and the establishment of research programme roughly along these lines, the riddle of the place of experience in science and world will continue to come back, either to be explained away or to be re-claimed as too hard, given what we know.
- The nature of 'hard' becomes reframed in two senses:
  (1) it is hard work to train and stabilize a new methods to explore experience,
  (2) it is hard to change the habits of science in order for it to accept that new tools are needed for the transformation of what it means to conduct research on mind and for the training of succeeding generations.

References

Abrams, D. (1996), *The Spell of the Sensous: Perception and Language in a More Than Human World* (New York: Pantheon).

Baars, B. (1988), *A Cognitive Theory of Consciousness* (Cambridge: Cambridge University Press).

R. Bernet, (1994), *La Vie du Sujet* (Paris: Presses Universitaire de France).

Calvin W. (1990), *Cerebral Symphony: Seashore Reflections on the Structure of Consciousness* (New York: Bantam Books).

Chalmers, D.J. (1995), 'Facing up to the problem of consicousness', *Journal of Consciousness Studies*, **2** (3), pp. 200–19 (reprinted in this volume).

Chalmers, D.J. (1996), *The Conscious Mind: In Search of a Fundamental Theory* (New York: Oxford University Press).

Churchland, P.S. and Sejnowski, T. (1992), *The Computational Brain* (Cambridge, MA: MIT Press).

Crick, F. (1994), *The Astonishing Hypothesis* (New York: Scribners).

Damasio, A. (1994), *Descartes' Error: Emotion, Reason and the Human Brain* (New York: Grosset/Putnam).

Davidson, R. and Sutton, S. (1994), 'Affective neuroscience: the emergence of a discipline', *Curr. Opinion Neurobiol.*, 5, pp. 217–24.

de Waal, F. (1996), *Good Natured: The Origins of Right and Wrong in Humans and Other Animals* (Cambridge: Harvard University Press).

Dennett, D. (1991), *Consciousness Exaplained* (Boston: Little Brown).

Dennett, D. and M.Kinsbourne (1992), 'Time and the observer: the where and when of time in the brain', *Behavioral and Brain Sciences*, **15**, pp. 183–247.

Depraz, N. (1996), *Incarnation et Transcendence* (Paris: J.Vrin).

Depraz, N., Varela, F. and Veermersch, P. (1996), *Exploring Experience with a Method* (forthcoming).

Dreyfus, H. (ed. 1982), *Husserl: Intentionality and Cognitive Science* (Cambridge, MA: MIT Press).

Dreyfus, H. (1993), Review of 'The Embodied Mind', *Mind*, **102**, pp. 542–6.

Edelman, G. (1989), *The Remembered Present: A Biological Theory of Consciousness* (New York: Basic Books).

Flanagan. O (1992), *Consciousness Reconsidered* (Cambridge, MA: MIT Press).

Globus, G. (1995), *The Post-Modern Brain* (New York: Benjamin).

Howe, R.B. (1991), Introspection: A reassesment, *New Ideas in Psychology*, **9**, pp. 24–44.

Husserl, H. (1962), *The Idea of Phenomenology* (The Hague: M. Nijhoff).

Husserl, E. (1966), *Zur Phänomenologie des Inneren Zeitbewusstseins (1893-1917)*, ed. R. Bohm (The Hague: M.Nijhoff). Partial English translation: *The Phenomenology of Internal Time Consciousness* (Bloomington: Indiana University Press, 1996).

Hut, P. and Shepard, R., 'Turning the hard problem upside down and sideways', in this volume.

Ihde, D. (1977), *Experimental Phenomenology* (New York: Open Court).

Jackendoff, R. (1987), *Consciousness and the Computational Mind* (Cambridge, MA: MIT Press).

James, W. (1912/1995), *The Principles of Psychology* (Cambridge: Harvard University Press).

Jeannerod, M. (1994), 'The representing brain: neural correlates of motor intention and imagery', *Behavioral and Brain Sciences*, **17**, pp. 187–245.

Johnson, M. (1987), *The Body in the Mind: The Bodily Basis of Imagination, Reason and Feeling* (Chicago: Chicago University Press).

Klein, P. and and Wescott, M.R. (1994), 'The changing character of phenomenological psychology', *Canadian Psychology*, **35**, pp. 133–57.

Koch, C. (1996), Review of 'The Conscious Mind', *Nature*, **381**, p. 123.

Langsdorf, L. (1985), Review of Dreyfus (1982), *Husserl Studies*, **3**, pp. 303–11.

Leder, D. (1991), *The Dissapereance of the Body* (Chicago: Chicago University Press).

Libet, B. (1985), 'Unconscious cerebral initiative and the role of conscious will in voluntary action', *Behavioral and Brain Sciences*, **8**, pp. 529–66.

Leopold, D. and Logothetis, N. (1996), 'Activity changes in early visual cortex reflect monkeys' percepts during binocular rivalry', *Nature*, **379**, pp. 549–53.

Lyons, W. (1986), *The Disappearance of Instrospection* (Cambridge, MA: MIT Press).

Lyotard, J-F. (1954), *La Phénoménologie* (Paris: Presses Univ. de France).

McGinn, C. (1991), *The Problem of Consciousness* (Oxford: Blackwell).

McInerney, P. (1991), *Time and Experience* (Philadelphia: Temple University Press).

McIntyre, R. (1986), 'Husserl and the representational theory of mind', *Topoi*, **5**, pp. 101–13.

Mangan, B. (1993), 'Taking phenomenology seriously: the "fringe" and its implications for cognitive research', *Consciousness and Cognition*, **2**, pp. 89–108.

Mazoyer, B. Ronald and Fox (ed. 1995), International Congress on the Functional Mapping of the Human Brain, *Human Brain Mapp.* **Suppl. 1**.

Merleau-Ponty, M. (1945), *La Phénoménologie de la Perception* (Paris: Gallimard).

Nagel, T. (1986), *The View from Nowhere* (New York: Oxford University Press).

Pessoa, L., Thompson, E and Noë, A. (1996), 'Finding out about filling in', *Behavioral and Brain Sciences* (in press).

Petitot, J. (ed. 1995), 'Sciences cognitives et phénoménologie', *Archives de Philosophie*, **58** (4), pp. 529–631.

Petitot, J., Roy, J.M., Pachoud, B. and Varela, F. (ed. 1996), *Naturalizing Phenomenology: Contemporary Issues in Phenomenology and Cognitive Science* (Stanford: Stanford University Press) in press.

Picton,T. and Stuss, D (1994), 'Neurobiology of conscious experience', *Current Biology*, **4**, pp. 256–65.

Posner, M.I. (1994), 'Attention: the mechanisms of consciousness', *Proc. Natl. Acad. Science (USA)*, **91**, pp. 7398–403.

Posner, M & Raichle, M (1992), *Images of the Mind* (New York: Scientific American Library).

Roy, J.M. (1995), 'Le "Dreyfus bridge": Husserlianism and Fodorism', *Archives de Philosophie*, **58**, pp. 533–49.

Searle, J. (1992), *The Rediscovery of the Mind* (Cambridge, MA: The MIT Press)

Smith, B.C. (1996), 'Who's on third? Subjectivity at the physical basis of consicousness', *Consciousness Research Abstracts*, p. 53.

Singer, W. (1993), 'Synchronization of cortical activity and its putative role in information processing and learning', *Ann. Rev. Physiol.*, **55**, pp. 349–74.

Spiegelberg, F. (1962), *The Phenomenological Movement*, 2 vols. 2ed. (The Hague: Martinus Nihjoff).

Thompson, E. and F. Varela (1996), *Why the Mind is not in the Head* (Cambridge: Harvard University Press, forthcoming).

Varela, F. (1979), *Principles of Biological Autonomy* (New York: North-Holland).

Varela, F. (1995), 'Resonant cell assemblies: A new approach to cognitive functioning and neuronal synchrony', *Biol. Res.*, **28**, pp. 81–95.

Varela, F. (1996), 'The specious present: A neurophenomenology of nowness', in Petitot *et al.* (1996).

Varela, F. J., Thompson, E. and Rosch, E. (1991), *The Embodied Mind: Cognitive Science and Human Experience* (Cambridge, MA: The MIT Press).

Velmans, M. (1996), *The Science of Consciousness* (London: Routledge).

Vermersch, P. (1994), *L'Entretien d'Explicitation* (Paris: ESF Editeurs).

Jonathan Shear

The Hard Problem:
Closing the Empirical Gap

I

The 'hard problem' of explaining consciousness, as David Chalmers puts it, is that of giving an intelligible account of why experience exists at all, and also of why it is found in intimate association with individual physical systems such as the nervous systems of human beings and other sentient creatures.

> Why should a physical system, no matter how complex and well-organized, give rise to experience at all? Why is it that all this processing does not go on 'in the dark', without any subjective quality? Right now, nobody has good answers to these questions. This is the phenomenon that makes consciousness a *real* mystery.*

Why is it that we do not have good answers to these questions? Simply put, there appears to be a huge conceptual gap between the subjective nature of our ordinary conscious experience and the nonsubjective nature of ordinary (i.e. nonconscious) physical objects. For the former are typically filled with sensory and other qualities ('qualia'), and the latter appear to be qualia-free spatial structures. Our experience is full of colours, tastes, sounds, and feelings, and no account of consciousness that fails to refer to such things could reasonably be held to be adequate. Yet the objective physical world, according to all common sense, has none of *these* sorts of things in it by itself. Indeed, our scientific accounts of the physical universe are formulated in terms of distributions of dynamic potentials to occupy and influence the occupation of space, with no reference to subjective qualities or qualia whatsoever. In short, while qualia are an essential, if not *the* essential, feature of consciousness, they play no role at all in our scientific accounts of the objective physical universe. And it would seem that however one might combine or otherwise manipulate colourless, soundless, feelingless spatio–temporal components, one will only get other colourless, soundless, feelingless spatio–temporal structures, and never any subjective qualia at all. Thus the hard problem of generating any coherent account of how and why the physical universe in general, and sophisticated nervous systems in particular, should generate consciousness and its qualia-filled content.

This paper will address the hard problem by arguing that it is, first and foremost, an empirical rather than a purely conceptual problem, and that a highly developed scientific

---

* This succinct expression of the 'hard problem' is from a summary of Chalmers' keynote paper privately circulated by its author prior to the publication of the full paper. The author's paper was originally published in the *Journal of Consciousness Studies*, **3**, No.1 (1996), pp. 54–68.

study of the phenomena of consciousness, complementing our physical sciences, can be expected to play a major role in any adequate resolution of the hard problem. It will then examine and reject some influential philosophical arguments implying that the problem cannot properly be approached empirically through research on the phenomena of consciousness. Finally it will suggest that developing a scientific exploration relevant to resolving the hard problem can be expected to profit by taking some cues from traditional eastern methodologies for exploring the internal phenomena of consciousness. It will not, however, attempt to directly solve the problem itself.

II

The hard problem, of course, has been formulated in many different, often highly technical, ways. But the simple formulation above captures, I think, much of the intuition underlying the hardness of the problem. If this intuition *is* our general one, and I think it is, then any good resolution may well have to be one that appears, at least initially, counter-intuitive. Thus many of the standard responses to this problem, ranging from reductionist claims that subjective consciousness is *nothing but* physical objects or structures (of one specific kind or other), or even that it *does not exist* at all (and thus need not be explained), to panexperientialist postulations of some form of experience or qualia as an all-pervasive component of the physical (and even inanimate) universe, are, to be sure, in fact highly counter-intuitive. David Chalmers' postulation of experience and 'information' as 'fundamental features' of the universe in general is no exception.

The defenders of the various attempted resolutions often argue, of course, that this counter-intuitiveness is not by itself any sufficient reason to reject their particular theories. For the history of science has made it abundantly clear that our ordinary intuitions about the world around us are often in fact simply wrong. We see the world around us as populated with solid objects. Yet we now know they are mostly empty space. (Indeed, the average neutrino is more likely to pass through a mile-thick slab of rock than to hit something and bounce off.) Until the early decades of the present century it had seemed *obvious* that biological processes such as nutrition, respiration and growth were full of *life* — and thus different *in principle* from mere inorganic mechanical ones — and that understanding them required reference to *something* (e.g. *elan vital*) other than mere mechanical components and processes. Yet now it seems apparent that such life processes can, in principle at least, be adequately accounted for in terms of mechanical interactions of DNA and its chemical environment. And it had certainly seemed intuitively unquestionable that space and time were the immutable contexts for the existence of physical objects, and that each physical thing in our environment occupied a definite spatial location at any given time. Yet we now all accept that these intuitions have been contradicted by what we know from relativity and quantum physics. The upshot of all this, then, has often been taken to be that our ordinary intuitions have so often proven unreliable that it is invalid to take them as reliable grounds for rejecting whatever postulated resolution of the hard problem is being defended, whether the physicalist extreme of functionalism or the subjectivist extreme of panexperientialism.

I have no quarrel with this general line of reasoning about the limitations of our ordinary intuitions — so far as it goes. But it contains an important, often overlooked asymmetry, highly relevant to attempts at resolving the hard problem. The intuitions called into question in the preceding paragraph are all intuitions about the objective world, rejected on the basis of our modern scientific knowledge. And this scientific knowledge is in turn the product of sophisticated empirical investigative methodologies capable of penetrating beyond our ordinary, superficial perception and displaying the deep, underlying structure of the physical world. Our discussions of the subjective nature of the contents of consciousness, on the other hand, almost all too often refer only to its components as we are ordinarily, commonsensically aware of them. This observation holds even for sophisticated psychophysiological studies; for even here, the correlations we typically make are between physiological structures and processes and the contents of subjective awareness (perceptions, thoughts, memories, moods, etc.) as we are ordinarily familiar with them. It is as if we were are attempting to tackle deep problems of consciousness using, on the side of consciousness itself, only what amount to superficial Aristotelian investigative methodologies. The result is that while our discussions about the nature of the outer, objective world are embedded in our contemporary scientific knowledge, our discussions about the phenomenological contents of consciousness often remain based on superficial, commonsensical perception, classification and under-standing of the contents of our inner awareness.

The relevance of all this to the 'hard problem' is quite clear. As it stands, there is a huge, seemingly unbridgeable conceptual gap between the subjective, first-person mental and the objective, third-person physical. Closing this gap will require cutting across deeply held commonsensical intuitions about reality. Thus if we want to come to an optimum, empirically sound understanding of the relationship (whether reductive, causal, dual-aspect, idealist, or ungraspable) of the physical world to the subjective realm of consciousness, it stands to reason that we should, to whatever extent possible, go beyond superficial 'Aristotelian' perception and intuitions to systematic scientific knowledge in *both* cases, subjective as well as objective. This is the project the present paper addresses, if only in a very preliminary way. As Wittgenstein noted, it is often valuable to step outside of our ordinary perspective and 'make the familiar strange'. The suggestion I will make is that we *can* step outside of the perspective of our ordinary everyday sorts of awareness, both conceptually and perceptually, in ways relevant to unpacking, and perhaps even resolving, the hard problem.

III

One more aspect of the hard problem ought to be noted here. The hard problem as articulated above is that of how colourless, soundless, feelingless spatio–temporal struc-tures could ever generate our consciousness with the qualia that fill them so richly. Another aspect of the problem involves the contrast between the spatial nature of the contents of objective, material world and the apparent non-spatiality of our minds. Thus, it is often asked, how is it that such essentially spatial objects could ever generate something fundamentally non-spatial, as our minds appear to be?

Descartes, of course, emphasized this contrast in his epoch-making articulation of dualism. His thesis of the essentially mathematizable spatiality of objective phenomena continues to dominate our scientific understanding of the material universe, and his thesis of the general non-spatiality of the contents of mind appears to accurately reflect fundamental aspects of our ordinary, commonsensical understanding of mind. As Colin McGinn, writing in the Cartesian tradition, puts it: to ask, for example, whether a thought is to the left or right, or north or south, of a hope, or to think of either as having spatially distributed parts, is simply to make a category mistake. For such questions simply do not fit the nature of thoughts, hopes, or so many other mental contents; they are not the *kinds of thing* that fall under spatial predicates. Consequently, as McGinn and others argue, the gap between the spatial and the non-spatial is so great that the notion that non-spatial minds evolved from spatial matter (particles and fields) is utterly incomprehensible, and the common, seemingly scientific notion that

> something essentially non-spatial emerged from something purely spatial — that the non-spatial is somehow a construction out of the spatial . . . looks more like magic than a predictable unfolding of natural law (McGinn, 1995, p. 101).

Thus, McGinn concludes, there must be some as-yet-unknown non-spatial aspect of the universe which is responsible for the generation of consciousness. But our empirical knowledge is, as yet, obviously inadequate.

> [W]ithout a more adequate articulation of consciousness we are not going to be in a position to come up with the unifying theory that must link consciousness to the world of matter in space . . . Clearly, the space of perception and action is no place to find the roots of consciousness . . . but we seem unable to develop a new conception of space that can overcome the impossibility of finding a place for consciousness in it (p. 107).

McGinn concludes, moreover, that our knowledge here is likely to *remain* inadequate. For, he argues, we have 'no access to' the 'real inner constitution' of consciousness, and our conception of space is limited by its connection to 'our space-representing faculties' which

> have a quite specific set of [evolutionary] goals that by no means coincide with solving the deep ontological problems surrounding consciousness and space (p. 108).

The situation may not, however, be as bleak as McGinn and kindred thinkers (dubbed 'the new mysterians' by their critics) would have it. For the notions of matter and space articulated by contemporary physics are very different from our surface, commonsensical ones, and as a number of articles in this volume make clear, some of the most interesting work in the attempts to resolve the 'hard problem' turns is that of theorists who have turned their attention to such non-commonsensical quantum-mechanical understandings of the deep structure of matter and space. Hameroff and Penrose (1996), for example, argue that if phenomenal aspects of information are in fact a fundamental feature of nature, as Chalmers suggests, then we need to go to the deepest stratum of the objective universe, space itself, before we are likely to understand how this could be; they then attempt to correlate the quantum mechanical nature of space with the mechanics of the nervous system that presumably underlie the contents of our awareness. Seager (1995) argues that information itself appears to be a fundamental feature of quantum dynamics underlying all events in space, and then attempts to resolve a long standing combinatorial problem facing panpsychism by reference to quantum-mechanical superposition. Clarke (1995) attempts to reduce the contrast between the local spatial boundedness of ordinary objects in the material world and the non-spatiality of consciousness by pointing out that while the material world is tightly localized at the surface level of everyday macroscopic phenomena, it, too, is radically nonlocalized at its quantum-mechanical base. And Hodgson (1996) argues that the conflict between the mechanical determinism taken for granted by classical physics and the freedom of choice we all (rightly or wrongly) feel to be a feature of our awareness can be resolved by reference to quantum-mechanical indeterminism underlying objective nature in general and our central nervous system functioning in particular.

Such approaches, whatever their individual merit, all attempt to reduce the contrast between our ordinary conceptions of the realms of consciousness and matter by utilizing our knowledge of the quantum-mechanical depths of the objective world to uncover features of space and matter which appear much more akin to those of consciousness than we would ordinarily expect. At the very least, they show that the spatial–non-spatial contrast between matter and consciousness, emphasized by thinkers from Descartes to McGinn, cannot simply be taken at face value. For physics has transformed our notions of the relationship between matter and space (portraying, among other things, matter as ultimately generally nonlocal), and makes it clear that our understanding of spatiality needs to be deeply re-evaluated before applying it to the 'hard problem'.

IV

It stands to reason, I think, that a well-developed science of the subjective phenomena of consciousness might turn out to transform our understanding of the hard problem in comparably unexpected ways. And it seems even more reasonable to think that whatever particular results it might produce, such a science ought to be an essential component, complementing our physical sciences, of any ultimate resolution of the problem, what-ever it might turn out to be.

First, however, some *in principle* objections to this approach need to be addressed. A variety of twentieth century thinkers have, of course, argued forcefully against the coherence of the notions of mind, mental contents, and introspection. In the present context of the 'hard problem', however, it may be most useful to focus on the objections raised by Searle (1992), who argues against the coherence of the notion of introspection without denying the existence of mind and its contents.[1] Indeed, he emphasizes their importance, arguing commonsensically both that '[c]onsciousness and intentionality are ineliminable' (p. 20) and that '[n]o description of . . . third-person, objective, physiologi-cal facts would convey the subjective first-person character of [for example a pain] simply because the first-person features are different from the third-person features' (p. 117). This anti-reductionist argument, he asserts, 'is ludicrously simple and quite decisive' (p. 118). Nevertheless, as Searle puts it,

> in the philosophy of mind, obvious facts about the mental, such as that we all really do have subjective conscious mental states and that these are not eliminable in favor of anything else, are routinely denied by many, perhaps most, of the advanced thinkers in the subject (p. 3).

Why is this?

---

[1] We can note in passing that the arguments of the following sections can readily be adapted to apply to major themes of the more radical critics such as Ryle and Rorty as well.

I believe one of the unstated assumptions behind the current batch of views is that they represent the only scientifically acceptable alternatives to the antiscientism that went with traditional dualism, the belief in the immortality of the soul, spiritualism, and so on (p. 3).

Searle, of course, shares this desire to be scientific and to avoid dualism. But, he argues, to do this one needn't go so far as to deny the existence of consciousness or the irreducibility of (aspects of) its contents. But this has 'no untoward scientific consequences whatsoever' (p. 124). For first-person phenomena of consciousness, while they exist and are irreducible, *cannot be observed at all*. He reaches this surprising conclusion by the following reasoning. The notion of observation, of seeing some thing,

> works on the presupposition that there is a distinction between the thing seen and the seeing of it. But for 'introspection' there is simply no way to make this separation. Any introspection I have of my own conscious state *is* itself that conscious state (p. 97: emphasis added).

Consequently,

> I cannot *observe* my own subjectivity, for any observation that I might care to make is itself that which was supposed to be observed (p. 99).

As a result, while we *can* use 'consciousness to study consciousness' and 'subjectivity to study subjectivity', our scientific models of 'studying', which all 'rely on the distinction between observation and the thing observed, do not work for subjectivity itself' (p. 99). In short, there is nothing that can properly be called introspective observation, there are no private objects to be introspected, and nothing like any 'private inner space . . . into which I can enter' to make introspective observations (p. 98). Consequently, 'consciousness is not known by introspection in a way analogous to the way objects in the world are known by perception' (p. 105) and neither introspective observation nor any supposedly introspected phenomena — whether irreducible or not — can have any significance for our scientific view of reality.

On the face of it, the 'hard problem' of explaining consciousness would appear to be an empirical one involving, among other things, understanding the causal and ontological relationships between two very different realms, the mental and the physical. Thus, given the historical intractability of the problem, we might expect that extended empirical examination of both of the very different, but obviously highly correlated, realms involved would be the most likely place to look for clues as to how the problem might be resolved. But arguments such as the above suggest that this approach would be misguided. For if they are correct, the mind and its contents are not in fact observable phenomena, and introspection cannot provide us with the appropriate empirical data.

V

One of the difficulties of understanding consciousness empirically, of course, is that we are attempting here to see ourselves, and self-reflection, like self-reference, can often be tricky. Searle's discussion of the observation–observed distinction is a case in point. But there is an empirical feature of self-reference that plays an even larger role in the intractability of the hard problem. As Descartes pointed out, there are ways in which it seems that consciousness is the most indubitable *given* of all of our knowledge and experience. Yet there is a considerable body of empirical knowledge, generated in the field of cognitive development, that indicates that the contents of our ordinary adult human consciousness are *not* simply given to us, but are instead the products of a regular sequence of stages of normal human development. Moreover, the structure of the earlier stages is significantly different from that of the ordinary adult awareness that our philosophical analyses and problems typically reflect.

Widely replicated experiments show, for example, that our ordinary notion of 'physical object' does not reflect a simple 'given' of very young children's awareness. For they have to learn to connect the visual and tactile experiences of an object as being of the same thing, to associate the rest and moving phases of objects as being of the same things, to recognize that physical objects continue to exist at times and places when they are not being observed, and then to learn that objects have to move through space and time in continuous paths and cannot exist in more than one place at a time. In short, behavioural studies have made it apparent that very young children (in the first two years of life) have to *construct* what we as adults would take to be the notion of solid physical objects as integrative foci of their attention and activities.

Further studies also make it clear that once the notion of abiding physical objects has been generated and become stable, the commonsensical distinction between what we call 'mental' and 'merely subjective' on the one hand, and 'physical', 'real' and 'objective' on the other, naturally emerges. As Kohlberg describes this process, our ordinary commonsense adult view develops through a regular sequence of steps over several years, with the normal child recognizing first that dreams are not 'real events', second that they cannot be seen by others, third that they take place 'inside' oneself, and fourth that they are 'caused by' oneself (Kohlberg, 1969, p. 357). Moreover, research over the past thirty years indicates that this sequential development of our ordinary, commonsensical adult mental/physical distinction is culture-independent, taking place in children in a wide diversity of societies, from modern industrial to traditional aboriginal. Indeed, the standard sequence of development is reported even in children in cultures where the prevailing adult view *opposes* this development (considering dreams, for example, as 'real' and dream experiences as real travel to other places), where the normal sequence is typically completed, but then (partially) reversed during adolescence as the prevailing cultural view becomes internalized (Kohlberg, 1969, p. 358).

Jean Piaget, the seminal researcher in the field of cognitive development, early on coined the term 'childhood realism' to refer to the thinking of children prior to their generation of the mental/physical distinction, arguing that dreams and other mentally-generated phenomena are perceived by children at this stage as external, palpable realities, potentially visible to others. This thesis has been quite influential in cognitive developmental thinking, and anyone who has gone into a small child's room after a 'bad dream' to reassure him or her that what had just been experienced was 'only a dream' and 'not real' can easily get a sense of its import. As traditionally articulated, the thesis holds that three-year-olds generally (a) have not yet generated any clear distinction between mental and physical and (b) regard all phenomena they experience, mental as well as physical, as physical and real — thus childhood 'realism'. Aspects of this 'childhood realism' thesis, however, have recently been called into question by the work of Wellman and others. Wellman's research is worth noting here. He began by articulating various paradigm features of our ordinary adult understanding of the mental/physical distinction, e.g. that thoughts are different from (physical) things; beliefs are different from actuality and can be false; desires and mental activities are different from physical actions and outcomes; mind is private and individual, etc. (Wellman, 1990, pp. 3–4.) He then isolated three 'obvious' criteria used by adults to distinguish mental entities from physical: behavioural-sensory evidence (e.g. one can see, touch and sit on a chair), public exist- ence, and consistent existence (objective constancy, etc.) (p. 18), and then tested three-, four-, and five-year olds to see how consistently they used these criteria to distinguish mental from physical objects and phenomena. His data showed (1) that children as young as three ascribe 'behavioural-sensory, public existence, and consistent existence status to physical objects but not mental entities' the overwhelming majority of the time, and (2) that 'when [these] children did make errors, they were as likely to ascribe not-real status to physical items as they were to ascribe physical status to not-real, mental items' (p. 19). Thus, Wellman concludes, contrary to Piaget, that children as young as three are not, in fact, childhood 'realists', taking all of their experiences to be physical, but instead even at this early age appear to have an operational 'theory' of mind as a 'container' or 'sum' of its thoughts, attitudes, etc. (p. 11).

'Theory of mind' is a lively topic of debate and research in cognitive development. Many follow Wellman's conclusions. Others, while accepting Wellman's research and critique of Piaget, argue that three-year-olds should not be described as having a 'theory' of mind, since the term 'theory' implies a not-yet-developed competence with second order reflexive concepts (representations of representations, etc.). Thus, on their account, what can properly be called 'theories' of mind develop only later on the basis of already developed first-order distinctions of experiential phenomena as mental — or — physical. (See, for example, Astington *et al.*, 1988.)

Nevertheless, despite such ongoing disputes about 'childhood realism' and the precise age at which a fairly well-structured 'theory of mind' enabling children to distinguish between mental and physical phenomena first appears, and despite the debates about the significance of the theories that do emerge (e.g. whether they are ontologically significant or mere 'folk theories') there appears to be a general, empirically-grounded consensus among cognitive developmental researchers that the young child (1) has various sorts of experiences, (2) learns (during the first two years of life) to integrate a subset of them according to the topological features characteristic of physical objects (including in particular continuity of spatio-temporal locations and abidingness even when unper- ceived), (3) finds (during the third year of life) that these topological integrations sometimes are and sometimes are not appropriately supported by the behaviour of other people, (4) generates accordingly the distinction between public physical and private mental objects of experience, and (5) then progressively (largely between the ages of three and five) learns to sort his or her experiences according to these categories of mental and physical, often making mistakes along the way,[2] with mental entities being negatively identified as those which are 'not real', 'cannot be touched or sat in', 'cannot be seen by

---

[2] Wellman found, for instance, one in four 3-year olds thinking, e.g. that hidden physical objects could be transformed by their mental effort, that their mental images could be seen by others, etc. (pp. 35–8).

others', etc. (p. 34). In short, according to standard research and accounts, our ordinary adult distinction between mental and physical is the product of the child's reflecting on his or her experience in terms of what amount to criteria of intersubjective accessibility, until the distinction between the two domains becomes (largely) habitual and automatic.[3]

VI

The significance of these cognitive developmental observations for Searle's analysis is straightforward. Searle had argued that the notions of introspection and internal observation are incoherent, inasmuch as the notion of observation presupposes the distinction between the act of observing and what is observed, and this distinction is necessarily absent in the case of first-person experience of mental phenomena. But cognitive developmental analyses indicate that introspective and external phenomena are not so different in kind as one might otherwise think. A small child, as we saw, has to *learn* which of his or her experiences are to be categorized as mental and which as physical, by observing and evaluating their various contents and relationships. Moreover, whether we are considering small children or adults, it surely seems arbitrary and inappropriate to insist, as Searle's thesis does, that the content of an experience describable phenomenologically as, for example, 'seeing the red convoluted pattern characteristic of a red rose', can be observed and examined only if the experience turns out to be an external, sensory one, with its object distinct from the experience itself.[4] For the experience is what it is, and can be observed, examined, evaluated, and judged (correctly or not) to be objective or subjective, quite independently of whether it ultimately turns out that it is an objective one (with object different from the experience itself) or not. We have no particular difficulty in fact either in saying, or understanding someone else's saying, 'I just observed what I took to be a rose, but I don't know if it was a real rose or if I was just dreaming or imagining things.' In other words, there is a perfectly good sense in which both an act of observation and the subsequent act of reporting it can be said to take place without requiring any presumption of the observation/object distinction Searle insists is required for all instances of observation. If this is correct, as common sense would hold, the category 'observable experiences' is properly broader than (and, according to cognitive developmental accounts, also prior to) the category 'objective experiences', and it is a mistake to hold that consciousness is not displayable by introspection

---

[3] This account is, to be sure, incomplete. For, as Wellman notes, the cognitive developmental research indicates that the child's notion of mind develops beyond the mere sorting of the contents of experience in terms of the above 'negative' features ('not real', 'cannot be seen by others', etc.) to the inclusion of positive features (e.g. transformability by mental effort alone) as well (p. 34).

[4] This would imply, for example, that a given act of examining the content of one's experience could be called 'observing' it only if the experience turned out to be an external one. Thus, if one's assessment of whether one had been experiencing a real rose or merely hallucinating one happened to fluctuate back and forth, one's report of what one had been doing would also have to fluctuate back and forth between 'observing the contents of one's experience' and 'not observing the contents of one's experience', without one's act (or memory of it) changing at all. This surely seems contrived, and much less satisfactory than simply saying one remembered observing the contents of one's experience, despite the fact that one at present remains unsure about whether the experience was a real sensory one or a mere (mental) hallucination.

in a way analogous to the way the physical world is displayed by perception, and a mistake to restrict the notion of observation to the latter alone.[5]

VII

Searle based his conclusion that the notion of introspective observation is incoherent on his claim that observation presupposes 'a distinction between the thing seen and the seeing of it.' We saw above how cognitive developmental research provides grounds for rejecting both this claim and Searle's conclusion. Nevertheless, it is clear that the notion of objectivity, crucial for scientific methodology and knowledge, *does* involve distinctions akin to those Searle refers to, and it will prove useful for our discussion of the possibility of a science of consciousness to examine, if briefly, these sorts of distinction from the perspective of cognitive developmental research.

According to standard cognitive developmental accounts, every normal child passes through a sequence of stages on the way to our ordinary adult perception and common-sensical conception of the world.[6] An important early component of the development of the child's idea of physical objects and objective reality is the generation of the notion of their existing independently of one's own awareness. The child, as reproducible experiments readily show, first comes to imagine objects as existing outside his or her perception (as when an observed object passes behind an obscuring screen), then to conceive objects as perceivable to others when he (or she) does not perceive them, and also in ways that can differ from his own perceptions. This then develops (despite paradoxes of the sort Hume raises) into the notion of objects as existing completely independently of all observers' perceptions. The child's notion of physical objects as existing independently thus develops in a regular sequence of stages, and, not surprisingly, his notions of appearance, reality and truth emerge and develop in tandem with this notion of independent existence. Finally, we can note that these notions become stabilized, and even (for some) formalized in adolescence, when the ability to think about thoughts systematically and to alter selected individual variables self-consciously (as in algebra and the kinds of causal experimentation that underlie scientific method) is typically gained.

Given the fundamental role of the notion of independently existing physical objects in the generation of our notions of appearance-and-reality, truth-and-falsity, and scientific experimentation, it should be no surprise that science has become so deeply wedded to the physical — even when many of its objects have become so abstract as to appear purely mathematical and hardly physical at all (compare, for example, the *in principle* unobservable 'vacuum fluctuations' of the fundamental quantum mechanical fields, the individual 'points' of which are complex mathematical functions, standard in quantum mechanics). But despite this natural ontogenetic connection, physicality turns out to be not at all essential to what it is to be 'scientific'. For, as scientists and philosophers of science have

---

[5] This above analysis, of course, ignores the difficulties raised by Wittgensteinian critiques of the possibility of private experience and language and questions about the possible significance of 'unverifiable' components of meaning, the examination of which would take us too far afield here.

[6] This developmental sequence was first discovered and articulated by Piaget. Research over the past twenty years has shown that Piaget's theory of discrete, internally unified, non-overlapping developmental stages was much too neat and tidy. But the general sequence outlined above has been widely replicated and remains the norm in the field.

both so often brought out, it is not *ontological* considerations such as the physicality of objects referred to that properly decide whether or not a claim is scientific, but *methodological* considerations of whether the claim can be (or has been) intersubjectively corroborated and/or falsified according to the proper sorts of experimental protocols.

Thus the independence of the observer that is paradigmatically relevant to scientific methodology, and thus science itself, is that of the *truth* of conclusions, rather than that of *objects* referred to — despite the importance of this latter sort of independence in the original cognitive developmental genesis of the appearance–reality, truth–falsity distinctions. This shift from an unreflective object orientation to an abstract truth-and-methodology orientation, where the relevant kind of observer-independence shifts from physical objects to the truth-status of claims, mirrors, of course, the move from concrete-operational thinking to the formal-operational thinking underlying scientific thought in general. Indeed, this shift in conceptualizing what science is about is just what cognitive developmental theory would indicate should naturally take place as science becomes fully mature. It is, moreover, precisely the move already standard in philosophy of science, where abstract methodological considerations of inter-subjectively accessible corroborations and/or falsifications, rather than considerations of the concreteness of particular objects studied or particular theories being developed, are taken to determine whether something is 'scientific' or not.[7]

The application of this observation to our discussion of the possibility of a science of consciousness is straightforward. For here, as elsewhere in science, the relevant question is not an ontological one of whether the *objects* studied are either physical or independent of the observer (notions which often become problematic in quantum mechanics, of course), but a methodological one of whether the relevant *claims of fact* are both intersubjectively corroboratable and independent of the claimant's possibly confounding subjective beliefs, expectations, etc. Thus, in the context of the possibility of a science of consciousness, the crucial factor is how well reports of inner experiences become systematically correlated with objectively observable phenomena in accord with standard objective scientific protocols — rather than, contrary to Searle' claim, questions of whether the internal phenomena observed can properly be thought to be independent of the acts of observation. In short, the relevant empirical data would include, for example, correlations of reports of specific experiences with specific physiological (especially brain) states and psychological and behavioural parameters of the kinds already studied in psychological and psychophysiological research. What is needed, then, is not so much new conceptualizations of science or new objective methodologies for exploring relationships of the phenomena of consciousness to physiology and behaviour (although these, of course, may always prove useful), but new systematic methodologies for the exploration of the subjective phenomena of consciousness.

VIII

In contrast to the west, eastern cultures have taken the idea of systematic exploration of the internal phenomena of consciousness seriously for quite some time. They have, accordingly, developed a wide variety of systematic exploratory methodologies, includ-

---

[7] See, e.g., Karl Popper's (1962) discussion of 'the demarcation between science and non-science'.

ing in particular those that can be referred to generically as 'meditation'. The major eastern meditation traditions are of course hardly monolithic, with different traditions (and subtraditions within traditions) often employing different exploratory methodologies, philosophical assumptions, and terminologies. Nevertheless, some common general features relevant to our present discussion can readily be noted. In the first place, it is widely accepted (in Yoga, Vedanta, Buddhism, Taoism, etc.) that the surface phenomena of consciousness emerge from deeper structures of consciousness which can be experienced directly, and that these deeper structures in turn emerge from an underlying 'ground' of consciousness which is also experienceable. This ground, moreover, is regularly described as the *simplest state* of awareness, consciousness *devoid of all its discrete activities and contents*. Thus, as the *Yoga Sutras,* the central text of Yoga, puts it, it is qualityless 'pure consciousness', experienceable only when all the discrete wavelike fluctuations of mind have 'settled down', leaving consciousness alone by itself in state of 'objectless *samadhi.*' In Buddhism, it is widely referred to as '*shunya*', the 'void', as well as 'pure consciousness', experienceable in meditation when all the activities of mind have ceased. Taoism uses the term '*wu*', or 'nothingness'. And Zen (Chinese, *Ch'an*) uses all of these terms, as well as the symbol of an empty circle (compare the famous 'Oxherding' pictures).

We can also note that while the procedures used in these different traditions may vary greatly, they all tend to display a common logic: removing attention from all phenomenal *objects of* consciousness until ultimately even the meditation procedure itself is left behind (or 'transcended'), leaving *consciousness* alone by itself.[8] Indeed, this feature of the relevant meditative procedures suggests why, as Hume and almost every empirically oriented (western) philosopher since has noted, no such ground of consciousness has proven locatable through ordinary introspective examination. For, on this account it *cannot* be found by *searching* for it, because as pure consciousness it must be devoid of all discrete activities and contents, including in particular the activity of searching for it and the experience of any imaginable thing searched for.

The eastern traditions referred to above of course differ on many points of theory and interpretation. But they all agree that experiences describable in the terms above occur when all of the mind's activity ceases, and agree that these experiences display the fundamental nature of human consciousness.[9] They also agree in their claims that the experience is associated with a uniquely settled metabolic state, characterized by complete cessation of voluntary muscular activity, reduced pulse and blood flow, and complete suspension of respiratory activity. And they also agree in their claims that the experience is properly regarded as a 'higher' state of consciousness, associated with a

---

[8] Compare, for example, Taoism's 'forgetting' everything; Yoga's 'settling all the activity of mind' (responsible for phenomenal contents); Zen's focusing on contradictory *koans* having no graspable content, and ultimately to be left behind themselves; Transcendental Meditation's repetition of meaningless *mantras*, ultimately to be forgotten, etc.

[9] Indeed, even the Hinayana Buddhists, famous for their *anatma*, or 'no self', doctrine, agree that the experience referred to above displays the foundational nature of our awareness, underlying our ordinary — if illusory — sense of self. And the Mahayana (Zen, Tibetan, etc.) regularly also add that it is the true 'Self' (as contrasted with, and underlying, our ordinary illusory, self-image-constituted sense of self).

global enhancement of the individual's psychological well-being, physical health, effectiveness in activity (compare, for example, the reputed role of the experience in the Chinese and Japanese martial arts), and also with further, even more enjoyable 'higher' states of consciousness said to occur when this experience comes to be a component of all of one's other, more ordinary sorts of experience.

These empirical claims, of course, are all debatable. Hermeneutical thinkers have disputed (on epistemological grounds) the very possibility of this (or any other) experience occurring in common across different cultures. Modern western philosophers have referred to the experience as inconceivable and in principle impossible.[10] The physiological claims are likely to appear odd, to say the least. The psychological claims of 'higher' states of consciousness are apt to appear even more unlikely. And the common claim that this qualityless experience displays the nature of the self is also likely to appear surprising.[11] These questions have been examined at length elsewhere by various thinkers (including myself), with varying results, and it will not be possible to address them here.[12] But enough has perhaps been said to gain some sense of the claims traditionally made, and to begin to explore some of their potential significance for the 'hard problem'.

IX

It was suggested at the beginning of this paper that knowledge of the depths of the inner, phenomenal realm ought to prove useful for attacking the 'hard problem', for it would seem reasonable that we would be likely to fully uncover the foundational relationships between matter and consciousness only when we have foundational knowledge of each. This kind of knowledge, in other words, can be expected to be a significant role in 'the more adequate articulation of consciousness' McGinn argues is going to be needed if we are 'to come up with the unifying theory that must link consciousness to the world of matter and space'. To this end, some major philosophical arguments against the possibility of developing a scientific study of the inner phenomena of consciousness were addressed and rebutted. It was then suggested that eastern meditative traditions offer what appears to be a good candidate for experience of 'pure' consciousness as the basis for further scientific understanding of the phenomena of consciousness.

---

[10] It is interesting to note that Kant, while certain that no one actually had such an experience of qualityless 'pure consciousness' (argued by him to be the rationally necessary but factually unexperienceable nature of the self), left open the logical possibility that other types of beings could have the appropriate experiential faculty though we ourselves could not form 'the least conception' of it.

[11] For a discussion of the pure consciousness experience in the context of western theories of self, see Shear (1996) and chapter 4 of Shear (1990a).

[12] We can note here, however, that contemporary research on westerners and easterners practising traditional eastern meditation techniques (Yoga, Zen, and TM) now appears to be corroborating some of the more modest of these empirical claims, in particular a uniquely settled physiological state and coherent central nervous system functioning and modest enhancement of psychological functioning in association with reports of the 'pure consciousness' experience. For some interesting physiological studies, see for example, Levine (1976), Dillbeck and Bronson (1981) and Farrow and Hebert (1982). For a discussion of hermeneutical issues, see the various articles in Forman (1990) and also Shear (1990b). A variety of other issues are discussed in the references cited in note 11.

All of this, of course, hardly constitutes even a prolegomena to any future science of consciousness. Many standard scientific methodological questions remain, but discussing them here would take us too far afield (cf. Harman, 1994). Let us therefore simply suppose that such issues have already been settled in favour of the possibility of a science of consciousness, and speculate a bit about the possible significance of 'pure consciousness' and other related experiences identified by eastern meditative traditions for the 'hard problem'.

The eastern meditative traditions in question, as noted, vary greatly in their ontologies, metaphysics, and meditation procedures. Nevertheless, if we confine ourselves to the logic (as contrasted with the mechanics) of the procedures and the phenomenology of experiences we find widespread descriptions of techniques for allowing all noticeable activity of mind to 'settle down'. These techniques, when successful, are said to result in a state of consciousness devoid of all determinate mental content (sensations, intentions, thoughts, and even any subjective spatio–temporal manifold in which such objects of awareness could appear). This state is commonly taken to display consciousness in its simplest state (hence the 'pure consciousness', 'pure Self', 'one's original face before one was born', 'Void', etc. of Yoga, Vedanta, Mahayana, Taoism, etc.). In time, this experience is reported first to become stable, and to then become perceived as the background of all of one's other experiences (thoughts, outer perceptions, etc.). One then reportedly can become aware of the subtle mechanics of the rise and fall of the 'fluctuations' of consciousness itself, which, as they become phenomenologically more concrete, give rise first to experiences of contentless extendedness and directionality (referred to in terms of unbounded, empty space in the Upanishads, Buddhist canon, Taoism, etc.) and then to the determinate content (sensations, thoughts, etc.) that typically fills this manifold and constitutes our ordinary awareness.

Let us now suppose for the sake of argument that such accounts do in fact accurately represent intersubjectively accessible, culture-invariant, intersubjectively corroboratable experiences of the ground, deep layers, and mechanics of the unfolding of consciousness, and also imagine that they express what at some future time come to be recognized as 'facts' of a science of consciousness. One of the first things we can note is the similarity of aspects of these accounts of the (presumed) deepest nature and mechanics of consciousness to those of the deepest aspects of objective space and its material contents in contemporary quantum theory. This similarity, of course, has been noticed and commented on, in varying degrees of detail, by physicists, yogis and philosophers since the founding of quantum mechanics, and has served as the springboard for all sorts of ontological and epistemological speculations.[13] The point of interest here, however, is only the qualitative similarities between the ground of consciousness and its (phenomenological) contents on the one hand and those of space and its (material) contents on the other. For if we take these qualitative similarities from physics and the imagined science of consciousness at face value, then some of the problematic contrasts between

---

[13] The remarks of founders of quantum mechanics such as Schrödinger and Heisenberg on this topic are well known, if rather limited. More detail can be found in the writings of physicists such as Lawrence Domash (working with Maharishi Mahesh Yogi) and Fritof Capra (reflecting Taoist as well as Hindu ideas) beginning in the early 1970s. See Chapter 7, 'Knowledge and the World', in Shear (1990a) for more details, references, and ontological and epistemological speculations.

consciousness and the objective universe underlying the 'hard problem' appear to be significantly reduced. Thus, on this account both matter and the usual contents of consciousness appear to emerge from an object-free, nonlocal, space-like 'ground state' and to manifest their phenomena (matter and phenomenological contents, respectively) through wave-like fluctuations of this ground (see, e.g. Bohm, 1980). And if quantum theorists such as Bohm and Wigner are correct, this spacelike ground appears, in both cases, to have a further, prespatial foundation ('quantum pre-geometry' and 'pure consciousness', respectively) containing no manifest content (whether space–time bound structures or qualia). Qualitatively speaking, then, the differences between these ultimate foundations becomes vanishingly small, if not simply nonexistent. In short, on this scenario contrasts between qualia-filled consciousness and spatially localized matter which led to Descartes' irreducible dualism and McGinn's argument that we may well never solve the 'hard problem', become recognized as reflecting surface appearances, inapplicable to the deepest levels of matter and consciousness — and no longer therefore presenting *in principle* obstacles to the possibility of resolution of the 'hard problem'.

One more result is worth noting here. Chalmers and others have responded to the 'hard problem' by suggesting that phenomenal experience must be a fundamental feature of nature, not to be explained *by* matter, but existing along with (or as an aspect of) it. To the extent that conscious experience is qualia-filled, however, this implies that contentful experience is an ubiquitous feature of nature, shared by even its most primitive (e.g. subatomic) components as well as complex animate beings. This suggestion, of course, is likely to be a difficult one to swallow, even if, as argued by a number of contributors to this issue, it seems forced on us by unflinching analyses of the 'hard problem'. The existence of the experience of 'pure consciousness',[14] however, allows us to modify this conclusion in a way that may make it intuitively less unpalatable.

This experience, in order to be remembered at all, would seeme to have to have *some* kind of quale associated with it, even if it is nothing more than some sense of an existing nothingness — a sort of 'void' quale. But logically it would have to be *the simplest possible* quale — one tantamount to a phenomenal nothing. Thus on this account, even if, as Chalmers and others argue, a phenomenological component has to be added to what we ordinarily take to be the nonconscious material universe as a pervading fundamental feature, what has to be added now, namely bare consciousness itself, turns out to be so simple and primitive that it adds virtually nothing. This, it would seem, might reduce our intuitive objection to the notion of atoms, etc. as having some kind of consciousness, however primitive, to the practically nothing as well.

The above reasoning reflects what might be called the 'natural' approach to the 'pure consciousness' experience, of the sort taken regularly, for example, by Yogis, Vedantins, and Vijnavadan Buddhists. There is, however, also another, more radical approach, taken, for example, by strict Madhyamika Buddhists and Shunyavadis (doctrine of 'voidness'),

---

[14] Since experience typically has the internal structure of I-experience-it, and the experience of 'pure consciousness' reportedly has neither any 'it' nor any internal structure in it, some contemporary commentators (cp. Robert Forman) prefer the stricter terminology 'pure consciousness event' rather then either 'experience *of* pure consciousness'. It should be noted, accordingly, that the 'of' in 'experience *of* pure consciousness' is used by me simply for stylistic naturalness, and not to suggest the existence of any intentionality within the experience (or event) itself.

who prefer to refer to the experience in question using only such locutions as '*neti–neti*' ('not this – not this'[15]) and 'suchness' (versus 'existence') in order to avoid even a hint of imputation of content. Clearly on this account, too, *adding* bare consciousness to matter would, as above, no longer involve problems of adding any of the contents of ordinary experience. Moreover on this more radical account in which consciousness can exist *entirely* independently of qualia, it is easy to see that the 'pure consciousness' experience would also show that the hard problem of understanding how (or whether) consciousness might be produced by matter could be at least logically independent of the problem of accounting for qualia. For if consciousness can exist independently of qualia, it may well be possible to account for its existence without needing to refer to qualia at all, leaving the problem of qualia as a separate problem *within* the field of consciousness.

X

In conclusion: the intent of this paper has been to argue (1) that a scientific study of the subjective phenomena of consciousness is likely to play a significant role in any adequate resolution of the 'hard problem', (2) that it could contribute to resolution of this problem by providing new sorts of perspectives on consciousness capable of at least narrowing, if not closing, the otherwise intractable conceptual gap between consciousness and the physical universe, (3) that traditional methodologies for exploring the contents and dynamics of consciousness developed in eastern cultures may well prove useful in the development of such a science, and (4) that the reported basic experience of 'pure consciousness' in particular may prove very useful here. This paper does not, of course, pretend to solve the 'hard problem'. Indeed, its analyses are potentially compatible with materialist, idealist, and nondualist resolutions, that is, with resolutions that account for consciousness as a product of matter, matter as a product of consciousness, or both as emerging from a common, further base. For they suggest only that matter and consciousness are much more similar, perhaps surprisingly so, at their bases than ordinarily thought — however these bases ultimately turn out to be related. Whether or not this suggestion turns out to be even remotely correct, and whether or not a science of consciousness ever develops along these lines, it seems apparent that a developed science of consciousness should be developed, and, along with our physical sciences, contribute significantly to the final disposition of the 'hard problem', whatever it might be.

References

Astington, J.W., Harris, P.L. & Olson, D.R. (eds. 1988), *Developing Theories of Mind* (Cambridge: Cambridge University Press).

Bohm, D. (1980), *Wholeness and the Implicate Order* (Boston, MA: ARK Paperbacks).

Chalmers, D.J. (1995), 'Facing up to the problem of consciousness', *Journal of Consciousness Studies*, **2** (3), pp. 200–19 (reprinted in this volume).

Clarke, C.J.S. (1995), 'The nonlocality of mind', in this volume.

Dillbeck, M.C. & Bronson, E.C. (1981), 'Short term longitudinal effects of the Transcendental Meditation technique on EEG power and coherence', *International Journal of Neuroscience*, **14**, pp. 147–51.

---

[15] That is, 'Neither this, nor that'.

Farrow, J.T. & Hebert, J.R. ((1982), 'Breath suspension during the Transcendental Meditation technique', *Psychosomatic Medicine*, **44**, pp. 133–53.

Forman, R.K.C. (ed. 1990), *The Problem of Pure Consciousness* (New York: Oxford University Press).

Hameroff, S.R. & Penrose, R. (1996), 'Conscious events as orchestrated space–time selection', in this volume.

Harman, W. (1994), 'The scientific exploration of consciousness: Towards an adequate epistemology', *Journal of Consciousness Studies*, **1** (1), pp. 140–8.

Hodgson, D. (1995), 'The easy problems ain't so easy', in this volume.

Kohlberg, L. (1969), 'Stage and sequence: The cognitive-developmental approach to socialization', in *Handbook of Socialization Research*, ed. D.A. Goslin (Rand McNally & Co.).

Levine, I.P. (1976), 'The Coherence Spectral Array (COSPAR) and its application to the study of spatial ordering in the EEG', *Proceedings of the San Diego Biomedical Symposium*, **15**.

McGinn, C. (1995), 'Consciousness and space', in this volume.

Popper, K. (1962), *Conjectures and Refutations* (New York: Basic Books).

Seager, W. (1995), 'Consciousness, information and panpsychism', in this volume.

Searle, J.R. (1992), *The Rediscovery of the Mind* (Cambridge, MA: The MIT Press).

Shear, J. (1990a), *The Inner Dimension* (New York: Peter Lang Publishing).

Shear, J. (1990b), 'Mystical experience, hermeneutics and rationality', *International Philosophical Quarterly*, **XXX** (4), pp. 391–401.

Shear, J. (1996), 'On the existence of a culture-independent core component of self', in *East–West Encounters in Philosophy and Religion*, ed. Ninian Smart, B. Srinivasa Murthy & Daniel Guerriere (Long Beach, CA: Long Beach Publications).

Wellman, H.M. (1990), *The Child's Theory of Mind* (Cambridge, MA: The MIT Press).

Response

David J. Chalmers

Moving Forward on the Problem of Consciousness

I: Introduction

I am very grateful to all the contributors to this symposium for their thoughtful comments.[1] The various papers reflect a wide range of approaches and of views, yielding a rich snapshot of the current state of play on the problem of consciousness. There are some interesting criticisms of my point of view, which I hope to address in this reply in a way that clarifies the central issues at hand, and there are also a number of intriguing positive proposals for confronting the problem. I am honoured to have provided an opportunity to bring such a thought-provoking collection of ideas together.

When I wrote my keynote paper, I had no idea that it would be subject to such close analysis. That may be a good thing, as all the hedges, qualifications, and citations I would have added had I known might have made the paper close to unreadable, or at any rate twice the size. But it also means that the paper — intended as a crisp presentation of some central issues, mostly for non-philosophers — skates quickly over some subtleties and has less flesh on its bones than it might. I will try to flesh out the picture in this article, while still keeping the discussion at a non- technical level. A more detailed presentation can be found in my book *The Conscious Mind* (1996), to which I will occasionally point in this response.

Because of the unexpected influence of the 'hard problem' formulation, I have occasionally received far more credit than I deserve. So let me state the obvious: the reason the formulation has caught on is that everyone knew what the hard problem was all along. The label just makes it a little harder to avoid. Any number of thinkers in the recent and distant past — including a number of contributors to this symposium — have recognized the particular difficulties of explaining consciousness and have tried to face up to them in various ways. All my paper really contributes is a catchy name, a minor reformulation of philosophically familiar points, and a specific approach to dealing with them.

The papers in the symposium are divided fairly evenly into those that take issue with aspects of my analysis, and those that provide positive approaches of their own. I will concentrate mostly on those in the first class, though I will make a few comments on those in the second. A quick glance at the relevant papers may give the appearance of much disagreement and a sprawling landscape of mutually contradictory points of views, but a

[1] Thanks to Gregg Rosenberg, Jonathan Shear and Sharon Wahl for helpful comments. This paper was originally published in the *Journal of Consciousness Studies*, **4**, No.1 (1997), pp. 3–46.

closer look reveals a more coherent picture. Once a few minor misunderstandings and verbal disagreements are cleared up, and the various contributions are aligned, one is left with a small number of central 'choice points' on which the central disagreements turn. I hope that my reply helps to clarify this landscape.

The reply has three main parts. In the first I consider the critiques of a generally reductive or 'deflationary' orientation; in the second I consider those of a generally nonreductive orientation; and in the third I make some comments on the various positive proposals.

II: Deflationary Critiques

Recall the main conceptual distinction between the easy and hard problems. The easy problems — explaining discrimination, integration, accessibility, internal monitoring, reportability, and so on — all concern the performance of various *functions*. For these phenomena, once we have explained how the relevant functions are performed, we have explained what needs to be explained. The hard problem, by contrast, is not a problem about how functions are performed. For any given function that we explain, there remains a nontrivial further question: why is the performance of this function associated with conscious experience? The sort of functional explanation that is suited to answering the easy problems is therefore not automatically suited to answering the hard problem.

There are two quite different ways in which a materialist might respond to this challenge. The *type-A* materialist denies that there is a 'hard problem' distinct from the 'easy' problems; the *type-B* materialist accepts (explicitly or implicitly) that there is a distinct problem, but argues that it can be accommodated within a materialist framework all the same. Both of these strategies are taken by contributors to this symposium. I will discuss the first strategy in the next two sections, and the second strategy after that.

1. Deflationary analogies

The type-A materialist, more precisely, denies that there is any phenomenon that needs explaining, over and above explaining the various functions: once we have explained how the functions are performed, we have thereby explained everything. Sometimes type-A materialism is expressed by denying that consciousness exists; more often, it is expressed by claiming that consciousness may exist, but only if the term 'consciousness' is defined as something like 'reportability', or some other functional capacity. Either way, it is asserted that there is no interesting fact about the mind, conceptually distinct from the functional facts, that needs to be accommodated in our theories. Once we have explained how the functions are performed, that is that.

Note that type-A materialism is not merely the view that consciousness is identical to some function, or that it plays a functional role, or that explaining the functions will help us explain consciousness. It is the much stronger view that there is not even a distinct *question* of consciousness: once we know about the functions that a system performs, we thereby know everything interesting there is to know. Type-A materialism subsumes philosophical positions such as eliminativism, behaviourism, analytic functionalism, and others, but it does not include positions, (such as those embraced by **Clark**[2] and **Hardcastle**), that rely on an *a posteriori* identity between consciousness and some

---

[2] Names in **bold type** refer to papers in this symposium.

physical/functional property. Positions of the latter sort accept that there is a real phenomenon to be accounted for, *conceptually* distinct from the performance of functions (the *a posteriori* identity ties together *a priori* distinct concepts), and therefore count as type-B materialism. Type-A materialism, by contrast, denies that there is a conceptually distinct explanatory target at all.

This is an extremely counterintuitive position. At first glance, it seems to simply deny a manifest fact about us. But it deserves to be taken seriously: after all, counterintuitive theories are not unknown in science and philosophy. On the other hand, to establish a counterintuitive position, strong arguments are needed. And to establish *this* position — that there is really nothing else to explain — one might think that extraordinarily strong arguments are needed. So what arguments do its proponents provide?

Perhaps the most common strategy for a type-A materialist is to deflate the 'hard problem' by using analogies to other domains, where talk of such a problem would be misguided. Thus **Dennett** imagines a vitalist arguing about the hard problem of 'life', or a neuroscientist arguing about the hard problem of 'perception'. Similarly, Paul Churchland (1996) imagines a nineteenth century philosopher worrying about the hard problem of 'light', and **Patricia Churchland** brings up an analogy involving 'heat'. In all these cases, we are to suppose, someone might once have thought that more than structure and function needed explaining; but in each case, science has proved them wrong. So perhaps the argument about consciousness is no better.

This sort of argument cannot bear much weight, however. Pointing out that analogous arguments do not work in other domains is no news: the whole point of anti-reductionist arguments about consciousness is that there is a disanalogy between the problem of consciousness and problems in other domains. As for the claim that analogous arguments in such domains might once have been plausible, this strikes me as something of a convenient myth: in the other domains, it is more or less *obvious* that structure and function are what need explaining, at least once any experiential aspects are left aside, and one would be hard pressed to find a substantial body of people who ever argued otherwise.

When it comes to the problem of life, for example, it is just obvious that what needs explaining is structure and function: How does a living system self-organize? How does it adapt to its environment? How does it reproduce? Even the vitalists recognized this central point: their driving question was always 'How could a mere physical system perform these complex functions?', not 'Why are these functions accompanied by life?' It is no accident that Dennett's version of a vitalist is 'imaginary'. There is no distinct 'hard problem' of life, and there never was one, even for vitalists.

In general, when faced with the challenge 'explain X', we need to ask: what are the phenomena in the vicinity of X that need explaining, and how might we explain them? In the case of life, what cries out for explanation are such phenomena as reproduction, adaptation, metabolism, self-sustenance, and so on: all complex functions. There is not even a plausible candidate for a further sort of property of life that needs explaining (leaving aside consciousness itself), and indeed there never was. In the case of consciousness, on the other hand, the manifest phenomena that need explaining are such things as discrimination, reportability, integration (the functions), *and experience*. So this analogy does not even get off the ground.

Or take **Churchland**'s example of heat. Here, what cries out for explanation are such things as: heat's abilities to expand metals, the causation of fire, heat transmission between substances, the experience of hotness. All but the last of these are clearly functions, and it is these functions that reductive explanations of heat explain. The existence of such functions is entailed by the microphysical story about heat: in any world that is physically identical to ours, such functions will automatically be present.

If someone were to claim that something were 'left out' by reductive explanations of heat (as Churchland suggests they might), or of light (as Paul Churchland suggests they might), what something might they be referring to? The only phenomenon for which the suggestion would be even remotely plausible is our subjective experience of light and of hotness. The molecular theory of heat does not explain the sensation of heat; and the electromagnetic theory of light does not explain what it is like to see. And understandably so: the physicists explaining heat and light have quite reasonably deferred the explanation of their experiential manifestations until the time when we have a reasonable theory of consciousness. One need not explain everything at once. But with consciousness itself, subjective experience is precisely what is at issue, so we cannot defer the question in the same way. Thus once again, the analogy is no help to a reductionist.

In his article 'The Rediscovery of Light' (1996), Paul Churchland suggests that parallel antireductionist arguments could have been constructed for the phenomenon of 'luminescence', and might have been found plausible at the time. I have my doubts about that plausibility, but in any case it is striking that his arguments about luminescence all depend on intuitions about the conscious experience of light. His hypothetical advocate of a 'hard problem' about light appeals to light's 'visibility' and the 'visual point of view'; his advocate of a 'knowledge argument' about light appeals to blind Mary who has never had the experience of seeing; and the advocate of a 'zombie' argument appeals to the conceivability of a universe physically just like ours, but in which everything is dark. That the first two arguments trade on intuitions about experience is obvious; and even for the third, it is clear on a moment's reflection that the only way such a universe might make sense is as a universe in which the same electro- magnetic transmission goes on, but in which no-one has the experience of seeing.

Churchland might insist that by 'luminescence' he means something quite independent of experience, which physical accounts still do not explain: but then the obvious reply is that there is no good reason to believe in luminescence in the first place. Light's structural, functional, and experiential manifestations exhaust the phenomena that cry out for explanation, and the phenomena in which we have any reason to believe. By contrast, conscious experience presents itself as a phenomenon to be explained, and cannot be eliminated in the same way.

A similar critique applies to examples such as Dennett's 'cuteness' (what needs explaining is the structure and functioning of cute people, and our experience and judgment of them as cute), his 'perception' (the functioning of perceptual systems plus the experience of perception), and so on. In all such cases, either the analogous arguments are not even *prima facie* plausible (as in the case of life), or at best, they gain their plausibility through pointing to experiential properties that reductive accounts omit (as in the cases of perception and light). So they can do no work at all in arguing for reductionism about experience.

Indeed, similar remarks can be made about *any* phenomenon that we observe in the external world. When we observe external objects, we observe their structure and function; that's all. Such observations give no reason to postulate any new class of properties, except insofar as they explain structure and function; so there can be no analogue of a 'hard problem' here. Even if further properties of these objects existed, we could have no access to them, as our external access is physically mediated: such properties would lie on the other side of an unbridgeable epistemic divide. Consciousness uniquely escapes these arguments by lying at the centre of our epistemic universe, rather than at a distance. In this case alone, we can have access to something other than structure and function.

2. Is explaining the functions enough?

So, analogies don't help. To have any chance of making the case, a type-A materialist needs to *argue* that for consciousness, as for life, the functions are all that need explaining. Perhaps some strong, subtle, and substantive argument can be given, establishing that once we have explained the functions, we have automatically explained everything. If a sound argument could be given for this surprising conclusion, it would provide as valid a resolution of the hard problem as any.

Is there any compelling, non-question-begging argument for this conclusion? The key word, of course, is 'non-question-begging'. Often, a proponent will simply *assert* that functions are all that need explaining, or will argue in a way that subtly *assumes* this position at some point. But that is clearly unsatisfactory. *Prima facie*, there is very good reason to believe that the phenomena a theory of consciousness must account for include not just discrimination, integration, report, and such functions, but also *experience*, and prima facie, there is good reason to believe that the question of explaining experience is distinct from the questions about explaining the various functions. Such *prima facie* intuitions can be overturned, but to do so requires very solid and substantial argument. Otherwise, the problem is being 'resolved' simply by placing one's head in the sand.

Upon examing the materialist papers in this symposium, such arguments are surprisingly hard to find. Indeed, despite their use of various analogies, very few of the contributors seem willing to come right out and say that in the case of consciousness, the functions are all that need explaining. Only **Dennett** embraces this position explicitly, and even he does not spend much time *arguing* for it. But he does spend about a paragraph making the case: presumably this paragraph bears the weight of his article, once the trimmings are stripped away. So it is this paragraph that we should examine.

Dennett's argument here, interestingly enough, is an appeal to phenomenology. He examines his own phenomenology, and tells us that he finds nothing other than functions that need explaining. The manifest phenomena that need explaining are his *reactions* and his *abilities*; nothing else even presents itself as needing to be explained.

This is daringly close to a simple denial — one is tempted to agree that it might be a good account of *Dennett's* phenomenology — and it raises immediate questions. For a start, it is far from obvious that even all the items on Dennett's list — 'feelings of foreboding', 'fantasies', 'delight and dismay' — are purely functional matters. To assert without argument that all that needs to be explained about such things are the associated functions seems to beg the crucial question at issue. And if we leave these controversial cases aside, Dennett's list seems to be a systematically incomplete list of what needs to be explained in explaining consciousness. One's 'ability to be moved to tears' and 'blithe disregard of perceptual details' are striking phenomena, but they are far from the most obvious phenomena that I (at least) find when I intro- spect. Much more obvious are the experience of emotion and the phenomenal visual field themselves; and nothing Dennett says gives us reason to believe that these do not need to be explained, or that explaining the associated functions will explain them.

What might be going on here? Perhaps the key lies in what Dennett has elsewhere described as the foundation of his philosophy: 'third-person absolutism'. If one takes the *third-person* perspective on oneself — viewing oneself from the outside, so to speak — these reactions and abilities are no doubt the main focus of what one sees. But the hard problem is about explaining the view from the *first-person* perspective. So to shift perspectives like this — even to shift to a third-person perspective on one's first-person perspective, which is one of Dennett's favourite moves — is again to *assume* that what needs explaining are such functional matters as reactions and reports, and so is again to argue in a circle.

Dennett suggests, 'subtract the functions and nothing is left'. Again, I can see no reason to accept this, but in any case the argument seems to have the wrong form. An analogy suggested by Gregg Rosenberg is useful here. Colour has properties of hue, saturation, and brightness. It is plausible that if one 'subtracts' hue from a colour, nothing pheno- menologically significant is left, but this certainly doesn't imply that colour is nothing but hue. So even if Dennett could argue that function was somehow *required* for experience (in the same way that hue is required for colour), this would fall a long way short of showing that function is all that has to be explained.

A slight flavour of non-circular argument is hinted at by Dennett's suggestion: 'I wouldn't know what I was thinking about if I couldn't identify them by their functional differentia.' This tantalizing sentence suggests various reconstructions, but all the recon- structions that I can find fall short of making the case. If the idea is that functional role is essential to the (subpersonal) *process* of identification, this falls short of establishing that functioning is essential to the experiences themselves, let alone that functioning is all there *is* to the experiences. If the idea is rather that function is all we have access to at the *personal* level, this seems false, and seems to beg the question against the intuitive view that we have knowledge of intrinsic features of experience. This is to miss the point, however: if Dennett can elaborate this into a substantial argument, that would be a very useful service.[3]

---

[3] One might look to Dennett's book *Consciousness Explained* (1991) for non-circular arguments, but even here such arguments for the relevant conclusion are hard to find. The plausible attacks on a 'place in a brain where it all comes together' do nothing to remove the hard problem. The book's reliance on 'heterophenomenology' (verbal reports) as the central source of data occasionally slips into an unargued assumption that such reports are all that need explaining, especially in the discussion of 'real seeming', which in effect assumes that the only 'seemings' that need explaining are dispositions to react and report. I think there may be a substantial argument implicit in the 'Orwell/Stalin' discussion — essentially taking *materialism* as a premise and arguing that if materialism is true then the functional facts exhaust all the facts — but even this ultimately comes to no more than 'if something more than functions needs explaining, then materialism cannot explain it', and I would not disagree. At best, Dennett's arguments rule out a middle-ground 'Cartesian materialism'; the hard problem remains as hard as ever.

In his paper, Dennett challenges me to provide 'independent' evidence (presumably behavioural or functional evidence) for the 'postulation' of experience. But this is to miss the point: conscious experience is not 'postulated' to explain other phenomena in turn; rather, it is a phenomenon to be explained in its own right. And if it turns out that it cannot be explained in terms of more basic entities, then it must be taken as irreducible, just as happens with such categories as space and time. Again, Dennett's 'challenge' *presupposes* that the only explananda that count are functions. (Tangentially, I would be interested to see Dennett's version of the 'independent' evidence that leads physicists to 'introduce' the fundamental categories of space and time. It seems to me that the relevant evidence is spatiotemporal through and through, just as the evidence for experience is experiential through and through.)

Dennett might respond that I, equally, do not give *arguments* for the position that something more than functions needs to be explained. And there would be some justice here: while I do argue at length for my conclusions, all these arguments take the existence of consciousness for granted, where the relevant concept of consciousness is explicitly distinguished from functional concepts such as discrimination, integration, reaction, and report. Dennett presumably disputes this starting point: he thinks that the only sense in which people are conscious is a sense in which consciousness is *defined* as reportability, as a reactive disposition, or as some other functional concept.

But let us be clear on the dialectic. It is *prima facie* obvious to most people that there is a further phenomenon here: in informal surveys, the large majority of respondents (even at Tufts!) indicate that they think something more than functions needs explaining. Dennett himself — faced with the results of such a survey, perhaps intending to deflate it — has accepted that there is at least a *prima facie* case that something more than functions need to be explained; and he has often stated how 'radical' and 'counterintuitive' his position is. So it is clear that the default assumption is that there is a further problem of explanation; to establish otherwise requires significant and substantial argument.

I would welcome such arguments, in the ongoing attempt to clarify the lay of the land. The challenge for those such as Dennett is to make the nature of these arguments truly clear. I do not think it a worthless project — the hard problem is so hard that we should welcome all attempts at a resolution — but it is clear that anyone trying to make such an argument is facing an uphill battle.

In **Churchland**'s paper, this sort of argument is even harder to find. Indeed, it is not always clear who Churchland is arguing with: she does not address the central arguments in the keynote paper at any point, and she often seems to be arguing with someone with views quite different from mine. Her arguments have *premises* that are consistently more plausible than Dennett's, but they do not come close to establishing the relevant conclusion. I include Churchland as a type-A materialist as she suggests that there is no principled difference between the 'hard' and 'easy' problems, but her position is sufficiently inexplicit that it is hard to know for sure.

Churchland asks for a systematic difference between the 'easy' and 'hard' problems, not mentioning the detailed analysis of this difference in my paper. The difference is, of course, that the easy problems are all clearly problems of explaining how functions are performed, and the hard problem is not. Perhaps Churchland, like Dennett, would deny this; unlike Dennett, however, she never addresses the question directly. If she truly holds that the functions (discrimination, integration, access, control, report, . . .) are all that we need to account for, then clearly some explicit argument is required. If she does not, then the relevant distinction is present right there.

Churchland notes correctly that phenomena such as attention have an experiential component. I am not sure how this is meant to deflate the problem of experience. Vision has an experiential component, too; that's the 'hard' part. We can give neural or cognitive accounts of the functions associated with these phenomena, but it remains unclear why the experiential aspect should accompany those functions. This isn't to deny that it *does* accompany them. There are deep and intimate links between the 'hard' and 'easy' phenomena, some of which I note in my paper, and more in my book. So when Churchland criticizes somebody's proposal for ruling out such links, it is not my proposal she is addressing.

Perhaps the problem is that Churchland sets up the 'easy/hard' distinction as the distinction between the problems of (e.g.) attention, learning, and short-term memory on one hand, and the problem of consciousness on the other. This is not quite my way of doing things: I set up the distinction as that between explaining how functions are performed and explaining subjective experience. It is plausible that the notions of 'memory', 'attention', and perhaps even 'consciousness' subsume elements both of functioning and of subjective experience, as Churchland in effect points out — so there are 'easy' and 'hard' aspects of memory, attention and consciousness. To keep things clear, it is best to set up the distinction directly.

Churchland is also right to note that it is not always obvious just where experience is present and where it is not, especially in fringe cases. But it is a philosophical truism that we should not let the existence of fringe cases blind us to the facts about clear cases. One goal of a theory of experience will be to clarify the status of those fringe cases; in the meantime, in cases where experience is clearly present, it is as hard to explain as ever.

And Churchland is also quite right that there is much about the 'easy' problems that we do not understand. 'Easy' is of course a term of art, and nothing substantial in my arguments rests on it. Churchland's point would be a relevant rebuttal to an argument that rested on it, or to an argument from ignorance, but my argument is nothing of the sort. Facts of the form 'we don't know' or 'I can't imagine' play no explicit or implicit role in my arguments. Rather, the key is the conceptual point: the problem of consciousness is not a problem about how functions are performed. No matter how much we find out about the mechanisms that perform these functions, the basic explanatory point is unaffected.

Contrast Churchland's case of sensorimotor integration. It's true that we do not know much about the mechanisms here. But we do know what we need to do to explain sensorimotor integration: we need to explain how information from different sensory areas is brought together and put to use in the control of action. This is a problem about how functions are performed: it is *guaranteed* that once we find the mechanism that performs the function and explain how it works, we will have explained sensorimotor integration. But for consciousness, this guarantee fails: it is not just functions that need to be explained. So the research programme that promises so much on the easy problems needs to be augmented where the hard problem is concerned.

So Churchland either needs to *argue* that functions are all that need to be explained, or she needs to face up to the disanalogy and the explanatory problem directly. Homilies about the progress of science do not carry much weight in this context. We have seen that 'normal' (function-explaining) science in the neuroscientific mode has limitations that have to be confronted, not ignored; and if one relies instead on a gesture in the direction of a major conceptual revolution sometime in the future, then one is in effect conceding that the hard problem is very hard indeed.

Proponents of the 'no problem' view sometimes like to suggest that their view is supported by the results of modern science, but all the science that I know is quite neutral here: I have never seen any experimental result that implies that functions are all that need to be explained. Rather, this view seems to be rooted in a *philosophical* claim. This claim does not seem to be supported either by empirical evidence or by non-circular argument; at the end of the day, it may be that the position is grounded instead in some sort of unargued axiom, such as Dennett's third-person absolutism. And to anyone who is impressed by the first-person phenomenology of consciousness, such an axiom will always beg the crucial questions. The position reduces to an unargued denial.

This is not to say that type-A materialism cannot be argued for at all. There are a few sophisticated arguments for such a position in the literature (for example, Shoemaker, 1975, and White, 1986), but even these ultimately come down to 'consider the alternatives', isolating the difficulties that one gets into if one accepts that there is a further phenomenon that needs explaining. There is no doubt that these difficulties (both ontological and epistemological) are considerable; life would be a lot easier if the hard problem did not exist. But I think these difficulties are solvable; and in any case, to deny the problem because of the difficulties has the flavour of solution by decree. So while I think such arguments need to be taken very seriously, they do little to actually remove the problem. To truly make the problem go away, one needs *positive* and *non-circular* arguments for the counterintuitive conclusion that the functions are all that need explaining; and such arguments are very hard to find.

Of course, type-A materialism is unlikely to disappear any time soon, and we will probably just have to get used to the fact that there is a basic division in the field: that between those who think the 'easy' problems are the only problems, and those who think that subjective experience needs to be explained as well. We can therefore expect two quite distinct sorts of theories of consciousness: those which explain the functions and then say 'that's all', and those which take on an extra burden. In the end, the most progress will probably come from internal advances in the respective research programmes, rather from the endless battle between the two. So beyond a certain point in the argument, theorists in these camps might just agree to disagree and get on with their respective projects. This way, everyone can move forward.

3. Type-B materialism

Type-A materialism offers a clean and consistent way to be a materialist, but the cost is that it seems not to take consciousness seriously. Type-B materialism tries to get the best of both worlds. The type-B materialist accepts that there is a phenomenon that needs to be accounted for, conceptually distinct from the performance of functions, but holds that the phenomenon can still be explained within a materialist framework. This is surely the most attractive position at a first glance. It promises to avoid the extremes of both hard-line reductionism and property dualism, which respectively threaten to deny the phenomenon and to radically expand our ontology.

I was attracted to type-B materialism for many years myself, until I came to the conclusion that it simply cannot work. The basic reason for this is simple. Physical theories are ultimately specified in terms of structure and dynamics: they are cast in terms of basic physical structures, and principles specifying how these structures change over time. Structure and dynamics at a low level can combine in all sorts of interesting ways to explain the structure and function of high-level systems; but still, structure and function only ever add up to more structure and function. In most domains, this is quite enough, as we have seen, as structure and function are all that need to be explained. But when it comes to consciousness, something other than structure and function needs to be accounted for. To get there, an explanation needs a further ingredient.

The type-A materialist gets around this problem by asserting that for consciousness, too, structure and function are all that need to be explained. But this route is not open to the type-B materialist. Given that we have accepted that something more than structure and function needs to be accounted for, we are forced to the conclusion that the 'further question' will arise for *any* account of physical processing: why is this structure and function accompanied by conscious experience? To answer this question, we need to supplement our story about structure and function with something else; and in doing so we move beyond truly reductive explanation.

So while many people think they can reject a Dennett-style 'no problem' view and still expect a purely physical explanation of consciousness one day, this view seems untenable for systematic reasons. An account of physical processing may provide the *bulk* of a theory of human consciousness; but whatever account of processing we give, the vital step — the step where we move from facts about structure and function to facts about experience — will always be an *extra* step, requiring some substantial principle to bridge the gap. To justify this step, we need a new component in our theories.

There is one route to type-B materialism that one might think remains open; this is the route taken by **Clark** and **Hardcastle**. These two are clearly realists about phenomenal consciousness, and they are equally clearly materialists. They reconcile the two by embracing an empirical *identity* between conscious experiences and physical processes. Although consciousness is not equivalent *a priori* to a structural or functional property (as type-A materialists might suggest), the two are nevertheless identical *a posteriori*. We establish this identity through a series of *correlations*: once we find that consciousness and certain physical processes are correlated, the best hypothesis is that the two are identical. And this postulated identity bridges the explanatory gap.

This is a popular approach, but it has a number of problems. The problems are all rooted in the same place: it makes the identity an *explanatorily primitive* fact about the world. That is, the fact that certain physical/functional states are conscious states is taken as a brute fact about nature, not itself to be further explained. But the only such explanatorily primitive relationships found elsewhere in nature are fundamental laws; indeed, one might argue that this bruteness is precisely the mark of a fundamental law. In postulating an explanatorily primitive 'identity', one is trying to get something for nothing: all of the explanatory work of a fundamental law, at none of the ontological cost. We should be suspicious of such free lunches; and indeed, I think there is something deeply wrong with the idea.

To evaluate the truth of materialism, what matters is whether all facts follow from the physical facts. As I argue at length in my book, in *most* domains it seems that they certainly do. The low-level facts about physical entities determine the facts about physical structure and function at all levels with conceptual necessity, which is enough to determine the facts about chemistry, about biology, and so on. The facts about genes 'fall out' of the facts about the structure and function of DNA, for example. A geneticist does not need a primitive Genetic Identity Hypothesis to cross the divide — 'what do you know, whenever there is some unit that encodes and transmits hereditary characteristics, there is a gene!' Rather, to encode and transmit such characteristics is roughly all it *means* to be a gene; so there is an *a priori* implication from the facts about the structure and functioning of DNA in a reproductive context to the facts about genes. Even Mary in her black-and-white room could figure out the facts about genes, in principle, if she was equipped with the facts about DNA and the concepts involved.

But the facts about consciousness do not just fall out of the facts about the structure and functioning of neural processes, at least once type-A materialism is rejected. As usual, there is a further question — 'why are these processes accompanied by consciousness?' — and merely repeating the story about the physical processes does not provide an answer. If we have rejected type-A materialism, there can be no conceptual implication from one to the other.

Clark and Hardcastle's answer is to *augment* one's account of physical processes with an 'identity hypothesis' (Clark) or an 'identity statement' (Hardcastle), asserting that consciousness is identical to some physical or functional state. Now, it is certainly true that *if* we augment an account of physical processes with an identity statement of this form, the existence of consciousness can be derived; and with a sufficiently detailed and systematic identity statement, detailed facts about consciousness might be derived. But the question is now: what is the relationship between the physical facts and the identity statement itself?

Neither Clark nor Hardcastle gives us any reason to think that the identity statement *follows* from the physical facts. When answering the question 'why does this physical process give rise to consciousness?', their answer is always 'because consciousness and the physical process are identical', where the latter statement is something of a primitive. It is inferred to explain the correlation between physical processes and consciousness in the actual world, but no attempt is made to explain or derive it in turn. And without it, one does not come close to explaining the existence of consciousness.

This identity statement therefore has a very strange status indeed. It is a fact about the world that cannot be derived from the physical facts, and therefore has to be taken as axiomatic. No other 'identity statement' above the level of fundamental physics has this status. The fact that DNA is a gene can be straightforwardly derived from the physical facts, as can the fact that H_2O is water, given only that one has a grasp of the concepts involved. Papineau (1996) argues that identities are not the sort of thing that one explains; I think this is wrong, but in any case they are certainly the kind of thing that one can *derive*. Even the fact that Samuel Clemens is Mark Twain, to use Papineau's example, could be derived in principle from the physical facts by one who possesses the relevant concepts. But even if one possesses the concept of consciousness, the identity involving consciousness is not derivable from the physical facts. (It might be objected that if one possessed an *a posteriori* concept of consciousness — on which consciousness was identified with some neural process, for example — then the facts about consciousness could be derived straightforwardly. But this would be cheating: one would be building in the identity to derive the identity. In all other cases — genes, water, and so on — one can derive the high-level facts from the low-level facts using the *a priori* concept alone. One does not *need* the identity between genes and DNA to derive the fact that DNA is a gene, for example: all one needs is a grasp of the meaning of 'gene'. That is, in all the other cases, the implication from micro to macro is *a priori*.)

We might call this the 'magic bullet' version of the identity theory: it treats identity as a magic bullet which one can use to kill off all our explanatory problems by drawing disparate phenomena together. But identities do not work like this: elsewhere, they have to be *earned*. That is, an identity requires an actual or possible explanation of how it is that two phenomena are identical. ('No identification without explanation.') One earns the DNA–gene identity, for example, by showing how DNA has all the properties that are required to qualify as a gene. The original identity theorists in the philosophy of mind (Place, 1956; Smart, 1959) understood this point well. They consequently buttressed their account with a 'topic-neutral' analysis of experiential concepts, asserting that all it means to be an orange sensation is to be the sort of state caused by orange things, and so on; this suffers from all the problems of type-A materialism, but at least it recognizes what is required for their thesis to be true. The type-B materialist, by contrast, posits an identification *in place of* an explanation.

Indeed, type-B materialism seems to give up on the reductive *explanation* of consciousness altogether. The very fact that it needs to appeal to an explanatorily primitive axiom to bridge the gap shows that consciousness is not being wholly explained in terms of physical processes: a primitive bridging principle is carrying the central part of the burden, just as it does on the sort of theory I advocate. Calling this principle an 'identity' may save the letter of materialism, but it does not save the spirit. When it comes to issues of *explanation*, this position is just as nonreductive as mine.

Elsewhere in science, this sort of explanatorily primitive link is found only in fundamental laws. In fact, this primitiveness is just what makes such laws fundamental. We explain complex data in terms of underlying principles, we explain those principles in terms of simpler principles, and when we can explain no further we declare a principle fundamental. The same should hold here: by positing a fundamental law, we recognize the price of explanatory primitiveness, rather than pretending that everything is business as usual.

One can draw out the problems in other ways. For example, once it is noted that there is no conceptually necessary link from physical facts to phenomenal facts, it is clear that the idea of a physically identical world *without* consciousness is internally consistent. (By comparison, a physically identical world without life, or without genes, or without water is not even remotely conceivable.) So the fact that physical processes go along with consciousness seems to be a *further* fact about our world. To use a common philosophical metaphor: God could have created our world without consciousness, so he had to do extra work to put consciousness in.

Type-B materialists sometimes try to get around this by appealing to Saul Kripke's treatment of *a posteriori* necessity: such a world is said to be conceivable but not 'metaphysically possible', precisely because consciousness is identical to a physical process. (Hardcastle embraces this line, and Clark says something similar.) But as I argue in my book, this misunderstands the roots of *a posteriori* necessity: rather than ruling conceivable worlds impossible, *a posteriori* constraints simply cause worlds to be redescribed, and the problem returns as strongly as ever in a slightly different form. The issues are technical, but I think it is now well-established that Kripkean *a posteriori* necessity cannot save materialism here. To declare that the relevant worlds are all 'metaphysically impossible', one would have to appeal instead to a far stronger notion of necessity which would put inexplicable constraints on the space of possible worlds. This is a notion in which we have no reason to believe.

So the problems of type-B materialism can be expressed both on intuitive and technical grounds. On the most intuitive grounds: it is a solution by stipulation, which 'solves' the problem only by asserting that brain states are conscious states, without explaining how this can be. On slightly more technical grounds: it requires an appeal to a primitive axiom identifying consciousness with a physical process, where this identity is not derivable from the physical facts and is thus unlike any identity statement found elsewhere. On the most technical grounds: it either rests on an invalid appeal to Kripke's *a posteriori* necessity or requires a new and stronger notion of metaphysical necessity in which there is no reason to believe.

On to some specific points. **Clark** suggests that the explanatory gap arises only from assuming that consciousness and physical processes are distinct in the first place, and he faults my use of phrases such as 'arises from' for begging that question. I think this misses the point: one can phrase the question just as well by asking 'Why are certain physical systems conscious?', or even 'Why is there something it is like to engage in certain processes?' Such questions are just as pressing, and clearly do not beg any questions against identity.

In fact, ontological assumptions are irrelevant to posing the explanatory question. All that matters is the *conceptual* distinction between structural/functional concepts and consciousness, a distinction that Clark explicitly accepts. (His talk of 'correlation' makes this even more clear, as does his observation that it *could* turn out that the functions do not correlate with experience.) Given that it is not *a priori* that the performance of these functions should be conscious, it follows that an explanation of the functions is not *ipso facto* an explanation of consciousness, and we need to supplement the explanation with some further *a posteriori* component. Clark's 'identity hypothesis' provides this extra component; but its primitive nature makes it clear that a wholly reductive explanation is not on offer. Indeed, Levine (1983), who introduced the term 'explanatory gap', embraces an 'identity' picture just like this, but he is under no illusion that he is providing a reductive explanation.

Hardcastle offers her own diagnosis of the roots of the debate, painting a picture of 'committed materialists' who can't take the issue seriously, and 'committed sceptics' who are entirely sure that materialism is false. I think this picture is far too bleak: in my experience the majority of people are more than a little torn over these issues, and there is plenty of common ground. In particular, I think Hardcastle does materialists a disservice: to characterize materialism as a 'prior and fundamental commitment' is to make it into a religion. Materialism is an *a posteriori* doctrine, held by most because it explains so much in so many domains. But precisely because of this *a posteriori* character, its truth stands or falls with how well it can explain the phenomena. So materialists cannot just circle the wagons and plead a prior commitment; they have to face up to the problems directly.

In any case, I think the basic intuitive divide in the field is not that between 'materialists' and 'sceptics', but that between those who think there is a phenomenon that needs explaining and those who think there is not: that is, between type-A materialists and the rest. The issue between Dennett and myself, for example, comes down to some basic intuitions about first-person phenomenology. But once one accepts that there is a phenomenon that needs explaining — as Hardcastle clearly does — the issues are more straightforwardly debatable. In particular, the problems of the type-B position are straightforwardly philosophical, rooted in its need for explanatorily primitive identities and brute metaphysical necessities.

Indeed, I think Hardcastle's defence of her identities makes straightforwardly philosophical missteps. Against someone who raises an explanatory gap question ('why couldn't these physical processes have gone on without consciousness?'), she responds with an analogy, pointing to a water-mysterian who asks 'why couldn't water have been made of something else?', and a life-mysterian who asks 'why couldn't living things be made from something other than DNA?' But such questions are disanalogous and irrelevant, as they get the direction of explanation backward. In reductive explanation, the direction is always from micro to macro, not vice versa. So even if life could have been made of something else, this blocks the DNA explanation of life not in the slightest. What matters is that in these cases, the low-level facts imply the high-level facts, with no primitive identity statements required. But this is not so in the case of consciousness; so Hardcastle requires a primitive identity of an entirely different kind, for which analogies cannot help.

For a truly consistent type-B materialism, one would have to face up to these problems directly, rather than trying to slide over them. One would have to embrace explanatorily primitive identities that are logically independent of the physical facts and thus quite unlike any identities found elsewhere in science. One would have to embrace inexplicable metaphysical necessities that are far stronger than any *a posteriori* necessities found elsewhere in philosophy. And one will have to make a case that such postulates are a reasonable thing to believe in. I am sceptical about whether this is possible, but it is at least an interesting challenge.

But even if type-B materialism is accepted, the *explanatory* picture one ends up with looks far more like my naturalistic dualism than a standard materialism. One will have given up on trying to explain consciousness in terms of physical processes alone, and will instead be relying on primitive bridging principles. One will have to infer these bridging principles from systematic regularities between physical pro-cesses and phenomenological data, where the latter play an ineliminable role. One will presumably want to systematize and simplify these bridging principles as much as possible. (If there are to be brute identities in the metaphysics of the world, one hopes they are at least simple!) The only difference will be that these primitive principles will be called 'identities' rather than 'laws'.

I think it makes far more sense to regard such primitive principles as laws, but if someone insists on using the term 'identity', after a while I will stop arguing with them. In the search for a *theory* of consciousness — the truly interesting question — their theories will have the same shape as mine. The epistemology will be the same, the methodology will be the same, the explanatory relations between principles and data will be the same, and all will be quite unlike those found in standard materialist theories in other domains. The names may be different, but for all explanatory purposes, consciousness might as well be irreducible.

4. Other deflationary approaches

A different sort of 'deflationary' approach is taken by **O'Hara and Scutt**. Their paper has the juicy title 'There is no hard problem of consciousness', suggesting a Dennett-like reductionism, but the substance of their paper suggests quite the opposite. In fact, they hold that the hard problem is *so* hard that we should ignore it for now, and work on the easy problems instead. Then perhaps all will become clear, in a decade or a century or two.

Now there is not much doubt that progress on the easy problems is much faster than progress on the hard problem, but O'Hara and Scutt's policy suggestion seems quite redundant. Researchers working on the easy problems already outnumber those working on the hard problem by at least a hundred to one, so there is not much danger of the world suddenly falling into unproductive navel-gazing. But if O'Hara and Scutt are suggesting that *no-one* should be working on the hard problem, this seems to move beyond pragmatism to defeatism. Granted that the hard problem is hard, it nevertheless seems quite reasonable for a community to invest a fraction of its resources into trying to solve it. After all, we do not *know* when a solution to the hard problem will come. Even if we do not solve it immediately, it may well be that the partial understanding that comes through searching for a solution will help us in the further search, in our work on the easy problems, and in our understanding of ourselves. It is in the scientific spirit to *try*.

Sociological issues aside, the substantive issue arising from O'Hara and Scutt's article is that of whether there is any chance of progress on the hard problem any time soon. O'Hara and Scutt do not really provide much argument against this possibility; they simply reiterate that the hard problem is very hard, that we are not assured of a solution, and that scientific progress has often made hard problems seem easier. All this tells us that the prospects for a solution are uncertain, but it does not tell us that they are nonexistent.

In my article I advocated a positive methodology for facing up to the hard problem. Pay careful attention both to physical processing and to phenomenology; find systematic regularities between the two; work down to the simpler principles which explain these regularities in turn; and ultimately explain the connection in terms of a simple set of fundamental laws. O'Hara and Scutt offer no reason to believe that this must fail. They reserve most of their criticism for reductive methods such as those of Crick and Edelman, but that criticism does not apply here. They very briefly criticize a specific suggestion of mine, saying 'it is impossible to understand how information can have a phenomenal aspect'. They do not substantiate this remark (for my part, I do not find it impossible to understand at all, as long as we realize that a fundamental law rather than a reduction is being invoked) but in any case the criticism seems quite specific to my theory. O'Hara and Scutt give us no reason to believe that a fundamental theory could not be formulated and understood.

I should also clarify a common misunderstanding. O'Hara and Scutt attribute to me the view that understanding the easy problems does not help at all in understanding the hard problem, and others have attributed to me the view that neurobiology has nothing to contribute in addressing the hard problem. I did not make these claims, and do not agree with them. What I do say is that any account of the easy problems, and indeed any neurobiological or cognitive account, will be *incomplete*, so something more is needed for a solution to the hard problem. But this is not to say that they will play no role in a solution at all. I think it is obvious that empirical work has enriched our understanding of conscious experience a great deal, and I expect that it will continue to do so. A final theory of human consciousness will almost certainly lie in a combination of processing details and psychophysical principles: only using both together will the facts about experience be explained.

So I agree with O'Hara and Scutt that research on the easy problems is of the utmost importance: it is here that the meat and potatoes of consciousness research resides, and attention to this sort of work can help even a philosopher in staying grounded. But to ignore the hard problem entirely would be futile, as understanding conscious experience *per se* is the *raison d'être* of the field. Some of us will continue to focus on it directly, and even those working on the easy problems will do well to keep the hard problem in sight out of the corner of their eyes. To paraphrase Kant and stretch things a bit, we might say: hard without easy is empty; easy without hard is blind.

Another proposal that could be construed as 'deflationary' comes from **Price**, who suggests that much of the problem lies in our heads. We should not expect to *feel* as if we understand consciousness, but this may be no big deal. There are similar explanatory gaps accompanying every causal nexus ('*why* does event A cause event B?'); it's just that in most cases we have gotten used to them. The explanatory gap in the case of consciousness is analogous, but we are not yet as used to it.

I agree with Price's analogy, but I think it ultimately supports my view of the problem. Why are causal nexi accompanied by explanatory gaps? Precisely because of their contingency (as Price says, there is no '*a priori* necessity' to them), which is in turn due to the brute contingency of fundamental laws. If we ask 'why did pressing the remote control cause the TV set to turn on?', we might get a partial answer by appealing to principles of electromagnetic transmission, along with the circuitry of the two objects, ultimately seeing how this causal chain is the natural product of the underlying dynamics of electromagnetism (for example) as it applies to the material in the vicinity. But this answer is only partial, as we have no answer to the question of 'why do those fundamental principles hold?' Those principles are apparently just a brutely contingent fact about the world, and this contingency is inherited by the causal chain at the macroscopic level.

If Price is right that the explanatory gap between brain and consciousness is analogous, then this suggests that the gap is due to some contingency in the connecting principles, because of underlying brutely contingent fundamental laws. Which of course is just what

I suggest. We have here an inter-level relationship that *could have been otherwise*, just as Price points to intra-level relationships in physics that could have been otherwise. Either way, this arbitrariness is ultimately grounded at the point where explanation stops: the invocation of fundamental laws.

It is worth noting that for other inter-level relationships — that between bio- chemistry and life, for example, or between statistical mechanics and thermodynamics — there is no explanatory gap analogous to the brain–consciousness gap. The reason is precisely that the high-level facts in these cases are *necessitated* by the low-level facts. The low-level facts themselves may be contingent, but there is no further contingency in the inter-level bridge. (Indeed, the inter-level relationship in these cases is not really causation but *constitution*.) Because there is no contingency here, the relationship between the levels is transparent to our understanding. Contra- positively, the lack of transparency in the brain–consciousness case is precisely due to the contingency of the psychophysical bridge.

In any case, Price's analogy between the brain–consciousness relation and ordinary causal relations is helpful in seeing why belief in an explanatory gap need not lead one to mysterianism. Rather than elevating the explanatory gap to a *sui generis* mystery, we recognize that it is of the sort that is ubiquitous elsewhere in science, and especially in fundamental physics. This case is unusual only in that here, the gap is found in an inter-level rather than an intra-level relationship; but the same strategy that works for intra-level relationships works here. Once we introduce fundamental psychophysical laws into our picture of nature, the explanatory gap has itself been explained: it is only to be expected, given that nature is the way it is.

A final view that might be considered 'deflationary' has been discussed by **McGinn**, not so much in his contribution to this symposium as in an earlier paper (McGinn, 1989) and most explicitly in his review of my book (McGinn, 1996). On McGinn's view, the explanatory gap also arises for psychological reasons, but his reasons differ from Price's. He suggests that there may be a conceptual implication from physical facts to facts about consciousness, which would be *a priori* for a being that possessed the relevant concepts; but we do not and cannot possess the concepts, due to our cognitive limitations, so we can never grasp such an implication. On this view, materialism turns out to be true, but we can never grasp the theory that reveals its truth.

This intriguing view seems at first glance to offer an attractive alternative to both dualism and hard-line reductionism, but in the end, I am not sure how much of an alternative it is. The problem lies in the concept (or concepts) which support the implication from physical to phenomenal facts. What sort of concept could this be? If it is a structural/functional concept, then it will suffer from the same conceptual gap with experiential concepts as any other structural/functional concept (the existence of a gap here is independent of *specific* details about structure and function, after all). If it is not a structural/functional concept, then there appear to be principled reasons why it cannot be entailed by the physical story about the world, as physics deals only in structure and function.

So we are still faced with the problem that structure and function adds up only to more structure and function. This claim holds true for systematic reasons quite independent of considerations about cognitive limitations, and I doubt that McGinn would deny it. So it seems that McGinn needs to assert either (1) that explaining experience *is* just a problem of explaining structure and function, if only we could grasp this fact, or (2) that something more than structure and function is present in fundamental physics. The first option would make McGinn's position remarkably like **Dennett**'s (the only difference being that Dennett holds that only *some* of us are limited in this way!), and the second position would fall into the category of expanding fundamental physics, which I will consider below. Either way, once made specific, this view is subject to the pros and cons of the specific position to which it is assimilated. So in the end, it may not open up a distinct metaphysical option.

III: Nonreductive Analyses

1. Conceptual foundations

I will now address some critiques from those who take nonreductive positions. It appears that I staked out some middle ground; having discussed objections from my right, it is now time for objections from the left. The intermediate nature of my position may stem from an inclination toward simplicity and toward science. Reductive materialism yields a compellingly simple view of the world in many ways, and even if it does not work in the case of consciousness, I have at least tried to preserve as many of its benefits as possible. So where reductionists think that I have over- estimated the difficulty of the hard problem, some nonreductionists think that I may have underestimated it, or alternatively that I have underestimated the difficulty of the 'easy' problems.

The latter position — that the hard problem is hard, but that explaining discrimination, reportability, and so on is just as hard — is taken by **Lowe** and **Hodgson**, for two apparently different reasons. Hodgson thinks these problems are hard because a physical account cannot even explain how the functions are performed; Lowe thinks they are hard because they require explaining more than the performance of functions. (It is possible that Lowe intends to make both points.) I will address Lowe's position first, and save Hodgson's for my discussion of interactionism and epiphenomenalism.

Why say that explaining reportability, discrimination, and so on requires explaining more than the performance of functions? Lowe says this because he holds that true 'reports' and 'discriminations' can be made only in systems which have the capacity for thought, which in turn requires consciousness. If externally indistinguishable functions were performed in a system without consciousness, they would qualify as 'reports' (and so on) only in a 'jejune' sense. So an account of non-jejune reportability requires explaining more than functions.

I have some sympathy with Lowe's position here; in particular, I find it plausible that there is an intimate relationship between consciousness and thought (Lowe suggests that I think otherwise, but I don't think that suggestion can be found in my article). But it seems to me that the issue about 'reportability' and so on is largely verbal. Does a sound uttered by a functionally identical zombie really qualify as a 'report'? The answer is surely: yes in one sense of 'report', and no in another. If Lowe objects to calling it a 'report' in any sense at all, one can simply call it a 'pseudo- report'. Then the easy problems are those of explaining pseudo-reportability, pseudo-discrimination, and the like. Nothing important to my article changes; the distinction between the easy problems (explaining functions) and the hard problem (explaining conscious mentality) is as strong as ever.

Lowe might reply that reportability, so construed, is not a problem of *consciousness* at all. Again I am sympathetic, but again I think that this is a verbal issue. Plenty of people who take functional approaches to these problems take themselves to be explaining aspects of consciousness in some sense; and there is little point getting into territorial arguments about a word. It's more productive to accept the characterization — if someone holds that 'consciousness' has *some* functionally definable senses, I will not argue with them — but to point out the key problems of consciousness that are being skipped over all the same.

The same goes for Lowe's concerns, shared by **Velmans** and **Libet**, about my use of the term 'awareness' for a functionally defined concept distinct from that of full-blown consciousness. Again, a word is just a word. As long as we are clear that 'awareness' is being used in a stipulative sense, the substantive issues should be clear. In particular, there is certainly no implication that humans are 'aware' *only* in this attenuated sense, as Lowe somehow infers; and it is hard to see how this terminological choice helps blur the 'function/sentience' distinction, as Velmans suggests. If anything, explicitly separating consciousness and awareness makes the distinction harder to avoid. Nevertheless, it is clear that enough people are uneasy about the terminology that it it is unlikely to catch on universally. Perhaps another term can play the role, although I suspect that any word choice that dimly suggests mentality would meet similar opposition from some. It's a pity that there is no universal term for this central functional concept; in the meantime I will go on using the term 'awareness', with the stipulative nature of the usage always made clear.

The exact relationship between consciousness and 'intentional' (or semantic) mental states — such as belief, thought and understanding — raises deep and subtle questions that I did not intend to address in my article. Lowe seems to have gotten the impression of a straightforward functionalism about these aspects of mentality, but such an impression was not intended. I am torn on the question of intentionality, being impressed on one hand by its phenomenological aspects, and on the other hand being struck by the potential for functional analyses of specific intentional contents. In my book, I try to hew a neutral line on these deep questions, noting that there is a 'deflationary' construal of concepts such as 'belief' so that even a zombie might be said to have beliefs (pseudo-beliefs, if you prefer), and an inflationary construal such that true belief requires consciousness. Over time I am becoming more sympathetic with the second version: I think there may be something in the intuition that consciousness is the primary source of meaning, so that intentional content may be grounded in phenomenal content, as Lowe puts it. But I think the matter is far from cut and dried, and deserves a lengthy treatment in its own right. For now, phenomenal content is my primary concern.

2. The roots of the hard problem

Robinson, **McGinn**, and **Warner** offer proposals about why the hard problem is hard. These are not direct critiques of my view, for the most part, but they fall into the general category of nonreductive analyses, so I will address them briefly here.

Robinson suggests that the hardness lies in the fact that some phenomenal properties — hue properties, for example — have no structural expression. I think there is a considerable insight here. Elsewhere in science, instantiations of structural properties are generally explicable in terms of basic components and their relations, and it seems to be precisely their structure that makes them explicable in this way. The structural properties of experience itself (the geometry of the visual field, for example) form an interesting intermediate case: while they are more amenable to physical explanation than other phenomenal properties, this explanation still requires a nonreductive principle to cross the gap. But these properties may be reducible to structureless *phenomenal* properties and their relations. If so, Robinson may be correct that the core of phenomenal irreducibility lies at the more basic level.

A few questions remain: for example, if it turned out that phenomenal properties had structure 'all the way down', might they not be irreducible to physical properties all the same? For reasons like this, I sometimes lean toward an alternative view which locates the irreducibility in an independence of the *kind* of structure found in the physical domain, and ultimately in the *intrinsicness* of phenomenal properties, which contrasts with the relational nature of all our physical concepts. But clearly these views are not far apart.

McGinn offers a closely related analysis. He locates the problem in the *non-spatial* character of consciousness: that is, in the fact that it lacks spatial extension and structure, and therefore does not fit easily into physical space. I think the overall intuition is very powerful. The detailed claim needs to be carefully unpacked, to avoid lumping in consciousness with less problematic non-spatial states and properties (e.g. the legality of an action, which is a complex dispositional property but not a spatial property; and possibly even the charge of a particle) while simultaneously avoiding the need to appeal more controversially to a non-spatial *entity* bearing the state or property (McGinn seems not to want to rest his case on this appeal; e.g. his footnote 3). I suspect that once this work is done —adding appropriate restrictions on the class of properties, perhaps — McGinn's analysis will be even closer to those above.

Warner locates the source of the problem in a different place: the *incorrigibility* of our knowledge of consciousness. I agree with Warner that there is some sense in which some knowledge of consciousness is incorrigible — I know with certainty that I am conscious right now, for example — but it is remarkably tricky to isolate the relevant sense and the relevant items of knowledge. Warner himself notes that plenty of our beliefs about our experiences are mistaken. He gets around this problem by limiting this to cases where our ability to recognize experiences is 'unimpaired', but this seems to come dangerously close to trivializing the incorrigibility claim. After all, it is arguably a tautology that an 'unimpaired' belief about an experience will be correct. Warner may have a way to unpack the definition of 'impairment' so that the claim is non-circular, but this is clearly a non-trivial project.

In Chapter 5 of my book (pp. 207–8), I make some brief suggestions about how to make sense of an incorrigibility claim. In essence, I think that experiences play a role in constituting some of our concepts of experience; and when a belief directs such a concept at the experience which constitutes it, there is no way that the belief can be wrong (in essence, because one's current experience has got 'inside' the content of one's belief).

Many or most beliefs about experience do not have this specific form, and are therefore corrigible; nevertheless, this may isolate a certain limited class of beliefs about experience that cannot be wrong. (This limited class of beliefs arguably can ground the first-person epistemology of conscious experience, but this is a further complex issue.)

In any case, Warner and I are agreed that there are *some* beliefs about conscious experience that cannot be wrong. What follows? Warner holds that it follows from this alone that experience cannot be physically explained, as physical science cannot countenance the necessary connections that incorrigibility requires. I am not sure about this. On my account, for example, the necessary connection between belief and experience is an automatic product of the role that the experience plays in constituting the content of the belief; and it is not *obvious* to me that materialists could not avail themselves of a similar account. Shoemaker (1990) gives an alternative account of incorrigibility from a functionalist perspective, relying on the interdefinition of pains and pain-beliefs. Perhaps Warner would object that neither of these accounts captures the kind of incorrigibility that he is after; but perhaps they capture the kind of incorrigibility in which there is reason to believe. So I am not yet convinced that incorrigibility is truly the source of the mind–body problem, but it is clear that there is much more to be said.

Warner uses these considerations about incorrigibility to suggest, like Lowe, that even reportability — one of my 'easy' problems — cannot be physically explained. My reply here is as before. I did not intend reportability to be read in a strong sense that *requires* the presence of experience. Rather, I intended it to require merely the presence of the reports, functionally construed, so in particular I did not intend it to encompass the incorrigibility of beliefs about experience. (If I were writing the article now, I would modify the wording in the list of 'easy' problems to make it absolutely clear that functioning is all that matters.) Certainly, *if* 'reportability' is read in a sense that requires conscious experience, then it cannot be reductively explained.

3. Fundamental laws

A further set of issues is raised by my appeal to fundamental laws in a theory of consciousness. **Mills** thinks that because I invoke such laws to bridge physics and consciousness, I am not really solving the hard problem at all (**Price** suggests something similar). At best I am providing a sophisticated set of correlations, and finding such correlations was an easy problem all along.

Mills reaches this conclusion because he construes the hard problem as the problem of giving a *constitutive* (or 'non-causal') explanation of consciousness in physical terms. If the problem is construed that way, Mills is quite right that it is not being solved at all. But to define the problem of consciousness this way would be to define it so that it becomes unsolvable: one might call *that* problem the 'impossible problem'.

I prefer to set up the hard problem in such a way that a solution is not defined out of existence. The hard problem, as I understand it, is that of explaining how and why consciousness arises from physical processes in the brain. And I would argue the sort of theory I advocate can in principle offer a good solution to this problem. It will not solve the impossible problem of providing a reductive explanation of consciousness, but it will nevertheless provide a theory of consciousness that goes beyond correlation to explanation.

A good analogy is Newton's theory of gravitation. The Newton of legend wanted to explain why an apple fell to the ground. If he had aimed only at correlation, he would have produced a taxonomic theory that noted that when apples were dropped from such-and-such heights, they fell to the ground taking such-and-such time, and so on. But instead he aimed for *explanation*, ultimately explaining the macroscopic regularities in terms of a simple and fundamental gravitational force. In Newton's time, some objected that he had not explained why the gravitational force should exist; and indeed he had not. But we take Newton's account to be a good explanation of the apple's falling all the same. We have grown used to taking some things as fundamental.

Something similar holds for a theory of consciousness. It would be deeply unsatis-fy-ing for a theory of consciousness to stop at 'complex brain state B is associated with complex experience C', and so on for a huge array of data points. As in Newton's case, we want to know how and why these correlations hold; and we answer this question by pointing to simple and fundamental underlying laws. Just as one can say 'the apple fell because of the law of gravity', we will eventually be able to say 'brain state B produced conscious state C because of fundamental law X'.

Because something is being taken as primitive, this does not yield as *strong* an explanatory connection as one finds in cases of reductive explanation, such as the explanation of genes in terms of DNA. But it is an explanation all the same. The case of gravity suggests that what counts in an explanation is that one reduces the primitive component to something as simple as possible, not that one reduces it to zero.

Mills suggests that this is no better than explaining why a sheep is black in terms of the fact that it is a member of the class of black things. But here the explanatory posit is just as complex as what needs to be explained; whereas in our case, the fundamental laws are far simpler than the data. If our 'explanation' was 'brain B yields experience E', or even 'certain oscillations yield consciousness', we would have a problem like Mills': these posits would be so complex and macroscopic that they stand in need of further explana-tion themselves. For a comprehensive explanation, our basic principles need to be so simple and universal that they are plausibly part of the basic furniture of the world.

Of course one can always ask 'why does the fundamental law hold', as Mills and also **Robinson** suggest. But we should not expect any answer to that question. In physics, we have grown used to the idea that explanation stops somewhere, and that the fundamental laws of nature are not further explained. That is what makes them fundamental. If my negative arguments about consciousness are correct, then we will have to do the same here. We will explain and explain and explain, and eventually our psychophysical explanations will be reduced to a simple core which we will take as primitive. So we do not get something for nothing, but we get a perfectly adequate theory all the same.

Mills is right that once we view things this way, there is a sense in which the hard problem becomes an easy problem (although not an Easy problem), in that there is a clear research programme for its solution and there is no reason why it should be intractable in principle. This I take to be precisely the liberating force of taking consciousness as fundamental. We no longer need to bash our heads against the wall trying to reduce consciousness to something it is not. Instead we can engage in the search for a construc-tive explanatory theory.

In any case, it seems that Mills does not disagree with me on the issues of substance. Whichever problems one takes to be 'hard' or 'easy', the deepest problem of consciousness is that of how we can construct an explanatory theory of consciousness which accommodates consciousness in the natural world. And a fundamental theory of consciousness, we agree, is the best way to do just that. I will be happy if we can come up with a theory of consciousness that is only as good as Newton's theory of gravitation!

4. Epiphenomenalism and interactionism

A number of contributors worry that my position may lead to epiphenomenalism, the view that consciousness has no effect on the physical world. If the physical domain is causally closed, so that there is a physical explanation for every physical event, and if consciousness is non-physical, then it can seem that there is no room for consciousness to play any causal role. Conversely, it can seem that if consciousness is non-physical and plays a causal role, then there will not be a physical solution even to the 'easy' problems. **Hodgson** and **Warner** spend some time discussing this issue, and **Seager** and **Stapp** allude to it. I discuss this issue at considerable length in my book, but will summarize the state of play as I see it below.

In essence, I think that (1) while epiphenomenalism has no clear fatal flaws, it is to be avoided if possible; that (2) the causal closure of the physical domain is not to be denied lightly; and that (3) denying causal closure does not really help solve the problems of epiphenomenalism, which run deeper than this. Most importantly, I think that (4) it may be possible to avoid epiphenomenalism even while embracing the causal closure of the physical domain, by taking the right view of the place of consciousness in the natural order. I will consider these issues in order.

First, is epiphenomenalism an acceptable view, or should it be rejected out of hand? There is no doubt that the view is counterintuitive to many, but it is also hard to find fatal flaws in it. While we certainly have strong intuitions that consciousness plays a causal role, our *evidence* for these intuitions lies largely in the fact that certain conscious events tend to be systematically followed by certain physical events. As always, when faced with such a constant conjunction, we infer a causal connection. But the epiphenomenalist can account for this evidence in a different way, by pointing to psychophysical laws, so our intuitions may not carry too much weight here.

Hodgson argues vigorously against epiphenomenalism, largely by appealing to 'common sense'. I think common sense should not be undervalued here, but it is also inconclusive. At best, it establishes a presumption against epiphenomenalism if other things are equal, not a solid argument against it if other things are not. Hodgson also points to various functions that he thinks could not be performed as well without consciousness, but his arguments all depend once again on a first-person intuition that consciousness is playing a causal role, rather than on an objective analysis of the functions themselves. He also makes an appeal to evolution, but an epiphenomenalist can account for the evolution of consciousness without too many problems: evolution selects for certain physical processes directly, and psycho-physical laws do the rest, ensuring that consciousness will evolve alongside those processes. Like all fundamental laws, these psychophysical laws are universal, so we do not need an evolutionary explanation of why these laws hold in the first place.

Other anti-epiphenomenalist arguments can be made by appealing to the relationship between consciousness and the things we *say* and *judge* about consciousness. It seems that the epiphenomenalist must hold that consciousness is causally irrelevant to our utterances about consciousness, which is at least very odd. Some argue that it is more than odd, suggesting that if consciousness were epiphenomenal we could not *refer* to consciousness, or that we could not *know* about consciousness; but I think that a close analysis, as I give in my book, suggests that these arguments do not go through, as our knowledge of and reference to consciousness depends on a relationship to consciousness that is much tighter than mere causation.

Warner gives a novel argument against epiphenomenalism, and against any other view that has a causally closed physical domain plus psychophysical laws. He suggests that psychophysical laws *must* interfere with physical laws, as they automatically entail violations of physical conservation laws. I do not see why this is the case: surely it is at least coherent to suppose that the physical picture of the universe might be supplemented by some psychophysical laws that introduce consciousness but leave the physical domain untouched, Warner's argument relies on the claim that the 'production' of experience by a physical process must involve a corresponding decrease in some physical quantity, but I see no reason why this must be so: there will be *some* physical criterion for the existence of an experience, to be sure, but this criterion may be one that can be satisfied perfectly well in a causally closed physical world. So the conceptual coherence of epiphenomenalism, and that of other views with causal closure plus psychophysical laws, is unthreatened.

Still, all this establishes at best that epiphenomenalism has no fatal flaws. It does not establish that epiphenomenalism is plausible. Not only does epiphenomenalism violate certain aspects of common sense; it also leads to an inelegant picture of nature, with consciousness 'dangling' on top of physical processes as a kind of add-on extra. If it turns out that every other position has fatal flaws, then we may have reason to embrace epiphenomenalism; but in the meantime, we have good reason to investigate alternatives.

There are two sorts of alternatives that one might consider. First, we might see if it is plausible to deny the causal closure of the physical domain, thus leaving room for a causal role for experience in an interactionist dualism. Second, we might see if a causal role for experience might be *reconciled* with the causal closure of the physical domain. The second alternative may sound paradoxical at first, but I think there is a very natural way to make sense of it, which may ultimately provide the deepest resolution of this issue.

But first: is the physical world causally closed? In the paper I accepted that it was, not because I think things *have* to be that way, but because to deny this is to go a long way out on a limb. One does not have to go out on that limb to embrace the irreducibility of consciousness, so I prefer to stay neutral, lest the baby of consciousness once more be thrown out with the bathwater of Cartesian dualism. Still, are there any good reasons to deny causal closure, and to assert that physical explanations of the various functions are incomplete?

Perhaps the most common such reason is an indirect one: 'It *must* be the case that physical explanations of the functions are incomplete, if consciousness is to play a causal role.' This reason has some force, although I think both of its premises can be questioned: we have seen above that it is not obvious that consciousness *must* have a causal role, and we will see below that consciousness might have a causal role even if the physical domain is causally closed. But in any case, I set this indirect reason aside: the question for now is whether there are any *direct* reasons. That is, if we set consciousness aside and take a third-person view of the world, is there any reason to believe that physical explanations of these functions are impossible?

Hodgson offers an array of reasons to deny causal closure, but they are mostly grounded in the indirect reason above. Hodgson does not deny that some physical system might perform the functions with which the 'easy' problems are concerned; he simply thinks that that is not the way that *we* do it, as consciousness plays a role in our own case. So his case that the 'easy' problems are hard depends largely on the existence of the hard problem, and not on considerations intrinsic to the easy problems themselves. Indeed, I think that 'objective' reasons suggesting that no physical systems could perform these functions are very thin on the ground.

The main place where third-person considerations may give reason to deny causal closure is in the intriguing case of quantum mechanics, which both Hodgson and **Stapp** appeal to. While there are interpretations of quantum mechanics on which it is causally closed — the interpretations of Bohm and Everett, for example — there are also interpretations on which the physical domain is not, and which leave a potential causal role for consciousness wide open. Stapp, for example, favours an interpretation on which consciousness is responsible for 'collapsing' the wave function, and Hodgson favours an interpretation on which consciousness determines certain apparent quantum indeterminacies.

Indeed, it can seem that quantum mechanics provides about as perfect a causal role for consciousness as one could imagine in a physical theory. Any indeterminism in quantum mechanics comes in at the point of 'collapse', which on the most common interpretations is triggered by 'measurement', and it can seem that consciousness is the only non-arbitrary way to distinguish a measurement from other physical events. If so, then consciousness may be present in quantum mechanics' very foundations. Such interpretations are controversial among physicists, but mainly because they presuppose that consciousness is non-physical; if we have already accepted this for independent reasons, this concern loses its bite. (It is interesting that philosophers reject interactionist dualism because they think it is incompatible with physics, whereas physicists reject the relevant interpretations of quantum mechanics because they are dualistic!)

On most days of the week, I lean toward a different interpretation of quantum mechanics (Everett's), but interactionist collapse interpretations have obvious attractions and are not to be dismissed lightly. (I lean toward them about two days a week, and toward Bohm's interpretation on Sundays.) At least it seems clear that interactionist dualism is not *incompatible* with physical theory, as we understand it today. But I think there is a deeper reason why an appeal to interactionist dualism does not really solve the problems of epiphenomenalism. This is because even interactionism is subject to an epiphenomenalist worry of its own! Perhaps it can get around this worry, but it turns out that the same move is available to theories in which physics is causally closed.

The worry is as follows: for any given interactionist theory, it seems that we can remove the facts about experience, and still be left with a coherent causal story. Take Eccles' theory on which 'psychons' in the mind affect physical processes in the brain.

Here, one can tell a perfectly coherent causal story about psychons and their effect on the brain without ever mentioning the fact that psychons are *experiential*. On this story, psychons will be viewed as causal entities analogous to electrons and protons in physical theories, affected by certain physical entities and affecting them in turn; and just as with protons and electrons, the fact that psychons have any experiential qualities will be quite inessential to the dynamic story. So one can still give a causal explanation of behaviour that does not involve or imply experience. The same would go for a Cartesian theory involving ectoplasm, for **Libet**'s proposal involving a 'conscious mental field', and even for the theories that Stapp and Hodgson advocate.

Consider **Stapp**'s view, for example. Presumably when this view is filled out, it will say that certain physical states P give rise to certain experiential states E, and that these states E bring about physical collapses in turn. But however this story works, the fact that the states E are *experiential* will be quite inessential to the story. One can imagine that a formally identical theory might be formulated from a 'God's-eye' point of view, invoking such states E in causing collapses, but never mentioning experience at all. So it is not easy to see how Stapp is giving experience an *essential* role.

Stapp has sometimes advocated his view by pointing to the 'zombie' possibility for classical physics: if physics is causally closed, there is a logical possibility of physically identical zombies with the same behaviour, suggesting that experience plays no essential role in our behaviour. But interestingly, a similar objection can be made to Stapp's own view. Given that physics works as Stapp suggests, there is a logically possible world with a 'quantum zombie'. In this world, instead of P causing experience E which causes collapse, P causes collapse directly. There is no consciousness in this world, but all the functions are performed just the same. So there is a sense in which the fact that *experience* is associated with collapses in our world is superfluous. One can tell a similar conceptually coherent 'zombie' story for any interactionist picture, whether Hodgson's or Eccles' — just move to a possible world in which any intermediate causal roles are played without any associated experience — thus suggesting that these problems are not unique to the picture in which the physical world is causally closed.

The real 'epiphenomenalism' problem, I think, does not arise from the causal closure of the physical world. Rather, it arises from the causal closure of the world! Even on an interactionist picture, there will be *some* broader causally closed story that explains behaviour, and such a story can always be told in a way that neither includes nor implies experience. Even on the interactionist picture, we can view minds as just further nodes in the causal network, like the physical nodes, and the fact that these nodes are experiential is inessential to the causal dynamics. The basic worry arises not because experience is logically independent of physics, but because it is logically independent of causal dynamics more generally.

The interactionist has a reasonable solution to this problem, I think. Presumably, the interactionist will respond that some nodes in the causal network are experiential through and through. Even though one *can* tell the causal story about psychons without mentioning experience, for example, psychons are *intrinsically* experiential all the same. Subtract experience, and there is nothing left of the psychon but an empty place-marker in a causal network, which is arguably to say there is nothing left at all. To have real causation, one needs something to do the causing; and here, what is doing the causing is experience.

I think this solution is perfectly reasonable; but once the problem is pointed out this way, it becomes clear that the same solution will work in a causally closed physical world. Just as the interactionist postulates that some nodes in the causal network are intrinsically experiential, the 'epiphenomenalist' can do the same.

Here we can exploit an idea that was set out by Bertrand Russell (1927), and which has been developed in recent years by Grover Maxwell (1978) and Michael Lockwood (1989). This is the idea that *physics* characterizes its basic entities only extrinsically, in terms of their causes and effects, and leaves their intrinsic nature unspecified. For everything that physics tells us about a particle, for example, it might as well just be a bundle of causal dispositions; we know nothing of the entity that *carries* those dispositions. The same goes for fundamental properties, such as mass and charge: ultimately, these are complex dispositional properties (to have mass is to resist acceleration in a certain way, and so on). But whenever one has a causal disposition, one can ask about the categorical *basis* of that disposition: that is, what is the entity that is doing the causing?

One might try to resist this question by saying that the world contains *only* dispositions. But this leads to a very odd view of the world indeed, with a vast amount of causation and no entities for all this causation to relate! It seems to make the fundamental properties and particles into empty placeholders, in the same way as the psychon above, and thus seems to free the world of any substance at all. It is easy to overlook this problem in the way we think about physics from day to day, given all the rich details of the mathematical structure that physical theory provides; but as Stephen Hawking (1988) has noted, physical theory says nothing about what puts the 'fire' into the equations and grounds the reality that these structures describe. The idea of a world of 'pure structure' or of 'pure causation' has a certain attraction, but it is not at all clear that it is coherent.

So we have two questions: (1) what are the intrinsic properties underlying physical reality? and (2) where do the intrinsic properties of experience fit into the natural order? Russell's insight, developed by Maxwell and Lockwood, is that these two questions fit with each other remarkably well. Perhaps the intrinsic properties underlying physical dispositions are themselves *experiential* properties, or perhaps they are some sort of *proto-experiential* properties that together constitute conscious experience. This way, we locate experience *inside* the causal network that physics describes, rather than outside it as a dangler; and we locate it in a role that one might argue urgently needed to be filled. And importantly, we do this without violating the causal closure of the physical. The causal network itself has the same shape as ever; we have just coloured in its nodes.

This ideas smacks of the grandest metaphysics, of course, and I do not know that it has to be true. But if the idea *is* true, it lets us hold on to irreducibility and causal closure and nevertheless deny epiphenomenalism. By placing experience inside the causal network, it now carries a causal role. Indeed, fundamental experiences or proto-experiences will be the *basis* of causation at the lowest levels, and high-level experiences such as ours will presumably inherit causal relevance from the (proto)-experiences from which they are constituted. So we will have a much more integrated picture of the place of consciousness in the natural order.[4]

---

[4] There may be other ways to reconcile a causal role for experience with the causal closure of the physical. See Mills (1995) for a different strategy that relies on causal overdetermination. But even if this view avoids epiphenomenalism, it retains a fragmented, inelegant picture of nature.

The Russellian view still qualifies as a sort of 'naturalistic dualism', as it requires us to introduce experience or proto-experience as fundamental, and it requires a deep duality between the intrinsic and extrinsic features of physical reality. But underlying this dualism, there is a deeper monism: we have an integrated world of intrinsic properties connected by causal relations. The view can even be seen as an odd sort of 'materialism', as it says that physical reality is all there is — but it says that there is much more in physical reality than physical theory tells us about! In the end the name does not matter too much, as long as the picture is clear. (I would be tempted by 'fundamentalism' as the most accurate coverall for the sorts of view I embrace, were it not for the associations!)

There are obvious concerns about this view. The first is the threat of panpsychism, on which more later. The second is the problem of how fundamental experiential or proto-experiential properties at the microscopic level somehow together *constitute* the sort of complex, unified experience that we possess. (This is a version of what Seager calls the 'combination problem'.) Such constitution is almost certainly required if our own experiences are not to be epiphenomenal, but it is not at all obvious how it should work: would not these tiny experiences instead add up to a jagged mess? I discuss some approaches to this problem later. *If* it can be avoided, then I think the Russellian view (which turns out to be particularly compatible with an informational 'it from bit' view) is clearly the single most attractive way to make sense of the place of experience in the natural order.

It is notable that even an interactionist dualism can be seen as a sort of Russellian view. It draws a slightly different picture of the causal network, and takes certain nodes in this network — the 'psychon' or 'collapse' nodes, for example — and colours them in. The differences are that not *all* nodes in the network are coloured in in this way (presumably there are some different, unknown intrinsic properties in fundamental matter), and that the experiential nodes in this picture are at a fairly high level. This may actually help avoid the problem above: instead of trying to constitute our consciousness out of innumerable *different* fundamental nodes, there might turn out to be a *single* node in each case (or just a few?) which carries the burden. (Though one may well wonder why this single node should have such a complex of intrinsic properties, in the way that our consciousness does!) This avoidance of the constitution problem may in the end turn out to be the greatest virtue of a quantum interactionism.

In the meantime, I think this question is wide open. There are at least three potential ways of seeing the metaphysics here: the epiphenomenalist version, the interactionist version, and the Russellian version. All have pros and cons, and I think the question of their mutual merits is one that deserves much further investigation.

5. *My psychophysical laws*

A few contributors made comments on the three specific proposals I made about psychophysical laws: the principle of structural coherence, the principle of organizational invariance, and the double-aspect view of information. Taking these in turn:

(1) The principle of structural coherence. This is the least controversial of the three proposals, and unsurprisingly there was not much argument with it. It has long been recognized that there is a detailed correspondence between structural properties of the information processed in the brain and structural properties of conscious experience (see the 'psychophysical axioms' of Müller (1896) and the 'structural isomorphism' of Köhler

(1947) for example). My slightly more specific proposal, specifying that the relevant information is that made available for global control, is also implicitly or explicitly present in much current research.

The only criticism is by **Libet**, who thinks that my equation of the structure of consciousness with the structure of awareness is either trivial or false. I think he is placing too much weight on the use of the word 'awareness' here, however; I use the term stipulatively to refer to global availability of information (availability for such processes as verbal report, among other things), and might easily have used another term instead. I suspect that when this verbal issue is set aside, Libet will not find much to disagree with.

(2) The somewhat functionalist principle of organizational invariance, and my arguments for it, met with a bit more disagreement. **Velmans** objects to it on the grounds that a cortical implant might produce a refined version of blindsight, with excellent perform-ance but no verbal reports of consciousness and hence no experience. But this is no counterexample to the principle: the very absence of verbal reports in these subjects show that they are functionally inequivalent to normal subjects. Perhaps they are 'functionally equivalent' in some very loose sense, but the invariance principle requires a much stricter isomorphism than this. The moral is that the processes involved in the production of verbal reports are just as much part of a subject's functional organization as the processes responsible for discrimination and motor action. Indeed, these aspects of organization may be among the prime determinants of conscious experience.

Similarly, **Libet** says that I rely on a 'behavioural' criterion for conscious experience, instead of more convincing criteria such as a subject's verbal report. But a verbal report is a sort of behavioural criterion in its own right; and in any case, it is clear that any subject who is functionally isomorphic to me in the strict sense that the principle requires will produce exactly the same verbal reports, and so will satisfy Libet's criterion. Libet is quite right that there are cases where performance on many tasks is dissociated from verbal report, but such cases are irrelevant to assessing the principle.

A fairly common reaction to these thought-experiments is to suggest that no silicon chip could in fact duplicate the function of a neuron, or at least that one should not beg that question. I agree that this is clearly an open empirical question. The principle says only that *if* a system is a functional isomorph of a conscious system, it will have the same sort of experiences; it makes no claims about just how such isomorphs might be realized. Silicon chips are just an example. If silicon isomorphs turn out to be possible, then the principle applies to them; if they do not, the scope of the principle will be more limited. Either way, the idea that functional organization fully determines conscious experience is unthreatened by this line of questioning.[5]

Hardcastle wonders if we can *really* know what will happen upon duplicating neural function in silicon. Here the answer is no and yes. No, we can't know for sure that neural function can be duplicated perfectly in silicon — that's the same open question as above. But we do know that *if* function-preserving substitution is possible, the resulting system will make just the same claims, the same behaviour, and so on, as the original system. In

---

[5] That being said: if the laws of physics are computable, a neuron's behaviour is in principle computable too, and it is not implausible that the relevant computations could be hooked up to electrical and chemical mediators with other neurons, at least in principle if not easily in practice. We already have seen artificial hearts, and people are working on artificial retinas; my own money is on the eventual possibility of artificial neurons.

fact we can know, in advance, precisely how the system will look from the third-person point of view. And even from the first-person point of view, I know that *if* some of my neurons are switched with identically-functioning silicon chips, I will come out swearing up and down that my qualia never changed. So, in the relevant sense, I think we already know as much as we will ever know about how such a system will be.

Indeed, I think that if such substitution is ever possible, nobody will doubt the invariance principle for long. All it will take is a couple of substitutions, with subjects asserting that nothing has changed, and we will hear that there is 'empirical evidence' that function-preserving substitution preserves conscious experience. The conclusion may be disputed by a handful of sceptical philosophers, but the subject's own word will be hard to resist. So I think that even now, the conditional assertion — if a functional isomorph is possible, *then* it will have the same sort of conscious experience — is at least as safe a bet.

Lowe thinks that the invariance principle 'sells out completely' to functionalism, but this is a misunderstanding. Even many dualists hold that two subjects with the same brain state will have the same conscious state; presumably they are not thereby 'selling out to physicalism', except in a highly attenuated sense of the latter. Consciousness is not reduced to a physical state; it is merely associated with one. By the same measure, to hold that two subjects in the same functional state have the same conscious state is not to sell out to functionalism, except in an attenuated sense. Consciousness is not reduced to a functional state; it is merely associated with one. Functional states, like physical states, turn out to determine conscious states with natural but not logical necessity. The resulting position, nonreductive functionalism, is compatible with the rich construal of mentality that reductive functionalism tacitly denies, precisely because a *logical* connection between function and experience is avoided.

Lowe may think that even a nonreductive functionalism is a bad thing, but to make that case, further reasons are required. For my part, I think that nonreductive functionalism stands a chance of capturing the most plausible and attractive elements of functionalist doctrines, while ignoring their reductive excesses.

Seager finds it odd that there should be laws connecting complex functional organizations to experience. I think that he is right and wrong to be worried about this. It would indeed be very odd if there were *fundamental* laws connecting complex organizations to experience (just as it would be odd if there were fundamental laws about telephones), but I do not claim that such laws exist. The invariance principle is intended as a non-fundamental law: eventually it should be the consequence of more fundamental laws that underlie it. Such laws need not invoke complex functional organization directly; they might instead invoke some simple underlying feature, such as information. As long as this feature is itself an organizational invariant (as information plausibly is), the invariance principle may be a consequence.

Seager also worries about the fineness of organizational grain required to duplicate experience. I discuss this in my book: the grain needed for the fading and dancing qualia argument to go through is one that is sufficiently fine to capture the mechanisms that support our behavioural dispositions, such as our dispositions to make certain claims, and also sufficiently fine to allow either (a) that any two realizations be connected by a near-continuous spectrum of realizations (for the fading qualia argument), or (b) that any two realizations be connected by a chain of realizations such that neighboring links in the chain differ only over a small region (for the dancing qualia argument). It is not impossible that a less fine grain will also suffice to duplicate experience, but the arguments will give no purchase on these cases. Seager worries that nature does not know about levels of organization, but again this would be a worry only if the invariance principle were held to be a fundamental law.

Finally, Seager thinks that the association of experience with functional organization leads to a particularly worrisome form of epiphenomenalism. I think it is clear, however, that the arguments he invokes apply to *any* association of experience with physical properties. There is indeed an interesting problem of 'explanatory exclusion' to worry about, as I discussed above, but nothing about this problem is specific to the invariance principle or to any of the psychophysical laws I propose.

(3) The double-aspect analysis of information is by far the most speculative and tentative part of my article, and it is surely the most likely to be wrong. Indeed, as I say in my book, I think it is more likely than not to be wrong, but I put it forward in the hope that it might help progress toward a more satisfactory theory. So I am far from sure that I can defend it against every possible criticism. That being said, I think that a couple of the criticisms of the information-based approach may rest on misinterpretations.

Lowe resists my invocation of Shannonian information as 'inappropriate for characterizing the cognitive states of human beings'. But as before, I am not trying to *reduce* mental states to information processing. Such processing is instead invoked as a potential key to the physical *basis* of consciousness. True, the double-aspect view implies that consciousness has formal properties that mirror the formal properties of the underlying information; I think this claim is clearly plausible from phenomenological investigation, but it is nowhere claimed that these formal properties exhaust the properties of consciousness. Just because the skeletal framework is syntactic, for example, there is nothing to prevent irreducible non-syntactic properties from being present as well. In fact, it is obvious that there are phenomenal properties over and above these formal properties: such properties are precisely what make the phenomenal realization of the information so different from the physical realization. Shannonian information at best provides a framework around which a theory of these intrinsic properties can be hung.

Varela is similarly 'dumbfounded' by my appeal to this sort of information, because of the 'outmoded cybernetic tradition' it invokes. I am not nearly as certain as Varela that Shannonian information (as opposed to the cyberneticist use of it) is outmoded; indeed, I think one can argue that information states of the kind I describe in my book play a central role even in the computationalist, connectionist, and 'embodied' frameworks that Varela endorses. These frameworks may add something to information states — such as a semantic content, or a context within the world — but all these frameworks invoke certain 'difference structures' and their causal roles in a cognitive system. And precisely because this difference structure captures an important formal isomorphism between aspects of conscious states and the under- lying physical states, the concept of information may provide a framework within which we can make progress. Once it is clear that experience is not being *reduced* to information, I think the way is cleared for information to play a useful formal role, and perhaps even to play a role in the underlying metaphysics.

Libet, **Hardcastle** and **Velmans** note that some information is nonconscious. As I discuss in my book, there are two ways to deal with this. The first is to find further constraints on the sort of information that is associated with experience; it is entirely possible that some such constraint may play a role in the psychophysical laws. (Velmans offers some interesting suggestions about such constraints, although none of them seem likely candidates to be truly fundamental.) The other possibility is to accept that all information has an experiential aspect: while not all information is realized in *my* consciousness, all information is realized in *some* consciousness. This is counterintuitive to many, but I do not think the possibility can be immediately dismissed. I will discuss it when I discuss panpsychism below.

The ontology underlying the informational picture (which **Velmans** worries about) remains open. I discuss a number of possible interpretations of it in my book. I am most attracted to a Russellian interpretation in which experience forms the 'intrinsic' (or realizing) aspect of informational states which are fundamental to physics but characterized by physics only extrinsically. There is at least a kinship between the informational model and the Russellian metaphysics here, and exploiting it would lead to definite double-aspect ontology. ('Physics is information from the outside; experience is information from the inside.') But I am not certain that this can be made to work, and more straightforwardly dualistic interpretations are also available.

I favour the informational view largely because when I look for regularities between experience and the physical processes that underlie it, the most striking correspondences all lie at the level of information structures. We have to find *something* in underlying physical processes to link experience to, and information seems a plausible and universal candidate. Perhaps the biggest concern about this view is that these informational structures do not lie at a *fundamental* level in physical processes; as **Bilodeau** (1996) notes, they are curiously abstract to play a role in a fundamental theory. On the other hand, there are ways of seeing information as fundamental to physics itself, so there may be ways in which a connection at a fundamental level can be leveraged to support this striking connection at the macroscopic level. But all that is very much in the realm of open questions.

IV: Positive Proposals

A number of contributors made positive proposals about how the hard problem might be approached. These divide into (1) neuroscientific and cognitive approaches; (2) phenomenological approaches; (3) physics-based approaches, and (4) fundamental psychophysical theories. I will not try to assess each proposal at great length, but I will say a few words about the approaches and their relationship to my framework.

1. Neuroscientific and cognitive approaches

Proposals with a neurobiological and cognitive flavour were made by Crick and Koch (1995), **Baars**, and **MacLennan**. The philosophical orientations of these range from reductionism to property dualism; this alone illustrates that a neurobiological approach to consciousness is compatible with many different philosophical views. Even if neurobiology and cognitive science *alone* cannot solve the hard problem, they may still play a central role in developing a theory.

Crick and Koch come closest to a reductionist view, although they are appropriately tentative about it. They first divide up the hard problem into three parts and offer an interesting solution to the third, concerning the incommunicability of experience. I think their idea here — that only relations are communicable because only relations are preserved throughout processing — is largely correct. That is, all that is communicable are differences that make a difference, or information states. Of course this is strictly speaking one of the 'easy' problems, but it clearly has a close connection to the hard problem; I expect that a good cognitive account of what we can and cannot communicate about consciousness will lead to some very useful insights about the hard problem itself. I develop this point and tie it to an informational view of consciousness in Chapter 8 of my book.

On the hard problem, Crick and Koch suggest that it may be promising to focus first on 'meaning'. I am less sure about this: meaning seems to be almost as difficult a concept as consciousness, and perhaps even more ambiguous. If one invokes a purely functional construal of meaning — so that meaning comes down to certain correlations with the environment and certain effects on later processing — then a neurobiological account of meaning may be forthcoming, but such a functional account will not tell us why the meaning should be consciously experienced. And if one invokes a richer construal of meaning — one on which meaning is more closely tied to consciousness, for example — then there is more chance that an account of meaning may yield an account of consciousness, but a functional explanation of meaning becomes much less likely. Nevertheless I imagine there are useful insights to be had by treading this path, whether or not it leads to a solution to the hard problem.

An intermediate line is taken by **Baars**, who argues that a functional theory can at least shed considerable light on subjective experience, but who does not claim that it will solve the hard problem. Indeed, he thinks the hard problem is too hard to be solved for now, because it involves an implausible criterion. I think that Baars misinterprets the hard problem slightly, however. To solve the hard problem we need not actually evoke all relevant experiences in ourselves (his 'empathy criterion'). The point is not to *experience* what it is like to be a bat (although that would be nice!), but rather to explain why there is anything it is like to be a bat or a human at all. And this seems like a perfectly reasonable scientific question.

Baars also notes that there are deep causal connections between 'easy' and 'hard' aspects of our mental lives. This is certainly correct; indeed, I pointed out some such connections in my article. There seems to be a tight connection between global availability and consciousness, for example, as Baars suggests. So this sort of connection is quite compatible with my framework: the distinction between the easy and hard problems is a *conceptual* distinction, not a claim that the two have nothing to do with each other.

In particular, even once these causal interconnections are granted, one can still ask how and why the 'easy' aspects are tied to the 'hard'. In conversation, Baars has suggested that one should just regard this as a brute fact, noting that psychologists are used to dealing in brute facts! So one might just take it as a brute fact that the contents of a global workspace are consciously experienced, for example. I think there is something to this, but one has to note that this brute fact has some strong consequences. For a start it implies that a theory of consciousness requires explanatorily primitive principles over and above the facts about processing. Even if 'easy' and 'hard' phenomena are two different aspects of the same thing, as Baars suggests, this still requires some further principle to tie the two aspects together, and indeed to explain why there are two aspects in the first place.

Of course it is most unlikely that the whole problem will be solved in one bite, so it is entirely reasonable for Baars to leave things at the level of a connection between the global workspace and consciousness. This reflects a common strategy for dealing with consciousness in those areas of psychology that take it seriously: take the existence of consciousness for granted, and investigate just how and where it maps onto cognitive processing. (The literature on the properties of conscious vs. unconscious processes can be read this way, for example.) This way the roots of consciousness may be located, and the path may be cleared for a theory of the underlying connection.

MacLennan aims to take the next step, searching for a simple theory that explains the connection. He accepts that there is an irreducible phenomenal aspect that is systematically associated with neural processes, yielding a property dualism similar to mine but with a neurodynamical flavour; and he develops some ideas about the 'deep structure' of the link between neural processes and experience.

I think MacLennan's idea of 'protophenomena' (or 'phenomenisca') as basic elements of consciousness is particularly interesting, and promises considerable rewards if it can be further developed. For a precise theory, I think we will need an account of (a) precisely when a protophenomenon is associated with a physical process, (b) what sort of protophenomena will be associated, depending on the characteristics of the physical process, and (c) the principles by which proto- phenomena combine into a unified conscious experience.

None of these questions is trivial, although MacLennan makes a start on all of them. His answer to (a) relies on a one-activity-site-one-protophenomenon principle; for my part I would be surprised if things were so straightforward. It might be that protophenomena are determined by informational states of the system that are not straightforwardly localized, for example. He does not have too much to say about (b) — precisely what makes for the difference between visual and auditory proto- phenomena, for example? — but he has a preliminary analysis of (c). I suspect that (c), an analogue of the problems faced by the Russellian metaphysics described earlier, may turn out to be the hardest question of all.

In any case, I see the central parts of the projects of Crick and Koch, Baars, and MacLennan as all being compatible with the research programme I envisage on the hard problem. At the nuts-and-bolts level, we must try to isolate the neural processes associated with consciousness, and to find detailed and systematic associations between these processes and characteristics of conscious experience. We should do the same at a cognitive level, where it may be that we will find 'cleaner' associations if less detail, along with a way of integrating key elements of the neural story into a big picture. A clean association between global availability and consciousness, for example, promises to help make sense of messier associations involving various specific neural processes. Finally, we should search for the fundamental principles that underlie and explain these associations, boiling things down to as simple a system as possible.

All this is compatible both with the scientific worldview and with the irreducibility of consciousness. Once released from the insistent tug of the reductive dream, we are free to engage in the project of relating consciousness to physical processes on its own terms. The resulting science may be all the richer for it.

2. *Phenomenological approaches*

Shear and **Varela** concentrate on phenomenological approaches to the hard problem. I think that such an approach must be absolutely central to an adequate science of consciousness: after all, it is our own phenomenology that provides the data that need to be explained! If we are to have a detailed psychophysical theory, as opposed to a mere ontology, then we will have to catalogue and systematize these data much as happens elsewhere in science; and to do this, patient attention to one's own experience is required.

Of course there are deep methodological problems here. The first is the old problem that the mere act of attention to one's experience transforms that experience. As we become more patient and careful, we may find that we are studying data that are transformed in subtle ways. This is not too much of a problem at the start of investigation — we have a long way to go until this degree of subtlety even comes into play — but it may eventually lead to deep paradoxes of observership. Phenomenologists from both East and West have proposed ways to deal with this problem, but I think it has a certain resilience. Even if there do turn out to be limits on the fineness of this method's grain, however, I have no doubt that coarse-grained methods can take us a long way.

The second problem is that of developing a language — or better, a formalism — in which phenomenological data can be expressed. In other areas, the advent of such formalisms has led to rapid progress. We still seem to be far from such a formalism here, however. The notorious 'ineffability' of conscious experience plays a role here: the language we have for describing experiences is largely derivative on the language we have for describing the external world. Perhaps, as Thomas Nagel has suggested, the structural properties of experience (e.g. the geometric structure of a visual field) will be most amenable to the possibility of formal expression, whether in informational, geometric, or topological terms, or in other terms entirely. I suspect that the residual non-structural properties will pose special problems.

The third difficulty lies in the failure, or at least the limitations, of incorrigibility: our judgments about experience can be wrong. I don't think this difficulty is as damning for phenomenology as it is sometimes made out to be; after all, our judgments about external data can be wrong, too, but science manages just fine. What is important is that our judgments about experience are accurate by and large, particularly when we are paying careful and patient attention. Our introspection must also be *critical*: we must take care to consider any ways in which it might be going wrong. But if our phenomenological judgments pass these tests, I think one is justified in taking them to be reliable.

Shear's and Varela's papers together make a strong case that a sophisticated phenomenological study is possible. In Shear's wide-ranging paper, the remarks about 'pure consciousness' are particularly intriguing. I confess that I find myself among the sceptics where this notion is concerned. I am not sure that I can imagine a consciousness without quality: would not even a 'void' experience have a certain voidish quality? (Shear's own position is appropriately cautious here.) But perhaps this is only because I have never experienced such a thing myself. The idea is appealing, at any rate, in the same sort of way that the Russellian idea of a physical world without intrinsic qualities is appealing: the appeal manifests itself both in spite of and because of its flirtation with incoherence. And the potential link that Shear suggests between this idea and a fundamental theory is certainly suggestive.

I am also sympathetic with much of Varela's discussion, in its shape if not in every detail. Varela takes himself to differ with me on some central points, but I am not sure why. The main difference between us seems to be one of emphasis: he emphasizes the phenomenological data, whereas I emphasize the systematicity in the relationship between these data and underlying processes. Perhaps he takes my 'extra ingredient' or 'theoretical fix' to be something more reductive than I intended. Varela himself seems to endorse the need for an extra ingredient in our theories — namely experience itself — which fits my programme well. He may differ by doubting the likelihood of simple underlying laws connecting the physical and phenomenal domains; but if so, he does not give his reasons in this article. In any case, the idea of 'neurophenomenology' sounds eminently sensible to me. The test will be whether it can be cashed out in the form of detailed results.

It would be overambitious to suppose that phenomenology by itself offers a solution to the hard problem. The ontological debates are as hard as ever, and phenomenology is largely neutral on them (except, perhaps, in rejecting type-A materialism). But it is absolutely central to the *epistemology* of the hard problem: without it, we would not even know what needs explaining. In most areas of science, we need an adequate epistemology to get a detailed theory off the ground, and there is no reason to suspect that the case of consciousness will be any different. If so, the sort of careful study advocated by Shear and Varela will be a central component in the path to a solution.

3. Physics-based approaches

In getting an empirical theory of consciousness off the ground, the two areas just discussed will play the central roles. Neuro/cognitive science will provide the third-person data and phenomenology will provide the first-person data. As all this goes on, theorists of all stripes will seek to systematize the connection between the two. In the early stages, this connection will be strongest at the 'surface' level: researchers will isolate correlations between fairly complex neuro/cognitive processes and relatively familiar characteristics of conscious experience. This high-level project may well be the solid core of consciousness research for many years to come. As the project develops, though, there will be an increasing drive to find the deep structure that underlies and explains these high-level connections, with the ultimate goal being a fundamental psychophysical theory.

We are not close to having such a fundamental theory yet, but this need not stop us from speculating about its form. Many contributors to this symposium do just that, offering proposals about links between consciousness and physical processes at the most fundamental level. In this section and the next, I will discuss these proposals. Those with conservative tastes might stop here: what follows is largely untrammelled speculation in physics and metaphysics about what may be required to bring consciousness within the natural order. I do not know whether any of this is on the right track, but there are plenty of interesting ideas with which I am more than happy to play along.

A number of contributors suggest approaches in which physics plays a central role. I expressed some criticism of physics-based proposals in the keynote paper, but mostly insofar as these were offered as *reductive* explanations of consciousness ('neurons can't do the job, but quantum mechanics can'). None of the current contributors offer that sort of account. Most of them instead offer proposals in which consciousness is taken as fundamental, and is related nonreductively to the entities in physical theories, in the hopes of finding a place for consciousness in the natural order. Such suggestions are not subject to the same sort of criticism, and they certainly cannot be ruled out *a priori*.

The difference between the two sorts of physics-based proposals is most apparent in the article by **Hameroff and Penrose**. Previous work had given me the impression that their aim was to explain consciousness wholly in terms of quantum action in microtubules; but this paper makes it explicit that consciousness is instead to be taken as fundamental. In essence, Hameroff and Penrose offer a psychophysical theory, postulating that certain quantum-mechanical reductions of the wave function, brought on when a certain gravitational threshold is attained, are each associated with a simple event of experience. They suggest a kinship with Whitehead's metaphysics; the view might also fit comfortably into the Russellian framework outlined earlier.

This is an intriguing and ambitious suggestion. Of course the details are a little sketchy: after their initial postulate, Hameroff and Penrose concentrate mostly on the physics of reduction and its functioning in microtubules, and leave questions about the explanation of experience to one side. Eventually it would be nice to see a proposal about the precise form of the psychophysical laws in this framework, and also to see how these billions of microscopic events of experience might somehow yield the remarkable structural properties of the single complex consciousness that we all possess. I am cautious about this sort of quantum-mechanical account myself, partly because it is not yet clear to me that quantum mechanics is essential to neural information-processing, and partly because it is not easy to see how quantum-level structure corresponds to the structure one finds in consciousness. But it is not impossible that a theory might address these problems. To know for sure, we will need a detailed explanatory bridge.

Stapp offers a very different sort of quantum-mechanical proposal. Instead of trying to constitute experience out of many low-level quantum-mechanical events, he takes consciousness as a given, and offers a theory of the role it plays in collapsing physical wave functions, thus showing how it might have an impact on the physical world. As I said earlier, this sort of 'collapse' interpretation of quantum mechanics needs to be taken very seriously — in the interests both of giving a good account of quantum mechanics and of giving a good account of consciousness — and Stapp's, as developed in a number of papers, is perhaps the most sophisticated version of such an interpretation to date. It certainly offers the most natural picture in which consciousness plays a role in influencing a non-causally-closed physical world.

Stapp's paper is neutral on some central questions that a theory of consciousness needs to answer. He says quite a lot about his mental-to-physical laws, characterizing the role of consciousness in wave-function collapse, but he does not say much about the physical-to-mental laws which will presumably be at the heart of a theory. Such laws will tell us just *which* physical processes are associated with consciousness, and what *sort* of conscious experience will be associated with a given physical process.[6] As it stands, Stapp's picture seems compatible with almost any physical-to-mental laws. Stapp offers some suggestions about such laws in his book (Stapp, 1993), where he proposes that experience goes along with 'top-level processes' in the brain; but perhaps it is a virtue of Stapp's broader proposal about the causal role of consciousness that many different psychophysical theories can benefit by invoking it.[7]

Clarke suggests a different connection between physics and consciousness, rooted in the nonlocality of both. The nonlocality of the former is less controversial, in a way: nonlocal causal influences are present in most interpretations of quantum mechanics, with the exception of those by Everett (1973) and Cramer (1986), and nonlocal constitution of physical states is present on most of these in turn. The sense in which mind is nonlocal is less clear to me. I am sympathetic with Clarke's point that mind is not located in physical space, but I am not sure of the link between these two sorts of nonlocality. Clarke argues that the physical structure that supports mind has to be nonlocal; but all that is clear to me is that it has to be *nonlocalized*, or distributed across space, which is equally possible on a classical theory. But perhaps nonlocal constitution of a physical state could be linked to the unity of consciousness, especially on a view which identifies consciousness with a physical state in such a way that unified consciousness requires a unified substrate: nonlocal physical constitution might unify the basis? The idea might also help in a Russellian metaphysics, though I am not sure that it is required.

Another appeal to physics is made by **McGinn**, who suggests that accommodating consciousness within the natural order will require a radically revised theory of space. A question immediately suggests itself: will this theory be forced on us to explain (third-person) empirical evidence, or just to accommodate consciousness? I suspect that it must be the latter. All sorts of revisions in our physical theories are made to explain the external world, but they always leave theories cast in terms of some basic mathematical structures and dynamics (whether Euclidean space, four-dimensional space–time, or infinite-dimensional Hilbert space). There are principled reasons why structure and dynamics is all we could possibly need to explain external evidence; and given *any* theory cast solely in terms of structure and dynamics, the further question of consciousness will arise.

So it seems to me that McGinn needs an empirically adequate theory of space to be revised or supplemented in some fundamental way to accommodate consciousness, while leaving its external predictions intact. But McGinn also strongly wants to avoid epiphenomenalism (see McGinn, 1996). I think that the natural way (perhaps the only way) to

[6] Of course, we know that experiences have 'actualizations' as a physical correlate; but given that Stapp wants pre-existing experiences to *cause* the actualizations, we need some independent physical criterion for experience. This would then yield a physical criterion for actualization in turn.

[7] One intriguing if far-out possibility: if Stapp's proposal were granted, it might even be that experimental physics could help determine the psychophysical laws, and determine which systems are conscious, at least in principle. It turns out that different proposals about the physical criteria for collapse have subtly different empirical consequences, although they are consequences that are practically impossible to test in general (see Albert, 1992, for discussion). So at least in principle, if not in practice, one could test for the presence or absence of collapse in a given system, and thus for the presence or absence of experience!

satisfy these requirements is along the Russellian lines suggested above: there is a pervasive intrinsic property of physical reality, a property which *carries* the structure and dynamics specified in physical theory but is nevertheless not revealed directly by empirical investigation, and which enables the existence of consciousness. This picture seems to square well with McGinn's remarks about a 'hidden dimension' of physical reality. Concentrating on space in particular, we might perhaps think of this property as the 'medium' in which the mathematical structures of space are embedded.

It seems clear, at any rate, that McGinn's 'hidden dimension' requires us to postulate *something* new and fundamental over and above what is empirically adequate. As such it seems that he is embracing option (2) of the dilemma I posed him earlier in this paper (p. 396). And this new fundamental property is a sort of 'proto-experience', at least in the sense that it enables the existence of experience. If so then McGinn's view, when unpacked, is in the same sort of ballpark as the views I am advocating. Of course McGinn *could* be right that we will never be able to form such a theory, for example because of our inability to grasp the relevant proto-experiential concept. On the other hand, he could be wrong; so I for one will keep trying.

Bilodeau takes the most radical physics-based approach, holding (I think) that we have to abandon the idea that there are objectively existing states in fundamental physics. Instead, physical reality crystallizes in some way as a product of experience and the process of inquiry. Once we see that experience is fundamental to the very nature of physical reality in this way, the hard problem may go away.

Bilodeau suggests that this picture is the most natural upshot of quantum mechanics, appealing especially to the writings of Bohr. Now I think this picture is certainly not *forced* on us by quantum mechanics — there are plenty of ways of making sense of quantum mechanics while maintaining the idea that fundamental physical reality has an objective existence, if only in the form of a superposed wave function. Bilodeau clearly finds these interpretations unappealing, but I (like many others) find them much more comprehensible. Given that macroscopic physical reality has an objective existence, it seems that its causal antecedents must have objective existence (otherwise why would it come into existence?), and in the process of explanation we are relentlessly driven to causal antecedents at more and more fundamental levels. So the only way I can make sense of the idea that fundamental physical reality does not have objective existence is as a form of idealism, on which *all* physical reality is present only within experience. Bilodeau disclaims this interpretation, however, so this may be a cognitive limitation on my part.

In any case it seems that even under Bilodeau's reasoning, there still needs to be an explanatory theory connecting experiences and brain processes. I am not quite sure what the shape of such a theory will be, but perhaps his version of the metaphysics will be able to give a natural version of it. It would be very interesting to see some of the details.

4. Fundamental psychophysical theories

Some of the most intriguing pieces, to me, are those that speculate about the shape of a fundamental theory of consciousness. Many of these proposals invoke some form of panpsychism. Panpsychism is not *required* for a fundamental theory; it is not written in stone that fundamental properties have to be ubiquitous. **Libet** and **Stapp**, for example, both invoke fundamental theories without invoking panpsychism. But the idea of a fundamental theory certainly fits well with panpsychism, and the proposals by **Hut and Shepard**, **Rosenberg** and **Seager** are all explicitly panpsychist.

Some contributors (e.g. **Mills** and **Hardcastle**) roll their eyes at the idea of panpsychism, but explicit arguments against it are surprisingly hard to find. Rosenberg and Seager give nice defences of panpsychism against various objections. Indeed, both upbraid me for not being panpsychist *enough*. I do not know whether panpsychism is true, but I find it an intriguing view, and in my book I argue that it deserves attention. If a simple and powerful predictive theory of consciousness ends up endorsing panpsychism, then I do not see why we should not accept it.

Panpsychist views need not ascribe *much* of a mind to simple entities. Sometimes the term 'panexperientialism' is used instead, to suggest that all that is being ascribed is some sort of experience (not thought, not intelligence, not self-awareness), and a particularly simple form of experience at that. And some versions do not even go this far. Instead of suggesting that experience is ubiquitous, such views suggest that some *other* property is ubiquitous, where instantiations of this property somehow jointly constitute experience in more complex systems. Such a property might be thought of as a *proto-experiential* property, and the associated view might more accurately be thought of as *panprotopsychism*.

Of course it is very hard to form a conception of protoexperiential properties. We know no set of *physical* properties can constitute experience, for familiar reasons. But perhaps some quite alien property might do the job. I was particularly intrigued by **Hut and Shepard**'s postulation of a property 'X', where X stands to consciousness as time stands to motion. That is, just as time enables the existence of motion, in combination with space, X enables the existence of consciousness, in combination with the basic dimensions of space–time. This offers an elegant picture of proto- experience quite different from the tempting picture on which proto-experience is 'just like experience but less so'.

In a way, Hut and Shepard's proposal has a lot in common with **McGinn**'s suggestion of a 'hidden dimension' of space which enables the existence of consciousness. As with McGinn, one can ask whether the dimension is truly 'hidden', or whether it will manifest itself in our external observations (the physics we have now does a pretty good job, after all). As before, I suspect that such a property *has* to be hidden, as an empirically adequate theory can always be cast in terms of structure and dynamics that are compatible with the absence of experience. Thus, as before, it seems that the new dimension will either (a) be epiphenomenal to the other dimensions (or at least to the projections of those dimensions that we have access to), or (b) relate to them as a sort of Russellian 'realizing' property, carrying the structure in one of these dimensions and making it real. The latter would be particularly compatible with the idea of turning the hard problem 'upside down', on which physical reality is itself somehow derivative on underlying (proto)experiences.

Rosenberg offers a detailed defence of panpsychism, and makes a number of points with which I am particularly sympathetic. He makes a strong case against the existence of fundamental laws that connect consciousness to mere complexity, to aspects of functioning, or to biological properties. While I think there is nothing *wrong* with the idea of a nonpanpsychist fundamental theory, Rosenberg's discussion eliminates some of the most obvious candidates.[8] And he begins to unpack what panpsychism might involve in a way that makes it clear that the idea is at least coherent.

Rosenberg also makes a strong case for an *integrated* view of nature, on which consciousness is not a mere tacked-on extra. My keynote paper may carry a flavour of the latter (except for the final paragraph of section VII), but I think the former is the ultimate goal. Perhaps the best path to such an integrated view is offered by the Russellian picture on which (proto)experiential properties constitute the intrinsic nature of physical reality. Such a picture is most naturally associated with some form of panpsychism. The resulting integration may be panpsychism's greatest theoretical benefit.

Seager also provides some motivation for panpsychism, and gives a particularly interesting accounting of its problems. I think his 'completeness problem' (a version of the epiphenomenalism problem) is mitigated by embracing the Russellian interpretation, on which the fundamental (proto)experiences are part of the causal order, although there will always be residual worries about *explanatory* superfluity. (Giving experiences certain anomalous effects doesn't help here; experience-free structural explanations are just as possible either way.) This view would also solve his 'no-sign' problem: we cannot expect to have external access to the intrinsic properties that underlie physical dispositions. A solution to the 'not-mental' problem must likely wait until we *have* a theory; presumably we will then be justified in attributing (proto-) mentality in certain cases precisely because of the theory's indirect explanatory benefits in explaining our *own* experiences. A version of the 'unconscious mentality' problem will apply to any view that postulates proto-experiential rather than experiential properties at the fundamental level (how does experience emerge from non-experience?), but this need not be quite as hard as the original hard problem. We know that physical properties cannot imply experience, because of the character of physics, but novel intrinsic proto-experiential properties cannot be ruled out in the same way.

This leaves the 'combination problem', which is surely the hardest.[9] This is the problem of how low-level proto-experiential and other properties somehow together *constitute* our complex unified conscious experiences. The problem could be bypassed altogether by suggesting that complex experiences are *not* constituted by the micro-experiences, but rather arise autonomously. This would hold true under many psychophysical theories, including some versions of an informational theory; its main disadvantage is that it once again threatens epiphenomenalism. To make experience causally relevant in the Russellian way, it seems that it *has* to be constituted out of the intrinsic natures of the fundamental causally relevant entities in physical theory. Unless we embrace an interactionist picture like **Stapp**'s where there is fundamental causation at a high level, it seems that integrating experience into the causal order leads inevitably to the combination problem.

To solve the problem, we have to investigate the principles of composition to which experience is subject. The 'problem' may well arise from thinking of experiential

---

[8] Another possibility worth considering, though: several simple laws might *combine* to imply that experience only comes into existence in certain complex cases.

[9] One might also think of it as the 'constitution problem', to avoid the implication that constitution must work by simple combination; consider Hut and Shepard's non-combinatorial proposal, for example.

composition along the lines of physical composition, when it might well work quite differently. I suggest in my book, for example, that something more like *informational* composition might be more appropriate. Alternatively, we may try to keep a closer isomorphism between experiential composition and physical composition, but investigate nonstandard manners of physical composition. Seager's invocation of quantum coherence is an intriguing example of such a strategy: in this case, physical composition yields a unity that might mirror the unity of experience. To the best of my knowledge, the evidence for widespread stable quantum coherent states at a macroscopic level in the brain is not strong, but this is nevertheless a strategy to keep in mind. A related quantum-mechanical strategy is discussed by Lockwood (1992), who also provides an illuminating discussion of the problem in general. There may well be other interesting ideas waiting to be explored in addressing the problem; it is likely to be a fruitful area for further inquiry.

Of course everything in these last two sections has the air of something put together in the metaphysical laboratory, to use Seager's phrase. It is all extraordinarily speculative, and has to be taken with a very large grain of salt. Like my own speculations about information, these suggestions have not yet been remotely developed to the point where they can be given a proper assessment — indeed, their largely undefined nature may be the reason that I am able to speak reasonably warmly of all of them! And most of them have not yet begun to provide a detailed explanatory bridge from the fundamental level to the complex experiences we know and love. I favour the informational view partly because it seems closer to providing such a bridge than proposals based directly in physics or elsewhere, but even this view is very sketchy in crucial places.

To have a fundamental theory that we can truly assess, we will need a fundamental theory with *details*. That is, we will need specific proposals about psychophysical laws, and specific proposals about how these laws combine, if necessary, so that ultimately we will be able to (1) take the physical facts about a given system, (2) apply the psychophysical theory to these facts, and thus (3) *derive* a precise characterization of the associated experiences that the theory predicts. As yet, we do not have a single theory that allows this sort of derivation. Indeed, as I noted above, we may first need to develop a proper formalism (informational, geometrical, topological?) for characterizing experiences before this project can get off the ground. And once we have such a formalism, it may well be extremely hard to devise a theory that even gives the right results in the simplest familiar cases. Once we *do* have a detailed theory that gives approximately correct results in familiar cases, however, we will know we are on the right track. The ultimate goal is a simple theory that gets things exactly right.

I imagine that it may well be many years until we have a good detailed theory. We will probably first have to concentrate on understanding the 'macroscopic' regularities between processing and experience, and gradually work our way down to the fundamental principles that underlie and explain these regularities. Most researchers are now working at the macroscopic level, insofar as they are working on experience at all, and this is as it should be. But we can at least speculate about the form of a fundamental theory, in our more philosophical moments, and there is no reason why we should not try to come up with some details. Perhaps we will prove to have been terribly premature, but we will not know until we try. And in the meantime, I am sure that the attempt will be enlightening.

V: Conclusion

Taking a broad view of the metaphysics of the hard problem, here is the lay of the land as I see it.

(1) The first 'choice point' is the question of whether there is a problem of consciousness at all, distinct from the problem of explaining functions. Some, the type-A materialists, deny this, though we have seen that there seem to be few good arguments for such a counterintuitive conclusion. Given that there *is* a further phenomenon that needs explaining, we have seen that one is forced to the conclusion that no reductive explanation of consciousness can be given, and that explanatorily primitive bridging principles are required.

(2) In a second choice point, some (the type-B materialists) try to preserve materialism by arguing that these principles are 'identities'. But we have seen that these explanatorily primitive identities are unparalleled elsewhere in science, are philosophically problematic, and require the invocation of a new and ungrounded form of necessity. In any case, the *form* of a theory of this sort will be just like the form of a theory that takes consciousness as fundamental, and these 'identities' will function in our explanations just like fundamental laws.

(3) All other theories take experience (or proto-experience) as irreducible, along with irreducible principles relating it to the physical domain. The next choice point is whether to hold onto the causal closure of the physical. Denying this, perhaps through an invocation of wavefunction collapse in quantum mechanics, leads to an interactionist dualism. But the advantages of this denial can be questioned.

(4) Given that the physical domain is a closed causal network, the next choice is that between views which put experience *outside* this network, with psychophysical laws that make experience epiphenomenal, or which put experience *inside* this network, by virtue of a Russellian monism on which the intrinsic properties of matter are proto-experiential. The latter offers the most attractive and integrated view, if the 'combination problem' can be solved.

(5) The final choice point turns on the *form* of the psychophysical laws in our theory. This is the meatiest question of all, and can be engaged by researchers in all fields: the earlier questions require some tolerance for metaphysics, but this question is more straightforwardly 'scientific'. Much work on this question will be independent of specific choices on questions (2)–(4), though some aspects of these choices may inform one's approach to this question.

Progress on the hard problem will likely take place at two levels. On the philosophical level, there will be an ongoing clarification of the issues surrounding (1)–(4), and the arguments for and against the various options at the various choice points. For my part I think the case for introducing new irreducible properties is hard to resist, but the choice points at (3) and especially (4) are still open. On a more concrete level, there will be progress toward specific laws as in (5). A combination of experimental study, phenomenological investigation, and philosophical analysis will lead us to systematic principles bridging the domains, and ultimately we hope to be led to the underlying fundamental laws. In this way we may eventually arrive at a truly satisfactory theory of conscious experience.

References

Albert, D. (1992), *Quantum Mechanics and Experience* (Cambridge, MA: Harvard University Press.

Chalmers, D.J. (1996), *The Conscious Mind: In Search of a Fundamental Theory* (New York: Oxford University Press). See also http://ling.ucsc.edu/~chalmers

Churchland, Paul M. (1996), 'The rediscovery of light', *Journal of Philosophy*, **93**, pp. 211–28.

Cramer, J.G. (1986), 'The transactional interpretation of quantum mechanics', *Review of Modern Physics*, **58**, pp. 647–87.

Dennett, D.C. (1991), *Consciousness Explained* (Boston, MA: Little, Brown & Co.).

Everett, H. (1973), 'The theory of the universal wave function', in *The Many-Worlds Interpretation of Quantum Mechanics*, ed. B.S. de Witt & N. Graham (Princeton: Princeton University Press).

Hawking, S. (1988), *A Brief History of Time* (Bantam Books).

Köhler, D. (1947), *Gestalt Psychology* (New York: Liveright Publishing Corporation).

Levine, J. (1983), 'Materialism and qualia: The explanatory gap', *Pacific Philosophical Quarterly*, **64**, pp. 354–61.

Lockwood, M. (1989), *Mind, Brain, and the Quantum* (Oxford: Blackwell).

Lockwood, M. (1992), 'The grain problem', in *Objections to Physicalism*, ed. H. Robinson (Oxford: Oxford University Press).

Maxwell, G. (1978), 'Rigid designators and mind-brain identity', in *Perception and Cognition: Issues in the Foundations of Psychology* (Minnesota Studies in the Philosophy of Science, Vol. 9), ed. C.W. Savage (Minneapolis: University of Minnesota Press).

McGinn, C. (1989), 'Can we solve the mind–body problem', *Mind*, **98**, pp. 349–66. Reprinted in *The Problem of Consciousness* (Oxford: Blackwell, 1991).

McGinn, C. (1996), Review of *The Conscious Mind*, *Times Higher Educational Supplement*, April 5, 1996, pp. vii–ix.

Mills, E. (1995), 'Interactionism and overdetermination', *American Philosophical Quarterly*, **33**, pp. 105–15.

Müller, G.E. (1896), 'Zur Psychophysik der Gesichtsempfindungen', *Zeitschrift für Psychologie und Physiologie der Sinnesorgane*, **10**, pp. 1–82.

Papineau, D. (1996), Review of *The Conscious Mind*, *Times Literary Suppl.*, **4864** (June 21, 1996), pp. 3–4.

Place, U.T. (1956), 'Is consciousness a brain process?' *British Journal of Psychology*, **47**, pp. 44–50. Reprinted in *Mind and Cognition*, ed. W. Lycan (Oxford: Blackwell, 1990).

Russell, B. (1927), *The Analysis of Matter* (London: Kegan Paul).

Shoemaker, S. (1975), 'Functionalism and qualia', *Philosophical Studies*, **27**, pp. 291–315. Reprinted in *Identity, Cause and Mind* (Cambridge: Cambridge University Press, 1984).

Shoemaker, S. (1990), 'First-person access', *Philosophical Perspectives*, **4**, pp. 187–214.

Smart, J.J.C. (1959), 'Sensations and brain processes', *Philosophical Review*, **68**, pp. 141–56. Reprinted in *The Nature of Mind*, ed. D. Rosenthal (Oxford: Oxford University Press, 1990).

Stapp, H. (1993), *Mind, Matter, and Quantum Mechanics* (Springer Verlag).

White, S. (1986), 'Curse of the qualia', *Synthese*, **68**, pp. 333–68.

Paper received November 1996